ISBN 978-1-331-03871-9
PIBN 10136831

1 MONTH OF
FREE
READING

at

www.ForgottenBooks.com

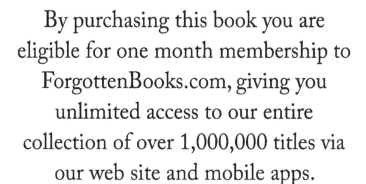

By purchasing this book you are eligible for one month membership to ForgottenBooks.com, giving you unlimited access to our entire collection of over 1,000,000 titles via our web site and mobile apps.

To claim your free month visit:
www.forgottenbooks.com/free136831

NAPOLEON'S BROTHERS

BY

A. HILLIARD ATTERIDGE

WITH EIGHTEEN ILLUSTRATIONS
AND SIX MAPS

LONDON

METHUEN & CO.

NEW YORK

BRENTANO'S

1909

PREFACE

THE story of Napoleon's four brothers is little known to the English reader. They are overshadowed by the greatness of the Emperor. We catch glimpses of them here and there in the popular histories of his career, as his mere satellites, but the narrative only takes note of such of their actions as brought them into direct relation with him. They all survived him. They lived comparatively uneventful lives after the downfall of the Empire had stripped them of their state and driven them into exile, but some of their sons helped to make history. Their story is worth telling from a point of view that does not so utterly dwarf them. We may trace the course of events from their standpoint, and see how Joseph and Lucien, Louis and Jerome played their parts; how some of them helped in their brother's marvellous rise to power; how they bore themselves in the days of prosperity, and in the darker times that followed the fall of the Empire; and how one of them survived to see Bonapartism again a factor in European politics, long after the first of the Napoleons had passed away.

SUMMARY OF CONTENTS

CHAPTER I

EARLY DAYS IN CORSICA (1768-1793)

CHAPTER II

THE RISE OF THE BONAPARTES (1793-1795)

CHAPTER III

FORTUNE AT LAST (1796-1797)

CONTENTS

CHAPTER VII

THE COMING OF THE EMPIRE (1802-1804)

CHAPTER VIII

MARRIAGE QUESTIONS (1804-1805)

CHAPTER IX

KING-MAKING (1805-1806)

CHAPTER X

JOSEPH, KING OF NAPLES (1806-1808) AND LOUIS, KING OF HOLLAND (1806)

CHAPTER XI

HOW JEROME WENT TO WAR AND GOT HIS KINGDOM AND ANOTHER WIFE (1805-1807)

CHAPTER XII

LUCIEN IN REVOLT—LOUIS AND HORTENSE—JOSEPH TRANSFERRED TO SPAIN (1807-1808)

CHAPTER XIII

THE TROUBLES OF THREE KINGS (1807-1809)

CHAPTER XIV

THE THREE KINGS IN THE WAR OF 1809

CHAPTER XV

THE FLIGHT OF LUCIEN AND LOUIS (1809-1810)

CHAPTER XVI

KING JOSEPH AND THE MARSHALS—WESTPHALIAN AFFAIRS (1809-1810)

CHAPTER XXI

THE END OF JEROME'S KINGDOM OF WESTPHALIA (1813)

CHAPTER XXII

THE DETHRONED KINGS AND THEIR AMBITIONS (1813)

CHAPTER XXIII

JOSEPH, LIEUTENANT-GENERAL OF FRANCE (1814)

CHAPTER XXVIII

NAPOLEON II.—THE DAYS OF EXILE (1815-1817)

CHAPTER XXIX

THE BONAPARTES IN EUROPE AND AMERICA—FIRST YEARS OF LOUIS NAPOLEON (THE FUTURE · NAPOLEON III.) (1815-1830)

CHAPTER XXX

DEATH OF NAPOLEON II.—STRASBURG—DEATH OF HORTENSE (1830-1837)

LIST OF ILLUSTRATIONS

xviii   •

LIST OF ILLUSTRATIONS

LIST OF PLANS

THE BROTHERS OF NAPOLEON

JOSEPH BONAPARTE, King of Naples and Spain . 1768-1844

LUCIEN BONAPARTE, Prince of Canino .   .   . 1775-1840

LOUIS BONAPARTE, King of Holland 1777-1846

JEROME BONAPARTE, King of Westphalia   .   . 1784-1860

THE HOUSE OF THE BONAPARTES AT AJACCIO

NAPOLEON'S BROTHERS

CHAPTER I

EARLY DAYS IN CORSICA

(1768-1793)

'AJACCIO is the prettiest town in Corsica. It hath many very handsome streets and beautiful gardens, and a palace for the Genoese Governor. The inhabitants of this town are the genteelest people in the island, having had a good deal of intercourse with the French.'

So wrote James Boswell in his account of Corsica, published in 1768. He had visited the island two years before, and his journey had made him famous. For in the middle of the eighteenth century Corsica was for Englishmen a barbarous, almost inaccessible, land. By the time the book appeared there was no longer a Genoese Governor at Ajaccio. The Republic had ceded the island to Louis xv., and with it handed over to the French the quarrel with Pasquale Paoli and the Corsican patriots. Boswell had visited Paoli at his headquarters in the interior of the island, at Corte, ' which,' wrote the Scottish explorer, ' is properly its capital, and will undoubtedly be one day a city of eminence.'

Corte has not fulfilled this prophecy. It is Ajaccio that has become world-famous. Boswell does not mention by name any of the ' genteel people ' he met there in 1766, but we know that prominent in the local society of the little place were two brothers—Napoleon and Lucien Bonaparte. Their family had been settled in the island for some hundreds of years. Napoleon, the elder brother, had a house in the town, a three-storied building, standing in a narrow street in the oldest part of Ajaccio.[1] Outside the town the Bonapartes

---

[1] The Bonapartes occupied the first and second story. The top story was sub-let to some of the Pozzo di Borgo family, a son of which entered the diplomatic service of Russia, and was one of the most persistent enemies of Napoleon.

owned a farm with a vineyard on the slope of the granite hills ; and they had another small house in the town let at a low rent. They were not rich, but then there were no rich people in Corsica. The island was still in a primitive state. Most payments were made in kind, purchases were regulated by barter, and very little coin circulated outside the towns. The younger brother, Lucien, was a priest, and archdeacon of the cathedral of Ajaccio. The brothers were joint guardians of their nephew, Charles Bonaparte. In 1766 he was a handsome young man of twenty. He had just returned from Pisa, where he had followed the course of law, and taken a degree at the University, and he had already played some part in local politics, throwing in his lot with the Corsican patriots, who looked to Paoli to make their island an independent state.

The young man's politics were not approved of by his uncles. Neither did they like his attentions to a pretty girl of fifteen, Letizia Ramolino, who had just left her convent school. The Ramolini could claim to be noble. They had come to Corsica from Genoa in the fifteenth or sixteenth century. Some of them had married with the Bonapartes, so that there was already a traditional connection between the two families. They were fairly well off. Letizia's dowry would be a vineyard and lands worth some seven thousand francs. One cannot surmise, therefore, what was the objection raised by the elder Bonapartes to the proposed marriage of Charles and Letizia. It could not well have been her tender years, for girls married at fourteen or fifteen in Corsica. In any case, Charles married without their consent as soon as he came of age in 1767. The death of his uncle, Napoleon, soon after made him head of the family. Lucien, the archdeacon, whose health was breaking down, shared his home in Ajaccio.

After the coming of the French, Charles and his young wife had been for a short time absent from the town, at Paoli's stronghold in the hills at Corte. But they soon returned to their home, for Charles Bonaparte had realised the fact that the struggle for independence was hopeless, and made his peace with the new rulers of his native island. His name appeared on the list of the four hundred nobles of Corsica drawn up by order of Louis XV. in 1771, and two years later he was appointed one of the royal councillors for the government of the town and province of Ajaccio.

There was still a party in Corsica that dreamed of independence. But Charles Bonaparte thought more of the interests of his household than of local patriotism. He gave no half-hearted allegiance to the new government. He cultivated friendly relations with the French commissioners in the island and the officers of the local garrison. He was full of projects for developing the resources and the trade of the province, projects that if he could only realise them would, of course, benefit himself. Full of these ideas he made journeys to Genoa, Pisa, Naples. He was chosen a member of the delegation sent to Paris in 1777 to discuss Corsican interests with the central government. These journeys cost money. The entertainments he gave to a growing circle of French and Corsican friends must also have been an expense. And the fees of his official position were trifling,[1] and his projects had no tangible result. That Charles Bonaparte was not a successful man of business is clear from the straitened circumstances in which he left Letizia and her children when he died in 1785. She could only afford one servant, an old follower of the family, whose wages were three francs a month, and she did much of the housework herself.

The family was a numerous one. The eldest son, Joseph, was born at Ajaccio in 1768. Next year the second son, Napoleon, was born. The two boys spent their years of early childhood together at Ajaccio, and left Corsica on the same day to go to school in France. In the old house they had lessons from their uncle, the archdeacon, a stay-at-home invalid. For recreation there were the boats in the bay, and visits to the outlying farm and vineyard, with rough-riding lessons on the backs of hill ponies. Joseph was stronger and more active than his brother, more successful too with his lessons, and Napoleon looked up to him as his guide and hero.

There was a little sister born in 1771, and another two years later, but both died as children, and the two brothers were separated by some years of seniority from the rest of the family. Their father, during his stay in Paris, obtained for them free places in French schools. When they left home

[1] The salary attached to the appointment was only 900 francs (£36) a year.

for school, there were two little brothers and a sister at Ajaccio : Lucien, three years old ; Maria Anna Elisa, born the year before ; and Louis, a baby in his mother's arms.

It was in December 1778 that Charles Bonaparte took his two sons to France. It had been decided that a clerical career would be best for the eldest son. He might some day be a dignitary of the cathedral like his uncle, so he was left at the college of Autun, to begin a classical course of studies. Napoleon was to be a soldier, and went on to the military school of Brienne. In neither case would the education of the boys cost their father anything. He had used his influence at Paris to secure them *bourses* in the college and the school.

In 1783 Charles Bonaparte came again to France to place his eldest daughter, Marianne, at St. Cyr, and Lucien with his brother at Brienne. On the way he visited Autun, and found Joseph was discontented with his position in the college, and anxious to give up his clerical studies and the future that had been marked out for him, and become an officer in the army. Arrived at Brienne he told Napoleon how disappointed he was with Joseph's change of mind. There is a letter of Napoleon's dating from this time, addressed to Fesch, his mother's step-brother. It discusses Joseph's future in a very old-fashioned way, and is obviously a repetition of what he had heard his father say. He is sorry Joseph is giving up his studies after having gone so far. If he would persevere, the Bishop of Autun would soon give him a good benefice, and how helpful this would be to the family. The Bishop had even encouraged him to stay on by telling Joseph he would not regret it. But it was no use. He wanted to be an officer. But what would it lead to ? Joseph had not the aptitude for mathematics required for the artillery or engineers. He would have to be ' a poor devil of an infantry officer,' with little to do and small pay, lounging about most of his time, perhaps going to the bad among an inferior set of men. Surely none of them would like this prospect for him. He hoped a last effort would be made to keep him at the seminary. If he must go, it would be better he returned with his father to Corsica, where he might be apprenticed to a notary. Joseph ended by returning to Corsica, but, as we shall see, he carved out a better position for himself than what his brother suggested for him.

MARIA LETIZIA BONAPARTE, "MADAME MÈRE"

Lucien and Napoleon spent a year together at Brienne. The younger brother did not hit it off well with the elder. He resented Napoleon's attempts to advise and direct him. He afterwards said that his feeling of opposition to Napoleon dated from this time. Next year (1784) the elder brother was transferred to the Military School at Paris, and Lucien was alone at Brienne. His father had been in very bad health for some time, suffering from cancer of the stomach. In 1785 Charles Bonaparte went to Montpellier, hoping to obtain some relief from the treatment of one of the professors of the famous local medical school. But he became rapidly worse, and died there in the same year.

By the death of his father Joseph Bonaparte became the head of the family. He had left Autun, and returned to Ajaccio. He was only sixteen, but though he was slower witted than his brothers he was able to think and act like a man, and under the sense of responsibility he matured rapidly. Two sisters and a little brother had been born since he went to Autun. They were Maria Paoletta, afterwards known as Pauline, born in 1780 ; Maria Nunziate, the Caroline of later years, born in 1782 ; and Jerome, the youngest of the family, born the year before his father died. Two of his brothers and the eldest sister were provided for for the present, Napoleon with the artillery regiment he had just joined, Lucien at Brienne, and Marianna at St. Cyr.

The household at Ajaccio was therefore made up of his mother ; his uncle, the archdeacon, who had a very small income from the cathedral ; Joseph ; the three little ones ; and the maid-servant, who worked for three francs a month. The family was in terribly straitened circumstances. Two years before, in order to provide the expenses of his journey to Brienne and Paris with his children, Charles had had to borrow twenty-five louis (500 francs) from M. de Beaumanoir, the French commandant at Ajaccio. There were no means of repaying the money, and Madame Bonaparte offered to give the friendly commandant the family plate as a pledge for an eventual settlement. Joseph, besides looking after the farm and vineyard, was able to earn something by continuing the superintendence of work that his father had undertaken to carry on for the provincial government, plantations of mulberry

trees and the draining of some salt marshes. At the same time
he gave some time to study, for he intended to visit Pisa and
obtain there the degree which would be required as a qualification for some legal appointment in the island. It must be
remembered to Joseph's credit, that while his more famous
brother was serving as an artillery officer in various garrisons,
he had to live through these months of monotonous work at
Ajaccio, keeping the old home together, and helping his
widowed mother in her poverty. Narrow as their means were,
the economies of the household were so rigid that the archdeacon
was able to save up something of his income. His bank was
a pocket in the mattress of his bed, where the golden louis
accumulated one by one. The hoard was an important resource
for the Bonapartes at a crisis of their fortunes later on.

It was in June 1786 that Napoleon came back to Corsica
on his first long leave of absence. He spent some months
with his mother and Joseph at Ajaccio. He had been a sub-
lieutenant of artillery for more than a year, and seems to have
been unprepared for the poverty he found in the old house.
He was still as devoted as ever to Joseph, and during these
summer days he had many a long ride or walk with him, and
discussed with his elder brother not only the hopes of the
family, but also his own political views and ambitions. Napoleon
was still more of a Corsican than a Frenchman. He was full
of the new philosophical ideas. He dreamed of Corsica again
asserting its independence under Paoli. He was thinking of
writing a history of the island, which would be at the same time
a plea for its ' rights ' and a call to action. Joseph was more
interested in home questions. He was the head of the family,
and had to think of providing for his younger brothers and
sisters. As for politics he had his father's ideas. There was
no need of a revolution in Corsica. He would be satisfied if
all local appointments were given to Corsicans, and if France
would fly its flag over the fortresses and find money enough
to make up the deficit of the Corsican budget, and ensure that
all salaries were promptly paid without unduly increasing the
local taxation. Napoleon made Joseph an offer which did
something to lessen his anxieties. The young artillery officer
had been greatly attracted to his brother Louis, now a bright,
active boy, nine years old. He would take Louis back to

CARLO MARIA BUONAPARTE

France with him. The boy would share his barrack-room, he would provide for him out of his pay, himself act as his tutor, teach him mathematics, and make an officer of him.

After more than a year at home Napoleon was recalled to France in October 1787. Louis did not go with him, for the reason of his recall was a rumour of war with Prussia. In December the war scare was over, his leave was renewed, and he returned to Corsica. Joseph took advantage of his return to leave him in charge of the household at Ajaccio, and go over to Pisa, to take his degree in law. Having succeeded in this, he came back to Corsica in May. In June Napoleon rejoined his artillery regiment at Auxonne. Joseph had returned from Pisa with his law degree, and was ready to accept some post if it could be found.

Before he had realised his modest ambitions there came troublous times. Politics were now every man's business, and there were magnificent opportunities for all who understood the art of fishing in troubled waters—elections for the States-General of 1789, anxious debate as to what claims could be put forward for Corsica in the *cahier* entrusted to the delegates sent to Paris, and then news of great events in France. None of the Bonapartes found a place among the delegates of the island. From his French garrison Napoleon wrote anxiously. He complained that they sent him letters at terribly long intervals. Postage was too expensive a luxury for frequent use. He asked especially for news of Louis. He had not yet realised his project of becoming his young brother's guardian and educator.

He got another long leave of absence and hurried back to Ajaccio. Joseph had just become a functionary of the local administration. It was a very small appointment, worth just 900 francs a year, not forty pounds, but it was a beginning, and in the actual state of the family budget 900 francs were a help. A National Guard was to be organised. Napoleon's position as an officer of the regular army gave him a right to be heard on practical questions as to its organisation. He was busy, too, bringing out a pamphlet on Corsican affairs, and collecting material for his projected history. He looked for support from Paoli, in return for the services he and his family could render to the cause of the patriots. Joseph was chosen president of the local provincial council at Ajaccio. It was an unpaid office, but it meant influence. He would be a candidate for the National Assembly at the next elections.

Lucien had not gone on to a commission, but some post would doubtless be found for him. When Napoleon went back to his regiment in January 1791 he took Louis with him, to provide for and educate the boy in his quarters in the barracks at Auxonne. It meant many sacrifices, rigid economies on his small pay as a lieutenant of artillery. But he felt a delight in taking care of and training his little brother. One can see his enthusiasm for this labour of love in his letters to Joseph. Louis is making good progress, learning to read and write French ; working hard at mathematics ; reading geography and history. The boy of twelve goes with his brother into the society of the garrison town, and all the ladies are delighted with his graceful manners. ' I can easily see,' writes Napoleon, ' that he will turn out a better fellow than any of the four of us. But then none of us had so fine an education.'

Little Louis was not quite so enthusiastic. He felt the strain of hard work. As he sat in the barrack-room at Auxonne, chasing the elusive x through tangled equations, or grappling with French irregular verbs, his thoughts went back to the home at Ajaccio, the boats on the sunny bay, their rides on rough-haired ponies at the farm. He wrote to Joseph suggesting that perhaps after all he might come home, but he left the decision to his elder brother. ' You have only to say the word,' he wrote, ' and I shall remain here. You have only to say the contrary, and I will come home. You must know well that after Napolione it is you I love and cherish the most.' Joseph wisely decided that he had better remain with ' Napolione.'

Lucien had been left at Brienne when Napoleon went on to the Military School at Paris, but he had only remained a year there after his more famous brother's departure. He had given up the preparation for a soldier's life. With some vague idea of future ecclesiastical preferment, through the influence of his namesake the archdeacon and the Grand Vicar of Ajaccio, Canon Fesch, who was his mother's uncle, Lucien was sent to study at the seminary at Aix. It was hoped that he might obtain a free *bourse* there that would provide for the expenses of his education, but Lucien failed to win it, and feeling no real attraction for ecclesiastical studies, he left Aix and came back to Ajaccio. He would be a politician. He saw that a tide was at hand when politics meant a career. Joseph soon found that, deferential as he was to the head of the family, it was no use trying to control him. Lucien had resented Napoleon's assumption of an elder brother's authority at Brienne. Joseph was too easy-going to provoke a conflict with the young man, who, full of the fashionable Liberalism of the day, passed hours reading his favourite authors, writing endless essays on liberty and the rights of man, composing ambitious orations and declaiming them to imaginary audiences.

In October 1791 the elder Lucien, the archdeacon, was dying, and Napoleon came back from Auxonne on another long leave of absence. In these first years of his career he spent more time on leave than with his regiment. On the 16th the old man died. He left the family a legacy of his savings, some few thousand francs. Joseph had been chosen a member of the Departmental Directory of western Corsica, with a salary of 1600 francs. The days of wealth were still to come. Even the scanty inheritance of the archdeacon had to be spent at once, for the officers of the National Guard were being elected, and it was considered good policy to secure the post of lieutenant-colonel and second-in-command of the Ajaccio battalion for Napoleon. Money had to be spent freely to secure votes and to entertain the valiant guardsmen and their friends. In a letter written on the evening of the election, Lucien tells how the house was packed with guests and the band of the regiment played in front of it. The election was followed by a fierce quarrel between rival factions, and disturbances and bloodshed in Ajaccio ; Napoleon narrowly risked losing his life in this affair, and his high-handed methods of securing his own position and that of his party led to denunciations of his conduct being sent to Paris. He alone was prominent in the affair. We hear nothing of his brothers.

But Joseph and Napoleon were working together hand-in-hand for the advantage of the family interests. Joseph would have adopted less enterprising methods, but the other believed in taking risks. Lucien was outside the combination. He had

an excessive idea of his own importance. He flattered himself
that he was the statesman of the family, and felt a glow of
Republican virtue and enthusiasm that placed him above the
narrower views of Joseph and ambitions of Napoleon. He
showed deference to the former as the head of the family, but
was in a state of permanent revolt against Napoleon's efforts
to control him. What did this officer of gunners mean by
dictating to him? Napoleon had not been well received by
Paoli, who did not approve of his pamphlet, his ' Letter to M.
Buttafuoco' on the affairs of Corsica, and would not give
him some papers he wanted for that projected great work on
the history of the island. Napoleon thought Paoli was annoyed
at receiving huge rolls of manuscript from Lucien, denouncing
this or that local politician, and generally teaching the old
dictator his business. Lucien was plainly warned by Napoleon
that his literary efforts were damaging the family interests,
and that he had better be more prudent. He took his revenge
in an outspoken letter to Joseph. ' I say to you in the fullest
confidence,' he wrote, ' that I have always seen in Napolione
an ambition that is not indeed altogether selfish, but which
influences him more powerfully than any love for the public
welfare. I think that in a free state he is a dangerous man.
He seems to me greatly inclined to be a tyrant, and I think
that if he were a king he would be quite capable of playing
that part, and that his name would be an object of detestation
to posterity and to every thoughtful patriot. I can see (and
it is not since yesterday only I have seen it), that in the event
of a counter-revolution Napolione would try to keep on top,
and I think he is quite capable of turning his coat to protect
his own interests.' When in his vexation he wrote this strange
letter Lucien could not foresee that in a few years his brother
would be making himself the despot of France, with himself
as a prominent helper in effecting this counter-revolution.

There was a Jacobin Club at Ajaccio. Lucien was a member,
and thanks to his studies and his boundless self-confidence and
ready tongue, this young theorist of seventeen was soon its
leading orator. For Joseph with his leaning to the calmly
respectable, and for Napoleon with his dislike for wild talk, this
must have been a source of annoyance, especially as Lucien
showed as little circumspection in his speeches as in the writ-

ings with which he had bombarded Paoli. It was the time when the orator of a local Jacobin Club might hope to become one of the lights of the terrible central club in Paris, and no doubt Lucien felt he was on a path that would take him to the front faster than his squire-like eldest brother, or that overbearing lieutenant of artillery and colonel of National Guards, who was rather under a cloud, for his proceedings at Ajaccio did not please the great men in Paris, and he would have to go to France and explain or excuse them. His brothers had tried to get Lucien appointed by Paoli one of his secretaries, but Paoli knew too much of him already from his writings, and would not hear of it. Lucien was not disappointed. The secretaryship would have extinguished his oratory.

Napoleon went back to Paris in May 1792 and stayed there till November. It was an anxious time. Thanks to his prolonged absence from his regiment and his somewhat irregular proceedings at Ajaccio, he found himself temporarily removed from the active list of the army, and was in danger of further hostile notice being taken of his conduct. Then St. Cyr, like other old-fashioned royalist institutions, was to be abolished. If Marianna could have completed her course there, she would not only have a free education, but would receive a small dowry on leaving the school. Now he must send his sister back to Corsica. But great changes were coming. On August 10th he was a spectator of the rising and the fight between the Swiss Guard and the Marseillais. He said later on that with a little better leading the Swiss and the Royalists ought to have routed the armed mob of National Guards. Watching the course of events he saw that the Revolution was going to more than hold its own. So far he had been more Corsican than French. It was now he began to abandon his old ideas of Paolism and Corsican independence, and become more like the thoroughgoing Republican Lucien.

At the elections in September held in Corsica Joseph was a candidate for the National Convention, but was not returned. But he was elected one of the five judges for the district. Napoleon arrived just after the contest, bringing Marianna with him from Paris.

The soldier-brother busied himself with his duties as lieutenant-colonel of the local National Guard. It was soon to have its baptism of fire, for there was to be a raid on Sardinia. In December a French squadron arrived to co-operate in the enterprise. It brought with it Sémonville, Commissioner from the Government at Paris. Neither he nor Admiral Truguet, who commanded the squadron, could speak a word of anything but French, and Lucien attached himself to them as their interpreter with the Italian-speaking Corsicans. Sémonville was received by the club, and Lucien, its favourite orator, rolled out the Frenchman's high-flown speech in sonorous Corsican Italian.

The expedition to Sardinia was a failure. Napoleon just saved the guns attached to his infantry detachment. Paoli was reported to be trafficking with the English, and preparing to betray the Republic. Sémonville had left Ajaccio for Toulon after the return of the raiders. He took Lucien with him as his secretary, and the young man was at the same time given credentials from the club to the Jacobin Club at Toulon.

It was in March 1793 that Lucien arrived at Toulon. He began at once to figure as an orator of the Jacobin Club, and only a few days after his introduction to it startled his new audience with a philippic against Paoli. He denounced him as the betrayer of Corsica to the English, the fomenter of a fratricidal war. He ended by proposing that the club should send an address to the Convention at Paris calling for the outlawry of Paoli. The address drawn up by Lucien was adopted unanimously, and transmitted to Paris by one of the deputies of the Department, who was just starting for the capital. On April 3rd, far away on the northern frontier, General Dumouriez had answered the summons of the Convention to its bar by arresting the National Commissioners and riding across the border to join the Austrians. On the same day Escudier, Deputy of the Var, laid before the Convention Lucien's address from Toulon. Treason in north and south. The Convention decrees that Paoli must be summoned to its bar to answer for his treachery.

While the address was still on its way northwards, Lucien had written an exultant letter to Joseph. 'I have struck a decisive blow at our enemies. You didn't expect I could do so much,' he wrote proudly. It never occurred to him that he

AJACCIO FROM THE PRÈS D'ALATA

had for the moment ruined his brothers. For three out of every four Corsicans Paoli was the patriarch of their race. An attack on him would rouse them to frenzy, and a Corsican could express strong feeling better with a knife or a long-barrelled gun than with an address.

Corsica was already in revolt. Joseph was with the Republican Commissioners at Bastia, where there was a French garrison. Ajaccio was menaced by the approach of insurgent bands. Napoleon with great difficulty succeeded in escaping from the town and reached Bastia. He had promised to return if possible with a force that would hold his native town. If not, he would bring round a small ship in which his mother and her children would be conveyed to a place of safety.

At first Letizia thought she was safe at Ajaccio. But she was warned that the patriots would sack the home of the Bonapartes if they seized the town. The peasants round it were declaring for Paoli. She sent Jerome and her youngest daughter to be hidden in the house of her stepmother, Madame Fesch, and with Louis, Marianna, and Pauline she made her way through marsh and forest to the tower of Capitello on the coast, escorted by a few faithful dependants of her family, herdsmen and vinedressers, armed for the occasion. On the way she heard that the house in the town had been plundered, and could see the smoke of her burning farm in the outskirts of Ajaccio.[1] After an anxious wait at Capitello, Napoleon arrived with a flotilla of coasting craft, and the refugees were conveyed in safety first to Bastia, and then to the house of some old friends at Calvi. Napoleon, after an attempt to retake Ajaccio, joined them there. The young children were sent to their mother by Madame Fesch. Joseph arrived from Bastia. All the family except Lucien were gathered at Calvi.

But they had no resources, and in Corsica it looked as if Paoli, now supported by the English, would soon drive the French out, and then the position of the Bonapartes would be hopeless. It was decided to take refuge in France. There Napoleon, now again in favour with the Government, could rejoin his artillery regiment with the rank and pay of captain.

[1] The Casa Bonaparte, the house in Ajaccio, was not burned, but was sacked. Three years later Letizia obtained a compensation of 16,000 francs for the 'devastation' of her furnished house (decree of 6 Pluviose, An. VI.).

Some appointment would be found for Joseph to compensate him for what he had lost by fidelity to France and the Republic. So Letizia and her sons and daughters embarked for Toulon. There was some risk of being captured by a British cruiser, but on June 13th they arrived safely in France—safe, but almost penniless. They were welcomed by Lucien, whose oratorical effort had precipitated the crisis and the ruin of the family. But they had no word of reproach for him. They had the true spirit of adventure these Corsicans, women as well as men. They had lost the first turn of the game, but it might have been worse. They were all safe with their lives, and Republican gratitude would surely not forget their sacrifices.

CHAPTER II

THE RISE OF THE BONAPARTES

(1793-1795)

FOR the moment Lucien Bonaparte was the great man of the family. He had made history. The Jacobin Club, of which he was one of the lights, was all-powerful in Toulon. It could even defy the local authorities and terrorise them with the menace of a denunciation at Paris. In the harbour the crews of two warships were in revolt and threatening to hang their officers for lack of proper Republican zeal. On land a revolutionary tribunal had set up the guillotine. After a few days in the town Madame Bonaparte was glad enough to leave it. She found lodgings with Louis, Marianna, and her young children at the village of La Valette, on the slopes of the hills a few miles away to the north-eastward. Lucien stayed with them, but made frequent visits to his club. Napoleon went to rejoin his regiment at Nice. He drew 3000 francs of arrears of pay and could provide for the needs of the family at La Valette. General du Teil, whom he already knew, commanded at Nice. He made Captain Bonaparte one of his staff-officers, and set him to work erecting batteries on the coast, with the result that Napoleon was soon in official correspondence with the War Office.

Joseph had gone to Paris, where he put himself in communication with the Corsican representatives, the most important of whom was Salicetti, an old ally of the Bonapartes and a member of the dominant Jacobin party. These were the days of the Terror. The Moderate Girondins had gone down before the extremists of the Mountain, and were prisoners or fugitives. Each afternoon Joseph could see the victim-laden carts rumbling along the Rue St. Honoré to the Place de la Révolution.

In Paris Joseph met a number of other Corsicans, the delegates of victims of the counter-revolution, who were now living in poverty in a score of towns in the south of France. On July 11th the Corsican deputation appears before the Convention and presents its petition. Joseph is amongst the delegates, applauded by the galleries as martyrs of liberty, and presently invited by the President to share the honours of the session, to sit for a while side by side with the rulers of the Republic. On the motion of Jean Bon St. André, seconded by Collot d'Herbois (both reds of the deepest dye), the Convention votes an immediate grant of 600,000 francs. Letizia and her children in that village on the hillside near Toulon will have some little share of it. So Joseph's journey to Paris has been a success. But how will it all end? Two days after, late in the evening, Joseph hears how an hour ago Marat, the 'friend of the people,' has been stabbed by Charlotte Corday. Next day is a Sunday, and the glorious anniversary of the Bastille, but for all true Jacobins it is a day of mourning, not unmixed with alarm, for there is news of a revolt in south and west. On the Wednesday Charlotte, glorying in her deed, goes to the guillotine. Joseph will remember this stay in Paris. He is soon to leave it, unregretfully, for it is not a very safe place even for the friends of the Government. On the very day of Charlotte's execution the Convention, on the motion of Salicetti, declares Paoli a traitor and an outlaw. Salicetti is at the same time directed to proceed to the south and embark as Commissary of the Republic with 4000 men of the Army of Italy for Corsica, relieve the towns still holding out for France, and reduce the island to submission to the Republic.

Salicetti engaged Joseph to go with him as one of his colleagues. So he was again employed, and in receipt of a salary larger than any he had yet drawn. The party set off for Toulon by way of Lyons, but had not gone far when they heard that Lyons was up in arms against the Terrorist Republic. They turned off to the eastward, passing through districts where they had to trust to the escort of General Carteaux's troops to escape capture by roving bands of rebels. At last they reached Marseilles, whence they intended to go on to Toulon. But Toulon itself was in revolt. On July 12th, the day after

Joseph had sat in the Convention as one of the martyrs of Corsica, and heard St. André and Collot d'Herbois orating in support of the grant of 600,000 francs, the National Guard of Toulon had mustered to beat of drum, suppressed the clubs, turned out the Republican administration, installed a local government, declared its determination to resist oppression to the death, and secured the support of the warships in the harbour.   There could be no reconquest of Corsica now.   First Lyons and Toulon would have to be taken.   Toulon above all, for the English fleet was coming to help the rebels with British redcoats and allied Neapolitans.

To add to the troubles of the Bonapartes this revolt of the south, and the consequent adjournment of the Corsican campaign, made the ruling powers in Paris forget all about that generous vote of July 11th.   Not a penny was paid on account of it.   There had been just four weeks of rest at La Valette, with hopes that the family troubles would soon be over, and then came the revolt.   During these four weeks Lucien, who had lost his secretaryship through Citizen Sémonville sailing as ambassador to Constantinople, had addressed a long petition to the Government asking to be sent to the East as one of the new ambassador's secretaries.   Louis, less practical, and already showing signs of the literary dilettantism with which he amused himself in after life, had written to Bernardin de St. Pierre from La Valette.   He wanted to know from the author himself how much of the touching story of *Paul et Virginie* was true, how much purely imaginary.   He had read the book.   He was about to read it again.   He would like to be able to ' console his sympathetic sorrow by being able to say, " This is founded on fact, but this mere imagination ! " ' Louis was very young, but unfortunately he was not much wiser when he was much older.

Considering that Lucien had been one of the fiery spirits of the local Jacobin Club, La Valette was too near the port to be a safe place for him and his people, now that Toulon was in red revolt against the Jacobin Republic.   The Bonapartes were once more fugitives, this time to Marseilles. Joseph, thanks to his influence as the colleague of a Commissary of the Republic, was able to provide for them.   They were billeted on one of the wealthy families.   They were given

B

rations from the public stores, and a grant of 1200 francs a month. They were Corsican refugees, and the vote of the Convention justified the expenditure.

Napoleon was in Marseilles just then, and doubtless his influence supported Joseph in providing for the family. He had been travelling about collecting guns and stores from various places for his coast batteries, and had been with Carteaux when he routed the rebels near Avignon. In September he went off to join the besieging army before Toulon, and made his first great step onward and upward in the rise to fame and power. On the 4th of the month Salicetti had secured for Joseph an appointment as Assistant-Commissary of the Republic with the army in the south of France. It was a fairly well-paid post—6000 francs a year in pay, besides rations, lodging, a horse, forage, and office expenses.

During this residence at Marseilles Joseph Bonaparte had made the acquaintance of his future wife, Mademoiselle Marie Julie Clary, the daughter of a wealthy silk-merchant and ship-owner of the town. How the Bonapartes and the Clarys became friends it is impossible to say with any certainty. Several stories are told of their first introduction to each other, but none of them will bear the test of a critical examination. The most likely theory is that Joseph had become interested in Marie Julie through meeting her when she tried to obtain the intercession of Salicetti as a Commissary of the Republic in favour of some of her people, who were suspected of being compromised in the rising of the south. There was a Revolutionary Tribunal which had set up the guillotine at Marseilles. There was a permanent Court-Martial. The prisons were crowded with suspects. François Clary, Julie's father, was ill, and in fact dying. His brother-in-law, an officer of engineers, had joined the insurgents and escaped by sea. One of his sons committed suicide in terror of being brought before the merciless Tribunal. Another son was consul at Naples, and was suspected of having helped to secure the landing of the Neapolitan contingent at Toulon. The Clarys were in danger of being denounced and imprisoned, and then there would be executions and confiscation of their property. However the acquaintance began, Joseph Bonaparte took up their cause and secured their safety. He introduced them to his

family, and his mother became a fast friend of Julie. Mademoiselle Clary was twenty-two. She was short of stature and
very plain featured, but she had something better to recommend her than beauty of face or form. She was well educated,
intelligent, and, better still, a devoted daughter, kind-hearted
and unselfish, brave, and ready to do her utmost not only to
help her own people, but also many of the other victims of
this terrible time, when half the people of Marseilles had fled
and the rest saw their lives and fortunes at the mercy of a
group of vengeful Terrorists. Joseph had never been involved
in any way in the proceedings of the extremists. He now
appeared as a deliverer, and it is no wonder that Julie welcomed
the addresses of the handsome young Corsican, who could
claim noble birth, and who had official rank, and could influence
the men in power in favour of all those she loved. Madame
Bonaparte liked the girl well, and there was for the prudent
Letizia the further recommendation that her son's bride would
bring him wealth. Her inheritance would be perhaps some
150,000 francs, or £6000, a vast fortune for a poor Corsican
family. So it was settled that Joseph should marry Julie.

When Joseph had been named an Assistant-Commissary of
the Republic, a much more modest position had been found
for Lucien. It was a place in the commissariat service as
one of the storekeepers at the supply depôt formed at St.
Maximin, a little town some twenty-five miles north of Toulon.
The pay was only 1200 francs a year, say £4 a month, with
rations. It was hardly the reward our young orator expected,
after his hopes of a diplomatic post in the East. But he had
to be content with it.

On December 19, 1793, the Republican tricolour was again
flying over Toulon. The British fleet, with the redcoats hastily
re-embarked, was standing out to sea, and in the inner harbour
the revolted warships fired by Sidney Smith were burning,
and the quayside warehouses were in a blaze. And it was
Napoleon's plan of attack and Napoleon's guns that had won
the victory. Three months ago he was Captain Bonaparte.
He was now a Brigadier-General and the coming man.

After all, there is to be an expedition to Corsica. Joseph,
the great man's brother, is directed to take up his residence
at Toulon. Most of the ships have been saved and are being

repaired. Not so the warehouses, and Joseph's task as commissary is to get together supplies for the fleet and the expedition. Happily he has nothing to do with those other commissaries who have set up the guillotine, packed the prisons with rebels and suspects, and are daily sending them out to be shot in batches or beheaded. Toulon is a horrible place for some weeks after our Corsican's great victory, for it is the Terror that has conquered.

Happily Madame Bonaparte and her children had not come there with Joseph. But before following their fortunes further let us see what Lucien was doing. His brother's success had brought him no promotion. He was living as best he could on his pound a week plus rations at St. Maximin. But checking deliveries of stores and signing vouchers was not sufficient employment for a young man of his aspirations. There was, of course, a club at St. Maximin, and Lucien renewed his oratorical successes of Ajaccio and Toulon. His Christian name was not good enough for him. He took the fine old pagan Republican name of Brutus. He pointed out to the club, too, that the name of the town was quite out of date. Why should a thoroughly Republican place be called after a saint? He moved that it should be renamed Marathon. The ruling powers approved, and he was Citizen Brutus Bonaparte, public storekeeper of Marathon and president of the local club. Popular election made him also president of the local revolutionary committee. He was now a terribly powerful man in his little town of Marathon. He had talked of his brother playing the tyrant, but he showed that such inclinations were no monopoly of one member of the family. Twenty of the most respectable people of the town and district were imprisoned as suspects by his orders. Happily he went no further. Later on he had the good grace to be somewhat ashamed of his proceedings. 'Fellows,' he said, 'in whose company I would have blushed to be seen, thieves and ex-convicts, had become my comrades.'

He lodged in one of the inns of the place. The innkeeper's sister, Catherine Boyer, a country girl who could neither read nor write, waited on him, and in the intervals of his official and patriotic labours the young storekeeper made love to her. They were married soon after his brother's victory at Toulon, to the utter disgust of Joseph and Napoleon when they heard the news. It was, of course, a civil marriage. The record tells how on the 15th Floréal of the Year II. of the Republic (May 4, 1794), in the presence of Jean-Baptiste Garnier, member of the Council-General of the Commune of Marathon (formerly St. Maximin), Brutus Bonaparte married Catherine Boyer, daughter of the late Pierre Boyer and of his wife, Rosalie Fabre. The bride's age was twenty-one, the bridegroom's nineteen.

Napoleon, now General Bonaparte, had come to Marseilles after the siege of Toulon, and established his headquarters there. Joseph paid frequent visits to the place. It was decided that Louis was to be a soldier; the General would be able to secure him rapid promotion. At Napoleon's suggestion he was provided with a passport, and started off from Marseilles to join the Artillery School of Instruction at Châlons. But he got no further than Lyons. Hearing there a report that the school had been broken up, he returned to Marseilles. In the first week of January 1794 Napoleon was appointed to command the artillery of the Army of Italy and the coast defences of the French Riviera, and transferred his headquarters to Nice. He attached Louis to his staff with the rank of sub-lieutenant. There was no march into Italy that year, but in the early spring the French drove the Piedmontese from the passes of the Little St. Bernard and Mont Cenis. In the hill fighting at Oneglia General Bonaparte commanded the artillery, and Louis was with him, and was under fire for the first time. Then, that he might learn something of practical gunnery, his brother attached him to a company of coast artillery at the battery of St. Tropez, or, as the place was then called, Heraclea, for saints' names were out of fashion.

Napoleon had his headquarters at Antibes, and he brought his mother with his sisters and Jerome to a small country-house on the coast in the outskirts of the town. For all the growing prosperity of the family, Madame Bonaparte kept to her homely ways, and long afterwards old people at Antibes used to tell how they had seen the General's mother helping to do the household washing in the brook that ran down from the hills near the house.

It was during her stay here that she heard of the marriage

of Lucien and Catherine Boyer. The whole family were
indignant, not the least Letizia, for even by the law of the
country Lucien should have asked her consent. For some
time to come the Bonapartes would have nothing to do with
Lucien. He had chosen his own course and must take the
consequences. The young husband had an anxious time.
The depôt of stores at St. Maximin was broken up, and his
employment came to an end. He was threatened with a denunciation to the authorities, for he was of age for military service,
and had not presented himself for the conscription. With
all his zeal for the Republic he had no wish to fight for it.
So he left St. Maximin, and succeeded in getting employment
at a small wage at St. Chaumans, near Cette. His employer
was an army contractor, and his duty was to inspect and
generally supervise the horses and carts he used in delivering
supplies for the Army of Italy, in which Lucien's brother was
a general. He had left his wife for a while in the inn at St.
Maximin, and the temporary parting was a serious grief to
him, for he was happy in his ill-assorted marriage. Catherine,
though she could not write her name, was a devoted, loving
wife.

Joseph, after being busy for months in the collection of
stores for the Corsican expedition, embarked at Toulon in
the first week of June, as one of Salicetti's civil staff. The
squadron, which was crowded with troops, was made up of
seven vessels under Admiral Martin. Joseph went on board
of the flagship, the *Sans-Culotte*. The fleet was only a week
at sea. Off the north of Corsica Admiral Martin cut off and
captured an English frigate and an armed brig. But this was
his only success. Before he could close with the land the
British Mediterranean fleet (sixteen ships of the line and
frigates) hove in sight, and the French squadron had to avoid
a fight that could only end in disaster. Chased by the British,
Admiral Martin succeeded in reaching the Gulf Jouan, the
deep bay west of Antibes, where he anchored under the
batteries, and Napoleon hurried up more guns to protect him.
The enemy, reinforced by a Spanish fleet, lay off the Gulf,
blockading the French, but did not attack. Joseph's Corsican
expedition had failed, and he landed and joined the family
at Antibes. A few weeks later he was married to Julie Clary.

Her father had died in January; perhaps this was why the marriage had been delayed. The civil ceremony took place at Cuges, near Marseilles, on the 14th of Thermidor, in the Year II. of the Republic (August 1, 1794), before the Mayor of the Commune. Madame Clary was present. By Julie's desire and in strict secrecy the religious ceremony followed. The priest who officiated was the Abbé Reimonet, who, like so many of his brethren, had risked his life by refusing to accept the civil constitution of the clergy, and who was therefore an outlaw. On account of the difficulty of obtaining the ministration of a priest in these times in France, even for Catholics the civil ceremony was allowed by the Church to be a valid contract of marriage. Joseph must have been very devoted to his wife to run the risk of the religious marriage being talked of, for to accept the ministrations of a priest who had not taken the oath was an offence against the Republic which might easily lead not only to the loss of his appointments, but also to his arrest and condemnation to death.

On the morrow of Joseph's marriage the south of France heard the tidings of the events of the 10th Thermidor and the fall of Robespierre. It was serious news for Napoleon, for he had been in close relations with Robespierre's brother and others of the extremists. He had been lately in correspondence with the party in Paris, and now that every friend of the Robespierres was suspected, he was in danger of a capital charge being trumped up against him. He was put under arrest, and his papers were seized and subjected to a rigid examination. A week later the Commissioners charged with the examination signed a report which exonerated him. Nothing that could compromise him had been discovered, and he could be relied on to do good service to the Republic. He was directed to organise another expedition to Corsica. At his suggestion Joseph was given a post at Toulon, where he was made director of the military and naval hospitals. He went there in September with his wife and her sister, Desirée Clary.

The expedition was not ready until the end of the winter, and then it came to nothing. The troops were more than once embarked on the transports, but Admiral Martin, who commanded the Toulon fleet and was to convoy the expedition, would report that the English fleet barred the way, and they would disembark again. At last, in March 1795, Martin went out with more than twenty sail to clear the way, and was so roughly handled by the Anglo-Neapolitan fleet of seventeen ships off Cape Noli, that he was glad to get back to Toulon. Once more all idea of a Corsican expedition had to be abandoned.

In May the new Government at Paris made a redistribution of commands, and Napoleon, to his great disappointment, was directed to give up his post as General of Artillery with the Army of Italy, and proceed to the west of France, there to take command of an infantry brigade acting against the insurgents of La Vendée. At the same time Joseph's post as Commissioner at Toulon was suppressed. This did not matter much to Joseph, who had his wife's fortune, but Napoleon felt that he would be wasting his time hunting down and shooting rebels in the west instead of commanding the artillery of an army in important operations. He set off for Paris, taking Louis with him, and continuing his lessons from day to day. He travelled slowly, made long halts on the way, and intended to do his best to avoid taking up this obscure infantry command. When at last he reached Paris he wrote to his brother Joseph that he was ill and was asking for a long leave of absence. It was really a diplomatic illness, contracted only to gain more time. He sent Louis to continue his studies at the Artillery School of Instruction at Châlons. Some of his biographers represent him as having had to live in extreme poverty during this stay in Paris, but it is certain that he drew over £100 of pay and travelling expenses as soon as he arrived.

His letters written during this summer of 1795 show how keenly interested he was in all that concerned his mother and his brothers and sisters. Writing to Joseph, after speaking of his disappointment at the uncertainty of his own position, he adds, ' You know I live only for the pleasure I can give to those who belong to me.' He wrote still in praise of Louis. The young man had delighted every one he met in Paris. He was doing well at Châlons. He was a *bon sujet* ; he had health, talents, wit, energy, tact, everything one could wish to see in him. Something must be done, too, for that unfortunate Lucien. He was half starving in his billet with the army

JULIE, QUEEN OF NAPLES, AND AFTERWARDS OF SPAIN, AND HER
DAUGHTER, AFTERWARDS PRINCESS OF CANINO

contractor, and his first child had been born.   He had been a
fool, but Napoleon would try to get some better paid employment for him.   Suddenly there came news that Lucien had been
arrested.   The municipality of St. Maximin, now no longer
Jacobin, had lodged an accusation against him on the ground
of his proceedings in the days when he was Brutus Bonaparte
of Marathon, and when as president of the local revolutionary
committee he was working with thieves and ex-galley slaves,
and sending respectable citizens to prison.   Joseph, Napoleon,
and their mother all exerted themselves on behalf of the black
sheep of the family.   His mother sent him 500 francs.   On
July 12th Napoleon was able to report to Joseph that, thanks
to his efforts, a courier was leaving Paris with an order for
Lucien's release, signed by the Committee of Public Safety,
also various testimonials in favour of his patriotic character.
Then he sent Lucien money and brought him to Paris, promising that he would find him some appointment.   He thought
also of bringing his younger brother to Paris.   Little Jerome
was now eleven years old.   Some arrangement might be made
for his education, if he was sent north.   On these and other
matters he wrote many letters to Joseph, assuring him that
he felt for him the same warm affection that he had cherished
since their boyhood at Ajaccio.   He seemed to take a delight
in insisting on his devotion to his elder brother.

Joseph was at Genoa.   He had gone to Marseilles for a
short time after handing over his official business at Toulon,
and had then gone to stay at Genoa, to arrange some private
affairs connected with the fortune of his wife and family, for
Monsieur Clary had had business relations with Genoese firms
and there were debts to collect.   From Genoa he also corresponded with Corsica, mainly with a view to recovering the
property of the Bonapartes there, but also in connection with
local politics.   There was some correspondence with Napoleon
on the chances of restoring the island to France.   This gave
the General an opportunity for putting before the Government
a statement of his eldest brother s services to the Republic,
and suggesting that he should be given a consulate in some
important maritime city of Italy.

From Marseilles, before he went on to Genoa, Joseph had
written to his brother telling him he had some idea of going

to Constantinople. With the capital he could now command
there would be an opening for good business there. The
project was vague, and Napoleon wrote a letter strongly dis-
suading him from it. In August Joseph was surprised by
receiving a letter from his brother full of a new and much more
definite plan for pushing the family fortunes in the East.
The Sultan had asked the French Government to give him
the services of a general of artillery and a military mission to
assist him in reorganising and training the Ottoman army
on modern lines. He hoped to obtain the appointment.
There would be a splendid salary attached to it. He would
get Joseph the post of consul at Constantinople. In a month
he would be in Genoa. They would go on to Leghorn together,
and there embark for the East. The decree giving Napoleon
the appointment was actually signed. Meanwhile he was
giving the War Office plans for the operations of the Army of
Italy.

But then came the sudden change in his fortunes. The
forces of the reaction in Paris were preparing for the October
rising of the National Guard against the Government. They
were going to try to sweep away the lately established Directory, and replace it by what ? Perhaps a Royalist restoration.
Barras, the Director, was named Commander-in-chief of the
Army of the Interior, the force that was to protect the
Government. But Barras was no soldier. He wanted a
second-in-command to do his work for him. He chose the
Corsican artillery general, and on the famous 13th of Vendémiaire (October 5, 1795) General Bonaparte's guns scattered the
insurgent National Guards in the street fight round the
Tuileries and the Church of St. Roch. At two in the morning,
before taking a well-earned rest, he wrote a hurried letter to
Joseph telling him of his victory. ' As usual,' he said, ' I
have not been hit.' Before the end of October he had been
twice promoted by the Government he had saved, first to the
rank of General of Division, then to that of full General (at
the age of twenty-six) and Commander-in-chief of the Army
of the Interior.

He had now money in abundance. There was not only his
pay : he had such large sums at his disposal that it would
seem that the Directors had substantially rewarded his ser-

vices. He sent remittance after remittance to Joseph to be forwarded to his mother, so that she and the family might, to use his own expression, ' want for nothing, and be abundantly provided for.' In November he noted in one of these letters that up to date he had sent some fifty or sixty thousand francs.

Louis was also provided for. His course of studies at Châlons had not been a long one. Immediately after the victory in the streets of Paris, General Bonaparte obtained for him a commission as lieutenant in the 4th Artillery. But he was not to spend his time in drills and parades in a garrison town, as his elder brother had done for years. He would soon see active service. Meanwhile he was summoned to Paris, and in November was attached to his brother's staff. He was his military secretary, continuing his professional education under the greatest master of war the world had seen for centuries. When General Bonaparte rode out to inspect his troops of the Army of Paris, Lieutenant Bonaparte rode beside him as his aide-de-camp, and the young General felt a delight in the idea that he would make a famous soldier of his brother. If Louis had been all that Napoleon imagined he was, what a beginning of a great career was in his hands !

Little Jerome was also brought up to Paris from the south before the end of 1795, and sent to school at Napoleon's expense. He was eleven years old. Lucien too was not forgotten. Citizen Fréron was being sent to· the south with a roving commission to deal with reactionists and malcontents, and generally ensure that there should be no opposition to the new Government. Napoleon induced Fréron to take Lucien with him as his secretary. In the course of the journey Lucien was able to pose as a great man at Aix, where he had lately been in prison, and in the towns of the Alpine border, where he had been for months a badly paid servant of an army contractor. When Fréron's mission ended, Napoleon found another post for Lucien, this time Commissary with the Army of the North in the Netherlands. Lucien waited a long time in Paris before going north. He felt such a delight in sitting in the gallery of the Assembly listening to the debates for hours, that he could hardly tear himself away from Paris. With the army he neglected his duties. Looking after supplies and transport and keeping accounts was dull work for a man of Lucien's conscious political genius. He scamped the work to find time for reading newspapers and pamphlets, writing essays, and indulging in endless discussion with any one he could get to listen to him. Napoleon had to exert his influence to save him from dismissal.

So all the brothers were provided for by the end of this fortunate year 1795. Their mother had all she could wish for, and need no longer do housework or trouble herself with petty economies. But she was of a frugal mind, could not believe this good fortune would last, and had begun to save up against possible evil days. Joseph was established at Genoa, with his wife and her sister, doing some business while waiting for the consulate, but rich enough to take things very easily. Napoleon was General in command of the Army of Paris, and adviser of the War Office as to the conduct of the campaigns in the Netherlands, on the Rhine, in the Alps. He could have a high command at the front as soon as he asked for it. Louis was Lieutenant of Artillery and the General's staff-officer. Lucien was more or less occupied with his duties in the supply department of the Army of the North, and well paid for doing very little. Jerome was a schoolboy, often visited by his soldier brothers, well supplied with pocket-money, and making satisfactory progress in Latin, mathematics, drawing, and music. The old days of Corsica must have seemed very far off. The dreams of independence for the island, of little posts under the Corsican Government, once the summit of a Bonaparte's ambition, had dwindled into insignificance. The brothers were all Frenchmen now, loyal subjects of the great Republic that was holding its own so well against coalesced Europe, and under the lately established Directory seemed to have reached the port of secure and stable government through many wild storms of revolt. Stranger things were coming for all these young Corsicans in the next ten years. The General would be the Imperial Dictator of Europe. That quiet, grave-looking, young business man, who amused himself with speculations in shipping at Genoa, and hoped for a consulate, would be a King. There would be other royal crowns for the Lieutenant and the school-boy, and even scapegrace, idle Lucien would be a Prince.

CHAPTER III

FORTUNE AT LAST

(1796-1797)

IN March 1796 Joseph Bonaparte received a letter from Napoleon that brought him surprising and disappointing news. It put an end to a dream that Joseph had long cherished. He had hoped that his soldier brother would marry his sister-in-law, Desirée Clary. Now came the news that, without having given a hint of what was coming to his favourite brother, the head of the family, without asking the consent of his mother, the General had married one of the great ladies of the Parisian salons, a star of that new and strangely mixed society to which his rapidly acquired rank had introduced him. The General's wife was Josephine Beauharnais, a West Indian lady, who had married as her first husband the Vicomte de Beauharnais. During the Terror husband and wife had been in prison, and the Vicomte had died on the scaffold of the Place de la Révolution. Josephine would have had the same end if the fall of Robespierre had come a few days later. Freed from prison, she had been content to take a place in the society of Republican Paris in the days of that strange outburst of extravagance and dissipation that followed the Terror. Paris talked freely of her adventures, and whispered that she had been more than the friend of Barras the Director. She had some money, and more influence, and could be very useful to the General, but it was not a mercenary match. Josephine and Napoleon really loved each other. She was much older than her husband. There were two children of the first marriage, Hortense, a beautiful girl, and Eugène Beauharnais, who was the schoolfellow of Jerome Bonaparte, and three years his senior.

Napoleon had married Josephine on the eve of his departure

for the Army of Italy, which he was about to lead in his first brilliant campaign. On the way to the front he stopped at Marseilles to make his peace with his mother, and obtain from her a friendly letter of congratulation for his wife.

In the beginning of April Napoleon's four divisions—a little army of 32,000 ragged, ill-shod men—was concentrated at various points along the western Riviera from Voltri, close to Genoa, to Albenga, where the General had his headquarters. The Austrian and Piedmontese outposts held the passes looking down upon the lower coast country. Genoa, on the very edge of the region of disturbance, was still allowed to stand neutral. Joseph's first child, a daughter, who was named Julie-Josephine after her mother and father, had just been born. On April 7th Joseph reached Albenga after passing along the coast road, and seeing on his way the camps of his brother's army. It was a long time since the brothers had met. ' My brother is here,' wrote Napoleon to Josephine from Albenga. ' He has heard of our marriage with pleasure. He ardently desires to make your acquaintance, and I am trying to persuade him to go on to Paris. His wife has just given him a little daughter. They send you a present of Genoese bonbons.' Joseph added a letter of congratulation, somewhat stiff and formal, for he was reconciling himself to a disappointment.

Three of the Bonapartes were together at Albenga, Joseph, the General, and Lieutenant Louis Bonaparte serving on his brother's staff, and doing his duty in a way that fully satisfied his chief, who spared him as little as any other of his officers when there was work to be done or risks to be taken. Joseph was easily persuaded to remain at headquarters for the first stage of the campaign, and saw as his brother's guest that marvellous campaign of April 1796, the fortnight of victory, in which, outnumbered by the allies, Napoleon misled the Austrians, stormed the passes of the Genoese Apennines, separated the Piedmontese from the Austrian army, drove them northward, and with Turin at his mercy dictated a separate peace to the King of Sardinia.

On the morrow of his triumph Napoleon sent his despatches to Paris. Junot was the bearer of a military report on the campaign addressed to the Minister of War, and in the ordinary course would have conveyed all the General's letters. But Napoleon sent Joseph with him, and Joseph was entrusted with a mission that at once made him a person of importance, almost an ambassador. Napoleon had fully discussed with him his policy, shown him why he had granted an armistice to the Piedmontese, and on what lines a peace could be concluded that would put the passes and fortresses of the Piedmontese Alps in the possession of France, and give a new and better line of communication for the army in his coming operations against the Austrians in Lombardy. This was all set out briefly in the despatch to the Directory with which Joseph was entrusted, and in his credentials Napoleon explained that his brother fully understood his views, and would give the Government what further explanations and information might be required. Joseph had two other letters. One was addressed to Josephine. Napoleon wrote in it of his lifelong affection for his eldest brother. ' I hope,' he added, ' that he will win your friendship. He deserves it. Nature has given him a heart that makes him always gentle and kind. He is full of good qualities. I have written to Barras to have him appointed consul in one of the ports of Italy. For he wants to live quietly with his little wife, far away from the great whirlpool of public affairs.'

This was the modest request contained in the other letter, addressed to Barras. But Joseph's mission gave him an experience of the possibilities opened to him by acting in public affairs as his brother's right-hand man when matters of high policy were to be arranged. His ambition was enlarged. Instead of a consulate he began to think of an ambassadorship, not of course immediately, but as soon as he had obtained some diplomatic experience. He wrote from Paris to his brother telling him that during his interviews with Charles Delacroix, the Minister of Foreign Affairs, the latter had offered to appoint him French representative at Turin as soon as the peace with the King of Sardinia was signed. Joseph prudently told the Minister that although he was anxious to enter upon a diplomatic career in the service of the Republic, he would rather not have so high a post to begin with.

Napoleon had asked him to escort Josephine to Italy when he returned from Paris, but he found the lady not very keen

about leaving the gay society of Paris for her husband's headquarters in the field.   It was not till the middle of June that
he persuaded her to start with him for Italy.   Meanwhile he
had found time to make useful friends in Paris, to lay the
foundation for a diplomatic appointment, and to buy some
landed property near the capital, that was being sold as a
bargain.   He thought that he and Julie might make their home
there later, after he had some years of life as an ambassador
to his credit, and a larger fortune at his disposal.   On June
24th he left Paris for Italy.   He travelled in state with quite
a caravan of post-chaises.   He had a valet to look after his
luggage, increased by a huge load of boxes belonging to his
sister-in-law.   Josephine had her maid and three other servants.   Then there was Joseph's brother-in-law, Nicholas
Clary, and two officers, one of them Colonel Junot, soon to
be one of his brother's marshals, now his staff-officer.   They
travelled through Savoy and over the Mont Cenis into Piedmont,
Joseph amusing himself with writing the first pages of a book
that he published two years later.   All the Bonapartes had
this ambition for literary distinction, and their books would
make a small library.   On July 9th the party at length reached
the General's headquarters at Milan.

Since Joseph left Italy with the despatches for Paris his
brother had won new victories.   He had forced the passage
of the Po at Piacenza, beaten the Austrians at Fombio, stormed
the bridge of Lodi, captured Pizzighettone, and occupied Milan.
Then he had overrun Lombardy and blockaded Mantua.   Louis
had borne himself bravely in the campaign.   He had been
with Lannes in the vanguard in the advance by Piacenza on
Fombio, and he had been among the stormers at Pizzighettone.
The General was thoroughly pleased with him.   Lucien had
for a moment made his appearance at headquarters during the
advance on Milan.   He had thrown up his post with the Army
of the North, spent some time in Paris, and then hurried on
to Italy to ask the General to give him an appointment more
to his liking.   Napoleon was furious.   Lucien had acted without orders, without consulting any one.   He was sent away
from headquarters the very day of his arrival.   But Napoleon
relented so far as to use his influence to get him appointed as
Commissary at Marseilles, a post in which he could find enough

perquisites and 'expenses' to add considerably to his salary. In a few weeks the General heard to his disgust that his erratic, self-willed brother had gone off to Paris without asking for leave of absence. He wrote from his headquarters in Italy to the Minister of War, Carnot : ' One of my brothers, a commissary of the War Department at Marseilles, has gone to Paris without permission. This young man has a· certain amount of talent, but at the same time a very ill-balanced mind. All his life he has had a mania for plunging into politics. At this moment, when it seems to me that a great many people are anxious to damage me, and a whole intrigue has been set on foot to give colour to reports that are as stupid as they are wickedly calumnious, I ask you to be so good as to do me the essential service of ordering him to rejoin the army within twenty-four hours. I would like it to be the Army of the North.'

Napoleon was in an angry mood when he wrote thus. His anger did not arise solely from his disgust at Lucien's repeated acts of indiscipline. He had found that he had gone to Paris to join his sister Pauline there, and to concert measures with her for bringing about a marriage between her and his old employer, Fréron. Fréron was a dissipated roué, and was under a cloud on account of his proceedings during the Terror. Napoleon, his mother, all the family regarded his proposal of marriage as an outrage and a folly. But Pauline, a girl of sixteen, with more beauty than brains, was writing warm love-letters to her scoundrelly suitor. No wonder Napoleon was angry. Carnot sent off Lucien to the commissariat department of the Army of the Rhine.

At the end of July the armies of Würmser and Quosnadovitch came pouring down by the shores of Garda to the relief of Mantua. At the crisis of the campaign Napoleon thought it would be well to send one of his staff to Paris to explain the situation and his own plans to the Government. He chose Louis for this mission. The lieutenant had already proved his courage in action, and he could afford to miss some of the fighting. In a letter to Carnot Napoleon spoke highly of his brother. ' This brave young man,' he said, ' deserves all the consideration that you may be so good as to show him.' Louis acquitted himself well of his task, and the War Minister promoted him to the rank of captain and made him a present of a splendid pair of pistols.

He returned to Italy in October and was beside his brother in the battles of November 1796, when Napoleon foiled the efforts of Alvinzi and Davidovitch to raise the siege of Mantua and save the army of Würmser. At Arcola, during the three days' battle, Captain Bonaparte had more than one occasion of distinguishing himself. Once his brother had an order to send to a detachment holding a position that could only be reached by a road exposed at short range to the Austrian fire. Louis was the only staff-officer beside him at the moment. He gave him the order. Louis galloped through a storm of balls and, without dismounting, explained to the officer in command what was required. Men were falling around them. And then there was another dangerous ride back. ' I thought you were killed,' said Napoleon as his brother rejoined him. In the famous rush for the bridge Louis was beside his brother and saved his life. As Napoleon, carrying the tricolour standard himself, rushed along the causeway leading to the bridge, the fire of the Austrian sharpshooters lining the further bank struck down several of the officers near him. One of them in falling knocked him down. He rolled down the slope into a deep ditch, where he would have drowned had not Marmont and Louis rescued him and borne him back to safety through a pelting storm of fire.

In October Napoleon was able to send his brother Joseph on a visit to Corsica. Leghorn had been occupied by a detachment from the Army of Italy. A brigade of Corsicans had been formed by selecting the men from many regiments, and under Generals Gentili and Casabianca it had successfully landed in the island, and a counter-revolution was making rapid progress. Bastia and Ajaccio were both held for the Republic, and Joseph, after a voyage from Leghorn to Bastia, was able to revisit his birthplace. He had hardly sailed from Leghorn when the Foreign Ministry of the Directory sent to Milan his official appointment as Resident representing the Republic at Parma, with 18,000 francs a year as his salary. It was the entrance into diplomacy that he had asked for in Paris. But he was too much occupied with his mission to Corsica to attend to the appointment.

How things had changed since the flight of the Bonapartes from Ajaccio only three 'years ago ! The French Republican party was ruling the island, backed by the brigade from Leghorn. Citizen Miot, the Commissioner representing the Paris Government, accepted Joseph as a colleague, and adopted every suggestion he made. He was the General's brother. That was enough. So Joseph filled the local administration with old and new friends, and took a prominent part in the reorganisation of the island government, at the same time recovering the Bonaparte property and adding something to it by purchase. He took possession of the whole of the old house in the Rue Bonaparte (as it was then called), and refurnished it, giving the Pianelli family, who now owned the upper story, a house in the Rue du Centre in exchange. He had more profitable work to do than going to Parma, and work that pleased him better. He had wealth, power, the sense of success. It was something to be able to return to the old home at Ajaccio, and live there for a while as the virtual ruler of Corsica. He stayed over the end of the year, but he needed a wider field of action than the island, and made his ascendency at Ajaccio the stepping-stone to further honours. Once before he had failed to obtain election to the National Assembly. In the early spring of 1797 there were elections to fill the gaps made in the Five Hundred, the lower house of the Parliament of the Directory, gaps mostly resulting from the *coup d'état* of the 18th Fructidòr (Sept. 4, 1796). Joseph announced his candidature. There could be no opposition to him. He ·was unanimously elected as one of the representatives of Corsica, and before going to Paris went once more to the headquarters of his brother the General.

Napoleon had reduced Mantua and had then directed the victorious advance through the Styrian Alps, the blow at the heart of Austria, menacing Vienna, that brought the war to a triumphant end. The terms of the peace were being discussed, and he had his headquarters at the castle of Mombello, near Milan, where he was holding a kind of court, surrounded by his relatives, his generals, and staff-officers, French and Austrian diplomatists, delegates from the cities of Italy. Napoleon's mother and .wife were there, Josephine making a graceful and tactful hostess, and already taking something of the airs of a queen. Captain Louis Bonaparte was among the staff-officers, but changed since Joseph saw him last. He was anxious and depressed. He had just recovered from a dangerous and severe illness, partly the result of his dissipations in the intervals of the campaign. He had been too ill to follow the General in his march into the Styrian Alps. He was often absent from the brilliant circle at Mombello, and spent much of his time in lonely walks, or in reading, and attempts at literary composition. The brilliant promise of his first campaigns was under a cloud. Little Jerome was there, and with him Eugène Beauharnais, the two school-fellows rejoicing in a holiday from their Paris college, and a first sight of the great world. There too were Joseph's sisters, Marianna, who now used her other name of Elisa, lately married to a Corsican officer, Major Bacciochi, a bad match, and disappointing to the family, now that there were such splendid prospects opening before it. Pauline was waiting for her affianced husband, General Leclerc, a good friend of Napoleon, to come from Paris, and then the marriage would be celebrated in high state at Mombello.

Only one of the family was absent—self-willed, headstrong, unmanageable Lucien. When in August 1796 Carnot, at Napoleon's request, had packed Lucien off to the Army of the Rhine, his adventures had not ended. He liked his humdrum commissary's work there no better than the same employment with the Army of the North. He wrote to Barras and to Carnot complaining that he was a victim of persecution. In October he begged the War Minister to let him leave the Rhine and find him employment at Marseilles. Carnot sent the letter on to Napoleon's headquarters in Italy, and the General made an outspoken reply. Under date of October 25th he wrote to Carnot :—

‘ I have received your letter of the 17th Vendémiaire, Year v. (October 8, 1796). You must have seen by merely reading his letter how hare-brained this young man is. He got himself into trouble many times in ’93 notwithstanding the good advice that I never ceased again and again to give him. He wanted to play the Jacobin, so that it was lucky for him he was only eighteen, and his youth could serve as his excuse ; otherwise he would have found himself compromised in common with that handful of men who were the disgrace of their country. To let him go to Marseilles would be dangerous, not only for himself, but also for the public interests. He would be sure to fall into the hands of intriguers, and besides his former connections in the neighbourhood are very bad. But Corsica being now free, you will greatly oblige me by ordering him to go there, if his disposition will not allow him to settle down with the Army of the Rhine. In Corsica he could be of service to the Republic.'

So Carnot sent Lucien the unwelcome order to proceed to Corsica. There was no promotion for him. He was to continue the same modest employment in the island, and draw the same small salary. It was banishment, temporary extinction. He hastened to Marseilles, but there his haste came to an end, and he delayed his voyage as long as he safely could. He wrote to old political friends, among others to Fréron, to tell them he 'was going back to his mountains,' but would keep in correspondence with them, and might yet be able to serve them. It was not till the middle of March 1797 that he at last went to Corsica and found that he was to be posted at Ajaccio. He was there at the time of Joseph's election, but his eldest brother shared Napoleon's view that Lucien was an ambitious blunderer, who must be kept in his place. When Joseph went away to northern Italy, Lucien found himself rather lonely at Ajaccio, with a dull office routine to look after, or get others to handle for him. Joseph had left an agent to supervise the family property. Lucien was a guest or a caretaker in the old house. Joseph had hardly departed when Lucien, feeling utterly bored, temporarily deserted his post, and took a voyage on a frigate, the *Platon*. The ship anchored near Hyères. The municipality and the officers of the local garrison were getting up a fête and a banquet to celebrate the triumphs of the Army of Italy. They sent a deputation on board the ship with a formal invitation to Lucien to be the honoured guest of the evening. It was a flattering invitation. Lucien was hailed as a ' young warrior,' though his brief campaigns had been inglorious, for he had been only a civilian among the baggage waggons, or seated at a desk. He was asked to act as the representative of his brother, the conquering general. In other circumstances he would have

revelled in the opportunity of delivering a high-flown oration!
But there would be a dangerous storm if Napoleon learned
that he had not only left his business at Ajaccio to take care
of itself, but also posed at Hyères as a representative of the
Army of Italy. Lucien declined the proffered honour in a
stately letter.

'In a republic,' he wrote, 'glory is purely personal. She
covers with her laurels the defender of the fatherland, without
extending such fame to the members of his family. If I
accepted the honour you offer to me, I should be violating this
sacred principle, the very basis of democracy. I should also
be acting in opposition to the positive wishes of my brother,
who recognises no festal laurels unless they are gathered on
the battlefield. Accept then my thanks in my own name, and
that of my brother, and include among your toasts our invariable
toast, "Honour to the generous sons of liberty, *Vive la
République* ! " ' Then he went back to his exile at Ajaccio,
and tried to busy himself with dockets and accounts, while
his brothers were holding high revel at Mombello. He was
soon joined by his eldest sister. Napoleon thought that her
husband, Bacciochi, did not make a very brilliant figure at
his improvised court, and got rid of him by promoting him to
the rank of Colonel and sending him to take command of the
citadel of Ajaccio. With them came the mother of the Bonapartes. Letizia did not feel at home amid the glories of
Mombello. She was anxious to revisit the old house in Ajaccio,
and see what Joseph had done to restore and refurnish it.
She was welcomed home by Lucien in June 1797.

Lucien's wife, Catherine, soon won her heart. Letizia
herself was homely enough, and she liked this simple country
girl, who was devoted to her husband, and who had had since
her marriage to live on narrow means, while the rest of the
family were famous and wealthy. Then there was Catherine's
daughter, a little grandchild for Letizia. And Lucien's wife
was expecting another child. They all hoped it would be a
son. It was decided that an attempt should be made to make
peace between Napoleon and Lucien, and Catherine, who had
now learned to write, ventured on a letter to the General.¹ It
was a touching letter, and one wonders who composed it. She
asked Napoleon to allow her to call him brother. 'My first

child,' she said, ' was born at a time when you were irritated
against us. How I wish that the little one could caress you
in order to make you some compensation for all the trouble
my marriage has caused you.' Then she went on to say that
in another month she hoped a son would be born to her. She
would make him a soldier. She wished he would allow her
to give the child his name, and that he would be its godfather.
Would he send a procuration to Bacciochi or any one else
to represent him ? ' Mamma ' would be godmother (this
to let Napoleon know his mother had made peace already
with Lucien and his wife). ' Do not despise us because we are
poor,' she added, ' for, after all, you are our brother,' and
then she ended by assuring him of the affection she and her
husband felt for him. The letter had the desired effect. The
son, who was to be a soldier, did not live more than a year,
but soon after his birth Lucien was, thanks to Napoleon's
good offices, appointed Commissioner of the Republic at Bastia,
a post that gave him extensive powers, with 11,000 francs a
year of pay and expenses, besides forage for three horses.
Lucien's troubles were over.

When Joseph left Ajaccio he had the choice of either going
on to Paris to take part in the debates of the Five Hundred
and push his fortunes in the capital, or of taking up his post
as Resident at Parma. At Paris the year before, in his conversation with Delacroix, he had refused an ambassadorship,
but the success of his brother in the field and his own growing
prosperity had enlarged his views. He had let Delacroix
know that he would accept a more important post than Parma.
The General had also exerted his influence in his favour and
suggested a larger field for Joseph's first essay in diplomacy.
Accordingly on May 6th the Minister of Foreign Affairs wrote
to him that the Directory considered that ' he could be of
more service to the Republic in a more important post than
that which had at first been assigned to him.' It had therefore taken the first opportunity that presented itself to ' make
use of his talents and add to the reward he had justly earned
by his previous services.' Joseph was to be appointed Minister
Plenipotentiary to the Vatican to complete the negotiations
for the treaty of peace that the Republic was concluding with
the Pope. A few days later there was a further communica-

tion. Joseph, instead of having a temporary mission, was to be ambassador of the French Republic at Rome. He would have 60,000 francs a year. At the end of May Delacroix sent two letters to Mombello. One addressed to Joseph set forth in diplomatic phrases the object of Joseph's mission. The other, addressed to General Bonaparte, and to be communicated by him to his brother, was a confidential despatch, plainly revealing the treacherous policy the Directory meant to pursue at Rome.

To Joseph Delacroix wrote : ' The Directory summons you,. Citizen, to continue a portion of your illustrious brother's glorious task, and to maintain with Rome the peace which he has just signed by treaty. The destiny of your family will be to serve the Republic, and to be useful to it in turn in war and in peace. Your name will remind the Romans how serious a matter it is not to be always friendly to the Republic, and the Directory trusts that your care, your prudence, and your zeal will lead the Holy See to forget the many sacrifices it has been compelled to make, and will draw closer day by day the ties that have been formed between the two peoples.'

Possibly the last phrase contains a covert allusion to the object which the secret instructions indicated to Joseph. This was nothing less than the working up of a democratic revolution in the State to which he was accredited as ambassador. He was directed to ' make every effort to establish at Rome a representative democratic form of government ; to do this without any violent outbreak or disturbance, but in such a way as to secure that there should be a call for French mediation to prevent the disorders that might accompany the Revolution in the Papal States.'

Joseph had gone to Parma to present his credentials, and did not receive his appointment to the Roman Embassy till he returned to Milan in July. He at once began to prepare for his journey to Rome, and to select his secretaries and his household. It was decided that, besides his wife, his sister Caroline and his sister-in-law, Desirée Clary, should go with him. The gathering at Mombello was breaking up. Jerome had been sent back to his school at Paris, and Napoleon was about to return to the capital to develop the further schemes of his policy, and reap the rewards of his Italian victories. He was thinking of the invasion of England, or of a dash for the East, and a repetition of Alexander's conquests, with the destruction of the British Empire in India as his final goal.

Joseph arrived at Rome on August 31, 1797. He surprised the Romans by selecting for his official residence an old Palazzo, that of the Corsini, in the working-class district of the Trastevere—perhaps to show his love for the democracy. The more than courteous, the thoroughly friendly reception given to him, must have made him feel a little ashamed of his treacherous mission. Without waiting for the arrival of his official credentials, Pius VI. welcomed him in a private audience on September 2nd. He sent him a present of six horses ; Cardinal Doria, the Secretary of State, sent him two more ; and Prince Chigi four, so that his stable was full. On the 28th he was received in state at the Vatican. In the evening he gave a reception at the Palazzo Corsini, and the Pope sent a detachment of his cavalry to act as a guard of honour at the French Embassy. The cardinals and the Roman nobles crowded his salons, and vied with each other in expressing their hearty welcome to the friendly ambassador of France. His courtly manners, his grave dignity, his perfect command of Italian, all made a good impression. The Pope's niece, Donna Braschi, came to present the Roman ladies to the ambassadress. A few days after the Pope welcomed Madame Bonaparte and Joseph's sister Caroline in a private audience. Then there were banquets and balls at the palaces of the Roman nobles. Every one seemed anxious to pay court to the new ambassador, and he was assured that the Pope had no desire to raise dynastic questions, and was ready to live in peace with the Republic, being concerned only to secure the free exercise of their religion for the Catholics of France and her dependent states.

So in this autumn of 1797 all the brothers might feel well satisfied with the gifts fortune had given them. Napoleon was all-powerful with the Directory, and had established his fame as a master of the art of war. For him no ambition could now seem extravagant. Joseph was a wealthy man and ambassador to the most venerable Power in Europe. Louis, notwithstanding his having missed the last phase of the victori-

ous campaigns in Italy, had distinguished himself in the field,
and might count on rising as his soldier brother rose.   Even
Lucien had got to the end of his troubles and was relatively
well off.   Jerome was approaching the end of his college days,
and had seen something of the brilliant scenes amid which he
might hope his lot would be cast.

CHAPTER IV

JOSEPH AND LUCIEN 'MAKING HISTORY'

(1797-1799)

NAPOLEON could influence, but could not control, the policy of the Directory in 1797. Barras was still in power, and the idea of provoking new troubles in Rome was his. Napoleon's whole inclination was to cultivate more friendly relations with the Pope, and use his influence to win the adherence of the French Catholics to the Republic. He was quite satisfied with the results he had obtained by the peace of Tolentino. If he had thought there was any gain in occupying Rome and setting up a democratic government there, he could have done it after the rout of the Papal army. But he had held his hand when the way to Rome was open, and the pretext for an occupation ready.

Joseph Bonaparte was therefore not carrying out his brother's ideas when he followed out the instructions of the Directory, and the embassy at the Palazzo Corsini became a meeting-place for the Roman Republicans, many of whom had only been released from prison on the signing of the treaty with France. Joseph himself was too well satisfied with the court that was paid him, and the dignified position he occupied, to have any desire to precipitate a crisis. If he had foreseen what was coming, he certainly would not have brought to Rome his wife, his sister Caroline, Madame Clary and her daughter Desirée. He put himself in communication with the more respectable of the local 'patriots.' But the chief work was done by his military subordinates, who were more eager than he was to bring about a disturbance that would call a French division to Rome. There were several officers of the army attached to the embassy, and others were coming and going, visiting Rome on their way to the various garrisons of central

Italy. Of the permanent staff the most active was General Duphot, a young, hot-headed man, who saw in a Revolution at Rome a chance of distinction. He was busy day and night corresponding with the malcontents, interviewing and encouraging them, and promising them the support of France.

The ' patriots ' were a very small body of men, and without Duphot's encouragement would have risked nothing. The crisis came very suddenly, in the Christmas week of 1797. On the evening of December 27th General Duphot gave a dinner to some of the Republican leaders. Several toasts were duly honoured, and at last the general made a speech that was interpreted by his hearers as a call to early action, a promise of French protection. As usual at such patriotic gatherings there was an informer present, and early next day the Roman guests of the Republican general heard that the Papal police knew all about the talk over the wine, and meant to make some arrests. There was a rush to the embassy. A crowd of frightened patriots came to beg for temporary hospitality at the Palazzo Corsini, and the protection of the ambassador's flag. Joseph did not like his guests, and was trying to reassure them, standing among them in the entrance-hall of his Palazzo, when a party of Papal gendarmes arrived. At once the patriots rushed in confusion into the inner courtyard of the building. The officer in command of the Papal troops appears to have come to the entrance of the Palazzo with his men, a very small armed party, probably to obtain what information he could and bar the exit of the refugees. Joseph came out to meet him. He was in uniform and wore a sword, and with him were Duphot and three other officers. He told the Papalini that they were within the limits of the embassy, and thus violating French territory, and insisted on their withdrawing. Seeing the ambassador and the four officers thus standing between them and the dreaded gendarmes, the crowd of patriots plucked up courage and came out, and as the Papal troops withdrew showed a disposition to follow and attack them. Joseph's own account of what followed is that, anxious to keep back the over-eager Republicans, he drew his sword to restrain and threaten them, and Duphot and the others followed his example. It was a most unfortunate act for a peaceful ambassador, at the very moment when his protest was being obeyed by the troops. The Papalini not unnaturally thought Joseph and his officers were encouraging the mob to attack them, and ready to lead the onslaught, all the more because the Republicans were now drawing pistols and flourishing stilettos. They faced about and fired a volley, firing in the air, so that no one was hurt. Duphot now lost his head completely. Calling on the armed crowd to follow him, and waving his sword, he dashed at the gendarmes. Joseph in vain called him back, and re-entered the embassy. The patrol retreated along the Lungara towards the Vatican, without firing again. Duphot and his mob followed them. Joseph makes a very lame attempt to show that Duphot was still trying to separate the two parties. At the gate at the end of the Lungara there was a post of troops. The guard turned out, and as the mob approached pursuing their comrades they opened fire. Duphot fell dead with a bullet through his brains. On the fall of their leader the patriots turned and ran back to the embassy, where they took refuge. Only for its friendly shelter they would have been in a perilous plight, for the workmen of the Trastevere, intensely loyal to the Pope, were turning out at the sound of the firing, and, with a miscellaneous collection of arms in their hands, would have rushed the embassy had not the Papal troops appeared in force and held them back.

Duphot's dead body was brought into the embassy, and the Palazzo was hurriedly put into a state of defence. If Joseph had meant to provoke a French intervention he would not have placed himself so clumsily in the wrong. But now that the unfortunate Duphot had set fire to the powder, he felt he had no choice but to go further, and he was desperately anxious to get the ladies of his household out of the Palazzo Corsini and the dangerously excited Trastevere as soon as might be. He sent messenger after messenger to the Cardinal Secretary of State to inform him that his embassy had been violated, one of his officers killed, and that he was now all but besieged in the Palazzo. He said he had no choice but to break off all relations with the Holy See, and he demanded his passports instantly. At two in the morning a Papal official brought them to him. At six, when Rome was waking up for the day, a row of carriages, escorted by Papal cavalry, started from the Palazzo Corsini and passed through the city and out by the Porta Nomentana, on the way to Florence. Joseph's first embassy was at an end.

He reached Florence on the 30th. Sending thence a despatch to General Berthier, who commanded in northern Italy, he himself went on to Paris. The Directory accepted his version of the affair and expressed their approval of his whole conduct. .Berthier's troops occupied Rome, and on February 15th the Roman Republic was proclaimed from the Capitol.

Napoleon, after examining the question of an invasion of England, and advising the Directory to defer the attempt, was preparing for his raid upon Egypt. Joseph was to remain in Paris, and take care of the interests of the family. While looking out for a place which he meant to purchase and make his home in the capital, he rented a furnished house in one of the streets on the south side, where he lived a few weeks with his wife and sister-in-law. He took his seat in the Council of the Five Hundred, and began to make friends among his colleagues there. His brother Lucien soon joined him in Paris as a fellow-member. On April 12, 1798, he was elected to the Five Hundred as representative of one of the districts of Corsica. His election was quite irregular. To begin with, he was only twenty-three, and by the Constitution of the Year III. a candidate for the Five Hundred ought to be at least twenty-five years of age. But under the Directory there were no scruples about ' driving a coach-and-four through an Act of Parliament.' On the occasion of the *coup d'état* of Fructidor the Government, with Augereau's help, had swept away a crowd of opponents in the Five Hundred by arresting and deporting them and filling their places with its friends. Since then it had been a common practice for the assembly to get rid of unwelcome members by invalidating perfectly legal elections, and to vote that other elections that were clearly irregular were perfectly valid. Lucien's case was so weak that Napoleon did not expect he would be allowed to take his seat, and told him that in that event he would provide for him by giving him some post in the Army of the East. But Joseph did some successful lobbying, and the Five Hundred overlooked Lucien's youth and the other defects in his election, and declared the return valid. The orator of the clubs of Ajaccio, Toulon, and Marathon-St.-Maximin took his seat and was soon a prominent figure in the legislature of the Directory. Till he could find a house of his own he took up his abode with Joseph.

Louis was to go to the East on his brother's staff. He did not like the prospect. He wanted to stay in Paris. He protested that his health was not good enough for Egypt. It would be better for him to remain in France, and take care of himself at some health-resort. Besides the after-effects of his illness in Italy, he had only just recovered from an accident. On his way back to France he had been thrown out of an overturned diligence in the Alps, and had hurt his knee. His real reason for wanting to stay at home was that he was thinking of marriage. He had paid some visits to a school at St. Germain where his sister Caroline Bonaparte and Hortense Beauharnais were finishing their education. There he had met and fallen in love with another Mademoiselle Beauharnais, a niece of Josephine, who was paying for her education. The girl was regarded as a poor relation, and her mother had made a foolish second marriage. Napoleon put an end to Louis's love-affair by taking the girl from her school and promptly marrying her to one of his adjutants, Lavalette. Long years after she became famous by rescuing her husband from the prison where he lay under sentence of death during the 'White Terror' after Waterloo. Louis in his disappointment plunged into reckless dissipation in Paris, but his imperious soldier brother carried him off to Toulon, told him he must stop playing the fool and talking about devoting himself to poetry and literature, and made him march reluctantly along the path of military glory.

Joseph accompanied his brother as far as Toulon when the General went there to embark for the East in May. Josephine was to see her husband sail, and it was intended that she should follow him to Egypt as soon as he was firmly established there. Her son, Eugène Beauharnais, was going to the East as a staff officer. Unlike the reluctant Louis, he was delighted with the prospect, proud of his sub-lieutenant's uniform, and looking forward eagerly to his first campaign.

The expedition sailed from Toulon on May 19th. Joseph escorted Josephine to the watering-place of Aix, where she

was to stay a while before returning to Paris. He went back
at once to the capital. He was a busy man now, with no time
to spare. His own fortune had grown considerably, and he
was to administer during his brother's absence the wealth the
General had already accumulated. He completed the purchase of the château of Malmaison for Josephine. It was a
pleasant place, a few miles west of Paris, looking down on the
windings of the Seine near Bougival. For himself he bought
a splendid town house in the Rue du Rocher. The street is
now a busy thoroughfare near the Gare St. Lazare. In 1798
it was beginning to be a fashionable place of residence, and some
large houses had been built there. The one that Joseph
selected had been built some years before by a rich banker
for one of the stars of the Opera. Joseph paid 66,000 francs
for it, and spent 28,000 more in repairing and decorating
it. He also bought a country house and estate. He was no
longer satisfied with the little suburban property he had bought
before he went to Italy. In October he purchased the château
and the extensive estates of Mortefontaine, some nineteen miles
north of Paris on the way to Chantilly. It meant a large
expenditure. The purchase-money was more than a quarter
of a million of francs (258,000), and there were charges on the
estate of 5000 francs a year. It had been neglected since its
late owner, the banker Duruey, had died under the axe of the
guillotine. Extensive repairs would be necessary, and once
the estate was in order it would cost something serious to
maintain it, though on the other side of the account there
would be some rents, and the income from arable and pasture
land and forest. But it was a bargain. For it was a princely
estate, with a wide stretch of country included in its boundaries,
with hills and woods and two beautiful natural lakes. To be
the owner of Mortefontaine was to take a place among the landed
gentry, and Joseph felt the time was come to assert himself.
An ex-ambassador, a member of the Five Hundred, with
friends in the Government, and a big balance at his bankers,
a town house in Paris, and all the fortune of the family under
his control, Joseph Bonaparte was no longer the Corsican
squire. He was a great man, and he fully appreciated his
own position.

He had an element of laziness in his character, a disposition to rest and quietly enjoy the good things he possessed in a dignified way. In the debates of the Five Hundred he took little part, and at the end of his term of membership he did not seek re-election. With Lucien, who had still his fortune to make, it was different. In any case, a young man who was so proud of his oratorical triumphs could not be silent with such an audience to listen to him, and with the reporters of the newspapers waiting to take down his words. He had not been many days in the Assembly before he mounted the tribune. His fiery southern temperament made him exaggerate the style of oratory that was then in fashion. His speeches were full of classical allusions. Had he not been Citizen Brutus of Marathon only a few years ago ? Then there were the stock phrases of Republican patriotism, which always drew a round of applause. But in his now frequent speeches in the Assembly there was much more than this decorative matter. He soon made his hearers feel that he had studied the subjects on which he spoke, and the range of topics he dealt with was a wide one. He must have worked hard to get up his facts. While Joseph, as became a wealthy landed proprietor with a record of official employments to his credit, was a supporter of the Government, anxious to see the excellent state of things, under which he was so prosperous, indefinitely prolonged, Lucien, the ex-Jacobin, with his fortune still to be made, posed as an independent critic of the Directory. There was room for criticism. The Directory, which had obtained power by one *coup d'état* and secured its permanence by another, existed by an organised repression of its opponents on the one hand, and by permitting its supporters to indulge in bare-faced jobbery on the other. And presently there was news of blundering and disaster with the armies in the field in Europe. Lucien took care not to go so far in his opposition as to provoke the direct hostility of the men in power. He protested again and again that he was loyal to the Directory and to the Constitution. He denounced as a traitor any one who would even think of changing the constitutional Republican régime. He showed a tact that proved he had learned something; and partly because he gave proof of so much capacity, partly because an official appointment sometimes moderates outspoken criticism, he had not been long a member

D

when he was chosen as one of the Secretaries of the Five Hundred. He used his new position to make himself even more prominent. On more than one great occasion, after the President had spoken in the name of the Assembly, Lucien would rise and ask leave to add a few words, and then speak not in his own name but in that of the whole Five Hundred. Joseph had supplied him with money when he came to Paris, and he had managed to add to his modest fortune. The year after his election he bought the country house of Plessis near Paris for 57,300 francs—rather more than £2000.

At first the news of the Egyptian expedition was good. Malta had been captured and annexed on the way. Then Alexandria had been occupied, the Mamelukes routed, Cairo taken. But then communication became more difficult, and after Nelson had destroyed the French fleet (August 1, 1798) it was only possible to correspond by two routes, both uncertain, and one of them terribly slow. Letters could be sent either by running the partial blockade kept up by the British in the Mediterranean, or by a land journey through Tripoli, Tunis, and north Africa. At starting Napoleon had told Joseph to take care of Josephine. He was to pay her a liberal allowance, and generally assist her in business affairs. But he was also to act as a brotherly censor, and protect her as far as possible against her own tendency to run into indiscretions. She had shown no great desire to follow her husband to Egypt, and after the battle of the Nile it would have been impossible. She was perfectly happy in the society of Paris, where her conduct soon began to give serious anxiety to Joseph. Napoleon, too, was unhappy about her. On his voyage he had questioned some of his staff who had lived in Paris when Josephine was the widow of Beauharnais, and had heard more than he knew before of the reputation she had then acquired. In a fit of depression at these revelations, and his suspicions of what might happen in his absence, he had written from Egypt a letter to his eldest brother, which had never reached him. The ship that carried it was captured by one of Nelson's cruisers, and Napoleon's letter became the talk of London society. A scandal was all the more welcome there because it affected the great enemy of England. The letter was dated from Cairo, on July 25th, six days before Nelson's victory. ' I may be back in France in two months,' wrote Napoleon. ' I have much domestic trouble, for the veil is quite torn away. You alone now remain to me in the world, and your love is very dear to me. To lose it and to be betrayed by you would leave nothing for me but to become a hater of mankind. . . . Arrange for me to have some place in the country when I come back, either near Paris or in Burgundy. I mean to shut myself up in it, and pass the winter there. I am sick of human nature. I want solitude and isolation. I am tired of greatness, my feelings are dulled, and glory has lost its savour. At twenty-nine years of age I have exhausted everything, and there is nothing left for me but to shut myself up in myself. I shall keep to my house, and never share it with any one else. I have nothing left to live for. Farewell, my only friend ! ' In later letters Napoleon showed he had recovered from the first shock of his discovery, whatever it was, but he still had doubts about his future.

In March 1799 Louis arrived home from Egypt. He had been present at the capture of Alexandria, but he had been ill again during the voyage out, and did not accompany his brother on the victorious advance on Cairo. He was still in Alexandria when Nelson swooped down on the fleet in Aboukir Bay, and he must have heard the thunder of the guns roaring through that hot August night. After the disaster he went up to Cairo, and passed a few weeks there, spending most of his time with savants of the expedition, visiting the Pyramids, and watching the excavations of tombs and temples. Napoleon decided to send him back to France. He was to present to the Directory his brother's despatches and the standards captured in battle with the Mamelukes. He was also to impress on the men in power the need of making an effort to regain command of the Mediterranean, so as to be able to support the army in the East and reap the full fruit of its first successes. On October 9, 1798, he left Cairo for Rosetta, where the brig *Revanche* was under orders to convey him to France. On the 16th he reached Rosetta. A heavy gale was blowing, so that in any case he would have to wait, but he wrote to his brother that he thought the *Revanche* was too small and unseaworthy. He would want a better ship for the voyage—a dangerous voyage, for he would have to evade

the chance of capture by the British cruisers.   Napoléon wrote
to Rear-Admiral Perrée, who was in command at Alexandria,
that his brother was a bad sailor, and suffered terribly from
sea-sickness, and feared he would have an unpleasant time on
so small a vessel as the *Revanche*.   Could he find something
better for him ?   The Admiral had a fast-sailing despatch-boat
at Alexandria, the *Vif*, and on board of her Louis set sail on
November 5th.

He had a long journey, and wasted a good deal of time on
the way.   He reached Taranto in a week.   There, in fear of
the plague being imported from Egypt, he had to undergo
a quarantine of nearly a month.   The wonder is that he did
not in half the time obtain leave to pass out of quarantine
and continue his journey.   He sailed again in December.
He was chased by British cruisers, and so hard pressed that
the captain of the *Vif* thought capture was inevitable.   Louis,
in fear of his trophies finding their way to London instead of
Paris, threw the Mameluke standards into the sea, and was
ready similarly to dispose of his despatches at the last moment.
But the *Vif* was worthy of her name, and at last got away,
and ran for safety under the batteries of Porto Vecchio in
Corsica.   Important as his business was, Louis took a holiday.
He landed and went over to Ajaccio, where he spent three
pleasant weeks in the old home with his mother.   It was not
till February 1799 that he crossed over to Leghorn, where he
arrived on the 20th.   His mother accompanied him.   At Leghorn there was another delay.   Instead of proceeding by land,
Louis and Madame Bonaparte waited for the convoy of a
couple of warships.   When at last he arrived in Paris on March
11th, it was five months since he had left Cairo and a little
more than four months since he sailed from Alexandria.   His
news was rather out of date.   He had left his brother at Cairo.
When he reached Paris Napoleon was campaigning in Syria.

He presented his despatches and asked for a step in promotion.   His name appeared in the Army List as captain in
the 5th Hussars, though he had done no regimental service
with the cavalry.   He told the War Minister that for his
conduct at the storming of Alexandria (July 2, 1798) his
brother the General had provisionally promoted him *Chef
d'Escadron* (Major of Cavalry).   There was nothing about this

in Napoleon's despatches, but after some delay the War Minister took Louis's word for it, and confirmed him in the rank he claimed on July 30th.

As soon as news came of the invasion of Syria and the siege of Acre, Louis, who had been away from Paris on two months' leave of absence, was most active in impressing on all whom he could influence the urgent necessity of sending help to the Army of Egypt. If he were a deputy, he said to Joseph, he would raise the question in the Five Hundred. He would agitate it in the press, but he feared to give information that might eventually help the enemies of France. He begged Joseph to press the urgency of the matter on the Government. He could not understand, he said, the utter carelessness of those in authority as to the fate of an army of 20,000 men and a valuable colony. If there was a disaster, the effect of it in Europe and in France would make the Directors regret that they had not done everything possible to avert it. ' Tell this to the Directors and to the ministry, my dear brother,' wrote Louis to Joseph. . ' Speak to them strongly, and without allowing yourself to be misled by their telling you, as they certainly will, that your brother will extricate himself from all difficulties. In saying this they know very well that there is a limit to human power, and talk like this tends to throw all the blame on him if there is a disaster. You and Lucien ought not to rest until you have obtained a promise that they will pay attention to the affairs of this army, and serious attention.'

Lucien, active as he was in the Council of Five Hundred, never said a word there on the war in the East, whatever he may have done in private. Joseph interviewed some of the ministers, but appears to have been less anxious than Louis, and perhaps more confident in his soldier brother's luck. He had just arranged a marriage between his sister-in-law, Desirée Clary, and General Bernadotte. He was also arranging for the publication of the book he had begun two years before on his journey to Milan. It was a story, bearing as its title the name of the heroine, *Moina*. It was a half-sentimental, half-philosophical romance, of the kind that the success of *Paul et Virginie* had made popular. Louis had shown the manuscript to the author of that famous story, and Bernardin de St. Pierre had praised *Moina*, and noted especially its pictures of the horrors of war, its denunciation of the evils brought on the world by the ambition of conquerors. Joseph's story of an idealised shepherd and shepherdess introduced as one of its main episodes the devastation of their Alpine valley by war, after which the hero of the story was made to serve as a soldier of the Army of Italy. Some of the later critics of this very poor production have argued that when he published it Joseph was separating himself from his brother's policy, and posing as the friend of peace in contrast to the mere soldier. But they forget that the whole atmosphere of this kind of literature prevented it from having any bearing on practical life. Joseph could amuse himself with the story of his imaginary and utterly unreal peasants, and make them talk in the style of Jean-Jacques Rousseau or Bernardin de St. Pierre in long-winded reflections on the blessings of peace and the horrors of war, without any need of reconciling these ideal opinions with his own position as the brother of a conqueror—just as no one expected him to give up the splendours of Mortefontaine and the comforts of his big house in Paris, because he said pretty things about the delights of a simple life in the poverty of an Alpine herdsman's hut.[1]

The news of the failure of the Syrian expedition had reached France early in the summer. And there was bad news of events nearer home as the year went on. The Austrians were victorious in southern Germany, and an Austro-Russian army had made itself master of all northern Italy except Genoa and the neighbouring Riviera. The spell of victory seemed to have departed from the armies of the Republic. Naturally these disasters increased the growing unpopularity of the

---

[1] Lucien also published a work of 'philosophical' fiction about this time. Its title, *La Tribu Indienne* (The Indian Tribe), suggests a Red Indian story, but the scene was laid in Ceylon. It describes the adventures of a young Englishman, who makes a voyage to the East on board the East Indiaman *Bellerophon*, and is shipwrecked on the coast of Ceylon. (The name of the ship is a curious coincidence.) Lucien's imaginary hero wanders in a forest and falls in love with a beautiful huntress, whom he first sees 'reclining on the skin of an elephant.' This attempt at local colour suggests a very hard and uncomfortable couch. The Brahmins of Ceylon are the evil genii of the story, and their plots against the lovers give occasion for numerous tirades against the evils of 'priestcraft.' The book was a poor performance, but Lucien was proud of it, and employed some of the first artists in France on illustrations for a projected *édition de luxe*, which, however, never appeared.

Directory. Sieyès, himself a Director, was busy with plans for a change of Government, and was thinking of securing Moreau's help as his military accomplice. Napoleon would have been the man for the work, for it was his victory in the streets of Paris that had made the Directors the rulers of France, but he was far away in Egypt, if indeed he was still maintaining himself there, for there had been no letters from the East for some weeks.

In the middle of October, when a crisis in the fortunes of France was rapidly approaching, Joseph suddenly heard that his brother the General had landed at Fréjus. He had come back from the East when he was least expected, and had announced his own arrival. The three brothers, Joseph, Lucien, and Louis, at once started for the south to meet him. Louis fell sick again on the way and had to stop at Autun, while his brothers went on.

They travelled back to Paris with the General. He brought news of victory, the complete destruction of a Turkish army in sight of the British ships that had covered its landing in Egypt. Everywhere he was hailed as the destined restorer of victory to the French arms in Europe. His journey northwards was a triumph. On the way Joseph and Lucien had much to tell him of what had happened in France during his absence of nearly a year and a half. What Joseph had to say of Josephine's conduct was not very reassuring, but Napoleon had something better to do than begin a quarrel that would have made the world aware of his domestic troubles, and interfered with his plans for the immediate future.

Napoleon arrived at his house in the Rue de Victoire at Paris early in the morning of October 16th. There was an angry scene with Josephine, but it was immediately followed by a reconciliation, and Napoleon was busy with conferences with Joseph and Lucien, and preparing for his next great step, from which all the brothers had something to gain.

Joseph and Lucien already had some knowledge of Sieyès' plans. Lucien had a few days before been chosen President of the Council of Five Hundred. Once the General was in France, not as a man who had failed, but fresh from a recent victory, there could be no question that he must be the chief military agent in any change of Government. If the conspirators could not secure his help, they could hardly venture to move at the risk of seeing him commanding the armed forces of the Directory against them, and repeating his success of three years ago, the fight of Vendémiaire, when his guns had decided the fate of France in the streets of Paris on October 13, 1795.

The full story of the *coup d'état* of Brumaire belongs to the history of Napoleon, but two of his brothers played a part in it—one of them a leading part. Sieyès saw at once that he must secure the great soldier's alliance, and used Lucien as his intermediary. After he had sounded his brother and found that he was ready to act, a meeting between Sieyès and Napoleon was arranged at Lucien's house in Paris on the evening of the 10th Brumaire, just two weeks after the return from Egypt. Sieyès began to explain his elaborate plans for the new Constitution. The ex-Abbé was a professional Constitution maker, and would have revelled in describing his elaborate system of checks and counterpoises to an interested hearer. But Napoleon cut him short. He would only discuss the practical details of how the Directory was to be got out of the way and the ruling power transferred to the conspirators, among whom he meant to be the leader. He approved of the general plan, the transfer of the Chambers to St. Cloud, to avoid all danger of a street insurrection in Paris; his own nomination to the command of the army which was to ' protect' the assembly at St. Cloud, influence its decisions, and secure the execution of what it decreed; the resignation of the Directors, and then? He would have no cut-and-dried paper Constitution voted in a hurry. No, there must be a provisional Government to arrange all details. That part of the business could wait. The practical point was to hustle the Directory aside and take its place as soon as possible. Sieyès soon saw that he must let Napoleon have his way. The conference lasted only an hour. Napoleon was the first to rise and go. Sieyès remained a while to exchange impressions with his host. ' The General seems to be quite as much at home in this business as on the battlefield,' he said to Lucien. ' We must act on his opinion. If he were to draw back now all would be lost. Our only chance of success is his accepting the provisional consulate.' He felt that Napoleon had taken command, and he suspected that once he was at the head of the provisional Government, he would keep his place in the definite régime. But he still hoped that his own complex system of constitutional checks on personal power would be adopted.

After this there was a busy week. Lucien thought he could answer for the majority of the Five Hundred. Joseph had friends in the Council of the Elders, the upper house. Napoleon, and those officers who had linked their fortunes with his own, could count upon the army. Two out of the five Directors— Sieyès and Ducos—were in the plot. Once the blow was struck France would welcome any change from the unfortunate and oppressive rule of the Directory.

Joseph did his part under cover of social gatherings in his Paris house and at Mortefontaine. He tried to secure the support of General Bernadotte, to whom he had given the hand of his sister-in-law, Desirée. But Bernadotte played for safety. All that could be secured was his neutrality. ' You are certain to fail,' he said to Joseph, ' but I can yet do you a service. By standing aside I shall be in a position to protect you from the consequences later on.'

On the 15th Brumaire both the Councils gave a banquet to Napoleon and Moreau. After it was over there was another meeting late in the evening between Sieyès and Napoleon, again at Lucien's house. There all details were arranged, and it was settled that the blow should be struck on the 18th (November 9, 1799). The first part of the scheme was carried out to the letter. Early on the 18th the Council of the Elders met at the Tuileries ; and on the pretext that there was a conspiracy for a rising in Paris, and in virtue of a provision of the existing Constitution, adjourned the meeting of both Chambers to St. Cloud for next day. Another resolution gave Napoleon the mission of protecting the assembly at St. Cloud with the Army of Paris, of which the Council gave him the command. In the course of the day Moreau (won over by promise of high command under the new Government) had taken possession of the Luxembourg, the palace of the Direc-tory, and while Talleyrand secured the signed resignation of Barras, the General made the two other Directors, who were not in the plot, prisoners in their apartments.

On the 19th the formal vote at St. Cloud was to establish the new provisional Government. The Chambers met under the protection of their guard, but the palace was surrounded by a formidable force under the command of Napoleon and his trusted lieutenants. Many of the officers and men were veterans of Italy. All hoped that their leader would put an end to the Government of lawyers and talkers, and lead them to new victories. But now Napoleon showed that, however much at his ease he might be on the battlefield, he did not know how to deal with a large audience when it came to a question of telling and persuasive oratory. Lucien would have done better. Even Joseph would not have failed like his soldier brother. He thought it would help matters if·he made a personal appeal to the two Councils. He went first to the Elders. They were quite prepared to vote for the resolutions establishing the new régime, and the resolutions ought to have been at once proposed by one of their own members, and carried by the majority. Lucien, presiding over the Five Hundred, was expecting the message from the upper house, asking for confirmation by his own branch of the assembly. He had an anxious time, for a movement of resistance was rapidly developing among the Five Hundred.

Meanwhile, in another room of the palace, Napoleon was delivering, or trying to deliver, a long-winded oration, appealing to the Elders to save the country from the ruin inflicted on it by the Directory. He made the mistake of allowing himself to be involved in disputes with interrupters. When at last he withdrew he left an impression of failure, and the Council hesitated to vote.

Meanwhile, what had happened in the other house ? Lucien's task placed him in a somewhat awkward position. In his most fiery attacks upon the Directors he had always declared his absolute loyalty to the Constitution of the Year III. Only two months ago, on September 15th, he had protested from the tribune of the Five Hundred against any attempt to subvert its authority. ' I declare,' he had said, ' that if a sacrilegious hand were raised against the representatives of the people, the authors of such an attempt should.all be doomed to death rather than the immunity of one of these representatives should be violated. There is a law which is still in force,

and which you must all call to mind. It is that which pro-
claims outlawry as the fate of whosoever assails the security
of the representatives of the nation.'

This speech had a strange echo before the sitting of the
19th Brumaire was over. It had been arranged that Lucien
as President should call on one of his friends, Citizen Gaudin,
to speak first, and that Gaudin should talk against time till
the decree of the Elders arrived for confirmation. But Gaudin
had not spoken long before interruptions, that rose into a
stormy outcry, began on the left. Presently he lost courage
and sat down. Lucien had tried in vain to obtain order.
The Left, encouraged by a first success, now demanded that
each member in turn should rise and renew his oath of fidelity
to the Constitution. Lucien, hoping that long before this
ceremony was over the expected message would arrive, and
seeing no way to oppose the proposal, which was cheered from
various parts of the room, agreed to it. He called the roll of
members as slowly as possible. Still no message. A letter
was handed to him. He read it. It was Barras's enforced
letter of resignation. There were cries that Barras was a
traitor. In the midst of this excitement the door opened and
there arrived, not the messenger of the other Council, but
Napoleon, looking pale and excited, and escorted by four
grenadiers of the Council Guard and a group of officers, as if
he either feared violence or was about to employ it.

There were cries, not from the left only, of ' Down with the
tyrant! Down with the dictator! Outlawry! (*Hors la
loi !*) ' Napoleon, pressing forward towards the tribune, tried
to speak, but could not make one word heard. Lucien was
calling in vain for order. A number of deputies rushed forward as if to attack the intruding soldier. It was said that
some of them drew daggers, and one of the grenadiers claimed
that he saved Napoleon's life by turning a stab aside. His
officers protected him as he retreated from the hall. Lucien
faced the angry assembly. His appeal so lately made to the
law of outlawry now found its echo. ' *Hors la loi !* ' came the
cry from the benches. ' Put his outlawry to the vote, Citizen
President! *Hors la loi! Hors la loi !* ' It was the outcry
that had heralded the fall of Robespierre. For a moment
Lucien quitted his presidential chair to whisper a word to

General Frégeville, who commanded the Guard of the Council. Then he returned to his place, called again for order, and sat anxious but undaunted while a wild orator denounced his brother as a traitor. Then, when he thought he had given Frégeville sufficient time to communicate with his brother, he himself sprang forward and ascended the tribune. His audience were used to listening to him, and there was a moment of silence. ' There is no longer any liberty left here,' he cried in his deep, sonorous voice. ' As I can no longer make myself heard and exercise my authority, you shall see your president, in token of his sorrow, lay down the symbols of the office given to him by the people.' He flung off his robe and scarf, and descended from the tribune. Some of his friends pressed round him, and at the open door Frégeville was waiting with bayonets of a party of his grenadiers glittering behind him. With this escort Lucien left the hall amid a storm of hostile outcries.

Outside he found Napoleon riding along the lines of his troops and telling them that his life had been in danger. They were furious. Between them and the doorway Frégeville's grenadiers of the Legislative Guard were drawn up. To these Lucien addressed himself, mounting the horse of one of the officers in order to be better heard by his audience. In a fiery speech he called on them, by his authority as President of the Five Hundred, to clear out that den of assassins, to disperse these ' representatives of the dagger.' Napoleon rode up to his side and gave the order. Led by Frégeville, with Murat on one side of him and General Leclerc [1] on the other side, the grenadiers poured into the hall with drums beating and bayonets at the charge. The deputies fled pell-mell by the windows, jumping out into the garden, and then running away, and disappearing in the gathering darkness of the November evening.

At nine in the evening a few of the Five Hundred were assembled again in the same room that had witnessed the decisive charge of the grenadiers. Lucien took his place as President. The Council decreed that sixty-one of the members had ceased to belong to it ; appointed General Bonaparte and

[1] Leclerc was the husband of Pauline Bonaparte ; Murat was soon to marry Caroline.

the ex-Directors Sieyès and Ducos to govern France as Provisional Consuls, and elected two committees to draw up a new Constitution. In a brief sitting the Council of the Elders confirmed these decrees, and the new Consuls were sworn in. Only one of them really counted. Napoleon was the ruler of France, which welcomed the change, and Lucien had taken a leading part in placing this power in his hands.

CHAPTER V

IN THE DAYS OF THE CONSULATE

(1799-1802)

THE new Constitution of the Year VIII. differed essentially from Sieyès' project inasmuch as it made the First Consul the real active ruler of the State. Napoleon did not allow the Commissions to waste time. He himself presided over their deliberations, and while the Constitution was being elaborated, busied himself also with reorganising the administration, putting his own adherents into the most prominent positions. The Constitution came into force on December 24, 1799. As a reward for the decisive part he had played on the 19th Brumaire, Lucien was appointed Minister of the Interior. Joseph was named a Senator, and in order that he might win further honours in the career of diplomacy, he was shortly afterwards selected as one of the three plenipotentiaries who were to arrange a settlement with the envoys of the United States. Louis had taken no part in the *coup d'état*, but even he shared in the advantages Napoleon had now at his disposal. Louis had been *chef d'escadron*, or major, in the 5th Dragoons since his return from Egypt in the spring of 1799, but had done no military duty with his regiment during these few months. He was nevertheless promoted *chef de brigade* in the 5th Dragoons, a rank equivalent to that of Colonel.

On January 19, 1800, there was a gathering of the Bonapartes at Joseph's château at Mortefontaine for the marriage of Murat and Caroline Bonaparte. Murat was in command of the Consular Guard. Napoleon early in the spring appointed him second-in-command of Berthier's ' Army of Reserve ' in the south-east of France, the army which in the summer he himself was to lead over the Alps to Marengo. Louis was not at the

NAPOLEON AS A GENERAL OF THE REPUBLIC

FROM THE PAINTING BY H. E. P. PHILIPPOTEAUX AT VERSAILLES

gathering at Mortefontaine. He had gone to Normandy, where his Dragoon regiment was engaged in suppressing a local revolt. On his return to Paris he was sent by his brother on a tour of inspection to Nantes, Brest, and Rochefort.

Lucien was not a very successful Minister of the Interior. He had no taste for the dry details of administrative routine. He left all the real work to his subordinates. He had a stamp made with which his secretary affixed his name to documents requiring the ministerial signature. The only department to which he paid the least attention was the one that brought him into touch with journalists and men of letters. It was part of the duty of the Minister to cultivate the acquaintance of such men, in order through them to influence public opinion. Lucien soon formed a kind of literary circle, and in discussing current affairs with them was not always discreet. He was by disposition an oppositionist, and in these gatherings he did not refrain from criticism of the First Consul's policy. What he said was repeated. Fouché, the Chief of the Police, heard of Lucien's conferences through his agents. They reported to him that the Minister of the Interior was carrying on a disloyal intrigue with enemies of the Government. On April 8th Fouché complained to Napoleon in Lucien's presence that the latter was becoming a centre of disaffection. Lucien protested that the Chief of the Police was going beyond his proper sphere of action in interfering with or criticising him. Fouché declared that, being responsible for the security of the Government, he was only doing his duty. ' I would have the Minister of the Interior himself arrested,' he said, ' if I found out that he was conspiring.' Napoleon calmed Fouché, and after his departure warned his brother to be more discreet.

Joseph too had his circle of literary protégés, but he was more prudent than Lucien. Bernadotte, who had married his sister-in-law, was a frequent guest at his house in Paris and at Mortefontaine, and Bernadotte was no friend of Napoleon. There were others in his circle who excited Fouché's suspicions, but the wily Minister of Police could never secure any compromising information against the First Consul's eldest brother. Still there was some friction between Joseph and Napoleon. It arose from the former having got deeply settled in his mind the idea that the Bonapartes had now a kind of family claim to be the rulers of France.' His mind was running on the question of what would happen if, for instance, Napoleon were killed in action in the coming campaign. Who was to succeed him ? Would it not be a solid gain to France to put an end to all possible intrigues for the succession by making his power hereditary ? There seemed now no prospect that Josephine would bear him a son. Could it not be arranged that one of his brothers should stand next in succession ? and in that case should not the eldest brother have the first claim ? Joseph was not the only one who was thinking of such questions. There was even some talk on the subject in political circles, and naturally it was spoken of among Joseph's friends, and Napoleon heard of these discussions. At the beginning of May, when he was preparing to leave Paris to take command of the army, he put all his business affairs into Joseph's hands, as he had done when he went to Egypt. Joseph then told him what were his ideas as to the succession. Napoleon apparently left the question open. For a few weeks later Joseph reverted to it in his letters to his brother, telling him he hoped it would be soon decided. If not, he might feel compelled to abandon public affairs and live a quiet country life at Mortefontaine.

In these days of May 1800 Lucien was in such serious trouble that he entirely abandoned all idea of doing anything at the Ministry of the Interior. His wife was dangerously ill at the end of April. On May 14th she died. She had been a most devoted wife to him, and her death was a heavy blow. He asked Napoleon to let him go with him to the army, so that he might have his mind occupied with new scenes and experiences, but the General told him he must remain in Paris. Then for some ten days he shut himself up in his country house at Plessis, and refused even to receive letters from the Ministry. Louis's regiment, the 5th Dragoons, was attached to the Army of Reserve under Napoleon, and one would have expected that its *chef de brigade* would have taken the field with it. But Louis, who since his return from his tour of inspection had been living in lodgings in Paris amusing himself with literary studies, declared that he was too ill for campaigning, obtained leave of absence, and went to take the waters at Aix. Strange to say, Napoleon none the less continued to believe in the future of his younger brother, whom he had educated, and whom he still meant to make into a soldier.

Jerome, the youngest of the brothers, had hoped to accompany the First Consul in the field, all the more because his schoolfellow, Eugène Beauharnais, went with Napoleon. Jerome had left his college in 1799, after Napoleon's return from Egypt. Since then he had spent his time with Napoleon and Josephine at the Tuileries or at Malmaison. Of all the brothers he was the only one who had never known hard times. His recollections were of pleasant schooldays, with that wonderful holiday at Mombello, when Napoleon held his court there after the campaign of Italy. He was something of a spoilt child with expensive tastes. If he saw anything he fancied in the Paris shops, he would order it and tell the shopkeeper to send the bill to the Tuileries. Napoleon looked on his wild investments as a joke, and paid the accounts. Josephine humoured him in every way. He was supposed to be still studying, but he spent most of his time in amusing himself. His ideas of campaigning were based on his boyish recollections of Mombello. He wanted to go to the army, but Napoleon thought he was still too young for the coming march through the Alpine snows, and left him with Josephine. Joseph wrote to Napoleon that his wife was spoiling the young man, and that he ought to have a tutor to look after him. But Jerome all the same had a holiday at Malmaison during the campaign.

It was the campaign of Marengo, the march over the Alps, the dash into the midst of the divided Austrian armies, the hard-fought battle that was first all but lost and then won, and won to such decisive effect that it made Napoleon master of northern Italy. After the victory Joseph joined his brother at Milan, and they travelled back to Paris together. When the conqueror returned to his home he found Jerome in a very bad temper, still disappointed that he had been treated as a mere boy. 'Come, make friends,' said Napoleon, jestingly humouring him. 'Make peace, and I will give you something.' 'What will it be?' 'Anything you like.' 'Well, give me the sword you wore at Marengo.' Napoleon was wearing it. He unbuckled it, and handed it to his brother.

Louis was still away at Aix. Lucien was in Paris. He had

E

recovered from the first shock of his grief, and plunged into a course of reckless dissipation. Paris was full of scandalous gossip about him. As for the Ministry of the Interior, he was neglecting it to such an extent that rumour talked of endless abuses and peculations being carried on unchecked by his subordinates. In August Louis came back to his Paris lodgings. He seemed to have become a valetudinarian dreamer. He worried himself about his health. He had a group of young literary friends, to whom he read his poems and a romance he was writing. They flattered him as a genius. His regiment saw nothing of him.

Jerome had not only been given the sword of Marengo, he was gazetted a second lieutenant in the Chasseurs-à-cheval, a *corps d'élite* which was a kind of cavalry branch of the Consular Guard. As if to prove that he was at last to be treated as a man, he picked a quarrel with another young lieutenant, a cousin of Davoût. There was a duel at Vincennes. Several pistol-shots were exchanged, and at last a bullet, luckily a small one, buried itself in Jerome's body, flattening on his breast-bone. He was taken back to the Tuileries. The bullet was so deep in the muscles that the surgeons decided it was better to leave it there, after they had made several attempts to find and extract it. Jerome recovered. The bullet was extracted long years after from his dead body when he died a Marshal of the Second Empire.

In the late summer and autumn after Marengo the question of the future of France, the successor of the childless First Consul, was still being discussed by all who had a direct interest in the problem. Already it had been suggested that the Consulate should be prolonged for his lifetime, though it was not until after the peace of Amiens that the plebiscite gave him this life-tenure of power, and the right to name his successor; but it was generally assumed that he might rule France as long as he chose to cling to power, and that any arrangement he proposed as to the succession would become law. There was, of course, a thoroughgoing Republican minority that looked forward to his being perhaps replaced by a popularly elected successor at the end of the first term of ten years, if there were not some sudden change of Government in the meantime. As for the Royalists, most of those who were still abroad, and many of those who made their peace with the new Government, clung to the hope that Napoleon would play the part that Monk had taken in England and bring back the exiled king. Louis XVIII. had written to Napoleon more than once before Marengo making this suggestion, and telling him that if he would take this part he had only to name the reward he would require for himself and his family.[1] Josephine had been, and still was, in communication with the Royalists. Her secret ambition was to see the old Royal House of France restored, and her husband a Duke and Constable of France, reviving the triumphs of a Turenne under the old flag, under which her father and her first husband had fought. She had strong personal motives apart from the traditions of her earlier life and education. It had been whispered already that it might be Napoleon's duty to sacrifice his personal feelings to the interest of the perpetuation of the régime he was establishing in France, and divorce her in order to marry a wife who would give him an heir to his power. It was on this account that she was so opposed to the projects of Joseph and Lucien. They were anxious that Napoleon should at the earliest possible moment take steps to secure the succession to one of the family, and Joseph as the eldest regarded it as his right. Fouché was Josephine's ally, and regarded the agitation carried on by the two brothers as dangerous to the stability of the Government. To let the world know that Napoleon was on the way to establish a dynasty would be to challenge opposition from those who still believed in the Republic, as well as from the Royalists. The result might be that some ardent Republican would try to play the part of Brutus against this new Cæsar. Lucien as Minister of the Interior thought he had in his hands the means of educating public opinion in the direction of his own views. In the days of the Toulon Club he had precipitated the crisis in Corsica, which at first had seemed to bring with it the ruin of the family, but had opened the way to fortune. He regarded the crisis of Brumaire, which had made his brother First Consul, as mainly his work. Without giving Napoleon even a hint

[1] Napoleon seems to have waited definitely to reject these overtures till after Marengo. It was on September 7, 1800, that he wrote to the Comte de Provence (Louis XVIII.), refusing to discuss any further proposals. 'Sacrifice your interests to the peace and welfare of France,' he wrote. 'History will put it to your credit.'

of what was in hand, without consulting any one but some of his literary friends, he set to work on a pamphlet on the question of the succession to the Consulate. He did not avow the authorship after it appeared, but it was clearly his work, though one or other of his literary circle may have touched up some passages. He had it printed, and sent from his Ministry to every prefecture in France, and to a large number of officials, while other copies were given to the journalists he inspired.

Joseph, who was so deeply interested in the question, had just been appointed by his brother one of the plenipotentiaries who were to conclude the peace with Austria at Lunéville. The negotiations were far advanced, the real work had been mostly done, but Napoleon meant that his eldest brother should have the credit of being the chief of the diplomatists who completed the treaty, and have also the solid rewards that fell to an ambassador on such an occasion. Lucien's pamphlet, published anonymously under the title of *Parallèle entre César, Cromwell, et Bonaparte* (' A Comparison of Cæsar, Cromwell, and Bonaparte '), was circulating through France. Published in the last week of October, it had not at first attracted much attention. Joseph left Paris at five in the morning of November 14th to proceed to the Congress at Lunéville. On the afternoon of the same day Lucien arrived in Paris. He had been summoned from his country house by Napoleon, to whom Fouché had shown a number of copies of the pamphlet. They had been sent to the Chief of the Police by various officials who had received them from the Ministry of the Interior, and in their accompanying letters these officials asked if the pamphlet was not a seditious publication that ought to be promptly suppressed. Fouché reported that in the departments the pamphlet was already giving rise to a dangerous agitation.

The anonymous pamphleteer, who must be either Napoleon's brother, the Minister of the Interior, or one of his protégés, argued that it was a danger for France that her future should depend on the life of one man. True, he was the greatest of men. He had done what Cromwell had done for England, Cæsar for Rome. He had restored order and prosperity out of a chaos of civil strife and ruin. He promised France a new era of glory and greatness. ' Happy would the Republic be if only he were immortal ! ' But he was subject to the same chances of death as common men—nay, his position exposed him to special dangers. Only discord and calamity could follow his disappearance. ' If suddenly Bonaparte were to be taken away from our Fatherland, where are his heirs ? Where is the system provided for the purpose of maintaining the great example he has given and perpetuating the work of his genius. The fate of thirty millions hangs on the life of a single man ! '

Then, after arguing that the rule of deliberative assemblies had always ended in cabals and discord, the writer asked what would be the result of France being handed over to the control of some congress without a directing chief ? There would be a scramble for power by ambitious soldiers. ' Where is the successor of Pericles ? ' he continued. ' Where is the hero whom the unanimous confidence of the people and the army would peacefully install in the Consulate, and who would be capable of maintaining himself in that position ? You would soon find yourselves under the yoke of a number of military chiefs, who would dethrone one another, and whose weakness would make them cruel. Remember how at Rome, when the greatest of men was basely assassinated, he was replaced by a Nero, a Caligula, a Claudius l ' What was the remedy ? To define the succession at once. And the readers of the pamphlet were given clearly to understand that the successor ought to be one of the great man's family.

Lucien went to the Tuileries to see his brother. Fouché was present, and there was an angry scene. Lucien would not admit that he had written the pamphlet. He granted he had circulated it, but he said he had given the general idea to his friend Fontanes, who had gone beyond his instructions. Fouché told him that in any case he was responsible. He was a mischief-maker. It was of a piece with all the rest, with the disorder, the waste, the actual peculations at his Ministry. Why could he not attend to his duties instead of wasting his time with actresses ? Fouché spoke plainly, and Napoleon let him speak. Lucien, instead of defending himself, attacked Fouché. He told him he was a cutthroat of the Terror, responsible for rivers of bloodshed, and that he was now making money out of his Police Ministry, by blackmailing gaming-houses. He was not the man to call him to account. At last Napoleon interposed. He brought the discussion back to the pamphlet. Much of it, he granted, was sound enough, but it was the act of a madman to send out the more outspoken pages with the official stamp of a Minister upon them. Fouché called attention to the attacks on the army, and said that many of the generals, Moreau among them, were angry at such insults. Napoleon saw this danger. Finally he told his brother that he must resign the Ministry of the Interior. But he allowed that he meant well, and had been only imprudent. He would give him a compensation in another direction. He should go as ambassador to Spain, and his brother-in-law, Bacciochi, who was a friend of his, might go as his secretary. Another brother-in-law, General Leclerc, was to go in command of an army of observation that was to co-operate if necessary with the Spanish army in forcing Portugal to abandon the English alliance and close her ports against the British flag. In Spain Lucien would have a better position than at the Ministry, and would be removed from the temptation of trying to direct French opinion.

Lucien left Paris a few days later, studying Wicquefort on *The Ambassador and his Functions* as his travelling-carriage passed by Orleans and Bordeaux and northern Spain on its leisurely journey to Madrid, where he arrived on December 6th. By this time there was none of Napoleon's brothers left in Paris. Joseph was at Lunéville, busy with treaty. Louis was travelling in Germany. He had suggested that a change of scene would be good for his health. He had left Paris in October, and gone to Berlin, where he had been well received by the King of Prussia and the court. He spent some time as the guest of his namesake Prince Louis at his Schloss of Rheinsberg. He did not return to France till the end of January 1801.

Jerome had started on a new career. Napoleon had decided that his youngest brother should enter the navy. It would be a good training for him, and later on he might be High Admiral of France. A squadron under Admiral Gantheaume was about to sail from Brest for a cruise in the Mediterranean. Gantheaume was one of the best sailors in France. He had become a fast friend of Napoleon during the expedition to Egypt, and had attached himself to the fortunes of the First Consul. For his correspondence he used paper on which was engraved a star with the letter ' B ' amidst its rays, and below, the motto, *Je navigue sous son étoile* (' I sail under his star '). Napoleon chose the admiral as his brother's teacher. On November 22nd Jerome left Paris for Brest. He was the bearer of a letter to Gantheaume in which Napoleon wrote : ' I send you the Citizen Jerome Bonaparte, who is to serve apprenticeship to the navy under your orders. You know that he must be kept strictly in hand, and has much lost time to make up. Insist on his exactly discharging all the duties of the profession which he has adopted.'

Jerome was eight months at sea on his first cruise. The fleet passed Gibraltar successfully and entered the Mediterranean. Its mission was to carry supplies to the army that was still holding out in Egypt and raise the blockade of Alexandria. Jerome served on board the flagship, the *Indivisible*,[1] had a seat at the Admiral's table, and became so familiar with him that he borrowed a good deal of money from him, for he had not left his expensive tastes behind him in Paris. Gantheaume sent to Paris friendly reports on his pupil, and Napoleon wrote to Jerome to express his pleasure and encourage him. ' I am glad to hear,' he said, ' that you are making yourself at home on the sea. It is there that you will now find the best chance of fame. Go up the rigging. Learn all about the different parts of the ship. When you come back from this voyage I want to hear that you are as handy as a good sailor-boy. Don't let any one do your work for you. I hope by this time you are able to keep watch and work out your course.' There was no serious fighting. Gantheaume found himself opposed to superior forces and would not risk an action. He captured some merchant ships. Twice he ran into Toulon. On June 24, 1801, the fleet fell in with and captured the British warship *Swiftsure*, 74. The British ship made a brief fight against superior numbers, and then struck her flag. On board the *Indivisible* two men had been killed and eight wounded,

---

[1] This curious name for a warship was taken from one of the titles of the Republic, which had been declared to be an 'indivisible state,' an allusion to the abolition of the old provincial administration of the Monarchy.

so that it was not a very serious action.   Gantheaume sent
Jerome on board the *Swiftsure* to receive the captain's sword
and take possession.   The squadron then entered the waters
of Elba, and Jerome obtained leave of absence and went on
to Florence, where Murat provided him with money and the
means of amusing himself.   While he was there Napoleon
wrote to Gantheaume that he was well pleased with Jerome's
conduct, and that he should come on to Paris and make a short
stay there before starting on a longer voyage.   So Jerome
left Florence to return home.

What had the other brothers been doing while the young
sailor was cruising with Gantheaume ?   For Joseph 1801 was
a year of dignified diplomatic employments and increasing
prosperity.   When he left Paris in November 1800 for Lunéville, preliminaries of peace with the German Emperor had
been settled, and it was expected that Joseph, as the representative of France, would have only to sign the definite treaty.
But the court of Vienna refused to accept the proposals as to
the fate of Italy, and the armistice was broken off while
Joseph was still on the road.   But the victory won by Moreau
at Hohenlinden on December 3rd left the Austrians no hope
of successfully prolonging the war.   The armistice was renewed, the negotiations at Lunéville were taken up again,
and on February 9, 1801, Joseph and his colleagues signed the
treaty.

While the negotiations at Lunéville were in progress the
enemies of the First Consul had made an attempt to blow him
up, exploding a barrel of gunpowder near his carriage as he
drove to the Opera on Christmas Eve.   His narrow escape
brought once more to every one's mind the question of the
succession.   Napoleon had already come to a decision on the
subject.   The very day after he had decided that Lucien
must resign the Ministry of the Interior and go to Spain, he
had said : ' There is no longer any need of our worrying our
minds about looking for my successor.   I have found one.   It
is Louis.   He has none of the defects of my other brothers,
and he has all their good qualities.'   The only possible explanation of such a choice is that he had a kind of infatuation for
his pupil.   He saw in him what he hoped for, not what Louis
really was.   Otherwise how could he have given such•praise

to the dreamy hypochondriac who, with every chance of distinction in the career that had been prepared for him, had done so little ? He had overlooked even the fact that while his regiment was marching to Marengo, Louis had thought that his precious health required him to take a holiday at a watering-place. It must, however, be remembered that much as Napoleon esteemed Joseph, he had a fixed idea that he would survive his eldest brother. Lucien had more than once been a source of trouble, and was now under a cloud. Jerome was a boy with a good deal of the spoiled child in his character. Thus by a process of exclusion Louis was left as his choice. But even so he hardly deserved such a eulogy.

At the time when Napoleon thus selected him as the hope of the family Colonel Louis Bonaparte was enjoying the hospitality of the King of Prussia. When he came back to Paris at the end of January 1801, he heard not only that Napoleon had fixed upon him as his probable heir, but also that Josephine had made up her mind that he ought to marry her daughter Hortense. The marriage would make France the joint inheritance of the Bonapartes and the Beauharnais. Hortense was a beautiful girl. She had a lively disposition and a keen intelligence, and at Madame Campan's school at St. Germain she had acquired all the ' accomplishments.' She danced gracefully, she was a clever musician, she could use her pencil. She shone in the court circle of the Tuileries, and more than one officer of rank and distinction, among those who had attached themselves to Napoleon's fortunes, aspired to her hand. But Louis felt no attraction for her at this time, and shunned the court in his dread that he might be hurried into marriage. He gave up his Paris lodgings, and bought the country house and estate of Baillon. It was a lonely place, far from any main road, in the midst of woods and marshes, on the little river Thève, the stream which ran westward from the lakes of Joseph's domain at Mortefontaine, from which it was some miles distant. He hid himself away at Baillon with his books. But he soon got tired of his retirement. His regiment, the 5th Dragoons, was at Bordeaux under orders to proceed to Spain and join the army of observation that was to be assembled on the Portuguese frontier under the command of his brother-in-law Leclerc. At the end of

March Louis suddenly made up his mind to join the Dragoons and serve in the campaign at their head. He made a leisurely journey to the south, and on April 19th reviewed and took command of the 5th Dragoons at Bordeaux. It was not till June that he joined Leclerc's army with the regiment.

Lucien had been in Spain since the beginning of December. Before he left Paris he had told his friends that he would only be a year away. Before he was a month in Madrid he had a letter from Fontanes, his collaborator in the famous pamphlet and much other literary work of his Ministry. It was written on the morrow of the attempt on his brother's life, and told him that he was too far away at Madrid. He ought to be in Paris, holding the second place in the state, taking the risks and awaiting the reward of such a position. But Lucien saw no way of returning at once, and was quite content to hold for a while a position in which he hoped to earn some credit, and at the same time saw a good prospect of making a fortune. As ambassador at Madrid he had a splendid income, and opportunities for rapidly acquiring wealth. It would be a stepping-stone to higher things. He had had a most flattering welcome. 'I am loaded with favours,' he wrote. 'All the barriers of etiquette are broken down. I am received in private by the King and Queen whenever I wish, and they discuss business directly with me, and the Prince of the Peace (Godoy), far from resenting this, is pleased that it should be so.'

He spared no expense on his establishment, and entertained lavishly. But he was already looking to the business side of things. He had brought two artists with him, who were picking up pictures and other objects of art for him, and making wonderful bargains. Within a few weeks of his arrival he could report to the Foreign Office that he had signed three treaties. True, they had been drafted and settled by his predecessor, but his was the credit of completing them. First there was the treaty of alliance between Spain and the Republic signed on January 29, 1801. The two powers agreed to join in invading Portugal if she did not break off her alliance with England and close her ports against the British flag. On February 13th there was a further treaty for joint action against England, especially with a view to succouring the French army in Egypt. Finally, on March 31st, there was the treaty creating the Kingdom of Etruria for the benefit of a Spanish infanta. It was the custom to give presents to the pleni-potentiaries who signed a treaty of peace or alliance. These gifts usually took the form of snuff-boxes set with diamonds. The presents that Lucien received were even more valuable. The King of Spain expressed his pleasure at the conclusion of the three treaties by giving him twenty pictures, works of great masters, from the Royal Gallery, and 200,000 crowns' worth of diamonds. Later on he sent him his portrait, with a warning to unpack it from its case himself. In the case Lucien found diamonds worth half a million of francs. The weak King evidently thought that in thus bribing the ambas-sador he was indirectly securing for himself control over the policy of France.

In April he got Lucien to sound Napoleon on a strange proposal. The ambassador wrote to the First Consul sug-gesting that as the question of an heir was all-important, Josephine might be induced to consent to a divorce, and the King of Spain would then be ready to offer Napoleon the hand of a Spanish princess, the Infanta Isabella. Napoleon at once rejected the idea. ' Why should I separate myself from this poor woman,' he said, ' because I have been fortunate. Had I failed, had I been thrown into prison, she would have stood by me. Besides, if I did think of another marriage, I would not seek an alliance with a royal house that has begun its decline.'

Leclerc's army had not yet reached the border, but in May the King, Godoy, and Lucien went to Badajoz on the frontier, where the Spanish troops were carrying on a half-hearted cam-paign against the Portuguese in a desultory fashion. In the first week of June the French were close at hand, Leclerc's army with Colonel Louis and his dragoons. Once they came into line there would be serious operations, and a march on Lisbon. The Portuguese did not want this, and they sent their envoys in haste to Badajoz to patch up a peace. Lucien was honoured by being given the direction of the negotiations for Spain as well as for France. It was said that the Portu-guese brought Lucien a present of a packet of splendid Brazilian diamonds to add to his collection. In a few days he had accepted all their proposals. On June 6th, just as Leclerc's army was coming into line, Lucien signed the treaty and sent it to Paris for ratification.

Napoleon was furious when he read it. He refused to ratify it. It was not, he said, in proper diplomatic form. Some of the articles were impossible. Lucien had acted without consulting his Government. What he had done could not be accepted. But, strongly as he felt, Napoleon took care in his own letters to Lucien, and in those which Talleyrand wrote in his name from the Foreign Office, to spare his feelings. He even flattered him. Surely, he said, Lucien, with his profound knowledge of men and of the world, could even yet convince the Spanish court that it had both the interest and the power to exact fuller concessions from Portugal. But Lucien had become so firmly convinced of his own importance that he was in no mood to stand even friendly criticism. If Napoleon did not like his treaty, let him send another ambassador. He was only anxious to resign the embassy and return to Paris. Louis, too, was tired of his short stay on the Portuguese frontier. With a treaty under discussion and no campaign in prospect, he asked Leclerc for leave of absence in July. After being presented by Lucien to the King and Queen of Spain at Badajoz he went to take care of his health at the watering-place of Barèges. It was not till September that he returned to Paris, seeing no more of his dragoons.

Napoleon insisted on Lucien remaining at his post. In September Lucien wrote to Joseph telling him that he had let the First Consul know that he absolutely insisted on being recalled, and added that if he did not get his letters of recall soon he would leave Spain without them. He thought he had been badly treated, and he must have some rest. At last, on September 29th, the treaty with Portugal, revised by Talleyrand, was signed. Lucien was told he must wait for the ratifications to be exchanged. But he lost all patience, and on November 9th, after bidding farewell to the King and his Spanish friends, he started for France. He was so much afraid that he might be stopped on the way to Paris that he travelled under an assumed name. He had passports prepared on which one of his secretaries was described as ' General

Thiébaut,' and he made the journey as the General's secretary. Travelling day and night, he reached Paris on November 14th.

Joseph had during the summer acted as one of the plenipotentiaries of France in the conclusion of the Concordat with the Pope. It was signed at his town house in Paris on July 12th. Four days before, his daughter Julie had been born. He had been adding to his estate of Mortefontaine by buying land in the neighbourhood, and in August he purchased a larger house for his Paris home. It was the Hôtel Marbœuf, a splendid mansion on the Faubourg St. Honoré, with a garden running back to the Champs Elysées. As usual Joseph made a good bargain. The houses and lands of the old aristocracy ruined by the Revolution went for small prices in these years after the Terror. For the Hôtel Marbœuf Joseph paid only 60,000 francs (£2400), and he spent another thousand pounds on decorating and repairing it, for it had been shut up for years. There was no house in Paris that Joseph would have been better pleased to make his own. When he was a boy at Ajaccio a Marbœuf had been governor of Corsica. When his father went to Paris it was with the introduction from the great man, and Charles Bonaparte had been a guest in this very house, and on his return had described its splendours to his family. Now it was one of Joseph's residences, the place where he entertained generals and diplomatists, men of letters and science, and, now that the Concordat was signed, prelates and distinguished churchmen.

Napoleon had offered him the Presidency of the Cisalpine Republic. But Joseph would accept it only on conditions to which his brother had no idea of consenting. Napoleon intended that the Republic should be garrisoned by French troops, who also held the passes of the Piedmontese Alps, so that this Republic in northern Italy was practically a French province. Joseph made his acceptance of the Presidency dependent on a less oppressive protection by the mother Republic over which his brother ruled. The French garrisons must be withdrawn, and the Cisalpine army, recruited among Italians, must supply their place. More than this, Piedmont must be added to its territory so as to carry its frontier up to the French Alps, and he must be allowed to reconstruct the frontier fortresses. Napoleon withdrew his offer. Joseph said he was quite satisfied. He preferred a quiet life with his family. He did not care to face the chance of some sudden change in France, followed by a wave of revolutionary·aggression pouring over the Alps and making itself master of a Republic, which he would rule without having the power to defend it. The supposition pointed to the question of the strange things that might happen if Napoleon disappeared without the affair of the succession having been settled—a problem that was always before Joseph's mind.

Lucien followed Joseph's example and set up an establishment and a kind of court of his own in Paris, but on a more splendid scale. On his sudden return from Spain he had gone at once to see Napoleon at the Tuileries. He expected an unfriendly reception and was ready for a quarrel. The interview lasted three hours, but Napoleon was in a more conciliatory mood than he expected, and it ended in a kind of treaty of peace. Napoleon had not forgotten how useful Lucien had been in the days of Brumaire, and he felt that he could be of service to him again when his decrees had to be forced through some reluctant legislative assembly. Joseph was a senator and a member of the Council of State. Lucien was a better speaker and debater than his eldest brother, and a place would be found for him. But for the present, he told Napoleon, he did not want any official appointment. He would rest a while, and live as a ' simple citizen of Paris ' until his brother needed his help in some step for the further consolidation of his power.

So Lucien turned his diamonds into cash and began to live as a wealthy man in Paris. A week after his return he took a three years' lease of the Hôtel de Brienne, a great house in the Rue St. Dominique, on the south side of the Seine. The rent was 12,000 francs, nearly £500, a year. Not so well situated as Joseph's mansion, it was larger and grander in every way. There was a courtyard in front, opening by a *porte-cochère* on the street. From the courtyard one entered the main building, with its suites of salons, and behind it there was a large garden. At the side other buildings, with rooms for a large staff of servants, stables, and coach-houses. Before taking possession Lucien spent lavishly on improvements and decorations. The masterpieces of painting and the other works of art he had collected in Spain were hung on the walls of his salons. The portrait of the King of Spain had the place of honour. In this palace Lucien gathered his friends around him. Fontanes and his other literary acquaintances were regular visitors. Some of the returned Royalists were also among his friends. Chateaubriand was often a guest at the Hôtel de Brienne. Outside Paris Lucien still had his country house. There he had installed a certain Madame de Santa Cruz, who was sometimes called the Marquise de Santa Cruz. He had made her acquaintance at Madrid, and she posed as a Spanish lady of rank, though some said she was a German adventuress. Lucien had invited her to follow him to Paris. The men of the Consulate were no better than those of the Directory, though there was more of an attempt to keep up appearances, and more show of outward decorum.

Jerome had left Paris. Just before the return of Lucien he had gone on a long voyage that opened up to him a new period of his life, and had far-reaching consequences. After the capture of the *Swiftsure* and his holiday at Florence he had been summoned by Napoleon to Paris, where he arrived in the first days of September 1801. He had a reception that might have turned the head of a young man, even if he had not been spoilt already. He was treated as a hero. Poems were addressed to him. One rhymester told of the wonder he felt in looking on the laurel-crownèd brow of the ' young conqueror ' and realised what ' three years of war ' had done for him. He had gone away looking like one of his sisters and he returned looking like his famous brother. In plain prose Jerome had had a fairly easy time with a squadron that, when it was at sea, was chiefly employed in dodging the British Mediterranean fleet, and which had only been in action when it had the good luck to find the *Swiftsure* cruising alone, and so had been able to secure a very cheaply won success to balance against its failure to land a single man or a single case of stores in Egypt. Jerome accepted the flattery offered to him, and posed as a veteran naval officer and an authority on maritime questions. At the Tuileries he lectured Napoleon and his officers on naval policy. His brother tolerated it with a little suppressed amusement, and Jerome thought he had made a good impression. In a letter to Admiral Gantheaume, eight days after his return, he boasted of it with a charming unconsciousness of his own absurdity. ' They call me here the " rough sailor," ' he said. ' It is because one day they were having a discussion with me. They reason like mere land officers, and after a lot of talk I took up my hat and said to them : " I am going ; for you argue like a lot of fools, and like people who are at their ease in arm-chairs ! " '

At first this kind of thing was amusing, but Napoleon soon got tired of it. He sent Jerome off on a tour of the north coast. He was to visit the ports from Boulogne to Dunkirk. At the end of October he sent him orders to go to Rochefort and join the squadron which was to proceed to the West Indies under Admiral Latouche Tréville. On November 6th Jerome reported himself at Rochefort. On the 29th he embarked on the flagship, the *Foudroyant*. The Rochefort squadron sailed on December 14th. It was made up of seven battleships and seven frigates and some light craft. It formed a junction with the fleet of Admiral Villaret Joyeuse in the waters of San Domingo on January 29, 1802.

Louis's fate had been decided for him. When he returned to Paris at the end of September he was invited to Malmaison, where Napoleon and Josephine were staying. Josephine had a long talk with him, urging that it was time for him to settle down and make himself a home, and that there could be nothing better for him than the marriage with Hortense, and the union of the hopes of the two families, with all the brilliant prospects it would open for him as Napoleon's heir. The First Consul himself came in and exerted his diplomacy. In the evening there was a ball. Louis danced with Hortense and proposed to her, and was of course accepted. The same evening it was even decided that the marriage should take place in January. In after years Louis protested that he had been hurried into the match against his will. But although he had been long averse to the project, he was now under the spell of Hortense's winning ways, and for three months he seemed to all who knew him a devoted lover. There certainly was no hurry. The marriage was to be a great event, and there must be due time for preparation.

LOUIS BONAPARTE

On January 3, 1802, the marriage contract was signed at the Tuileries. Louis declared his property to be the estate of Baillon, and money and movable property to the value of 180,000 francs. Napoleon put at his disposal the house where he himself had first made his home with Josephine in the Rue de la Victoire. To the bride the First Consul gave a dowry of a quarter of a million of francs. Josephine added a hundred thousand more. Next day in the evening, towards nine o'clock, the civil ceremony took place before the Mayor of the Tuileries district of Paris. Among the witnesses were Madame Letizia Bonaparte, the mother of the bridegroom ; Lucien ; his sister Madame Bacciochi ; and his sister Caroline, with her husband, General Murat. Then there was a gathering at the house in the Rue de la Victoire for the religious ceremony. A large room had been converted into a temporary chapel. The legate of the Pope, Cardinal Caprara, was waiting to bless the marriage. The whole family came with the bride and bridegroom from the Tuileries, all except Jerome, who was far off on the Atlantic. Napoleon was there with his mother and his wife, the mother of the bride. Joseph had come from Mortefontaine. He was about to start for Amiens to settle the peace with England. There, too, were Lucien and the sisters of the Bonapartes. Elisa, now Madame Bacciochi, Caroline with Murat, and Pauline with her husband, General Leclerc, who had returned from Portugal and was about to go to San Domingo to take command there. Amongst the crowd of generals and courtiers was Lavalette with his wife, the poor cousin of the Beauharnais whom Louis once wanted to marry. The Cardinal, wearing cope and crozier, performed the ceremony. Then Murat came forward with Caroline. He told Caprara that on account of the state of things prevailing at the time of his marriage there had only been the civil form ; he and his wife now wished their union to be blessed by the Church. So there was a second marriage ceremony. Then supper, and early in the morning Louis and Hortense drove out of Paris to spend the honeymoon at the lonely château of Baillon, which he had bought as a refuge from Josephine's schemes for the marriage that had just taken place.

Thus the year 1802 began for the Bonapartes. Napoleon was holding almost a royal court at the Tuileries. He was the master of France, the arbiter of western Europe, the restorer of peace.   Joseph and Lucien were wealthy men.   Joseph was about to be associated with the final success of the treaty with England.   Louis, after all his mistakes, was the husband of Hortense, the probable heir of all his brother's power. Jerome was voyaging to new adventures beyond the Atlantic.

CHAPTER VI

THE ADVENTURES OF JEROME

(1802-1803)

WITHIN a few days of the arrival of the fleet in the West Indies (January 29, 1802), Jerome was in action for the second time. But again it was not a serious affair. The squadron co-operated with the land forces in the capture of Port au Prince, the ships driving the negro gunners of Toussaint L'Ouverture's army from the seaward batteries. Jerome then went ashore at Cape Haitien to spend some time at the headquarters of General Leclerc, his sister's husband, who had taken command of the land forces and brought his wife with him. So far Jerome had served as an *aspirant de marine*, or midshipman. Admiral Villaret promptly promoted him *enseigne de vaisseau*, a grade between aspirant and lieutenant. He owed his promotion to the name he bore.

In a few weeks he had seen enough of Haiti and was anxious to get back to Paris. He persuaded his brother-in-law to ask the Admiral to send him home with despatches. Villaret wrote to the Minister of Marine, Decrès, that the General had expressed a wish that his despatches should be entrusted to an ' active and intelligent officer, who could add to his report details that he might have overlooked.' This was flattering for Jerome, who had only been five weeks in San Domingo. On March 4th he sailed on board the *Cisalpin*, the smartest frigate in the fleet. She reached Brest in thirty-seven days, and on April 14th Jerome was back again in Paris.

He handed in his despatches, but instead of troubling himself about ' further details,' proceeded to amuse himself in ways that made Napoleon anxious to send him away as soon as possible. In a few days he was ordered to go to Nantes and return to the West Indies on board the corvette *Epervier*, which was fitting out for sea. It was, however, nearly six months before the *Epervier* started. At first she was not ready; then Jerome succeeded in adding delay to delay, notwithstanding repeated orders from Paris. Meanwhile there was a round of amusement, balls, dinners, suppers and the rest. In one of his letters urging his departure Napoleon told Jerome that he was sorry to hear that he was neglecting the profession which should be his path to fame. He ought to be at sea. He could console himself if he heard that his brother had died young doing his duty, but it would be a wretched thing to live even sixty years of useless life. One might as well have never existed.

Jerome did not take things so seriously. He was second-in-command of the little *Epervier*, her commander being Captain Halgan, an old friend of his, who allowed him to do just what he liked. Difficult as it seems to imagine such a burlesque absurdity, it is said that Jerome, not liking the quiet naval uniform of his rank, had taken with him a hussar uniform to wear at balls in the West Indian ports, and, impatient to swagger about in this striking costume, appeared sometimes on the deck of the *Epervier* as a lieutenant of cavalry, in a sky-blue jacket and a scarlet waistcoat. After six weeks at sea the corvette reached St. Pierre in Martinique. Halgan was so ill that he went ashore, and Jerome was put in command of the *Epervier*. As he had this responsibility he was given the provisional rank of lieutenant, which Admiral Villeneuve, who commanded on the station, confirmed on November 27, 1802. At the same time the Admiral advised Lieutenant Bonaparte to take his profession a little more seriously. He told him frankly that in any case he would be an admiral some day, but added that it depended on his conduct whether he would be a mere figure-head or a fighting admiral, who would be a credit to the navy.

At the end of November Jerome sailed to Santa Lucia, and made an excursion to the volcanic crater with its smoking *soufrière*, which is one of the sights of the island. The day was hot. He suffered from a touch of sun, and when he came back to St. Pierre he was in a state of collapse. The Admiral, alarmed at his illness, sent him ashore for some weeks. He stayed in the house of a Martinique planter named Lecamus, whose son, Auguste, became attached to him, and was for many years to come his secretary and companion. In January 1803 he put to sea again and visited Guadeloupe, and the English island of Dominica, where the governor gave him almost a royal reception. After this yachting excursion he brought the *Epervier* back to Martinique, laid her up to be overhauled and painted, and went ashore for another holiday with his friends. In April there were rumours of a rupture with England. The *Epervier* was ready for sea, and Admiral Villeneuve urged that Jerome should go back with her to France before war began and British cruisers again made the Atlantic unsafe.

But Jerome had other plans, and did not consider he was under the Admiral's orders, for he had been sent from France only to visit the French West Indian colonies and obtain some sea experience. On April 15th he wrote to Joseph : ' In the next fortnight I shall sail for San Domingo. I intend to spend three days there, and then go on to New England. I will sail up the Delaware and anchor at Philadelphia. Thence I shall go by land to New York and Boston, and from that port I shall proceed to France. My voyage will have been a long one, very laborious, and above all, very instructive for me.' It really had been so far a kind of pleasure trip, and he had spent weeks ashore. But he was quite satisfied with himself, and went on to sketch out his future. ' On my return I shall get command of a smart frigate, and if war should break out, a thing I in no way desire, I shall be in a position to take command in two years' time of a fine squadron, or I shall die the death of honour. If, as I hope, the good fortune of our family does not desert me, I shall succeed, and you will have the pleasure of seeing your youngest brother worthy of the name he bears.'

While Jerome was still planning his excursion to the United States, Villaret, who commanded at Martinique, received from Napoleon formal orders to send back his brother to France at once, as war was more than likely. When on May 31st the *Epervier* stood out of the harbour of St. Pierre bound for Brest, war had actually begun in Europe, though the news had not yet reached the West Indies. Next day, June 1st,

the *Epervier* again anchored at St. Pierre.   Jerome had come
back with a report of an exploit that alarmed Admiral Villaret.
He told how in the strait between Martinique and Dominica
he had met a large ship under a full sail, which he took to be
a merchantman.   He had shortened sail and signalled to her
to lie to, but as she held her course he ran up to her and fired
a shot into her sails, ' to let her know he wanted to speak
with her.'   The stranger then lay to, and as the *Epervier* came
within speaking distance an officer called out to Jerome that
the ship was British, a king's ship.   He was apparently an
exceptionally good-tempered type of the British naval officer
of those days, and, according to Jerome's account, the Englishman assured him that things were going well and everything
pointed to peace.   Jerome explained to Villaret that he
thought it worth while to come back and tell him the good
news.   He was thinking that after all he might go to the
United States.   But one of Jerome's officers let the Admiral
know that a better sailor than Lieutenant Bonaparte must
have known at once that it was a British warship, for her flag
was flying.   ' You have committed a folly,' wrote Villaret to
the young man.   ' You must be away from Martinique before
the protest that will certainly come reaches me.   You must
set sail as soon as you get this letter, see the First Consul,
and give him your explanation of this affair.'

Jerome sailed, but he went no further than Guadeloupe,
where he remained a fortnight.   To another letter from
Villaret, insisting on his immediate departure for France,
Jerome sent a very cool reply.   ' I have received your letter,
my dear Admiral,' he wrote.   ' Our opinions differ, but I am
ready to subordinate my views to yours.'   Then, instead of
saying he was ready to start, he went on to argue that the
best course for him was to put a local French merchant ship
under the Danish flag, and take passage in her to France.   If
the Admiral insisted he would go in the *Epervier*, but he foresaw that in that case he would be made prisoner by the English.
Villaret would be responsible.   This very letter would prove
the event had been foreseen.   Meanwhile he stayed at Martinique.   In July he sent the *Epervier* off to Brest on his own
authority, remaining on shore himself with one of his officers
Ensign Meyronnet, his secretary Lecamus, his doctor, and his

servant. The *Epervier* was captured by a hostile cruiser. Jerome and his suite embarked as passengers on board of an American pilot boat and reached Norfolk in Virginia on July 20th.

From Norfolk he sent Meyronnet to Philadelphia with orders to charter an American vessel for his return to France. With the rest of his suite he went on to Washington, and sent Lecamus to inform Pichon, the French ambassador, of his arrival and tell him to come·to his hotel. Pichon was surprised at the First Consul's brother thus suddenly arriving in Washington, without even a letter to herald his visit. But he waited on him, promised to do all he could for him, and complied with his request for a large advance in dollars. He advised Jerome to remove to a more respectable hotel, and introduced him to a friend of his, Joshua Barney, who provided him with more comfortable quarters.

Joshua was a strange character. He had been in France when the navy, suddenly deprived of most of its officers, sons of old Catholic and Royalist families of Brittany and Normandy, was promoting boatswains to command warships, in the hope that their Republican zeal would make up for their lack of knowledge. Barney was a good sailor, and, introduced to the Admiralty by one of his friends as a countryman of Paul Jones, he was given a commission, and actually commanded two frigates which appeared in American waters. Hence he was known as ' Commodore Barney.' He left the navy, and having made some money, opened hotels at Washington and Baltimore, and dabbled in politics. The Commodore became Jerome's guide and friend. He took him off to his Baltimore hotel and introduced him to local society, where the First Consul's brother became the lion of the season.

Pichon urged that Jerome should at once take a passage to France. ' My opinion absolutely differs from yours,' came the reply, and Jerome went on to tell him that he had sent Meyronnet to France with a report, and would await the orders of the First Consul and the Minister of Marine. Pichon was also anxious at hearing that Jerome was now entirely in the hands of the Commodore, who had the reputation of being something of an adventurer. He wrote a letter of warning. The only result was that Jerome told the ambassador to mind his own business. ' I thank you, Citizen,' he wrote, ' for the particular interest you are so kind as to take in all that concerns me, especially in my choice of my acquaintances. But I have a principle, from which I shall never depart, and that is, to judge men entirely by their conduct, and so long as Citizen Barney acts in my regard as he has so far done, I shall not change my opinion of him. Although I know very little of the language of this country, I am perfectly well acquainted with its manners and usages, and, as I have always done, I am quite capable of choosing my own line of conduct.'

Among the families with which Jerome had cultivated friendly relations was one which stood in the front rank of the society of Baltimore. It was that of a wealthy merchant, William Patterson, who had emigrated from Ireland as a boy of fourteen and had made his fortune in Maryland. His daughter Elisabeth, born on February 6, 1785, and thus just three months older than Jerome, was an exceedingly beautiful woman, with charming manners, and Jerome had fallen in love with her almost at their first meeting. For Elisabeth Patterson the handsome young officer, who was the brother of the most famous man in Europe, and had served in two naval expeditions, was a hero. She was well educated and spoke French, learned from French nuns in her convent school. Jerome could only speak a few words of English, so the language, too, helped to draw them together. Jerome had made up his mind that there should be a marriage, and when in August the French frigate *Poursuivante*, commanded by Captain Willaumez, anchored at Baltimore, and Pichon suggested that Jerome should take this opportunity to return to France, he again refused to go.

He went up to Washington with Willaumez, and told Pichon he would wait till he heard from his brother. The ambassador presented Jerome and the Captain to the President, one of the great men of American history and one of the makers of the United States, Thomas Jefferson. He had negotiated with the First Consul the purchase of Louisiana, which then included the greater part of the Mississippi valley. He was glad to welcome the great man's brother. Jerome took the airs of a prince, and made a little speech in which he expressed his desire for the continuance of most friendly relations between France and the United States. In the evening he was Jefferson's guest. Next day the ambassador tried again to persuade him to embark on the frigate. He refused. Willaumez then gave him a formal order to do so, pointing out that he was his superior in rank. Jerome flatly denied his right to give him orders, and returned to Baltimore.

A few weeks after, Pichon heard from Jerome that he was engaged to Elisabeth Patterson. He vainly remonstrated. Jerome replied by telling him the marriage was fixed for November 3rd, and inviting him to be present in his official capacity. Pichon at first agreed to come; then reflecting that the First Consul was not likely to approve, he refused, and sent to the French consul at Baltimore, to Mr. Patterson, and to Jerome himself a protest, pointing out that by the law of France Jerome himself being under age, and not having the consent of his surviving parent, could not be legally married abroad. Jerome wrote him an angry letter. Mr. Patterson was anxious about his daughter's future, and had insisted on the marriage being at least deferred. Meanwhile he sent Elisabeth away to visit some friends in Virginia.

On November 22nd the ambassador was delighted at hearing from Jerome's secretary, Lecamus, who had come from Baltimore, that the engagement was at an end. Jerome would go to New York and sail for Europe. He begged the ambassador to hand back to him all the correspondence on the subject, and not to write about it to Paris. Then came a further message. Notwithstanding what he had already borrowed, he was short of money and deep in debt. Would Pichon lend him 10,000 dollars to make some payments and arrange for his voyage? Pichon was himself short of money, but he found the dollars, and Jerome went as far as New York. But in the first week of December the ambassador was disappointed by receiving another letter from him, dated from Baltimore on the 1st, and asking for more money—2000 dollars. There were some further debts he really must pay. Pichon sent him a thousand and promised to send more, and again pressed him to lose no time in embarking.

But Jerome had given up the idea. He had resumed his relations with the Patterson family. One wonders if the

engagement was ever definitely broken off.   If so, it was
renewed.   Mr. Patterson was quite content to have the marriage take place, provided it was a valid one in the eyes of the
Catholic Church.   The law of the United States would recognise it.   Jerome pledged himself to use every effort to have
it validated in France, and assured Patterson that there
could be no doubt that he would be successful.   On the eve
of the marriage a contract was drawn up, which was intended
to make the binding nature of the morrow's ceremony absolutely unassailable.   The best lawyers had been consulted,
and the local French consul had agreed to be present at the
marriage.   By special licence it was celebrated on Christmas
Eve, 1803, the officiating priest being Dr. Carroll, Archbishop
of Baltimore, a prelate whose memory is still venerated among
the Catholics of America.   He was the brother of ' Carroll of
Carrollstown,' one of the signatories of the Declaration of
Independence.

On Christmas Day Pichon had a characteristic letter from
Lecamus, Jerome's secretary.   He had ' the honour to inform ' the ambassador that the marriage had taken place,
and he asked him to make a further advance of 4000 dollars
to meet the pressing expenses that Jerome would have to
incur.   He told Pichon that he understood he had promised
this loan, and added that Jerome was ' expecting it with
impatience.'

It was a thunderbolt for Pichon, who thought he had put
an end to the affair.   He believed that Napoleon would never
consent to the marriage, for his star was now rising fast, and
Jerome might have hoped for the hand of a princess.   So
Pichon could only renew his protests.   Jerome himself was
anxious as to how his family would receive the news.   Meyronnet had not yet returned.   He had reached Paris, but it was
only in January 1804 he had embarked again for America
bearing a letter directing Jerome to return at once.   It
would be some weeks before the letter could arrive.   Meanwhile the *Poursuivante* still lay at Baltimore, ready, if Jerome
wished, to convey him to France over the sea now swept by
the English cruisers.   But Jerome was the centre of Baltimore
society, and was telling his friends that he expected to make
a prolonged stay in America.   It was probable, he said, that

he would be appointed ambassador of the French Republic to the sister Republic of the United States, and would set up house with his bride at Washington.

But if he had really such hopes they were doomed to speedy disappointment. Other fortunes awaited him. But before following further the story of his married life we must see how his brothers had been faring during these two years.

CHAPTER VII

THE COMING OF THE EMPIRE

(1802-1804)

THE great events of the years 1802 and 1803 were the conclusion of the peace with England at Amiens, the signing of the various treaties which placed the relations of the Republic and other Powers on a friendly footing, and the completion of the agreement with Rome by the ratification of the Concordat by the Legislature. This last step rallied to the Government the large number of Frenchmen who had so far regarded the Republic as synonymous with religious persecution. The restoration of religious peace was celebrated by a *Te Deum* at Notre Dame, and the event was notable as being the occasion of the first state progress through its streets that Paris had seen since the fall of the King. The First Consul went from the Tuileries to the Cathedral surrounded by liveried servants and splendidly uniformed court officials, through streets lined with troops. No monarch of France had ever been the centre of a more brilliant display.

The treaties and the Concordat assured to him the position he had won as ruler of France, and at the same time they indirectly guaranteed and recognised the rank and wealth obtained by all who had risen on the tide of change, and secured to the peasant who had come into possession of his land and to the speculator who had bought national or ecclesiastical domains the undisturbed enjoyment of his property. A period of war, anxiety, and disorder was at an end, and the great majority of the French people saw in the personal rule of Napoleon the best hope of security against further troubles like those of the past. So it was easy for him to consolidate and extend his power. The Consulate for life with the right to choose his successor was granted to him by a plebiscite.

JOSEPH BONAPARTE

The way was then clear for the organisation of the Empire, which, like the earlier Empire of the Cæsars, associated absolute power with Republican forms. The change prepared in the closing months of 1803 was completed in the spring of 1804. Meanwhile the treaty of Amiens had proved to be only a truce, and France and England were again at war in May 1803.

We have not to trace the history of these great events, but only to see how they affected the fortunes of Napoleon's brothers, and what part Joseph, Lucien, and Louis had in the new development. We have already seen how Jerome was faring beyond the Atlantic.

In the opening weeks of 1802 Joseph had held at Amiens the position of chief plenipotentiary of France in the negotiations with England. The treaty was signed on March 25, 1802. It was the most important of those that Joseph had been employed upon, and he had now considerable experience of the methods and traditions of diplomacy. The services he had thus rendered to the Republic added to his own sense of his importance as head of the Bonaparte family and a great landed proprietor. He felt more strongly than ever that he had a right to take the foremost place in France in case of his brother's death, and the conduct of Louis made him ready to believe that sooner or later Napoleon's eyes would be opened to the unfitness of his younger brother for such high destinies.

For Louis's conduct was such that Napoleon had good reason to be disappointed with him. After a brief stay at Baillon he had returned to Paris, to the house in the Rue de la Victoire. Within a few weeks of his marriage his old dreamy restless mood had come back upon him. Though Hortense tried to conceal it, her friends could see she was anxious and unhappy. At the beginning of March 1802, within two months of the marriage, he left her alone in Paris, and went off to his regiment at Joigny. No one believed that it was any zeal for his military duties that took him away. In April he made a brief visit to his house in Paris and then returned to Joigny, which he left in May to go to the watering-place of Bagnères-de-Bigorre, writing to Hortense that he was ill and the doctors advised his going there. Some of his more intimate friends ventured to remonstrate with him. He wrote to them that he was unhappy and discontented with the position that had been made for him, and it was better he should follow his own course. In these letters he only once mentioned Hortense. It was to explain to a friend, whom he had asked to sell Baillon for him, that his wife was as anxious as he was to get rid of the property.

Hortense, thus abandoned by her husband, spent much of her time with her mother and Napoleon at the Tuileries or at Malmaison. She had resumed something of the position she had occupied in their home before her marriage. The continued absence of her husband was made the pretext of scandalous stories against her. Whispered in Paris they found an echo in London, and took a still more malicious form when in the summer it was reported that Hortense would be a mother before the end of the year.

For the First Consul and Josephine this was a new claim to their affectionate care, for if the hoped for child was a boy he would be educated to be the heir of Napoleon's greatness. The old house in the Rue de la Victoire was a very small one. In the same street there was a larger house, built in the last days of the old monarchy for one of the reigning beauties of the Opera, designed by an artist, and having a large garden with a wonderful array of kiosks and summer-houses, statues and grottoes, ponds and fountains and little water-courses crossed by toy bridges. It was a fairy palace in miniature. Napoleon bought it for Hortense, and in the summer she took up her residence there with a large suite of servants and ladies-in-waiting. At the end of September Louis was persuaded to come back to Paris, and on October 10th Hortense's first child was born, a son, who was given the names of Charles Napoleon, after his grandfather and his uncle. Napoleon had already formed his plans for the future of the child. He would watch over the boy's education. He would formally adopt him as his heir. He hoped he would one day be Napoleon II., for already he was vaguely thinking of the coming empire.

He had called to his aid Lucien's parliamentary talents to smooth the way. In 1802 one-fifth of the members of the Senate, the Tribunate, and the Corps Législatif retired. Napoleon took care that the lists of retiring members should be so drawn up as to weed out the opposition, and he replaced them by men who could be relied upon to support his own ideas.

In the negotiations to this end Lucien showed himself an able and tactful politician. For once he worked heart and soul with his brother. He became a member of the Tribunate. In Sieyès' original scheme for the constitution this body was to act as a check on the two other houses, and had large powers of criticism and revision. Its duties were now modified, so that its office was primarily to study and put into proper form the measures to be proposed to the Senate and the Corps Législatif. Lucien's business thus became that of seeing that every step the First Consul wished to propose should be initiated in the Tribunate and presented in the best form to the other legislative bodies.

One of the first of the important measures he had thus to champion was the establishment of the Legion of Honour. In Napoleon's idea it was not to be a mere machine for distributing decorations. It was to be an organisation of fifteen ' cohorts ' or groups, each made up of some four hundred officers and legionaries. Each member was to be chosen because he had done service to the state, preferably in war. His entrance into the Legion was to be a pledge of his future fidelity, nominally to the Republic, really to Napoleon. Each was to watch over and be answerable for the conduct of his comrades. The Legion would thus be a band of some six thousand picked men, bound to the First Consul by the honour conferred on them and the pension it carried with it. Naturally the opposition, feeble as it was, was inclined to protest. Lucien declared that they were misrepresenting the ideals of the Government. In a speech addressed to the Tribunate he proclaimed that to misrepresent and caricature the intentions of the Government was an act of disloyalty, if it was not a folly like that of Don Quixote setting his lance in rest against windmills which he imagined to be giants. He, who had once been the readiest to oppose the proposals of the Directory, now held that to challenge the policy of the Consulate was a proof of disaffection or of want of understanding. As the delegate of the Tribunate he successfully championed the proposal in the Corps Législatif. On the formation of the Legion Joseph was named a Grand Officer and member of its Council. Lucien, after some hesitation on Napoleon's part, was given the same distinction. The dignity of Grand

Officer conferred ex-officio membership of the Senate, so both Joseph and Lucien became senators under the revised Constitution of the Year x. (1802).

In carrying through the revision Lucien had again done good service to his brother. After lengthy negotiation between the various branches of the legislature and the leading groups of politicians, and after more than one dispute between Napoleon and Joseph, who had still deeply fixed in his mind the idea of his own paramount claims, at last the French people were asked to decide by plebiscite whether Napoleon was to be Consul for life with the right of choosing his successor. And by an overwhelming majority they answered ' Yes.' At the same time the Senate placed at his disposal an annual civil list that enabled him not only to maintain a splendid court, but also to provide liberally for his family and his chief supporters.

In January 1803 Napoleon proposed to Joseph that he should accept the office of chief of the military department of the Swiss Confederation, then under French protection. Joseph declined the honour, and suggested that General Lannes should have the appointment. He did not wish, he said, to break up his home in France. He divided his time between Paris and Mortefontaine. Besides his official duties as senator and member of the Grand Council of the Legion of Honour, he occupied himself with literary and scientific questions at the Institute and at learned societies, to several of which he and Lucien both belonged. Lucien was very prominent as a patron of art and letters. He was adding to his picture-gallery by frequent purchases. He assisted more than one young author with funds for the publication of a first book, and when he was elected a member of the Institute, he at once assigned the annual allowance to which his membership entitled him to the poet Béranger, who had lately applied to him for assistance.

Later on in life Lucien asserted that at this time there was a growing opposition between him and the First Consul, arising from his old love for Republican institutions making him hostile to the absolutist policy of Napoleon. But neither his letters nor any other contemporary record gives any evidence of such friction. On the contrary, until his second marriage

Lucien appears to have had the most cordial relations with Napoleon. There was far more of friction between Joseph and Napoleon. It led to brief quarrels, followed by a speedy reconciliation, because Napoleon felt still his old love and respect for the trusted companion of his boyhood, and because Joseph's disposition was too placid to allow of his anger ever being more than a passing feeling. He was in sharp opposition to Napoleon over the sale of Louisiana to the United States in April 1803, but before the month was over he was employed by the First Consul in delicate negotiations with the English ambassador, Lord Whitworth. Mutual accusations of bad faith in the matter of the execution of the treaty of Amiens had strained the relations between France and England almost to breaking point. Whitworth had bluntly said that he could not continue the discussion with Talleyrand, because it was no use talking to him unless one had money in his hand. At Napoleon's request Joseph conferred with Whitworth and tried to clear up the position. But his efforts led to no result. On May 14th Joseph was one of the deputation appointed by the Senate to wait upon the First Consul, and assure him of the support of all France in the war with England, for Whitworth had been given his passports. At this moment the brothers were fast friends. A few weeks later there was an angry scene between them at Mortefontaine, resulting from Napoleon's insisting on Josephine taking precedence of Madame Joseph Bonaparte at her own table and in her own house. But next day there was a reconciliation.

But while, notwithstanding such passing clouds, Joseph and Napoleon remained united, and the eldest brother held an assured position, the three others had enough of self-willed obstinacy to set themselves more or less at variance with the First Consul. Louis, whom he had promoted to the rank of brigadier-general in April 1803, had left Paris in March and spent six months at Montpellier, going through a prolonged cure and worrying himself about trifles of all kinds. Napoleon had helped him by purchasing Baillon from him and presenting the place to one of his generals. He was disappointed in the brother on whom he had once built so many hopes.

Lucien was taking a course that was soon to lead to an open rupture between him and his all-powerful brother. The

' Marquise de Santa Cruz ' had long since left his country
house, but Lucien's affections had been won by another lady,
Madame Jouberthou.   Her maiden name was Marie Alexandrine Bleschamp, she had been married at the age of nineteen to Jean François Jouberthou, a Paris stockbroker.   He
had made a fortune by daring speculations, and was living
in a splendid mansion on the south side of the Seine, when
his daughter Alexandrine was born in 1799.   Two years later,
by one of those sudden turns of fortune that are the lot of
daring speculators, Jouberthou found himself all but ruined.
His fine house was sold up, and leaving his wife and her little
daughter with very scanty resources in Paris, he sailed for
San Domingo, where he hoped to make some money in
connection with supplies for the army.   A report soon came
that he had fallen a victim to the deadly climate.

Lucien met Madame Jouberthou at a friend's house in the
early summer of 1802, and soon after she was staying with him
at his country house at Plessis near Paris.   There was little
secrecy about the affair.   Fontanes, Lucien's old literary
colleague, wrote to a friend that the lady was pretty, coquettish,
and somewhat grasping.   But it was supposed that, like the
' Marquise,' she would presently disappear.   When Lucien
went back to Paris he took a house for the lady near his own.
There, on May 24, 1803, a child was born, a boy, whose birth
was registered next day under the name of ' Jules Laurent
Lucien.'   On the same day (May 25) there was a secret
marriage.   By the Canon Law and the law of France such a
subsequent marriage of the parents would legitimatise the
child, and Lucien, though he could not yet venture to make his
intentions public, had determined to unite his lot for life with
that of Alexandrine Jouberthou.   A priest, the Abbé François
Perier, and two trusty witnesses were brought to the house,
and the Abbé signed a certificate dated 5th Prairial, Year XI.
of the Republic (May 25, 1803), to the effect that at nine A.M.
that day he had baptized a child, Jules Laurent Lucien, born
the evening before at No. 67 Place du Corps Législatif, ' the
offspring of a legitimate marriage ' which he had celebrated
between the Senator Lucien Bonaparte and the Lady Marie
Alexandrine de Bleschamp, widow of François Jouberthou de
Vambertie, adding that both parties to the marriage had made

oath before him that 'they could not immediately declare their marriage before the civil authorities on account of an absolute necessity of a political character, but promised to do so as soon as it could be done without danger.' Afterwards Lucien's enemies alleged that he could have had no proof that Alexandrine was really a widow. But the Abbé Perier could not have acted without some proof on this point, and Madame Jouberthou must have had letters and papers establishing the fact. As a formal certificate of the local authorities, afterwards produced by Lucien, showed, Jouberthou had died at Port au Prince, San Domingo, on June 15, 1802, nearly a year before.

Within a few days of the secret marriage Napoleon sent for Lucien. He had a brilliant proposal to make him. On May 27th Louis I., King of Etruria, had died at Florence. Etruria was the central Italian kingdom founded that the Spanish Infanta, who had married Louis when he was only Duke of Parma, might be a queen. It was part of the Franco-Spanish policy embodied in the treaties Lucien had signed as ambassador at Madrid. His brother now proposed that he should go to Florence to act as French resident there, and advise and assist the widowed Infanta. She was childless, and Napoleon pointed out that if Lucien would only play his part a marriage could be arranged next year, and he would be a king, ruling at Florence, once, it was said, the home of a branch of the Bonapartes, some thought the place of their origin. To Napoleon's surprise Lucien refused the offer. He used many arguments to combat the First Consul's views, but he did not say that he had a wife and son on the other side of the Seine. Napoleon was disappointed, and somewhat annoyed. His first plan of king-making had come to nothing, on account of what looked like mere self-willed opposition on Lucien's part. But there was no rupture between the brothers. On the contrary, in July Napoleon conferred a new favour on Lucien. He sent him to visit Belgium and the lands of the Moselle and Rhine, telling him to select a district which he would represent as senator and of which he would be a kind of protector. These territorial senatorships gave a right to a residence in the district and 25,000 francs a year for expenses. Lucien selected Trèves as his district, and so had

as a country seat on the Moselle the château of Poppelsdorf,
a fine house with picture-gallery, library, concert-room, and
a beautiful park.

In September Napoleon offered Joseph the post of chancellor
of the Senate and Lucien that of treasurer. Both brothers
refused the appointments.   The reason of their refusal appears
to have been that there was just then some friction between
them and the First Consul on the question of the succession.
They wanted their rights as his brothers defined, and were
jealous of his project to make the son of Louis his heir.   Next
month Lucien, tired of concealing his marriage, and believing
he was now in a position to hold his own against the displeasure
of the First Consul, took a step which would soon put an
end to all secrecy.   On October 26th he went through the
formality of the civil marriage before the assistant-mayor
of Chamant, near Plessis, at the same time recording his
declaration of the legitimacy of his son.

Joseph and Napoleon were both thunderstruck at the news.
Once more it seemed to them Lucien, as in the case of Catherine
Boyer, had made a foolish marriage, at a time, too, when he
could have waited to choose among the highest in Europe,
and by a wise choice help forward the rising greatness of their
house.   Napoleon was especially angry at his brother's long
silence.   He saw now that he had rejected a favourite plan of
his own for the sake of an irregular union with the widow of
a broken-down stockbroker.   He would not have minded if
he had taken Alexandrine as his mistress.   He was furious
at the thought that she was his wife. Joseph, too, was heartily
opposed to Lucien.   How could they press forward the plan
for hereditary right, he asked, with this child among the
possible claimants to the future sovereignty of France? ' It
seems,' he said, ' that Destiny is blinding us, and means to
use our blunders to give France back to her old rulers.'

Joseph was employed by Napoleon to try to bring Lucien
to reason.   He was to offer him a *modus vivendi*, a compromise.
It was suggested that Lucien should write to Napoleon giving
an undertaking that for the present his wife should not bear
his name, or be presented to his relations, and that he would
not publicly acknowledge the marriage until the First Consul
judged the time was opportune and had given his consent.

On these conditions Napoleon would agree to receive Lucien as if nothing had happened and would not object to his living quietly with his wife. Lucien was persuaded by Joseph to write the letter. But he almost at once regretted it. To an invitation from Joseph to dine at his house at Paris, an invitation in which his wife was not included, he replied by a refusal. He did not want such entertainments, he said; he complained of being 'rejected by the family after having served its interests and won honour for it'; he was sorry he had been guilty of 'the baseness of writing that letter to the First Consul, agreeing that his wife should not bear the family name.' 'Every one,' he added, 'is only too willing to give her the name, and so my promise has no practical effect. I only wish that all the women who bear the name did as much honour to it as she does. My wife, my son, my daughters, myself are all one, and public opinion sees this and will do us justice.' The result was a rupture with Napoleon. On December 4th Lucien left Paris with his wife. He wrote to Joseph that he was going to Florence, Rome, and Naples. He would resign his seat in the Senate, and he suggested that Bernadotte should be proposed for it (perhaps because Bernadotte, the husband of Joseph's sister-in-law, was always unfriendly to Napoleon). 'Do not do anything during my absence to make peace for me with the First Consul,' he added; 'I am going away with hatred in my heart.'

He travelled by the Rhineland and Switzerland to northern Italy; then to Florence, Rome, and Naples and back to Venice, visiting picture-galleries and buying some more pictures for his collection. His mother had taken his part and exerted her influence in his favour with Napoleon. At the end of February 1804 he was back in Paris, and it was thought some kind of a reconciliation might be patched up.

Meanwhile news had come of Jerome's marriage. His messenger, Meyronnet, had arrived in France in the winter of 1803, and in January 1804 started again for America bearing a letter from the Minister of Marine ordering Jerome to return at once on board a French warship, and on no account under a neutral flag. Meyronnet was on the Atlantic when, through news from America published in the English papers, Paris heard of Jerome's marriage. On February 18th the

Paris *Débats* published the report without giving entire credence to it. 'We read in some of the English papers,' ran the paragraph, 'that Jerome Bonaparte, the brother of the First Consul, has been married at Baltimore to Miss Elisabeth Patterson, the eldest daughter of Mr. William Patterson, a rich business man of that city, and that the marriage ceremony was performed by the bishop. But for the last year there have been so many false reports circulated about Jerome Bonaparte that one may perhaps doubt this story.'

The news was likely to make Napoleon more difficult to reconcile with Lucien, and the reconciliation effected by Madame Letizia Bonaparte did not go very far. She was about to visit Italy, and she suggested that Lucien should spend some time there, thus avoiding any chances of further friction with his brother at Paris. Napoleon was to give him a letter of introduction to the Pope, so as to let the social circles of Rome suppose there was no quarrel. In his letter to Pius VII. Napoleon recommended Lucien to him, and explained that he was going to make a prolonged stay in Rome in order ' to devote himself to the study of antiquities and history.'

But Lucien seemed in no hurry to leave Paris. On March 14th, the day after Napoleon had given him the letter to Pius VII., Robert Patterson, the brother of Jerome's wife, came to see him. He had just arrived in France, sent by his father to ascertain what view the Bonaparte family took of the marriage. He had gone first to Lucien, and he had an encouraging reception. Lucien assured him that all the family, with one exception, approved of Jerome's marriage. It was true that ' for the moment ' the First Consul was displeased, but he stood alone. As ' the first magistrate of a great nation ' he looked at things from a political point of view, with which the rest of the family had nothing to do. They were ' simply citizens,' and as such, judging by all they heard of the lady, they were ' proud and happy at the news of their brother's choice.' He thought that Jerome and the Pattersons should not attach too much importance to the displeasure of the First Consul. ' I myself,' he continued, ' though I am of an age to be my own master, and though I have occupied high positions in the Government, have also incurred his displeasure by my recent marriage. So Jerome does not stand alone. But as in marrying we have in view our own happiness and not that of another, it is a matter on which no one has a right to talk to us of his approval or disapproval. Our general wish just now is that Jerome should remain where he is, and take the necessary steps to become a peaceful citizen of the United States as soon as possible.' He was told that Jerome would in that case have to take the oath of allegiance to the United States and renounce all claim to noble rank. ' Of course he should do so,' said Lucien. ' The high honour of becoming a citizen of the United States is well worth it. His position is greatly to be preferred to ours. We are yet out on a stormy sea. He is safely anchored in harbour. We are taking steps to secure that he will have a pleasant future.' Then he hinted that he might go to America himself with his wife and children before long.

Though he thus spoke in the name of the Bonaparte family, there is no doubt that Lucien expressed only his own feelings inspired by sympathy for a brother whose case was so like his own, and by resentment against Napoleon. Joseph certainly did not share his views. Louis was utterly indifferent. Madame Letizia was anxious for peace, she always took the part of her sons, and defended Jerome as she defended Lucien himself. Robert Patterson soon found that the First Consul would not hear of any friendly arrangement. A few days later the First Consul sent an official despatch to Pichon at Washington warning him that he must not advance 'another dollar to Jerome, and an order to Jerome himself to return to France at once. on a warship, with the further information that orders had been given to all captains of French ships on the Atlantic that they were on no account to receive on board the ' young person ' with whom Jerome had gone through the form of marriage, and that if she landed at any French port she would be forced to re-embark.

Notwithstanding his projected visit to Rome, Lucien had lingered on in Paris, because in this month of March 1804 the final steps were being taken that were to lead to the establishment of hereditary power and the proclamation of the Empire. A great conspiracy against Napoleon, which included in its ranks royalist zealots like Cadoudal and Republican generals

like Pichegru and Moreau, had been crushed, and Napoleon
had tried to strike terror among his enemies by the murder of
the Duc d'Enghien.   Joseph and Lucien had a common bond
of action in their joint opposition to the project of their exclusion from all claim to the succession in favour of the son of
Louis.   Their younger brother had returned from his ' cure '
at Montpellier, and had taken command of a brigade of dragoons at Compiègne, which included his own regiment.   Hortense had gone there, and was acting as a graceful hostess at
the entertainments which General Louis Bonaparte gave to
his officers and to the social notabilities of the little town.
During the discussions which followed the vote of the Senate
on March 28, 1804, calling for establishment of hereditary
government, Louis had come up to Paris from Compiègne.

On April 4, after some preliminary conferences with Joseph,
in which Napoleon made no definite proposals, he told his
eldest brother that he meant to assume the title of Emperor,
and at the same time adopt Charles Napoleon, the son of
Louis, as his heir, naming Joseph guardian of the boy and
regent, in case he himself should die while his heir was still
a minor.   Joseph met the proposal with a protest against his
own exclusion from all hope of succession.   After the interview he consulted his friends.   They thought he ought to accept
Napoleon's scheme of succession, but Joseph clung to his old
idea of his paramount right as eldest brother and head of the
family.   On the 7th Napoleon and Josephine went to see
Louis at his house, and Josephine explained to him what was
proposed.   Louis seemed inclined to accept, but hesitated
to give a definite answer.   Next day he went to consult Joseph
about the proposal.   Joseph put the matter in the worst
possible light.   He told Louis he would be sacrificing his own
claims, and would see his son taken from him to be brought
up by Napoleon and Josephine, and that the mere suggestion
was an insult.   It meant that Louis himself was held unfit
to reign.   It was the outcome of the jealousy of the Beauharnais against the Bonapartes, an outrage on all the family.

Louis was easily led to take this view.   Joseph went to
Lucien, and the two brothers exchanged their ideas on the
subject.   Both saw in the proposal an attack on their own
claims.   They agreed that Louis must refuse at once, and

Joseph took the young man with him to the Tuileries, anxious that he should speak while he was still under the influence of what he had said to him that morning. Louis broke out into an angry remonstrance with Napoleon. ' What,' he asked, ' had he done to deserve to be disinherited ? What would be his feelings at seeing his own son set above him, made independent of him, taught to despise him ? He would never agree to it. He would rather renounce all his hopes for the future. He would leave France, taking little Napoleon with him, and then ' we shall see if even you will dare in the face of the world to tear the son away from his father.' Napoleon tried to argue. Louis would not listen to him. He saw that for the present he must give up his favourite project.

There was another conference. Napoleon consented that Joseph should stand first in succession. He did not so much mind yielding the point, for Joseph had only daughters, and in any case he believed he would certainly outlive his eldest brother. He proposed to exclude Lucien. Then Louis and his son would stand next. Joseph insisted that Lucien himself should not be excluded, and Napoleon was ready to accept this provided that Lucien's rights should not descend to the son of the Jouberthou marriage. He sent for Lucien and offered him this compromise. It was one evening in April when the First Consul was staying at St. Cloud. After dinner Lucien went into Napoleon's study about nine o'clock. The discussion lasted nearly three hours. Lucien would not hear of any compromise. ' My wife, my son, myself,' he repeated, ' stand together.' Napoleon in vain urged reasons of state, argued, almost entreated. Then, when Lucien would not yield, the brothers parted in anger. It was midnight when the First Consul came back alone to the drawing-room, where Josephine was waiting to hear the result. ' It is all over,' he said, ' I have just broken with Lucien and driven him from my presence.' Josephine suggested that after all peace might yet be made. ' It is good of you to plead for him,' said Napoleon, ' but it is all over.' Then he told her how he had exhausted in vain every argument. ' It is hard,' he said, ' to meet with such opposition when such great interests are at stake. It looks as if I must isolate myself from every one, and count only on myself. Well, I can stand alone, and you,

Josephine, will be there to console me.'   Within two days after,
on April 14th, Lucien and his family left Paris.   He travelled
with a suite of servants, secretaries, artists in four big lumber-
ing carriages, that rolled away on the road to Lyons bound for
the Mont Cenis and Italy.

A few days before, as if to show that he had no quarrel with
Louis, Napoleon had promoted him to the rank of general
of division, and made him a member of the Council of State.
He now suggested to Joseph that, if he was to take his place
as possible successor to a military empire, he must not remain
a mere civilian.   What was his object in persuading his eldest
brother, a portly, respectable country gentleman, who prided
himself on his broad acres at Mortefontaine and his achieve-
ments in diplomacy, to pose as a soldier ?   Was it to convince
him that he was not fitted to be the ruler of an armed empire ?
Or was it simply to keep him away from Paris while the
constitution of the new empire was being put into shape ?
Whatever was his motive, he succeeded in bringing Joseph
to accept the new career he offered him.   The Army of
England was encamped at Boulogne, and flat-bottomed
boats for its transport across the Channel crowded every
harbour and creek along the north-west coast.   On April 18th
Napoleon informed the Senate that their colleague, ' the
Senator Joseph Bonaparte, Grand Officer of the Legion of
Honour, had expressed a desire to share the perils and glories
of the army encamped at Boulogne.'   He went on to speak
of the important services Joseph had rendered to the state,
the wise counsels he had given, the tact and ability he had
shown in important negotiations.   He considered, he said,
that it was for the good of the state that Joseph should be
placed in a position where he ' would share in the vengeance
of the French people ' on its great enemy, and at the same time
obtain a new claim to the esteem of the nation.   He said that
his brother had served with him in his first campaigns, and he
had remarked his aptitude for a military career.   This was
hardly true.   Joseph had been a mere spectator of the first
stage of the campaign of Italy, and at an earlier date had been
with his brother before Toulon in a civil capacity.   But
Napoleon had to say something to justify his next announcement.   Joseph was to be appointed Colonel, and to take

command at once of the 4th Infantry of the line, one of the most distinguished regiments of the army.

With his commission Napoleon prepared for Colonel Joseph Bonaparte a wholly fictitious record of service, a strange document which may be thus summarised :—

Student of artillery	1783
Staff-officer	1792
Major and adjutant-general . . .	1793
Campaigns	1793, 1794
Wounds. Slightly wounded at the siege of Toulon.	

The basis of all this was his employment during the war as a commissary, busy with stores and supplies. Of the wound at Toulon there is no record elsewhere. Strangely enough, Joseph's presence with the army in 1796 is not referred to. But the commission and a grant of 300,000 francs for expenses were solid realities. On the 25th Joseph in full uniform left Paris for the camp. On the 30th he took command of the 4th Infantry at Boulogne, and worked hard to learn the elements of his new business, while at Paris debates were in progress in which he was deeply interested and in which he could not say a word. The episode had the unfortunate result that years after in Spain the ex-colonel of Boulogne imagined he was a heaven-inspired general, and tried to over-rule the plans of men who had commanded armies for years. He was not happy at Boulogne. In May he wrote to his wife that he sometimes thought of abandoning all plans for a great future and living quietly among his fields at Mortefontaine. While Joseph was thus writing to his wife, the Council of State and the Senate had adopted a project for the constitution of the Empire that gave Napoleon indirectly all he wanted. The succession to the Imperial Crown was to be the right first of Joseph, then of Louis and of their male descendants, *but* Napoleon as the First of the Emperors was to have the right of adopting as his heir any Prince of the Imperial family on his attaining the age of eighteen. He could thus after all place Charles Napoleon in front of Joseph and Louis, when the time came. Their rights might prove to be merely nominal.

Joseph was disappointed, but he had some consolations. He would be a Prince of the Empire, with a civil list of a million francs, and Grand Elector, with the palace of the Luxembourg as his residence and an allowance of one-third of a million. Further, Napoleon secured for him a grant of 350,000 francs more for expenses at the outset. As Grand Elector he would stand next to the Emperor. He would on certain great occasions preside over the Senate as his representative. He would direct the working of the very limited constitutional machinery belonging to the new order of things. There was a splendid official costume for the Grand Elector, a white tunic embroidered with gold and a mantle trimmed with ermine for great days, and for those of less importance a blue velvet tunic with a broad scarf of gold, a velvet mantle studded with golden bees, a court sword and a plumed hat. Everything was carefully regulated to make the theatrical side of the Empire as gorgeous as the old monarchy had been even in the days of 'le Roi Soleil.'

Louis was to be Grand Constable of the new Empire, a military title, recalling that of the Constables of France in the warlike days of the older monarchy. As Prince of the Empire he too had a million of francs a year, and a third of a million more added to it as Constable. But it gave him only ceremonial rank, and no direct command. It indicated Napoleon's hope that he would still prove himself a soldier, and some day be fit to lead armies in the field. For the present his effective rank was general of division, and the Marshals of France, veterans soon to be rewarded with this revived rank, had a first claim to actual command. Besides his office of Constable Louis was appointed Colonel-General of the Carbineers, the cavalry of the Emperor's guard. In 1804 he was able to spend more than three-quarters of a million in purchasing the Hôtel St. Julien, a large mansion in the Rue Taitbout, to which he moved from the house Napoleon had bought for Hortense in the Rue de la Victoire; and two other properties in the country north of Paris beyond the forest of Montmorency, namely, the château and lands of St. Leu, and an adjoining estate. In the summer he was chiefly occupied with putting these new possessions in order, but he was still anxious about his health, and went for a while to take the waters at Plombières.

In August Joseph obtained leave of absence from his military duties, came to Paris, and as Grand Elector received in state at his house in the Faubourg St. Honoré addresses of congratulation presented by the Council of State, the Senate, and the Corps Législatif.   The spokesman of the Senate assured him that all knew his love of simplicity, and that he valued rank and title only because his position gave him the opportunity of serving the nation and his fellow-men.   The address of the lower house expressed the joy of the French people at having at their head 'a family that united in itself the art of conquest and the art of government, the talent for negotiations, the gift of eloquence, the splendour of heroism, the grace of intellect, and the charm of courtesy.'   Joseph could take most of these praises as addressed to himself.

In the autumn there was again some friction between him and his brother — discussions over the choice that he had made of his household, which Napoleon thought ought to have included more of the old aristocracy of the days of royalty and of the new military element—and further disputes as to the position his wife was to occupy on the great day of the coronation.   But at last everything was arranged.   The Pope had come to Paris, and on December 2nd there was the solemn inauguration of the Empire at Notre Dame.   Joseph, the companion of those boyish holidays so long ago at Ajaccio, stood beside him as the first of his subjects, in the midst of such a display of ecclesiastical, courtly, and military pomp as France had never seen till then.   Just before he went up to the altar where the Pope waited to give him the crown of his new Empire, Napoleon turned to his brother and whispered to him, 'Joseph, if our father could only see us now!' Louis was there, too, trying to look his part as Constable of France, the representative of her armed Imperial might. The other brothers were far away, Jerome still beyond the Atlantic, Lucien in Italy with 'hatred in his heart.'

CHAPTER VIII

MARRIAGE QUESTIONS

(1804-1805)

WHILE he was still arranging the stately ceremonial of his coronation Napoleon had been thinking of erecting tributary kingdoms, to be the satellites of his new Empire. The 'Cisalpine Republic' was to be transformed into the 'Kingdom of Italy,' and his first idea was to offer its Iron Crown to Joseph. Though he had already taken some steps in this direction, and sounded the Emperor Francis on the subject, it was not till the end of December that he made the flattering proposal to his brother. Joseph at first seemed disposed to accept it, but when everything was nearly settled he refused, because his renunciation of all claim to the Imperial succession was made a condition of his wearing the crown of Italy. It was in vain that his friends pointed out to him that his right to the succession was more imaginary than real, and that it would be better for him to be King of Italy at once than wait for the Imperial crown, which Napoleon could put beyond his reach by sooner or later devising it to an adopted son. Joseph persisted in his refusal.

Napoleon then proposed to assume in his own person the rule of the new kingdom, adopt Charles Napoleon, the son of Louis, transfer his right to Italy to the boy, proclaiming him King under the title of Napoleon II., and governing the kingdom for him till he came of age. This plan also had to be abandoned, for Louis obstinately refused to hear of his son being ' preferred before him,' or of his being adopted by Napoleon before the age fixed by the decree of the Senate.

Although he was thus once more thwarted by Louis in a favourite scheme, Napoleon continued to distinguish his brother by special marks of his goodwill. He clung to the idea that, disappointing as Louis himself had proved to be, the succession to the Empire would be secured in his line. A second son of Louis and Hortense had been born in October 1804. The child was baptized and given the name of Napoleon Louis on March 24, 1805. The baptism was made the occasion of an elaborate state ceremonial, with more of ostentatious display than had ever graced the christening of an heir to the old monarchy. The ceremony took place at St. Cloud. All the great dignitaries of the Empire were present. Pope Pius VII. was the officiating priest. Louis had complained that his health suffered in Paris and northern France, and said he felt the need of a warmer climate. Napoleon appointed him governor of the 'Departments beyond the Alps,' portions of the former territory of Piedmont and Genoa, now annexed to France. He was to reside in the former palace of the Sardinian kings at Turin. But he was in no hurry to take up his new post. He looked on it as a kind of exile. In any case, he said, he would not go there till after the coming coronation of Napoleon as King of Italy at Milan, which was to take place in May 1805.

The Emperor, after the failure of two successive combinations for giving the Iron Crown to one of his kindred, had decided to assume it himself. His brother Lucien, after a short visit to Rome, had gone to Milan in November 1804. The preparations were being made for the Emperor's coronation at Notre Dame, and Lucien had a lingering hope that at the last moment he would be invited to be present. But no invitation came. On December 1st, the eve of the great day, a daughter was born to him at Milan, to whom he gave the name of Letizia. In March he heard that Napoleon would soon be in the capital of Lombardy for his second coronation, and he left Milan for Pesaro, in the Papal States. On the eve of his journey he wrote to the Emperor a letter which he hoped would open a way for a reconciliation. His mother and brother Joseph were ready to use their influence on his behalf. And he had a new ambition. He had heard of Napoleon's attempts to secure the co-operation of Joseph and of Louis in the government of the Italian kingdom, and he knew that the question of the appointment of a regent was being discussed. If he could make friends with the Emperor, he might hope to be regent of Italy.

' I think it my duty to inform your Majesty that I am going to Pesaro,' he had written from Milan. ' There I shall continue to cherish the same feelings of inalterable devotion to your cause, a devotion that cannot be affected by the disappointments that are my lot. Any mark of your goodwill, Sire, would be precious to me, for if past events have excluded me from the political family circle of princes of the Empire, I do not think that I have deserved, and I beg that you will spare me, anything that might appear to signify your dislike.'

Early in April Lucien had a letter from his mother. She told him that his letter had produced an excellent impression on the Emperor. On the eve of his departure from Paris for Italy there had been a family debate on the matter, and she was delighted to think her sons would soon be reconciled. She begged Lucien to make every possible concession, and not let this chance pass by. It might be the last. The same post brought a letter from Joseph. He had been talking with the Emperor, and Napoleon had said he would be glad to meet Lucien at Milan. But then he went on to explain that on one point Napoleon was immovably resolved. He had no objection to Lucien arranging for his wife to reside on one of his properties, but he had said to Joseph that he would never see her, never recognise her as his sister-in-law. He was pleased with Lucien, and excepting this he would make any concession to him. ' Lucien has brains,' he added ; ' tell him to use them to make the best of the position in which he has placed himself. With this one exception I am ready to do anything he asks.'

Lucien wrote in reply to the Emperor that Joseph's letter was a serious disappointment to him. ' It informs me,' he said, ' that your Majesty is ready to do for me anything that is not inconsistent with the firm resolution you have taken not to acknowledge my wife. That resolution, Sire, profoundly grieves me, for it excludes me for ever from the honourable public career which I hoped your Majesty would open to me. I can assure you, Sire, that any dignity that would be accompanied by an open manifestation of the disfavour that weighs upon the dearest half of myself would only debase me in my own eyes. A title that I could not share with the mother of my children would be a fatal gift, that would poison all my life.'

Napoleon did not at once close the correspondence. He left it to Talleyrand to try to bring Lucien to reason, but Lucien, to his honour, refused to sacrifice his wife. Meanwhile the Emperor had become involved in another matrimonial discussion with Jerome. He had stopped at Stupinigi in Piedmont, in the last days of April, to make the final arrangements for his coronation at Milan. Here on April 22nd he received the news that Jerome and his American wife had arrived at Lisbon on the 9th.

It was some sixteen months since his marriage at Baltimore, and more than a year since the first rumours of the event had been published in the Paris newspapers. When the marriage took place Lieutenant Meyronnet was crossing the Atlantic with orders to Jerome to return instantly to France. Jerome replied in a letter addressed to Talleyrand. Not a word did he say of his marriage. He regretted that he had not sooner received the First Consul's orders. He would lose no time in acting upon them, and would take the first opportunity of returning to France. At the same time he wrote a letter to his mother. He began by telling her that no doubt she had already learned from his previous letters to her the news of his marriage. Of these earlier letters there is no trace whatever. It is possible that they may really have been written and then lost at sea, but it seems more probable that the allusion to them was a fiction on Jerome's part, intended to make Madame Letizia believe that he had lost no time in informing her of the step he had taken. He went on to tell her that he hoped soon to present his wife to her. He hoped she would be pleased with his choice. Meanwhile he was sending her Elisabeth's portrait.

Notwithstanding his talk about returning at once, Jerome made no effort to secure a passage to France. He was waiting on in the hope that his mother and his brothers would make his peace with Napoleon. At the end of June 1804 Pichon had informed him that he had received express orders from the Ministry of Marine directing Lieutenant Jerome Bonaparte to leave the United States for France without further delay, and that at the same time he had been himself warned not to supply

H

him with funds except for this journey, and to intimate to him that his wife would not be allowed to enter France. At the same time he handed Jerome a letter containing a personal appeal to him from the Minister, Admiral Decrès. Decrès asked him how it was consistent with his honour and duty as a naval officer to remain idle, thousands of miles away, while France was at war. All might yet be repaired by a prompt submission. If he would return to France *alone*, the First Consul would pardon his errors on account of his youth, and open to him a career in which he might win himself a name. Jerome told Pichon he would start at once. Two French frigates were at New York, but a strong British squadron was coming up the coast to blockade their exit. Jerome pretended he was anxious to avail himself of this chance, but delayed his start for New York until the hostile squadron had arrived, and it was impossible for the frigates to put to sea.

Pichon had cut off supplies; but Jerome had received some large remittances from a friend who had succeeded in raising a loan for him in Paris, so he was able to stay on at Baltimore. The late summer and the early autumn brought news from France that made him anxious. The Empire was to be proclaimed, but his name was left out of the list of Imperial Princes; the Paris papers had published an officially communicated note to the effect that there could be no truth in the report of Jerome's marriage; he was under age and could not contract a legal marriage without the consent of his family, though ' it was possible he had involved himself in an affair with a mistress, which was probably the origin of the report.' He had appealed to Joseph to intervene in his favour, but Joseph sent a guarded reply. ' Tell Madame Bonaparte,' he wrote to Jerome, ' that once she has been received by the head of the family she will have no more devoted brother than myself.' In October he resolved to go to Europe. He embarked with his wife and his suite on a brig which was wrecked at the mouth of Chesapeake Bay. Jerome and his wife and friends escaped, but had to abandon most of their property. Early in December he again prepared to start, but had to give up the idea on learning that British cruisers were watching the mouth of the Chesapeake. His money was running out, and his position was becoming desperate. The rumour that he was about to leave America had reached Europe early in 1805. The Emperor obtained his mother's signature to a protest against the marriage, proclaimed it null and void, and forbade any official of the state to recognise it.

His father-in-law, Mr. Patterson, now placed at Jerome's disposal one of his ships, a fast-sailing clipper, the *Erin*, and on March 3, 1805, he embarked at Baltimore accompanied by his wife, a brother-in-law William Patterson, and his secretary. On April 9th the *Erin* cast anchor at Lisbon, and Jerome landed and asked the French ambassador for passports for himself and his party to France. The envoy told him that he could give him a passport, but that ' Miss Patterson ' could not be allowed to enter France with him. He went on board the *Erin* with Jerome, and when he was introduced to his wife, he asked, ' Is there anything I can do for *Miss Patterson* ? ' ' Tell your master,' she replied, ' that *Madame Bonaparte* is ambitious, and demands her rights as a member of the Imperial family ! ' Then she turned away angrily, and left Jerome to continue the discussion.

He decided to accept the passport for himself and his secretary Lecamus, and go on to Italy and personally plead his cause with Napoleon. Meanwhile the *Erin* with the rest of his party proceeded to Amsterdam, where Elisabeth was to await the result of his journey. On the way he wrote to her telling her to have no fear for the future. ' The worst that can happen to us,' he said, ' is only that we may have to go to some foreign country and live there quietly, and as long as we are together we are certain to be happy.' Travelling day and night he reached Turin on April 24th. It was only the day after Napoleon had heard the news of his arrival at Lisbon. On the 23rd the Emperor had sent orders to Jerome to come at once to Milan by a defined route. If he went elsewhere he would be at once arrested. If his wife entered France she was to be expelled. To his mother Napoleon wrote to inform her of these orders. He said he would call Jerome to a strict account. If he was obstinate he would perhaps send him for trial to a court-martial, and his fate would be a warning to young officers not to abandon their duty.

Jerome was confident that if he could only see the Emperor he would persuade him to pardon everything and recognise his marriage. But Napoleon sternly refused to receive him. Jerome was officially informed that unless he made a complete surrender he would be severely dealt with. Though not under arrest, he was made to feel that he was in serious danger. He wrote to his brother entreating him to make some concession, begging for an interview. The only reply was a cold reminder that the Emperor was inflexible, and that if Jerome delayed his submission it might come too late. At last, on May 5th, his courage broke down. Flattering himself that he would yet gain his ends, and that his surrender would be only a temporary expedient, he wrote to the Emperor that he was ready to obey him in everything.

Next day Napoleon replied. He was about to make his state entry into Milan. He invited Jerome to come to see him at Alessandria. He was ready to forgive everything. ' Your union with Miss Patterson,' he wrote, ' is null in the eyes of both religion and the law. Write to her to go back to America. I will grant her a life-pension of 60,000 francs, on condition that she does not bear your name, to which the invalidity of her union with you gives her no right. Tell her you cannot change the nature of things.' This done, he was ready to restore him to favour and give him a career.

The interview took place. Jerome was all abject submission. Napoleon declared that he was satisfied and would treat him generously. He would arrange for the payment of his debts, assign him an income of 150,000 francs a year and give him a naval command. Lecamus was sent off to break the news to Elisabeth. But Jerome was feebly playing a double part. He had not Lucien's courage and determination, and he sent Elisabeth a private letter protesting that he would be true to her, and that before long he would still persuade the Emperor to acknowledge their union. Meanwhile they must have patience.

When Lecamus reached Amsterdam he learned that Elisabeth was in England. When the *Erin* arrived in Dutch waters the authorities had refused Madame Bonaparte permission to land, for under the Batavian Republic Holland was practically French territory. After waiting for some days the *Erin* had sailed for Dover, where Madame Jerome and her brother landed on May 19th. A curious crowd witnessed the disembarkation and cheered the Americans. They proceeded by postchaise to London. They took lodgings at Camberwell. The district is now a mass of busy streets. It was then in the country, 'a village, two miles from London,' visited by tourists, who came to see the famous Dr. Lettsom's Park and Botanic Garden, and to enjoy the 'fine view over the metropolis and the surrounding country.' Here Elisabeth received Lecamus's bad news and Jerome's confidential letter. When Napoleon heard that she had taken refuge in England, and thus put herself under the protection of his enemies, he was more than ever enraged against her.

Jerome had gone to Genoa to take command of a squadron of two 44-gun frigates and two brigs. He had been promoted to the rank of *capitaine de frégate*. From Genoa he wrote to Elisabeth on July 29th. 'God sees my heart,' he said, 'and knows that I only love and live for my good wife.' When he would again have the joy of seeing her he would tell her all that had happened when he met the Emperor. 'My brother,' he went on, 'is as good and generous as he is great, and if for the moment political reasons compel him to adopt this line of conduct, the time will come when all this will change.' He begged her to be patient, and above all not to refuse the pension offered by the Emperor. It would be ruin for them all to provoke an open quarrel. She must seem to accept the new situation of affairs, and if she did not hear from him to the contrary within two months, she must return to America. She could take a house at Baltimore, and he would write to her, but she was to allow no one except her mother to know of the correspondence. No one else must hear of it, or he would be ruined beyond remedy. Again and again he insisted on the absolute necessity of concealment and dissimulation, begging her to trust him, and to believe that it was all for her sake and the sake of their child, who he thought must be born by this time. He hoped it was a son. He sent her drafts of letters she was to copy and address to the Emperor and Empress. She was to sign them simply 'Elisa,' a non-committal form of signature. She was to take care to say nothing against Napoleon. Whatever she said would be reported to him. With patience all would be well sooner or later. He ended with protestations that he thought only of her, and longed to be reunited to her.

Three weeks before this letter was written Elisabeth had given birth to a son at Camberwell on July 7th. The child was afterwards named Jerome Napoleon Bonaparte. Elisabeth and her brother, with a view to future eventualities, had the certificate of birth registered by a notary, and countersigned by the ambassadors of Austria and Prussia at London. These precautions were taken with the intention that later the rights of an Imperial Prince should be claimed for the son of Jerome and his American wife. The two months named in her husband's letter from Genoa passed by, but she remained in London, still hoping the Emperor would relent.

But Napoleon regarded the affair as settled, and had not the remotest idea of reconsidering his decision, which he believed that both Elisabeth and Jerome had accepted. As there was no civil registration of the marriage in France, he considered that there was no need of its being declared invalid by any French tribunal. But in order to obviate possible scandals, and destroy any ground for future claims on behalf of Jerome's son, he was anxious to obtain a decree of an ecclesiastical court declaring the religious ceremony of no avail. He had mentioned this wish of his casually to Pius VII. when the Pope was in Paris for the coronation. In May, after Jerome's submission and on the eve of the coronation at Milan, the Emperor forwarded the documents containing a statement of the case to the Pope, with a letter in which he assumed that the Papal judgment must be in his favour.

This letter is a curious document, strangely tactless, full of misstatements on points of fact, and arguments that prove nothing. These arguments were helped out by a veiled threat to override an adverse decision by an appeal to ' the Gallican Church,' and by an attempt to play upon what he supposed would be the Pope's feeling against a marriage with a Protestant.

' I have spoken more than once to your Holiness,' wrote Napoleon, ' of a young brother of mine, nineteen years old, whom I sent on a frigate to America, and who after only a month's stay there,[1] although he was not of age, married at

---

[1] Jerome had been in the United States *more than five months.* He arrived on July 20, 1803, and was married on December 24.

Baltimore a Protestant, the daughter of a United States business man. He has just come home, and fully recognises his fault. I have sent his so-called wife back to America.[1] According to our laws the marriage is null. A Spanish priest[2] so far forgot his duty as to bless it. I would like to have from your Holiness a Bull annulling the marriage. I send your Holiness several reports on the question, including one from Cardinal Caselli, which you will find throws much light on the subject. As the Gallican Church does not recognise marriages of this kind, it would be easy for me to have it annulled at Paris ; but it appears to me to be better to have this done at Rome, if only as a warning to reigning Houses against contracting marriage with a Protestant. Will your Holiness be so good as to have this arranged privately? I shall not issue the civil decree annulling the marriage until I hear you have been so good as to settle the point. It is also important for France that there should be no Protestant daughter of my house after me ; and it is dangerous that a minor of nineteen, a young man in such a distinguished position, should be exposed to the temptation of acting thus against the civil law and against considerations of all kinds.'

The Pope replied that the matter would have the most serious attention. He took no notice of threats or of the Emperor's strange plea for his intervention. After weighing all the circumstances, he finally declared the marriage held good in the sight of the Catholic Church. Later on, when Napoleon, notwithstanding his assumed dislike for mixed marriages, was arranging that Jerome should wed a Protestant princess, he obtained a declaration against the marriage from servile French ecclesiastical lawyers. The incident was the first step towards his rupture with Pius VII., a rupture completed when he found that he could not persuade the Chief of Christendom to descend to the position of the leading ecclesiastical official of his Empire.

Jerome had meanwhile risked giving new offence to the Emperor by his conduct at Genoa. He thought the rank of

---

[1] She was still in Europe, but Napoleon assumed that what he ordered must have happened.

[2] Napoleon had a copy of the certificate of John Carroll, Bishop of Baltimore, declaring that he had personally celebrated the marriage, and must have known that the Pope would have the same information, yet he makes this stupid misstatement.

capitaine de frégate was not high enough for the commander of a squadron, and without any authority but his own impulsive ambition he assumed the higher grade of *capitaine de vaisseau*, put on the uniform, signed official documents with this new title, and promoted some of his midshipmen to the rank of lieutenant, without even going through the formality of proposing their names to the Admiralty. Napoleon sent him a sharp reprimand, and the officers he had promoted were reduced to their old rank. Then the Emperor showed he had pardoned this lack of discipline by writing to Jerome more than one encouraging letter. He told him he had talent enough to do great service to France, and he looked forward to his soon holding high command. Meanwhile he provided for him an opportunity of easily winning distinction without running any risks. On July 1, 1805, after adding a third frigate to Jerome's little squadron, he directed him to proceed to Algiers and demand the immediate liberation of all the French and Italian prisoners held captive among the Dey's galley-slaves. Jerome had been amusing himself in the midst of the social pleasures of Genoa, and he was in no hurry to complete his preparations for sailing. It was not till August 7th that he put to sea with his three frigates and two brigs. Bad weather drove him into Toulon, and it was not till the 18th that he anchored under the batteries of Algiers. If he had to enforce his demand, it would have been a daring challenge with so small a force. But although nothing was said of this private arrangement in the accounts of Jerome's expedition published at the time, the French consul at Algiers had already settled to pay the Dey 450,000 francs (£18,000) for the ransom of 231 French and Italian galley-slaves. Jerome had merely to take them on board of his ships. On August 20th he set sail again for Genoa, where he arrived on the 31st. There was such fear of importing the plague from Algiers that the squadron remained a fortnight in quarantine. Then there was a day of triumph such as might have been given to Jerome if he had conquered Algiers. He landed amid the roar of saluting cannon. He went by flag and flower decked streets and quays to the Cathedral of San Lorenzo, escorted by his sailors and the liberated prisoners. There was a *Te Deum*, and then a banquet at the Governor's palace. Decrès,

JEROME BONAPARTE

FROM THE PAINTING BY BARON A. J. GROS AT VERSAILLES

the Minister of Marine, wrote to him that the eyes of the navy, of France, of all Europe were turned to him. The Emperor promised him promotion, and employment in more important operations. He gave up the command of his squadron and went to Paris.

His wife was still in London. Jerome wrote to her from Paris urging her to go back at once to Baltimore. He loved her dearly, he said;. he longed to see her and their son, but for the present they must wait patiently while he did his work as an officer of the navy, serving his country, and preparing the way at the same time for a complete reconciliation with the Emperor. At last in October Elisabeth and her infant son sailed for America. She had written home that Jerome was not free to act as he wished, and they must not judge him harshly. No doubt all would come right in the end.

But strongly as he protested his affection for Elisabeth and his grief at being separated from her, he was as fond of, and as ready for, amusement at Paris as he had been at Genoa. The plain fact was, that whatever he might write in his letters to Baltimore, he was gradually getting used to his new existence, and reconciling himself to his brother's wishes. He was the most light-headed and selfish of the family, and he had not the courage to risk his expected position as a Prince of the Empire for the sake of Elisabeth.

Lucien was a man of a very different temper. Of the four brothers of Napoleon he was in every way the strongest character. Again and again he had chosen his own course, and till now he had finally succeeded in every case in inducing Napoleon to accept the situation he had created. Joseph was always ready to take his part, discreetly, it is true, and without risking anything. His mother was devoted to him : it almost seemed as if he were her favourite son. He was ambitious. The wealth he had won for himself made him to a certain extent independent of the Emperor's goodwill, but he did not care for the position of a mere wealthy patron of art and literature. He believed he could play a part in the great game of king-making, and he wanted to have his share in the destinies of the new Empire.

While the negotiations were still in progress between Pesaro and Milan, and Talleyrand was discussing with him the conditions of a reconciliation with the Emperor, some of Lucien's friends were urging him to temporise, to make an apparent submission, and trust to gain all he wanted later on. They told him that if he played his part well, he might secure the Regency of Italy, perhaps even its crown. Let him make for the moment any and every concession to Napoleon, and ask in return for the rule of Italy. Then he could identify himself with the national movement, secure the support of the Pope, who was friendly to him, and of foreign powers, which were jealous of Napoleon, and he might dictate his own terms. There are some indications that Massena, himself an Italian, was among these friendly advisers. But with all his ambition Lucien would hear of no terms that would sacrifice the position of his wife and her children. Napoleon wanted him to annul the marriage, and promised him that if he would do this he would have everything he could hope for. The Emperor would not even object to Lucien bringing ' Madame Jouberthou ' to France and living with her, but she must not assume the name of Bonaparte. Lucien would not hear of an arrangement that would dishonour his wife, his children, and himself. The most he would concede fell far short of what the Emperor demanded. In a dignified letter to his brother Lucien set forth the irreducible minimum of what he would agree to.

' I respectfully submit to your Majesty,' he wrote, ' as the unalterable basis of any settlement, that my wife must bear my name, even though she is not recognised by your Majesty as having any dynastic rights. Since my name belongs to me and to her, my children can bear no other, for they are my legitimate offspring. This name is sufficient for my wife and children, for it ratifies and defines their position before the law. . . . Charles, Letizia Bonaparte, and Alexandrine Bonaparte cannot be other than what they are, and all that your recognition can give them and ought to give them is the title of " Highness." ' He went on to say that he would be ready to agree to his wife not bearing this title. It would be no disappointment to her, for such was her love for him that she set more value on the mere name of ' Madame Bonaparte.' Nor would he claim any rank for her children, though those of his first marriage, already recognised by

Napoleon, ought to have the title of Highness. He would be quite ready to fulfil the duties of any office assigned to him, but he would not appear at court unless on occasions of official ceremony, and his wife would never appear there.

This was Lucien's ultimatum. Napoleon broke off the negotiations. If he were a private individual, he said, he might have agreed to recognise his brother's marriage, but he was the head of a state, and questions of succession had to be considered. Lucien had taken a course that shut him out from a great career.

Lucien left Pesaro for Rome, where he rented a palazzo, hung up his collection of pictures, and gathered a literary and artistic circle around him. He seemed to have made himself a home there, and Roman society welcomed his wife. But to his friends he spoke of leaving Europe for America, and becoming a citizen of the United States. In the autumn another attempt was made to arrange a reconciliation between him and Napoleon. Joseph used his good offices on the side of Lucien, but nothing came of the negotiation. Napoleon insisted on a complete surrender; Lucien, to his honour, refused to sacrifice his wife to his ambition.

Before the year ended Napoleon was preparing thrones for his brothers, for 1805 was the year of the ' king-making victory ' of Austerlitz. But Lucien was content to remain uncrowned, without even the rank of an Imperial Prince.

CHAPTER IX

KING-MAKING

(1805-1806)

WHILE Napoleon was engaged in these disputes over the marriages of Lucien and Jerome he was preparing for the series of military triumphs that made him the master of Europe. At Milan in the early summer he was still dreaming of the conquest of England. The army destined for the invasion was encamped at Boulogne, and Villeneuve's fleet was engaged in its far-reaching manœuvre for securing the temporary command of the Channel. It was the diversion of the British fleets to the Atlantic that enabled Jerome to make his expedition to Algiers in the summer without fear of molestation.

Before going to Italy Napoleon had ordered Joseph to rejoin his regiment at Boulogne, and told him that he had still much to learn before he would be fit to command the 4th Infantry in action. Joseph spent only a few days in camp. He would have been much happier on his estate at Morte-fontaine, or in his newly furnished palace of the Luxembourg at Paris, holding his court there as Grand Elector of the Empire. He took advantage of this office to get rid for a while of his military duties. The electors of the department of the Dyle in Belgium were to meet to choose their representa-tives, and Joseph resolved to preside over the election at Brussels, which was also the district from which he took his title as senator. His journey through Belgium was some-thing like a royal progress. At Brussels, Antwerp, Ghent, and Bruges he had a state reception. He poured out money with a lavish hand. He gave two francs to each soldier of the guards of honour paraded on his arrival. He distributed one franc each to the soldiers of the garrisons which he reviewed. He invited the officers to lunches and dinners. He listened to grievances, promised to support with his influence claims for promotion. Napoleon wrote to him that it was a folly to spend a hundred thousand crowns a month in largesses and entertainments. He replied that he had had only given a few presents to the military bands that played for him and the detachments sent to serve as his escort.

He made a short visit to the camp, and complained to the Minister of War that he had not been received with due honour as a Prince of the Imperial family. At reviews and inspections he was not the mere colonel of the 4th, but Prince Joseph, and taking post beside the General in command he seemed to claim the honours of the day. Napoleon wrote to remind him that all this was a disregard of military discipline, that in camp the General in command came first and he was only one of his colonels, notwithstanding his princely rank. Joseph showed how little he cared for discipline and how much he thought of his own importance by starting off on another journey without troubling himself with the formality of a leave of absence.

He passed through the cities of French Flanders and Belgium, then along the Rhine by Cologne, Coblentz, Mayence and Strasburg, and then to Nancy, where he arrived in the beginning of June. He had a number of travelling-carriages, and a suite of officers in uniform and servants in livery. In each city he posed as a Prince of the Empire, reviewed the troops, received the civil authorities, entertained the generals and officials, and again scattered his largesses with a generous hand. His wife had been taking the waters at Plombières. She joined him at Nancy, and together they returned to Mortefontaine. He wrote to the Emperor that he awaited his further orders.

When Napoleon returned from Italy Joseph went to meet him at Fontainebleau. The Emperor tried to make his brother realise how irregular his conduct had been. Joseph listened to his lecture on military discipline with the tolerant air of a superior person who was quite satisfied with himself, and could afford to let his soldier brother make the most of his professional prejudices. Then he calmly told him that he could not sink the Prince in the mere colonel of the 4th.

He always remembered what was due to his real rank.   And then he added that he was quite ready to go back to his regiment, and suggested that, instead of making trouble about what was past and gone, the best thing they could do was to return to camp together, and let no one see that there was any difference of opinion between them.   In the presence of such sublime self-possession even Napoleon was conquered. The Emperor and the Prince rode into Boulogne camp together, and Joseph shared the honours of the reception.

The Emperor had intended that Louis should go with him to Italy, be present at the coronation at Milan, and then take over his governorship of the ' Departments beyond the Alps.'   But Louis had pleaded ill-health.   He was laid up at his new country house at St. Leu.   He had partly lost the use of his right hand, and was suffering from acute rheumatism. A confirmed hypochondriac, he exaggerated his illness.   The doctors had advised that he should try the hot mud-baths of St. Amand (not the village which ten years later was the scene of some of the hard fighting of the battle of Ligny, but a town on the northern frontier of France some twenty miles south-west of Lille).   Napoleon still clung to the hope of making a soldier of Louis.   The reserve of the Army of England was concentrated about Lille.   It was made up of two infantry divisions and two regiments of Carbineers, the mounted *corps d'élite* of which Louis was Colonel-in-chief.   He directed him to take command of this reserve corps.   He might establish his headquarters at St. Amand, and try the cure there.   So Louis, with Hortense and her children, left St. Leu for the quiet little northern town.   He left all military duties to his staff, and gave his undivided attention to his health, which seemed to benefit by the mud-baths.   But, as he had found during the voyage to and from Egypt he was a bad sailor, he doubted if he was sufficiently recovered to face a voyage across that terrible Channel and the fatigues of a campaign in England.

However, he was spared the trial.   The great naval combination had failed.   Villeneuve, instead of sweeping the narrow seas, had taken refuge under Spanish batteries.   And England had brought a new coalition into being.   Austria and Russia were allied with her and preparing for war.   Prussia was inclined to join them.   In August, after a few days of hesitation, Napoleon broke up the camp of Boulogne and began that wonderful march of which the stages were Ulm, Vienna, and Austerlitz.

The map of Europe was to be redrawn. Before he left Boulogne the Emperor had told Joseph that he would soon offer him a kingdom, probably Naples, for the Bourbons of the Two Sicilies were throwing in their lot with the coalition, and he would make an end of that ' perfidious dynasty.'

At first it had been intended that Joseph at the head of his regiment should share the dangers and the glories of the war. But on second thoughts Napoleon decided to leave him in France. Perhaps he doubted his brother's capacity for command in action, not without reason. Perhaps he hesitated to risk the life of his most capable successor, as well as his own. In any case, Joseph was directed to return to the Luxembourg, and as Grand Elector preside over the Government in his brother's absence. Josephine went with her husband as far as Strasburg, and there awaited the event of the campaign.

Louis, as Grand Constable, was to take command of Paris, and was nominally responsible for the maintenance of order in the capital, the forwarding of reinforcements to the field armies, and such measures as might be necessary for the defence of France during the war.

Jerome had no sooner returned to Paris after his Algerian expedition than employment was also found for him. He was given the rank of *capitaine de vaisseau*, and directed to take command of a battleship in a squadron with which Admiral Bouet-Willaumez was to go to sea to prey upon English commerce, while the British navy was occupied in blockading the fleets of France, Spain, and the Batavian Republic.

Louis was at first inclined to plead his ill-health as a reason for not taking over the military governorship of Paris, but his friends persuaded him that he must accept it. Joseph held high state at the Luxembourg. He presided over the Senate and the Council of Ministers; he had his guard of veteran soldiers; he gave banquets, concerts, theatrical entertainments in his palace; he had plenty of opportunities for displaying his portly person in his splendid official uniforms. But in the midst of all this there was an unpleasant suspicion that he was a mere figure-head. The Emperor had so arranged matters that all effective control in civil affairs was in the hands of Cambacérès, who was nominally Joseph's right-hand man. Military matters were outside his province, and belonged to that of Louis and the Ministry of War. Little was left for him but ceremonial display. He even complained that important news from the seat of war only reached him, the head of the home government, at second hand, after having first gone to the Empress at Strasburg, and then become common property through being published there. But though he fretted and fumed, he must have realised that after all it was more comfortable for an easy-going man like himself to be holding high state at the Luxembourg as Grand Elector of the Empire, instead of sleeping in the mud of half-frozen bivouacs, or leading bayonet charges as colonel of the 4th Infantry. And then he had only to be patient for a while. There was a crown waiting for him, and at the Luxembourg he could rehearse the part he would soon have to play as a king.

Prince Louis, General in command of the Army of Paris, was displaying unwonted energy, under the impulse of responsibility and the encouragement of the great news that came from beyond the Rhine. For him too a kingdom was being made ready, though he had not been let into the secret. In fact, his ignorance of what the Emperor had in view for him led him to overdo his part on a critical occasion. It was well known that England, Austria, and Russia were all urging Prussia to join the coalition. In November, when Austerlitz was still unfought, there were rumours that the Prussian army was about to take the field, and invade northern France through the Netherlands while the Emperor's main forces were occupied with the Austro-Russian army in Moravia. As a matter of fact Napoleon knew well that the Prussians were not ready to march, and that Frederick William was hesitating between the peace and the war party, and weakly watching for the result of the struggle in Moravia. But the Emperor made the alleged danger in the north from a Prussian intervention the pretext for marching French troops into the territories of the Batavian Republic. Louis was to direct this occupation of the Netherlands, and though he did not know it, the real object of the operation was to prepare the way for abolishing the Republic and proclaiming him king of the country he would thus appear to have protected from foreign invasion.

On November 8th, by a decree.dated from Linz in Austria, Napoleon directed the Grand Constable of the Empire to form an Army of the North, to protect the northern departments and co-operate in the defence of Antwerp and the Batavian territories. Napoleon intended that while others did the real work, Louis should appear to the public to be the directing spirit of the operation. He had arranged all the details. Kellerman and Lefèbvre, who commanded the reserves at Mayence and Strasburg, were ordered to send what troops they could spare into the Netherlands. A trusted staff officer was despatched from the Imperial headquarters to see that the French troops were brigaded with the regiments of the Batavian Republic under the command of French generals of division, so that the control of all the armed forces in the Netherlands would be in French hands, and French troops would form part of every garrison.

But Louis took the rumour of a Prussian invasion seriously, and displayed a sudden energy of which his brother probably believed he was incapable, and against which he had therefore taken no precautions. Louis sent urgent orders to every northern garrison from Brest to Verdun to despatch every available man and gun that could be spared to Belgium. Although there were always elements of disorder in Paris, he almost stripped the capital of troops. Nearly the whole garrison, including detachments of the Imperial Guard, was in full march for the north. At the end of the month, forgetting all his complaints of ill-health, Louis himself left Paris to take command of the Army of the North, which was now growing to a force that Napoleon had never dreamed of employing in this direction.

On December 4th, the morrow of Austerlitz, Louis reached Antwerp, and reviewed the garrison and the troops concentrated there. Then he visited in turn the strong places and the cantonments of his army, conferred with the Batavian Ministers of War and of the Navy, and established his headquarters at Nymeguen. On the 19th he received orders from the Emperor to send two mixed divisions of French and Batavian troops under the French General Colaud from Antwerp to· garrison Amsterdam, thus securing a hold on the Dutch capital. On the 30th he had a letter from Berthier, dated nine days before, from the palace of the Austrian Emperor at Schoenbrunn.

' The Emperor directs me to inform you,' wrote Berthier, ' that you need not have any serious anxiety about the north. His Majesty orders you to send back to Paris all the detachments of his Guard that you have moved to Holland. The Emperor expects to return to Paris at any moment, and besides does not wish his Guard to be employed in mere detachments. As I have informed your Highness, the Emperor has come to an arrangement with Prussia which greatly changes the northern situation.

' His Majesty orders you, *mon Prince*, to remain in Holland, place your army in cantonments there, and maintain it on a fairly strong footing. Holland must furnish all the pay and supplies of the Army of the North ; it must also buy and supply you with all the artillery and transport horses you may need, and for these purposes your Highness is to draw nothing from France, for the Army of the North is not to cost the Emperor anything. . . .'

A week later came the news of the peace of Pressburg, by which Austria abandoned the coalition. No sooner had Louis heard of it than, despite the formal order to remain in Holland, he handed over the command of his army to General Colaud, made a flying visit to Amsterdam and The Hague, and then returned to Paris as quickly as relays of post-horses could convey him. After a brief halt there, he travelled with the same haste to Strasburg, where Napoleon was expected on his way back from the war. The Emperor was astonished and disappointed at meeting his brother there on January 22nd (1806). He told Louis that he ought to have remained in Holland, and Louis replied that as all danger of war there was over, he thought that as Grand Constable he ought to be in France to receive the Emperor on his return. The brothers travelled back to Paris together, Napoleon now giving Louis some information as to his plans for a kingdom of the Netherlands,

Joseph had already left Paris to take possession of his kingdom. Austria had no sooner been struck down than Napoleon proclaimed his intention of driving the Bourbons from Naples. On the last day of 1805 he had written to Joseph : 'I intend to take possession of the kingdom of Naples. Marshal Massena and General Saint-Cyr are marching upon it with two army corps. I have appointed you my lieutenant and commander-in-chief of the Army of Naples. You will start within forty-eight hours, going by way of Rome, and let your first despatch bring me the news that you have driven this perfidious court from Naples, and subjected that part of Italy to our laws.'

Joseph received this letter on January 7, 1806. He had long been aware of the Emperor's plans for Naples and his own personal interest in them, and by the same messenger he sent back his brief reply that very day. He noted the receipt of the Emperor's letter, and added : 'I thank your Majesty for the confidence you repose in me, and I shall start in forty-eight hours.' He left Paris on the night of January 8th accompanied by two members of his household, who were to act as his staff officers. He did not reach Rome till the 25th. There he had an interview with the Pope, and reported to his brother that he had had a friendly reception. The troops Massena had sent down from northern Italy and Saint-Cyr's contingent were concentrating between Rome and the northern frontier of Naples. Joseph established his headquarters at Albano, a few miles from Rome, and on January 27th issued the proclamation to the Army of Naples which the Emperor had sent to him. 'Soldiers,' wrote Napoleon, 'my brother marches at your head. He knows my plans and is invested with my authority. He has all my confidence, sustain him with yours.'

At Albano Joseph received from the Emperor the formal offer of the Crown of Naples. In a letter dated January 19th Napoleon wrote to him : 'My intention is that the Bourbons shall cease to reign at Naples. I will place on the throne a Prince of my family. I offer it you in the first place ; if this does not suit you, it will be given to another.' On the 31st Joseph wrote in reply that he was entirely at his brother's disposal, and ready to accept any arrangement that he considered of advantage to his interests and those of his Empire. He reminded him that in their conversations at the camp of Boulogne he had already agreed to this very proposal.

The letter did not reach the Emperor till February 9th. Meanwhile, in his anxiety to have the matter settled, Napoleon had begun to fear that Joseph might raise difficulties, as he had done when he was offered the crown of the north Italian kingdom. On January 30th he had directed a special envoy, Miot, to travel post-haste to Joseph's headquarters and explain his views to him. He was to repeat to him the offer of the Crown of Naples, making it clear to him that he would still remain Grand Elector, and retain all other rights he held as a Prince of the Empire. He was to tell him that he must accept or refuse at once. If he hesitated Napoleon had in his mind another whom he would adopt, give the name of Napoleon, and place on the throne. When Miot reached southern Italy Joseph had already given his reply. There was no reason for him to hesitate. When he was offered the Iron Crown of the North he had refused because its acceptance entailed the surrender of his rights in the Empire and the shadowy chance of succession to the Imperial Crown. No such conditions were now imposed. He had obtained the Crown of Naples on his own terms.

In the first week of February his army of 30,000 veterans, commanded by trusted and experienced leaders, moved towards the frontier. No serious resistance was expected, for the court of Naples, which had counted on a Russo-Austrian victory in Moravia, was panic-stricken at the downfall of Austria, and instead of the help of a strong Russo-Austrian corps had only been reinforced by small Russian detachments from Corfu and a few British troops from Malta. The Russians were withdrawing. The British were being sent to Sicily, where the Bourbon court was to take refuge under the protection of England. Gaeta, and some of the minor fortresses of the mainland, were garrisoned, but there was no adequate force for the defence of the capital, and a considerable part of its population were ready to welcome the invaders.

Most of the regiments of the French army were clad in worn-out uniforms and shod with broken shoes. But like the Army of Italy in 1796, they were looking forward to finding all they needed in the country they were about to invade. But Joseph ordered that there should be no requisitions, and that marauding should be sternly repressed. It was a new way of making war for these soldiers of the old Republic and the new Empire. Joseph did not mean to allow the Napoleonic method of making war support itself to be used at the expense of his future subjects. He hoped to be welcomed as a popular ruler, and he arranged for all supplies to be furnished by contractors from the Papal States.

On February 8th he crossed the frontier. He issued two proclamations, one to his army, calling on the soldiers to observe strict discipline and treat the Neapolitans as friends; the other to the people of Naples, declaring that the French came as protectors and allies, not as conquerors, and were enemies not of the people, but of the Bourbons only. The proclamations were signed ' JOSEPH NAPOLEON, Prince and Grand Elector of the Empire, Lieutenant of the Emperor, and Commander-in-chief of his Army of Naples and Sicily.'

The assumption of the name of ' Napoleon ' in addition to his own is a notable event. Till then Joseph had never used it. But it was the name under which he was later to assume the throne. The Emperor meant to found subsidiary dynasties of ' Napoleons,' not of ' Bonapartes.'

On the 14th Joseph with the main body was at Capua, and the advanced guard, a brigade under General Parton-neaux, had pushed forward and occupied Naples without firing a shot. The forts surrendered. The Royal family had fled to Sicily. The army had retired to the Abruzzi and the south to co-operate with the bands of peasants who were rising in the name of King Ferdinand, or to Gaeta where a German officer, the Count of Hesse-Philipstadt, was in command, and had refused a summons to surrender.

From Capua Joseph sent a despatch to Napoleon to inform him of the occupation of Naples, and next day (February 15, 1806) he made his entry into the city at the head of a column of French troops. He was, on the whole, well received by the people, for all the more zealous supporters of the old government had fled with the court. On the 16th he went in state to the Cathedral. Then came a proclamation announcing that though there would be a change of dynasty, all the local authorities and officials who accepted the new state of affairs would retain their posts ; there would be no confiscations, no war contributions. A ministry was formed, which was composed almost entirely of Neapolitans. The Corsican Salicetti, an old friend and ally of Joseph, was put at the head of the police. Joseph was not yet proclaimed king, but he was beginning to reign and defining his policy.

He thought he was already becoming popular. He wrote to Napoleon that he had gone out on foot and without escort among the lazzaroni, and had been welcomed by them. At Gaeta the Bourbon flag still flew. In the Abruzzi war had been proclaimed against the invaders, but in most of the Neapolitan provinces there was no sign of hostility to the French. Joseph was preparing for his formal proclamation as king, and meanwhile was making himself at home in his palace, looking out upon one of the most beautiful scenes in the world. A few years ago he had been hoping for a consulate in one of the ports of Italy.

Louis Bonaparte was also to be provided with a kingdom. The Emperor had not consulted him about the choice of it. He would no doubt have preferred Naples, for he had a fixed idea that he could never be well in the north, and a home among the Dutch canals was hardly the best place for a rheumatic patient. But his opinion was not asked. At Strasburg, on the return from the Austerlitz campaign, Napoleon had given his brother the first hint of what was arranged for him, but he was not brought into the negotiations for the formation of the new kingdom till everything was settled.

Early in January 1806 Talleyrand had written to the Grand Pensionary or President of the Batavian Republic expressing his regret that his failing health would make it necessary soon for him to resign his office into the hands of a new president, and the fear that his successor might not be so devoted to France, and might even be under the influence of the English party. He asked the Republic, therefore, to send to Paris an envoy with full powers to discuss with the Emperor's government the steps to be taken ' to establish in Holland a new régime which would permanently secure its independence and prosperity,' and he added that the Emperor would be pleased if Rear-Admiral Verhuell was appointed to this special mission. The Dutch President and his ministers knew what was coming, and made an attempt at resistance. They sent Verhuell to Paris, but his instructions directed him ' to accede to the Emperor's desire to exercise a greater influence in the election of the head of the Batavian Republic, but at the same time to offer an unyielding opposition to any proposal to introduce an hereditary monarchy to the profit of some prince of the Imperial family.'

Admiral Verhuell reached Paris towards the end of February. He found he had to deal not with Talleyrand, but directly with the Emperor, and in the first interview Napoleon presented an ultimatum. He told the Admiral that it was essential that the policy of Holland and of France should be in close accord. The defence of northern France depended on the security of Holland. The position of Antwerp made it essential that it should be in the hands of the friends of France. He could not, therefore, feel satisfied with an electoral system that left the policy of Holland at the mercy of what might be a chance decision, subject too, it might be, to foreign and unfriendly influences. Some more stable and reliable system must be substituted for that of the Batavian Republic, and after mature consideration he had decided that only one of two courses was possible. Holland must either be annexed to the Empire, or preserve its independence by accepting the rule of one of the Imperial princes as its king, and ' in order to give the Dutch people a pledge of his interest in their welfare and his goodwill towards them ' he would offer the crown to his brother Prince Louis.

Verhuell reported the interview to his government. They knew that resistance was hopeless, and of two unwelcome alternatives they chose that which would at least leave some semblance of national independence to their country. In April they sent a deputation to Paris to discuss the constitution of the new kingdom, and to secure the best possible terms from Napoleon. The Emperor refused to enter into any discussion of details with them, and referred them to Talleyrand. The Minister opened the debate by telling them that before any points of detail could be discussed they must undertake that, as soon as the draft of a treaty between France and Holland and the outlines of the new Dutch constitution were settled, the people of the Netherlands would invite Prince Louis to accept the crown. In the face of the threat that otherwise there would be an annexation of their country they gave the required pledge.

They obtained assurances that no French officials would be appointed except in the King's household; that liberty of worship would be maintained, and the existing Dutch system of law would remain in force; and that the crowns of France and Holland would never be united on one head. They could only secure a doubtful declaration as to their claim that no French troops were to be stationed in Holland. It was when these points had been settled that Napoleon at last told Louis all was arranged and the Dutch delegates were ready to offer him the crown. He was to have a civil list and a royal domain that would give him two millions of florins a year, with a quarter of a million more for Hortense, and he was to retain his office of Grand Constable of the Empire with its emoluments.

At first he showed some hesitation about accepting the offer. He was allured by the idea of royal state and the prospect of increased wealth and influence, but he was held back by the timid, lazy, comfort-loving side of his character. As King of Holland it would not be so easy for him to disappear from time to time to some health-resort and spend idle days in following out some cure for his ailments, real and imaginary. Hortense would have been glad if he had refused. A life of ceremonial state at The Hague and Amsterdam had no attraction for her. She had become reconciled to her husband's periodical absences. She liked her quiet life at Paris, where she amused herself with lessons in music and painting from some of the first artists of the time, and expeditions to her old school at Madame Campan's house at St. Germain, where she played the part of a patroness. Then there were the pleasures of shopping at Paris, where every month she spent part of her income in adding to her collection of jewellery, for which she had almost a mania. And then, too, she would have to give up her close association with her mother, Josephine, and her circle of old friends. With Louis, however, Hortense's ideas counted for little, and his personal hesitation was soon conquered by the Emperor's strong will.

The offer of the crown was declared to represent the wishes of nine-tenths of the people of Holland. The instructions of the government to Verhuell that the proposal should be resisted at all costs remained for the present a secret of diplomacy. At last on June 5th all had been settled, and the formal proclamation of Louis took place at the Tuileries. After the Dutch delegates had been introduced, and had made the offer of the crown, Napoleon told them that France was so generous as to renounce all right of conquest over their country, but could not acquiesce in its government passing into any but friendly hands, for Holland secured the defence of the north of France. Then, turning to Louis, he expressed his pleasure at his acceptance of the crown of Holland. He reminded him that he was still a French prince. The dignity of Constable of the Empire would keep him in mind of his duty, which would be to cherish the alliance between the two nations, and maintain a soldierly spirit among the brave troops of his new kingdom, some of whom had been in action at Austerlitz and had won the admiration of the Emperor by their conduct. In his reply Louis referred proudly to his having been employed in protecting Holland from the threat of invasion the year before. He had then, he said, learned to know the people of his new kingdom and could appreciate the honour of being called to reign over them. He relied on the Emperor's protection, and assured him that ' his people ' would share his own feeling of love and gratitude to France and to her ruler.

After this exchange of compliments the party adjourned to the large salon, where there was to be a public audience, and the diplomatists, generals, and officers of state were to offer their congratulations. Louis led the way, and the chamberlains announced him as ' The King of Holland.' A week later he left Paris to take possession of his kingdom.

Crowns had thus been found for two of the brothers. Jerome, now cruising with Bouet-Willaumez on the Atlantic, would have a kingdom provided for him a few months later, as part of the remodelling of Germany that was to follow the campaign of Jena and the downfall of Prussia in the coming autumn.

The remaining brother, Lucien, might have had a crown if he would but surrender to Napoleon. Lucien, however, had no idea of submission, and bore himself proudly in his exile in Italy. Joseph, passing through Rome to take possession of Naples, was surprised at the state his brother displayed. In Rome he had a palazzo, with picture-galleries that were famous even in that centre of art, and a theatre where in the winter he gave a series of plays, concerts and operettas, in which the performers were the best that could be engaged, and the audience was made up of the nobles of Rome and the most distinguished foreign visitors. Lucien had wealth enough at his disposal to play the part of a liberal patron of art and literature and a generous host. When in the summer Rome became hot and unhealthy he had his villa at Frascati, to which he transferred the hospitality of his Roman palace.

He was not like his brothers an Imperial prince, but he had everything of a prince but the name, and this deficiency Pius VII. supplied. In the summer of 1806, hearing that the papal exchequer was not over abundantly supplied, Lucien offered the Pope a large loan. Pius VII. refused to accept it, but told Lucien that the money would be welcome if it could be made the purchase price of the lands and fief of Canino. By this arrangement Lucien became a Roman prince, and set himself to develop the resources of his little principality. He reorganised and restarted the local ironworks, and cleared out the once famous mineral springs and established baths. He resided for part of the year in the old castello of the Princes of Canino, set to work to improve the tillage of farms and vineyards, and to his delight discovered the buried remains of a Roman villa, rich in works of art, and carried on excavations which added some treasures to his collection. Best of all he was his own master; and though his brother Joseph and his mother were still making occasional suggestions for a reconciliation with Napoleon, Lucien Bonaparte, Prince of Canino, was in no hurry to become one of the puppet kings with whom his famous brother was surrounding his upstart Imperial throne.

CHAPTER X

JOSEPH, KING OF NAPLES (1806-1808) AND
LOUIS, KING OF HOLLAND (1806)

WHEN Joseph established himself at the royal palace of Naples in February 1806, as Napoleon's lieutenant and destined successor of the banished Bourbons, his views as to the immediate future were very different from his brother's. Joseph was a man of a kindly, easy-going disposition, somewhat of an optimist, and his optimism, in the first place, made him entertain a very high opinion of his own capacity. So far he had in his own way been eminently successful. He had been the first of the brothers to obtain position and competence by his fortunate marriage. He could look back upon easily won diplomatic successes. He had more than once held his own against Napoleon in matters of policy, where his personal interest was concerned. Socially he had been a success, and had won many friends. There was no trace about him of the rough manners of camp and barrack. He had a courtly bearing, and was well fitted to appear in the part of a king. He was taller than Napoleon, and though ease and good living had made him somewhat portly, his stature prevented him from having the corpulent appearance of the Emperor. His handsome features bore a kindly expression of self-satisfied benevolence.

In his palace at Naples he was dreaming of a popular reign. He would be the protector of the Neapolitans, their deliverer, not their conqueror. He would make as few changes as possible, and spare them the burdens and the hardships of military rule. The welcome he had received in these first days, the gratitude expressed for his having refrained from levying any contributions to support the army, the readiness

with which the officials of the old régime accepted the continuance of their functions and promised their support—all
this made him believe that his dream would come true, and
that Naples would flourish under his kindly rule when he was
proclaimed king.

But for Napoleon Naples was a conquered country. Joseph,
even when he was crowned its king, was still to be his lieutenant, ruling, not in the interest of the Neapolitans, but
in that of the Empire. When Joseph's despatches arrived,
he said his brother was living in a fool's paradise and did
not know how to govern. Joseph had asked for remittances
to pay and provide for the French troops. Napoleon held
that an army of occupation should not cost France one
centime, but should live, and live comfortably, at the expense
of the occupied country. Joseph had reported that he had not
confiscated the British and Russian goods in the warehouses
of Naples. Their total value, he said, was not great, and the
seizure, while doing little harm to the enemy, would inflict
serious loss on the Neapolitan merchants to whom they were
consigned. There could be no addition to the taxes, wrote
Joseph, and he had promised that there should be no war
contributions. He felt, he said, that he must make the people
realise that they had gained, not lost, by the change of rulers.

Napoleon replied in a warning letter. He did not approve
of Joseph's kindly methods. He could not understand them.
Nothing would be gained by them. *Dans un pays conquis
la bonté n'est pas l'humanité* (' Forbearance is not humanity
in a conquered country '), and Naples should be considered
as a conquered country. The people should be disarmed,
the palace kept in a state of defence, and well guarded. The
forts should be held by French troops. Sooner or later there
was always a rising in a conquered country. The insurrection
might come any day, and then it must be sternly repressed.
Whatever promises he had made, there ought to be a war
contribution of at least thirty million francs levied on the
Neapolitans, so as to make the army contented. It was
ridiculous that after making themselves masters of Naples,
they should not be able to live at their ease at the expense
of the Neapolitans.

In another letter he suggested to Joseph that he should

take the first opportunity of confiscating the possessions of the adherents of the Bourbons. The insurrection he had forecasted would give the occasion for doing this. These lands should be given as fiefs to Frenchmen, generals and colonels of the army of occupation. He would thus have a military aristocracy to support him. Some of them would marry Neapolitan wives, and in a few years this French element would give him a real hold on the ' conquered country.'

Joseph considered that the Emperor would have formed a different opinion if he were on the spot. He was further confirmed in his idea of his own popularity by the reception given to him when in April he made a journey to the south, after Reynier had forced the remnant of the Bourbon army to abandon Calabria and embark for Sicily. He wrote to his brother that in the towns of Campania, Basilicata, and Calabria he had been received with acclamations, and the people vied with each other in protesting their loyalty and promising their support. At Reggio on April 13th he received the decree, dated March 30, 1806, by which Napoleon transferred to him the kingdom of Naples, which ' had come into the possession of the Emperor by right of conquest and formed a part of the Empire.' He was to reign under the name of Joseph Napoleon, retain his office of Grand Elector and his rights to the succession ; there was no tribute to be paid to France, no provision, as to supplying a contingent to the Imperial armies. But there was an indirect military contribution, for Napoleon would not permit that the Army of Naples should go without reward. Pensions to the amount of a million of francs, secured on the revenue of Naples, were to be provided for the French officers and soldiers ; and further, six military duchies were to be created in the kingdom, and held as fiefs of the Empire by those whom the Emperor might select. Each fief was to have a revenue of 200,000 francs. Napoleon made a beginning by annexing the districts of Ponte Corvo and Benevento, little territories within the Neapolitan boundary which had belonged to the Holy See since the middle ages, and without consulting the new King of Naples made Talleyrand Prince of Benevento, and Joseph's brother-in-law, Marshal Bernadotte, Prince of Ponte Corvo, this being a reward for his part in the victory of Austerlitz.

Joseph returned to Naples, where he was proclaimed King amid the wildest rejoicings. Everywhere, except at Gaeta and the little coast fortress of Amantea in Calabria, resistance to his rule was at an end. Yet all danger was not over, for it was the year after Trafalgar, and Sidney Smith, cruising off the coast with a frigate and a squadron of small vessels, was master of the sea, and might at any moment ferry over an expedition from Sicily to raid some undefended point of the long coastline. But Joseph had an army of 45,000 French veterans to uphold his throne, and was reorganising the Army of Naples. Marshal Jourdan had come from France to assist him in this department. Joseph was forming a royal guard, recruited among the sons of the Neapolitan aristocracy, and in his confidence in his new subjects had rejected his brother's advice to trust for his personal safety to a guard of Corsicans and Frenchmen. His wife Julia and her daughters were still at Mortefontaine, for it had been decided that they should not go to Naples till the state of the kingdom was thoroughly settled, and Napoleon refused to credit his brother's optimistic reports that that period had already arrived.

Joseph was organising his household and his court, and busying himself with endless details of ceremonial. He had chosen as his armorial bearings the arms of Naples with the addition of the Imperial eagle. For his flag he had fixed upon a tricolour of red, white, and black, the last colour being chosen because the mountaineers of Calabria wore black, and he had been persuaded of their devotion to his cause. He had written to the Emperor that all the people were on his side, from the proudest duke of the nobility down to the brigand Fra Diavolo. He was inviting his literary friends in France to visit him at Naples. They could assist him in planning the Academy he was about to establish. Then he interested himself in the arrangements of the Opera, and proposed to provide a subvention for a French theatre, to which Talma and the stars of the Paris stage would be invited. Already the royal palace at Naples was becoming the centre of a brilliant society, and Joseph flattered himself that the nobles of southern Italy were rallying to his throne, and were ready to aid him in developing the resources of his kingdom.

He had taken no part in the military operations in the

Abruzzi and the south.   Napoleon had written to him that he ought to show he was ready to share the dangers of the soldiers, who were fighting for him, and he spent one night in the trenches before Gaeta.   Seventeen thousand were engaged in the siege, but the sea front was open, supplies were thrown into the place by Sidney Smith, and Hesse was declaring that he would never surrender.   Joseph, after this brief experience of war, went back to his palace.   There, in the end of the first week of July, he received tidings from the south that rudely awakened him from his optimistic dreams and for a moment almost reduced him to a state of panic.

General Reynier, who had driven the Bourbon troops from Calabria before Joseph's progress through the south in April, was in the province of Calabria Ultima, with some 8000 French troops, engaged in a desultory brigand hunt in the hills.   On July 1st Sidney Smith ferried across the straits from Sicily a column of British and Neapolitan troops under Sir John Stuart.   The little army was less than 5000 strong.   There were five British battalions,[1] 12 guns, and no cavalry.   They landed on the 1st and 2nd in the Gulf of Santa Eufemia, near the village of Maida.   On the 4th Reynier attacked them with nearly 8000 men, mostly French troops, but including some Swiss and Polish regiments of the Imperial army.   He expected an easy victory, but he was badly beaten after a hard fight at close quarters, in which bayonets were crossed.   Leaving on the field some 3000 killed, wounded, and prisoners, he retreated through the hills to Catanzaro, and then continued his retirement northward, harassed at every step by the mountaineers, for all the south was blazing out into insurrection at the news of his defeat.   Reggio welcomed the victors, and all Calabria was lost at a blow, and then the rising spread into the Basilicata.   Reynier had to fight his way to the northwards.   The tocsin was ringing from every village bell-tower in the south, and the men who had acclaimed Joseph in April were cheering for the Bourbons and the English.

Joseph heard the news of disaster late on July 7th.   Next day he wrote a despairing letter to his brother.   ' Sire,' he said, ' you must come to our assistance.   The state of this country is deplorable.   The treasury is empty.   Trade does

---

[1] The 20th, 27th, 58th, 78th, and 81st Regiments.

not exist. The army is in want of everything, and I have no means of providing for it. I am working day and night. I do not complain of any one, but we cannot meet the needs of a state of war when we have neither money nor commerce. Will your Majesty remit six millions to me as soon as possible. The enemy is showing himself at all points on the coast, and the army is losing heart.' Next day he wrote again, urging the instant need of money and reinforcements.

Happily for him, although he spoke of ' the enemy appearing at all points on the coast,' there had been only the descent of Stuart's brigade in southern Calabria. Though they had full command of the sea the English ministers failed to realise their opportunity. It was still the period when England engaged only in isolated enterprises that led to nothing. Stuart had to content himself with seizing Reggio and rousing the south. And the veteran generals who commanded the French army rose to the occasion. Reinforcements were provided by Massena by the simple expedient of vigorously pressing the siege of Gaeta. On the 10th Hesse was wounded, and a less able commander took his place. On the 17th the main rampart was breached, and on July 18th Gaeta surrendered, thus setting free some 17,000 men for operations against the insurgents.

Then came months of civil war. From the Abruzzi to Calabria French columns were hunting down the rebel bands, dispersing them only to find that they gathered again like a swarm of flies. There were stormings and burnings of villages, courts-martial and military executions, confiscation and pillage. Peace was maintained in the capital by the proclamation of martial law, a civic guard was formed, and all the French civilians were armed. To fill the empty treasury a forced loan was imposed on the wealthier classes ; crown lands were sold ; all feudal privileges and exemptions were abolished with a stroke of the pen in order to make taxation and administration more effective.

General Stuart's brigade, wasted with the malarial fevers of the district of Santa Eufemia, had been soon withdrawn to Sicily, and beyond the help in arms and ammunition that had been distributed to them by the raiders, the insurgents were left unsupported. Gradually they were reduced to submission in district after district, but it was a costly process. The French lost more men by sickness and exposure than by wounds in action. At one time more than 12,000 of the 45,000 men of the Army of Naples were in hospital. Officers and soldiers were alike disgusted with a warfare that brought no distinction. Theirs was a campaign of endless marches and obscure skirmishes, while their comrades of the Grand Army were triumphing under their Emperor's eyes at Jena and Auerstadt. And yet it was a war that had its own dangers. Columns were ambuscaded and massacred. Stragglers were cut off. Quarter was neither asked nor given. The insurgents were described as 'brigands.' Some of them deserved the name, and all under this general condemnation fought with ropes round their necks. In December 1806 General Verdier had to raise the siege of the Calabrian walled town of Amantea, after having failed in three attempts to storm it, and lost hundreds of men. A second siege, begun in January 1807, ended a month later in the fall of the place, and cost Verdier 600 more of his men. In the spring Hesse, the defender of Gaeta, crossed over from Sicily with some 5000 Neapolitan troops and relighted the flickering flame of insurrection in Calabria. Reynier routed him, and besieged Cotrone. The garrison held out for a month, causing heavy loss to the besiegers, and were then embarked for Sicily by Sidney Smith. At the end of the year the Bourbons still held Reggio, and Reynier's columns were pursuing bands of 'brigands' in the Calabrian mountains. It was not till February 2, 1808, that he made himself master of Reggio. The Bourbon flag still flew on the fortress of Scylla, near the entrance of the Strait of Messina. It was evacuated on February 17, 1808, and the twenty months of civil war were at last ended.

But notwithstanding the war Joseph was decidedly popular with at least a considerable proportion of his subjects. The fighting went on chiefly in a few mountainous districts, in Calabria and the Abruzzi for the most part, where there was always trouble with brigand bands, and the war against the rebels was carried on almost entirely by troops of the Imperial army. Part only of the exceptional taxation fell upon the Neapolitans, and this affected only the wealthier classes. For the great majority of the people the good ad-

K

ministration introduced by Joseph's friend, his French Minister of Finance, Rœderer, resulted in a slightly decreased burden of taxation, at least for the present. France bore the real strain of the Neapolitan war, in the form of continual reinforcements for the Army of Naples, subventions to Joseph's treasury, and loans raised in Paris.

At Naples Joseph was personally popular. It was acknowledged by all but the thoroughgoing partisans of the Bourbon régime that he was anxious to protect his adopted country from being treated as a conquered province, and was trying to govern in the interests of the people. Even the somewhat extravagant expenditure of his court was, if anything, a source of popularity. Its cost was defrayed by loans, and the money circulated in the capital, which enjoyed a brief period of artificially sustained prosperity. Even when the civil war in the provinces was at its worst, Naples was tranquil and Joseph went about freely, with only a ceremonial escort.

His brother-king, Louis of Holland, had had an easier task. For him there was no red menace of civil war. The Dutchmen had been compelled to bow to the imperious will of Napoleon and put an end to their Republic, endeared to them by the memories of the heroic days of its first foundation, and the long struggle for the preservation of their hard-won liberties. But to the foreign king they gave a loyal welcome, striving to make the best of the new situation forced upon them. It was on June 5, 1806, that Louis was formally proclaimed King at Paris in the presence of the Dutch envoys. The Emperor intended that he should start for Holland next day. But Louis spent a week in preparations, organising an elaborate household for himself and his Queen, so that when they left Paris early on June 12th, a whole expedition was *en route* for Holland, men and women of all ranks from the King's chamberlains and aides-de-camp down to his lackeys, while the Queen had her ladies-in-waiting and her maids. So anxious was Louis to provide for every eventuality that he even took a French expert in gardening with him to Holland, the land of gardeners.

Royal salutes, guards of honour, addresses of congratulation presented by the local authorities, welcomed Louis and Hortense at every stage till they entered their kingdom, and there the Dutch people gave them a reception that augured well for the popularity of the new régime.

In the quaint old towns guards of honour of armed burghers paraded to welcome them. They had been organised for the occasion, and each town vied with its neighbours in the display it made. The burgher guard of The Hague in its scarlet uniforms with epaulettes of gold lace was the most brilliant of all. It paraded with detachments of Dutch and French regulars to meet the newly arrived sovereigns on June 18th, and escorted them to the old palace in the park outside the town, the ' House in the Wood,' there to await the state entry into their capital.

June 23rd had been chosen for the great day. The Hague was crowded with visitors from all parts of Holland and Belgium. Flags flew out in the bright summer sunshine, and the streets were adorned with arches of green foliage and strewn with leaves and flowers. The line of route was kept by French and Dutch troops, and deputations of burgher guards from the great cities. At noon the royal procession left the ' House in the Wood,' and passing down the long tree-shaded avenue of the Park entered the broad streets of the town amidst the booming of cannon and the music of carillons pealing from every church steeple.

The Dutchmen noted with pleasure, and the French with some suspicious jealousy, that except a few officers of his household Louis had not allowed any of the French to take part in the procession. Dutch cavalry formed the escort. Then came heralds in rich tabards mounted on quaintly caparisoned horses. Then the long line of state carriages, conveying the admirals, the ministers, and the council of state. Then the royal carriage, drawn by eight white Flemish horses. Lastly the carriages of the generals of the army, and the ladies and gentlemen of the royal household, and another body of Dutch dragoons.

Arrived at the palace, the quaint old Binnehof, with its memories of half the triumphs and tragedies of Dutch history, Louis entered the great hall, and seated on his throne surrounded by his ministers and his officers he received the homage of ' their High Mightinesses ' the representatives of the Dutch people, the successors of the old States-General, who had held themselves to be the equals of kings. He made a long, carefully prepared speech to his new subjects. He told them that he had accepted the crown offered to him by their delegates with full consciousness of the difficult task before him, resolved to devote himself to the welfare of the people, and encouraged by the promises of support from the great functionaries of the state. He had been still more encouraged by the reception that he had met with in Holland. Then he entered into an argument to show that freedom and progress could be best secured under the settled system of a monarchy. He assured them that he would reign in the interest of Holland, which was now his adopted country. There was a passing allusion to the protection of the Emperor, but not a word to indicate that Louis ruled, not by the will of the Dutch people, but by the choice of his soldier brother.

A state banquet ended the day. Louis had made a good impression, and Hortense had charmed every one by her kindly courtesy. She had looked forward with dismay to a life in Holland, but in the midst of the loyal welcome of the Dutch people she forgot her fears ; and in the summer sunlight the green polders, the tree-shaded canals and highways, the old-world cities of the Netherlands looked very different from the foggy land of swamp and ditch that she had imagined. She wrote to her mother the Empress expressing her pleasure at the welcome she had received. She told of an excursion to Rotterdam, where she had presided at the launch of a battleship, and where every one seemed anxious to do her honour. There was also a visit to Amsterdam. She had added to her collection of jewels. She bought some almost every month, and at Amsterdam, the capital of the diamond trade, she spent more than 20,000 francs one afternoon.

King Louis had already begun to busy himself with a hundred plans for the government of his kingdom and the securing of due splendour for his court. He wrote to the Emperor asking for the withdrawal or reduction of the French garrisons, at the same time asking to be allowed to select a number of officers and men to be incorporated in his guard. He proposed a treaty of commerce, with special advantages for Holland. He sketched out the statutes of two orders of chivalry, so that he might have decorations to give away. He proposed to introduce the rank of marshal into his army. Finally, he suggested a loan from the Imperial treasury. Napoleon wrote in reply to this last proposal that Louis must look to his own subjects for supplies. ' My expenses are heavy,' said the Emperor, ' and I am not in a position to help you, as I would otherwise like to do. You had better let your Council clearly understand that there is no hope of my sending money, otherwise it will never provide the means you require in order to meet the needs of your position. I have no money to spare, and am just able to meet my immense expenses.' He consented to recall all the French troops except two regiments, and allowed Louis to select the recruits he wanted for the Royal Guard. He told his brother to set to work quietly and patiently, warning him that to increase the resources of the country would be the work of years. It could not be the result of a few weeks. He himself had had to wait a long time for any improvement in the condition of affairs in France.

But Louis's nervous temperament made him feverishly impatient. And soon the novelty of his position began to wear off, and he felt wearied by his outburst of activity. Within a week of his entry into his capital he was writing to Napoleon that he was suffering from the dampness of the Dutch climate and must soon take a holiday at some health-resort on the Rhine or in France. Within a month he quitted The Hague for Wiesbaden, leaving his ministers to govern without him. He spent two months travelling to various health-resorts with Hortense. He visited Aix-la-Chapelle, Mayence, and Aix, writing many letters to Napoleon on the affairs of Holland, and elaborating various projects for the future. It was not till September 18th that he returned to his kingdom.

It was the eve of the rupture with Prussia. Napoleon, while still prolonging the negotiations, was massing the armies that were to conquer at Jena and Auerstadt, and then march on to new battles on the borders of Russia, and force the Czar to become his ally. Notwithstanding all his disappointments he clung to the idea he had cherished since the days when Louis was first his pupil and then his staff officer, that he could make a successful soldier of his younger brother.

He had planned for Louis a part in the coming campaign.
He was not to share the dangers and glories of the main-
operations, but he was to hold an independent command,
at the head of a Franco-Dutch army, which was to have the
relatively safe and easy mission of effecting annexations in
north-western Germany, while the Emperor with the Grand
Army was marching on Berlin.   Louis was to concentrate
two divisions composed chiefly of Dutch troops, but including
a French contingent, at Wesel on the lower Rhine.   He was
to take no risks, but wait till the Grand Army was well on its
way to Berlin, and then invade and occupy Westphalia, and
send a detachment to seize Emden and East Friesland.   It was
not likely he would meet with any resistance.   A column
under Mortier from Mayence was to occupy Cassel and depose
the Elector of Hesse-Cassel, but Louis was warned by Napoleon
that he did not want him to take a personal part in this
operation, apparently because it might be regarded unfavour-
ably by his own subjects.   Later Napoleon intended that
Louis should occupy Hanover and the rich cities of the Hanseatic League, Bremen, Hamburg, and Lubeck.   Here there
might be some show of resistance, but Louis would be able
to pose as a conqueror, and on his return to The Hague the
boundaries of his kingdom were to be enlarged by a share
of his conquests.

On the eve of the war Louis was still hesitating.   At the
end of September he wrote to the Emperor that, with all his
goodwill, he doubted if his health would allow him to take the
field for an autumn campaign, that might go on into the
winter.   He would be very sorry to give up his place at the
head of an army, but his poor health might compromise the
success of its operations.   But at the last moment he decided
that he would go to Wesel.

He arrived there on October 7th, and superintended the
construction of a bridge of boats over the Rhine, while
his two divisions were concentrating.   Next day Napoleon
put the Grand Army, 200,000 strong, in movement for its
advance on Berlin from South Germany.   The Prussians
under the Duke of Brunswick were gathering north of the
Thuringian hills to bar his way.   But King Louis at Wesel
was alarmed by wild reports that the enemy was strong enough

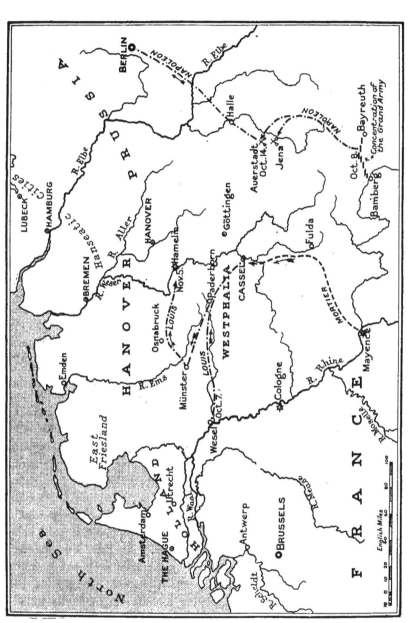

THE CAMPAIGN OF 1806 (NAPOLEON'S MARCH ON BERLIN—KING LOUIS' OPERATIONS)

to detach a huge force, which was to come sweeping down on the lower Rhine, join hands with a British army suddenly thrown into Holland, and then strike for France, cutting Napoleon's communications with his own country. He ought to have known that the enemy had neither the numbers nor the time for such a wild operation. The crisis must come in a few days far away to the north-east of the Thuringian forests. Unless Napoleon was beaten, Louis was safe enough at Wesel. But he prepared to meet the wholly imaginary danger in his own way. He ordered a good half of his army to remain in Holland to wait for the chimerical British descent. He called up part of Mortier's corps from the middle Rhine. He sent urgent messages to Paris asking that he might be at once reinforced with troops, mobilised national guards, gendarmerie, all that fighting material that could be got together. Mortier refused to march. Cambacérès wrote from Paris that he would move no troops without an order from the Emperor. In the midst of Louis's alarms came the news, that in two battles fought on the same day (October 14th) at Jena and Auerstadt, the Prussian armies had been hopelessly routed. Soult and Murat were in hot pursuit of the remnant. The way to Berlin was open, and the Emperor would be there in a few days.

With the news came orders for Louis to advance. He was to occupy the western provinces of Prussia, and march on Göttingen, combining with Mortier in a further advance for the seizure of Hesse-Cassel. Louis sent forward detachments to occupy Münster and Osnabrück, to pull down the Prussian and hoist, not his brother's, but his own flag. It was not till the end of the month that he himself stirred from Wesel. On October 30th he was at Paderborn. The Emperor had been at Berlin since the 25th and was growing impatient at the sluggish way in which Louis was reaping the fruits of the double victory. He had written to him to send forward one of his divisions to assist Mortier in securing Cassel and disarming the troops of the Elector, but suggesting that the King of Holland should not take any personal part in the deposition of the Prince, *mission un peu délicate*, an unpleasant task better left to Mortier alone.

Before this letter reached Louis one of Mortier's officers

had come to Paderborn to ask for the loan of a Dutch division. He refused to part with it, and marched himself at its head to the neighbourhood of Cassel, and on October 31st he bivouacked a few miles from the place. Here he was visited by the Baron von Gilsa, an envoy of the Elector. According to his own account, written many years after, he told the Baron that the Elector had better not leave Cassel. If he did his country would be annexed. If he held on and pleaded that he had been neutral in the great struggle, matters might yet be arranged. When he gave Von Gilsa this advice he had the Emperor's orders to co-operate in driving the Elector out of Hesse-Cassel, Napoleon's alleged justification for the step being that he believed the Elector was his enemy, and had only been deterred from openly declaring himself by his fears for the result of the war. It was the first deliberate step of Louis in his policy of asserting his own independence of his brother's views.

The very same evening Mortier's corps was in Cassel and the Hessian troops laid down their arms. Louis heard the news next morning. He had an angry interview with Mortier, in which he told the Marshal that he should not have acted without communicating with him. Mortier showed him the Emperor's orders, and evidently did not care much for the displeasure of a mere king of Holland. Louis marched off his division to the northward on his way back to Paderborn. He wrote to the Emperor telling him he had occupied Westphalia, and proposing that he should take over the command in Cassel as well, adding, however, that if the weather got worse he might have to go back to Holland.

The Emperor at Berlin fully believed that his orders to Louis had been obeyed : that the King of Holland had left a division to help Mortier and pushed on with the other to Göttingen. While Louis was on his way to Münster a despatch rider was conveying a letter addressed to him at Göttingen, in which Napoleon put Mortier and his corps under his orders and directed him to march with the combined Dutch and French forces and seize Hanover and the Hanseatic cities. When Louis's letter of November 1st reached him on the 5th, Napoleon wrote : ' I am annoyed at your having gone in person to Cassel. The nature of the business to be done there was such that I did not want you to be mixed up with it. The idea of your returning with your troops to Münster is an utter piece of folly. You will find nothing of that kind in your orders. They directed you to proceed to Göttingen and await my further orders there.'

Louis was busy at Münster organising Westphalia as a province of Holland, setting up the Dutch arms on the public buildings, appointing officials, convoking a local assembly. He wrote to Napoleon that he had retired there from Cassel because he heard that 4000 Prussians from the old fortress of Hamelin were about to make a dash at his communications with Holland. Before this explanation reached the Emperor General Loison arrived at Münster from Berlin with orders to assume the government of the district in the Emperor's name. He handed Louis another angry letter from Napoleon. ' They tell me,' wrote Napoleon, ' that you have taken possession of Münster and other districts on the right bank of the Rhine in your own name, and that you have set up the arms of Holland. I do not believe these reports. They are too absurd.' Napoleon knew they were true enough. He ended by telling Louis that he must march. He wished him to have the credit of occupying Hanover.

Louis advanced as far as the village of Ertzen near Hamelin. Some Prussian cavalry made a dash from the town, and there was a skirmish between them and the 2nd Regiment of Dutch Hussars, in which a few men were wounded. It was the only fight of Louis's campaign. He halted at Ertzen, and wrote to the Emperor that he could not advance without reinforcements, and that he would meanwhile stand on the defensive. Napoleon knew perfectly well that Louis had in front of him only a weak detachment holding an out-of-date fortress; that he had only to summon Hamelin and it would surrender, and then he could march into Hanover without firing a shot. Utterly disappointed, he wrote to his brother that he had better hand over the command to Mortier and return to Holland.

Louis's brief campaign had shown only his unfitness for command. All the Emperor's old illusions were gone. But he took care to protect as far as possible his brother's credit. He announced that Louis had given up the command only on account of ill-health, and that his services would be rewarded by the annexation of East Friesland to his kingdom. He wrote to him telling him he ought to make a public entry into Amsterdam, and that perhaps further additions would be made to his territory.

So Louis went back to his kingdom as a conqueror. Some of the splendours of his brother's triumphs were reflected on his tributary crown. So little was known in Holland of the details of current events that Louis was hailed as one of the leaders who had helped to humble Germany, and there was the solid manifest fact that out of the wreckage of Prussia he had secured a new province for Holland, a district inhabited by men of kindred blood. So Amsterdam hung out its tricolours and acclaimed his return. But already a rift had begun to open between him and Napoleon.

CHAPTER XI

HOW JEROME WENT TO WAR AND GOT HIS KINGDOM AND ANOTHER WIFE

(1805-1807)

KING LOUIS was not the only one of Napoleon's brothers who played some small part in the campaign of Jena. Jerome, the spoilt child of the Bonaparte family, was with the Grand Army, and on the very day that Louis ended his campaigning Jerome took command of an army corps. Before telling how this twenty-two-year-old captain in the navy became, in the course of a few months, first a general and then a king, we must see what he had been doing since he left Genoa for Paris in September 1805 after his expedition to Algiers.

He was only to make a short stay in the capital, for the Emperor had ordered him to proceed to Brest to take command of a line-of-battle ship in a squadron of six vessels, which was being fitted out by Admiral Bouet-Willaumez, and was to start for a cruise of more than a year's duration to prey on British commerce in the Atlantic.

Jerome was not particularly attracted by the prospect of this long voyage. He talked of going to Germany to discuss matters with Napoleon. Decrès, the Minister of Marine, with great difficulty persuaded him to abandon the idea and to set out for Brest. On October 7th he told Decrès he was getting ready and would leave Paris next week. But next day he said he was short of money, and there were debts he must pay. He asked for an advance of 40,000 francs. Besides his annual allowance of 150,000 francs, paid each month, he had since midsummer received from Napoleon nearly 200,000 francs—some £8000. It was all gone. Jerome was always hopelessly extravagant, but at Genoa and now in Paris he must have been squandering money even more lavishly than was his wont. He was given the 40,000, and went to Pont-sur-Seine to pay a farewell visit to his mother, but on his return to Paris he spent another month amusing himself. Decrès protested. He really must obey orders. Jerome replied that he was most anxious to start, but he had spent his money. He must have 60,000 more to settle those bills and have something in hand. Again the money was found for him, this time as a loan. Napoleon was furious when he heard of it. Jerome, he wrote, had more money than any prince in Europe. He must not have another centime. If he could not pay his debts, let him go to prison. ' One cannot imagine,' he said, ' how much this young fellow costs me, and with it all he only gives me disappointment after disappointment and is no use in my plans.'

Jerome was at last on his way to the fleet. From Nantes he wrote to his wife at Baltimore on November 21st. He began his letter with a piece of amusing boastfulness. He was only a *capitaine de frégate* about to serve under Bouet-Willaumez, who had received strict orders from the Emperor to keep him in his place, and make him do his work and learn his business. But writing to Elisabeth he posed as an admiral.

' I have arrived here,' he said, ' on my way to Brest, to take command of a squadron. I shall sail on the *Veteran*, a ship of 84 guns. I hope my expedition will be successful.' Then he went on to assure her of his unfailing devotion. ' The object of every step I take, my one care, my constant anxiety is to see once more my good Elisa, my dear little wife, without whom I could not live, and my little Napoleon Jerome; that is the name of our son. If you could imagine how I tremble at the thought of anything happening to him ! '

Those who saw him daily did not imagine he had any troubles or anxieties. He revelled in the entertainments provided for him at Brest, where, despite the Emperor's orders, he had a kind of public reception. Bouet-Willaumez allowed him to select his own officers. As second in command of the *Veteran* he chose Halgan, under whom he had served in the West Indies. Halgan was a good officer of his own rank, and Jerome, who was quite ignorant of anything beyond the elements of his profession, relied on him for the navigation of his big battleship. Then he had Meyronnet, who had been with him at Baltimore, and his secretary Lecamus of Martinique. Besides his officers he had quite a staff of valets and cooks. The cruise was to be as like a yachting trip as possible.

The fleet sailed on December 13th. Napoleon hoped that this prolonged sea service under the best of his admirals would make a man of Jerome. On the last day of the year he wrote to Joseph that he had great plans for their youngest brother, and when he came back he would have a princess ready to marry him.

Off Madeira the squadron made prizes of two large English merchantmen. Willaumez, instead of keeping a strict hand on Jerome, was letting him do very much as he liked, and evidently thought, that whatever were the Emperor's orders, it would be useful for him to flatter this young prince, who would soon be High Admiral of the Empire. On January 1, 1806, he signalled to the fleet that henceforth Captain Jerome Bonaparte, the Emperor's brother, would take precedence of the other captains, and act as commander of the second division. The fleet was sailing into the South Atlantic in the hope of intercepting a convoy of Indiamen as it rounded the Cape of Good Hope.

On February 17th, when about one hundred and fifty miles from the Cape, Willaumez chased and captured an English corvette, and learned from her captain that the Indiamen had passed days before and were safely on their way to England. The Admiral then sailed across the Atlantic to Brazil, and on April 3rd anchored in the harbour of Bahia.

The greater part of the month of April was spent at Bahia. Jerome passed part of the time on shore as the guest of the Portuguese commandant, but gave several dinner-parties on board of the *Veteran*. Before sailing he wrote to Elisabeth at Baltimore. He begged her not to believe any disquieting reports she might hear about him. ' You know me, Elisa,' he said, ' and you can feel certain that nothing can ever separate me from you.' He asked her to have her own and her baby son's portraits painted and sent to France for him.

Leaving Bahia at the end of April the squadron sailed northwards, and on May 15th anchored in the harbour of Cayenne. It was to remain there a fortnight. Before the time was up Jerome suddenly put to sea without telling the

Admiral what were his intentions. Bouet-Willaumez, after waiting a few days for his return, set out in search of the missing *Veteran*. He was haunted by the idea that she might fall in with a superior English force, and that Jerome would be taken prisoner. After an anxious cruise of nearly three weeks in the West Indian seas, the Admiral entered the harbour of Fort de France in Martinique on July 24th, and saw the *Veteran* lying safely at anchor under the guns of the batteries. Jerome had been there since July 5th. He had run across from Cayenne to Martinique to see his old friends there, and give Lecamus the pleasure of visiting his home.

Jerome had written to Baltimore from Cayenne, and again from Martinique. At Cayenne he had gone on board an American schooner to arrange about his letter being conveyed to the United States, when the Captain told him he had come from Baltimore and had seen Madame Jerome Bonaparte only a few days before looking well. ' Imagine my delight,' wrote Jerome to his wife. ' I assure you it was my first moment of happiness since we parted.' He then went on to argue that the sacrifices he had made were a proof of his devotion to her. ' If I had renounced you,' he said, ' I would now be in command of his Imperial Majesty's fleet. For an ordinary naval officer the position I hold is very good, especially considering my age ; but what is it for me who with one word could have everything ? Believe me that if I had consented to separate myself from you and my son, who are the objects of all my affections, I would be at this moment not a subject, but a sovereign. . . . I have preferred you to a crown, and I would rather have you than all the world.'

He went on to say that after the war was over he would leave Europe for the United States, live happily with her, and forget that he had been a prince and had possessed a fortune. No sacrifice for her sake would be too great. Then he insisted on the need of prudence and secrecy, and begged her not to bring up their child as an American, but as a Frenchman. Let the first word he learned be the name of Napoleon. Tell him the great man was his uncle, and he would be a prince with a famous career. It was rather a self-contradictory letter, and Jerome, when he wrote it, must have felt that he was playing a part, without quite knowing how the tragicomedy was to end.   From Martinique he wrote to Elisabeth a story that he must have known well was mere fiction.   He told her as a profound secret that three days after she left Holland, the Emperor had decided that she should be acknowledged as his brother's wife, and it was only on account of her flight to England that Napoleon had changed his mind.   It was a foolish and unfeeling attempt to make her feel the responsibility for the miscarriage of his schemes, and it can hardly have deceived Elisabeth.

Jerome was already tired of the long cruise, and anxious to be again in a position to push his fortunes in Europe.   At Martinique he suggested to Bouet-Willaumez that some means might be found for arranging his return to France.   He might be sent home with despatches.   The Admiral would not hear of it.   On July 1st the squadron put to sea, and for the rest of the month was cruising north of the West Indies, on the look-out for English traders.   On the 27th a small privateer struck her colours to the *Veteran*.   Instead of sending a full prize crew on board Jerome took her in tow.   This so reduced the speed of his ship that by sunset the squadron was hull down on the horizon, and next morning was out of sight. Then, instead of making for the rendezvous appointed in his orders in case he lost touch of the fleet, Jerome first steered northwards towards Newfoundland, and then set his course for the Azores.

Off the islands he captured a British brig, and heard from a Russian captain that a large convoy of slow sailing British ships was straggling away to the northward.   He slipped in amongst them next night.   The ship that was convoying them was, with five of the best sailing ships, well away from the rest.   Jerome gathered up eleven prizes in the early morning, and got away with them, reached the north-east of Spain, and made for L'Orient.   He was chased by an English squadron, but escaped, and took his prizes safely into the port of Concarneau in Brittany.

He started in a few days for Paris, taking with him Lecamus and Meyronnet.   He was a little anxious as to his reception by the Emperor after taking on himself to leave the fleet. But he had come back at a propitious moment, and his luck in falling in with the badly guarded convoy off the Azores had enabled him to represent his dash across the Atlantic as a successful exploit in the war upon English commerce. It so happened that Napoleon, busy with the preparations for the Jena campaign, and planning a remodelling of Germany, had already taken the first steps to arrange a marriage between Jerome and a German princess, and destined a crown for him. If he had not returned he would soon have been recalled. It was all the better for the Emperor's plans that the official press was able to announce to the public that British merchantmen to the value of five millions of francs had been taken by a daring stroke of his Imperial Highness Prince Jerome. It was the first time he had been given the title. Napoleon received him with open arms, gave him the Grand Cordon of the Legion of Honour, and told him that without asking for his consent it was all but settled that he was to marry the Princess Catherine of Würtemberg, and that the marriage was to be the stepping-stone to a throne. He was to go to Germany with the Emperor, and further opportunities of distinction would be offered to him in the coming war. The naval officer

> That never set a squadron in the field
> Nor the division of a battle knew

was to be suddenly transformed into a general.

Jerome forgot all his protestations of affection for the wife he had married at Baltimore, the mother of his son. Dazzled by the prospects opening before him, he agreed at once to all the Emperor's plans. His marriage with Elisabeth Patterson would be declared invalid by a servile French ecclesiastical court accepting the judgment of the civil authority. Besides, his destined bride was a Protestant princess, for whom the judgment of the civil law would be sufficient.

Before the Revolution her father had been one of the electoral princes of the German Empire. On the outbreak of the war with Austria in 1805 he had thrown in his lot with Napoleon, and had been rewarded by the erection of Würtemberg into a kingdom. He had welcomed the suggestion that the hand of his daughter Catherine should be given to the brother of his protector, and the negotiations for the marriage treaty had begun at Stuttgart in August 1806, when it was supposed that Jerome was still in the West Indies and no one had any idea that in a few days he would arrive in France.

Catherine of Würtemberg was between twenty-three and twenty-four years of age, nearly two years older than her intended husband. She was the daughter of Frederick William of Würtemberg and his first wife, a princess of the ducal House of Brunswick, and had been born and spent her first years at St. Petersburg, when her father was serving in the Russian army, in days when he had not much prospect of ever being either duke or king, for more than one heir stood between. When he became the ruler of Würtemberg in 1797 the little state was committed to the anti-French policy of Austria, but after Hohenlinden Frederick of Würtemberg realised that he was not on the winning side, and threw in his lot with the France of Napoleon, with the result that he gained extensions of territory and promotion to a kingly crown. His daughter Catherine grew up in the ceremonious court which he maintained at Stuttgart a typical German *fräulein*, not tall, and made to appear somewhat shorter by her stout build, but with small hands, a pleasant face, blue eyes and light flaxen hair. Frederick William's predecessor had been somewhat of a spendthrift, a builder of huge rambling palaces, the cost of which and the expense of unsuccessful wars had emptied his treasury. His successor was economising, and fond as he was of his daughter he spared her hardly any money, and left her with a limited wardrobe and few amusements. Much of her time she spent in reading, and she could talk many languages, including French, which she spoke with a touch of a German accent. Like a dutiful German princess she was ready to accept the husband provided for her by her father's policy. On September 9, 1806, the marriage treaty was signed at Stuttgart, and it was hoped the wedding would take place in October, but the course of events delayed it till the following year.

On September 19th Jerome, who had already been recognised as an Imperial Prince, was promoted to the rank of Rear-Admiral. Two days later Napoleon informed him that as a Prince of the Empire he would have an annual allowance of a million francs, beginning from October 1st. He was to have a household, nominated partly by the Emperor, partly at his own choice. Amongst those whom Napoleon named were the chaplain-general, Cardinal Maury, and the chamberlain of the household, General d'Hédouville, a son of a noble family, who had at an early date joined the Republican army, and had served on the staff of General Hoche. Amongst those whom Jerome himself selected were his secretary, Lecamus of Martinique, and his faithful henchman Lieutenant Meyronnet and some other young naval officers. On October 6th an ecclesiastical commission named by the Emperor pronounced the Patterson marriage invalid. A few days later Napoleon wrote to the King of Würtemberg that he feared his brother's marriage with Catherine would have to be deferred, as Jerome was about to take part in the campaign against Prussia.

Napoleon had left Paris for Mayence at the end of September. Jerome went with him, accompanied by a kind of staff made up of General d'Hédouville, Lecamus, Meyronnet and some other of his naval friends. There was some talk of a flying visit to Stuttgart, in order that Jerome might make Catherine's acquaintance, but the young man was not anxious for the meeting, and was satisfied with an exchange of portraits. For the moment he was much more interested in the campaign, in which the Emperor was to provide him with some opportunity for distinguishing himself.

On October 8th, the day on which the general advance of the French army began, Napoleon named Jerome commander of a new *corps d'armée*, the 9th Corps of the Grand Army, which was to be composed of three divisions, two of Bavarians and one of Würtembergers. He was destined for a German throne and he was to lead Germans to victory, including some of his future father-in-law's troops. Next day he went to Cronach in South Germany to take command of his corps, but found that only one Bavarian division was actually assembled. The rest could not be mobilised and concentrated for some time to come. On the 13th he wrote to the Emperor a letter which did him more credit than most of his correspondence :—

' I beg,' he wrote, ' that your Majesty will not keep me away from the battlefield, but will allow me to be near your person. You know better than any one else that what I most

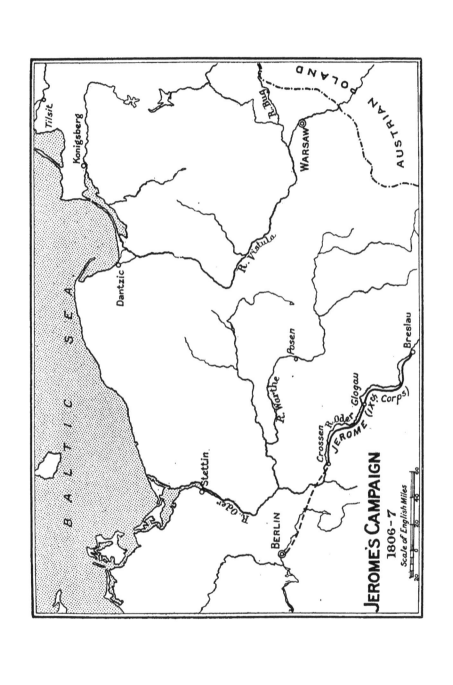

JEROME'S CAMPAIGN

1806–7

Scale of English Miles

need now is to win some glory. How greatly I would be to be pitied if on my return from the campaign the most I could say would be, " I commanded the Bavarians and was all the time with the rearguard." '

Napoleon received the letter on the morrow of the double victory of Jena and Auerstadt. He sent word to Jerome to come and join his headquarters. But it was too late for him to witness any fighting. He had only the satisfaction of riding beside his victorious brother in the triumphal entry into Berlin.

. However, the war was not quite over. Murat and Soult were pursuing and making prisoners of the wreck of Brunswick's army. But a single corps had retired with the Prussian king beyond the Vistula, where a Russian army was gathering to support Frederick William, all too late. Silesia was held by Prussian garrisons, and Napoleon assigned to Jerome the conquest of this province. It would be a series of sieges. His corps was complete, and had been moved up to Crossen, south-east of Berlin on the main road into Silesia by Glogau and Breslau. It was nearly twenty-five thousand strong, and included the two Bavarian divisions of Generals Deroy and Minucci and the Würtemberg division of General Seckendorf, with three small cavalry brigades commanded by Mezzanelli, a Bavarian officer, and the French generals Lefèbvre-Desnouettes and Montbrun.

Leaving Berlin on November 2nd, Jerome took command of the 9th Corps at Crossen on the 5th, and, marching along the south bank of the Oder, appeared before the old fortress of Glogau on the 12th.

The Prussian commandant refused to surrender, and Jerome showed he had not even the most elementary ideas as to how to reduce the place. After a short cannonade, which did no appreciable damage to rampart or ditch, he ordered General Deroy to storm the fortress with his Bavarians. Deroy respectfully refused to make the attempt. If the rampart were breached he was ready to lead an assault, but against intact fortifications, protected by a deep ditch, and with open ground to cross, it would be madness. ' I could not count on my men following me,' he said. Jerome wrote to Napoleon reporting Deroy's refusal. It was most painful, he said, for him to find that he could not inspire with his own zeal the troops he commanded. At the last moment Deroy had brought to a dead stop an operation on which he had counted as the means to a brilliant success. He wished he had a few French regiments with him to give an example to these South German allies. It was rather a shock to Jerome to receive in reply, instead of words of approval from the Emperor, a cold official letter from Berthier, the chief of Napoleon's staff, taking the side of the Bavarian general.

' His Majesty,' wrote Berthier, ' considers that the remarks made to you by General Deroy were quite proper. One cannot storm a town when one has not breached the wall, and when there is a ditch with its scarp and counterscarp still intact. His Majesty thinks that those who advised such an assault were quite wrong, for the only result would be to incur a heavy loss of life without any result.' He then went on to inform Jerome that Napoleon was detaching General Vandamme from Ney's corps, with orders to proceed to Glogau and direct the siege operations.

Jerome felt hurt at this rebuke and this partial supersession. When Vandamme arrived he marched off to Lissa with his Bavarians, leaving the General only the Würtemberg division. Vandamme brought up some heavy artillery, began regular siege-works, and breached the rampart. On December 2nd Glogau surrendered to him, and he reaped the success intended originally for Prince Jerome.

Next day the Prince received new orders from his brother, giving him another opportunity. Napoleon directed him to march on Breslau. ' The place,' he wrote, ' has not one-fifth of the garrison required for its proper defence. The general in command has said that he cannot hold out if he is blockaded for even a few days by infantry alone. A hundred shells thrown into this large and splendid city will make him surrender. I want you to have the honour of taking it in person.'

Jerome accordingly set the 9th Corps in movement for Breslau, but the march had hardly begun when he wrote to his brother (then at Posen, on his way to occupy Warsaw) asking to be allowed to spend some time at his headquarters. He was apparently not too confident in his own capacity for command, and in bad humour at having Vandamme sent to take care of him. Berthier wrote to him in the Emperor's name on December 17th, telling him to join headquarters at Warsaw about the 21st or 22nd, and meanwhile to leave Vandamme in charge of the siege operations against Breslau, and detach Deroy's Bavarian brigade on other duty.

Jerome set off for Warsaw, taking Lecamus and some others of his little court with him, but disregarding the Emperor's orders, he directed his chief of the staff, General d'Hédouville, to command the operations against Breslau, and kept Deroy to blockade it on the right bank of the Oder, while Vandamme was to control only the operations on the left bank. D'Hédouville was to send reports to the Prince at Warsaw, and act under his directions '.as far as possible.' Jerome left Warsaw with the Emperor and on December 23rd joined the army which was operating against the Russian General Benningsen on the banks of the Narev. He only spent a few days in camp and bivouac, and saw no fighting ; part of the time he accompanied Murat in a rapid march, before which the enemy retired without ever making a stand. But Napoleon, with the foundation of the Westphalian kingdom in view, was determined that Jerome should have some military reputation, so in the bulletin which announced the victory of Golymin and the retreat of Benningsen, there appeared a little bit of fiction about Jerome : ' His Majesty,' ran the despatch, ' desirous that Prince Jerome should have the opportunity of gaining military experience, summoned him to his headquarters from Silesia. The Prince took part in all the engagements that have occurred, and was frequently on the outpost line.'

By his absence in Poland Jerome had just missed a chance of being present at a brilliant victory of his own troops. On Christmas Eve the Prince of Pless, the Prussian Governor of Silesia, had attempted to come to the help of the besieged garrison of Breslau. Minucci's Bavarian division and Montbrun's cavalry had met and beaten him, taking five hundred prisoners and six guns. Next day Vandamme took advantage of this success once more to summon Breslau to surrender, but the place held out. Jerome had returned to Warsaw when he heard the news. He wrote to Vandamme, his senior in years, services, and military rank, telling him he was much annoyed at his having taken it upon himself to

summon the governor of Breslau. He reminded him that
he (Vandamme) was serving under his orders. It was not
his place, but that of the Prince's chief of the staff, D'Hédouville, to communicate with Breslau. He hoped he would not
again have to blame him in this way. It was painful to him,
all the more because he had a high opinion of Vandamme,
and 'had had the pleasure of reporting favourably to the
Emperor on his talents, zeal, and energy.' He ordered him,
in the event of Breslau surrendering, not to enter the place,
but to march off with the Würtembergers and part of the siege-
train to attack Schweidnitz on the Austrian border of Silesia.

Vandamme replied with a dignified protest. 'During the
fifteen years that I have been a general,' he said, ' I have
never received from any of my superiors such a severe reprimand as your Highness has addressed to me.' On January came
the news that Breslau was on the point of surrendering. Jerome
hurried up from Warsaw, signed the capitulation, sat proudly
on his horse surrounded by his staff as the Prussians marched
out and laid down their arms, and then made a triumphant
entry into the capital of Silesia. Horace Vernet, then a young
artist just beginning to specialise as the painter of the
military triumphs of Napoleon, was commissioned to produce
an historical picture of the ' Taking of Breslau ' with Jerome
as the central figure.[1] It was cheaply purchased fame, for
the Prince had not been present during one hour of the siege
and was reaping the laurels of Vandamme, Deroy, and Minucci.

Vandamme was sent off with the Würtembergers to reduce
Schweidnitz, and Deroy with his Bavarians to besiege the
little fortress of Brieg. Jerome remained at Breslau. He
occupied the old palace, surrounded himself with a court,
entertained, appeared at the theatre, amused himself, squandered money freely on a crowd of parasites and flatterers, and
engaged in love-affairs that showed how little he thought either
of his wife in America or his destined royal consort at Stuttgart.
He took it on himself to suggest to the Prince of Pless that
there should be an armistice in Silesia. Napoleon, as soon as he
heard of it, stopped the negotiations and wrote to Jerome :—

---

[1] Vernet lived to add to his war pictures of the First Empire others celebrating
the earlier triumphs of the Second, amongst them a picture of the Battle of the Alma,
in which the most prominent place is given to Prince Napoleon, Jerome's son.

' I cannot understand how, at your age and with your desire to obtain a military reputation, you can be so anxious for an armistice. The persons you have about you may wish for it, but even they should have reminded you that your duty would not allow you to conclude it without my orders.' Jerome replied in a letter that, considering what his military record had so far been, was a piece of sublime absurdity. ' Your Majesty,' he said, ' has addressed to me a reproach I do not deserve. I am passionately fond of war. Eager for glory I fear no danger in my efforts to obtain it, and I venture to say to your Majesty that even though in your army there are as many brave men as there are soldiers, there is not one who is braver than I am.'

All the same he remained at Breslau, making only flying visits to the camps of his troops in order to pose again and again as the conqueror of Silesia. On January 16th he went to Brieg to receive the surrender of the place which Deroy had reduced. On February 5th he was for a few hours in Vandamme's lines before Schweidnitz. He came back again on the 16th to see the garrison march out. Kossel and Neiss, two other small fortresses, were then besieged, and Jerome returned to his amusements at Breslau, leaving Vandamme and Deroy to do his work. This did not prevent Napoleon from announcing in one of his bulletins that ' Prince Jerome was reducing in succession all the strong places of Silesia.'

The Emperor can hardly have been misinformed about Jerome's proceedings. We have proof of the contrary in the letters of remonstrance he addressed to him from time to time. Yet there are indications of a kind of self-delusion about his brother in other parts of his correspondence. Thus a little later we find him writing to King Joseph of Naples : ' Prince Jerome is doing well. I am very well pleased with him, and, unless I am greatly mistaken, he has in him the making of a man of the very first rank. Of course I don't let him get this idea of himself into his head, for all my letters to him are scoldings. He is adored in Silesia. I have purposely pushed him into an isolated position as a commander-in-chief, for I don't believe in the proverb that one must know how to obey in order to be able to command.'

Notwithstanding the scoldings, Jerome, a spoilt child from

the first, had a very exalted idea of his own merits. And this was encouraged by the way in which he was advertised in the bulletins of the Grand Army, and by his promotion to the rank of general of division on March 14th (1807).

In the middle of April Von Görtzen, who had succeeded Pless as Governor of Silesia, got together some 6000 men, and marched with them to raise the siege of Kossel, which was still holding out. Lefèbvre-Desnouettes barred his way with an inferior force. The news of Görtzen's advance reached Breslau on the 15th, and Jerome started with reinforcements for Lefèbvre. On the morning of the 17th the reports of cannon in his front told him that Lefèbvre was heavily engaged with the Prussians. As he marched on the firing became less heavy, and when he arrived on the field Von Görtzen was in full retreat. He reported this success to the Emperor, telling him at the same time that he was about to return to Breslau. Napoleon wrote to him : ' I wish you had been under fire instead of Lefèbvre. . . . Why need you go back to Breslau ? Remain in camp. You ought to be living in a hut in the midst of your troops. You should have them under arms at two in the morning with yourself in the middle of them, ready to receive the reports of reconnoitring parties sent out in all directions. I can't see yet that you are really making war. How is it that Hédouville and Deroy don't give you a hint ? I suppose it is because every one is ready to flatter a prince, and likes his own ease. But with all this kind of thing you will never gain any experience. One can only learn war by going under fire.'

Jerome wrote in reply, not from the camp before Kossel but from his palace at Breslau, that his brother was not doing him justice. He explained that he really deserved credit for the recent success. He had sent Lefèbvre orders to manœuvre so that Von Görtzen would be caught between the two columns of troops, but the Prussian had beaten a retreat just too soon. He assured the Emperor that he was working day and night, and looking only for a word of approval from him as his reward. The date ' Breslau ' at the top of the letter was a sufficient commentary on Jerome's protests of soldierly zeal.

On May 10th there was again news that Von Görtzen was advancing. This time Jerome resolved to be in time for the fight, and proceeded to Lefèbvre's headquarters. The Prussian general made a feint at Jerome's camp with a part of his force, and just when the Prince thought he had won a victory there came news that Von Görtzen with his main column was making a dash for Breslau, held only by a weak garrison under the French General Dumuy. Jerome sent Lefèbvre forward towards Breslau and followed at a more leisurely rate to support him. Lefèbvre's detachment was roughly handled by the Prussians, and lost some of its guns, but they were recaptured, and failure turned into success by the veteran Dumuy arriving from Breslau in the nick of time. Napoleon told Jerome frankly that he had made a bad mistake and nearly incurred a disaster by dividing his forces.

Neisse, Schweidnitz, and Kossel now surrendered in succession, and Jerome concentrated all his corps to invest the entrenched camp formed by Von Görtzen at Glatz. On May 24th the works were stormed by two columns under Vandamme and Lefèbvre. While these veterans led the stormers, Jerome directed the attack from a position that commanded a good view but was almost out of range of the Prussian guns, if we are to believe the letter of one of his staff. Three cannonballs fell some twelve paces in front of the group, so they were under fire. Horace Vernet painted another picture, ' Prince Jerome at the storming of the entrenched camp of Glatz.'

Silesia was conquered. Jerome asked for the Legion of Honour for Lecamus, Meyronnet, and the rest of his personal retainers, but Napoleon did not want to make the coveted red ribbon and bronze star too cheap, and refused it. But there was a shower of Bavarian and Würtemberg decorations for everybody. In June came the victory of Friedland. Napoleon was on the Niemen, and Russia was ready to sign first peace and then the Alliance of Tilsit. Prussia lost all her territories west of the Oder. From these lands a kingdom would be marked out for Jerome, the victorious conqueror of Silesia, the hero of sea and land, and Catherine of Würtemberg would be a queen. ' My brother,' Napoleon wrote to Jerome from Tilsit, ' I have just signed the peace with Russia and Prussia. You have been recognised as King of Westphalia. This kingdom will include all the states of which you will find the list hereto annexed.' The list included the old Prussian province of Westphalia, Hesse-Cassel, a considerable part of

Brunswick and several minor principalities, much of the territory being what Louis had prematurely annexed to Holland.
He had to be content with East Friesland.

On his way back to France Napoleon met Jerome at Dresden.
He brought him the Grand Cross of St. Andrew set with diamonds, as a gift from the Czar. They travelled to France
together, the new King listening respectfully to the Emperor's
plans for the organisation of his German kingdom. Paris
was reached on the 27th, and Jerome was given rooms in the
Tuileries. The next event was to be the celebration of his
marriage with Catherine.

According to the treaty of the year before there was to be a
marriage by proxy at Stuttgart, then the Princess was to
enter France by way of Strasburg, and there would be a second
celebration when she reached Paris. Her father was to provide a dowry of 100,000 florins, and jewels to the same amount.
Napoleon and Jerome were to give her more jewellery to the
value of 300,000 francs, besides providing for the annual
expenses of her household on a befitting scale, and giving her
a further annual allowance of 100,000 francs.

On August 1st Bessières started for Stuttgart, where he
arrived on the 10th, as special ambassador for the marriage.
Next day there was a state reception, when Bessières presented
his credentials and formally asked the hand of the Princess
for Jerome, in whose name he spoke at the marriage by proxy
celebrated on the 12th according to the Lutheran rite, followed
by a state banquet and ball. On the 14th Catherine bade
farewell to her old home and reached Strasburg on the 15th,
where a suite of the ladies and gentlemen of her future household were waiting to escort her to Paris.

Though she travelled by easy stages, the heat was oppressive;
and Catherine was very tired, and suffered too from home-
sickness. On the 21st a short morning drive ended at the
château of Le Raincy on a wooded slope above the forest of
Bondy, a few miles east of Paris. It was then the country
house of Junot, the Governor of Paris, and Madame Junot
was waiting to receive the bride. There she was to see for the
first time her destined husband. The afternoon was passed with
Madame Junot. At dinner-time Jerome arrived accompanied
by Cardinal Maury, Lecamus, and the officers of his household.

Louis Napoleon   *Princess Élisa*   *Empress Joséphine*   *Napoleon*   *Mme. Mère*   *Jérome*   *Princess Pauline*   *Murat*

Princess Cath. of Würtemberg   *Princess Caroline*

THE MARRIAGE OF JEROME BONAPARTE AND THE PRINCESS CATHERINE OF WÜRTEMBERG (AUGUST 22, 1807)

Catherine was tired, ill, embarrassed. After dinner she actually fainted. Madame Junot thought her pretty, but rather too cold and dignified. Jerome's impressions were not enthusiastic. ' The princess,' he wrote to an intimate friend, ' seems very good-hearted, though she is not beautiful—*elle n'est pas mal*,' which we may translate, ' she will do very well.' The dinner had been purposely fixed for an early hour. After it, in the cool of the evening, the party drove into Paris in a long train of carriages. At nine the Tuileries were reached. Through a double hedge of bearskin-capped veterans of the Imperial Guard, and amid the red light of hundreds of torches, her carriage drove up to the grand entrance, and at the foot of the staircase the Emperor surrounded by his court was waiting to welcome her.

She wrote to her father next day her impression of her meeting with the conqueror of Europe: ' I threw myself at his feet. He raised me up very graciously, and kissed me tenderly. Then he led me through the state apartments into the Empress's salon, where we found her with Madame, the Emperor's mother, the Queen of Naples,[1] the Grand Duchess of Berg,[2] and the Princess Stéphanie.[3] The Emperor presented me to all these princesses and then took me to the rooms where dinner was served. He talked much with me, and forced me to take some wine, to give me courage, as he said. It is true that I had need of it, though I felt much less nervous with the Emperor than when I met the Prince. After dinner the Emperor went back with us to the salon, where we remained a good hour. He chatted with the princes and princesses, but above all he was extremely kind and amiable to me.' Then, late as it was, there was a drive by the Champs Elysées to the border of the Bois de Boulogne, the Emperor taking her in his own carriage. Then another conversation in the salon, and at last the Princess was shown her room next to the Empress's. It was half-past one and Catherine was tired out and anxious to go to sleep, but the Empress came in and asked to see her jewels.

Next morning early another meeting with Napoleon and Josephine. The Empress brought in the casket containing

---

[1] Madame Joseph Bonaparte.   [2] Madame Murat.
[3] Stéphanie Beauharnais, daughter of Josephine by her first marriage.

the Emperor's presents to the bride, and Napoleon himself
put on her a diadem of brilliants and her necklace and earrings,
and told her she was 'papa's dear child.' Then Jerome
arrived, and had a long talk with Catherine, during part of
which Josephine was present. In the evening a court was
held, princes, marshals, generals, officers of state and the
representatives of the Legislative Assembly were all present,
and the civil marriage was registered. On the following evening there was another gathering for the religious ceremony,
which was celebrated in the chapel of the Tuileries, the officiating prelate being one who was more of a politician than a priest,
Karl Theodor Dalberg, Prince Archbishop of Mayence, Pri-
mate of Western Germany, and formerly Chancellor of the old
German Empire. He had been for years a staunch ally of
Napoleon, and Jerome was to be his neighbour as a German
king. As the long procession of princes and courtiers left
the chapel for the Galerie de Diane, where a state banquet was
ready, a thunderstorm burst over Paris. Later the rain ceased,
and after midnight Napoleon and the Empress drove off to
St. Cloud, leaving Jerome and Catherine to spend the first
days of their honeymoon at the Tuileries.

On the 25th Jerome and Catherine appeared at a gala performance at the Opera. Then there were visits to the Emperor
and Empress at St. Cloud, and to the Queen of Naples at Mortefontaine. On September 4th they were back at the Tuileries,
where Catherine had to spend some lonely days, while Jerome
went to Rambouillet to discuss the future of Westphalia with
Napoleon. Then Catherine had a few days at Rambouillet,
and when she returned to Paris with Jerome they were the
guests at a garden-party which the Murats gave in their honour
at the Elysée. A surprise had been prepared for Catherine.
In the garden a little village of quaint wooden cottages like
those of her native country had been erected. Dairymaids
in German peasant costume saluted her and wished her happiness. They were ladies of the opera who had rehearsed their
parts. Then there was a long visit to the Emperor at Fontainebleau, and at last, after a few days more in Paris, Jerome
and Catherine started on November 18, 1807, to take possession
of their Westphalian kingdom.

CHAPTER XII

LUCIEN IN REVOLT—LOUIS AND HORTENSE—JOSEPH
TRANSFERRED TO SPAIN

(1807-1808)

NAPOLEON was now at the summit of his power. He had reshaped the Continent, and made every state from the Ural Mountains to the Atlantic his obedient vassal or his enforced ally. England alone held out against him, but he hoped to combine with the Czar in a raid upon Asia that would destroy her eastern empire, and sap the chief source of her wealth. Meanwhile he had closed the Continent against her trade.

Three of his brothers were kings, Louis in Holland, Joseph in Naples, Jerome in Western Germany, and the marriage of the last with a princess of one of the old ruling houses of Europe was a recognition of the fact that he had raised his family to a permanent place among the imperial and royal races that form a small ruling caste in Europe. But one brother stood stubbornly outside the system he had established, and of them all Lucien was the one whom in his own heart he believed to be the ablest, the most daring and energetic, the best fitted to play a great part in the consolidation and perpetuation of his empire.

At Rome Lucien maintained a princely state that seemed to proclaim to the world that he had little or nothing to gain by becoming one of his brother's satraps—a provincial governor disguised as a king. He was a Roman prince, busy developing his fief of Canino, improving the tillage of the lands, digging up pavements and sculptures from the buried villa he had discovered, introducing manufactures, showing on a small scale that, if he had been so inclined, he could have ruled a larger territory. He had other properties in the country, including a pleasant villa at Frascati, and in Rome he had purchased as his home the Palazzo Nuñez, and made it one of the chief social centres of the Eternal City. On the evenings when he entertained company his salons were crowded with cardinals and monsignori, Roman nobles and distinguished foreign visitors, ambassadors, artists like Canova, men of science and letters like Humboldt. In the theatre of the palace concerts and dramatic entertainments were frequently given, and on one noted occasion a mixed company of professionals and amateurs presented Voltaire's tragedy of *Zaïre*. One of the most striking situations in the play is that where the hero Orosmane defies the crusading king to separate him from his beloved Zaïre. Lucien himself took the hero's part, his wife was Zaïre, and the brilliant audience rose and made the roof ring with their ' Bravos ' when, holding her hand, Lucien thundered out his defiance at once to King Lusignan on the stage and to his brother the Emperor—

> ' Pour Zaïre, crois-moi, sans que ton cœur s'offense,
> Elle n'est pas d'un prix qui soit en ta puissance.
> Tes chevaliers d'Europe et tous leurs souverains
> S'uniraient vainement pour l'ôter de mes mains ! '

For once the stilted theatrical verses rang with a real meaning.

Nor was it only thus that Lucien accentuated his position. In his old Jacobin days he had written his romance of Ceylon to set forth his hostility to priests of all kinds. Now he was engaged on a more ambitious literary effort with a diametrically opposite purpose. He was writing an epic, *Charlemagne,* in which the great Pope Leo III. was the real hero, and the Papacy was represented as the fountainhead of civilisation and law in Europe. It was some years before the long heroic poem was completed, but as soon as the first book was ready in manuscript, he read it to the Pope and a circle of the cardinals at the Vatican. In more than one passage could be traced a declaration for Pius VII. against Napoleon's claim to subject even the papal power to his own Imperial rule, and in *Charlemagne* Lucien described an ideal emperor, placing his sword at the service of the Holy See, leaving it to his audience to supply. the contrast with the would-be Charlemagne of their own day. Pius VII. showed his great friendship for Lucien in many ways, notably by granting him a mark of honour rarely given even to reigning sovereigns, when on the birth of a little daughter the Pope asked to be her godfather, and chose for her his own mother's name.

Lucien made no further attempts to arrive at a reconciliation with the Emperor. This passive attitude strengthened his position. Overtures were made to him from time to time by other members of the family, but Lucien was inflexible on the one point on which Napoleon had insisted from the first. Whatever offers might be made to him, even though it were a kingdom, Lucien would not hear of any arrangement that would put a slight upon his wife.

About the time of Jerome's marriage with Catherine of Würtemberg his mother and his brother Joseph wrote to Lucien suggesting a compromise. His uncle, Cardinal Fesch, tried to persuade him to give way. To his mother and to Joseph Lucien wrote a polite refusal of their intervention on his behalf. But to Fesch he sent a scathing reply : ' Have you forgotten all honour, all religion ? ' he said. ' I wish you would have at least sufficient common sense not to think I am like Jerome and to spare me the useless insult of your cowardly advice. In a word, don't write to me again until religion and honour, which you are now trampling under foot, have dissipated your blindness. At least hide your base sentiments under your purple robes, and follow in silence your own path along the highway of ambition.' Madame Mère wrote to her son that Fesch did not deserve such treatment. She begged him to write to his uncle in a more friendly tone. As for herself she would say no more on the subject, but the breach between her sons would fill her life with sorrow and desolation.

After the Würtemberg marriage Napoleon came to northern Italy to settle various matters in the peninsula, to confer with the Viceroy Eugène and with Joseph, and to discuss with them the affairs of Rome and the growing tension with Pius VII., who refused to close his ports to the English flag, declaring that he was a man of peace, the enemy of no Christian nation. The Emperor decided to make a last effort to reduce Lucien to submission during this visit to Italy.

He felt he had need of him. He was forming his plans for

the remodelling of the Spanish peninsula. They were still vague and undecided, and at the moment he leant to a project suggested to him by the friends of Ferdinand, Prince of the Asturias, that the heir of the Spanish crown should be betrothed to a daughter of the Bonapartes, as a first step in the new policy. The eldest daughter of the family—though even she was still a child—was Charlotte, one of Lucien's daughters by his first marriage. Napoleon thought seriously of selecting her as the future bride of the Spanish prince, and made the proposal to Lucien through Joseph, adding as a condition that Charlotte should be sent to Paris to complete her education, under the care of those the Emperor might select.

Joseph saw Lucien during a short visit he made to Rome, and endeavoured to persuade him that this proposal would open a way to a reconciliation with the Emperor. It was agreed between the two brothers that Lucien should go to northern Italy for an interview with Napoleon, and discuss not only Charlotte's future, but his own position. But in the letter in which Joseph announced this decision to Napoleon he made it quite clear that on the main point in dispute Lucien was as inflexible as ever. 'No matter what arguments I urged him with,' wrote Joseph, ' I could never get from him anything but a declaration that he felt his honour was concerned in not disavowing his wife or any of his children, and that it was impossible for him to disgrace himself in his own eyes.' At the same time he protested that he was only anxious to find a way in which he could co-operate with the Emperor, and be of service to him. In other words, Lucien wanted peace, but it must be on his own terms. Napoleon flattered himself that when they came face to face he would be able to overcome his brother's resolution, and he agreed to the meeting.

It took place at Mantua. The brothers met late in the evening of December 12, 1807, and the debate went on far into the night. Napoleon flattered Lucien, alluded to his past services, especially to that stormy day in Brumaire that had been the crisis of his own fortunes, and told him that he counted on him for greater things in the future. Lucien protested that he would only be too happy to break away from his present inactive life, take part in the great events of the day, and serve the Emperor to the best of his ability.

But when it came to fixing the terms of the proposed alliance, neither of these two strong-willed men would yield on the central point that divided them. Napoleon thought he was making generous concessions when he told Lucien that he would arrange a royal marriage for Charlotte, recognise Lucien as an Imperial Prince, probably offer him a crown, and recognise the daughters of the second marriage as his nieces, but all this Lucien rejected because it was to be granted only on two conditions : (1) that he should divorce [1] Madame Jouberthou (as Napoleon persisted in calling her) ; and (2) that the Emperor should not be asked in any way to recognise her son Charles Lucien, born on the eve of the marriage, but legitimatised by it both according to French and to Canon Law. Napoleon would not hear of the boy having even the most remote prospect of being included in the Imperial succession through the concessions offered to his father. And Lucien would accept neither of these conditions. There was no advantage, he said, that the Emperor could offer him great enough to induce him to sacrifice his wife or son.

After nearly six hours of conversation both were wearied out, and an agreement seemed as far off as ever. Lucien at last said it was no use continuing the debate. He would return to Rome in the morning. Napoleon urged him to spend a few days with him at Mantua, but Lucien was not to be persuaded. After a short sleep he started on his homeward journey.

From Milan, on December 17th, Napoleon wrote to Joseph telling him that he thought he might with advantage intervene in the negotiation and persuade Lucien to accept the proposals made to him at Mantua. Joseph sent one of his equerries to Rome to urge upon Lucien the advisability of reopening the negotiation, but without any result. Lucien was firmer than ever. He would not even hear of Charlotte being sent to Paris. ' What,' he exclaimed, ' can they expect me to put my child into the hands of people who will poison her mind against my wife ? ' So Lucien maintained his independence, and as the relations between the Emperor and the Pope became

---

[1] In the course of the conversation Napoleon told Lucien that if he consented to a divorce he would not be the only one of the family to take such action, for he (Napoleon) was thinking of divorcing his own wife for reasons of state.

M

more and more strained, he sided more and more openly against his brother. Jerome had given up his wife and his child to obtain the petty German kingdom of which he was just taking possession ; Lucien remained true to the mother of his children even at the cost of a crown.

Let us now see how it had fared with the other two brothers, Louis of Holland and Joseph of Naples. When we last heard of Louis he had just returned in triumph to Amsterdam after his somewhat inglorious conquest of Westphalia, which, though he wanted it for Holland, was finally to be assigned to his youngest brother. The winter of 1806-7 was beginning, and Louis began again to complain of the rigours of the Dutch climate. His ill-health was no doubt in part the result of his disappointment at the outcome of his campaign. He resented the way in which his actions had been criticised and his orders overruled. Above all, he was irritated at seeing the Dutch troops retained in Germany under the command of French generals. He thought that it was part of a plan of his brother's for making him a mere puppet king, and he proceeded to assert himself by a restless activity.

Day after day decrees came pouring from his study in the old Binnenhof at The Hague. He promised his subjects a new code of law, a thorough reorganisation of the administrative machinery, public works on an enormous scale. He set to work with the Dutch admirals on a scheme for the reconstruction of the navy. He published the statutes of two new orders of chivalry, the Order of the Union and the Order of Merit, which would place at his disposal stars, crosses, and ribbons in abundance. He announced the introduction of the rank of marshal not only into the Dutch army, but also in the navy.

Napoleon did not want to have marshals of Holland set up beside his marshals of France. He wrote to Louis on January 2, 1807 : ' Do you think a French general of division would take orders from your Dutch marshals ? You are aping French organisation, though your circumstances are utterly different. Why not begin by establishing the conscription and having a real army ? ' And again on the 7th : ' You have instituted the rank of marshal. If you have as yet named no one, make no such nomination. There is nobody in Holland fit to hold such high rank.' Louis was deeply offended, and persisted in his plans.

His wife, Hortense, had been at Mayence with her mother, the Empress Josephine, during the campaign. She remained there for nearly three months after Louis's departure from the army, and did not return to The Hague till near the end of January 1807. Louis felt hurt at her prolonged absence, and there was an immediate quarrel between husband and wife, which soon became the subject of much malicious gossip. Hortense was angered by Louis's attention to one of the Dutch ladies of his court. Louis retorted with jealous complaints of his wife's conduct : her choice of friends, even of her partners at the court balls. Letters from The Hague brought the gossip of the court to Napoleon's knowledge, and he wrote a kindly letter of remonstrance to Louis. He should try to make his young wife happy, he said. ' You have the best and most virtuous of wives, and you make her miserable. Let her dance as much as she likes ; it is only right at her age. I have a wife of forty, and from the battlefield I write to her that she must go to balls ; and with a wife who is only twenty and naturally wishes to live her life and has still some of the illusions of youth, you want her to live as if she were in a convent, or to be busy always like a nurse with her children ? You yourself are too much shut up in your study and not about enough in public business. I would not say all this unless I thought so much of you. Make the mother of your children happy. You have only one way of doing this, and that is by showing her a great deal of esteem and confidence.'

Louis replied that tale-bearers had misrepresented him to the Emperor. The quarrel went on, but before long a terrible sorrow united Louis and Hortense for a while. In April he had been making a visit to some of the Dutch cities. On the 29th, when he returned to The Hague, his eldest son Charles Napoleon was ill. The boy had long been regarded as the destined heir of the Empire. Josephine and Napoleon were devoted to him. Even from his camps and bivouacs on the eve of great battles Napoleon would send a message to him. He expected to find in the letters of Josephine and Hortense little stories of his childish pranks, and was disappointed if there were no such news.

At first the doctors were not quite sure what was the matter with the child. On the 30th they declared that his life was in danger. There was a panic at the Binnenhof. Louis summoned now this now that doctor from Amsterdam and Utrecht, and grave professors of medicine from Leyden. Quite a crowd of doctors gathered at the palace, but they were evidently puzzled, and with each new arrival some different remedy was tried. On May 3rd a messenger was sent off post-haste to Paris to bring back with him the famous Corvisart. But before he arrived the child expired in a fit of convulsions, at midnight on May 5th.

Hortense gave way to such a frenzy of grief that the doctors feared for her mind. With difficulty she was removed from the room where the child had died, and Louis was told that it would be better to take her away from the palace. A carriage was sent for. Hortense, almost insensible, was carried out of the Binnenhof, and Louis drove away with her to a villa among the woods outside the town, the property of one of his Dutch courtiers, who had lately been appointed chief huntsman of the court, and whose wife was one of the Queen's ladies of honour. There Hortense passed the night between life and death, often recognising no one, sometimes calling plaintively for her son.

Next day she was better. Caroline, the wife of Murat, arrived and took her across the frontier to the palace of Laeken near Brussels. Louis joined her there, bringing with him their surviving son, little Napoleon Louis, but the sight of the boy threw Hortense into a fresh transport of grief—she seemed to hate the sight of him, and would not stay in the same room. There were new fears for her reason.

Josephine arrived at Laeken and escorted her daughter to St. Cloud, and after a brief stay there it was decided that Hortense should go to one of the watering-places of the Pyrenees. At the end of May she travelled by Orleans and Bordeaux to Cauterets.

Napoleon had sent Louis leave of absence from his kingdom in order that he might rejoin her there. After naming a council of regency, and arranging for the embalmed body of little Charles Napoleon to be escorted to Paris, where it was to be entombed at Notre Dame, he left Holland in the first week of June, and after a passing visit to his château of St. Leu, came to St. Cloud on June 5th on a visit to Josephine. The Empress was rejoicing in the idea that now there would be a permanent reconciliation between Louis and her daughter. In this there would be some consolation for the loss of the grandchild she had loved so fondly. She had no suspicion that the death of the boy meant years of sorrow for her ; that the loss of his destined heir would set Napoleon thinking of a ·divorce, a marriage with a younger wife, the daughter of an imperial house, and the hope of a son of his own.

. Travelling incognito as General Van den Spiegel, Louis went on from Paris to the Pyrenees, but again selfish thoughts of his own health and convenience took him not to Cauterets, but to Eaux Bonnes, the waters of which his doctor had specially recommended to him. But they seemed to do him no good, and at last he went to Cauterets and stayed a while with Hortense. Then his restless humour came upon him again, and he went to try the springs of St. Sauveur and Ussat while the Queen made excursions through the beautiful Pyrenean country, sometimes on foot with guides, sometimes in the saddle. Cauterets was the centre of these excursions, until the beginning of August. A little court gathered round Hortense, French and Dutch visitors to the Pryenees, among them Decazes, one of the few Frenchmen to whom Louis had given a legal appointment in Holland, and Carl Hendrik Verhuell, the Dutch ambassador to Spain and brother of Marshal-Admiral Verhuell, the chief of the Dutch admiralty and one of the great men of the kingdom. Decazes and Verhuell were assiduous in their attentions, and Louis was angrily jealous when he heard of this. But his health had improved at Ussat, and when on August 11th he met Hortense at Toulouse they seemed ·to be again on the best of terms. Travelling slowly by way of Lyons they reached St. Cloud on August 27th.

There little Napoleon Louis was waiting for his mother, and she was pleased to see him. All fears as to her mind were now dissipated, but Josephine was anxious about her general health. She was thin and haggard-looking and coughed continually, and there was a prospect of the birth of another child. She persuaded Napoleon to arrange for her daughter to remain with her, while Louis returned to his kingdom. Josephine took Hortense and Napoleon Louis to stay a while with her at Fontainebleau.

Louis delayed his departure from Paris. He stayed on to discuss with Napoleon questions which later on were to lead to an open rupture between the brothers. He wanted to have Flushing handed over to him. Napoleon insisted on a French commandant, and at least a partly French garrison, for the place which watched the approach to Antwerp, now growing into the chief naval arsenal of his empire. He wanted more men from Holland. Louis protested that it was impossible to raise and equip a large force in a country the whole trade of which was crippled and ruined by the Berlin decree closing the ports to English goods even under a neutral flag. Some liberty of trade must be granted to Holland. Napoleon replied that there was in Holland a general conspiracy to smuggle in English goods, and that, instead of complaining of the Berlin decree, Louis would do better if he tried the effect of enforcing it. In the end nothing was settled, and Louis went back to The Hague full of the idea that he and his little kingdom were being sacrificed to Napoleon and his great empire.

He did not remain long at The Hague. The Binnenhof was associated now with a tragedy. It was too near the dangerous sea where the British ensign was flying. He decided to make quaint old Utrecht his capital. There was no building that could serve as a palace. A number of large houses were bought. Masons, carpenters, decorators were set to work to open communication between them, break down walls and provide salons and halls of audience on a grand scale, and construct a state entrance. At last all was ready. The ambassadors and officials came to Utrecht and found houses or lodgings for themselves. The city rejoiced in a coming era of prosperity. But suddenly King Louis changed his mind. After all he would be cramped at Utrecht. Historic Amsterdam would be a better capital. His palace would be the great *stadhuis*, the town-hall built by Burgomaster Tulp in the days when the Dutch burghers made victorious war on kings, with its carved gables celebrating in sculptured designs the glories of the northern ' Queen of the Seas,' and its tower crowned by a gilded ship.

All was arranged, and a deputation of citizens came to Utrecht to beg King Louis to make Amsterdam his capital and accept as a gift from the city the famous Stadhuis. Louis, who had settled the address of the deputation, graciously consented, and on April 20, 1808, he made his state entry into his new capital. His carriage, drawn by eight horses and escorted by his Dutch cuirassier guard, passed over the endless bridges of the northern Venice, and by the quays of sleepy canals overhung by gabled houses gay with flags, till at last, amid the clang of bells and the roar of cannon, he alighted at the Stadhuis, and held high festival till late at night to celebrate his coming.

Four days after he had taken possession of his new capital, the city echoed to the booming of 101 guns, and a proclamation announced that another son had been born to the royal house. The happy event had taken place at Paris on the 20th, the same day on which Louis had made his state entry into Amsterdam. The child was named Charles Louis Napoleon, the names of his grandfather, his father, and the Emperor. He was to have a strange career. Like his great namesake he was to grasp at power, and build up a Second Empire on the ruins of a future republic, revive for a brief period the glories of the First, and then disappear amid disasters greater than those of Leipsic and Waterloo. The son of Hortense was the future Napoleon III.

Joseph's rule in Naples was nearing its end, and this just at the time when the country had become reconciled to its Corsican king and was beginning to feel the good effects of his administration. It was in many ways a misfortune that Napoleon looked on his brothers rather as governors of provinces, whom he might move from country to country as he moved about his marshals and generals. He did not believe that these brother-kings personally counted for anything. If they succeeded, it was because he was at their back. If they failed in any way, it was the result of their own deficiencies. Any one he named would do equally well. This was how, in an evil hour for them both, he thought of sending Joseph to another kingdom, and finding a substitute for him at Naples.

The civil war was at an end, but it was still necessary to maintain a large French force in southern Italy, because

Sicily, held by the Bourbons and the English, would be a source of danger if the French army were withdrawn. With the majority of his subjects Joseph was popular enough, and this precisely because he had taken a line of his own, and refused to listen to Napoleon's advice and make Frenchmen of the Neapolitans. Joseph ruled as an Italian king, and tried to identify himself with Neapolitan ideas. He would not introduce the Code Napoleon ; he kept up the old-fashioned divisions of the coinage instead of worrying the people with francs and centimes ; he refused to suppress the Franciscan monasteries, or to meddle with the traditional titles of nobility in the name of democratic equality. He was even busy with the elaboration of a scheme of representative government, which had more of reality in it than anything of the kind that then existed in any of the great states of the Continent. Taxation was somewhat lighter than under the Bourbons, and there were fewer administrative abuses.

Personally Joseph was somewhat extravagant, but his capital, which prospered through the expenditure of the king and his court, did not blame him for this. There had been no queen at Naples. Julia was not seen there till almost the eve of her husband's departure. She shrank from the idea of posing as a queen and being the centre of a court, and clung to her quiet life at Mortefontaine, where she was educating her daughters, making occasional visits to Paris. At first she urged as the reason for her absence the civil war and the insecurity of Naples. Then she pleaded her health : she could not face that terrible journey over the Alps and life in a hot climate. More than once Napoleon told her plainly that she ought to be beside her husband. Joseph did not seem much troubled by her absence. The gossip of the court linked his name with that of a noble Neapolitan lady, on whom he lavished grants of land and money from his civil list.

At the end of 1807 the Emperor had decided on his plans for the absorption of the Spanish peninsula into his Imperial system. The Braganzas had been driven from Lisbon by Junot. The French army under Murat, coming in the guise of allies, held Spain to all appearance at its mercy. The Spanish Bourbons were quarrelling amongst themselves, and the scandals of the royal family had disgusted even their own supporters.

Murat had impressed on the Emperor his own view that Spain was ready to welcome a new régime, and to accept any sovereign he might propose. Napoleon had given up his first idea of a marriage between the heir of the Spanish throne and a daughter of the Bonapartes, and then a kind of French protectorate disguised as an alliance. He was looking out for a king for Spain, and perhaps he would name another for Portugal later on.

If Lucien had submitted, there is little doubt that the crown of Spain would have been offered to him. Murat, whose wife was a Bonaparte, fully expected that he would be named. But Napoleon thought this was too high a promotion for one of his marshals, even though he was his brother-in-law. Jerome was out of the question. Even Napoleon could not think of sending a Protestant queen-consort to Madrid. Joseph and Louis remained. At the beginning of 1808 he made the offer to Joseph. The future of Naples was left undecided. In earlier days the kings of Spain had ruled Naples through their viceroys. This might be done again. Or some other chief might be found to take Joseph's place in southern Italy.

But Napoleon did not propose to hand over all the Spanish dominions to his brother. The country north of the Ebro was to be annexed to France, and part at least of Spanish America was to be added to the French colonies. After a very brief consideration Joseph refused. He rightly judged that with a proud people like the Spaniards he would have no hope of popularity if the very beginning of his reign was to be associated with the dismemberment of their country, and the loss of the historic border lands which had been the citadel of Christendom against the first flood of the Moorish invasion; the lands where Spain had rallied for the reconquest, and the cession of which to France would give away to a stranger country the mountain barrier of the Pyrenees. He said he preferred to remain at Naples. Napoleon gave some relief in his disappointment and ill-humour at the refusal by peremptorily ordering Julia to leave Paris, and take her place beside Joseph at Naples.

The Emperor then offered the crown to Louis, telling him time pressed and he must answer ' Yes ' or ' No ' at once. Louis answered ' No.' Writing his memoirs, years after, he said he was disgusted at the idea of being moved about like a mere official; and he felt he was pledged to Holland, and had no right to think of throwing in his fortunes with those of any other people. Napoleon was surprised at his refusal of what he considered a most brilliant offer.

He turned once more to Joseph. This time he made no reservations. Might he propose him as king to the Spanish notables at Bayonne. King Charles of Spain had agreed to abdicate. Prince Ferdinand would not assert any counter-claim, but was ready to become the pensioner of France. There would be no cession of territory. Joseph would be chosen King of Spain and the Indies, and the people were ready to welcome him as the herald of better days. The letter conveying this offer was dated April 18, 1808. It reached Joseph in the last week of the month. He accepted. His letter was not in Napoleon's hands till May 10th. While it was on its way Madrid had risen in fierce revolt against the French, but Murat had swept the streets with grapeshot, and reported to the Emperor that only the rabble had joined in the movement, and the position was now better than ever.

Only the official story ever reached Joseph, and that much later. If he had even suspected the truth, that Spain was on the eve of widespread insurrection, he might well have hesi-tated about leaving that fair palace looking out on the Bay of Naples. But he saw everything from the official point of view, and dreamed of new triumphs as a popular king of Spain. On the 21st came Napoleon's reply to his acceptance, written the very day he received it. It was an order bidding Joseph come with all speed to Bayonne to accept his new crown..

Next day there was a great feast at the court in honour of Queen Julia, so Joseph did not leave Naples till the 23rd. He was still king of his Italian kingdom, and hoped to retain it, so there were no farewells.

In February the French under General Miollis had occupied Rome, and Lucien had given new offence to the Emperor by his open demonstrations of loyalty to Pius VII. and his refusal to meet the French officers of the army of occupation except on the most rigidly formal terms. His position in Rome, now under his brother's rule, became so difficult that he talked of going with his family to the United States. But wealthy as he was, he had maintained such an expensive state, and locked up so much money in his palazzo, his pictures, his villas, his factories, his schemes of improvement at Canino, that he was short of cash, just when he needed it most in order to be free to act. He had appealed to his brothers the three kings, and Joseph, Louis, and Jerome had each lent him 200,000 francs, so that he had the equivalent of some £24,000 at his disposal. He had left Rome first for Florence, then for Bologna, undecided what further course to take. At Bologna, on May 27th, Joseph interrupted his journey northwards in order to have a talk with him.

The brothers discussed various possible plans for Lucien's future, Joseph suggesting arrangements for which he thought he might later on obtain Napoleon's consent, though, as he explained in reply to a question from Lucien, they were his own ideas and he had no authority from the Emperor to put them forward. Would Lucien care to be King of Portugal or of Naples ? No, said Lucien, he would prefer a small state like Tuscany, where he would not be interfered with, and could really govern as he thought best. Then Joseph suggested another possibility. He might be his viceroy for the Spanish possessions beyond the Atlantic. His son might marry one of Joseph's daughters, and as the Salic Law prevailed in Spain, this would keep the succession in the family. Lucien liked the idea. The brothers agreed to work together for its realisation when a favourable opportunity presented itself. It was a ' castle in Spain,' never to be heard of again, for Joseph never had a viceroyalty of the Indies at his disposal.

Resuming his journey, Joseph made another halt at Turin to see his sister Pauline, Princess Borghese. He did not reach Bayonne till June 7th. Impatient at the delays in his journey, Napoleon had already announced in the Madrid *Gazette* that Joseph was at Bayonne, and on the day before he arrived, June 6th, he had proclaimed him King of Spain and the Indies. The proclamation explained that he took this course in response to an invitation of the Spanish notables to put an end to the interregnum, and he guaranteed to the Spanish crown the integrity of all its possessions in Europe, Asia, America, and Africa. Murat, as Lieutenant-General of the kingdom, was ordered to give effect to the decree.

Joseph issued a proclamation of his own on the 11th, announcing his accession to the Spanish people, and declaring his intention to direct all his energies to securing their welfare. The very form of the proclamation asserted his intention to pose as the legitimate successor of the old kings of Castille and Leon, not as a king made by the Revolution. He signed *Yo el Re* and described himself as ' Don Joseph, by the grace of God, King of Castille, Aragon, the Two Sicilies, Jerusalem, Navarre, Toledo, Valencia, Galicia, Majorca, Minorca, Seville, Cordova, Murcia, Santiago, the Algarves, Algesiras, Gibraltar, the Canary Islands, the West and East Indies, the Islands of the Ocean and Terra Firma, Archduke of Austria, Duke of Burgundy, Brabant and Milan, Count of Hapsburg, Tyrol and Barcelona, and Lord of Biscay.' It was the traditional roll of titles dating from the empire of Charles v., and Joseph had placed it at the head of his proclamation without asking the advice of the Emperor, who thought it somewhat ridiculous.

He confirmed Murat's appointment as Lieutenant-General, and at the same time issued a number of important decrees as King of Naples, regardless of the fact, of which his brother must have already informed him, that Murat had been for a month nominated as his successor in southern Italy. On May 2nd—the very day on which Murat was sweeping the streets of Madrid with salvoes of grapeshot and charges of cavalry— Napoleon had written to the marshal to inform him that Joseph would be King of Spain, and going on to tell him that he must at once choose for himself either the crown of Portugal or that of Naples. He advised him to choose Naples, promising to secure Sicily for him later in addition. Meanwhile he was to continue his functions of Lieutenant-General of Spain. He told him that in becoming a king he need not cease to serve in the Imperial army. Alluding to his opinion of his sister Caroline's talents, he added, 'With a wife like yours you can be absent from your kingdom when war calls you to my side.'

Murat replied that ' on no consideration ' would he go to Portugal. He chose Naples, but only on condition that it was not to separate him from the Emperor. Regardless of this arrangement Joseph issued from Bayonne decrees charging the revenues of Naples with gifts of various sums, small and large, to all who had helped him, to all his friends in his old kingdom, including a parting gift of nearly half a million ducats to the Duchess of Atri. Then there was a shower of orders and decorations, and finally, on June 20th, he issued a proclamation giving to the kingdom of Naples the constitution on which he had been long at work. By its last article it was guaranteed by the Emperor, so that he must have acted with Napoleon's consent in thus securing for himself the credit of a liberal act, instead of allowing Murat to inaugurate his reign by establishing representative government. It was only on July 5th that he signed the deed by which he resigned the kingdom of Naples to the Emperor, to dispose of it as he might judge fit.

A constitution had already been drafted for Spain. Joseph took part in the final deliberations upon it. The King was to govern with the help of a Senate and Council of State, and the Cortes, representing all classes of the people, was to meet at least once in three years, and vote a triennial budget. The colonies were to send deputies to the Cortes. All internal custom-houses on the borders of the old provinces were to be suppressed. The Inquisition was abolished. Only Spaniards were to be appointed to public offices and employments. The Catholic religion was proclaimed to be that of King and people, and the Church was guaranteed the enjoyment of its property and revenues. In the presence of the Spanish notables Joseph swore to maintain the constitution, and received their oaths of allegiance in return. Joseph declared he would be a Spanish king, and gave most of the appointments in his household to Spaniards as an earnest of his intentions.

On July 9th he left Bayonne. The Emperor accompanied him as far as the French bank of the Bidassoa. On the further side of the river the royal carriages were waiting with a cavalry escort. Joseph had been allowed to hear nothing of the serious development of the Spanish insurrection. He was told his escort of 1500 men was a mere guard of honour. So he was full of hope for a brilliant future, as he bade farewell to his brother, took his seat in the state barge, and stepped ashore on Spanish territory amid the acclamations of his escort and his courtiers. Then the long line of carriages formed up, the King and his suite took their places, and the escort began to move forward *en route* for Madrid.

CHAPTER XIII

THE TROUBLES OF THREE KINGS

(1807-1809)

BEFORE Jerome left Paris in the winter of 1807 Napoleon had tried to impress upon this spoiled child of the Bonapartes the necessity of making a new start and taking the business of life somewhat more seriously now that he was a king. Jerome had suggested as a desirable preliminary to this turning over a new leaf that he should be assisted to pay his debts. Lavishly as he had been supplied with money, he admitted that he owed nearly two millions of francs, or about £80,000, to French creditors. He did not trouble his brother by bringing into the account minor debts still unpaid in America. The Emperor obtained for him a loan of 1,800,000 francs from the Imperial treasury, which was to be repaid by annual instalments out of his civil list as King of Westphalia, amounting to five million francs a year, and he brought the sum up to the round two millions by advancing to him part of his allowance as a Prince of the Empire, which had been fixed at a million francs. Thus relieved from present embarrassments, Jerome promised to keep his accounts in better order in the future.

The Emperor had prepared a constitution for Westphalia. The Westphalians under the rule of Prussia and the Hessians under the Prince Elector had lived under absolute governments. Jerome was to be a constitutional king, with a Council of Ministers, a representative assembly of the Estates of his kingdom, a budget, the Code Napoleon, trial by jury, equality of all before the law. Again and again Napoleon urged upon him the necessity of trusting and employing men of the middle class, and making his new subjects feel that every office in the state was open to merit. There was to be an army gradually formed on the French model, but to assure Jerome's position, and at the same time to diminish the burden of the local conscription, half of it would be formed for the first few years of French troops, paid by the Westphalian exchequer. To organise the ministries of the Interior, Justice, and Finance the Emperor lent his brother the services of three French experts, all of them men of high standing and long experience.

In his household the new King found well-paid places for the group of young men who had followed his fortunes and subsisted on his purse and credit since his first appearance as a naval officer. Meyronnet, the lieutenant of the navy, who had been his envoy from Baltimore to Paris after his first marriage, was appointed Grand Marshal of the court. Alexandre Lecamus, his secretary, whom he had picked up in Martinique, became Grand Chamberlain, and there were a crowd of others, whose names there is no need to catalogue here. Lecamus's younger brother Auguste was summoned from Martinique to have his share in the pleasant times that were coming. He was directed to travel by way of the United States and see Elisabeth Bonaparte, or, as she was called in official correspondence, Elisa Patterson, at Baltimore. Jerome had written to her from Paris after his marriage with the Princess, protesting that he was the victim of public policy and had made an unwilling sacrifice to his brother's ambition, and announcing the visit of Auguste Lecamus. To Lucien he had written some feeble excuses of the same kind. He felt his brother's conduct presented a striking contrast to his own, and he told Lucien that he hoped he would not judge him harshly, for he was more to be pitied than blamed.

On November 22, 1807, the King and Queen of Westphalia with their suite left Paris for Germany, and after a visit to the court of Catherine's father, the King of Würtemberg, at Stuttgart, they reached Cassel on December 7th. It had been chosen as the capital of the new Westphalian kingdom. Not far from the city there was a ready-made palace that might have accommodated the splendours of even a more ambitious court than Jerome's. In the course of the eighteenth century every petty German prince had constructed for himself a lordly pleasure-house and park, inspired by the glories of Versailles. Had not Thackeray's Duke Aurelius of

Pumpernickel, with his territory ten miles across, his palace of Monplaisir, with ' gardens arranged to emulate those of Versailles, where amid the terraces and groves there were huge allegorical waterworks, which spouted and frothed stupendously upon fête-days.' William of Hesse had begun his Versailles when the ministers of George III. were supplying him with plenty of good English guineas in return for shiploads of his subjects, sent across the Atlantic to fight George Washington, and he had carried on his work imperturbably through the years of revolutionary war upon the Rhine. The great park with its groves and statues, fountains and cascades, grottoes and temples, was the setting for a splendid palace, and Wilhelmshöhe, as it was called, was famous in Europe. Jerome changed its name to Napoleonshöhe. Strange turn of fortune,—a prince, who was then a boy at the court of Prussia, lived to be the conqueror of France some sixty years later, to be proclaimed German Kaiser in the real Versailles, and to send Jerome's nephew, Napoleon III., to spend his days of captivity in this second-rate Versailles, once Napoleonshöhe, now Wilhelmshöhe again.

But there was no presentiment that the fortunes of the Bonapartes had reached their highest and would soon be on the wane, no shadowy fear of a Waterloo or a Sedan, on the bright frosty day of December 7, 1807, when Jerome made his state entry into Cassel, amid cheering crowds, and when the early darkness of the evening was brightened with a general illumination, and showers of rockets burst up from the terrace of Napoleonshöhe.

Before the New Year, within three weeks, Jerome had shown that he did not intend to pay much attention to the advice the Emperor had given him at Fontainebleau, but that he would govern his kingdom in his own way, and that he found account-keeping too troublesome a business. There were banquets and fêtes at Napoleonshöhe, and balls, including one in which all the guests appeared in old German costumes of the seventeenth century. Jerome did not like the old-fashioned furniture of his palace, and ordered new fittings and decorations regardless of cost. He remodelled the ministry, dismissed some of the trusted administrators whom the Emperor had placed at his disposal, substituted his young friends, making

Alexander Lecamus Secretary of State, ennobling him with the title of Count of Fürstenstein, and giving him one of the royal domains with which to support his new dignity. Early in the New Year he found himself once more in debt and short of money. He wrote to Napoleon telling him how painful it was to send away distressed creditors empty-handed, but the Emperor felt he had done enough in advancing those two millions, and refused further supplies.

Herr Jacobsohn, a wealthy banker of Cassel, was called to the palace, and on strict business lines, with an ample margin for profit, promised to find all that was wanted; and soon Jerome counted among his creditors the Jews of Westphalia and some of the great men of the old Jüdenstrasse at Frankfort, where the Red Shield hung over a little house that was the cradle of kings of finance. A royal guard was formed, uniformed on the model of the Würtemberg guards he had reviewed at Stuttgart, not on that of his brother's war-worn veterans, and they were all Germans. Napoleon had in vain urged him to form his bodyguard, at least in part, of picked officers, men from the French contingent in Westphalia. 'It is a great folly,' he wrote to Jerome, 'thus to put your household at the mercy of a band of foreigners. But you have all the self-confidence of a young fellow of twenty, and it will be fatal to you.'

Then, without consulting his brother, Jerome began to name ambassadors to the Powers. Napoleon thought his own envoys could very well take care of the foreign interests of Westphalia, which in his eyes were identical with those of France. And there was further cause of disappointment with his brother in the fact that Jerome was already giving fresh cause for scandalous gossip. An actress whom he had made much of during his stay at Breslau in the campaign of Silesia was summoned to Cassel; nor was she the only lady of doubtful reputation who figured among his guests at the fêtes of Napoleonshöhe.

Jerome thought he was popular because Cassel basked in the splendour of his court, and now that the Jews had supplied the funds, a crowd of shopkeepers were making money. But Napoleon warned him that under the surface there were signs of disaffection, the first whispers of a possible storm of

N

patriotic German opposition to foreign rule. Jerome treated
all this as alarmist prejudice, and Napoleon, who was fond of
his youngest brother, clung to a touching hope that as he
grew older he would be wiser, and would still do something
worthy of his name. In this hope he risked his own success
in Germany on his support of the self-willed, pleasure-loving,
light-headed young man he made King of Westphalia. It
would have been better for both the brothers if the Emperor
had not broken up the American marriage, in order to give
Jerome the hand of a princess and make him a petty king.

In the spring of 1808 Auguste Lecamus arrived at Cassel,
bringing a letter from Elisabeth and a portrait of her son, little
Jerome Napoleon Bonaparte. Auguste was sent back to
America on a confidential mission. He was not to see the
French ambassador at Washington, but go straight to Baltimore and deliver to Elisabeth and her father letters from
Jerome requesting them to entrust the boy Jerome Napoleon
to the envoy, so that he might be brought back to Europe
to be educated ' as befitted his rank ' and the career destined
for him. To Mr. Patterson Jerome wrote in formal, official
style. To Elisabeth he repeated his protestations of affection,
his regrets that reasons of state had separated them, and
then asked her to ' make one more sacrifice ' for the sake of
their son by sending him to be educated in Europe, adding
some vague talk about the changes a happier future might
bring.

The letters were dated from Cassel on May 16, 1808.
They were personally delivered by Auguste Lecamus in Baltimore on July 9th. A few days later Elisabeth gave Lecamus
two letters to take back to Westphalia. One purported to
be written to him by his son, but as Jerome Napoleon was only
four years old, it must have been written for him. The boy
was made to say that he refused ' to break mamma's heart ' by
leaving her and going away to Europe. Elisabeth's letter
informed her faithless husband of the steps she had taken on
receiving the message of Lecamus.

She had communicated directly with General Turreau, the
Emperor's ambassador at Washington. She had denied a
rumour that her parents were anxious to marry her to a wealthy
Englishman, but told Turreau that Sir Sidney Smith, the

Emperor's old enemy, had invited her to London and promised her a friendly reception in society there. She had refused : she would never take a step that would be unfriendly to Napoleon. More than this, she was ready to do anything he thought best, provided he would put an end to her difficult position by allowing her to come to France, giving her a title to replace the name she had resigned at his behest, and an income that would provide for her wants and enable her to educate her son. It was as much as informing Jerome that she no longer believed in him and his vague promises, and preferred to trust the Emperor.

Jerome replied with a long letter dated from Cassel on November 22nd. More protestations of regretful affection, assurances that ' his Elisa and his Jerome had a place in his heart that no power on earth, no considerations of policy could take from them.' What was the use of appealing to the Emperor ? It could only do harm. The constitution of the Empire made it impossible for their son to be recognised as a French prince. She had sadly misjudged him, and was making it more difficult for him to carry out the plans he had formed for her own welfare and that of the boy. He tried to alarm her by going on to say that he would rather lose his kingdom and his life than place his son in the power of people to whom the boy's early death would be more useful than his life. He would not separate his son from her. He made her a new proposal. Let her bring little Jerome to Westphalia. He would give her the domain of Smalkalden on the Saxon border, with a revenue of 200,000 francs. She would be Princess of Smalkalden, her son a Prince, and they would be safe and happy in Westphalia under his protection. He added that he made this proposal with the Emperor's approval, which was a deliberate falsehood, for Napoleon knew nothing of it. The letter was signed, ' Yours devotedly for life, Jerome Napoleon.'

Elisabeth replied that ' the Kingdom of Westphalia was not large enough to contain two queens,' and continued her negotiations with Turreau and the Emperor. All that she obtained for some time to come was a grant of money that made her independent of her father's help. Jerome was disappointed at his failure, and angry at Elisabeth's correspondence with

Turreau, but he soon recovered from his ill-humour. All his troubles sat lightly on him.

It was different with Louis, King of Holland. His self-centred, hypochondriac temperament made him exaggerate everything, suspect every one. Napoleon had to remonstrate with him on rumours that he was contemplating an open rupture with Hortense. He was annoyed at her prolonged absence, listened to scandalous gossip about the stay at Cauterets, seemed ready to believe that Charles Louis Napoleon was not his son. He was annoyed at French agents being sent to Holland to report on the observance of the decree against English goods, and infuriated by special orders being given to the customs officials of France along his land frontier to stop or seize all British colonial produce that might have been landed in Holland, and prevent its introduction into the Empire. He said the trade of his country was being ruined, his people impoverished. To a proposal to cede part of Dutch Brabant and Zeeland in exchange for German territory, in order to give France more complete control of the Scheldt, he replied that he could do this only with the consent of his people, who would never hear of it. He began to dismiss his French officials, and replace them by Dutchmen. He told his friends there was a regular conspiracy to ruin Holland in the interest of France, and reduce him to the position of a cipher. He added that the Emperor's foolish adventure in Spain would end only in disaster.

Involved in this Spanish adventure, the third of the three Bonaparte kings, Joseph, had the most serious anxieties of all. When he gave up pleasant Naples and accepted the crown of Spain he was the victim of illusions resulting from a blind faith in official bulletins. On that July day when he crossed the Bidassoa and set forward for Madrid he still had no doubts about his future. But strange and unwelcome surprises were waiting for him.

He travelled by easy stages through the north. At San Sebastian and Tolosa he remarked that his reception was not enthusiastic, very different from the acclamations that had hailed him in southern Italy. But he suggested that the French army of occupation had been too exacting, and directed that orders should be sent to the generals to spare the people as much as possible in the matter of contributions, and repress all indiscipline among the troops.

At Vittoria, on July 12th, there was disquieting news. The Spanish Generals Cuesta and Blake, with an army of 40,000 men, regulars and insurgents, were at Medina de Rio Seco, near Valladolid ready to bar his best road to his capital. But Joseph still clung to his illusions. He despatched two of his Spanish officers with orders to see Cuesta, assure him of the high opinion that both the Emperor and the new King entertained of him, point out to him that he was taking a mistaken course, and invite him to join Joseph, who would take his troops into his service, and give him and his officers a reception they would never regret. Before Joseph's envoys could deliver their message, Marshal Bessières, who commanded the French Army of the North and fully understood the realities of the situation, had hurriedly got together some 14,000 men and, reckless of mere paper odds, had marched to clear the way. On July 14th he attacked Cuesta and Blake at Médina, and after six hours of sharp fight and fierce pursuit dispersed the patriot army, which left a thousand dead on the field, and all its guns and baggage and 6000 prisoners in the hands of the victor. The way to Madrid was open, and something too had been done to open Joseph's eyes.

Napoleon wrote to him that Bessières had secured him his crown, and suggested that he should send the Marshal the Order of the Golden Fleece as his reward. Joseph, disappointed at his reign being inaugurated by the slaughter of his subjects, refused the decoration to the victor. He went on to Madrid, where he was solemnly proclaimed King on July 24th, and where the French party had organised a welcome that for the moment reassured him.

But then came swift news of disaster. A French squadron of five battleships and a frigate lay at Cadiz. The city had risen in revolt, the insurgents had manned the forts and fired on the fleet. The Spanish warships in the bay had joined in the cannonade, and the French squadron had surrendered. An English force was being hurried to the help of insurgent Cadiz. Worse still, on July 21st, General Dupont with all his army had been beaten at Baylen in Andalusia, and had surrendered to Castaños. With news like this, the rising against the French and their King was spreading like wildfire from province to province.

Joseph could only spend a few days in his capital. The generals told him that they could not answer for his safety there. In the first days of August he retired to Burgos, where he was safe behind the bayonets of Bessières, while Castaños entered Madrid in triumph, and the British under Wellesley made their first descent on Portugal. Napoleon's letters to Joseph took a desponding tone. Dupont had disgraced the flag. What folly and baseness! He had to remain in Paris, for he had to look after the affairs of Germany, Italy, Poland, and he was sorry he could not be beside Joseph and at the head of his soldiers. But by the autumn everything would be regained. Perhaps after all, he said, Joseph did not care much about ruling over Spain.

It was quite true. Joseph had been rudely awakened from the dream into which his brother had lulled him, and was regretting Naples, and wondering if by any chance he could even now return there. On August 9th he wrote to the Emperor from Burgos :—

' This is what I should like to do : retain the command of the army long enough to beat the enemy ; re-enter Madrid with it, just as I marched out with it ; and then from the capital issue a decree to the effect that I decline to reign over a people which I have had to reduce by force of arms, and that being still free to choose between such a people and that of Naples, which is capable of appreciating my rule and doing justice to my character, I prefer the people who know me, and return to Naples, expressing my best wishes for the welfare of Spain, but devoting myself to labouring for that of the Two Sicilies. I would resign to your Majesty the rights I hold from you, so that you might dispose of them as your wisdom would suggest. I therefore beg that your Majesty will delay any steps that are being taken as to Naples. As for this country, I am convinced that the new arrangements will meet with more resistance than your Majesty thinks, and that on the whole they will be of no advantage to any one.'

A few days later—on the 14th—without waiting for Napoleon's reply—he wrote again to him. It must be evident, he said, that after having reigned at Naples and abdicated the crown of Spain, he could hardly be asked to drop back into private life. And it would be still more unbecoming to give him the crown of some third country, after he had failed to keep that of two others. But what would best befit his Majesty the Emperor, the Neapolitans, and himself would be to leave him the crown of Naples, which after all he had not abdicated either *de jure* or *de facto*. He then proceeded to argue that while still King of Spain he had issued decrees for Naples, as King of that country; that he only renounced Naples on condition of being put in real possession of Spain; surely his Majesty would not wish him to suffer through having trusted to his fraternal affection, and neglected strict diplomatic forms and conditions; for, after all, his renunciation of the crown of Naples could not take effect until he was put in possession of the Spanish monarchy. Now Joseph knew very well that on July 15th the crown of Naples had been given to Murat, and that King Joachim had been proclaimed there by the officials on August 1st—a fortnight ago. But he suggested that compensation could be found for the Marshal elsewhere. These Bonapartes thought of marking out kingdoms on the map of Europe, and setting up thrones, much as company promoters think of registering companies and allotting shares, and even his recent experiences had not opened Joseph's eyes to the fact that his brother would soon find it more difficult to play the part of king-maker.

Napoleon merely acknowledged Joseph's letters. His real reply was to send orders to the Imperial Guard and the best corps of the Grand Army and his most experienced generals to leave their cantonments in Germany, and march across France for the Pyrenees. He was staking all his fortunes on the Spanish cast of the dice of war. He was all the more determined because the news of Vimiera and Roliça had come from Portugal, and Wellesley had driven Junot from Lisbon.

But one all-important element was lacking to his armies in Spain. He had sent his best leaders, his best troops to Joseph; Marshal Jourdan had been summoned from Naples to assist the King of Spain in the direction of the war; but Napoleon himself could not come, and it needed his authority to control personal jealousies and divergent views, and his genius to bring order out of chaos and prevent the war degenerating into a series of unconnected local operations. He must have recognised this, but he had to grapple with even a greater danger. Europe was taking fire at the news that the soldiers of the Empire were no longer invincible. Germany was restless, rumour said that Austria was arming. The Emperor had to take steps to prevent a general upheaval in central Europe, if only for a while. He invited the Czar to meet him, and hastened to Erfurt, where he renewed the alliance of Tilsit, and took measures which gave him some breathing time. It was only in the late autumn that he was free to deal personally with the affairs of Spain.

In the first week of November 1808 he crossed the Pyrenees. Joseph came to meet him at Vittoria on the 5th. Things had not gone well during the three months since the evacuation of Madrid. The tried soldiers of the Empire had indeed inflicted many defeats on the Spanish patriots; but trampled out in one place, the flame had burst forth in another. The very dispersion of the Spanish armies, after they had failed to win pitched battles against the French, had only made the situation more difficult by multiplying the guerilla bands and giving a wider extension to a murderous partisan warfare. And the French marshals had acted on no settled plan, and had failed to combine their operations effectively.

They were jealous of each other, and discontented at being asked to take orders from King Joseph, whom they regarded as a mere civilian, and his chief of the staff Jourdan, whom they voted out of date. Joseph, with all the self-sufficient courage of an amateur, drew up plans for the campaign, which he took to be inspirations of genius, and Jourdan thought he had more to gain by flattering than by criticising him. The marshals, however, refused bluntly to act on plans written in obvious ignorance of the real state of affairs. ' This order,' said Ney, in reply to one of Jourdan's communications, ' is drawn up by some one who knows nothing of our business. The Emperor has given me an army corps, to conquer with it and not to capitulate. You may tell the King that I have not come here to play the part of Dupont.' Moncey sent back the officer who brought him his orders, bidding him tell the King that they would endanger the existence of his army, but if knowing this the King still insisted, the Marshal would obey. The Emperor, informed of Joseph's plans, had written him a scathing condemnation of them, trying, however, to spare his brother's feelings by presuming that he had been mis-informed and ill-advised by others. ' With such schemes,' he said, ' one could not count on success even with an army entirely made up of men like those of the Guard and led by an Alexander or a Cæsar—far less with such an army as you have actually in Spain.' Now he was on the spot to take the command out of Joseph's inexperienced hands and give orders that no marshal would hesitate to execute. The need was pressing. An English army under Moore was advancing to support Castaños at Madrid,—a small army, but it would be a solid nucleus of resistance on the patriot side.

Napoleon struck swiftly and sharply. The Somo Sierra pass was stormed, and on December 4th the French were again in Madrid. Moore heard of the loss of the capital and the rapid approach of the enemy in overwhelming numbers just in time to begin his retreat across the snowy plateaux of Leon. The Emperor pursued till the English reached the mountains of Galicia, and then left it to Soult to follow them up to Corunna. Except in Andalusia and the south, the French were everywhere victorious, and Joseph could feel again that he had a hope of being really King of Spain.

Throughout the brief campaign Napoleon controlled and directed everything. There was no longer even a pretence of Spanish interests being kept in view. Spain was being conquered. And this introduced a certain amount of tension into his relations with Joseph. From the day of their meeting at Vittoria in November the Emperor complained that his brother was too fond of his own opinion, too self-willed. The fact was that Joseph rightly realised that there would be no chance of his being accepted as King by the mass of the Spanish people, unless there was at least some show of respect-ing his independence, and giving him some active part in the direction of affairs ; and he thus was led to resent the Emperor's dictatorship and the way in which his generals dominated everything. In Naples there had been a long civil war, but every act had been done in the King's name : he had let it be distinctly seen that he meant to be a Neapolitan

king, not a mere French viceroy, and he had ended by winning real popularity. Now, when he surrounded himself with
Spaniards, insisted on Frenchmen who joined his service
wearing the red Spanish cockade instead of the tricolour,
protested against the severities ordered by the Imperial
generals, Napoleon complained that he was not acting like a
French prince. Joseph, terribly handicapped as he was by
his brother's military policy, was really making a desperate
attempt to prepare the way for a possible reconciliation with
the Spanish people. French writers still ridicule his ' weakness,' his ' illusions,' but it was the only chance he had, and he
showed a touch of statesmanship in his effort to repeat his
Neapolitan policy in Spain.

When Madrid surrendered, on December 4th, Joseph refused
to enter his capital and live there as a mere cipher, while all
executive power remained in the hands of a French military
governor. He went to stay first at El Pardo, and then at
Aranjuez. On December 8th he wrote to Napoleon, telling
him that he declined to be a mere nominal king with no
authority. ' I blush with shame,' he said, ' in the presence of
my so-called subjects. I beg that your Majesty will accept
my resignation of all the rights you have given me to the
Spanish crown. I shall always prefer honour and probity to
power purchased at so dear a price.' Napoleon after some
hesitation gave way, told Joseph he could not hear of his
abdication, promised he should very soon be put in possession
of the executive power at Madrid, and handed over to him
and his lieutenant Jourdan the direction of the two *corps
d'armée* of Victor and Lefèbvre. He told him that as soon
as he had disposed of the English invaders he would leave
Spain himself, so that Joseph would have a freer hand.

On January 22, 1809, King Joseph again entered Madrid.
He had in his suite some of the representatives of the old
nobles of Spain, and his staff was largely composed of Spanish
officers. Before going to the palace he made a visit to the
Church of San Isidoro, where a *Te Deum* was sung. Addressing
his scanty court he declared that he hoped to rule as a
patriotic Spanish King. ' When I accepted the crown,' he
said, ' the conditions of the oath I took were the unity of our
holy religion, the independence of the monarchy, the integrity

of its territory, the freedom of its citizens. The dignity of the Spanish crown shall not suffer while I wear it.'

There is no doubt he meant every word he said, but for all his goodwill there remained the fact that he was the nominee of a minority of the nation, supported by the foreigner. And so far the foreign aid given to the insurgent majority had been trifling, so that they could regard the insurrection as a purely Spanish movement, in the success of which the national pride was involved, and the sanguinary repression of the movement by the French marshals had put a blood-feud between the unfortunate King and the majority of the people. Joseph was destined to struggle unsuccessfully either to win the loyalty or to overcome the resistance of his ' so-called subjects.'

CHAPTER XIV

THE THREE KINGS IN THE WAR OF 1809

ON the day after Joseph re-entered Madrid, Napoleon had arrived at the Tuileries after travelling in hot haste from Spain. He had hardly arrived when a courier brought the news of Corunna, fought on January 16th. Soult reported the battle as a victory. The English, he said, had been driven to their ships, their gallant leader was dead, the tricolour flew on the citadel of Corunna, six English guns were among his trophies. The Spanish insurgents were holding out only in the south.

The Emperor flattered himself that one great danger was at an end. But there was another to be faced at once. Austria was arming. He had hurried back from Spain to meet the peril in central Europe, to appeal to the ordeal of battle against his old enemy with an army largely composed of young conscripts, and with his best generals and his war-tried battalions left beyond the Pyrenees.

The menace from Austria stirred all the patriot spirits of Germany. The times were not yet ripe for the great national upheaval of the War of Liberation, but there was an ominous stirring below the surface in Jerome's kingdom. He and Catherine had been with Napoleon and the Czar at the congress of Erfurt in the autumn, and the Emperor had forgotten his many causes of complaint against his brother, and urged him to do all that was possible to place the Westphalian army on a war footing in the new year, when there would probably be one more chance of his winning distinction in the field. Jerome had provided a small reinforcement for the army in Spain, and promised to have a division of infantry, with cavalry and artillery, ready for the coming war in Germany.

The Emperor had hardly returned to Paris from Spain when

an envoy of Jerome's came to ask him for financial help. He was deeper than ever, in debt; how could he be ready for the campaign unless he could find some money? Napoleon refused to discuss the matter with the envoy, and wrote to Jerome that if he would put an end to his reckless extravagance, his endless fêtes, and attend to business he would have money enough. He could give him nothing. Jerome found some resources in a forced loan to which all his wealthier subjects had to subscribe, receiving government bonds in exchange, and in the suppression of five minor universities and the confiscation of their endowments. The students of the rest of Germany sent addresses of sympathy to the youth of Westphalia, and the subscribers to the forced loan nursed their resentment in secret. A further advance of six million francs was obtained from a group of bankers at Amsterdam in return for mining concessions. Much of this money was wasted, but some of it went to complete the equipment of the Westphalian army.

By the middle of March 1809 it was plain that war with Austria was inevitable. The statesmen of Vienna thought that with part of the Grand Army locked up in Spain, and Germany throbbing with discontent, the moment was come to strike. Three armies were being formed. The main army under the Archduke Charles was to invade South Germany; two others under the Archduke John and the Archduke Ferdinand d'Este were to operate in Italy and the Grand Duchy of Warsaw. The English, besides supporting the Spanish insurgents, were to make a diversion by attacking Antwerp.

Leaving the defence of Italy to Eugène, and of Warsaw to Poniatowski, Napoleon was concentrating his main army on the upper Danube in Bavaria. Jerome, whom he still trusted after all his failures in the field, and still hoped to make into a successful soldier, was given a comparatively easy task. He was put in command of a reserve corps to be formed of his own Westphalians, some of Louis's Dutch troops who were at Hamburg, and part of the garrison of Magdeburg.

The war was begun by the Archduke Charles crossing the Inn on April 3rd. A week before this Jerome had had a warning that, instead of taking part in the main operations, he might have to deal with hostile movements in his own kingdom.   On the night of April 2nd an ex-Prussian officer, Captain Catt, raided his eastern frontier at the head of an armed band, made prisoners of the police and annexed the public funds in a couple of small towns, but finding the peasants afraid to rise, and a hostile force moving to attack him, retreated safely into Prussia, after a two days' campaign. Catt's raid was the prelude of other attempts at insurrection, and the first menace of the future German rising.

After a visit to Frankfurt, where he stayed at the house of his financial friend Jacobsohn, Jerome returned to Cassel and issued a proclamation to the soldiers of the Westphalian army.   The Emperor was closing on the Archduke, but all Germany expected victory for Austria.   But on the 22nd Napoleon conquered at Eckmuhl and the Archduke was in full retreat.   Before the news could reach Cassel, Jerome had an anxious time, for on the very day of the battle his police discovered the existence of a widespread plot.   The conspirators meant to act that very night.   Officers and soldiers of his own personal bodyguard were implicated. After dark Colonel Dornberg, commanding the Chasseurs of the Royal Guard, was to seize the palace, make Jerome a prisoner and hurry him off to the coast, where a ship was ready to take him to sea and hand him over to the English. The same evening there was to be a rising in town and country, and many of the officials were ready to declare for the insurgents.

The treachery of Dornberg was a shock to Jerome, for the Colonel had been lavish of his protestations of loyalty, and formed one of the inner circle of the court.   Jerome acted with more energy than one would have expected.   Dornberg and several other leaders were arrested before they could move.   The Chasseurs of the Guard were paraded with other regiments, and Jerome, on horseback and surrounded by his French supporters, told them the traitors were in prison and called on them to stand by him.   There was no one to give the signal of revolt, and they remained faithful.   But he had prepared for emergencies.   His servants and his French employés had been hastily armed, and formed an inner guard for the palace.   'Jerome was awake and on the alert all night.

The morning brought news of popular outbreaks in all directions. Columns of troops were sent out under trusted leaders to disperse the rebels. But even next day the situation seemed so doubtful that Queen Catherine was hurried off to Strasburg, and a lot of the royal treasures were sent under escort with her. Then came the news of Eckmuhl, and the insurrection, disorganised from the outset by the arrests at Cassel, rapidly flickered out.

Then there was another alarm. Major Ferdinand von Schill, who commanded a hussar regiment at Berlin, made a raid upon the borders of Jerome's dominions in the hope of drawing Prussia into the war. Schill was one of the popular heroes of Germany, for after Jena he had refused to surrender, and had carried on for a while a guerilla warfare against the French. Picking up 300 infantry on his way from Berlin, he crossed the Elbe above Magdeburg on May 1st. Gathering adherents as he went, he first struck southwards, then made a rapid march northwards, playing a game of hide and seek with the troops sent after him. Pursued by the Westphalians under General D'Albignac, headed off by Louis's Dutch troops from Hamburg under General Gratien, he evaded both of them, and seized Stralsund. By that time his original force of 500 had multiplied tenfold. At Stralsund he expected help by sea, but none came, and on May 30th the place was stormed by Gratien's Dutchmen and a Danish division under General Ewald, and Schill was killed.

His raid came at a critical moment. On May 10th Napoleon had seized Vienna, but on the 22nd he had failed at Aspern, and retired into the Isle of Lobau. When Stralsund was stormed the fortune of war still trembled in the balance on the Danube. Wagram was not fought and won till more than a month later. Jerome was so anxious that he collected about Cassel all the troops he could summon to his aid, Westphalians, Dutch, and French.

While Schill was retiring on Stralsund one more effort to create a diversion in Germany had been made by the patriots— the fourth, and in some ways the most formidable of these isolated and ill-directed enterprises. The Duke of Brunswick appeared in Saxony at the head of a force of volunteers, old soldiers who had served in the armies of Brunswick and Hesse,

some 1700 infantry and 600 cavalry, and the Austrians sent
a strong column under General Kienmayer to support him.
Brunswick seized Dresden, Kienmayer marched on Leipzig,
and to Cassel there came an alarming rumour that a force of
15,000 men was on the move in Saxony and would soon be
across the border of Westphalia.   Napoleon, still camped in
the Isle of Lobau, sent orders to Jerome to attack the enemy
in Saxony with his forces, now known as the 10th Corps of the
Grand Army, and told him he would be supported by a corps
under Junot.   On May 20th Jerome replied that he was about
to march, but he did not start till June 16th.   He took a whole
household with him, including a crowd of secretaries of state
and the ministers accredited to his court.   On the 22nd
he was skirmishing with Kienmayer's advanced guard, and
scored a small success.   On the 25th the Austrians evacuated
Leipzig, and next day he entered the city in triumph.

On the 27th he moved out on the Dresden road, and caught
up and defeated the Austrian rearguard.   Junot was coming
up, and had he pressed the pursuit and combined his operations
with those of the Marshal, he could have destroyed both the
Austrians and Brunswick.   But now he hesitated, for news
had come of a minor rising of peasants in Westphalia, and he
was anxious to return to Cassel.   Finding his hands free,
Kienmayer turned on Junot and beat him.   Jerome, alarmed
about Westphalia and exaggerating the Austrian force in his
front, began to retreat.

On July 8th Napoleon, who had thoroughly beaten the main
Austrian army at Wagram two days before, and was sure that
Jerome was in full march on Dresden, ordered him, after
securing that place, to enter Bohemia.   On the 17th, still
unaware of his retreat, Napoleon wrote again telling Jerome
to concentrate all his available force about Dresden, and send
25,000 men into Bohemia.   He must obey orders.   'During
the war,' he said, 'you must act neither as King of Westphalia nor as the Emperor's brother, but only as a general
commanding an army corps.'   It would be ridiculous to act
otherwise.   He should be first, secondly, and lastly a soldier.
What was the good of dragging ministers and diplomatists
about and keeping up a court.   'You should bivouac and
march with the advanced guard, be on horseback day and

night. Otherwise you had better remain in your palace. You are making war like a Persian satrap.' 'Is it from me, Bon Dieu,' he continued, 'that you have learned such ways? from me, who, with an army of 200,000 under me, am to be found in the firing line, and leave secretaries of state at Munich or Vienna! Cease making yourself ridiculous. Send the diplomatists back to Cassel, get rid of baggage and attendants, and have only one table. Make war like a young soldier, who has need of glory and renown, and try to deserve the rank which you have attained.'

It was a sharp lesson. What would Napoleon have said if he had known that, instead of being at Dresden, Jerome was that very day at Erfurt in full retreat for Cassel, where he arrived on July 20th? Luckily Kienmayer had heard the news of the Austrian disaster at Wagram, and evacuated Saxony. But Brunswick still kept the field, and the danger of a German rising was not yet at an end.

It was not till the 25th that Napoleon received a despatch from Jerome telling him he was at Cassel and trying to explain his retreat. He blamed Junot for not helping him; he exaggerated the troubles in Westphalia; he talked of the danger of the great English expedition preparing against Antwerp being diverted to Hanover and his own states. Napoleon wrote a long reply, reminding Jerome of his previous failures and blunders. 'You commanded a battleship,' he said, 'and abandoned your admiral without orders. You made excuses that I saw through but accepted, because one ship more or less mattered little and I had other views.' But he went on to tell him that 20,000 men in the wrong place might mean the loss of a campaign, and, though he did not want to disgrace him by depriving him of his command, he could not risk the fortune of his armies on disobedience to clear orders, even though the culprit was his own brother. 'Twenty thousand men more or less may change the face of Europe. If, then, you mean to go on as you have begun, surrounded by men who know nothing of war like D'Albignac, or Rewbell, or Fürstenstein (Lecamus), having no man who can give you good counsel, sending me romances, you may as well stay with the women in your palace. Please to understand that as a soldier I have no brothers, and you cannot hide the real motives of

o

your conduct under futile and ridiculous pretexts. So that you may not risk further results of this kind, I shall be pleased to hear that you have handed over the troops under your command to the Duke d'Abrantes (Junot).' Then, as if regretting the blow this summary dismissal would be to Jerome, and despite all he had said about running fresh risks of disappointment through his affection for his brother, he continued : ' If you retain the command of your troops, move at once to Dresden. I will send you a chief of the staff who has some common sense. Concentrate at Dresden the Saxon and Dutch troops, and those of the Grand Duchy of Berg, with your own. If hostilities recommence,[1] the theatre of war will be in Bohemia, and you will have an active part in it. If the war is not resumed, the concentration of a large number of troops at Dresden and Bayreuth may facilitate the negotiations.'

In letters written at the same time to Reinhard, his diplomatic representative at the court of Cassel, the Emperor made all manner of excuses for his brother. He believed he was clever enough, but he was misled by the crowd of young men who had been his flatterers and boon companions, and whom he had made into officers of state and generals of his army, and decked out with Westphalian titles. Reinhard was told to let these people, Lecamus, Count of Fürstenstein, Meyronnet, Count of Wellingerode, D'Albignac and Rewbell, Westphalian generals, and the rest of the group, understand that if they did not take things more seriously, and exert a better influence on their master, it would be the worse for them. Meanwhile the Emperor trusted that Jerome would act like a soldier after all, and occupy Dresden forthwith.

But Jerome remained at Cassel, for despite the armistice there was still war in Westphalia, war carried on by a bold partisan leader with an insignificant force that ought to have been easily swept aside, if these improvised Westphalian generals knew their business. On hearing of the armistice the Duke of Brunswick, with his 1800 infantry and 600 horse, decided to carry on the war on his own account, and make one more effort to raise Germany. On July 21st he started on a

---

[1] An armistice had been signed at Znaim on July 12, and the negotiations were in progress which ended with the treaty of Schönbrunn (October 14, 1809).

raid, the objective of which was his own old city of Brunswick.
On the 25th he bivouacked in the suburbs of Leipzig, and then
he made a dash across Westphalia by Halle and Halberstadt.
Tenfold forces were closing round him. General Thielmann's
Saxons and Gratien's Dutchmen were following him up. A
French brigade from Magdeburg was closing on his right
from the northward. A Westphalian division, 6000 strong,
under Rewbell was moving in his front, and other detachments
of the Westphalian army were being despatched from Cassel,
where, as if he were confronted by a formidable invasion,
Jerome was accumulating a reserve.

On the 29th Brunswick scored his first success, with dire
disaster to one of Jerome's oldest friends, his henchman the
ex-naval officer Meyronnet, now Grand Chamberlain of his
kingdom, Count of Wellingerode and Colonel of the 5th Westphalian infantry. Meyronnet had reached Halberstadt with
his regiment, and had gone to rest in one of the houses. In
the market-place arms had been piled, and the adjutant of
the 5th was calling the roll of the regiment before telling off
the men to their billets. There were no outposts, no scouts
sent eastward, no precautions. Brunswick was close at hand.
His cavalry dashed into the town, the infantry followed.
The 5th Infantry were captured without firing a shot, taken
without arms in their hands. Meyronnet was made a prisoner
as he ran out into the street. Brunswick continued his march,
and on July 31st entered the city from which he took his title,
and where he had reigned before Jena.

Next day Gratien and Thielmann occupied Halberstadt.
Rewbell was approaching Brunswick city. The Dutch general
sent Rewbell word that he had better combine with him and
Thielmann to capture the Duke. But Rewbell thought that
with his 6000 he could take Brunswick, and would not wait
for his friends. He would storm the city single-handed. But
Brunswick with less than half his force came out to meet him,
2500 against 6000, and thoroughly routed him, capturing guns
and colours. Then by a rapid march northwards he eluded
the pursuit of Dutch, Saxons, and French, and on August 7th
reached Elsfleth on the estuary of the Weser, where a British
squadron was waiting for him. He embarked his troops and
his trophies in safety. He had become one of the national

heroes of Germany, and his raid was one more incentive to the future national rising.

Rewbell was dismissed from the army, and went to the United States with his American wife, whom he had married at Baltimore in the days when Jerome was courting Miss Patterson. The Emperor, bitterly disappointed at Jerome's failure to obey his orders, and at the hopeless mismanagement of the situation caused by Brunswick's raid, still tried to spare his brother's feelings and save his reputation. By an order issued on August 11th he left him the nominal command of the 10th Corps, but it was to consist only of his Westphalians and other garrison troops, which were not to be moved except by the Emperor's orders. All the French, Dutch, Saxon and other German troops in Westphalia, Saxony, and South Germany were put under the command of Junot, and in case of the war being resumed he was to form them into a *corps d'armée*. The peace of Schönbrunn made it unnecessary to do this.

The war of 1809 had also had its influence on the fortunes of Louis and his kingdom of Holland. It had been intended that, as a diversion in favour of Austria, and to destroy a dockyard that was a menace to the Channel, an English expedition should be sent to seize Antwerp. From the first the enterprise was mismanaged. A hopelessly incompetent general, Lord Chatham, received the command, merely because he was a Lord and the brother of Pitt. There were such endless delays that the expedition was not ready to sail till after Wagram had been fought, and when Napoleon was discussing the terms of peace in the Austrian Emperor's palace of Schönbrunn. By the middle of July 41,000 men were embarked on a huge fleet of transports, escorted by 37 battleships, 23 frigates, and more than a hundred sloops and gunboats. The armada, as it lay in the Downs, was like a floating city. The troops embarked were just twice as many as Wellesley could put in his battle line in Spain. Had they been sent there Joseph might have been driven from Madrid. Had they been at once pushed on to Antwerp, the place must have fallen almost without a blow. On July 28th at last the expedition sailed. On the 29th the estuary of the Scheldt was white with their sails.

Antwerp and Holland were at Chatham's mercy, and were only saved by his incompetence. Since April Louis had been warning his brother of the dangers of the situation. He pointed out to the Emperor that Antwerp, with its fortifications out of repair and held only by 2000 old soldiers and coastguards, invited attack. Antwerp, however, was a French fortress, and Louis could not interfere there. Flushing, on the island of Walcheren at the river mouth, was a Dutch place, but Napoleon had insisted on its being held by a French garrison, in order to be better able to prevent English goods being run into the Scheldt. When Louis reported that he had visited Flushing, found the place in bad order, and thought General Monnet, the commandant, was incompetent, Napoleon thought he was inspired by jealousy at the fortresses being no longer in Dutch hands. But even if Flushing had been in the best of order, there was nothing to prevent a hostile fleet sailing past it. There was only a gunboat squadron in the river higher up. At Antwerp there were some larger ships under repair, and several building.

But Louis's whole kingdom was defenceless. Napoleon had taken one division from him for service in Spain ; another (General Gratien's) for Westphalia. Both had fought well. Including his personal guard he had not quite 9000 soldiers left in Holland. He could add somewhat to these numbers by calling out the National Guard, but he said, ' With such insignificant forces at my command I cannot guarantee the safety of The Helder, Helvoetsluys, Walcheren, or even Amsterdam itself from a sudden attack,' and he pointed out that the English were collecting a very formidable force on the other side of the narrow seas. He suggested that at least Gratien's division should be sent back to him.

The Emperor with 300,000 men locked up in Spain, 300,000 more in action against Austria, besides the numerous garrisons of the Empire, with conscripts called out in advance and his resources strained to the uttermost, affected to believe that the English expedition, which had been talked about for years, was a mere empty menace. He left Louis to shift for himself as best he could. He did not even take the obvious precautions that were quite within his power. Warned in April he did nothing, and when the danger became a reality nearly four months later, he tried to make Louis the scapegoat of his own negligence.

Louis no sooner heard the English were in the Scheldt than he acted with a vigour that did him credit. But nothing he could have done would have saved Antwerp, only for the fact that Chatham stupidly set to work to occupy the island of Walcheren and reduce Flushing before going further up the river. On July 30th Strachan began landing his troops on Walcheren, occupied Middelburg, and set about a regular siege of Flushing. Louis made good use of the respite thus given to Antwerp. Claiming, as Grand Constable of the Empire, the right to command the French troops at Antwerp, or within reach of it, as well as his own whom he brought up from Holland, he had 7000 Dutch troops in or near the place by August 3rd, and had also called in various French detachments and set large bodies of workmen to repair, extend, and arm the defences along the river. The old works on the narrow bend of the Scheldt below the city, Fort Lillo on the right and Liefkenshoek on the left bank, were not even armed. Louis brought heavy guns from Antwerp citadel and mounted them in the forts, and erected and armed five other batteries to sweep the narrows, and flooded the country covering the rear of his forts and the approach to the city. The flotilla was sent scouting down the river. Orders were issued for calling out the National Guards in Holland. Antwerp was safe for the moment from being rushed. Chatham was bombarding Flushing, where he burned half the town, but it was not till August 16th that Monnet surrendered the place, and Chatham announced that he would advance on Antwerp.

It was too late. On this very August 16th Louis handed over the command at Antwerp to Marshal Bernadotte, who had arrived with considerable reinforcements. By the end of the month there were 30,000 men guarding Antwerp, and the English were dying of fever and ague, and in no position to press the attack. They tried to hold on at Walcheren, but were driven out by the fearful toll levied by the marsh fevers. When at last the expedition withdrew it left thousands of graves behind the island dykes.

Napoleon's correspondence with Louis during the anxious days of the English expedition does not show the Emperor in a favourable light. He was afraid that a disaster on the Scheldt might embarrass his peace negotiations at Schönbrunn. He had laughed at the danger which now threatened, and he had neglected the simplest precautions. Anxious and irritated, he tried to make a scapegoat of Louis, to throw on him the blame for his own neglect. Instead of thanking him for his energetic efforts, he blamed him for presuming to give orders as Constable of France to French troops. He told him his office of Constable was purely civil and honorary, and gave no right of command. He asked him how he thought any one was going to respect his independence if he did not provide better for the defence of Holland. His kingdom was a sham, if it had not an army, and was open to the first comer. He seemed to forget that it was not Holland, but his own possessions on the Scheldt, that had been left open to attack, and saved by the English general's stupidity and his own brother's energy. Louis complained that he was being very unjustly treated, and told Napoleon that in dealing thus with him, and threatening to overrule his authority in Holland, he was not taking an honourable course. He had heard of a project for annexing Holland and garrisoning it with French troops, and he was indignant that the Emperor should allege as possible motives for such action, negligences of which not Louis but Napoleon himself had been guilty, and to which Louis had in vain called his attention.

The third of the three kings, Joseph of Spain, had seen something of war on a grand scale during the campaign of 1809. When Napoleon returned to France at the beginning of that year, in order to prepare for the war in central Europe, he left his brother in nominal command in Spain, so that Joseph had under his orders 200,000 men divided into several army corps and commanded by six marshals of France and a crowd of generals. It was an army of many nations, gathered from all parts of the Empire, officers and men having for the most part little interest in the war, beyond such as might arise from personal motives, which often meant the opportunity for pillage. So true was this that, especially among the Germans and other non-French contingents, there were many desertions to the side of the Spanish insurgents.

This heterogeneous army had to be divided into numerous detachments to deal with the various centres of resistance, and to protect the hnes of communication and garrison the fortresses. This dispersion made it possible for Wellesley with a very small British force to make a successful advance from Portugal into the very heart of Spain in the campaign of 1809, though his small numbers, and the failure of the Spaniards to co-operate with him, obliged him eventually to retire with his little force to the fortified lines of Torres Vedras.

To give unity to the operations of the French army, thus divided and carrying on simultaneously half a dozen minor campaigns, would have required a high order of military talent, linked with equal determination. Joseph was not a military genius, and Jourdan, his chief of the staff, was one of the second-rate generals of the day; but whatever chance the King had of successfully directing the war was marred by the arrangements invented by the Emperor for keeping some personal control of the course of events beyond the Pyrenees. First from Paris, then from his headquarters in South Germany, and later from the palace of Schönbrunn, he sent orders on orders, either direct to Joseph or through the Paris War Office.

He had himself ridiculed, at an earlier date, the attempt of a Council of War in Vienna to control and direct the Austrian armies in Italy and on the Rhine. He was making the same mistake himself. In vain Joseph pointed out that it would be better to send general directions as to the military policy to be adopted, leaving the men on the spot to choose the means of carrying them out, instead of sending detailed orders, which, when they reached Madrid, might indeed apply admirably to a state of things that existed a fortnight ago but were now out of date, and misleading. Napoleon made matters worse by not only sending orders to Madrid, but also communicating directly at times with the marshals without telling Joseph and Jourdan what he had done. The result was contradictory or confusing directions coming from two different quarters, and when to this was added the strong inclination of some of the corps commanders to act on their own responsibility without recking much of orders from Madrid, Paris, or Schönbrunn, and without giving any clear report of their proceedings, one can imagine the kind of chaos that prevailed in French military affairs in Spain, a state of things for which most of the blame was very unjustly laid upon Joseph.

In the spring of 1809 Wellesley (soon to be Wellington) had taken command of the little British army at Lisbon, and in concert with Beresford's Portuguese corps had driven Soult out of northern Portugal. Then he had come to the rescue of Cuesta, whose army had been roughly handled by Victor, and rallying the Spanish general's army, 40,000 strong, to his own 20,000, he moved up the Tagus valley in the early summer, threatening Madrid. In July Joseph marched to meet him with some 56,000 men, soldiers of many nations, but mainly French and under French general officers. Jourdan was with him as his chief of the staff, and of the subordinate commanders Marshal Victor was the senior, and took a leading part in the executive work of the campaign. The first encounters with the allies were successes for the French. It was by the merest accident that Joseph missed having Sir Arthur Wellesley as his prisoner. When at last, after the allied outposts had been driven in, the two armies faced each other at Talavera de la Reina, and most of Cuesta's 40,000 broke in hopeless rout at the first onset of the French, it looked as if Joseph had a great victory in his hands.

At the council of war held in the French lines on the morning of July 28th, Jourdan was strongly in favour of merely watching the British position until reinforcements came up, when by a threat against the British flank and line of communications Wellesley might be forced to retire, or if he held his ground would have to meet overwhelming numbers. Joseph was in favour of this very prudent course, but Victor urged immediate attack. Now that Cuesta had proved a broken reed, Joseph had more than two to one against the English. If he attacked he must win. If he hesitated, Wellesley would give him the slip, and get safely behind his fortifications in Portugal. Joseph was afraid of being condemned by Napoleon if he did not accept Victor's view, and he ordered the attack. During the hard-fought day he was under close fire, and all acknowledge that he showed a perfect coolness, as if he had been a soldier all his life. But though victory more than once seemed to be in the hands of the French, all their attacks were beaten off, and they suffered so heavily that in the night it was decided to fall back and take up a defensive position on the road to Madrid.

Wellesley could not follow up his advantage. Outnumbered, and abandoned by his allies, he retreated into Portugal. Jourdan, as chief of the staff, sent Napoleon a despatch in which he claimed a victory for Joseph : Cuesta's army routed, Wellington's march stopped, guns and colours taken from the Spaniards, Madrid saved. It was some time before Napoleon could find out what had really happened. The British retreat gave colour to the claim for victory. Even in England some of the opposition writers, notably Cobbett, protested that Talavera must have been lost by the allies. ' A pretty victory,' wrote Cobbett, ' which results in our general marching back to Portugal as fast as he can go.' Popular French writers of to-day still talk of Talavera as an indecisive action, or a drawn battle.

Joseph, turning aside to scatter a large Spanish force of irregulars and secure plenty of guns and colours as trophies, marched back to Madrid, where he made a triumphal entry and there was a *Te Deum* for his success. The outlook in Spain seemed better. The British were holding Portugal, or part of it, thanks to their fortified lines. Their fleet secured Cadiz for the insurgents, but, except in the south, the French seemed to be mastering the insurrection. For Joseph, however, mere defeats of Spanish armies and slaughtering of his ' so-called subjects ' did not help much to secure his throne. And the position was made all the more difficult because the French generals levied contributions, winked at plunder, shared in it themselves, and perpetuated the blood-feud by wholesale executions.

In his correspondence with his brother, Joseph, still hoping against hope for the day when he could act as a Spanish king and make a bid for the loyalty of the people, pleaded for the abrogation of martial law, the establishment of civil courts, the fulfilment of the promises made to the notables at Bayonne. Napoleon replied that he was taking an ideal view of the situation and disregarding unpleasant facts. He explained to Joseph that at Bayonne he had been put forward as a constitutional king, governing with a Spanish ministry and the consent of the Cortes. But he had been driven from Madrid. He had been reinstated, and he was maintained by French bayonets. The constitutionalism of Bayonne was out of date, mere ancient history. Spain was a conquered country, and he must make up his mind to give a free hand to the soldiers on whom his throne depended.

Joseph still persisted that if he were only given a free hand himself, he could still be ' King of Spain, not by force of arms, but through the love of the Spaniards.' He blushed, he said, at being a mere cipher in the hands of military commandants whom he could not control. ' Let me,' he continued, ' either be King in the way that befits a brother of your Majesty, or let me return to Mortefontaine, where the only happiness I shall ask for is to live without humiliations and to die with a peaceful conscience.'

Napoleon did not take this offer of abdication seriously. And he was right. Joseph clung to power, hoping still that the moment would come when the opposition of the Spaniards would be tired out and the English be driven away, so that civil government would replace martial law, and he could rule according to his own ideas.

After the peace of Schönbrunn it seemed for a while that this hope might be realised. The Emperor was again to all appearance Dictator of the Continent. The ally of Russia, the conqueror of Austria, he was able to divorce his first wife, and persuade the proud Hapsburgs to allow him to put an Archduchess in her place. But his very success had blinded him to the dangers caused by the continual strain of aggressive war : Spain was the open wound of his Empire, England was as doggedly hostile as ever, Germany was awaking, Russia was becoming tired of an alliance that meant only the destruction of her trade and the embarrassment of her finances. And with the hope of having a son to whom he would hand on his power, the Emperor began to deal in a more arbitrary way with his brothers, and between pressure from without the Empire and dissension within the family the reigns of the three Bonaparte kings had even a shorter lease of life than the Empire itself. Lucien, the man who would not be king, was soon to throw in his lot openly with the Emperor's enemies.

CHAPTER XV

THE FLIGHT OF LUCIEN AND LOUIS

(1809-1810)

WHILE the three kings, his brothers, were ruling their states and commanding armies, Lucien was living the life he had chosen in Italy ; and despite well-meant attempts of others to close it up, the breach between him and the Emperor was becoming wider and deeper as the years went on. Nothing had come of the proposals made by Joseph when he met Lucien at Bologna in May 1808, for the King of Spain was never in a position to offer his brother the viceroyalty of the Indies. A few weeks later, when Lucien had gone to spend the summer at Florence, his mother wrote to him suggesting that he should send her his eldest daughter Charlotte, and holding out hopes that she would find a prince as the girl's husband, and use the marriage as a step towards a reconciliation between the brothers. But for a while this proposal also led to nothing.

At Florence Lucien lived in state, as he had done in his Roman palace, spending money freely, buying pictures and statues, and seriously diminishing the 600,000 francs he had collected from his brothers for his long-talked-of journey to the United States. He still spoke of leaving Italy at an early date, but he stayed on, hoping that some change in the general situation of affairs might make it possible for him to remain in Europe. In the autumn he returned to Canino and busied himself once more with his estate, his excavations and the factories, and the continuation of his epic of *Charlemagne*. On November 3rd his second son was born there, and was given the name of Paul-Marie in honour of Pope Paul III., who was a native of Canino.

In 1809 he carried out works and improvements on such

a large scale at Canino that it seemed as if he had abandoned the idea of leaving Italy, and this though the annexation of Rome and the imprisonment of Pius VII. made his position there more difficult, for he was now living in the territory of the Empire. He had introduced the cultivation of cotton, bringing peasants from southern Italy to teach his people the work. Iron was imported from Elba for his foundries. The castello was repaired, and some houses that interfered with the view removed ; a new gate and a fountain were given to the little town.

In the summer there was the news of Wagram ; in the autumn that of the Emperor's triumph at Schönbrunn, and then letters from his mother, from his uncle Fesch, and from his sister Pauline, all insisting that the time was come for making his peace with Napoleon on favourable terms, for a new situation would soon be created for the family by the coming divorce of Josephine and the marriage of the Emperor with a princess. This would mean a rearrangement of all Napoleon's plans for the Bonaparte family, and now or never Lucien must secure his position for the future. They would use all their influence in his favour. The proposal that he should send Charlotte to Paris to his mother was revived, and it was suggested that her sister should accompany her.[1]

In December 1809 Napoleon had convened all the members of his family at Paris to be witnesses of the new arrangements he was making, the separation from Josephine, to which she gave her consent ' for motives of public policy,' and the consequent resettlement of their affairs. Joseph could not leave Madrid, the rebel Lucien had not been invited, but Jerome and Louis were there, and Napoleon's mother and sisters, with Eugène and Murat. For Louis the visit to Paris was a time of critical negotiations. Napoleon had made up his mind to annex Holland, and was trying to force his brother to abdicate. Louis was making a hopeless struggle to preserve at least some show of independence for his adopted country, and gradually drifted into a position of open hostility to the Emperor. This dispute did not smooth the way for the

---

[1] Charlotte and her sister were the daughters of Lucien's first marriage with Catherine Boyer, which had been recognised by Napoleon.

negotiations on which Lucien ventured, encouraged by his mother, uncle, and sister.

In December he sent two confidential envoys to his mother at Paris. They were a Corsican named Campi, who had been with him at the Ministry of the Interior during the Consulate and had since acted as one of his secretaries, and his brother-in-law Boyer, the brother of his first wife Catherine, who had for a long time been one of his trusted agents. He had not given them power to settle anything definitely. They were to discuss matters with his relations in Paris, find out how far the Emperor was prepared to go, keep him informed, and submit some proposal for his consideration, but he gave them plainly to understand that he could not accept any proposition that would imply separation from his wife.

The negotiations dragged on for weeks. They would not have lasted many days only for the fact that Madame Mère, in her anxiety for peace, gave Napoleon the impression that Lucien would yield, and when the Emperor declared he was ready to make some arrangement, Lucien in his turn was misled into thinking that Napoleon was giving way and he could dictate his own terms. As a pretext for the coming of the envoys the first question discussed was the future of Charlotte. Madame sent word that she would receive her and provide for her education, and that the Emperor would see that she was offered the hand of a prince. Only then Lucien's own position was discussed, and after much diplomatic fencing the Emperor consented to see Campi on the subject.

The interview took place on February 3, 1810. We know what passed from Campi's detailed record of the conversation. Napoleon spoke plainly. If Lucien was ready to make his submission, let him come to Paris. He would see him with pleasure, but let him not come if he meant to continue his opposition. Campi showed him a letter of Lucien's, in which he expressed his desire to be of service to the Emperor. ' What do you make of it ? ' asked Napoleon. ' I don't see in it any intention of coming into line.' Campi reminded him of Lucien's letters to his mother. ' Yes,' said Napoleon, ' he has also sent me a letter full of fine phrases. It 's not the time for phrases. I don't mean to recognise a woman who has been brought into the family in spite of me. Lucien has always deceived me. He promised Joseph, and you know it, that he would never make Madame Jouberthou his wife.'— This, by the way, was not true.—' I blame myself,' the Emperor went on, ' for having recognised even his first marriage, and for not having had Madame Jouberthou arrested. But Christine Boyer had some good in her, and the times were different. But now that I am Emperor of the French, giving the law to kings, am I to yield to this woman ? I have never received an act of submission from her.'

' She did not dare to write to your Majesty,' Campi put in. ' I know how she has acted,' the Emperor continued. ' There can be no change in my policy. If she loves her children, if she loves Lucien, she will get him to agree to a divorce.' Campi tried to argue. ' King Jerome,' he said, ' and Madame Mère have told me that your Majesty did not insist on a divorce.' The Emperor replied that if Lucien would not have a divorce, it would only end in his refusing altogether to recognise the marriage. Then he could do nothing for the children. A divorce would indirectly recognise the rights of the children, except of course the earliest, born while Monsieur Jouberthou was still alive. ' No,' protested Campi, ' the first husband was dead fourteen months before the boy was born.'

' That has to be proved,' said Napoleon. ' In any case he was born before the second marriage.' Napoleon affected to regard this as an intolerable scandal, forgetful of his own conduct. But he would leave Lucien no pretext. He would provide even for the eldest born. But he was master, as head of the Empire he must choose who should belong to the Imperial family. If Lucien would not submit now, he would not have another chance. Why not let Lucien come to Paris and discuss the matter ? asked Campi. No, said Napoleon. He did not want a repetition of the useless interview at Mantua. If Lucien was not his friend let him go and join the English. ' Your Majesty has no better friend,' said Campi, and then Napoleon burst into a storm of invectives against his brother.

Campi nevertheless proposed that he should be given a letter for Lucien. ' No,' said Napoleon, ' tell him from me that when the interests of the world are at stake one must sacrifice family affection. Such sacrifices are necessary.

Look at the Empress. I had lived long with her ; I loved her ; at my age why should I think of another wife ? But my position made it necessary to part with her, and I have done so. Lucien has been the cause of that divorce, for it was his obstinacy made me think anxiously of the future, and then I hoped for heirs who would not make my inheritance a source of trouble. I thought only of the happiness of my people. The Empress has been the victim of my policy. I will take care of her. I never abandon the victims of my policy. Look at Jerome's first wife. She was misled, she wrote to me. I am giving her 20,000 crowns, and I shall make her forget her misfortune. If Lucien agrees to a divorce I shall see in his wife only a sufferer by my system, and I shall think only of benefiting her. I don't tell you all I shall do. Would she like to go to America, I will give her the means. Would she prefer to remain at Rome, I agree. I will do everything to make her life happy. . . . If Lucien agrees to give up his wife, let him come here with all his children. I shall forget all the wrong he has done, and place him in his proper rank. But if he prefers his wife to the happiness of his children, the peace of our family, the great projects I have in my mind, then he is no longer my brother, and I don't want to hear any more about him. Let him go to America. I will have a ship got ready for him at Naples, and let there be an end of this business of his. Otherwise he may expect to be arrested with his wife and children and to die in prison. If I once take rigorous measures, there will be no resource left for him. It will be called tyranny, but what matters what men say ? ' And then came more threats and reproaches against Lucien. He even talked of arresting him, if he stayed at Canino. Finally he told Campi to go back to Lucien and tell him how matters stood ; meanwhile he would like to have Charlotte sent to Madame Mère. He also told Campi to find out privately from Lucien's wife if she would accept a divorce and persuade her husband to it in return for certain advantages.

When Lucien received the report of his envoy he was deeply disappointed. ' I am very unfortunate,' he said to Campi. ' Mamma misled me when she told me that the Emperor would not insist on a divorce. The news you bring me destroys all my hopes. . . . I cannot without dishonouring myself divorce a wife who has borne me four children. I shall go to America.' He did not want to embark from Murat's territory, so he hoped a ship would come from Naples to Città Vecchia to receive himself and his family, and that the Emperor would take over his property, and give him a pension instead, as he had no means of supporting himself if he left Europe. As the Emperor had no quarrel with the children of the first marriage he would send Charlotte and her sister to his mother, so that they might be spared the troubles of exile.

Lucien thus discussed the future with Campi, who delayed reporting to the Emperor until he could have an opportunity of a private interview with Madame Lucien. At last he was able to meet her while her husband was temporarily absent from Canino. He put before her the Emperor's proposals, telling her that in Napoleon's opinion she would best serve not only the Emperor, but her husband and her children's future, by persuading Lucien to accept a divorce, and that if this were done Napoleon would give her an Italian duchy and an assured rank and revenue for life. Parma was named as the territory to be conferred on the lady, if she would give up her husband.

Alexandrine wrote a letter to the Emperor in reply, without consulting Lucien or letting him know of the negotiation. Campi was to convey this reply to Paris. It was a very dignified document. She thanked the Emperor for his expressions of goodwill conveyed by Campi, and for his offer of rank and fortune, but at the same time ' regretted she could not conform to what his Majesty described as political necessities.' Even if she could recognise such necessities, she could not bring herself to give up a beloved husband like Lucien. ' Here on earth it is beyond the power even of the mighty Emperor whom I address to compensate me for such a sacrifice. No, Sire, the Duchy of Parma, any other sovereignty, any earthly advantage, would only serve to put into a stronger light the black ingratitude with which I would be repaying the love, esteem, and confidence of the most generous of men, and would be no gain to me, for I could never stifle the voice of conscience. . . . Sire,' she continued, ' I throw myself at your feet. It is as impossible for me secretly to separate myself from Lucien as for him publicly to abandon me. We belong to each other for life, till death. It only remains for me to ask of you, for the first time, the one favour that Lucien has ever begged from your Majesty. Sire, allow us to live in peace in some corner of your empire.' She ended by hoping that some day her children might be of service to the state and its chief, and that he would overlook the fact that their mother had been ' in her youth so unfortunate as to give offence to his Majesty.'

Thus Lucien was immovable, and the attempt to influence him through his wife had failed. After Campi had started on his return journey to Paris, taking Charlotte with him, Alexandrine showed Lucien a copy of her reply to Napoleon. He was delighted with it, and said it was an admirable letter. Campi was the bearer of another letter from the husband refusing with equal firmness all idea of a divorce.

Campi arrived in Paris on March 8th, and at once handed over Charlotte Bonaparte, a bright girl of nearly fifteen, to Madame Mère, who welcomed her grandchild, and, making the wish the father to the thought, took her coming to mean that Lucien was yielding. She went with Fesch to Napoleon and told him that the separation between Lucien and Alexandrine would be arranged. When Campi gave the Emperor the letters next day, he saw that his mother's report was mere guesswork. He told Campi that he did not blame Alexandrine. It was Lucien who was in fault. If his brother thought that he would be touched by his sending his daughter, and would change his policy, he was mistaken. Charlotte would be provided for, but her father had better leave Europe, as he had talked of doing. Campi asked would the Emperor give him a passport ? No, said Napoleon, he must apply to the Ministry in the ordinary course. Napoleon really thought that Lucien could never tear himself away from Italy, where he had so many interests and such extensive property, and that at the last moment he would ask for terms. He thought he must be only bluffing when he talked of going away, and he tried to bluff in reply by pretending to be, if anything, anxious that he should go.

On the same day Campi had interviews with other members of the family, Madame Mère, Cardinal Fesch, King Louis. Madame and Fesch suggested that a way out could be found by Lucien agreeing to a divorce by the civil power only. The

Emperor would be content with this, for he did not want Lucien to marry any one else. The religious marriage would stand, and Lucien could live with Alexandrine privately. They wrote letters to Canino setting forth this scheme, which had the weak point that it was not the Emperor's idea, but a compromise which they thought possible. King Louis told Campi that, though he had been on Lucien's side at an earlier period of the affair, he now strongly advised him to accept the divorce, submit to the Emperor, and come to Paris to take his place as an Imperial Prince, when the new Empress arrived from Vienna. Divorce was in the air at Paris just then. The Emperor had set the example. He was trying to force it on Lucien, and Louis, disputing with his brother as to what shreds of independence might be left to Holland, was all the while thinking of a divorce from Hortense, who had been estranged from him since they parted after the Pyrenean holiday. This was perhaps why he had changed his mind as to what Lucien should do.

Campi reported to Lucien that the Emperor was not to be moved, and that the rest of the family, even those who had first opposed Napoleon, were now taking his side. He himself advised Lucien to surrender. With his letter there came another from Madame Mère addressed to Lucien's wife begging her to submit to the inevitable, and for the sake of the future of her husband and her children agree to a divorce. Once Madame Mère had been the champion of Lucien and Alexandrine, but now she too had despaired of successful resistance to the Emperor's arbitrary demands. She tried to make surrender easier by holding out the hope that the so-called divorce would be a mere civil formality.

Lucien, with Alexandrine's full approval, refused to hear of even a nominal divorce. He sent Campi a reply for the Emperor, in which he expressed his readiness to serve him in any capacity, where the question of hereditary rank, and therefore of his marriage, would not be involved. To his mother he wrote an angry letter of remonstrance. Why had she turned against him ? He told her to send back his daughter at once to him. He would not leave Charlotte in the hands of people who were acting like his enemies. If the family had only remained true to him, Napoleon would have been forced by this time to come to terms, but they had abandoned him, and he would leave Europe and shift for himself.

It was not till April 10th that Campi was able to present Lucien's letter to the Emperor, whose time had been taken up with the reception of his new Empress. Napoleon rejected at once the idea of finding some subordinate post for Lucien. If he was to be any use for his policy, he must come into the family system on an equal footing with his brothers. He spoke of all his disappointments about Lucien, minimised his services, said that his uncle, the old Archdeacon Lucien, had predicted that his namesake would turn out to be the ' *mauvais sujet* of the family.' Lucien must accept his orders or go.

On April 12th Campi left Paris for Italy. He had letters from Madame Mère to Lucien begging him to make peace by a surrender, even at the last moment. But Lucien had resolved to leave Italy and the Empire. He wrote to his mother telling her that Napoleon had threatened him with imprisonment, and the negotiation was at an end. Let Charlotte be sent back. He had allowed her to go to Paris only in the hope of an arrangement being made to put an end to all dissensions in the family.

Lucien's daughter left Paris on June 4th. According to some of her grandmother's letters the girl had charmed every one and made many friends. But other accounts point to her having had an uncomfortable time at Paris. One hears of her being involved in disputes with people who had the bad taste to speak lightly of her parents in her presence. In her letters to her father she made outspoken and unfriendly comments on many of her distinguished relatives. Unlike more important communications, such as those between the brothers and their agents, which always went by special couriers, Charlotte's gossiping letters were put in the ordinary post, and in the post-office there was the confidential police bureau, the *cabinet noir*, where letters were opened, copied, and resealed. Even Charlotte's schoolgirl talk was thus noted, and Napoleon had the collection of notes sent to his study as a means of perhaps detecting some family secret of his brothers. It was one of the meannesses of the ' Grand Empire,' as bad as listening furtively at keyholes. Poor Charlotte had no idea that her expressions of discontent with her reception, her childish jests at Madame Mère and the great man himself, were thus being reported by the secret police. But she cannot have had a pleasant time at court, or she would not have said to her father when she came back to him at Canino, ' You are quite right not to go to these people. We shall be much better off in America ! '

At Campi's request the Minister of Police issued on June 1st two sets of passports allowing Lucien, his family and secretaries and servants, to pass the frontiers of the Empire. One set was made out in the name of the Senator Lucien Bonaparte ; the other, to be used in case he travelled incognito, was in the name of Monsieur Fabrizi, ' a man of business ' (négociant). This precaution of having duplicate passports was a very ordinary one at the time. Napoleon of course knew that the passports were issued, but he did not believe Lucien would venture to use them, and regretted that they had been granted, when, too late, he found his brother was in earnest and was not merely bluffing.

Lucien was already making his preparations. He spread the report that he was going to Corsica, but he meant really that the first stage of his journey should be to Cagliari in Sardinia, where, driven from Turin, the Sardinian king and court were living under the protection of the British fleet, just as the Bourbons of Naples were holding their court in Sicily. He managed to communicate with the King of Sardinia and the British Minister at Cagliari by pretending that a messenger he had sent to Corsica had been captured at sea, taken to Cagliari, and then released. There was some peril in these communications, and the reply of Hill, the English envoy, was not encouraging. He could not pledge his government either to favour Lucien's voyage or to welcome him in English territory. This meant that at sea, even under a neutral flag, Lucien ran a certain amount of risk of being made a prisoner of war if he met a British cruiser. However, he decided to go to Cagliari and communicate thence with the British government. He was thinking of taking refuge in England, instead of crossing the Atlantic.

How was he to get a ship to convey him ? Under the French flag he could not feel safe, or under the flag of a tributary state of the Empire, or its allies. This excluded

most European flags.   No British ship could enter the
harbour of Cività Vecchia.   But with the help of his brother-
in-law Murat—now King Joachim Napoleon of Naples—he
found a solution for the problem.

At Naples there was a large American ship, the *Hercules*,
Captain Edward West of Salem, Massachusetts, which was
under arrest for alleged violation of the continental blockade.
Murat was at the moment not very well disposed towards
Napoleon, against whom he had many grievances, real or
imaginary.   He therefore readily responded to Lucien's
suggestion that he should be allowed to charter the *Hercules*,
ostensibly for a voyage to America.   Murat not only released
the American ship, but he advanced a considerable sum of
money to have her fitted out without delay, and when she
sailed for Cività he sent his corvette, the *Achille*, a ship of ten
guns and eighty men, to escort her.   On July 21st the two
ships anchored in the harbour of Cività Vecchia, and the
Hercules began to embark Lucien's baggage.   He had mort-
gaged his property and many of his pictures, and sold many
of his jewels to provide himself with funds, but he had packed
up a considerable quantity of portable valuables, including
many works of art, which could either be turned into money
or used to adorn his new home in a strange country.

On August 7th he embarked with his party.   The Governor
of Rome, General Miollis, came to see him off.   His passports
were in order, and no one imagined that the Emperor had any
objection to his departure.   With Lucien were his wife and
her children, Anne Jouberthou, the daughter of her first
marriage, and Charles, Letitia, Jeanne, and Paul Bonaparte,
the eldest a boy of seven, the youngest a baby in arms.   Then
there were Lucien's daughters by his first marriage, Charlotte,
aged fifteen, and ' Lili,' two years younger.   There was
the chaplain, the Abbé Maurice Malvestito, who was generally
known as Père Maurice ; a French doctor, M. Defrance ;
Lucien's brother-in-law, André Boyer, and a secretary, M.
Servières, who had his wife and little son with him ; then there
was the tutor to the children, M. Charpentier, and an artist,
M. de Chatillon.   Besides, there were twenty-three servants,
ten women and thirteen men, mostly Corsicans, who looked
on Lucien more as a chief of a clan than a mere employer.

Early in the evening the *Hercules* put to sea.   Murat's little warship escorted her out of the harbour, and then parted company.   Under the Stars and Stripes in the open sea Lucien could feel he was free.   It was a fine night, but next day the weather was stormy.   Lucien told Captain West to steer for Caghari, and to the relief of the crowd of passengers, most of whom were terribly sick, the *Hercules* anchored in the shelter of the bay.   The first stage of Lucien's exodus was accomplished.

Before following his fortunes further we must tell the story of the departure from the Empire of another of the four brothers, Louis of Holland.   It was a mere coincidence that in the same summer two out of the four brothers should have openly broken with the Emperor, and shaken the dust of the Empire from their feet, for Louis's exodus from Holland had nothing to do with the culmination of Lucien's revolt.

When Louis came to the family council at Paris in December 1809, Napoleon had already made up his mind to bring Holland more completely under his own rule, and either deprive Louis of the crown by persuading him to abdicate like Charles IV. of Spain at Bayonne, or, if he remained king, make him little more than a nominal ruler.   Many of the throughgoing eulogists of Napoleon—French writers especially—argue that the Emperor was forced to adopt this policy by Louis's own incompetence as a ruler, his weakness of character, his changeful, capricious temperament; and they further suggest that Napoleon was made more hostile to his brother on account of Louis's neglect of his wife Hortense, whom, since his marriage with her mother, Napoleon had treated as a favourite daughter. But at this moment, when he was divorcing Josephine, the Emperor paid little attention to the troubles of Hortense, who moreover was quite as much to blame as Louis, and had shown for months something like positive dislike to her husband.   As for the affairs of Holland, if Louis had been a man of stronger character the difficulties created between him and the Emperor by the situation of the tributary kingdom would have been, if anything, still more serious, and would probably have come sooner.

The crisis was inevitable, and it had been aggravated by

Napoleon's own mistakes in 1809. Louis was not to blame. If the Emperor had paid attention to his reports, Antwerp and the Scheldt would not have been at the mercy of the British. When the danger came, it was Louis who had saved the situation by taking full advantage of the delay caused by Chatham's stupid operations in the Isle of Walcheren. But Napoleon, though he must have known the true facts of the case, and though he had stripped Holland of Dutch troops, taunted Louis with the defencelessness of his little kingdom, and told him that a French army of occupation would have to provide for its safety.

But it was not on military grounds that he thought of a French occupation. He wanted to hold the coast from Dunkirk to the Elbe, in order to enforce the exclusion of British goods from the Continent. For Holland the strict enforcement of the system meant ruin, all the more because the Dutch colonies were now in English hands, and unless some modification of Napoleon's blockade decrees were permitted, the whole import trade of the country would cease. In two ways the decrees were evaded. First, there was a vast system of smuggling, at which the Dutch authorities undoubtedly connived. Secondly, American ships crowded into the Dutch ports, and under the neutral flag kept up a commerce with the British colonies, landing their products under the disguise of American goods. It was to stop this double current of contraband trade that Napoleon established a customs line along the land frontiers of Holland, with strict orders to confiscate all goods of British origin. This was ruining the Dutch transit trade, for this inner customs line prevented goods being sent not only into France, but also up the Rhine and into Germany. During the winter months, when the Baltic was ice-bound and even the northern ports of Germany were not always open, goods for Russia used to pass through Holland, and Russian exports were forwarded by Dutch agents. The course of trade is now quite different. In former times this transit trade was one of the chief sources of wealth of the merchants of Amsterdam and Rotterdam. The Emperor meant to destroy it. Not content with his inland customs line, he insisted on taking advantage of a clause in the commercial treaty between France and Holland, by which he was allowed to have customs agents at the mouths of the Dutch rivers. He contended that 'river' included 'canal,' and ordered Louis to admit the French customs officers to every little fishing-village along the Zuyder Zee. In order to ensure the repression of the contraband trade there were to be French garrisons along the coast. It would be a veiled annexation of the kingdom followed by the impoverishment of its people.

Louis felt, and was justified in feeling, that if he was to remain King of Holland he must not be a mere puppet presiding over the ruin of the country ; that if he was to have any hope of popularity, of handing on his crown to his son, it could not be as the royal chief of a French custom-house organisation. This was why he made a last effort to gain time, to preserve some shreds of independence, in the hope that perhaps peace with England would put an end to an intolerable situation.

Although it is anticipating the course of events, it may be well to note here that before the end of this same year 1810, Napoleon, by his efforts to compel the Czar to enforce the blockade against American ships conveying British goods, took the first step towards the rupture with Russia that led finally to Moscow and the horrors of the winter campaign of 1812. It was the Czar's determination not to consent to the commercial ruin of the Baltic ports which brought on the war. Alexander pursued the same policy as Louis, but unlike the weak King of Holland, the ' Czar of All the Russias ' was able to defy the would-be dictator of Europe.

Before leaving Holland Louis, who was fully aware that the crisis was at hand, had taken certain precautions. He might be forced to temporise, so he told his ministers that they must not consider any despatch signed ' Louis ' to be his free act. They were only to regard as genuine expressions of his ideas letters signed with his Dutch name ' Lodewijk.' In case the French army should advance from Antwerp or Brussels to occupy his fortresses, unless they had his orders to the contrary, the commandants were to offer a passive resistance, withdraw all detachments inside the works, close the gates and raise the drawbridges. He foresaw the possibility of a repetition of the policy Napoleon had adopted in Spain : occupation of the fortresses by French troops and forced abdication of the king.   The President of the Council of Ministers, Van der Heim, was to act for him in his absence, and he left him full instructions for various eventualities.   Roell, his Minister of Foreign Affairs, accompanied him.

His first interview with the Emperor was a mere matter of ceremony.   At the second meeting Napoleon spoke of his projects with brutal frankness.   He told Louis he meant to annex Holland.   If he agreed, he might either return to live in France as a Prince and Constable of the Empire, or he would find him another throne in Germany.   If he resisted, it would be war, and no compensation for his dethronement.   ' Holland,' he said, ' is nothing but an English colony, more hostile to France than England herself.   I mean to eat up Holland ! ' Louis asked for time to consider his policy.

On December 3rd the Corps Législatif opened.   The King of Holland was given a hint that he had better not be present. It would be embarrassing.   He acted on this advice.   In his speech from the throne the Emperor said : ' Holland, situated as it is between England and France, is in difficulties with both. It is the outlet of the chief waterways of my Empire ;   changes will have to be made there ; this is an inevitable necessity for the safety of my frontiers, and for the interests of my Empire viewed in their true light.'

For two days Louis kept away from court.   Then the Emperor sent for him, and told him he would have to abdicate. Forty thousand troops of the Army of the North, commanded by Marshal Oudinot, were under orders to march into Holland.

Thus challenged, Louis suddenly lost his courage and tried to move the Emperor by protestations of his devotion to him, and suggested a compromise.   The annexation of Holland would, he said, be a calamity for both countries.   Even France would be a loser in the end.   He was ready to accept the Emperor's policy as to the blockade and cede to him all the country up to the left bank of the Maas.   In exchange he hoped to have the Grand Duchy of Berg, which the Emperor had already assigned to the heir of the crown of Holland, Napoleon Louis, reserving the actual administration of the duchy for himself till the Prince came of age.   •

The orders for the occupation were suspended.   Napoleon

seemed willing to negotiate, but for a few days he was taken up with the formalities of the divorce from Josephine, which was declared on December 15th. Instead of attending exclusively to the affairs of his kingdom, Louis was ill-advised enough to petition the Emperor, two days later, to allow him to arrange a formal separation from Hortense. She raised no objection to this, leaving the decision entirely to the Emperor. He referred it to a family council, which met, of all days, on Christmas Eve, and decided that a public decree of separation would cause unnecessary scandal ; husband and wife might agree to live apart, and the Emperor could settle what was to be the share of Hortense in her husband's property. Napoleon ended the matter for the present by deciding that Hortense might live on in Paris, and giving her the custody of her two sons, an income of half-a-million francs, and certain of her husband's French estates. Louis was deeply disappointed at not having the custody of his eldest son, to whom he was strongly attached. He saw too late that he had made a mistake.

As for Holland, the Emperor made a new offer to his brother, telling him at the same time that he doubted if he would be able to observe the conditions he imposed, and predicting that the compromise would only delay the annexation for a while. Louis was to cede to France all his territory up to the left bank of the Rhine ; he was to forbid all trade and all communication with England ; he was to maintain an army of 25,000 men, and build and keep up a fleet of 14 ships of the line, 7 frigates and 7 smaller craft. Finally, he was to suppress the rank of marshal in his army and navy, and abolish all privileges of nobility. On these conditions he would remain King of Holland north of the Rhine, and the Emperor would withdraw his customs agents. On the first failure to observe the new treaty Holland would be occupied.

Louis told his brother that he had no other course open to him but to accept these terms. Roell, his minister, could arrange all details with Champagny, the Emperor's Minister of Foreign Affairs ; meanwhile he would go back to Holland and take his eldest son with him.

Napoleon turned sharply on him. The boy must remain in France, and he himself would not be allowed to go till all was signed. 'Do you mean to set your police agents on me and stop me?' asked Louis. 'Yes,' said Napoleon, 'if you try to go. What are you going for? Is it to raise a revolt against me?' Louis had been in communication with the Russian ambassador, sounding him as to the possibility of foreign support. He must have wondered if the Emperor's secret police had got wind of his intrigue. He told Napoleon that though he wished to ·be in Holland, he would submit to delay his departure.

Then through Roell he fought the treaty line by line, asking for concessions, modifications, in every clause. To Holland he sent by a trusted messenger orders to his ministers to be prepared for passive resistance to a French invasion, to concentrate a force of his troops at Amsterdam, and be ready to send the gold in the bank of Holland out of the country. He personally pressed the Emperor to give Holland some territorial compensation for the cession of the left bank of the Rhine. He protested that though personally willing to accept the new treaty, he ought to have the consent of his people, and should be allowed to go to Holland to consult them. Napoleon replied that he could summon, say, thirty leading men from Holland to come to Paris, as the representatives of the people. This was just the way in which the Spanish Notables had been brought to Bayonne to witness the abdication of Charles IV. and the proclamation of King Joseph. With that precedent in his mind Louis rejected the proposal. The Emperor saw that he was trying to gain time, and decided to act in order to force his brother's hand.

On January 14, 1810, Oudinot informed the governors of Bergen-op-Zoom and Breda that he was directed by the Emperor to take possession of these two cities. The Dutch officers replied by closing their gates, and refusing to admit French troops within their walls except by order of King Louis.

Napoleon was furious when he heard the news four days later. He made his Minister of War send Louis a letter telling him that a grave offence against the Emperor had been committed; that no commandant of the allied troops had a right to close his gates against a Marshal of France; and that he himself, as Constable of the Empire, should be ready to welcome French troops to any of his cities. He must at once direct his governors of Breda and Bergen-op-Zoom to allow Oudinot's troops to be quartered in their towns.

To the Emperor Louis pointed out that it was not a mere question of giving a hospitable reception to French troops ; if it had been there would have been no difficulty. But Oudinot had talked of seizing Breda and Bergen. ' Oudinot is a fool,' said Napoleon. ' He ought to have stormed both places and hanged the commandants. I shall have to hang them myself.' ' If any one is to be hanged it should be your brother,' replied Louis, and told the Emperor his officers had acted by his orders. If it was not a seizure of the fortresses, but a matter of allowing French troops to occupy them side by side with his own, it was different. Oudinot's troops could be admitted. He would send orders at once.

Napoleon had already directed Oudinot to occupy the country between the Scheldt and the Meuse ; to take under his command the Dutch troops in Brabant as well as his own ; to leave the Dutch authorities in possession of their offices, but to supersede their action by proclaiming martial law. Louis was told that if there was any resistance, he would be responsible for the bloodshed that would follow. Louis could not hold out against such a threat. He directed his officers in Dutch Brabant to place themselves under the Marshal's orders.

Thus part of Louis's kingdom was gone, but if he could gain time, there was still a faint hope of saving most of it. There were rumours of a possible peace with England. The Emperor was negotiating, and the Dutch ministers sent an agent to London to watch over their interests. If there was peace, the reason for the annexation of Holland would be removed, for trade would be reopened. But though the negotiations dragged on for some time, they never went beyond the stage of inconclusive preliminaries.

Meanwhile, in the beginning of February, Fouché came to Louis. The Emperor had asked him to take the Dutch business in hand, and he said he could get more favourable terms for the King of Holland. The Emperor would be content with the left bank of the Meuse, and he could convince him that Holland could not afford to maintain 28 warships and 25,000 men. The terms must be made lighter. Why Fouché was brought in is not clear. His intervention made Louis hopeful, but suddenly came news that made the poor King fear he was being played with, and that the Emperor would take everything. French troops were being moved into Holland from Germany ; they were marching on Nymeguen. Not the Meuse, but the Waal, was to be the limit of the French occupation. Louis wrote to his ministers to put Amsterdam in a state of defence. He left it to them to decide whether they would hold the capital against the French in case of a further advance.

The ministers formed a committee of defence calling admirals, generals, and burgomasters into their council. They brought up guns, and prepared to lay the neighbouring country under water. La Rochefoucauld, the French ambassador, protested, and told them they must stop work. They replied that they would consult the King. He reported to the Emperor that the Dutch were preparing for a revolt.

Before he received the report of his ministers Louis had written another letter to them, telling them that all he wanted was a show of defence, which would make Napoleon hesitate to go to extremities. He knew the Emperor did not want to give Europe the spectacle of an army of invasion shooting down his brother's troops. Nor did Louis mean that there should be bloodshed. As soon as the French showed they meant to attack Amsterdam, they were to be admitted under protest. When Napoleon received his ambassador's report he told Louis that if the preparations at Amsterdam did not cease, he would tell Oudinot to occupy the whole of Holland and proclaim the annexation. Again Louis gave way. He even pretended his ministers had gone beyond his orders, and dismissed two of them. He declared he would be content with a settlement that would leave him Holland north of the Waal.

Then again he began to waste time over long discussions of details, though Champagny, the Emperor's minister, told him the sooner a treaty was signed the better. The Emperor might lose patience at any moment. For some days nothing was done. Louis was ill, broken down by anxiety, he said, and would see no one. Napoleon thought it was a diplomatic illness. Champagny was directed to draft the treaty. Louis saw that further delay was impossible.

On March 16th he signed the arrangement that handed over to France the country up to the Meuse ; made him a mere provincial governor of the rest of Holland, with the title of King ; imposed French control on his policy, and placed French garrisons on his coasts to stop all trade with England. Then after he had figured in the fêtes for the arrival of Marie Louise, as a Prince of the Empire, Napoleon allowed him to return to Holland, but on condition that Hortense accompanied him, so that there might be no scandal.

On April 11th he reached Amsterdam. He had sent word that there was to be no demonstration on his arrival, and he had shown his discontent with the new state of things by dismissing most of the French members of his household. Hortense followed him, accompanied by Napoleon Louis, but leaving her younger son in Paris. She arrived at Utrecht in the middle of April, made a stay of ten days there, and rejoined Louis at Amsterdam on the 24th. Louis made no secret of the fact that her coming was a mere ceremonial visit forced upon him.

The French were not only occupying the coast. It seemed as if only Amsterdam would be left to the Dutch. French troops entered The Hague and Utrecht. To Louis's protests Napoleon replied that Holland was such a labyrinth of water-ways that effective surveillance could not be exercised by mere detachments on the seashore. On May 5th Louis went to Antwerp to see the Emperor, who, accompanied by Marie Louise, was making a progress through the northern departments. The interview was disappointing. Louis learned that all hope of an arrangement with England was at an end, and Napoleon told him he would insist on the strict execution of the treaty, and reproached him with encouraging hostility to France in Holland. Louis had already told his ministers that he was ready to abdicate rather than prolong the existing situation, but they had replied that as long as he was king, and some vestige of independence remained, they could still hope for a change for the better. His abdication would only mean complete annexation.

On May 16th Hortense suddenly left Amsterdam, and, after a short visit to the château of Leu, went on to Plombières. It was her final parting with her husband. The tension in

Holland rapidly became more acute. At Amsterdam the coachman of the French envoy was stoned by a mob. At Utrecht and Rotterdam French officers were insulted. The French customs officials, not content with keeping a strict watch on the coasts and in the ports, began to stop, search, and seize barges on the canals far inland, on the plea that they were conveying English goods. Very few of them could speak Dutch, and this made their interference a still greater source of trouble. The resistance of the people to their action was not infrequently supported by King Louis's officials. The movement of French troops created a general feeling of unrest.

There were renewed rumours that Amsterdam would be occupied. Louis demanded of the French agent, Serrurier, a pledge that this would not be attempted, telling him that he could not answer for the peace of the city in the presence of such an aggression. He had already removed from office Van der Poll, the Burgomaster, on account of his French leanings, and he had protested against a column of French troops marching through Haarlem while he was staying at his villa in the suburbs of the town.

At last in June Napoleon wrote to Serrurier a letter, which showed that he had determined on making Louis's position impossible, and forcing on the abdication. He directed his envoy ' to keep the quarrel open,' and to press for reparation for the insults offered to the French uniform and the livery of the embassy. The leaders in the attack on the coachman ought to be arrested and hanged. Van der Poll was to be reinstated in his office. As for the King's threat to oppose the occupation of Amsterdam by French troops, and his protest against their march through Haarlem, it was an insult to the French army. ' His eagles ' were welcomed in every city of the Empire from the Ebro to the Vistula. It was intolerable that an Imperial Prince, the Constable of France, should show hostility to them, even if he were King of Holland, a kingdom that owed its existence to the French army. Orders had been sent to Oudinot to occupy Amsterdam if full satisfaction was not at once given to the Emperor's demands.

The Dutch ministers replied to Serrurier that they could not identify the people who had attacked his servants, and

Louis hinted that the affair had been greatly exaggerated. He reinstated Van der Poll as Burgomaster, but he refused to invite a French occupation of his capital, and protested that the treaty was being enforced with unnecessary rigour, and in a way that must alienate all sympathy with France in Holland. He was informed by Serrurier that the Emperor had decided on sending a French contingent to Amsterdam under Oudinot's orders, the reasons alleged being the insults to French officials and the danger of the capital becoming a centre of revolt. Oudinot would march in on July 4th, and had orders to send to France all the guns that had been mounted on the defences of the city. Serrurier pointed out that resistance would be impossible, and the best course for the King was to arrange with the municipality to give a public welcome to Oudinot's troops.

Louis had gone to Haarlem. In the last few days he had thought vaguely of an appeal to the European powers, to Russia and to Austria. He had talked with his generals and his ministers of the possibility at the last moment of meeting this aggression with armed resistance. The soldiers told him it was too late. Before the French occupied the country north of the Waal, the dykes could have been opened, and all the might of France defied, at least until the winter made the flooded country passable for troops, as in the days when Pichegru overran Holland and captured a fleet frozen in the ice at Texel with his dragoons. Before the ice came England, and perhaps other Powers, might intervene. But it was now too late for such a daring policy, for the French controlled most of the sluices. The ministers informed him they could hold Amsterdam, but only for a few days, and the result would be the ruin of the city.

Louis told Serrurier that Oudinot would not be welcomed, but there would be no resistance. On the day he entered Amsterdam the King of Holland would cease to reign. He would not prolong a humiliating situation for a day longer.

It was on June 28th that Louis was informed of the coming occupation of Amsterdam. Beyond his statement that this meant the end of his reign, he gave no information as to his plans, and to the last moment Serrurier hoped he would accept the new position of affairs. But in private the King was busy

Q

with a few trusted friends, his Minister of Police, Hugenpoth, and his two aides-de-camp, General Travers and Rear-Admiral Bloys van Treslong. He sold through a banker some of the Dutch estates he had bought. He handed his diamonds to a business agent to be sent out of the country. He left his son at Amsterdam with the Grand Marshal of the Court, to whom he gave sealed directions for his conduct. He drew ten thousand francs in gold from the bank, and sent one of his equerries to see that relays of horses were ready up to the eastern frontier. Hugenpoth provided a series of passports with the names in blank.

All day long on the 1st and 2nd of July he was busy writing in his study at Haarlem. On the 3rd, late in the day, he sent a courier to the ministers at Amsterdam, to hand them three documents. First, his formal act of abdication in favour of his son Napoleon Louis, and failing him of the Prince's brother Charles Louis Napoleon; secondly, a protest against the occupation of his capital and the other acts of the Emperor, including what he described as the forced signing of the treaty of March 16th. He declared that the independence of Holland was being destroyed by acts of violence, which were an outrage on the law of nations. Finally there was a proclamation to the people of Holland, which was to be posted on the walls of Amsterdam at dawn on the 4th, before the entry of the French troops. It bade ' his people ' farewell, informed them of his abdication, repeated in briefer terms his protest, told them he had striven in vain to guard their independence, and commended his son to them.

After having despatched these documents, and with the help of his two officers put together his papers and some personal belongings, he sat down to dinner. There were several guests, and after dinner the evening was passed in the usual way. A number of officers and courtiers and their wives were in the salon of the château. There were card-tables set out, music, conversation, the unpleasant topics of the moment being avoided, except where men exchanged impressions outside the general circle. At half-past ten, when the party broke up, no one except General Travers, the Admiral, and the King knew what was going to happen.

At eleven a carriage with four horses mounted by postilions

drew up in a lane near the château, on which a small doorway in the garden wall opened. Outside the wall there was a muddy ditch, crossed by a bridge of a single plank, leading to the little door. The door opened, and out came the King and his two officers. They had no servants with them, and they carried the light baggage for the journey themselves. A postilion held a lamp. Suddenly, just as all was ready, Louis remembered a portfolio he had left in his study, and went back for it. A favourite dog followed him out. But as the King walked across the narrow plank he slipped and fell into the ditch. He was helped out, wet and covered with mud. It was proposed that he should go back and change. But he refused. No more time should be lost. The party, with the dog, got into the carriage. The postilions mounted, and the carriage started through the dark night by the willow-bordered road along the canal bank towards Amsterdam. It passed by the outskirts of the capital, and then the postilions turned inland, avoided Utrecht and the outposts of Oudinot's army, and disappeared into the flat lands of Guelders round sleeping Amersfort. At the posts where horses were changed it was stated that the party were three officers travelling on public service. At one of these changes the dog was run over and killed. Louis was greatly distressed at the loss of his favourite. It was, he said, part of his bad luck, that now haunted him everywhere. As the early dawn came the travellers were far towards the German border.

Next day as Oudinot's troops marched into Amsterdam, where they were received in sullen silence, the rumour spread that the King had disappeared. The ministers were told that they must take no step till the Emperor's will could be known, and when Napoleon's orders came his will was declared to be the annexation of Holland. Prince Napoleon Louis was to be sent to St. Cloud.

For a fortnight Napoleon could learn nothing of his brother's movements, beyond the fact that he had crossed the German frontier and passed through Osnabrück. He feared that Louis might attempt to embark for America, or still worse for England. The North German ports were guarded. Inquiries were made in every possible quarter. But in these days there was no network of telegraph wires, no army of newspaper correspondents eager to solve a mystery. A fortnight went by after Louis's disappearance before the Emperor learned that he was at the baths of Töplitz, in Bohemia.

Thus in the summer of 1810 Lucien and Louis sought refuge in foreign lands. Lucien had been long in revolt, but Napoleon had thought up to the very last that Louis was too weak to break openly with him.

CHAPTER XVI

KING JOSEPH AND THE MARSHALS
WESTPHALIAN AFFAIRS

(1809-1810)

OF the three Bonaparte kings two still remained: Jerome at Cassel, playing the part of a would-be *Roi Soleil* in his sham Versailles of Napoleonshöhe; and Joseph at Madrid, struggling to uphold his insecure throne, threatened at once by native revolt and foreign intervention, and, as he judged, endangered as much by his brother's policy as by the opposition of the Spanish patriots.

After the victory of Wagram Napoleon thought of himself taking command in Spain, and more than once in the next twelve months he actually made preparations for leaving Paris for the Peninsula; but first the business of the divorce, then his second marriage, and after this the new organisation of his Empire, detained him month after month in his capital, till at last the centre of interest for him changed from the Spanish peninsula to northern Europe.

But though he did not come in person, he sent to Spain some of his most trusted generals and all the troops that could be spared from the vast army of many nations that had to be maintained to garrison the provinces of his Empire. A hundred thousand men, veterans or conscripts, crossed the Pyrenees. Tens of thousands of them had marched across half Europe before they reached the Spanish border. An army of 80,000 under Massena descended the valley of the Tagus and invaded Portugal, pressing Wellington and the British back to the fortified lines of Torres Vedras, where for long months of 1810 they stood at bay, safely supplied from the sea, while their enemy, depending on a long line of communications on which his convoys were at the mercy of the guerillas, could only maintain his army with difficulty, and lost thousands by disease and privations. But with the British thus shut up in a corner of Portugal, the French had for a while a free hand in the rest of the Peninsula.

For a short time it looked as if King Joseph might hope to bear down all opposition, and even win a great part of the Spanish people to his side. But the chances of success were crippled by divided command and disunited policy. The movements of the French armies were directed partly by Napoleon through the Paris War Office, partly by King Joseph and Soult, who was now his chief of the staff, and a much more efficient helper than Jourdan had ever been. The limits of these two authorities, Paris and Madrid, were ill defined and were continually varying. At the beginning of 1810 Napoleon looked for the chief result to Massena's operations, which were directly controlled by his Minister of War. The position repeated on a vaster scale the situation at Toulon in 1793. Then, as now, the local resistance depended on the co-operation of the British. If they could be driven away, the native revolt must collapse. Everything therefore turned upon Massena's success, and the soldier Emperor thought only of this all-important operation, and considered that all the resources of the French in Spain should be directed to supporting it.

Joseph had formed a plan of his own. He was concentrating four *corps d'armée*, 60,000 men, in an ' Army of Andalusia,' that was to attempt the conquest of the south under his personal command. Joseph's army was moving through the snowy passes of the Sierra Morena before Soult's reports enabled the Emperor fully to realise what was intended, and he did not interfere with the operation, though he disapproved of it. French historians too readily assume that Joseph's southern campaign threw away the one great chance of expelling the British from the Peninsula. If, they say, these 60,000 men had been united to Massena's army; if he had crossed the Portuguese frontier with 140,000 men instead of 80,000, he would have driven the British into the sea. It is difficult to judge of what might have been, and easy to construct imaginary campaigns, but what actually happened in Portugal makes one seriously doubt if Massena would have

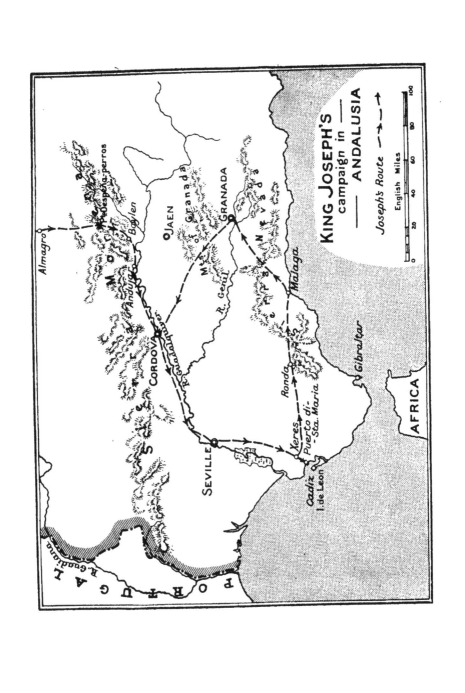

KING JOSEPH'S
campaign in
ANDALUSIA

Joseph's Route

English Miles
0   20   40   60   80   100

PORTUGAL

R. Guadiana

Almagro

Puerto-de-perros

Bojlen

JAEN

Mts. of Granada

GRANADA

Andujar

R. Genil

CORDOVA

R. Guadalquiver

S I E R R A

M O R E N A

S I E R R A   N E V A D A

Malaga

Ronda

Xeres
Puerto di-
Sta. Maria
Cadiz
I. de Leon

SEVILLE

Gibraltar

AFRICA

done any better with a larger force. One thing is certain. He found it so difficult to supply his 80,000 men that his army was half starved before the hnes of Torres Vedras, and it seems, therefore, not unlikely that a larger force would have only fared worse, and been forced by its miseries to retire sooner.

However this may be, not only Joseph, who was something of an amateur commander, but Soult, who was as good a soldier as any of the marshals and better than most of them, thought that Massena had quite as large an army as could be usefully employed in Portugal, and Joseph's plan for the southward march of the 60,000 had much to commend it. The Junta, which claimed to govern Spain, had been long established at Seville, which had thus become a rival capital to Madrid. In its cathedral hung the eagles and standards captured from Dupont at Baylen. To drive out the Junta and conquer the rich lands and historic cities of the old kingdoms of Granada and Jaen, Cordova and Seville, would give Joseph the prestige of success; and he believed that there was in Andalusia a large party which was tired of the war and ready to rally to his government on the morrow of a victory, if they could only be assured of generous treatment. That any serious resistance could be opposed in the field to his 60,000 men there was not the least reason to expect. So sure was he of triumphal entries into the cities of Andalusia that he took with him most of his ministers, his chamberlains and equerries, his carriages and plate, the ceremonial uniforms for his guard, rich hangings for improvised halls of state. The royal headquarters was made up of a crowd of courtiers and officials, as well as soldiers, and the personal baggage-train of King Joseph was a huge convoy in itself.

On January 8th the King joined the headquarters of his army at Almagro, a hundred miles south of Madrid, and ordered the general advance in three columns across the Sierra Morena. It was a few days before all was ready, and then the movement through the difficult hill country was somewhat tedious, but on the 22nd the army had passed the Sierra. Joseph himself had traversed the wild defiles of the Despeñaperros, and had occupied Baylen. The army of the Junta had been routed, almost without a serious stand, and had left in his hands 6000 prisoners and 25 cannon. He was able to date

the despatch which announced his success to his brother from
Baylen, hitherto associated only with disgrace and disaster.

Three days later he was at Andujar. Delegations from
the historic cities of Cordova and Jaen had come to meet him
there, bringing the keys of their town gates and declaring
their readiness to accept him as their king. Granada was
ready to submit. One of Joseph's Spanish officers, the Count
of Azanza, was sent with a detachment to receive its surrender.
On the 27th Joseph entered Cordova in triumph. There
other deputations were waiting for him, and a message from
Seville told him the Junta had taken refuge at Cadiz, where
with the sea around them they could look for protection to
the English. Seville would welcome him. Perhaps it might
be possible to arrange even for the surrender of Cadiz itself.

After a skirmish on the 31st with some bands of patriots,
who tried to harass his march, Joseph entered Seville on
February 1st. It was a scene that might well make him believe
that he was at last the popular king of the Spanish people.
As he rode through the narrow Moorish streets at the head
of his Spanish guard (mostly Frenchmen in Spanish uniforms),
flowers fell in showers from roofs and balconies, bright carpets
hung from the windows, the lofty tower of the Giralda rocked
to the pealing of its twenty bells. At the Cathedral he dismounted and entered for the singing of a *Te Deum*. The
bishop and canons welcomed him, and gave back to him the
captured eagles and banners that Dupont had lost at Baylen,
and which had since been hanging in their choir. Deputations
of the religious orders were there also, and were promised the
King's protection. Then he went on to the palace, the old
Moorish Alcazar, second only in its splendours to the famed
Alhambra. There he was greeted by deputations from the
cities of Andalusia ; delegates of its four ancient kingdoms
of Seville, Granada, Jaen and Cordova, nobles and commons,
clergy and laity. In the courtyard were the gifts of some of
the noble houses that now declared for him, fighting bulls,
guarded by gaily dressed *toreros*, and richly caparisoned horses
led by pages in old-world costumes.

From the Alcazar of Seville Joseph addressed a triumphant
despatch to Paris, and gave the officer who carried it the
eagles of Baylen to be restored to the Emperor. He issued a

proclamation to the French army that had followed him, in which, addressing them as the 'soldiers of Talavera, of Almonacid, of Arzobispo, of Ocaña, and of the Sierra Morena,' he told them he would never forget their services, and bade them regard as brothers the Spaniards, whom they had freed from those who had misled them.

To the people of Andalusia he announced an amnesty for all who abandoned the Junta and accepted his rule, even for deserters from the royal army who had joined the guerillas. Those who wished might return to their homes. All prisoners would be liberated. Those who chose to serve in the royal army would retain their rank. All civil officials who took the oath of allegiance would be retained in their employments. For the maintenance of order in Andalusia, volunteers were called for to join a civil guard to be formed in each of the four kingdoms of the south.

Cadiz, and the island of Leon on which it stands, were now all that remained unconquered in Andalusia. On February 14th Joseph established his headquarters at Puerto de Santa Maria, on the opposite side of the bay of Cadiz, and attempted to open up negotiations for the surrender of the city. The committee of five to whom the Junta had handed over the conduct of affairs replied, ' The City of Cadiz, faithful to its principles, recognises no king but Ferdinand VII.' For ten days he tried in various ways to find a basis of arrangement with the provisional government at Cadiz, then on February 25th he left Puerto de Santa Maria and travelled by Xeres and Ronda to Malaga, where he arrived on March 5th. On the 2nd, in the hills near Ronda, there was an attack on his line of march by a party of guerillas. The King was himself under fire, and the enemy was repulsed by a charge of the royal guard and a squadron of French hussars. Apart from this unpleasant incident his journey was a peaceful progress, and he was welcomed in every town and village.

But now to the disappointment at Cadiz there were added other reasons for anxiety. In his reports to the Emperor Joseph had praised the discipline of the French army, but now he was every day receiving complaints of the misconduct of men, officers, and even generals, and the Spaniards were begging for protection and redress. Within sight of the royal headquarters the troops had behaved fairly well, and Joseph had too readily concluded that they were everywhere ' treating the Spaniards as brothers.' But they had all been trained in the Napoleonic school of ' making war support itself,' and with their pay in arrear and no reward for their efforts beyond a laudatory proclamation, they were levying contributions, making requisitions or openly plundering, and plunder led to other excesses, murder, incendiarism, and outrages of the worst kind.

Apart from any considerations of law and morality, this conduct of the Army of Andalusia had the serious result of making all King Joseph's well-intentioned efforts at conciliation useless. Among the people, who only yesterday hailed him with acclamations, a fierce hatred of the foreigners and their king began to blaze out anew. The prisoners he liberated, the civil guards he armed, deserted to the guerillas, the civil guardsmen taking with them the brand-new muskets and bayonets they had just received from French arsenals.

It was in vain that Joseph asked Napoleon to recall and disgrace some of the worst offenders. The Emperor was not much pleased with Joseph's bulletins of cheaply won victories, and the high-flown accounts of his progress through the cities of Andalusia. In fact he was somewhat irritated. He did not like his brother's independent action. He was annoyed at Joseph having, without consulting him, marched off 60,000 men paid out of the Imperial revenues, on an enterprise which he himself judged to be of no serious importance in the general plan for the conquest of Spain. Even the gift of the recaptured eagles of Baylen did not soothe him. He would rather they had been sent back by a French general, one of his own.

It was the time when he was coercing Louis and negotiating with Lucien. The divorce, his marriage with the Austrian archduchess, the hope of a son—all this, combined with his troubles with Louis and Lucien, made him think less than ever of his brothers as necessary to his success, and he was displeased at Joseph taking a line of his own. His displeasure increased when Joseph's despatches and the copies of his proclamations told him how far the policy of conciliation was being carried. He wrote to his brother that it was a folly to release prisoners, who ought to be sent to French fortresses ;

to pardon deserters, who ought to be brought before a court-martial; to put arms in the hands of Spanish volunteers, who would carry them off to the hills and join the rebels. He told him that in recognising rank given by the Junta he was putting false money into circulation. ' I cannot,' he said, ' have men serving in the royal Spanish army beside my own troops after having reddened their hands with French blood.' Joseph's complaints of French misconduct he disregarded. He even promoted men his brother had denounced. Spain must be treated as a conquered land; the army must live upon the country. To Joseph's requests for money he replied that he had none to spare. The generals must raise war contributions in the usual way.

Joseph saw that his policy of conciliation was being deprived of its only chance of success. The Emperor seemed determined to make him feel that he was only his viceroy. That there might be no mistake about it, Napoleon issued a decree, which by a stroke of the pen took possession of all the north and placed it directly under French military government. It was not as yet a complete annexation of the provinces of the north, but it pointed in that direction. Napoleon was enlarging the Empire he directly governed, at the expense of the tributary states. Before the end of the year he took Holland from Louis, Catalonia from Joseph, and the northern part of the Westphalian kingdom from Jerome, marking out all these lands into departments governed by French prefects.

In the refusal to listen to his complaints against the French freebooters, the rejection of his request for further financial help, and finally this partial annexation of one-fourth of his territory, Joseph saw a threat to make his whole position impossible—a menace made all the more formidable by rumours that Napoleon was tiring of the Spanish struggle and might perhaps try to make peace with England by throwing his brother over, offering him another kingdom, and sending the Prince of the Asturias to govern as Ferdinand vii. a Spanish kingdom, which would give to France the lands north of the Ebro and take Portugal in exchange.

Joseph, after his first successes, had written to his wife Julia to come and join him in Spain. In the presence of this new crisis he sent as a special envoy to Paris his minister Azanza, whom he had made Duke of Santa Fé and Knight of the Golden Fleece after the surrender of Granada. Azanza took with him another letter to Julia, a very remarkable document. Joseph told her that she must come to him, and before leaving France she must raise as much money as possible, selling property if need be, and obtaining from his bankers bills and drafts payable abroad, no matter where so long as the paper was sound, for he wanted to have funds at his disposal in a portable form. The fact was, he foresaw that he might find himself obliged to threaten his brother with an abdication, or Napoleon might force it on him, and in that case he meant to break with the Emperor and go abroad.

His friend and adviser, Miot, was already urging him to take this course. Miot did not believe in the possibility of permanent success in Spain. He told Joseph abdication was the best way out of a difficult position, and there could be no better time than the present. 'You should seize this opportunity,' he said, ' to separate your fortunes before all Europe from the Emperor's, and cast upon their real author the responsibility for the misfortunes of Spain. Fortune herself seems to have arranged this favourable opportunity for you. A brilliant campaign, the welcome given to you in Andalusia, the humane and moderate policy you have pursued, would all combine to make your retirement appear to be an act inspired by reason and self-sacrifice, and perhaps the people will do you the honour of expressing some regret for your departure, or at least will give you their sincere good wishes.'

Joseph hesitated what course to take. He still flattered himself that he might be able to impose his own ideas on the Emperor and retain his kingdom; and again, between such a success and an open breach with his brother, he saw a third possibility, the pleasant life of a country gentleman in France, with perhaps excursions at times into the field of diplomacy, the life he had led before his brother presuaded him to pose as a colonel at Boulogne and then accept his first crown in Italy.

Julia shrank from leaving Mortefontaine, and pleaded her bad health as a reason against going to Spain. Joseph, after a visit to Granada, had gone to Cordova in the middle of April. Thence he wrote to his wife : ' If the Emperor means to disgust me with Spain, I shall have to give it up without delay. In that case all I want is quiet. It is enough for me to have tried two kingdoms, and I don't want a third. For I want either to live peacefully on a property I shall buy far away from Paris, or to be treated properly as a king and a brother.' But it was for the second of these alternatives he still hoped.

It would have been better for him if he had boldly adopted the first, instead of clinging to a mere shadow of power. For Azanza's mission to Paris proved a failure. Instead of doing anything to satisfy the requests made by the ambassador, Napoleon issued order after order still further restricting Joseph's sphere of action. Berthier wrote to him that the Emperor could not allow him to interfere with orders sent to the marshals in the various provinces of Spain. Soult was to take supreme direction of military affairs and chief command of the armies everywhere except in Castille and a few districts round Madrid, to which Joseph had returned on May 15th. He found himself in command only of the royal guard and some minor French detachments of garrison troops, while the Emperor placed province after province under French military administration. Napoleon was still hoping for some result from Massena's campaign against Wellington in Portugal. In Spain itself the resistance of the patriots was at a low ebb. The marshals were fiercely trampling down all opposition, but at the same time making all Joseph's earlier attempts at conciliation seem to have been mere empty, if not treacherous, protestations of goodwill.

In July Joseph learned that Louis had fled from Haarlem and Holland was annexed, and then came news that Lucien too was in revolt and on the point of leaving Italy. The news from Holland ought to have been a clear warning to himself. On August 7th, the day that Lucien embarked at Cività Vecchia, Joseph sent another of his Spanish adherents, Hervas d'Almenara, to Paris with letters for the Emperor. He would wait at Madrid for Napoleon's reply, he said, but he begged that it might not be long delayed, for events were moving fast. The treatment he had received was alienating his supporters. He could not go to the army, where all right to command had been taken from him. At Madrid he was in charge of what—the hospitals, the depôts of the field troops, his guard, and the mere form of a powerless government. It would be useless for him to remain, unless the whole situation was changed. If his proposals could not be accepted, he must go.

'In that case,' he continued, 'I can only return to France and ask your Majesty to allow me to rejoin my family, from which I have been separated for years, so that I may find once more in the obscurity of my home the love and peace of which my throne has deprived me, without giving me anything in exchange, for to me it has been only a place of suffering from which I have had passively to look on at the devastation of a country I had hoped to make happy.'

His proposals were summed up under four heads : (1) that the French army should be under his orders ; (2) that he should have the right of sending away officers who conducted themselves badly ; (3) that he should be authorised to reassure the Spanish people by contradicting the reports, that were coming every day from Paris, as to an impending change in the government and the dismemberment of the kingdom by the annexation of the north to France ; (4) that the Emperor would show him the confidence he deserved, by allowing him to speak his mind to the Spanish people on all matters in the way he thought best befitted their position and his own without putting an unfriendly interpretation on his acts and words. If these concessions were made, he thought he could safely promise that the French army in Spain would not cost more than the two million francs a month which Napoleon was ready to pay—Spain would find the rest ; that the country would very soon be pacified, as the kingdom of Naples had been on the same system ; and that Spain would soon be a help to France instead of being, as at present, a source of loss and danger to the Empire.

To his wife Joseph wrote, a fortnight later, telling her he still hoped the Emperor would accept his proposals. If this were done, Spain would be pacified within a year ; 'but if the present system is not changed, Spain will soon be a blazing furnace, from which no one will be able to extricate himself with honour. They do not understand this nation,' he continued. 'It is a lion which one can lead with a silk thread by acting reasonably, but which a million soldiers cannot reduce by force. Every one here is a soldier, if one tries to govern by military force ; but every one will be a friend, if one speaks to them of the independence of Spain, the freedom of her people, the Constitution, the Cortes. This is the truth. Time will prove what I have said. Keep this letter, for it is prophetic.'

Almenara was no more successful than Azanza, and Champagny, the Minister of Foreign Affairs, told him plainly that the Emperor meant to annex the north of Spain as some compensation for the endless advances he had made to Joseph's treasury and the enormous cost of the military operations. Portugal would be given to Spain as a compensation ; but this was selling the bear's skin, for Massena had not yet driven the English into the sea, and no one was very sanguine about his succeeding.

Almenara returned to Madrid in the middle of November, just when Massena had abandoned all hope of forcing the lines of Torres Vedras, and was beginning his retreat into Spain after losing 30,000 men. This alone made it useless for Joseph to take any action on a proposal, brought from the Emperor by his envoy, that he should try to reopen negotiations with the Junta at Cadiz. He had lost the best opportunity for resigning, but even now it would have been wise for him to have acted on the alternative he had offered to Napoleon and refuse to remain after his proposals were rejected. Rumours of coming war in the north of Europe induced him to stay. If the Emperor took the field, he himself might hope for a freer hand in Spain. He clung feebly to his royal dignity, and was even weak enough to make the impossible suggestions to Napoleon, that if he left Madrid he might perhaps be allowed to resume his old place at Naples.

Jerome was the only one of the four brothers who was not forced into conflict with the Emperor, for, though there was more than one cause of dispute between Napoleon and his youngest brother, Jerome always submitted to the inevitable after a mere show of resistance. When he came to Paris at the end·of 1809, on the occasion of the divorce of Josephine, Napoleon informed him that he would add Hanover and some other minor territories to the Westphalian kingdom, subject to certain conditions, the chief of which was that out of the revenues of Hanover Jerome should provide for the pay, clothing, food and forage of a French division stationed in his new territory, as well as for that of the garrison of Magdeburg. He accepted the offer, and rejoiced at obtaining an increase of territory that would make Westphalia equal to Saxony or Bavaria, and give him ports on the seaboard and an opening for maritime trade. Always extravagant, he looked for an addition to his own personal resources now that his kingdom was thus enlarged, and he spent money and incurred debts on the most lavish scale during his visit to Paris, buying amongst other things a splendid royal crown, and ordering new state carriages.

On his return to Cassel he was disappointed at finding that the cession of Hanover was to be a very small gain, possibly even a source of loss to him. Lecamus, Count of Fürstenstein, had been left in Paris to settle the treaty of cession with Champagny, and the Emperor insisted on various charges being levied on the revenues of Hanover, which would leave no surplus after the maintenance of the French troops had been provided for. Jerome had expected to be asked to maintain about 12,000 French infantry besides his own Westphalian army, now more than 20,000 strong. But he found that besides some 12,000 men, troops of the line, he would have to pay for a division of French cuirassiers, 6000 strong, the most expensive arm of the service.

When he returned to Paris, to be present at the marriage of Napoleon and Maria Louisa, he tried to obtain some modification of these conditions, and explained to his brother that, anxious as he was to meet his views in every way, there was a limit to his own resources. He was in debt, and instead of being a help to him Hanover would be a new burden. The Emperor told him he must economise at Cassel. Why did he keep up a court that was more expensive than any in Germany ? This was the real cause of his difficulties.

Jerome knew that this was true. At Napoleonshöhe there was a continual round of costly entertainments, banquets, dramatic performances, masked balls, costume balls, and Jerome was trying the patience of Catherine of Würtemberg by his all but open amours with opera-singers and actresses, on whom he squandered enormous sums of money.   Even in Paris he was buying whatever took his fancy, mostly on credit. His two visits cost him something like a million and a half of francs.

However, he finally accepted Hanover, and made a visit to his new province.   He had hardly done so, when Napoleon informed him that there must be a redistribution of territory. It was the summer of 1810.   Holland had just been annexed, and in order to enforce the blockade of the Continent the Emperor wanted to have under his direct control all the coast of the North Sea from the Zuyder Zee to Hamburg.   He sent Jerome a map drawn up in the Foreign Office at Paris, showing all the coast districts of Hanover and all the Hanoverian and Westphalian territory along the frontier of Holland and the Lower Rhine annexed to the Empire, and divided into French departments.   Jerome was told that the changed situation in Europe and the interests of the defence of the Empire made this rearrangement necessary.

Napoleon's demand had an unpleasant resemblance to the proposal made to Louis to cede to France Zeeland and Dutch Brabant—a proposal which had been the first step to the annexation of Holland.   For a moment Jerome thought of resistance, but his ministers and his queen joined in urging him to avoid a quarrel with the all-powerful Emperor.   It was during this period of hesitation that an emissary of one of the German patriotic leagues proposed to him to act as a German prince, form an alliance with the other sovereigns of the Confederation of the Rhine and South Germany, appeal for help to the Czar and defy the Emperor.   He showed how little he was inclined to take such a desperate course by promptly informing Napoleon of the overtures made to him.

He told the Emperor he would conform in everything to his wishes, but he pointed out that not only was the best part of Hanover taken away from him, the richest lands, the mouths of the rivers, the ports, but that he was also being deprived of part of the old Westphalian territory, and he asked for compensation elsewhere.   Napoleon replied through Champagny that the cession of Hanover had never been ratified. True, the King of Westphalia had taken formal possession of it, but he had not fulfilled his obligations.   The pay of the French

R

troops in his territories was in arrears, and the generals were complaining that they were ill fed and badly provided. Repayments of advances made to Jerome by the French treasury, both principal and interest, were months in arrear. To hand over Hanover to the King of Westphalia would only increase his financial difficulties. He could not therefore ask any compensation for the loss of a territory that really did not belong to him. He was asked to cede part of Westphalia to the Empire, and in return he was to be given part of Hanover. This was abundant compensation. The Emperor could not hear of any further concessions.

Jerome felt that he was the victim of something like sharp practice, but he was helpless, and after a long correspondence and many appeals to Napoleon not to humble him in the sight of his fellow-sovereigns of Germany and his subjects, he gave way, and in a proclamation to the people of the ceded provinces bade them farewell and exhorted them to be loyal subjects of the great Empire.

New difficulties arose as Westphalia and central Germany felt the pressure of the strictly enforced coast blockade, but Jerome avoided anything more than the mildest of remonstrances. The Russian war-cloud was gathering, and Napoleon encouraged him with hopes of a better time to come, after new victories, perhaps a more important throne than that of Westphalia. Despite the disappointing experience of previous campaigns, the Emperor still clung to the hope that Jerome would some day prove himself a great leader in the field, and promised him an important command in case of war.

The outbreak of the conflict was still far off, but Jerome found a new amusement besides the masked balls and banquets of Napoleonshöhe. He formed a camp of exercise, reviewed his Westphalian troops, and ordered a magnificent uniform for the coming campaign. He would ride at the head of his army as a cuirassier. An artist was commissioned to design a helmet and breastplate. The plumed helmet was of silver, the cuirass of glittering steel was inlaid with enamels. While waiting for the war to begin, Jerome had the satisfaction of posing as a conqueror in his new helmet and cuirass at the reviews at Cassel. Considering that Napoleon promised him a high command, it is no wonder he believed that he possessed

Napoleonic talents for war, and if he ever had any doubt on the subject there were Vernet's pictures hanging on the walls of his gallery at Napoleonshöhe : the surrender of Breslau, with the Prussian garrison laying down its arms at Jerome's feet, the storming of the entrenched camp of Glatz, with the Prince riding under fire close up to the storming columns. So he forgot his debts, his troubles over Hanover, the wife and son beyond the sea, the menaces of German patriotism in Westphalia itself, and dreamed of battles to be won beyond the Vistula, and a crown as the reward of victory, perhaps the historic crown of a restored Poland stretching from the Carpathians to the Baltic shore.

CHAPTER XVII

THE EXILES—LUCIEN IN ENGLAND
LOUIS IN AUSTRIA

(1810-1811)

WHEN on that August day in 1810 the good ship *Hercules* of Salem, Massachusetts, anchored in the harbour of Cagliari, Lucien had no doubt whatever that he and his family and suite would be welcomed by the King of Sardinia and the English minister to his court. He had already written from Città to Hill, the English envoy, asking for passports for England or the United States, for without these documents he might be made prisoner at sea by the first British cruiser he met. In these days England did not recognise the principle, admitted at Paris in 1856, that the neutral flag covered either enemy's goods or persons belonging to a hostile state. Neither did the United States. The Stars and Stripes were therefore no protection for the party on board the *Hercules*.

Before venturing to land, Lucien sent ashore a letter to Rossi, the Sardinian premier, asking for permission to make some stay at Cagliari, and another to Hill announcing his arrival and asking him to support his request to Rossi. The replies were disappointing. Hill could not intervene in his favour. Rossi feared his residence in the island might lead to complications. To add to Lucien's anxieties the English frigate *Pomona*, which was in the bay, shifted her station and anchored near to the *Hercules*, keeping a close watch on the American ship. If he put to sea he would be quickly made prisoner. All that Lucien could obtain was permission to land, on condition that he remained under surveillance at the lazaretto or quarantine station.

Thence he sent further letters to the King and Queen of

Sardinia, enclosing letters of recommendation he had received from Pius VII. He also wrote to Prince Koslovski, the Russian ambassador, asking for his good offices. Instead of helping him, the Prince told the King that, as his master the Czar was the ally of Napoleon, he must oppose permission being given to Lucien to stay in Sardinia.

On August 14th the British frigate *Salsette* arrived in the bay, having on board Sir Robert Adair, the English ambassador to Turkey, a diplomatist who had already been employed on many important missions and was known to be the trusted confidant of the British ministry. The whole question was referred to his decision, and he went to see Lucien at the lazaretto. Sir Robert told him that he could not take up his residence in Sardinia, and when he said that he only meant to make a short stay and then proceed to the United States, the ambassador said this also was out of the question. The British Government could not allow it. General Moreau was already in the United States, where he had been in exile since he was involved in Pichegru's conspiracy against Napoleon in 1804. Moreau had been a friend of Lucien's. The Government feared that possibly Moreau and Lucien might venture on some enterprise in Spanish America, especially if there was any truth in the rumours of a peace between Napoleon and Ferdinand VII. Lucien protested in vain that he was done with politics. Sir Robert told him that the best thing he could do would be to go to England as a prisoner of war. He would be well treated, and allowed to set up his home there. Lucien asked for a passport to Plymouth, and suggested that as Adair was on his way home the *Hercules* with Lucien's party on board might sail in company with the ambassador's ship, the *Salsette*, and under her convoy, but Sir Robert would not take the responsibility of any such arrangement.

Adair sailed for England on August 16th. Lucien was still trying to obtain leave to stay in Sardinia, and talked of returning to Italy if it were refused. At last, finding his efforts useless, he told the British envoy that he was prepared to surrender as a prisoner of war, trusting to the generosity of the English Government to give him exceptional treatment. On the morning of August 22nd both the *Hercules* and the *Pomona* set sail. As soon as they were out of the territorial waters of Sardinia, the frigate fired a shot across the bows of the American ship, and her captain dipped his flag and lay to while a lieutenant and a prize crew came on board. Both ships then set their course for Malta, where they anchored on the 24th.

While awaiting the instructions of the British Government Lucien and his party, after a few days' stay in Fort Ricasoli, were allowed to reside at San Antonio, an estate which had formerly been the country seat of the Grand Master of the Knights of St. John. A company of infantry was stationed on the estate to keep guard over the party, and Lucien had to confine his walks within narrow limits and to give his word that he would not carry on any correspondence unknown to the Governor. Apart from these restrictions he was free to live as he wished amid very pleasant surroundings.

After he had been nearly three months at San Antonio, the orders of the British Government reached Malta. Lucien and his family were to proceed to England on board of a frigate; the *President*, which had been specially fitted out so as to provide for their comfort on the voyage. Arrived in England he would be allowed to choose a country residence, and would be subjected only to such surveillance as would assure the Government that he could not suddenly leave the country. After having reduced the numbers of his suite Lucien embarked with his party on board of the *President* on November 20th, and arrived at Plymouth on December 12th. It was blowing a heavy gale when the ship arrived, and in the evening the *President* dragged her anchors and was for a while in serious danger. Lucien had unpleasant impressions of his first sight of England.

Next day the weather had improved, and Lucien and his family landed. An immense crowd had gathered at the landing-place, and he was received with loud cheering as he made his way to the ' King's Arms,' where he was to stay a few days. His revolt against the Emperor, the great enemy of England, had made him a popular hero. At the hotel he received messages of welcome, offers of hospitality, from many of the great men of the country. He accepted the offer of Lord Powis to place temporarily at his disposal his country seat in Shropshire, Denham House, near Ludlow, at a nominal rent.

LUCIEN BONAPARTE

The English newspapers celebrated the arrival of the Emperor's brother as a triumph. They said that such was his tyranny that even his own kindred could not endure it ; and when they fled from his dominions, where did they find refuge ? —under the British flag, in the home of true freedom. Then there were self-approving comments on the generosity of a great people in giving hospitality to the victims of ' Bonaparte.'

The news that Lucien had taken refuge in England, and had received an enthusiastic welcome there, was a heavy blow to Napoleon. When his brother was preparing to leave Italy the Emperor had at first refused to believe that he was in earnest. At the last moment, on August 4th, he had changed his view as to Lucien's intentions, and written to General Miollis, the Governor of Rome, telling him that Lucien had been in correspondence with the enemies of the Empire, and might try to embark in order to surrender himself to the English. If he attempted to do so, he was to be arrested. The letter reached Miollis just five days after Lucien sailed from Città Vecchia.

As soon as he heard that Lucien had surrendered to the captain of the *Pomona*, Napoleon ordered his brother's name to be struck off the roll of senators. Lucien was further deprived of his annual income as senator and of other revenues derived from France, and neither he nor any of his family were to be permitted to re-enter the territories of the Empire. Lucien was in fact outlawed. Napoleon believed that he had from the first intended to settle in England, and now suspected that he must be plotting against him with his enemies.

Lucien was doing nothing of the kind. After a short stay at Ludlow he bought the estate of Thorngrove in Worcestershire, and settled down there to live the quiet life of a country gentleman. He soon had many friends, for there was a disposition to lionise the Emperor's brother, the exiled Prince of Canino. But he kept carefully aloof from politics. He gave some of his time to the completion of his great epic of *Charlemagne*. His wife Alexandrine, after reading her husband's verses, came to the conclusion that epic-maingk was not such a difficult matter, and set to work on a poem of her own, on the subject of the story of Bathildis, the Christian Queen of.Clovis the Frank. She wrote it in secret. It was to be a surprise for her husband.

Besides these literary labours and the education of his children, Lucien amused himself with arranging at Thorngrove the art collections that had been part of the cargo of the *Hercules*. There were pictures, statues, busts, bronzes, objects of antiquity from the Canino excavations, portfolios of engravings, cabinets of gems. Thorngrove became famous for its art treasures, and in the place of honour was displayed a bust of Pius VII., the gift of the Pope. There was not much Catholicity in the England of 1811, but Pius was popular, for he had refused to close his ports against the British flag, and the fact that he had been the friend and protector of Lucien made the Prince all the more welcome among his English neighbours.

He had not been long at Thorngrove when he found himself seriously embarrassed for money. His departure from Italy, his residence at Malta and Ludlow, with his suite and servants, the purchase of Thorngrove, the furnishing of the house and the installation of his collections, had made serious inroads on his purse, and then came a disaster. He had deposited some £8000 with a French banking-house in London, which closed its doors and stopped payment. He would have lost everything, only that he had received a warning from his friends the Barings and drawn out all the money that was on immediate call. But he was seriously embarrassed. Just then he received an offer of help from his brother-exile Louis. The ex-King of Holland had not heard of the failure of the London bank, but he thought that Lucien might be in need of his help, and without being asked he wrote to offer him a large loan.

Louis had been in Austria since his flight from Haarlem in the summer of 1810. On his arrival at Töplitz he had written to the Emperor of Austria asking for permission to reside in his states, and to the French ambassador at Vienna. In both these letters he announced that he had ceased to be King of Holland, and had assumed from his French property the title of Comte de St. Leu, the name by which he wished henceforth to be known. Then he wrote to Jerome and to his mother, telling them of his flight. In these letters, written a few days after his letters to Vienna, there were signs that he was still hesitating as to what his future policy was to be. He spoke of perhaps being allowed by Napoleon to live as a private individual either at the château of St. Leu or in the south of France, and seemed to be expecting some communication from him before definitely fixing his plans. More than a week after his arrival at Töplitz he had a new idea. On July 20th he wrote to Cardinal Fesch asking if he could not arrange to take over Fesch's property in Corsica and reside there, with the Emperor's permission. But he said he feared Napoleon would not agree to this.

Whilst thus professing to await Napoleon's decision as to his future arrangements, Louis drew up two solemn protests against the annexation of Holland and his own deposition, and forwarded them to the Emperors of Austria and Russia. He wrote to his ministers and agents in Holland telling them to collect various sums deposited in the Dutch banks, and realise certain properties, and transmit to him the money thus got together. Most of these letters were intercepted by the French police, and the French resident at Amsterdam informed Louis's correspondents that they must not touch any funds coming from the civil list, and that various properties claimed by Louis did not belong to him personally, but to the state. However, he was sufficiently well provided. He had brought a considerable sum with him ; more was sent from Holland, and his fine collection of diamonds, which had been placed in friendly hands, reached him safely. He offered to sell this treasure to Jerome for half a million of francs. Anxious as Jerome was to oblige him, and glad as he would have been to add the diamonds to his collection at Cassel, he had not funds at his disposal, and to buy them on credit—his usual way of obtaining what he wanted—would not have helped his brother.

At Töplitz Louis was following the cure at the local hot springs. It was the hope of obtaining some benefit from these that had made him choose the place when he left Holland. All his life, since he had wrecked his health by wild dissipation in Paris, he had been trying one cure after another. At Töplitz anxiety as to the future, irritation arising from the immediate past, had reduced him to a nervous state that partly explains his indecision and his frequent changes of plan.   His mother and his uncle Fesch were anxious to arrange for his return to France, and employed as a negotiator M. de Decazes, who had been in the service of Louis in Holland for a while, and had since acted on many occasions as an agent of his in Paris.   Decazes wrote to him that all his family were anxious to see him back at St. Leu and Paris, that the interests of his sons would be best served by his return, and that the Emperor would be ready to give him a friendly reception and make acceptable arrangements for his future position as a Prince of the Imperial family.

Louis's irritation had been increased by hearing of decrees published in Holland suppressing the civil list, confiscating much of what he considered his own personal property, and taking possession in the name of the Empire, not only of the palace of Amsterdam and château of Loo, but also of the improvised palace at Utrecht and the country house and park he had bought at Haarlem.   Decazes could get nothing from him by letter but complaints of the way in which he had been treated, so he left Paris for Töplitz to carry the negotiation on by personal interviews.

He reached the Bohemian watering-place on September 24th.   He spent a week there, and then accompanied Louis to Marburg, where the latter went to try a grape cure.   Decazes, speaking as the envoy of Madame Mère, Fesch, and Louis's other friends, urged that whatever might be his grievances in the past, there was still a future for himself and his sons as Princes of the Great Empire.   Would it not be better to make peace with the Emperor, and return to France ?   It was suggested that Louis might let it be supposed that he had quitted Holland in order to avoid any personal disputes over the annexation and to facilitate the fulfilment of the Emperor's policy.   His protests had not been published. They could be suppressed.   His stay at Töplitz could be explained as, not a flight from the Empire, but a visit to the watering-place for the sake of his health made with the Emperor's consent.

While Decazes was arguing with Louis at Marburg, La-blanche, the secretary of the French embassy at Vienna, arrived there bringing something like an ultimatum.   It was a letter from the ambassador, in which Louis, though addressed as a King, was summarily required to return to France. ' Sire,' wrote the ambassador, ' the Emperor orders me to write to your Majesty in the following terms. It is the duty of every French Prince and every member of the Imperial family to reside in France, and not to be absent from that country without the Emperor's permission. Since the reunion of Holland to France the Emperor has not objected to the King of Holland residing at Töplitz, as it appeared that the waters were necessary to his health, but the Emperor now requires that Prince Louis, as a French Prince, and a high dignitary of the Empire, shall return to France by December 1st next, at latest, under pain of being considered as disobedient to the Constitution of the Empire, and to the head of his Family, and of being treated as such.'

This summons did not make Decazes' task any the easier. Louis simply acknowledged the letter, but after an outbreak of irritation Decazes persuaded him to write a note to the effect that, if the Emperor would allow him to live quietly in some part of France or Italy, he would leave Austria. Having obtained this much the envoy hastened back to Paris. Louis did not remain many more days at Marburg, but when he left it, it was to settle down at a place still further away from France. He went to Gratz, the capital of Styria, a pleasant little city among the hills nearly a hundred miles south of Vienna.

In 1809, during the campaign of Wagram, a French army had been there under Eugène and had dismantled its old citadel. But this was the only trace left by war, and there was pleasant society in the place, in and round which there were many houses of the nobles of the province, besides the residences of retired Austrian officers ; and there was further the society provided by the garrison, the provincial authorities, the bishop and chapter, the university. The Archduke John, a soldier brother of the Austrian Emperor, was living there, and there was a little colony of French émigrés, some of them old soldiers of Condé's army of Mayence. Gratz was a miniature capital, with a pleasant life of its own, surrounded by beautiful country, with endless woods darkening the hillsides. It was to be Louis's home for some years to come. After a short stay at one of the inns he rented a country house in the suburbs, belonging to an Austrian officer, General Jordis, and took up his residence there, and, as the Count of St. Leu,. he paid a round of visits, introducing himself to the Archduke and the other leaders of local society.   He seemed to have quite given up the idea of returning to France.

On November 25, 1810, less than a week before the last day named in Napoleon's ultimatum, Decazes came back from Paris, bringing a passport for Louis, and the news that the Emperor would not ask him to take any part in state functions, but would allow him, as he had requested, to live quietly in any part of the Empire he might choose.   At the same time Decazes told him his family would like to see him near Paris, and added that no time should be lost in returning.   But Louis, though his conditions had been granted, would not hear of leaving Gratz.   In vain Decazes argued the point with him, and even implored him to return to France for his own sake, that of his children, and of his mother, who was so anxious to see him again.

Louis replied by harping upon his past grievances.   He would not trust the Emperor.   He could not become again a mere Prince of the Imperial family, and forget he had been a king.   He could not forget the ill-treatment of Holland or pardon it.   In France, under his brother's rule, he would only have to endure new humiliations and disappointments.   It was better he should live in obscurity as a private individual abroad, where there was no danger of his ever again being brought into conflict with the Emperor or sacrificed to his schemes.   For days Decazes tried to move him, told him he was conjuring up imaginary troubles in the future, exaggerating the grievances of the past.   At last he had to give up all hope of persuading Louis to yield, and he returned to Paris with the news that the ex-King of Holland was in a state of nervous depression, in which he looked at the darkest side of everything, and was not in the least disposed to take any step towards reconciliation with the Emperor.

On December 15th the *Moniteur* published the decree annexing to the Empire Holland and the north coast of Germany. It was also decreed that the ex-King of Holland should retain the personal title of King, besides the dignity of Imperial

Prince and Constable of the Empire, and should have, in compensation for the civil list he had given up, a revenue of two million francs charged on the treasuries of France and Holland, and the possession of certain estates. Louis protested anew against the annexation, refused all compensations, and wrote to his wife Hortense telling her she must accept no estates or revenues purporting to be given in compensation for what she had lost in ceasing to be Queen of Holland.

Hortense paid no attention to her husband's veto. She made no difficulty about accepting from Napoleon their house in Paris, all rights to the estate of St. Leu and a yearly grant of half a million francs. Her sons were at St. Cloud, and their education the Emperor would provide for. She had definitely parted from her husband, and soon it was hardly a secret that she had found a lover in a brilliant staff officer of the Emperor's, one of the young nobles of the old régime who had rallied to his victorious star, the Comte de Flahault, colonel on the staff, with a brilliant record of war service, and soon to be a general. At Gratz Louis became for some time almost a hermit, seeing few people except his doctors. He changed them from time to time, quarrelled with them, and offended the orthodox practitioners by accepting the treatment of one whom they regarded as little better than a quack. He amused himself with literature, writing poems, mostly of a melancholy kind,[1] and planning a more important work, a book on Holland which would be a defence of his policy. He corresponded with friends in Holland and in France and with his brothers. His letters were opened and resealed by an Austrian *cabinet noir*, and a secret police report noted his expressions of disapproval of Napoleon's attempts to coerce Pius VII. For Lucien, his colleague in exile and revolt, he felt a special sympathy, and this was how he came to offer him

---

[1] Here is a typical stanza from one of these poems, written at Gratz, but not published till many years later :—

> ' Victime de ma confiance,
> Sous d'injustes nœuds gémissant,
> Loin des amis de mon enfance,
> Je souffre et meurs à chaque instant.
> Jeté sur la rive étrangère
> Par un sort que je dois haïr,
> Hélas ! pour comble de misère
> Je ne dois ni ne puis mourir.'

further financial help out of what he had saved from the wreck of his fortunes in Holland.

In his first letter to Lucien Louis had offered to place in his hands his diamonds and a loan of 250,000 francs, half of a sum of half a million which he said he intended to leave him as a legacy. Lucien sent a trusted agent to Gratz to bring back the diamonds and the money, and the messenger handed to Louis a letter, in which Lucien said he hoped sooner or later to obtain permission to sail for America and hoped Louis would accompany him. But before the messenger reached Styria Louis's fit of generosity had cooled down, and he had changed his fickle mind. The agent came back empty-handed, bringing only a letter from Louis. He would like to know, he said, to what part of America Lucien intended to go. He thought that the United States would be the best refuge for them both, but he foresaw difficulties. He could not pass through any territory of the Empire, and even if he went he would have to return, if in a changed state of affairs France or Holland again asked for his services. The hermit of Gratz still dreamed at times of regaining his lost crown. As to the money and the diamonds, he said Lucien had misunderstood him. He only meant that he would leave him this wealth in case he died before his brother, which with his broken health was quite possible. He was sorry that at the moment he could not spare anything. His resources were barely enough for his needs.

Lucien, disappointed in this quarter, appealed to his mother, and she gave him 50,000 francs. The money was sent across the Channel with the help of a smuggler and paid to General Lefèbvre-Desnouettes, who had been made prisoner in a fight with the British cavalry in the Peninsula, and was living at Worcester on parole. Lucien was not named in the correspondence carried on through this secret channel. He was mentioned as 'Mr. Douglas.' An attempt was made to represent the payments as being on account of contraband goods, and Lefèbvre figured in it as being in negotiation with the smugglers in order to effect his own escape. In spite of these elaborate precautions the French secret police were able to report the whole affair to the Emperor, but he did not interfere with his mother's benevolence for Lucien, and pretended to know nothing of it. But he put a stop to another attempt of Lucien's to obtain valuable property on which he could have raised money in England. An agent had been sent to Italy to forward to Lucien cases containing some eighty valuable pictures and a number of statues and other works of art, which he had left ready packed at Rome and Naples. Napoleon had an embargo placed upon all these art treasures, ' lest they should be sent out of the country and fall into the hands of the English.'

In the early spring of 1811 Louis at Gratz heard the news of the birth of the son of Maria Louisa and Napoleon at Paris on March 20th. There was a direct heir for the Empire, and the sons of Louis fell into a secondary place. Till now in his more sanguine moments he had looked forward to the time when his own eldest son would reign as Napoleon II., and he himself would be the guiding mind of the Great Empire. Broken though he was in health, Louis hoped to survive to see this day, the coming of which might be hastened by the chances of war. The birth of the King of Rome made him feel more embittered than ever against the Emperor, who, he said, had robbed him of his throne, deprived him of the care of his children, and ruined his life. For his eldest son he had a strong feeling of affection. The boy, now titular Grand Duke of Berg, was being educated with his brother at St. Cloud. Louis looked on the child of Napoleon as the robber of his son's rights, and was for a while so miserable that even poetry and querulous complaints to his other brothers brought no relief.

The two brothers who were still kings were invited to Paris for the baptism of the heir of the Empire. The King of Spain was to be one of the godfathers, sharing that honour with the Emperor of Austria.[1] When the news of his nephew's birth and the invitation to Paris reached him in April 1811, Joseph was threatening to leave Spain for good unless the Emperor gave him more real authority. He had written to his wife, announcing his early departure, but he had already so often made the same announcement, that she did not take his message very seriously. The Emperor's invitation opened out

---

[1] The Emperor Francis did not come to Paris, but was represented at the ceremony by the Grand Duke of Würzburg.

a new possibility for him. He could go to France without definitely deciding as to whether he would return or not. That would depend on how far Napoleon was prepared to go in the way of concessions. To the Emperor he wrote that he would return to Spain if Napoleon thought it right he should do so, but he must put before him a clear statement of the circumstances that had made his position difficult, humiliating, all but impossible, and unless there was a prospect of things being made easier in the future, he was quite ready to abdicate and retire into private life.

After having held public rejoicings for the birth of the King of Rome—a review, a bull-fight, and a general illumination of Madrid—he left his capital, escorted by the royal guard, on April 23rd, and reached France by way of Valladolid and Burgos. In both of these cities he made a short stay, held a court, and delivered a speech that was meant to silence rumours as to his impending abdication and the annexation of Spain to France. He was pleased with the loyal addresses he received, and the welcome given to him by the Spaniards on the way. His friend the Duke of Frias had taken care that there should be no unpleasant incidents, and had organised these loyal demonstrations.

He reached Paris on May 15th, and took up his residence at the Luxembourg, which belonged to him as Grand Elector of the Empire. He stayed a month in France, and found time to make a visit to Mortefontaine, where he saw Julia again for the first time since her short stay at Naples. The baptism of Napoleon's son took place at Notre Dame on June 2nd.

There was some friction between Joseph and Napoleon arising from the Emperor's efforts to make his brother appear merely as a grand dignitary of the Empire, who happened to be also King of Spain, and Joseph's determination to keep up the fiction that he was an independent king visiting his Imperial brother of France. More important matters than these questions of ceremony were discussed between the brothers in two visits which Joseph paid to Napoleon at Rambouillet. They were hours together, with no minister or secretary present. Of what passed there is therefore no reliable record. On one occasion, when the brothers were

THE KING OF ROME

six hours together, those who waited in the anteroom could hear them raise their voices, and judged that for a while the discussion was an angry dispute. Joseph gained something, but not all he asked for. The Emperor granted him a subsidy of half a million francs for the next two months, and then a million each month till the end of the year, and after this had been settled made him a gift of two millions more. He would not extend his command beyond central Spain, but consented to a Spanish commissioner being attached to the general commanding each district, the Spaniard representing the King and having a voice in the civil government of the province and control of the administration of justice. The Emperor promised that attention should be paid to any well-founded complaints as to the conduct of his officers, and held out a hope of still further extending Joseph's powers as the situation improved from a military point of view. Though the British had been lately victorious at Sabugal, Fuentes d'Onoro, and Albuera, the outlook was not by any means hopeless. There were 300,000 of the Imperial troops in Spain, and they had complete control of several of the provinces, and many of the cities were, not indeed particularly friendly to the new régime, but tired of the war and anxious for peace and settled government. Joseph agreed to be patient and hope for the best, and on June 15th he left Paris for Madrid.

Jerome had also had various grievances to discuss with his brother, mostly complaints that the support of the French garrisons and the Westphalian army was bringing him perilously near to bankruptcy. The Emperor consented to do something to lighten his burden, and encouraged him with the hope of great things in store for him after the successes of the impending war with Russia, in which Jerome and his Westphalians were to play a great part. So he too returned to his capital in good humour. The Emperor had not made many concessions to the two kings, but he had made them hopeful for the future. It was his interest to let the world see that they were still his close allies. After the defection of Lucien and Louis the abdication of Joseph would have made a very bad impression in Europe.

CHAPTER XVIII

JEROME WITH THE GRAND ARMY IN THE
CAMPAIGN OF RUSSIA

(1812)

WHEN Jerome returned to Westphalia after the fêtes at Paris in the summer of 1811, he found that, whatever the Emperor might have promised, the burdens of his tributary kingdom were to be increased rather than diminished. With the shadow of coming war deepening on the Vistula, central Germany was becoming an armed camp for the Grand Army. Each week saw new battalions, squadrons, batteries arriving, and a considerable part of these forces were cantonned in Jerome's dominions. Davoût, who commanded at Magdeburg,' and had the general superintendence of the French concentration in central Germany, had never been on good terms with King Jerome, and not only insisted on money being found for his paymasters by the treasury at Cassel, and supplies collected from the country, but also took it on himself to set up military tribunals to bring to trial any one who resisted the exactions of his foraging parties. Jerome's protests only obtained a slight diminution of the contributions levied on his exchequer and his subjects, and could do nothing to prevent measures of harsh severity that prepared the way for the future revolt that was to cost him his throne. Thus, when on the report (which some of the French officers themselves considered baseless) that one of his soldiers had been ill-treated by some roughs at Brunswick Davoût sent a large force to live at free quarters in the city and threatened to sack it. When Napoleon was appealed to, he supported the Marshal, and declared that any place where French soldiers were assaulted would be put outside the protection of the law.

Jerome had promised to have 20,000 in the field for the coming campaign, and to leave 14,000 at the command of the council of regency at Cassel for the preservation of order. In maintaining this force and finding money for Davoût he had made his treasury bankrupt, and could only meet current expenses by raising loans on ruinous terms. But he consoled himself with the hope that he would not have long to trouble himself with the financial difficulties of Westphalia; and that as Joseph had been promoted from Naples to the more important throne of Spain, so he would soon resign his German kingdom for a more extensive territory, to be provided when the map of eastern Europe was redrawn after the coming victories over Russia.

On one point he did not allow lack of money to trouble him. The court of Cassel, the palace of Napoleonshöhe, were never the scene of more brilliant fêtes than during these months of the autumn of 1811 and the following winter. Balls, concerts, banquets, hunting parties, reviews followed each other day after day, and night after night. He had important guests to honour. Marshal Bernadotte, now chosen Crown Prince of Sweden, passed through Cassel on his way to the Baltic coast, and was received with such honours that Napoleon, who had always disliked the Marshal, wrote to Jerome an ill-humoured letter of remonstrance. Madame Mère also made a stay at Cassel, and Jerome took a special pleasure in showing his mother all the splendours of his court. He lost two of his old friends during this peroid. Meyronnet, Count of Wellingerode, his faithful companion since the days of his first adventures in the navy, had been exchanged for some British officers, and had returned to his post as Chamberlain of the court at Cassel. There was a quarrel over a matter of accounts, and Meyronnet resigned his post. He had hardly done so when his mind broke down, and he died soon after in a *maison de santé* at Paris. He had hardly left Cassel when General Morio, whom Jerome was about to appoint to the vacant post, was murdered by a groom, whom he had dismissed from the royal stables.

With the new year of 1812 all doubt as to the imminent outbreak of the great war was at an end. Jerome was to command not one corps, but the left wing of the Grand Army, which was to march through Poland, the land which he hoped would be his future kingdom. He set to work on his preparations for taking the field. This time he would go to war as a king, and his headquarters would be equipped regardless of expense. He had forgotten Napoleon's lessons of his last campaign, the warning that he should do his campaigning like a soldier and not like an eastern satrap. He was not the only commander of the Grand Army who tried to take into the field all the luxurious splendour of a court. Murat, King of Naples, was also about to make war like a satrap, but there was this difference. Murat was an old dragoon, ready on the day of battle to do his share of the hand-to-hand fighting like the youngest of his officers, and to leave all his wonderful array of tents, plate-chests, travelling kitchens, cooks and chamberlains behind him, and sleep beside a bivouac fire and make his supper of a biscuit if it was a question of a forced march or a swift pursuit. Jerome had never made war seriously. He had managed in most cases to have his headquarters in the palace of some city, and with the prospect of war on the Russian steppes he tried to take a movable palace with him, and made his own comfort and the ostentatious display, that he considered due to his rank, his first thought in preparing for his new command.

He was deep in debt and, as usual, the treasury was empty, but his good friends the Jews were ready to find supplies on business terms, and after a brilliant campaign there would no doubt be money in abundance to settle the accounts. His baggage for the field formed quite a formidable transport-train, with as many horses, waggons, and men as a brigade of artillery. The wardrobe alone took up seven heavy waggons, guarded by a staff of nine valets, besides the drivers and grooms. The catalogue of their contents, if given in full, would fill whole pages. There were uniforms of all kinds, every branch of the Westphalian army was represented. Of the plain uniform of the infantry of the line there was only one specimen, but there were four splendid uniforms of the body-guard, stiff with gold lace, and no less than seventeen cavalry uniforms. There were full dress and undress uniforms of a French general of division, uniforms of the Grenadiers and Chasseurs of the Imperial Guard, and besides these court dresses, hunting costumes, and plain clothes. There were sixty pairs of boots, and an immense stock of underwear, including two hundred shirts. There were 318 silk pocket-handkerchiefs. Besides these each waggon conveyed a supply of bedding and bedclothes, so that his Majesty might not run the risk of having to sleep wrapped in his cloak, even if part of his baggage-train were delayed on the road; and with the bedding there was packed in each case a silver toilet-service, and a dressing-case with gold-stoppered bottles, and ivory-backed brushes with the royal monogram and crown in gold. Several dozens of *eau de Cologne* completed the toilet equipment.

Then there were the waggons with tents, carpets, folding tables and chairs, mirrors, enough to set up a miniature palace at an hour's notice. And further waggons were set apart for the service of the table, a *chef* with his *batterie de cuisine* and his silver-lined saucepans was in command. He had his staff of assistants and waiters. There were chests of plate, table-linen, china and glass, and cases of champagne.

Then there was the master of the horse, with his grooms in charge of the royal horses, and the waggon-loads of saddlery, and the travelling-carriages for the King, his secretaries, his doctor, and his staff. One of the secretaries had the care of a cabinet containing a whole museum of decorations, stars, grand crosses, and the rest; and among the swords, of which there was a remarkable collection, there was the sword the Emperor had worn at Marengo, and which Jerome had got from him when as a boy he saw his brother on his return from the campaign of Italy. With the sword of Marengo, and such a splendid campaigning kit stretching over half a mile of road behind the royal headquarters, Jerome felt he was going forth to victory and glory.

Having thus made all the necessary preparations for facing the hardships of a Russian campaign, Jerome appointed his Queen chief of the council of regency, and left Cassel for Glogau in Silesia, the scene of some of his exploits of six years before. The two divisions of the Würtemberg *corps d'armée* were already marching eastward, and were to unite in Silesia with the Saxons, who were also to be under his command. The grooms, valets, and cooks with the waggon-train of his head-quarters had also been sent on in advance. For the present he was in command only of the 8th corps (Westphalians and contingents from other German states). But as soon as the war began he was to take command of the right of the Grand Army, formed by combining the Polish, Saxon, and Westphalian corps—a force of over 100,000 men.[1]

At Kalisch in Silesia he joined the 8th corps on April 10th. Notwithstanding the disputes he had with Vandamme in his former Silesian campaign, Jerome knew that he was a good soldier, and had agreed to the Emperor's proposal that when the three corps of the right wing were united Vandamme should act as corps commander of the Westphalians. He was in command at Kalisch, and with him was General Marchand, a French officer who was to act as Jerome's chief of the staff. The Emperor relied on Marchand to be a useful adviser to his brother, in whose own talents for command he still had some lingering faith, notwithstanding his previous experiences of 1806-7 and 1809.

Jerome only made a flying visit to Kalisch. He had orders

---

[1] Though we have to do only with Jerome's part in the campaign, it may be of interest to note how the force under his command fitted into Napoleon's general scheme. The enormous mass of men which he concentrated along the Russian frontiers between February and May 1812 was a European army of many nations, the French being a minority. The extreme left was on the Baltic, the right on the Carpathians, the line of the river Vistula marking the general front. The arrangement can be best shown by a diagram :—

Extreme Left (north).—10th Corps, Prussians (Königsberg).

Left Wing.—1st Corps from Hamburg.		
2nd ,, ,, Holland.		The Emperor.
3rd ,, ,, Metz. ·		
Main mass of cavalry under Murat.		
Centre.—4th Corps, Italians from Verona.		The Viceroy
6th ,, Bavarians.		Eugène.
Right Wing.—5th Corps, Poles (Poniatowski).		
7th ,, Saxons (Reynier).		
8th ,, Westphalians (Vandamme).		King Jerome.
4th division of cavalry (La Tour Maubourg).		

Main army of operations under Napoleon.

The Imperial Guard at Posen (to join main army as it advanced into Russia).

Reserve Corps.—9th at Berlin } in process of formation.
11th at Mayence }

Extreme Right (south).—The Austrian army about Lemberg, under Prince Schwarzenberg.

from his brother to make a rapid reconnaissance of the Cracow district, travelling incognito, so he set off with Lecamus and some of his staff officers, leaving Marchand and Vandamme in charge of the troops. The reconnaissance was a pleasant excursion. Amongst other places he visited the famous salt-mines of Wieliczka. Amongst the workers was a negro who recognised the King, told him that he had been for a while in his service in San Domingo, and was made happy with a handful of silver. On the 26th the excursion came to an end. Jerome received a despatch from the Emperor, ordering him to move up the 8th corps (Vandamme), the 7th Saxon corps (Reynier), and the 4th cavalry division (La Tour Maubourg) to Warsaw, actually occupied by the 5th Polish corps (Prince Poniatowski), and take command of the united force, the right wing of the main army of operations against Russia.

He sent orders to the generals to join him at Warsaw with their troops by May 2nd. There was already trouble with Vandamme, who being a practical soldier could not understand Jerome's way of commanding an army. He complained that the King's chief supply officer, a certain M. Dupleix, an official of the Cassel War Office, was neglecting his business, so that the troops were starving in a friendly country, and officers who had other work to do were at their wits' end trying to find food and forage, and forced to requisition them. At the same time Napoleon wrote complaining that he heard that Vandamme's troops were plundering the country. A letter from Berthier ordered Vandamme to shoot any soldiers who were caught pillaging, and to send back to Westphalia any officers who were implicated. And at the same time the bewildered general received a letter from the Count of Fürstenstein (Jerome's secretary and minister Lecamus) telling him that the King considered he had no cause of complaint against Dupleix.

When the march to Warsaw began Vandamme thought matters would be easier. His corps would leave a district that had been stripped of supplies. But there were now fresh difficulties. Marchand gave him an order of march for his divisions, and Vandamme issued the necessary orders. Hardly had he done so, when he received a different set of orders direct from Jerome, who neither knew nor cared what his chief of the staff had done. Vandamme protested that sudden changes like this meant confusion, overwork, discouragement and fatigue for men and officers. Jerome reminded him by letter that he must obey orders and not discuss them. The campaign was not beginning well.

In the first week of May the three corps were concentrated in the Warsaw district, Reynier's Saxons on the Vistula to the south-east, Poniatowski's Poles in the city and to the north of it, Vandamme's Westphalians away to the south-west. The cantonments and camps of the army were spread over a line of about fifty miles. Jerome made a rapid inspection of his army, travelling with six carriages and an escort of hussars. Horses for the royal train were requisitioned from the landed proprietors and peasants, forty or fifty for each stage, for the roads were heavy. After this rapid tour he returned to Warsaw, occupied one of the palaces, and began a series of receptions and entertainments. He was thinking of the hoped-for time when the Grand Duchy of Warsaw would be transformed into a kingdom, and meanwhile he had set up his court, which was brilliant with the uniforms of his officers and the national costumes of the Polish nobles, who came to welcome the brother of their liberator.

Prominent in the court circle was the Abbé de Pradt, the Emperor's ambassador to the Grand Duchy. Jerome spent many long hours in private interviews with the Abbé, asking him about Polish affairs, but listening impatiently and spending most of the time giving the veteran politician his own ideas. ' He talked everlastingly,' wrote De Pradt in his memoirs, ' and nearly always it was empty talk. He spoke enthusiastically of his brother, and I could see that he had a strong attachment for his wife and his relations. He seemed to me to have a most ardent ambition. He aspired to the throne of Poland, and he said to me one day, speaking of the King of Saxony, "That poor king! he thinks all this is for him ! " He did not speak well of the Poles, whom he characterised as " Gascons " and " poor creatures." He is showing his vanity at every turn, and told me he thought he had made a master-stroke of policy in selecting the Brühl palace and not the old royal palace as his residence, so as not to have the air of taking premature possession. . . . With a little more of legitimate claim to royalty and a little less of boyish vanity Jerome might have passed for a distinguished prince.'. The ambassador was evidently annoyed at being lectured for hours on high policy by a young man of twenty-seven, even though he was a Bonaparte.

But Jerome had other interests besides talking politics. Most of his time was given to his court, some of his amusements recalled the scandals of Cassel, and he spent money with open hands. Spendthrift as he was, however, he sometimes surprised his Polish friends by a touch of stinginess. One day a feeble old man was led into the circle of the court, leaning on the arm of a Polish noble. It was Naroski, a peasant who claimed to be more than a hundred and twenty years of age, the oldest man in Europe, born in the last years of the sixteenth century, when Louis XIV. reigned in France and Poland was one of the great powers of Europe, her bulwark against Turk and Cossack, against both of whom this old man had fought in far-off wars a century ago. He had been presented to Napoleon five years before, and the Emperor had given him a pension of 2000 francs. Jerome asked him some questions, listened to his broken replies, and dismissed him with a compliment.

The Emperor was at Dresden, holding his Congress of Kings. He had letters from Warsaw telling of Jerome's doings. Catherine of Würtemberg was at Dresden with her father. One day Napoleon told her to write to her husband that he was wasting his time. ' Before I gave him this command,' said Napoleon, ' I said to him, " If you intend to go to the army as a King, you had better remain at home." Why, then, has he come ? He had only to remain where he was.'

On June 5th all was ready for the general advance, and at last the Emperor sent Jerome definite orders to leave Warsaw. He was to march by Pultusk and Ostrolenka on Grodno, with the Poles and Westphalians and the cavalry, sending Reynier and the Saxons on a parallel line of advance more to the right, so as to keep touch with Schwarzenberg and the Austrian army. Bagration and the second Russian army was in his front. If Bagration awaited the attack, Jerome might look for the co-operation of Eugène and the central mass of the Grand Army. If, however, Bagration, as was expected, made a dash into Poland, Schwarzenberg would fall back before him and Jerome was to hang on the flank of the Russians, cut in behind them, and then, caught between his army and the Austrians, they would be surrounded and forced to surrender like Mack at Ulm. Jerome was not to consider himself bound by the letter of these orders ; they indicated the general plan to be adopted ; he must use his own discretion, according to how matters developed.

The more one thinks of these campaigns of King Jerome, the more one wonders at Napoleon's touching faith in his brother's military genius, and his persevering efforts to give the young man an opportunity for becoming famous as a victorious general. Napoleon was a judge of men, a supreme master of the science of war. Everything depended on a successful opening of the campaign. The destruction of Bagration's army might change the whole course of history. The Emperor had beside him men whom he could trust to do the best, marshals who had won their rank by a long series of victories, and whose very names were a pledge of success. Yet after all Jerome's previous failures he entrusted this delicate operation to the judgment of a young man, who was a mere amateur in war, and who would not have had command even of a brigade if his name had not been Bonaparte.

The march was to begin on the 15th. Meanwhile the Westphalians closed up on Warsaw. Before leaving the city Jerome gave orders that the Brühl palace should be kept ready for his return to the city. A trusted officer was left in charge of it. So busy was Jerome with these and other matters that the start was made three days late. It was not till the 18th that he began his advance, at the head of 80,000 men, with Reynier's corps some miles away to the eastward. He was to be at Grodno by the end of the month. Northwards the Emperor with the mass of the Grand Army was marching on Wilna, with the main Russian army under Barclay de Tolly in his front.

The Niemen at Grodno was the frontier line between Russia and the Grand Duchy of Warsaw, but before the river was sighted there was some skirmishing between venturous bands of Cossacks and Poniatowski's Polish lancers. Bagration had left only a small detachment to hold Grodno, and his army was to the south-eastward, on Reynier's line of advance, and looking as if he was contemplating that dash into Poland which Napoleon had conjectured to be his probable plan.

On the 29th Jerome was before Grodno. He ordered a column formed of three Polish regiments to storm the town, but instead of leaving the command of these troops to their beloved general, Poniatowski, the hero of the Wars of the Partition, he sent the Westphalian artillery general Allix to lead the attack, and reap the laurels of an easy victory. For the Russians only made a show of resistance. Can it have been because Prince Poniatowski was the national candidate for the Polish throne that Jerome thus took his battalions away from him, and deprived him of the first success ?

Time was now all-important. Bagration was retiring, followed up by Reynier, and the Austrians were pushing forward. By a swift advance Jerome might fall on Bagration's flank and force him to battle. But he wasted time. He entered Grodno on June 30th. From the captured town he sent off letters to the Emperor and to Queen Catherine announcing that he had opened his campaign with a splendid victory. Then he remained there for six days.

He quarrelled with Vandamme, deprived him of the command of the Westphalian corps, and directed him to return to Warsaw and await the Emperor's orders there. To Berthier, the Emperor's chief of the staff, he wrote complaining of Vandamme's conduct. The general's only mistake had been to report that he could get no supplies from Jerome's commissariat officers, and that his corps was being thrown into confusion by contradictory orders. Proud of his victory, and imagining himself already a great commander, Jerome actually sent Prince Schwarzenberg directions as to the movements of the Austrian army. The Prince replied that he had already given full orders to his army, and added with a touch of sarcasm, ' I am charmed at finding that his Majesty the King appears to approve of the movement I have prescribed for my army corps.'

From the Imperial headquarters, now at Wilna, came—not the congratulations on his victory which Jerome expected, but letter after letter expressing Napoleon's disappointment at his lack of energy and disapproval of his methods. On July 3rd Berthier wrote to him that the Emperor regretted that Poniatowski had not been left in command of his own troops in the attack on Grodno. ' General Allix had no business whatever there.' Generals should lead their own troops, otherwise there would be ill-feeling and lack of hearty co-operation. Next day the Emperor himself wrote that when he opened the last despatch from Grodno he hoped for news of Bagration's movements, and to hear that Poniatowski and the Poles were after him, but he found only complaints against General Vandamme. ' I cannot tell you,' he said, ' how annoyed I am at the little information you give me. It is impossible to make war in this way. You only occupy yourself with trifles, you talk of nothing else, and I am pained at seeing that with you everything is littleness. You are endangering the whole success of the campaign on our right. It is impossible to make war in this way.' The repetition shows how agitated the Emperor was as he wrote.

The next day the Emperor wrote Berthier a letter to be forwarded to Jerome. ' You will let the King of Westphalia know,' he said, ' that I am extremely annoyed that he has not sent all his light troops under Prince Poniatowski's orders in hot pursuit of Bagration to harass his army and delay his march. Tell him that after arriving at Grodno on the 30th he ought to have at once attacked the enemy and pursued him actively. Say to him that it is impossible to manœuvre in worse fashion than he has done, and that by disregarding all the rules of war and my instructions he has managed to give Bagration plenty of time to make his retreat, which he is carrying out at his ease.' He went on to tell Jerome that he had detached Davoût with part of his corps, and sent him off to the south-eastward of Wilna to try to head off Bagration, but Davoût would not be strong enough to stop the Russians, if they were not pressed by other troops from the westward. Prince Poniatowski was therefore to be hurried after Bagration with all the cavalry and light infantry. ' Tell the King of Westphalia,' Napoleon added, ' that all the result of my manœuvres, and the most splendid chance that ever presented itself in war, have been lost by his strange forgetfulness of the most elementary notions of war.'   .

Jerome had no idea that he had blundered so badly. On July 6th, after his long halt, he left Grodno, and before he marched off he wrote a self-satisfied letter to Queen Catherine. ' The Emperor,' he said, ' entered Wilna on the same day that I entered Grodno. So I hope he cannot fail to be pleased with what his right wing has accomplished. The few days I have halted here cannot have done any harm whatever.' But what Napoleon had foreseen had happened : Bagration was safe on the upper Niemen. He had left Reynier far behind him, and passed safely and at a considerable distance across the line of Davoût's advance. He had moved so quickly, that the Marshal never saw anything of his troops except a cloud of Cossack irregulars flung far to the north to screen the Russian retreat.

On this same July 6th Napoleon at last realised that he was risking far too much on his belief in Jerome. But even so he hesitated to do anything that would publicly disgrace the incompetent commander of his right wing. As a precaution he sent Davoût orders, which were to be kept secret for the present. The Marshal's operations must soon put him in touch with the King of Westphalia's army. In that case, but only ' if the good of the service should require it,' he was empowered as the senior officer to take supreme command of Jerome's three corps and his cavalry division and unite them to his own force.

He went still further. Jerome in reply to his complaints had written that he had not all his army concentrated at Grodno till the 3rd. That they were fatigued, and he therefore ordered a halt on the 4th, but had sent some of his troops forward on the 5th. If he had made a mistake, he hoped in the future to make up for the past. Napoleon in a published despatch explained that not only were the troops fatigued, and short of supplies, but a great storm had made the country impassable, so that the halt of the right wing at Grodno was unavoidable. In thus screening Jerome he forgot to explain how it was that this ' great storm ' had not delayed Bagration's retreat.

But in his private correspondence with Jerome he returned again and again to the subject of his failure. On the 7th he complained that the King sent him no useful information, that he had given the wrong direction to Reynier's march, and that even now his orders to Poniatowski were ill-judged. ' The two or three days your troops have lost,' he said, ' have perhaps saved Bagration.' Next day he sent him information obtained by Davoût as to the Russian retreat, and repeated that Jerome's blunders had lost for him, the Emperor, the results of calculations that would have secured a brilliant opening for the war. ' But you know nothing,' he went on, ' and not only do you consult no one, but you allow yourself to be influenced by the merest trifles.' He ended by exhorting him to try even now to act with energy, and not to be afraid to consult the experienced soldiers who were with him.

The letter reached Jerome early on July 9th at Bielitza, a village where he had his headquarters, to the south-west of Minsk. Davoût had occupied Minsk the day before. All that Jerome's army had seen of the Russians were the rubbish of their abandoned bivouacs, the bands of Cossacks retiring slowly across the level plain, or prowling on the edges of the pine-woods to snap up a straggler. The Russian army, which he was to have destroyed as the Emperor had trapped Mack at Ulm, was safe, several marches away to the eastward. Jerome knew nothing of his coming supersession, but he felt he had failed. His victory at Grodno had brought him, not congratulations, but day after day these terrible letters from Napoleon. He thought he was badly treated, and began to think of the pleasant, easy-going days at Cassel. Even all these waggon-loads of tents, wardrobe, plate, champagne and *eau de Cologne* could not make this wilderness of level wastes, dark pine-woods, and tumbledown dirty villages like Napoleonshöhe, especially if one was to find a scolding in every despatch from the Imperial headquarters.

He thought of going home. He found a possible pretext to explain his leaving the army. On July 9th he wrote to Catherine that he heard (whence or how he did not say) that the English were preparing for a descent on the Continent, so it was likely that ' after he had driven Bagration across the Dnieper ' the Emperor would send him to defend Hanover and Westphalia. To Napoleon he wrote the same day expressing his regret that with the best intentions he had failed to please him, and protesting that his reproaches were undeserved, and he spoke of perhaps leaving the army. The Emperor, losing patience, replied with a curt note. If Jerome chose to go, no obstacle would be put in his way.

On July 10th there was some fighting. Napoleon had a few days before ordered Jerome to use his cavalry to press the Russian rearguard. Instead of sending forward all La Tour Maubourg's division with its horse artillery, Jerome sent on only the light cavalry. They came on a superior force of Russians at Mir, and were driven in with a loss of five hundred men. When he heard of the defeat, the Emperor sent through Berthier another reprimand to his brother. ' Tell the King of Westphalia,' he wrote, ' that I am very much displeased with the affair of the 10th ; that his army is the only one that is not doing its duty ; that if General La Tour Maubourg had been at the head of his whole division he would have been able to lead it effectively ; that it is a thing unheard of, that it is showing an ignorance of the first elements of war, to pursue 6000 Cossacks and 4000 cavalry of the line, that is, some 10,000 to 11,000 horsemen, with a single division of light cavalry. That the King himself ought to be with his advanced guard, for nothing can replace the chief ; that the other commanders are not acting as he does.'

Before he received this letter Jerome had repaired the disaster. He occupied Mir, finding it abandoned by the Russians, and sent on La Tour Maubourg with the whole of the cavalry and horse artillery in pursuit. They encountered the mass of the enemy's cavalry at Neswies, drove them in, and entering the town with them, cleared them out of it, making many prisoners.

From the scene of the victory Jerome sent a despatch to Davoût. It was the first time he had written to him during the campaign. He had old grievances against the Marshal, the result of long-continued disputes as to the contributions to be levied on Westphalia and the treatment of its people during Davoût's command of the French troops quartered at Magdeburg and other places in Jerome's kingdom. It was unfortunate that of all the marshals it should have been Davoût who had been sent to co-operate with Jerome, and ' if the good of the service required it ' to supersede him. A more tactful commander, who had no record of past disputes with the King of Westphalia, might have arranged the coming transfer of command more dexterously. Jerome's letter, written late on the evening of the 12th, was very courteous. He addressed the Marshal as *Mon cousin*, the form the Emperor used to indicate that his marshals were the equals of princes. He suggested that if Davoût moved with his three divisions to the crossing of the Beresina at Bobruisk, he might stop Bagration's retreat there. Jerome would press him as he retired, and the Saxons were coming up. This combined operation would turn the Russians back to the southward.

Bagration's known object was to get away to the north-east and join forces with Barclay de Tolly, and Jerome's general idea was sound enough. The Russian general would be stopped if Davoût struck at the flank of his line of march while the King of Westphalia followed him up with his cavalry and the two corps he had in hand. Not being used to calculating questions of time and distance, Jerome made an error of detail. Bagration would be past the Beresina in four marches, and Davoût could not catch up with him till some point further eastward. (By the way, the Marshal had been wasting some days at Minsk, and might easily have been further forward.) Perhaps he felt hurt at the young King sending him a plan of operations; possibly the memory of last year's disputes still rankled in his mind. However this may be, he replied to Jerome's despatch by sending him a copy of Berthier's letter of July 6th, with a covering letter in which he spoke of it as an order to take command of the whole right wing as soon as Jerome's troops were in touch with his own, an order leaving him no discretion. ' In giving me the direction of your Majesty's troops,' wrote Davoût, ' the intention of his Majesty the Emperor and King, my master, is to secure unity in the operations against the enemy. The sentiments that animate both of us with regard to your august brother, and the respect I have for your Majesty, ought to be an assurance to the Emperor that there will be the greatest concord in our operations against his enemies.'

Jerome received Davoût's reply at Neswies in the afternoon of the 14th. He was waiting there for it, but he had pushed on La Tour Maubourg's cavalry to the eastward, and that day they were driving the Russian cavalry out of Romanova.

He had the feeling that he had at last begun to succeed, and he was counting on a friendly promise of co-operation from the Marshal. Instead came the order that put him and his army under Davoût's command.

He was wild with anger and disappointment. He decided without a moment's hesitation to resign his position in the army, and he wrote at once to Davoût, to Berthier, and to the Emperor, announcing his determination. The letter to the Marshal was studiously courteous and correct. He acknowledged the receipt of his letter; told him that, as under this arrangement his own services would be no longer necessary, he was about to resign his command; that he was taking with him only his personal guard, and if there was a battle within the next three days he would take part in it as an individual. Meanwhile his chief of the staff, General Marchand, remained at Neswies and awaited the Marshal's orders.

To Berthier, as chief of the staff of the Grand Army, he made the same announcement. He said that in the communication he had just received he saw proof that the Emperor had no confidence in him, and wished deliberately to inflict a humiliation on him, especially in choosing Davoût, against whom he had so many causes of complaint, to supersede and command him. He hoped his Majesty would accept his resignation. Some day he would appreciate the devotion of the brother he now dishonoured. He had told his generals that he was called to another occupation, and they were now under the command of the Prince of Eckmuhl (Davoût).

To the Emperor he wrote that ' quite apart from any feeling caused by the treatment he had just experienced, he had made up his mind not to serve as the subordinate of any one else '; that in any case, his notorious difficulties with Davoût at an earlier time would make it a special trial to serve under him. As to his conduct at Grodno, no one who was not on the spot could realise all his reasons. Davoût was now losing a still greater opportunity by his interference, after he (Jerome) had won successes that went far to regain anything his earlier delays had lost. However, he bowed to his Majesty's will. He did not murmur against it. He asked him to believe that nothing would change his love for him, or diminish his constant desire for his prosperity.

So far Jerome was acting with a certain amount of dignity. He made, however, the mistake of checking La Tour Maubourg's pursuit, and of causing some further delay by sending despatches from Berthier unopened to Davoût, instead of handing them to Marchand.   To the Queen he sent a short letter telling her what had happened.   ' After all,' he said, ' the first part of the campaign is ended, and has ended brilliantly.   The enemy is headed off on all sides ; Poland is entirely evacuated ; and the Russians are powerless to do anything but what the Emperor forces on them.'   On the 15th he assembled his guard, and had his baggage-train put in order, and next day he left Neswies on his homeward march.   Several of his officers tried in vain to persuade him to remain with the army.

On the 17th, in the course of his second day's march, he received Napoleon's reply to his letter of resignation.   The letter has been lost, but from Jerome's answer one gathers that it was a remonstrance against the course he was taking.   He replied the same day complaining that he had not had the least warning of the blow that had fallen on him ; that the Emperor's note of the 10th, saying that if he went no one would stop him, seemed to be a clear hint that he was not wanted ; that every one knew Davoût was his enemy, and he could not serve under him ; and that, finally, his having failed to satisfy the Emperor was an additional reason for his resignation. He protested his undying devotion to his brother's cause. He could not resume his command, but the Emperor could save his reputation by giving him a command elsewhere, for instance that of the troops that guarded the coasts of the North Sea.

The Emperor did not yet know that Jerome had actually left his headquarters, and thought his letter of the 14th would persuade him to remain with the right wing.   He actually sent him orders next day for a combined operation against Bagration.   Davoût meanwhile was trying to persuade him to reconsider his decision.   On the 15th he wrote to Jerome that by throwing up his command he was risking the success of the campaign.   He, Davoût, could only send general orders from a distance.   He entreated his Majesty to continue to direct in detail the operations of his three corps and his cavalry,

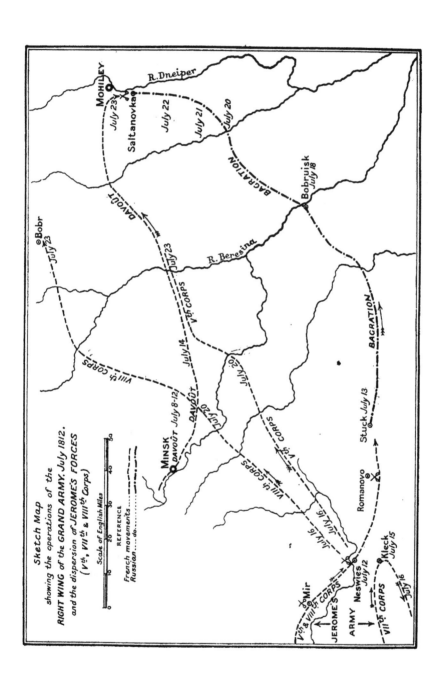

Sketch Map

showing the operations of the
RIGHT WING of the GRAND ARMY, July 1812,
and the dispersion of JEROME'S FORCES
(V.th, VII.th & VIII.th Corps)

Scale of English Miles

REFERENCE

French movements ....
Russian .... do ....

MOHILEV
R. Dneiper
July 23
Saltanovka
July 22
July 21
July 20
BAGRATION
Bobruisk
July 18

Bobr
July 23
DAVOUT
R. Beresina
July 23
V.th CORPS
July 14
VIII.th CORPS
DAVOUT July 8-12
July 20
MINSK
DAVOUT July 8-12
July 20
July 20
BAGRATION
Stuck July 13
V.th CORPS
VIII.th CORPS
July 16
Romanovo
July 16
Mir
V.th & VIII.th CORPS
JEROME'S CORPS
Neswies
July 12
ARMY
Kleck
July 15
VII.th CORPS
July 16

and then he explained the plan to be carried out. The fact was that Davoût was not sure that an open breach with the Emperor's brother would serve his own interests. Jerome wrote in reply that he could only serve under the Emperor, and no one else. ' His Majesty,' he continued, ' who is such an excellent judge of men, reposes in you a confidence which is justified by your talents and your past services, but as I have already told you, my cousin, whether it is you or any one else makes no difference to me, and I cannot act otherwise than I have done.' Davoût sent him another letter urging him to return, but Jerome continued his journey to Warsaw.

Before following further the story of Jerome's retirement from the army, it is necessary to discuss a point of military history. One of the latest historians of these events, who like so many French writers endeavours to show that the brothers of Napoleon were largely the authors of his ruin, and is far more severe upon Jerome than he deserves, argues that the King of Westphalia's sudden retirement prevented Davoût from destroying Bagration, and thus led to the Russian general being ultimately able to effect his junction with the northern army under Barclay de Tolly.

' On July 23rd,' he says, ' Davoût gave battle to Bagration near Mohilev, and, glorious as the day was, it was not decisive, because the corps of the Right Wing having been halted for five days for want of orders in the midst of operations, which, to give a good result, ought to have been continually pressed forward, did not take any part in the engagement.' [1]

This must have been written without taking the precaution of noting the actual positions of Jerome's three corps, when he resigned his command, and their subsequent movements. Jerome received the news of his supersession from Davoût on July 14th, in reply to his proposal for a joint operation against Bagration written on the 12th. On the 16th Jerome left Neswies. Now on that day by superior orders the right wing was broken up. Let me make this quite clear.

On the 15th the 7th corps, Reynier's Saxons, had reached

[1] ' Le 23 juillet Davoût a livré sous Mohilew à Bagration un combat, qui, pour glorieux qu'il fut, n'a point été décisif parce que les corps de la droite, immobilisés durant cinq jours, faute d'ordres, au milieu d'opérations qui pour être fructueuses devaient être constamment actives, n'y ont pris aucune part' (Frédéric Masson, *Napoléon et Sa Famille*, vol. vii. p. 324).

Kleck, a few miles to the south of Neswies. They were ordered to turn back and join Schwarzenberg, who had found that the Russian army of the south under Tormassov was more formidable than he had expected. On the 16th Reynier was marching away to the south-westward, and henceforth operated with the Austrians. He was badly beaten by Tormassov at Kobrin on July 27th.

This leaves only two of the three corps of Jerome's army available, the 5th (Poles) and the 8th (Westphalians). They both marched out of Neswies on the 16th, moving off to the north-eastward on diverging roads. The 5th or right column was to join Davoût; the 8th, the left column, was to join the central mass of the Grand Army. Napoleon was in touch with Barclay, and the hard fighting about Krasnoie, Witepsk, and Smolensk was coming. Bagration was moving eastward, trying to gain upon Davoût, who was marching on a parallel line to the north of him.

On the 21st the Russian turned sharply northward, marching on Mohilev along the left bank of the Dnieper. On the 23rd Davoût, advancing from Mohilev with his corps of French veterans, met and drove him back from the battlefield of Saltanovka. That day the 5th Polish corps was crossing the Beresina fifty miles away to the westward. It could perhaps have been up in time to join at a point of concentration even so far east as Mohilev if it had marched as rapidly as the 8th. Jerome was not a great commander, but a modification of his suggestion that he and the corps of the right wing should follow up Bagration, while Davoût tried to join in about Bobruisk, might have given more decisive results.

On the day of the battle of Saltanovka the 8th Westphalian corps was at Bobr, fifty miles north-west of Mohilev, on its march to join Napoleon. It is clear, then, that Jerome's departure did not 'immobilise' his corps; that even if he had remained with the army the dispersion of the right wing would have taken place, for Napoleon ordered it on account of the growing resistance of the Russians north and south; at most he would have had the Poles and the cavalry. If Davoût had not so abruptly taken command of the right wing, these troops would have been following up Bagration. To move off the Poles to the north-east was undoubtedly a mistake, but it was not Jerome's. He had mistakes enough to his account without trying to show that it was his fault that Davoût did not destroy Bagration at Saltanovka, and there is at least a chance that if his own suggestion had been followed the decisive result might have been obtained.

Jerome's second stay at Warsaw was a different experience from that of the days, only a few weeks before, when rumour pointed him out as the future King of Poland. He was a fallen star, and there was no crowd of courtiers hurrying to the Brühl Palace to salute a rising sun. De Pradt was unfriendly and uncommunicative. The Emperor wrote refusing to cover his brother's retreat by giving him a command in Germany of an army to defend Hanover against an imaginary invasion.

From Cassel came letters from the Queen. She was strangely devoted to her inconstant husband. As yet a childless wife, she trembled at the idea that reasons of state might lead to her marriage being broken up like Josephine's, or like that of the American. She had condoned all Jerome's infidelities. She was sad in his absence, but consoled by the idea that he was going to win laurels and fame in Russia. She had a horror of perhaps having to leave Germany for a foreign kingdom in Poland, but consoled herself with a rumour that the King of Saxony was to have Poland, and part of Saxony was to be given to Westphalia. Eager as she was to see Jerome again, she was startled by his letter of July 9th, telling her of a possible return, when the campaign had hardly opened. She wrote to him begging him not to make such a mistake, to remain with the army till at least some brilliant success had been obtained. The letter reached him at Warsaw, followed by others written when Catherine heard the first news of his resignation of his command.

Her advice came too late. Jerome replied with long tirades against the Emperor, Davoût, Poniatowski and the Poles. There was a conspiracy to ruin and disgrace him. Could he have acted otherwise? Late on the night of August 11th Jerome rejoined her at Napoleonshöhe. Under the influence of her affection for him she refused to believe he had really failed. She welcomed and consoled him, and told her friends that it was true that there was a conspiracy against her husband. The generals were jealous of his talents for war, and had spared no baseness to remove such a rival from the army.

In Cassel the official version of what had happened was that his Majesty's health had broken down under the hardships of the campaign. But this did not prevent the round of pleasures and fêtes beginning again. Never were Cassel and Napoleonshöhe more gay than during the autumn and the terrible winter of 1812. There were the same splendours as in the past, the same lavish expenditure, though the kingdom and the king were on the verge of bankruptcy. The King's mistresses appeared openly at his court,—a whole chronicle of scandal dates from this year of Moscow.

In the advance against the old Russian capital, the 8th corps, Jerome's Westphalians, had borne themselves well. In the great battle of Borodino two of its generals were killed, four wounded; 149 officers were killed or wounded severely. Cassel celebrated the news of victory with a *Te Deum*, and salutes of artillery and fireworks, and went on dancing and feasting.

In November there was another fête, on the occasion of the unveiling of a marble statue of Napoleon in front of the royal palace at Cassel. It was on November 13th, the day before the terrible retreat of the Grand Army from Smolensk had begun. By the end of the month the remnant of the Westphalian corps was struggling through the icy swamps of the Beresina, at the very place where it had crossed the river in July on its march to join Napoleon after Jerome left the army. In December came the news that the Emperor had passed through Dresden hurrying back to Paris, and that the Grand Army had been destroyed.

Jerome sent an envoy to Paris offering to come there if he could be of any service to his brother. For the first time since Jerome had left Warsaw the Emperor wrote to him. There was no allusion to the past. He simply told him that he could be of more service to him in Westphalia than in Paris. ' There is nothing left,' he said, ' of the Westphalian corps of the Grand Army.' He asked what troops his brother could raise. There would be a crisis in the coming spring.

Would Jerome do all he could to get men, horses, guns together, and strengthen the defences of Magdeburg ?

So Jerome's failure was eclipsed by the greater catastrophe. The homes of Westphalia were in mourning for their sons, dead under the Russian snows. Germany was quivering with eager readiness for revolt. The bankrupt throne at Cassel was tottering, but still there was feasting at Napoleonshöhe.

CHAPTER XIX

JOSEPH, LOUIS, AND LUCIEN IN 1812

THAT disastrous year for the Bonapartes—1812—had seen the beginning of the end in Joseph's kingdom as well as in Jerome's. In the summer of 1811, when Joseph returned to Madrid, after the baptism of the Emperor's son, he had obtained only a small part of the concessions he asked for, and he would have been wiser if he had insisted on his original demands, and stayed at Mortefontaine for good, if they were not granted. He had secured only a moderate amount of financial help, the confirmation of his command of the troops in Castille (where Jourdan was again to act as his chief of the staff), and an order to the generals in other districts to send him reports, while the check placed on their proceedings by Spanish commissioners being appointed in each province was merely nominal. The French marshals and generals in Spain had, in the absence of the Emperor, come to regard themselves, and to act, as petty kings in a conquered country. Each resented any interference with his proceedings in his own district, and thought chiefly of enriching himself and his favourites among his subordinates at the expense of the unfortunate people. Joseph might report upon their misconduct ; his commissioners might lend all their authority to the complaints sent up to Madrid by the victims ; but the unfortunate King of Spain had no power to right the wrongs of his subjects, and could neither censure nor remove their oppressors.

How powerless Joseph was may be judged from the fact that even Napoleon himself was unable to compel these military satraps to recognise his own authority. Catalonia had been placed under a different system from the rest of Spain. Marshal Suchet, who commanded there, did not report to Madrid, but directly to the Paris War Office, and there was no Spanish commissioner at Barcelona. On January 25, 1812, Catalonia and part of the neighbouring province of Aragon were virtually annexed to the Empire and divided into four departments, to which Napoleon proceeded to appoint French prefects. This meant the substitution of civil for military government. The prefects and their staffs of officials arrived. They were welcomed by the people, who saw in them protectors, but the French officers showed that they resented their interference. From the first they offered open obstruction to the new régime. M. Roujoux had taken up his residence at Gerona, as the prefect of the new department of the Ter. He found out that the garrison were plundering the people, and complained to the commandant, General Prost. The general entered Roujoux's office, drawing his sword as he came in, and told him he would run it through him if he forwarded to Paris any accusations against his men. At Olot a drunken soldier fired a shot into a peaceful group of Spaniards, and was roughly handled. The sub-prefect in vain protested that this soldier had caused all the trouble and that the town was absolutely quiet and loyal to the French. The troops were sent to sack the town for an hour, and the municipality was fined 60,000 francs. The French prefects were everywhere powerless to prevent such outrages, in what was now officially French territory under regular civil administration. What could a Spanish official do to check a general in a district under martial law ?

The generals even defied the King, and levied contributions on the money forwarded to him from Paris. From a convoy of 500,000 francs in gold and silver, passing through northern Spain on its way to the capital, a general requisitioned nearly a quarter of the amount, 120,000 francs, ' for the immediate needs of his army.' Joseph protested in vain. As the war with Russia drew nearer, the Emperor ordered some tens of thousands of his best troops to march from Spain into Germany to reinforce the Grand Army. The Army of the Centre, which was at the personal command of the King, was especially weakened in this way. These drafts were partly replaced by sending some thousands of young conscripts across the Pyrenees. But the final result was to strip the French armies in the Peninsula of a large proportion of their best officers and men, and send as a poor substitute for them half-pay officers, recently promoted sergeants, and boys who had yet to learn the elements of their drill.   This too at a moment when a serious crisis was approaching : the guerillas were again becoming active on all sides, and Wellington was no longer standing on the defensive.

To add to Joseph's difficulties, he was short of money.   The monthly million of francs promised when he was at Paris had not been sent to him regularly, and the pay of his guard, his officials, and his household was woefully in arrear.   He wrote to his brother that he had had to raise money on his property in France and on ' what was left of his diamonds,' for such was the misery around him at Madrid that some of his officers had to go without fire in the bitter winter weather. His complaints only obtained for him a very small supply. Once more he talked of abdicating.

But on the eve of the Russian war he had news from his brother that for a while reconciled him to his position, and gave him a glimmer of hope for the future.   At the end of March 1812 he was appointed commander-in-chief of all the armies in Spain.   Jourdan was to act as his chief of the staff. The direction of all the political and military affairs of the kingdom was to be in the hands of the King.   So ran Napoleon's letter.   But Joseph soon found to his disappointment that the extension of his powers was more nominal than real.   Marshal Soult, who commanded in the south, still acted as if he were King of Andalusia, and the other generals showed that they felt themselves bound to pay only a limited respect to the orders that came from Madrid.   They still sent reports to the Paris War Office, and were ready, if need be, to appeal to the Emperor, who was now so occupied with his task in Russia that he could pay no attention to the affairs of Spain.   In any case, Joseph had no power to remove them from their commands, however much they might disregard his authority.   The most he could do was to send an adverse report through General Clarke at the War Office in Paris to his brother, and it would be months before a reply could come from eastern Europe, even if his remonstrance ever reached the Emperor's hands.

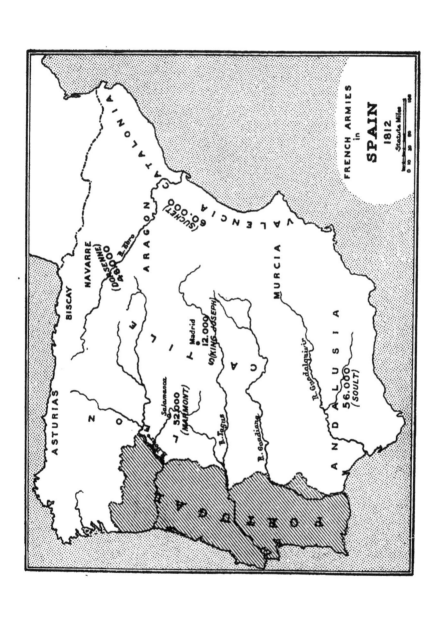

Almost at the eleventh hour Napoleon tried to patch up a peace with England on the basis of mutual concessions in Spain. Joseph was to convoke a Cortes, and to invite delegates of the insurgent government at Cadiz to join it, and then secure a vote recognising him as King of Spain. Catalonia was to be retroceded to Spain. The House of Braganza was to be restored in Portugal. The British and French armies were to evacuate the Peninsula. The whole plan had to be abandoned, almost as soon as it had been formed, for the British Government replied to the Emperor that they could enter into no negotiations for a settlement of the affairs of Spain except on the basis of the recognition of Ferdinand VII. as King. The Emperor had at an earlier date thought of the restoration of Ferdinand as a way out of his Spanish difficulties, but to accept it as a basis of negotiation now would have been a surrender. He went to Russia, leaving Joseph to hold his own in Spain with the help of generals who thought more of their own individual interests than the success of the enterprise to which they and the King were committed.

Though the drafts for the Grand Army had considerably reduced the French forces, Joseph when he assumed command in April 1812 had nearly 230,000 men nominally under his orders. This large force was thus distributed :—

Army of the Centre (Madrid, etc.) . . .	12,000
In the west, Army of Portugal (Marmont). .	52,000
In the south, Army of Andalusia (Soult) . .	56,000
In the east and north-east, Armies of Aragon, Catalonia, etc.	60,000
Army of the North (Dorsenne)	48,000
	228,000

Wellington had stormed the two border fortresses of the Spanish-Portuguese frontier—Ciudad Rodrigo in January, Badajos on April 6th—and was advancing into Spain with some 50,000 men. On paper King Joseph had an overwhelming superiority. Marmont had been directed by Napoleon himself to protect Salamanca. Wellington could not follow his old line of advance by the Tagus while the French at Salamanca were in a position to menace Portugal. He therefore advanced into Leon, and Marmont was able to bar his way with 52,000 men.   It would seem that it ought to have been a simple matter for Joseph to reinforce Marmont from the other armies, and so secure the defeat of the English ; and this was what he had decided to do, but he failed to secure a superiority of numbers at the critical moment for two reasons.

First, the local resistance of the Spaniards in some of the provinces was again so serious and active that the generals could not spare any men ; and secondly, Joseph and Jourdan from Madrid could not secure obedience for their orders. The generals were able in some cases to oppose to Joseph's commands contradictory orders which had been sent from the Paris War Office direct to them.   Dorsenne in Aragon declared he was not under the King's command, but responsible to Paris, and that in any case the most he could do was to hold his own without sending help to others.   Suchet in the north-east declared that he too held an independent command and had not a man to spare.   It was difficult to correspond with Soult in Andalusia.   It was not certain for a while that he had even received instructions to take his orders from Madrid, and he had withdrawn a number of posts he had maintained for a while in the Sierra Morena and La Mancha, forming a line of communications with Madrid, so that it was by no means easy to send a despatch in safety to him.   Perhaps he had broken up this line of posts in order to prevent his local independence being interfered with.

Joseph's Army of the Centre was so weak that it just sufficed to garrison the neighbourhood of Madrid.   The only resource left to him was to look to Soult's 60,000 men in the south for reinforcements.   He had no sooner taken command than he wrote to Soult to send a division into the Tagus valley.   A month later, on May 7th—as Soult had done nothing—he sent him an order to send at once Drouet's division to combine with Marmont in operations against Wellington.   Joseph was an amateur, Soult one of the best of professional soldiers, but in this case the amateur took a perfectly sound view and gave sound orders, and the professional soldier defended his disregard of them by alleging thoroughly unsound reasons for the mistaken course he took.

Joseph acted on the true strategic principle that all minor operations must be subordinated to the attack on the enemy's main army. ' In the existing state of affairs,' he wrote to Soult, ' there can be no doubt that your attention should be continually fixed upon the English army. We must keep in touch with it, and try to fight it with all the advantages on our side. I cannot agree to any other operation of mere detail being undertaken in the south any more than in the north, if it diverts you from this main objective.'

Soult was busy with projects against Cadiz and Tarifa and the Spanish army of Ballesteros. It was not till June 8th, a month later, that he replied to Joseph. He told the King that he was certain that if he detached any of his forces, Wellington would at once swoop down on Andalusia. He believed the English general had orders to this effect, for he was in continual correspondence with the Spaniards at Cadiz. Instead of sending a division to reinforce Marmont, he ought himself to be reinforced from Marmont's army and the Army of the North.

Before receiving Soult's letter Joseph—tired of waiting— had, on May 28th, sent direct orders to Drouet to march northwards. Soult stopped him. He told Drouet to remain where he was. If he marched to the Tagus, he, the Marshal, would have to concentrate his army and abandon the south to the enemy. To Joseph he wrote that he would resign his command if the King sent orders to his subordinates, and then he went on to tell what he meant to do in the south, as if Andalusia had nothing to do with the main campaign in central Spain.

Joseph repeated his orders. He told the Marshal the safety of Spain, the honour of the Imperial arms, were at stake. He must obey or resign. But he was not strong enough to insist on the Marshal's resignation, when Soult, after causing further delay by proposing that instead of reinforcing the north the French army should concentrate in Andalusia, at last gave a grudging obedience, and when it was too late set a division of infantry and a cavalry brigade in motion towards Castille.

Despairing of any help from Soult, Joseph had obtained a promise of reinforcements from the Army of the North, and reducing the garrisons of Madrid and Toledo to a mere handful of men, had himself mobilised a division formed out of the Army of the Centre. With these troops he marched from his capital on July 21st, crossing the great pass of the Guadarama next day. He had sent forward some days before messengers to Marmont with the news that he was coming to his assistance, and that reinforcements were also on the way from the north.

For a month Marmont had been facing Wellington on the river Tormes. The British had occupied Salamanca. Marmont did not feel strong enough to attack them, and contented himself with occupying positions that would enable him to fight a defensive battle if Wellington advanced. Wellington, too, hesitated to risk an engagement while the Marshal held such advantageous ground. For days the two adversaries faced each other, manœuvring so as to offer battle with the maximum of chances in hand, but neither risking an attack. In the third week of July Wellington's supplies were running short, and he was preparing to retire once more into Portugal. A captured despatch to a Spanish general revealed this to Marmont. He saw in the Duke's coming retreat a confession of inferiority. He knew that in a few days he himself would be superseded on Joseph's arrival. He tried to snatch a victory. On the morning of July 22nd he abandoned his cautious tactics and advanced from his strong position, to throw himself across Wellington's lines of communication. 'He wished to cut me off,' said the Duke. 'I saw that in attempting this he was spreading himself over more ground than he could defend. I resolved to attack him, and succeeded in my object very quickly. One of the French generals said I had beaten forty thousand men in forty minutes.' Marmont's army was defeated in detail, the left cut off, then the centre and right routed. Two eagles, eleven guns, and 7000 prisoners were left in Wellington's hands as trophies of one of his greatest victories. Marmont was wounded.

King Joseph heard the news of the disaster on the night of July 24th, when he halted at Blasco Sancho, two days' march from Salamanca. First a peasant brought a vague report. Then came despatches from Marmont, and his lieutenant Clausel. They were retiring north-eastward towards Valladolid with the wreck of the army, leaving the direct way to Madrid open to Wellington, and nothing to bar his advance but Joseph's few thousand men.

The King retreated to Segovia, where he arrived on the 27th. He halted there in the hope that Clausel, with Marmont's army, would join him, but the beaten troops continued their northern retreat. From Segovia he sent orders to Soult to evacuate Audalusia, and march with all his army to Toledo. 'This is the only means,' he said, 'of re-establishing our position.' He hoped the 10,000 men whom he had ordered Soult to send northwards a month before would be at Madrid by this time. On August 5th he re-entered his capital. There were no reinforcements from Soult, no news that he was coming.

On the 8th Joseph heard that the British were in Segovia ; next day that they were crossing the Guadarama, and that their cavalry was in touch with his own in sight of Madrid. On the 10th, for the second time, he had to abandon his capital to the enemy.

There was a panic in the city, the result of vague rumours that there would be a wild outburst of insurrection while the place was left without a government after Joseph's departure and before Wellington could arrive. The French colony took to flight with the King, and with them went crowds of Spaniards who had thrown in their lot with the invader and feared the vengeance of their compatriots. The King's troops had to escort a wretched train of fugitives, a multitude of men, women, and children, with some two thousand carriages and carts, besides long lines of laden pack-animals. It was an exodus, and the long column trailed for miles on the dusty sun-scorched road to Leganez.

Two days later Wellington rode into Madrid amidst the acclamations of the people. Joseph had halted at Aranjuez, hoping against hope that Soult would appear. Instead came another proposal from the Marshal that the King should abandon the rest of Spain, and stake everything on concentrating the army in the south for the defence of Andalusia. More than one historian of the war has described this as a brilliant plan. But Napoleon, who understood something of war, had always insisted that without safe communications through the north with France the army must be in a hopeless condition.

Had Joseph accepted Soult's proposals, and shut himself up in Andalusia, with the English holding the command of the sea, and the north and centre in the hands of Wellington and the guerillas, the campaign of 1812 would have ended in a Sedan.

On August 15th it was clear that Soult would not come ; the English at Madrid were dangerously near ; and there was news of a descent of a Neapolitan army from Sicily on the east coast. Joseph abandoned Aranjuez, and escorting his cumbrous convoy marched for Valencia, where he arrived on the 31st. Suchet had already defeated the Sicilian expedition, which had re-embarked. Joseph handed over the Army of the Centre to the Marshal.

Soult in Andalusia found his own position rapidly becoming dangerous. After one more letter from Joseph, in which the King again gave him the choice of obedience or supersession, he began his retreat on August 25th, and moving first eastward and then northward through the province of Murcia, reached Valencia. The whole of the west, centre, and south of Spain had been lost by the French. The disaster was not the fault of Joseph, but of Soult. The meeting between the King and the Marshal was all the more unfriendly because Joseph had discovered that Soult had been writing to the Emperor denouncing him, and even trying to prove that his brother was planning a treacherous arrangement to make peace with the Spaniards at the expense of the Empire. But with that strange weakness he showed in all his dealings with the rebellious Marshal, Joseph accepted his excuses and made peace with him.

For a while his throne was saved. Wellington, after spending a fortnight in Madrid, which might perhaps have been better employed, turned north, besieged Burgos, failed to take it after a siege of a month, and then found he had again to withdraw towards Portugal. The French had had breathing time, and Masséna had been sent from Paris to reorganise the resistance. There was another turn in the tide of war.

In the beginning of October, while Wellington was still before Burgos, Joseph had held a council of war at Valencia, at which Marshals Soult, Suchet, and Jourdan were present. This time it was Soult that proposed the best course of action.

He pointed out that out of the combined Armies of the Centre, the South, and Catalonia now concentrated in the east of Spain, a large field army might be formed to strike at Wellington through Castille while he was still engaged in the operations against Burgos, and face to face with the Army of the North. But Joseph, supported by Jourdan, overruled this plan. He wanted to reoccupy his capital as soon as possible. Suchet was left to hold the eastern provinces, and the march on Madrid began. Joseph re-entered the city on November 2nd. Following up the English retirement, but without ever venturing to bring his opponents to battle, he reoccupied Salamanca on the 22nd, and after a brief stay there returned to Madrid. In the city which had so lately welcomed Wellington he could hardly try to persuade himself or any one else that the position of a popular king was still possible for him. And the disaster of Salamanca, the evacuation of the south, the temporary loss of Madrid, had all gone far to diminish the prestige of the French, when to ruin it utterly there came the news of the destruction of the Grand Army and the failure of Napoleon himself in Russia.

Louis, in his retirement at Gratz, had been from afar an interested spectator of the great disaster of 1812. For once he had shown enough insight into coming events to forecast the unfortunate results of the Russian expedition even before the advance of the Grand Army began. Perhaps his predictions of failure were inspired more by pessimism as to his brother's affairs than any grasp of the military and political situation. Van Capellen, formerly one of his ministers, who had come from Holland to act as his secretary, tells how Louis ' repeated a hundred times that the Russian war would bring his brother to his ruin.' During the fatal year he occupied himself with literature. He printed for circulation among his friends a little volume of original poems and translations from Horace, and completed and read the proofs of a long-winded feeble romance, *Marie ou les Peines d'Amour*. The heroine was a Dutch girl, and one of the most striking scenes was the inundation caused by a flooded river overflowing the dykes, but beyond this everything in the dreary story reflected French ideas and manners. In some of the characters critics

U

saw suggestions of real people, and thus it had some of the interest of a *roman à clef*. Some of Louis's characteristics were seen in the hero, and a lady, who was not the heroine and who played a very unamiable part, was supposed to be an ill-natured sketch of Hortense. The proof-reading was a toilsome business, for the manuscript, after having been recopied by Capellen from Louis's somewhat illegible manuscript, was set up by Styrian compositors who knew no French, and made mistakes in every line.

That Louis was able to do the work at all showed a certain amount of dogged energy, for his state of health was more unsatisfactory than ever, notwithstanding endless consultations with learned professors and self-advertising charlatans, and trials of every remedy that could be suggested. A tour through Styria in the summer did him more good than all other methods of treatment, but for most of the year he was suffering from a partial paralysis of the right hand. To write he put on a glove to which a pen was attached. He could not hold it in the ordinary way. Yet he would write for hours. Not only was he busy with his books, but he also had a large correspondence. His mother and Fesch were still trying to induce him to make peace with the Emperor and return to France. He discussed their arguments and rejected their proposals. He wrote scores of letters to his eldest son, for whom he had a real affection, and sent to his tutors advice as to his studies and amusements. For the youngest son, the future Napoleon III., he seemed to feel no interest. He persisted in believing that Hortense had been faithless to him and that Louis Napoleon was no son of his, and in her subsequent conduct he saw confirmation of his suspicions. It was his feeling towards his Queen that kept him from any idea of returning to France. She had her house in Paris, the estate of St. Leu, and a large revenue from the Imperial treasury, and her life was a round of amusements, some of which gave rise to ill-omened rumours. The Emperor had refused to hear of a divorce, and Louis preferred to remain in exile.

He was also in correspondence with his brother-exile Lucien. The Prince of Canino was living the life of a country gentleman in Worcestershire. He had to practise a rigid economy, for since the failure of the bank he had been able to make ends meet only with the help of his mother's remittances. With Lucien at Thorngrove, as with Louis at Gratz, literature supplied an occupation. The great epic of *Charlemagne* was approaching completion. Chatillon, one of the artists Lucien had patronised in his days of prosperity, and who was now with him at Thorngrove, was engaged on a series of drawings to illustrate the poem, and an English engraver was busy reproducing these illustrations for the press. Arrangements had been made for printing and publishing the work in London. Byron had seen part of the manuscript and praised it. Three English versifiers, now all forgotten, were occupied on a translation, and Lucien's chaplain was making an Italian version. Not content with these coming triumphs, Lucien had sketched out a second epic on the subject of the liberation of Corsica from the Moors. Somewhat naïvely he wrote to a friend that it would be to the *Charlemagne* what Homer's *Odyssey* was to his *Iliad*. These Bonapartes took their literary labours very seriously.

Besides his poetic labours, Lucien found occupation in writing the first part of his memoirs. They were intended for the instruction of his children, and in one remarkable passage, written before the disaster in Russia, he noted that perhaps when they were old enough to read them, there would be no reason to envy the fate of their uncle Napoleon, and they might feel they had been more fortunate in being educated in free England instead of being Imperial princes.

But literature was not his only occupation. The ex-diplomatist of the Consulate flattered himself that he might use his talents for negotiation to influence the course of events. Early in the year he had some thoughts of returning to France, and had suggested to his friends there an arrangement for an exchange of himself and his suite for some English prisoners of rank, but this suggestion led to no result. In the summer he was in correspondence with Lord Castlereagh and was endeavouring to serve his brother Joseph's interests. He wrote to the minister, then Foreign Secretary, and the soul of the coalition against Napoleon, proposing that in the event of a peace between England and France, the Bourbons should not be restored in Spain, but Joseph should be retained as King. He endeavoured to prove that the arrangement would be welcomed by the great mass of the Spanish people, who would see in a constitutional monarchy under his brother an improvement on the old Bourbon régime, and he insisted that the change would be no loss, but rather a gain, to England. Joseph would be no longer a mere viceroy of Napoleon. There would be a treaty of commerce with England, an understanding that neither Napoleon nor any of his descendants should ever rule in Spain ; a guarantee of the independence of Portugal. Joseph would be a national king and the Pyrenees a barrier against French ambition. Several letters were exchanged, but Castlereagh would not commit himself to anything.

When the news arrived of the Russian disasters, and rumours that Napoleon was ill and dying, and when in Paris itself there was a formidable conspiracy against the Emperor, Lucien again exerted himself on Joseph's behalf. Through Colonel Leighton, the English Government commissioner who resided near Thorngrove, and had the general supervision of the little French colony, he suggested to the Ministry that in case of Napoleon's disappearance, leaving only a child in the cradle as his heir, Joseph, who till the birth of the King of Rome had stood next in succession, might be proclaimed Emperor. It would be a compromise acceptable to all moderate men in France. The Imperialists would be ready to welcome a Bonaparte. The hostility created by the restoration of the Bourbons, with their traditions of the old régime, would be avoided. Spain would be given back to Ferdinand VII. The new Emperor would be no menace to the peace of Europe, for Joseph had no military ambitions. It was an academic proposal, and never had any chance of success with Castlereagh, whose ambition was the sweeping away of the whole Bonapartist system, and for whom the Emperor and his brothers were a group of parvenus. The incident is only notable as showing the bent of Lucien's mind at this time.

With the winter it was evident that the end was coming. The destruction of the Grand Army ; the gathering spirit of revolt in Germany.; the new outbreak of patriotic resistance in Spain, all produced a state of things in which the only hope of anything of their power and state being saved for the Bonapartes lay in the chance of the Emperor raising new armies and winning new victories.

CHAPTER XX

THE DOWNFALL OF KING JOSEPH

(1813)

IT is difficult for us at the present day to realise the state of feeling in Europe in those dark days of the winter of 1812-13. Since the closing years of the eighteenth century the star of Napoleon had been in the ascendant in the world, and it was now eclipsed by a catastrophe almost unparalleled in history. We know that even before the Russian crisis the Bonapartist system was breaking up, but the men of the time did not perceive this, and to them it seemed as if the snows of Russia had overwhelmed a power that, strong against men, failed only when it defied the giant forces of nature.

Yet such was the glamour of Napoleon's genius, the prestige won by years of marvellous success, that even now men hesitated to believe the end was come. Statesmen felt so little assured of success against him, that they were still ready to negotiate and consider some compromise that would leave him a part of his power, and soldiers hoped for victory only if they could meet him with overwhelming numbers. It was this feeling that gave him a breathing-space in which to work out new combinations for the preservation of his Empire. But his own faith in his star was broken. To him it was plainer than to his enemies that the chances were terribly against him. It seemed to him that his best hope was in his infant son. He might perhaps be able to detach Austria from the new coalition against him, and arrange a peace through the good offices of the Emperor Francis, in order to secure the immediate or the eventual succession of Napoleon II., the child of his Austrian Empress. But meanwhile he must make ready for war with such scanty resources as were still left to him, and with the hostility of Europe rising higher each day, no longer a movement of princes and cabinets, but an uprising of the peoples, tired of war and military rule, everywhere except in Italy, where the name of Napoleon was still linked with national aspirations. And the irony of the position was that if Austria was to save him, he would most likely have to sacrifice Italy, the one land beyond the old frontiers of France that was still loyal to his name.

To his two brothers who were still kings, Joseph and Jerome, he sent orders in the first days of the new year. On January 3rd his Minister of War (General Clarke, Duc de Feltre) wrote to Joseph advising him, on the part of the Emperor, to confine his efforts only to holding the north of Spain. His headquarters ought to be at Valladolid, the old capital of the country. A detachment on his extreme left might hold Madrid, but the possession of that city was now a minor matter. His efforts should be directed chiefly to pacifying Biscay, Aragon, and the province of Santander. Even in the north the insurgents were now aggressive and had small armies in the field. They had even made raids through the Pyrenean passes and violated French territory.

Soult was recalled to France, as it was evident that he could not give the King the whole-hearted co-operation that was required.[1] Joseph and his right-hand man, Jourdan, had complete control of the military operations, except in the Basque provinces and along the Pyrenees, where General Clausel was given a certain independence of action and command, with the mission of destroying Mina's army of guerillas and guarding the all-important communications with France. Reinforcements, made up largely of mobilised national guards, were sent to hold the Pyrenean passes, but at the same time the armies in Spain were gradually stripped of some of their best officers, sergeants, and veteran soldiers, recalled week after week by the Emperor to stiffen the new armies of conscripts he was forming for the coming struggle in central Europe. So completely was Napoleon's attention riveted on the German theatre of war, that after a while he ceased to send

[1] Soult passed through Madrid on March 2nd on his way to France, having with him 'a large number of waggons conveying objects of value which he was bringing back from Andalusia.' The other generals plundered, but the Marshal had the monopoly of a province with many famous cities in it—hence the length of his personal baggage-train.

Joseph orders or advice, took little notice of his correspondence, in fact left him to shift for himself. Perhaps an additional reason for this was the difficulty of rapid communication. Despatches could not pass through the north of Spain without a formidable escort. Napoleon's orders sent to Joseph in the first week of January 1813 did not arrive at Madrid till the middle of February, after having been weeks on the way. This is enough to show what was the condition of the country.

Jerome had been warned by the Emperor that a crisis would come in Germany with the spring of 1813, and with an impoverished exchequer, a sadly diminished credit, and a people who were beginning to show unmistakable signs of patriotic agitation against his rule, he was endeavouring to form a new army to replace the Westphalian contingent that had been all but annihilated in Russia. He looked forward with anxiety to the coming struggle, the scene of which would be the borderlands of his kingdom. At the New Year of 1813 he had sent his chamberlain, M. Cousin de Marinville, to confer with the Emperor at Paris, and to obtain financial help for recruiting and equipping the new Westphalian army. Marinville suggested that the King should come to Paris to treat of these matters in person, but was told that Jerome would be more useful at Cassel. To leave his kingdom at this moment might be supposed to be a sign that he was anxious about its future. But without consulting his brother, Jerome took a step which was an open admission of his doubts as to the security of Cassel. On March 11th Marinville informed the French authorities that he had been informed by Jerome's secretary that Queen Catherine would arrive in Paris in a few days, bringing with her her household, her carriages, and all her personal property. He was anxious to arrange at once that she should be received in a befitting way and provided with a residence. A suite of some fifty ladies of honour, secretaries, equerries, maids and servants would accompany her.

In January Jerome had suggested to Reinhard, the French resident at Cassel, that, as there was talk of the Empress and the little King of Rome being solemnly crowned at an early date, the Emperor might invite Catherine to Paris for the proposed ceremony, and thus avoid her departure from Cassel being regarded as a flight from danger. Reinhard transmitted this suggestion to Paris, but no invitation came.

A month later Jerome renewed his proposal, adding that if Catherine did not go to Paris, he would send her to her father's court at Stuttgart. On March 2nd the Emperor wrote to his brother that for the present the Queen must stay in Westphalia. Only in the event of the Czar or the Russian commander-in-chief entering Berlin or Dresden, but not before, he was to send her to France. On February 17th the treaty of alliance between the Czar and the King of Prussia had been concluded, and on the same day the Russians under Wittgenstein had crossed the Vistula. At the beginning of March the Viceroy Eugène had evacuated Berlin. On the 7th Jerome heard a report that Wittgenstein had occupied the Prussian capital three days before. His preparations for Catherine's departure had been made long in advance. On the 10th the Queen and her suite left Cassel on their way to Paris.

Her departure encouraged the patriots in Westphalia. They said openly that Jerome would soon follow her. Napoleon was disappointed at the news, for he did not believe Cassel was in any real danger yet. He sent one of his chamberlains, M. de Canouville, to meet Queen Catherine, and to tell her not to come any nearer Paris than Compiègne. Canouville met her at Peronne, and escorted her to the château of Compiègne, where suites of rooms had been hastily prepared for her and her numerous suite. Thence she wrote to the Emperor, telling him that she had only consented to leave Cassel several days after the news had arrived that the enemy was at Berlin, and she had done so much against her will, and had only quitted her husband's side in order that Jerome might have all his troops at his free disposal, instead of having to detach any of them for her personal protection. She had brought with her in her suite members of some of the noblest families of Westphalia and Hanover, who would be so many hostages for the conduct of their relatives, so she suggested that her coming to France might be an advantage to the Emperor's policy.

Napoleon replied that she was welcome, though her husband had misunderstood his instructions as to her departure. He thought he had made it plain that it was only to take place if the Russian main army under the Czar and Kutusoff was at Berlin. Jerome had taken alarm and sent her away when only some of the Russian advanced cavalry had reached Berlin, and his action had caused unnecessary alarm. Her departure from Germany was not yet known to the public in Paris. This he explained was why he had asked her not to come there. He had hoped to visit her at Compiègne, but was too busy to go so far, and he therefore invited her to come with a few of her attendants to pay him a visit at the Trianon at Versailles. But Paris soon knew of the Queen's flight, and after his interview with Catherine at the Trianon, Napoleon arranged that she should take up her residence at the château of Meudon, in the pleasant outskirts of the capital.

Louis had been in correspondence with the Emperor since the beginning of the year. From Gratz, on January 1, 1813, he sent, under cover of a letter to his mother, another to Napoleon. He told him that he felt ' profoundly afflicted ' by the disasters of the Grand Army ; that he realised what an anxious time it must be for his brother, how important it was that every possible aid should be given to him in the coming struggle ; and he went on to say that he offered to France and to the Emperor ' the little strength that remained to him, and whatever service he was still capable of rendering, provided he could do this with honour.'

This clause was all-important. It implied conditions to be accepted by Napoleon. And Louis proceeded to explain what was in his mind. He felt, he said, that he still belonged to Holland. He could not consent to be separated from the land of his adoption, which he had only left after having prolonged his resistance to the point when, as a Frenchman and the Emperor's brother, he could go no further. The commercial questions that had led to the dispute between him and Napoleon in Holland were now of minor importance. Might not the Emperor consider the advisability of restoring him to his kingdom ? In that case he would be ready to answer for Holland giving a loyal support to the Empire, and assisting France in the coming conflict.

Louis was so convinced of the importance of this offer and of the probability of its being accepted, that he sent the Austrian

Emperor a long memoir on his policy as King of Holland, the circumstances of his departure, and his claims to restoration, suggesting that his efforts in this direction should have the support of the Austrian influence, which, like so many others, he expected would be exerted to secure the position of the Empress Maria Louisa, and indirectly that of her husband.

On January 16th Napoleon wrote to Louis, thanking him for the kind expressions of his New Year letter, and reminding him that at an earlier date he had more than once let him know how much he desired that he would return to France. His duty to the head of the family, to France, to his children, required that he should not persist in remaining in exile in Styria. ' Your sons are growing up,' he said, ' and have need of their father's presence. Come back, then, without any further delay, and I shall receive you, not as the brother you offended, but as the brother who educated you. As to your ideas of my affairs, they are incorrect. I have a million men under arms, and two hundred million francs in my treasury to uphold the integrity of the territory of the Confederation of the Rhine and of my allies, and to win success for the plans I have formed for the happiness of my people. Holland is French for ever. It is the outcome of our territory, the delta of our rivers ; it can be prosperous only with France, and it knows this well. If you remain in France, you are not separated from Holland, but if by separating yourself from Holland you mean renouncing all claim to govern it, you have already by your own act abandoned it when you abdicated.'

With the letter Louis received another from Madame Mère, in which she begged her son to return to France, assuring him that he would be heartily welcomed by the Emperor. She used every argument to persuade him, even flattery. ' Your return at this crisis,' she wrote, ' will call forth the same admiration throughout Europe that was evoked by your firmness of character three years ago. The public will applaud your noble act of self-devotion.' But Napoleon's frank refusal to discuss the restoration of Holland had for the moment determined Louis to remain in Styria. He wrote to his mother that since 1806 Holland had become his country. He would consent to return to France, and even live there as a private individual, if one of his sons were made King of Holland ; but to return without any restoration of the kingdom of the Netherlands would be to appear to admit by his presence in France that he thanked the Emperor for having robbed him and his children of their throne. He had been forced to leave Holland. But, granting this, had his son abdicated his rights ? Why should he be disinherited ? ' No, dear mother,' he concluded, ' I would suffer a thousand times more if I came, back instead of remaining abroad, and I would rather endure a thousand deaths than do what is contrary to my conscience and my duty. Do not say anything more to me on the subject ! '

Lucien also seems to have had some thoughts of returning to France. With all his grievances against his brother he felt drawn to him by the dangers and troubles of the moment. He sounded his mother on the possibility of an arrangement being made, but the matter went no further. Lucien remained at Thorngrove, occupied with his literary labours, to which he had added the study of astronomy. He had made the acquaintance of Herschel, and was in correspondence with him. Instruments were purchased, a telescope mounted, a little observatory installed in the grounds of Thorngrove, and Lucien busied himself with systematic observations, his chaplain, Père Maurice, helping him with the mathematical part of the work.

On January 4, 1813, his third son, Louis Lucien Bonaparte, was born at Thorngrove. He was to inherit his father's literary and scientific bent of mind, and, born in England, he was destined to pass most of his later life in London.

At the end of January Lucien was again in correspondence with the British Ministry. He once more suggested his former plan for an arrangement that would maintain Joseph as King of Spain, and tried to obtain permission to go to Paris in order to discuss it with Napoleon. Castlereagh courteously declined his proffered mediation. The English ministers were at last quite persuaded that Wellington would soon be able to dispose of King Joseph and the French marshals in the Peninsula. Wellington's position was strengthened by his appointment as commander-in-chief of the Spanish, as well as the Portuguese and British armies. He prepared carefully for the great effort which he intended to make in the early summer, visiting Cadiz to confer with the Spanish Junta, and accumulating magazines of supplies on the Portuguese frontier. Napoleon had foreseen the direction that would be given to the new advance into Spain, and had therefore advised Joseph to make Valladolid his headquarters. At the same time he had urged upon him the necessity of taking advantage of the respite given by Wellington's preparations, and using it to crush the insurgents in the north, and so secure his own line of communications with France.

It was not till May 13th that Wellington began his advance, but Joseph had not acted upon the Emperor's instructions, and had wasted four months that he might have employed to make his position in the coming struggle somewhat more favourable. He had remained at Madrid till the middle of March. The Emperor had repeated his orders again and again. In a note to Clarke, the Minister of War, on January 18th, he had written: 'Reiterate my orders to the King of Spain to transfer his headquarters to Valladolid, only to occupy Madrid with the extremity of his line, and send back considerable forces to the north and to Aragon in order to reduce northern Spain to submission.' Six days later he wrote again, 'Send order after order to the King of Spain to retire to Valladolid.' On February 10th he complained that his orders were neglected, and time was being lost. Unless the north were made secure at once, it would be too late.

Joseph clung to Madrid. He wrote to his brother that to abandon his capital would produce the worst impression in Spain, and be regarded as a first step towards abdication. When Soult passed through Madrid in the beginning of March, Joseph wrote to the Emperor that the Marshal agreed with him that there was no need of his leaving the capital. At last he consented to go to Valladolid, but even then he would not make up his mind to abandon Madrid. He informed the people in a proclamation that he was going to take personal command of the operations in the field, but he left in the city a large number of officials with a whole division of his troops to protect them. A little later, when there was a report that insurgent bands were menacing the capital, he moved three more divisions of the Army of the Centre to his left to protect it, and thus further weakened the main army in the field.

Leaving Madrid on March 17th, he reached Valladolid on the 23rd, and the city was for a few weeks like a temporary capital, with a court, state ceremonial, and a crowd of officials installed in temporary offices. Under pressure from Paris, Joseph at last consented to reinforce strongly Clausel's Army of the North, but instead of communicating directly with the General, he marked his dislike for the arrangement by sending the necessary instructions through the War Ministry at Paris, a loss of many days. He had been angered at Clausel being allowed to be largely independent of him. He complained, often with good reason, that though he was commander-in-chief in Spain, the generals were frequently able to produce contradictory orders from Clarke at the War Office, and the result was that they showed only a limited respect for his commands. He had complained of this to Napoleon. The Emperor replied that he would get on much better with the French generals if he was not continually using Spanish officials as his intermediaries, and communicating with them through his Spanish Minister of War. In directing the army he must henceforth act as a French commander-in-chief, not as the King of Spain.

Joseph and his chief of the staff, Jourdan, had intended to make a stand on the Douro and the Tormes, and fight another campaign of Salamanca, with better results, when Wellington advanced. Burgos, which had stopped the English march to the north after the defeat of Salamanca, was again to be the centre of resistance, if the first line was forced, and for this purpose considerable supplies were being accumulated there. But by the tardy despatch of several divisions to reinforce Clausel in the north, the sending of three more divisions to the neighbourhood of Madrid, the detention of one division in the capital, and the stretching out of a long line from Madrid on the left by Segovia and Valladolid to Salamanca and Zamora on the right, Joseph had so dissipated and frittered away his forces, that when at last, in the middle of May, Wellington began his advance, the King of Spain had not more than 30,000 men available under his immediate command.

Wellington's army was in movement on May 13th, but

Joseph's intelligence department was badly organised, and it was not till the 20th that he heard of the hostile advance, and realised the danger that threatened him.   To make a stand at Salamanca, or even at Valladolid, would be to fight with very inferior numbers and court disaster.   He decided to retire, and concentrate for battle further east, and the retreat had to be north-eastward towards Burgos.   To attempt to cover Madrid would be to lose touch with the reinforcements he could recall from the Army of the North, and to risk being cut off from France.   He had to order the evacuation of Madrid. From that direction and from Clausel's army in the north reinforcements would join him as he retired.   Now at last he must have seen how well judged were the Emperor's orders to keep his army in hand about Valladolid, neglect the holding of Madrid, and use the time before the English advance to clear the north of the enemy.

Thanks to the mistaken policy he had adopted, his difficulties had only begun.   He had hesitated for some days to give the now obviously necessary order for the evacuation of Madrid, and as the main road from the capital ran through Valladolid, he must hold on there till Lewal's division, which formed the garrison of his capital, could join him.   All his available cavalry was detached to protect Lewal's retreat, which was encumbered and delayed by the fact that the troops had to escort a crowd of officials and refugees, with some thousands of carts and carriages conveying their property.   It was a convoy miles long that struggled for days through the pass of the Guadarama and then moved slowly by Segovia to Valladolid.   Salamanca had been abandoned only just in time by General Vilatte's division, which was retiring on Valladolid hard pressed by the British cavalry.   Joseph could not possibly find supplies even for a few days at Valladolid for the retiring troops and the emigration from Madrid.   He sent away his court, the civil officials who had accompanied him, and a crowd of hangers-on of his temporary capital, and they too were accompanied by a huge waggon-train with a military escort.   He directed them to halt at Burgos.

They did not march from Valladolid till June 2nd.   Arrived at Burgos, they began to eat up the supplies collected for the garrison.   Lewal's division, with the crowd of refugees and the long convoy from Madrid, reached Valladolid on the 4th, and was ordered to move on at once for Burgos. Clausel had been directed to send back all available troops from the north. Thus, instead of making a stand against the British advance, Joseph had to devote all his energies to the evacuation of whole districts, and a rearrangement of his forces while retiring in face of the enemy.

Gathering his forces together as he went Joseph followed the retreat of the convoys. Twice there was some talk of making a stand, and twice the idea was abandoned. On June 9th the army halted round Burgos. The refugees had emptied the stores of supplies collected there. The retreat must continue, and, worst of all, instead of leaving Burgos well prepared to play the same part as in the preceding year, and so gain a breathing-space for the French army, the hope of defending the fortress had to be given up, for the garrison would be starved out in a few days. Burgos must be evacuated. Orders were given to continue the retreat, and make the next halt at Vittoria. There Clausel's divisions would have joined, and a battle might be risked. But even this decision was not taken until three days of hesitation had been wasted in discussing the possibility of a stand near Burgos.

The orders for the retreat were given on the 12th. Next day the magazines of gunpowder and shells in the citadel were blown up, and the business was so clumsily managed that a large number of officers, soldiers, and civilians were killed and wounded. On the 15th the army was at Pancorvo, where a council of war was held. It was there that, the year before, Clausel, retiring with the remnant of the defeated army of Salamanca, had halted and made a successful stand. But the position was different now, for the fortress of Burgos, before which Wellington had failed in 1812, no longer existed. Nevertheless some of the generals urged that the Pancorvo position should be held, and a battle fought. Jourdan pointed out that Wellington need not attack it. There were good roads by which he could work round it, seize the Vittoria road, and cut the army off from France. It was decided that the retreat must be resumed.

At last, on June 19th, the convoys, the refugees, the crowd of officials and courtiers poured into Vittoria, and a few miles west of the town the army halted along the heights above the Zadora, and took up positions for battle, covered by the line of the river. The various divisions halted as they came up, so that there was no methodical plan of battle, and, though the Zadora was unfordable, the numerous bridges that crossed it were not even prepared for demolition. There was no vigorous mind in command. The King was wearied and discouraged with the long retreat. Old Marshal Jourdan was suffering from fever, and there were no subordinate staff officers capable of supplying the places of the chiefs. Clausel's expected reinforcements had not arrived, and instead there was a letter from him saying that if he was to hold the north, he could detach at most only some 4000 men.

Hours were important, for the British were close at hand, yet the day of June 20th was wasted. Jourdan was resting in the city, lying down part of the day. Joseph, too, was not on the heights with the army, but idling in Vittoria, paying his court to the Marqueza de Monte Hermoso, who had followed him from Madrid to Valladolid, and then to Vittoria. Once, indeed, he sent word to Jourdan that he would like to go with him and reconnoitre the positions held by the army, but the Marshal replied that he was too ill with fever to mount his horse. Something was done to relieve the overcrowded city by sending a number of Spanish refugees with a large escort towards the French frontier, but the greater part of the convoy remained, and encumbered the streets and open places of Vittoria. A train of heavy artillery from Burgos and other abandoned fortresses was halted on the highroad to France, blocking the main line of retreat in case of a disaster. But it was not expected that Wellington would be able to attack until the 22nd, and the King therefore counted on having another day in which to move off the heavy guns and the rest of the enormous convoy, and rearrange the order of battle of his army.

But late in the afternoon of the 20th the English cavalry were driving in the French posts left beyond the Zadora, and in the evening Joseph and Jourdan knew Wellington might attack at dawn next day. Hurried orders were given to move the convoy, and all night carts were driving out of the town; but still thousands of vehicles remained, and the heavy

guns lay beside the road on the north-east of the city, im-
mobilised, for generals anxious to put their waggon-loads of
loot in safety had borrowed the gun horses.

At four A.M. the King rode out to the army accompanied
by Jourdan, who was still very ill. As Joseph reached the
heights the day was beginning. A heavy mist lay along the
Zadora and veiled its further bank, but up out of the river mist
came the rumble of gun-carriages, and the far-off sound of
bugles and the pipes of the Highlanders told that the British
were on the move. An aide-de-camp, sent by Joseph to the
general commanding on the left to tell him to come to the King
for orders, rode back with the message that the general could
not leave his troops as they were in contact with the enemy,
and then heavy firing from the same direction told that the
battle had begun ; and as the rising sun scattered the mist the
British attack was seen stretching over miles of ground,
already across the Zadora on the left, and advancing against
the bridges on the French right and centre.

The great battle lasted all through the long midsummer
day. King Joseph was under close fire for hours, and displayed a calm courage that was worthy of his race, but his
inexperience did not allow him to do much to control or direct
the defence of eight miles of hilly ground, and Jourdan was too
ill to give him any effectual assistance. The French were
gradually driven back upon Vittoria, while Graham, breaking
in upon their right, threatened to cut off their retreat. Reille's
division fought desperately to hold him back, and, though
defeat could not be averted, he saved Vittoria from being for
France a Baylen or a Sedan.

Napier describes with vivid touches the last stand before
sunset. ' Many guns,' he says, ' were taken as the British
army advanced, and at six o'clock the enemy reached the last
defensible height, one mile in front of Vittoria. Behind them
was the plain on which the city stood, and beyond the city
thousands of carriages and animals and non-combatants, men,
women, and children, were crowding together in all the madness
of terror ; and as the English shot went booming overhead,
the vast crowd started and swerved with a convulsive movement, while a dull and horrid sound of distress arose. But
there was no hope, no stay, for army or multitude. It was

x

the wreck of a nation. However, the courage of the French soldier was not yet quelled : Reille, on whom everything now depended, maintained his post on the upper Zadora ; and the armies of the south and centre, drawing up on their last heights, between the villages of Ali and Armentier, made their muskets flash like lightning, while more than eighty pieces of artillery, massed together, pealed with such a horrid uproar, that the hills laboured and shook and streamed with fire and smoke.'

As this last battle-line gave way, and retreat degenerated into rout, Joseph extricated himself from the press, and accompanied by Jourdan rode round the outskirts of the city—to traverse the confusion in its streets would have been impossible —and gained the road to France. But here further progress for the King and his party was difficult, for the road and the ground on both sides of it was covered with a mass of fugitives, making their way slowly forward amid the encumbrance of abandoned guns and waggons. It was suggested that the party should strike across country, avoiding the main road and retreating by that to Pamplona by Salvatierra. A native of Vittoria offered to show the way. But as he turned from the panic-stricken crowd Joseph narrowly escaped capture. A body of English cavalry that had penetrated to the north of the city came riding down on the crowd, a squadron of the 10th Hussars in front. They passed so close to the King that some of his party were ridden down. He was saved partly by General Jamin coming up to his help with the light horsemen of his guard, partly because the victors did not recognise the prize that was within their grasp, and were more anxious to capture the waggons and guns on the road than cut off a small party of horsemen.

The King's carriage, personal property and regalia, Marshal Jourdan's baggage with his jewelled baton, were taken by the British, with the greater part of the convoy, some 1500 waggons. 150 guns had been captured with about 400 artillery tumbrils. In the convoy were waggons laden with the military chest of the army, nearly a million sterling, besides the endless variety of valuables that represented the plunder of Spain by the French army during the last two or three years. Thousands of prisoners were taken with the convoy. The wreck of the army escaped by abandoning all these impedimenta to the victors.

After a difficult ride across broken country, Joseph and his party reached Salvatierra a little before midnight. A small French garrison held the town. He was too exhausted to send off even the shortest of despatches to Paris. Jourdan remarked that after all it was only one more battle lost. Joseph must have suspected that he had lost not only a battle, but his crown and kingdom. Next day he continued his flight under a deluge of rain over difficult mountain roads, and after a short march halted at a village in the hills. On the 23rd he reached Irurzun, in the mountains north-west of Pamplona, where he was safe from pursuit and on a good road, by which he could communicate with his generals and with France.

He spent some hours writing letters and orders. He knew so little about the actual position since he had left the panic-stricken army outside Vittoria, that he could only send off at haphazard some suggestions for the defence of the extreme north against the further advance of the victors. To Clarke at the Paris War Office he wrote that Jourdan would send him a full report on the battle. Meanwhile, summing up what had happened, he asserted that he had been attacked by forces that doubly outnumbered his own (the wildest of exaggerations), and that, after inflicting on the enemy as much loss as it suffered, the army had had to retire on Salvatierra. Unfortunately, he explained, nearly all the artillery and equipages of every kind had had to be abandoned, only the teams were saved. (A delicate way of telling that the drivers had cut the traces and galloped off, leaving guns and tumbrils to the enemy; in other words, that there had been a rout, not an orderly retirement.) He had just ordered Reille, who commanded the retreating army, to move to Tolosa, and get into communication with Clausel (Army of the North) and Suchet (Army of Catalonia). Then came an appeal for help. ' The army,' wrote Joseph, ' has neither bread nor artillery. The loss in men is not enormous, but a great effort will have to be made to re-arm the artillery ; the teams have been saved. It is of the most pressing necessity that the Emperor should give his attention to the armies in Spain. They are in want of everything.'

To Julie he wrote telling briefly of his defeat, and hinting at the failure not being all his fault. He asked her to let the Emperor know that, after concentrating the armies for the defence of the frontier, he intended to go back to Mortefontaine. ' I think I ought to have gone there,' he added, ' after the affair of Salamanca.' His money had been lost with the convoy, and his treasurer killed. Her brother, the banker Nicholas Clary, must arrange to send him at once 100,000 francs to Bayonne. He would soon be in France. He would not stop at Paris, but go straight to his old home at Mortefontaine.

Leaving Irurzun, Joseph reached Pamplona on the 24th. But parties of the enemy were in the neighbourhood, and to stay there would be to risk being blockaded. So next day he rode northward by mountain paths into the Pyrenees. On June 27th he was at the frontier village of Vera, where he slept that night. It was the last he spent in his kingdom. Next day he was at St. Jean de Luz in France.

ǰ His flight was a virtual abdication, though he did not yet realise it. He was recovering from the first shock of defeat. Even his lack of military science made him misread the situation and see gleams of hope. As he rode away from the lost battle, he had imagined that Wellington would be able at one swoop to rush forward to the frontier. Now that the generals were rallying and combining what was left of the French armies, he flattered himself with expectations that they would yet be able to make a successful stand under the shadow of the Pyrenees.

To the Emperor he wrote from St. Jean de Luz a long despatch defending his own conduct, and throwing the blame of failure on others. At the moment there was an armistice in Germany. At the end of April Napoleon had marched against the Russians and Prussians with an army of 170,000 men, largely composed of new levies. He had won the battles of Gross-Görschen and Bautzen and established himself at Leipzig and Dresden. Austria was still neutral. The armistice arranged on June 4th had been followed by negotiations. So Joseph, whose failure at Vittoria was now having a disastrous influence on these negotiations in central Europe, but who did not realise this and still thought of his brother as all-powerful at the head of his armies, asked Napoleon to help him.

' I am having San Sebastian armed and provisioned,' he wrote, ' for it had not been put in a state of defence. Bayonne is also in an unsatisfactory state, and steps are being taken to arm and provision it. It is important that your Majesty should direct remittances of funds to meet such large expenses, and should also send here officers and conscripts, and some generals who have not yet been employed in Spain, men who will bring with them some of your Majesty's spirit, and possess your confidence, and who have witnessed your successes in the north.' He ended by saying, that now that it was a question of defending France, he only regretted that he could not bring more military knowledge and experience to the task.

On June 30th he wrote another letter to the Emperor, and entrusted its transmission to Saxony to his friend Miot, who was to give Napoleon any further explanations he might require, and generally discuss the situation with him. In this letter he asked the Emperor to provide out of the French treasury for the pay of the royal guard, ' which now consisted of more officers and sergeants than soldiers,' and for that of the Spanish officers who were with him, and a number of Frenchmen in his service. He asked for certain promotions of these officers to be confirmed : to five he had given the rank of general of division, to five that of general of brigade. He was still King of Spain though he had taken refuge on the French side of the frontier, and Commander-in-chief though he had only his escort and his staff with him, and Clausel, Suchet, and the other generals were shifting for themselves. But though there were moments when he flattered himself that all might yet be regained, he still saw that the chances were that he would have to go back to Mortefontaine. In a letter to his wife, on the same day that he sent Miot away with his despatch for the Emperor, he wrote :—

' I do not think that the position in Spain can be resettled except by a general peace. I am remaining here because the frontier is threatened, but as soon as the first panic is at an end, and the defence has been put on a secure basis, my presence here will be useless, and I shall be glad to retire either to Mortefontaine or some place in the south. I imagine two armies will be formed here under two different chiefs ; and I do not believe there will be anything for me to do, after the first effects of the defeat have passed away, and the Emperor has made his arrangements.'

Long before Miot could reach Saxony the Emperor had decided on the steps to be taken. It was on July 1st that he heard of the disaster of Vittoria, and the news came at a most unfortunate moment when he was trying to force the allies to accept the basis of a treaty of peace. Soult was with him at his headquarters. He ordered the Marshal to proceed at once, post-haste, to Paris. He was only to spend twelve hours there. He was to confer with Clarke at the War Office, and then start at once for the north of Spain, where he was to have the title and powers of lieutenant-general of the Emperor and commander-in-chief. Soult was given an autograph letter of Napoleon to Joseph directing him to hand over to the Marshal all the troops under his command, including his guards and his Spanish officers. But this letter was only to be presented if Joseph made any difficulties. Napoleon did not know what had happened since the battle. If Joseph had done anything to regain lost ground, he was to be treated with more consideration. In any case, in order to avoid friction between him and his old enemy Soult, his friend the Senator Roederer was to go to the frontier, and explain to Joseph that the Emperor felt obliged to entrust the conduct of the war to a veteran leader in whom he had confidence. But if Joseph had done nothing to repair the disaster, he must stay at Pamplona, San Sebastian, or Bayonne, and wait further orders.

When Napoleon wrote these instructions he had no idea that his brother was already a refugee in France. But he realised that he might have quitted Spain, and he ordered him not to go north of the Loire till he had his permission. But supposing he had already come so far, he must proceed in the strictest incognito to Mortefontaine, and remain there. He must neither visit Paris, nor communicate with any high official of the Empire, or interfere in any way with the Regency of the Empress. Cambacérès, as Arch-Chancellor of the Empire, was directed to employ force, if necessary, to secure Joseph's observance of these restrictions. The Minister of War was not to communicate further with the King of Spain ; the Minister of Police was to keep his movements under observation.

In a private letter to Clarke, which Napoleon handed to

Soult, he blamed himself for the disastrous result of the Spanish campaign. 'All the blunders in Spain,' he said, 'are the result of my own ill-judged consideration for the King, who not only does not know how to command an army, but in addition to this cannot take a just view of his own powers and leave the command to a soldier.' When he wrote he complained that he was so badly informed as to what had happened in Spain, that he himself could form no idea of what was the real situation there. But he gathered there had been a decisive defeat.

When Soult reached Paris and showed his instructions to Clarke and Cambacérès, they tried to break the blow that was about to fall on Joseph. Roederer was sent off first to the frontier to see him and prepare him for what was coming. A staff officer, Major Verdun, was to follow immediately with a letter from Clarke, as Minister of War, veiling the Emperor's stern commands for Joseph's supersession in courteous and diplomatic phrases. Then Soult was to follow. In this they were really doing what Napoleon wished, for he still felt an affectionate respect for his elder brother, and was anxious to spare his feelings, but at the same time he was determined not to sacrifice his own fortunes to Joseph's vanity. In his letter to Clarke Napoleon, who thought that Julie, Joseph's wife, was at Paris (she was actually at Vichy), had directed the Minister of War to see ' the Queen of Spain ' and persuade her to use her influence with her husband to induce him to take what was to be done in good part.

Roederer did not reach the frontier till July 11th. He found Joseph at the château of St. Pée de Nivelle, a few miles to the south of Bayonne, whence he was sending off orders to the French generals on the other side of the Pyrenees. Roederer's news was no surprise to him, for rumour already reported that Soult was coming to take command. While Joseph and Roederer were talking of the changed situation, Major Verdun arrived and handed the King the official letter of the Minister of War. He did not open it till the Major had gone, and he was again alone with his old friend. Roederer tells how Joseph broke the seal, read the letter through twice, then sat staring at it, holding it in both hands, and finally passed it to him without a word.

Roederer had already seen the letter in Paris at the War Office. Indeed, he had helped Clarke to compose it. It was the letter of a courtier. Clarke explained, in neatly turned phrases, that after hearing of the defeat of Vittoria, the Emperor judged that it would be impolitic to involve a prince of his family in the difficulties that must result from this unfortunate event, and to make him appear in the eyes of France responsible for any further disaster that might be entailed by the first failure ; and he thought that in the interests of his Royal Majesty's own personal reputation and also in those of the Imperial family, it was better that the direction of the operations on the frontier should be entrusted to an experienced soldier, a marshal of the Empire. ' If you look into the Emperor's motives,' wrote Clarke, ' your Majesty will doubtless not fail to perceive that first of all the Emperor has been inspired by the deep attachment he feels for his august brother.' Only after this preface the name of Soult was mentioned. Then Clarke went on to explain that the serious negotiations in progress in Germany might be prejudiced by the King of Spain suddenly appearing at Paris, and this would also produce a discouraging effect on French opinion. The Emperor therefore desired that he should remain at St. Sebastian, Pamplona, or Bayonne. He would hand over his guard and the Spanish contingent with the other troops to Soult, and none of his officers or the civil members of his administration was to come north of the Garonne. The Spanish refugees would be collected at Auch and other places in the extreme south. The stay of the King of Spain on the frontier would appear to be his own voluntary act, for the fact that the Emperor had given these orders would be kept secret. Clarke expressed in conclusion the hope that Joseph would realise that the Emperor was acting as much in his brother's interests as in his own, and suggested that the arrangements made were such as Joseph himself would desire under the circumstances.

Roederer read the letter, then looked up and said quietly, ' This is really only what I have already been explaining to you. The only difference is that I brought an informal message from the Emperor to his brother, and here is the official communication to the King of Spain, the Lieutenant-General of the Emperor, the Commander-in-chief.'

Joseph burst out into a furious protest. ' What ! ' he said, ' this Soult is the man who denounced me to the Emperor, said I was trafficking with the English. He has evidently talked over my brother, made him listen to these infamous calumnies, and now he is sent to arrest me. This order to stay at Bayonne, to give up my guard, what does it mean but that I am to be the prisoner of Marshal Soult ? ' He went on to say that if the Emperor was thinking only of his abdication, there was no reason why he should not be allowed to go back quietly to Mortefontaine, and live, as he had long desired, in peace at home with his wife and daughters. But there was a deliberate attempt to insult and humiliate him. As to his conduct, he was ready to defend it before the most hostile judges, but he protested against being made to figure as ' the prisoner of Soult.'

Roederer had known Joseph long enough to feel no surprise at such an outburst. He let him talk for a while, and then began to reason with him. He argued that the Emperor, in insisting on his remaining on the frontier, really had in mind the possibility of maintaining his position as King of Spain. If he wished for his brother's abdication, surely Napoleon would have sent him instead an order to retire to Mortefontaine. As for the question of the guard, of course the new commander-in-chief would leave with the King a detachment sufficient for his personal escort and the military service of his household, but it was a tribute to its value as a fighting force that every man and horse that could be spared should join the army in the field. Surely Joseph could not object to this.

Gradually the first fit of anger passed away. Joseph listened to his friend, and at last said he was ready to do all that his brother wished. If necessary he would resign not only the command of the army, but also his crown. ' You know,' he said to Roederer, ' that I was not upset at hearing of the Marshal's appointment. You heard me discuss it quite calmly until I got this letter from the Minister of War, which seemed to mean that I was to be dethroned.' Then with the reference to the letter there came one more angry outbreak against Soult. Roederer interposed again, and Joseph spoke more quietly, and began to talk of a visit to the waters of Barèges, and of a property near Bayonne that he might buy as a temporary residence.

In the afternoon Joseph drew up a general order to the army, announcing that the command was to be transferred to Marshal Soult, Duke of Dalmatia. Next day the King was to meet the Marshal, and Roederer came again to the château, ready if necessary to throw oil upon the waters. Joseph showed him a letter he had written to the Emperor, in which he told his brother he would follow all his directions and stay at Bayonne, though it was with regret he gave up the idea of paying a short visit to his family at Mortefontaine, after such a long separation. After lunch Soult arrived. The two enemies met, and both acted with a courteous correctness that gave no hint of the storm of the day before. Joseph told the Marshal that his guard was at his disposal, with the exception of a few officers and men whom he would like to keep with him, and to this Soult agreed.[1]

But under the surface politeness Joseph felt a continual sense of suppressed anger against the soldier, in whom he saw a successful rival, and to whose earlier action he attributed his own failure. He left St. Pée for the château of Poyanne near Bayonne, and entered into business negotiations for its purchase. He kept up a court there. He had a picket of the grenadiers of his guard on duty at his gate, a cavalry escort when he drove out. Half a million francs had been remitted from Valencia. Possibly the money ought to have been turned over to the military chest of the army, but the treasurer of Joseph's household got possession of it, and as King of Spain he used most of it to pay the arrears of salary of his household and staff and of the detachment of the guard on duty at Poyanne, and used the rest to relieve the Spanish refugees at Auch, all that were left of his subjects. Roederer he had sent away on the 13th, on a mission to the Emperor. He was to arrange for

---

[1] The Royal Guard, though wearing the Spanish uniform and the red Spanish cockade, was, like the guard Joseph had formed at Naples, really French, composed of picked officers and men from the Imperial Army. Its full establishment was:—

Infantry.—Three battalions, each of 1200 men.

Cavalry $\begin{cases} \textit{Light Horse.} \text{—500 men} \\ \textit{Gendarmerie.} \text{—50 men} \end{cases} 550.$

Artillery.—A battery of Horse Artillery and another of Field Artillery.

Military Train.—Two transport companies.

regular payments to be made to Joseph from the French treasury, to enable him to live in befitting state at Bayonne, and provide for his retainers and the refugees, till better times came.

Roederer had hardly gone when Joseph became involved in a dispute with Soult, who had his headquarters at Bayonne. Joseph had sent one of his staff to the chief of the police to ask for passports for ·himself, under the name of ' General Palacios,' and for a suite of ten. He wished, it was explained, to go to the watering-place of Barèges. The official went to Soult, and told him that there was a rumour that Joseph was preparing to go away to Mortefontaine. Soult sent word that he could not consent to the King going to Barèges. It was too near the border; he might be captured there some night by a raiding band of Spanish guerillas. Joseph was indignant at the Marshal thus controlling his movements. He felt he was ' the prisoner of Soult.' He wrote to his wife that he would soon be at Mortefontaine.

It is probable that he'would have gone north without permission, relying on his belief that French prefects would hesitate to stop or arrest the Emperor's brother. But while he was still contemplating flight there arrived a permission from the Emperor for him to return incognito to Mortefontaine if he wished. The letter had been written by the Emperor on July 11th, the same day on which Roederer arrived at St. Pée and broke to Joseph the news of his supersession. Napoleon had learned from copies of Wellington's despatches the full extent of the disaster of June 21st, and had heard of Joseph's flight and his failure to do anything to repair the defeat. He felt that for him to stay any longer at Bayonne would be only to prolong a situation in which the King of Spain would be only a source of embarrassment to Soult, instead of a help to him.

Joseph lost no time in making his preparations for his return home. The French officers of his household were mostly to rejoin the army. His guardsmen were delighted at the news that they would be transferred to the Imperial Guard. He distributed gratuities to all who had served him, giving away a large number of splendid horses and mules, besides other property. On July 24th, accompanied by a small suite, he rode away from Poyanne in the early morning, and a few miles away took a postchaise at the village of Campagne, on the Bordeaux road. He was at Bordeaux that evening. The Marquesa de Monte Hermoso, who had escaped from Vittoria during the battle, had been in Bordeaux since July 2nd. She had left it that same morning *en route* for Paris.

Travelling north by Orleans, ' General Palacios ' reached St. Denis on the night of July 29-30, but instead of stopping there he changed horses and went on. In the morning twilight the carriage drove by the lakes and avenues of Mortefontaine to the château. He was still in name King of Spain, but he must have realised that his Spanish kingdom was as much a thing of the past as his reign at Naples. Long years had gone since he thought that as the seigneur of Mortefontaine he had reached the summit of his ambition. Weary with the long journey, he was like a man rousing himself from restless dreams of unreal greatness. But, after all, the sunny palace by the Bay of Naples and the more gloomy state of Aranjuez and Madrid were not as pleasant places as this homely old château amid its woods and lakes, and the nightmare of Vittoria would be forgotten in the welcome of Julie and her daughters.

CHAPTER XXI

THE END OF JEROME'S KINGDOM OF WESTPHALIA

(1813)

WHEN Joseph reached Mortefontaine on that summer morning the great disaster in Germany was yet to come, but his brother Jerome's throne was already in serious peril, and it was not without good reason that Queen Catherine of Westphalia had been sent to a safe retreat in the outskirts of Paris. The King of Spain, the Queens of Spain, Holland, and Westphalia were all in France, and the ex-King of Holland was a refugee in Austria. The break-up of the Napoleonic Empire had made terrible progress. Of the three brother-kings Jerome alone was still reigning. But war was on his borders, and his kingdom was seething with disaffection.

Napoleon was still at the head of a great army, whose young soldiers had gained confidence in recent victories, and he was still able to negotiate with the Allies as an equal. When he left Paris in April 1813 for the spring campaign in Germany, Jerome, whom he had repeatedly refused to see since his unauthorised departure from the Grand Army in Russia, had asked for an interview, but Napoleon put it off till the latter part of May, when he had reached Dresden after his first successes.

During the earlier months of 1813 Jerome had been working with unwonted energy and intelligence, and in the face of exceptional difficulties, to promote his brother's interests and his own. After the destruction of the Westphalian army in Russia [1] he had less than 5000 men available—his guard,

[1] In the four years before 1812 Jerome had raised a total force of 36,000 men for the Westphalian army. Of these a division 6000 strong had gone to Spain, and 25,000 had marched into Russia. The Westphalian contingent had suffered heavily in

some garrison troops, gendarmerie, regimental depôts and invalids, a mere nucleus for an army.   There was hardly a field-gun left in the kingdom, and the treasury was empty. He had raised more than one loan and obtained some help from his brother, less in the way of money than in the form of supplies of muskets, cartridges, and equipments from the French arsenals, and he had responded to Napoleon's call upon him to prepare for war in the spring.   Allix, his general of artillery, had turned one of the Westphalian foundries into an improvised arsenal and manufactured forty field-guns. By March Jerome was able to report that he had got together 20,000 foot, 2500 cavalry, and 50 guns.   .

But this was only one part of his task.   He had also to provide supplies for the garrison of Magdeburg and other French detachments stationed within his borders.   But Napoleon was not satisfied with his finding the necessary supplies from week to week.   He told Jerome that Magdeburg must be provisioned for a siege.   At first he asked for three months' supplies for 15,000 men, then he raised his demand to supplies for 20,000 for six months, and a little later said that he must have a year's food and forage in the magazines of Magdeburg for 15,000 men and 2000 horses.   He was really thinking, not so much of a possible siege, as desirous of having at Magdeburg a huge reserve depôt of supplies for his army in the field.

Jerome replied that with all the goodwill in the world he could not secure these millions of rations, because he had no money with which to buy them, and did not want to treat Westphalia as if it were a hostile country, and requisition them. Napoleon answered that there ought to be no objection to a system of requisitions.   He himself had fed the Grand Army by requisitions in France itself during his rapid march from the camp of Boulogne to the Rhine in 1805.   Surely what France had accepted was good enough for Westphalia.   But Jerome might have reminded him that in 1805 the receipts given by his supply officers for the requisitioned food and forage had been promptly redeemed in notes and cash by the French treasury,

the Russian battles of 1812, and had been all but destroyed in the retreat.   Two fragments of it remained, some 1500 men shut up in the fortress of Dantzic, and not quite 1000 more in the fortress of Kustrin.   All the available field artillery had been sent to Russia, and the guns had been abandoned in the retreat.   '   .

but now the Westphalian treasury was all but empty, and he could only offer unredeemable receipts to the farmers and peasants.

Jerome asked for money, the Emperor replied that he had none to spare, but he must have the supplies at Magdeburg all the same. Driven to his wits' end Jerome did what he could. Some small quantities of supplies were paid for, much more was practically requisitioned against unredeemable treasury paper. Between the requisitions and the conscription the Westphalian people in town and country felt that they were being hardly treated. They looked for the Allied armies as deliverers, and the growing discontent began to find voice in local disturbances.

The occupation of Berlin by the enemy and the retreat of Eugène had brought the Allied armies into dangerous proximity to the borders of Jerome's kingdom. In March the Russians under Wittgenstein were on the lower Elbe, threatening Magdeburg. The Cossack General Czernitcheff was with him, and crossing the Elbe with his wild horsemen, he carried on a guerilla warfare in Hanover and northern Westphalia. With the Cossack flying columns were a number of German partisans under Prussian officers, whose business it was to raise an insurrection of the peasants, and the direction of this work was in the hands of a former officer of Jerome's who now held a Russian general's commission and served on Czernitcheff's staff. This was no other than Dörnberg, who as colonel of the Chasseurs of the Westphalian Royal Guard had nearly succeeded in his plot for making his master a prisoner in his own palace in the year of Eckmuhl and Wagram.

Davoût kept the insurrection down by ruthless military executions and prevented the Cossacks from becoming masters of the districts they raided, but the whole north was disturbed, and not only did bands of student volunteers join the enemy, but Jerome's newly raised troops began to desert, and even detachments of his guard slipped away in the night from Cassel and Napoleonshöhe, taking their arms and ammunition with them, to join the rebels. In the last days of March disquieting rumours were in circulation at Cassel. The censorship of the press in the little capital made people distrust officially published news, but there was talk of wholesale deser-

tions of Jerome's newly raised troops, and whispers that the
Cossacks would soon come riding into the town. Even the
patriotic young Germans were half afraid of seeing these half-
savage spearmen masters of the place, but among the French
colony and Jerome's thoroughgoing German supporters there
was a dread of sack and massacre. In the first of April the
alarm became a panic.

The French officials began to send away their wives and
families and their portable property to Mayence, and men
joined in the flight. Horses and carriages could only be bought
or hired at panic prices. Each day saw long lines of vehicles
rolling away towards the French frontier. It was said that the
north was all in the hands of the insurgents, and that from the
eastward through the defiles and woods of the Harz Mountains
the terrible Czernitcheff was advancing on Cassel at the head
of an army. Rumour said King Jerome was packing up and
would soon disappear. He denied it. Whatever happened
he would remain. But it was plain that things were taking a
serious turn. General von Hammerstein, the King's aide-de-
camp, had marched out towards the Harz with infantry, light
horsemen, and twelve of Allix's new guns to meet the invaders.
The panic increased when rumours spread that Von Hammerstein was retiring on Cassel, and that his troops were desert-
ing from their colours. Frightened country folk came crowding into the town, driving their cattle and bringing with them
their few household goods piled on farm carts.

Jerome tried to allay the panic with official denials of the
bad news, and to show his confidence in the outlook gave
a state banquet at the palace. But both he and Reinhard,
the French envoy, were living anxious days. The King had at
Cassel and Napoleonshöhe five battalions of infantry, 700
horse and eighteen guns. But he could not rely upon them.
Deserters went away every night. If the enemy appeared his
troops might declare against him. He sent off messenger
after messenger to old Marshal Kellerman, who commanded
the reserves at Mayence, asking for reliable French troops to
be sent to his assistance. ' My troops,' he wrote, ' are entirely
made up of new recruits, and I don't know up to what point
they would stand fast, if they are to act by themselves.' Reinhard backed up his request, and wrote even more frankly.

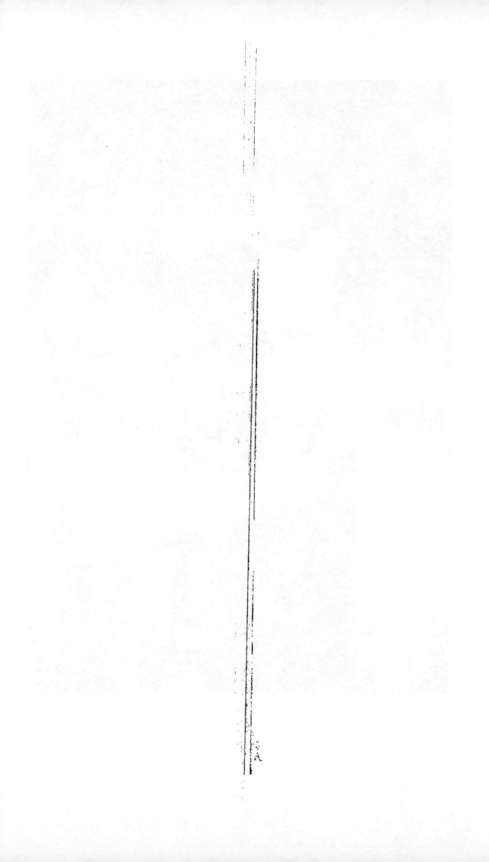

He told Kellerman that he must send reinforcements; 'above all, to stop the desertions of the Westphalian troops '—even two battalions if no more could be spared; and he added words that showed how little reliance could now be placed on soldiers from the tributary and allied states of the crumbling Empire —let them be 'French troops from the old departments,' that is, men of the old France such as it was before Napoleon's conquests added new departments in Germany and the Netherlands, French only in name.

On the 18th Napoleon was at Mayence, and the news allayed the panic. With the Emperor's arrival the great struggle was soon to begin. The Allies must concentrate for battle and cease to trouble themselves about such minor enterprises as a swoop upon Cassel. The pressure on Von Hammerstein diminished. News came from Mayence that General Teste was coming to Cassel with two French battalions, to be followed up by Dombrowski's Polish brigade of four more, men who so thoroughly hated the Cossack and the Russian that they could be thoroughly relied on. Cassel breathed again. Even the most patriotic Germans were glad their Cossack liberators were no longer at their gates. Later on they hoped to welcome their good brothers of Prussia, with one of Frederick William's generals to take care that due order would be kept.

To Jerome his brother wrote from Mayence that he must now see that it would have been wiser to have had a reliable Royal Guard of French veterans, such as Joseph had maintained in Spain and Murat now had at Naples. Jerome expressed a wish to come to see him. Napoleon replied that for the moment he had better remain at Cassel; they could meet later. He swept Von Hammerstein's division into the ranks of the Grand Army, and told Jerome that when Teste had been joined by more of his French battalions in May he might unite with them some of his Westphalian troops, and so form a corps, of which he would give him the command.

Jerome had hoped to be given high command from the outset, and did not realise how his former escapades in the campaigns of Silesia and Russia had shaken the Emperor's long-enduring confidence in his ability as a general. He had worked hard to form a Westphalian army, which he expected that his brother would allow him to lead to battle, and now this army, sadly diminished by weeks of desertions, was being frittered away in detachments, brigaded with Frenchmen, locked up in garrisons. The one complete division, that of Von Hammerstein, had been handed over to a French marshal. At Cassel, when Teste's battalions arrived, most of the Westphalian garrison had been sent off to the fortresses of the Elbe. Jerome had only the two battalions of his Westphalian guard left at Cassel and Napoleonshöhe, and elsewhere in his kingdom two infantry battalions and a regiment of cuirassiers. He was a mere spectator of great events, in which he had hoped to have a part. The Emperor's refusal to see him he felt as a rebuff, and he was still more disappointed when his request to be allowed to be present as an individual at one of the battles of the campaign was answered by a repetition of the advice to stay at Cassel.

In his disappointment he left cares of state to others, and again devoted his attention to organising week-end parties, dramatic performances, and other amusements at Napoleonshöhe. Reinhard complained to the Emperor that the personal conduct of the King ' made a bad impression on public opinion,' and was the subject of scandalous gossip. The gossip was well founded. The Princess von Löwenstein was installed at Napoleonshöhe as the King's guest, and it was even said that he was thinking of divorcing his childless Queen and marrying the favourite who had replaced her.

These were the days of Napoleon's last victorious campaign. Advancing swiftly on Leipzig at the end of April, the Emperor defeated the Russo-Prussian army at Gross Görschen on May 2nd in the hard-fought action which is sometimes known as the battle of Lutzen. The want of cavalry prevented him from reaping the full advantage of his success, but it gave him the possession of Leipzig, and by the 8th he was at Dresden. Other successes followed. On May 21st the victory of Bautzen was won. On June 4th the Allies, who were astounded at the energy of Napoleon, the large force he put in the field, the terrible blows he had struck, agreed to an armistice, and negotiations were opened, which though at one time they gave hopes of a settlement, at last, after a long struggle between the peace and war parties in the Allied councils, ended in a renewal

of the war, with Austria as a member of the Coalition, and all
the chances of war against the Emperor.

During this victorious advance of the Emperor into Saxony,
there had been another alarm in Westphalia. But it was soon
over. Czernitcheff had made a raid across the Elbe, and
seized the town of Halberstadt. He retreated promptly on
the approach of General Teste at the head of a flying column
from Cassel. But during the raid Jerome had taken it upon
himself to summon a detachment of Polish troops to his capital,
writing to their commander that he was ' acting with the
Emperor's authority and by his instructions.' This was a
deliberate fiction, and when the Emperor sharply reproved
his brother, and told him he must not indulge in such fabri-
cations, or interfere with troops not under his orders, Jerome
naïvely explained that he pretended to have instructions from
the Imperial headquarters, because he knew that otherwise
he would not have been obeyed. He promised not to offend
in the same way again.

Then came an order from Napoleon to have the rest of the
Westphalian regiments sent to Dresden to be incorporated
in the Grand Army. Jerome made a struggle to keep this
little remnant of his army. He did not like the idea of seeing
Westphalia entirely garrisoned, his very palaces guarded,
by Frenchmen and Poles. He would give his troops the order
to march, he said, if the Emperor insisted, but it was painful
to him to see them all taken away to garrison the capital of
the King of Saxony. He renewed his request for an interview,
and the armistice having now been concluded, the Emperor
told him he might come to Dresden. He arrived there late
in the evening of June 21st—just at the same time that his
brother Joseph was riding through the darkness by the hill
tracks to Salvatierra in flight from the rout of Vittoria. The
aide-de-camp on duty told him the Emperor was asleep and
could not be disturbed. He received Jerome next morning.
Times were changed since the brothers had last met at Dresden
in the spring of 1812 on the eve of the Russian campaign.
Then Napoleon held his court at Dresden with kings for his
courtiers.

In this, and in subsequent meetings with Napoleon during
the nine days that Jerome spent at Dresden, he discussed

the affairs of Westphalia and his own personal interests. He complained of the way in which his army had been broken up ; referred to the hopes the Emperor had held out to him of having a command in the field ; and said he still desired it in case the armistice did not end in a peace. Napoleon told him that for the present he must give up the idea of having a command. He could best serve both their interests by holding his position at Cassel, but he would not be secure there with only a West-phalian guard. Even at the eleventh hour he must consent to forming a Royal Guard composed of reliable French veterans; the Emperor would provide the officers and men. He ought to have done it years ago. Jerome agreed to this.

Then he raised a more personal question. It was typical of his utter lack of character and judgment that, at this most critical moment in his brother's fortunes, he should try to make into an affair of state an amour that had lately been the scandal of Cassel. With two marriages on his record, Jerome was dreaming of a third, and thought that Napoleon, with his own divorce and re-marriage of such recent date, would be persuaded to second his views.

He had lately been reminded of the existence of his American wife. We have seen how after his accession to the throne of Westphalia and his marriage with Catherine of Würtemberg he had tried to induce Elisabeth to cross the Atlantic with his son, and take up her abode in his kingdom as ' Countess of Smaalkalden,' and how she had replied that Westphalia was not large enough to contain two queens. When she accepted a pension from the Emperor, Jerome had written to her pro-testations of undying affection, and complained that she should ask help from his brother instead of from himself. Of this letter she had taken no notice, unless indeed there is foundation for a tradition, supported by no documentary evidence, that she wrote to him that ' she would rather find shelter under the wings of an eagle than be kept hanging at the beak of a gosling.' To an offer of the Emperor's to provide for the education of her son, she had replied that he was yet too young to be sent away to Europe.

On the eve of the Russian campaign Jerome, after a long silence, had tried to reopen correspondence with her, by send-ing her a letter containing empty and transparently absurd assurances of his affection.[1] She did not reply. In the autumn—but before any news of the disasters in Russia had reached the United States—she petitioned the Congress of Maryland for a divorce. In answer to an inquiry as to her motives made by the French ambassador at Washington (who was in frequent official communication with her, as he paid her the Emperor's pension of 5000 francs a month), she explained that it was a mere formality, intended to put her in a legal position to realise some property in land coming to her from her father. Her attention had been called to the fact that a law would soon be in force by which no one receiving a pension from a foreign prince could enjoy the rights of an American citizen. She had been advised, therefore, to turn her landed property into cash, and she could not as a married woman do this unless her husband acted for her. This was certainly her only reason for applying for a divorce to the civil authority, for she continued, in right of the religious ceremony, to assert her claim to be Jerome's wife. Congress granted the divorce (January 2, 1813), she realised her property, and she wrote to the Emperor asking him to receive her and her son in France, and arrange for the boy's education. She also suggested that she might be given a title, that would assure her future position and her son's. Napoleon was too much occupied with more pressing matters to deal with this petition.

Jerome had heard of the American divorce when he met his brother at Dresden, and he proposed another. The only motive he could allege was Napoleon's own argument for his divorce from Josephine, reasons of state, the desirability of replacing a childless consort by one that would give him hope of an heir to his crown. But the reason of state would count for little in Jerome's case. His throne was tottering, and to

---

[1] The letter, dated February 20, 1812, was addressed to 'Madame d'Albert, *née* Elisabeth Patterson.' This name had been used to cover earlier secret correspondence between Jerome and his wife. 'My dear Elisa,' he wrote, 'What a time since I have had any news of you or of my son ! Yet in the whole world you cannot find a better or more affectionate friend than I am. There are many things that I would like to write to you, but as I have reason to fear that this letter may be intercepted, I confine myself to letting you hear from me, and asking you for news of yourself and of my son. You may be quite sure that sooner or later everything will be arranged, for the Emperor is certainly the best as well as the greatest of men. Your affectionate and good friend, JEROME NAPOLEON.'

send Catherine of Würtemberg back to her father's palace at
Stuttgart would be an insult to a German sovereign that
would add to the growing hostility of all Germany to the
Empire. Jerome had been as faithless to Catherine as he had
been to Elisabeth. Notwithstanding all this she was most
devoted to him, and showed a patient tolerance of his conduct,
that can only be explained by the fact that she had been
taught, as a German princess of the period, that a queen must
appear to be ignorant of scandals that are known to all her
court. Her latest rival was the Princess von Löwenstein, the
daughter of one of the noblest houses in Germany. Jerome
wanted to dismiss Catherine and make the Princess his queen.
He even urged that the matter should be quickly settled,
so that a child of hers might be born in wedlock. Napoleon,
who himself showed scant respect for the moral law in his
own private conduct, did not regard Jerome's infidelities to
Catherine as a serious matter, but he scouted the suggestion of
her being divorced, above all at this moment. Jerome was
told to dismiss the idea from his mind. He might do what
he liked for the Princess von Löwenstein in the way of giving
her castles or lands in Westphalia, but to talk of making her
his queen was folly.

So after appearing at a round of court festivities, Jerome
left Dresden on June 30th and returned to Cassel, not over-
pleased with the reception his brother had given him. The
armistice lasted for some six weeks more. From the depôts
in France and the Army of Reserve parties of sergeants and
men arrived for the formation of the new Royal Guard, but
they came in slowly, and it was not till the beginning of August
that the first troops of Cavalry of the Guard could be formed.
Meanwhile further drafts of the few Westphalian troops in
the kingdom had been called up to the Grand Army, and
Teste's battalions had marched away, so that Cassel was left
almost without defenders.

The armistice ended on August 16th, and the war was
renewed, with Austria no longer neutral but on the side of the
Allies. Hostilities had lasted hardly a week when the 1st and
2nd Westphalian Hussars, attached to the extreme right of
the Grand Army, marched off in the night with their officers
at their head and joined the Austrians. Their commander

was the Baron Colonel von Hammerstein, a brother of the general of the same name, and an officer whom Jerome thought absolutely reliable. Napoleon at once ordered that the other Westphalian cavalry units with the army should be dismounted, and their horses turned over to the French cavalry corps. To Cassel he wrote that no more Westphalian troops were to be raised; 'it is only providing recruits and arms for the enemy,' he said, 'and there is no use shutting one's eyes to the fact that now no Westphalian can be trusted.'

The war had begun badly for Napoleon. Threatened from all sides by superior forces, he tried to win the terrible game by successive strokes from his central position, now at one, now at another army of the Allies. He had beaten back Blücher and the Army of Silesia. But his lieutenants were not so successful. Macdonald was defeated; Oudinot failed in a counterstroke against Berlin and was badly beaten by the Swedes and Bülow's Prussians. Vandamme was defeated and taken prisoner at Kulm. Bernadotte, once Marshal of France and now Crown Prince of Sweden, who commanded the northern army of the Allies about Berlin, found himself strong enough, after Oudinot's defeat at Gross Beeren, to send a column from the north into Jerome's kingdom to co-operate with Czernitcheff's Cossacks, and Cassel was once more in danger.

It was at this moment that Czernitcheff found means of communicating secretly with Jerome, and sent him a letter suggesting to him that he might yet save his throne by abandoning his brother's cause, posing as a German prince, and declaring for the Allies at the head of his Westphalians. By his marriage, wrote Czernitcheff, Jerome had become the son-in-law of the King of Würtemberg, the cousin of the Czar. The Allies would have no quarrel with him, if he would act as the patriot King of German Westphalia, for their quarrel was only with Napoleon and the aggressive French Empire. Jerome replied in a dignified note. He owed his throne, he said, to the victories of France, he was the brother of the Emperor, and he could not think of maintaining his present position at the cost of the misfortunes of Napoleon and the Empire. He sent copies of the correspondence to the Emperor.

But though he acted thus in the presence of a great temptation, the knowledge that he might treat separately with the Allies influenced him more than once. He could easily re-open this avenue to safety if he wished, for the wife of his trusted henchman Lecamus, now Count of Fürstenstein and Minister of Foreign Affairs, was a sister of Hardenberg, the chief minister of Frederick William of Prussia. We see some indication of momentary leanings towards revolt in a conversation he had with Reinhard, the French envoy at Cassel. Reinhard had spoken to him of the growing danger of an attack on his capital by the Allies. Jerome complained that the Emperor had taken away nearly all his Westphalian troops, withdrawn Teste's French brigade and Dombrowski's Poles, taken no notice of his request for other troops to replace them, and so left Cassel at the mercy of a hostile raid. ' Of course,' said Reinhard, ' in that event your Majesty will have to go.' ' What if I were to do like the other minor princes of Germany ? ' asked Jerome. ' What if I were to stay here ? My intention is to stay.' Reinhard did not at once see his meaning, and urged that to stay would be to run serious risks. ' Of course,' said Jerome, ' unless the enemy agreed to it.'

His words were inspired by a bit of ill-humour—perhaps, too, by some idea of making the Emperor understand that he was still worth conciliating. But he really had no intention of staying in Cassel as the vassal of the Prussians or Austrians. He was already, unknown to Reinhard, unknown even to the ubiquitous agents of Fouché's police, making secret arrangements for the coming crisis. He had found speculators to take the risk of privately buying some of the crown lands from him, and was lodging the proceeds of the transaction, some hundreds of thousands of francs, in the Bank of France under an assumed name. He was inquiring for an estate in France, and had already begun negotiations for the purchase of the château and park of Stains, near St. Denis. He was looking forward to a pleasant life in and near Paris after the war, with his million francs of yearly revenue as an Imperial Prince, supplemented by an indemnity for the loss of Westphalia.

In September the enemy had again crossed the Elbe and relighted up the northern insurrection, and in the middle of the month Czernitcheff was reported to be on the march through the Harz Mountains *en route* for Cassel, at the head of a column variously estimated at from 4000 to 6000 men, chiefly Cossack cavalry, with ten or twelve guns. The people were rallying to him, and provided him with the most complete information, and with guides who knew every by-road and forest path. If Jerome had had a moderate force of reliable troops he might have defied the raiders, but he had only a handful of doubtful defenders. General Zandt was sent out to Münden, a short day's march to the northward, to watch the approaches on that side, with four companies of chasseurs and 200 dragoons, less than 600 men in all, and these men Westphalians, who were not certain to fight. General Bastineller was sent out to Heiligenstadt, to hold the main road from the eastward with 1100 men, cuirassiers and light infantry. In Cassel, under his sturdy French General Allix, Jerome had his Westphalian bodyguard of 150 men, the grenadiers of the Westphalian Guard, 500, and all that was yet arrived of his new French Royal Guard, 400 thoroughly reliable men, two companies of Westphalian chasseurs and a couple of field-pieces. His whole force did not amount to 3000 men, and he had broken them up into three bodies at Cassel, Münden, and Heiligenstadt, so that the defence was weak everywhere. He sent urgent messages to the nearest French commanders asking for help, but they had other orders from Napoleon, to hurry all the men they could spare to Leipzig, and they could not send him any reinforcements.

On September 25th Czernitcheff, advancing from the eastward, was in touch with Bastineller's detachment. The Russian could have crushed him, but he merely kept him occupied with a false attack made by clouds of Cossack skirmishers ; and marching with his main body to the southward by country roads pointed out by his Westphalian guides, he got between him and Cassel. At dawn on the 28th a gendarme came spurring into the city with the news that the Cossacks were only a few miles away. An order sent to Bastineller to rejoin the King at Cassel failed to reach him, nor could he send back any news. It was supposed that he was captured. A reconnaissance of the French hussars was sent out. It was a hot day and the mists lay like a fog along the Fulda valley.. The hussars disappeared into it, but soon came galloping back with wild-looking spearmen at their heels, who only gave up the pursuit when the chasseurs who supported the hussars fired in their faces. The crisis had come at last.

There was a wild panic in Cassel. In the courtyard of the palace the royal carriages were being hastily packed with Jerome's baggage. Officials, French residents, all the hangers-on of the court, were hurriedly preparing for instant flight. Of the townsfolk some were talking of welcoming their deliverers, but most were barricading doors and windows. Jerome, who was never wanting in a certain cool courage, took a good breakfast, during which he sent for Allix and told him that he must remain and defend Cassel. For this purpose he could only spare him the two companies of Chasseurs of the Guard, a couple of hundred of the French hussars, whose horses had not yet arrived, and who would fight on foot, and the two guns. He had sent orders to Zandt to come in from Münden with his 600 men. As the escort of the royal retreat 200 mounted hussars, the bodyguard, and the grenadiers were to accompany Jerome.

After breakfast Jerome mounted his horse and rode out by the west of Cassel, with his escort and baggage-train, following the road that runs by the bank of the Fulda, and then turns off south-westward to Wetzlar and Coblenz. That road and the north-western highway towards Paderborn and Münster were already dotted with carriages conveying fugitives, in mortal fear of being cut off by the Cossacks.

The enemy had already occupied the eastern suburb of Cassel beyond the Fulda, opened the gates of the prison there, and liberated a number of Westphalians, whom Jerome had imprisoned as political suspects. Allix had barricaded the bridge over the Fulda, and defended the river crossing with his two guns and his handful of men. Above the town a party of Cossacks crossed by a ford and made a dash for Jerome's column, but they were driven back by a charge of the French hussars and the fire of the Westphalian guardsmen, who proved true. The grenadiers even pursued them to the ford, and Allix thought that if Jerome had followed up this success by crossing and falling on the flank of the enemy's attack, there might have been a victory. But the King took no unnecessary risks. He recalled his escort and continued his retreat.

Allix held his own during the 28th, for the attacking party

was only Czernitcheff's Cossack vanguard. The Russian general had led his main body to fall upon Bastineller, whom he hoped to trap while he was retiring on Cassel. But Bastineller's force was melting away, and by evening all except a handful of officers had either deserted and were on their way to their homes or had joined the enemy. Zandt, too, saw his men leaving him at every mile on the way back to Cassel from Münden. Early on the 29th he reached the city with less than half his force. At its gates some of these mutinied and deserted, and he rejoined Allix with only a couple of hundred Westphalian hussars.

On the morning of the 29th Czernitcheff announced his arrival by opening fire with twelve guns. A strong column forded the Fulda, and stormed the barriers at the Leipzig gate. Allix fell back on the palace, and held that and the neighbouring buildings. A Russian officer with a white flag summoned him to surrender, offering to allow him to march off with arms and baggage. Allix, though the position was desperate, refused the offer. The fight went on. Most of his Westphalians had abandoned him. The enemy was being helped by disbanded soldiers and insurgent citizens. Allix had only his French hussars with him, and half of these had been killed or wounded. In his admiration for this dogged resistance Czernitcheff sent another summons, and Allix surrendered, but only on condition that he should leave his guns, but take away with him his handful of men, with arms, baggage, colours, and as many of the diplomatic corps and the officials as wished to rejoin the King.

He marched out on the 30th, and Czernitcheff occupied the place, established his headquarters at the palace, seized the treasury, issued a proclamation in the name of the Crown Prince of Sweden (Bernadotte) announcing that the kingdom of Westphalia had ceasèd to exist, and established a provisional government. Guards were posted, and most of the Cossacks were kept outside the barriers of the city, so that Cassel escaped the dreaded sacking by its liberators, but a mob of patriots plundered some of the houses which the French officials had abandoned, burned a woollen factory that Jerome had established, and broke the nose and an arm off the statue of Napoleon in front of the palace.

The rioters and the members of the provisional government were soon sorry that they had jumped so quickly to the conclusion that all was over.   On October 3rd news arrived that Allix was coming back, accompanied by a French division under General Rigaud, despatched by Marshal Kellerman to recapture Cassel.   Czernitcheff hastily evacuated the city, and disappeared in the direction of the Harz Mountains.   It was a Cossack raid, not a conquest.   On October 7th Allix and Rigaud reoccupied Cassel without firing a shot.

Where was King Jerome ?   On September 30th he had reached the château of Montbauer near Coblenz.   He rested there till October 3rd, and then moved into Coblenz and occupied the prefecture.   He had sent word to Kellerman that he would remain on the Rhine till he was assured that troops were available to check the progress of the enemy and reoccupy his capital.   At Coblenz he entertained the Princess of Löwenstein and the Countess of Fürstenstein (Madame Lecamus), who had fled from Cassel by way of Münster.   To the Emperor he wrote from Coblenz reminding him that he had asked in vain for a French garrison for Cassel, and throwing on his brother the responsibility for what had happened.   As soon as he heard that Allix was marching on Cassel he wrote to him that the insurgents should be sternly dealt with.   Everything that was plundered must be restored.   The members of the provisional government must be put in prison.   Those who had broken the statue of the Emperor must be hunted out and hanged in front of it.   The leaders in the disorders were to be tried by court-martial.   Allix must act with vigour, and pay no attention to ' the outcries of old women.'

There were some executions.   The members of the provisional government, however, were lightly dealt with.   They pleaded that they had acted only to preserve order, and it was found that among them were friends and relatives of Jerome's most loyal supporters, amongst others the old Count of Hardenberg, the father of Madame Lecamus.   Jerome wrote to Allix to release them, and blamed him for acting precipitately, though he had only obeyed his orders.

Jerome left Coblenz on October 13th, and travelling by easy stages reached Cassel on the 17th.   He ordered that there should be no addresses of welcome by the authorities, but he posed as a conqueror, riding in at the head of his escort, meeting a column of Westphalian troops under Allix at the barrier and leading them to the palace. In the evening the streets were illuminated, ' by order.'

While Jerome was riding into Cassel the greatest battle of the century, the ' Battle of the Nations,' was being fought round Leipzig, and the Emperor's star was going down in disaster. But the King of Westphalia had no idea the end was so near. Guarded by 8000 French bayonets, he was not alarmed at the reports that the Cossacks were again showing themselves within a few miles of his palace. But on October 24th one of his French staff officers, Colonel Lallemand, arrived from Leipzig with the news of the great defeat. He had himself escaped with difficulty, after seeing the Emperor and the Imperial Guard marching out amid a confused mass of fugitives, and more than once during his long ride he had narrowly escaped being taken by the Cossacks.

At first Jerome spoke of remaining till he received orders from the Emperor. But next day he was making his preparations to depart. On the morning of the 26th he rode away, escorted by three battalions of French infantry, detachments of cuirassiers and dragoons, and his Westphalian bodyguard. On November 1st he reached Cologne. General Rigaud, with the 5000 Frenchmen who were left under his orders, remained for some days longer at Cassel quite undisturbed, and evacuated it only when he received orders from Napoleon to join the Grand Army in its retreat to the Rhine.

Jerome's departure had been a little premature, and showed unnecessary alarm. But even if he had stayed, he would have added only another week to his reign. He still considered himself King and set up his court at Cologne, but this time the kingdom of Westphalia had ceased to exist, and Jerome's late subjects were giving a frantic welcome to the Allies ; while his soldiers, the enthusiasts who had already taken up arms against him, and the more prudent patriots who had waited to declare themselves, were swelling the ranks of the armies that would soon be marching into France.

CHAPTER XXII

THE DETHRONED KINGS AND THEIR AMBITIONS

(1813)

THE three Bonaparte kings had now all lost their kingdoms, and the Imperial crown of their brother was in serious danger. But with a strange blindness to the obvious facts of the situation, Joseph, Louis, and Jerome all clung to the hope of restoring their fallen thrones, and insisted that they were still kings, whose rights both the Emperor and the hostile Coalition against him ought to recognise. When Napoleon reached Mayence on November 2nd at the head of 70,000 men saved from the wreck of his army, he found a letter from Louis awaiting him there, in which his brother formally asserted his claim to the kingdom of Holland, and suggested his immediate restoration, as a means of strengthening the Emperor's hands by securing the loyal support of the Dutch people.

Louis had left, Gratz in the early summer for a ' cure ' at the waters of Neuhaus. He returned to Gratz on July 8th. The armistice had then put a temporary stop to the war in Germany, and there were hopes of a peace being arranged. He wrote to various friends in Austria suggesting that in any redrawing of the map of Europe his claim to Holland should not be forgotten. Nothing came of this correspondence, and towards the end of July Fouché, who passed through Gratz on his way to the Illyrian province of Napoleon's Empire, had an interview with Louis, and appears to have persuaded him that he ought to make an effort to effect a reconciliation with his brother. At the beginning of August it was plain that the peace negotiations would break down, and Austria was preparing to join the Allies in the coming campaign. Louis declared that, as a Prince of the Imperial family, he could not avail himself of the invitation sent to him by the Emperor Francis to remain peacefully in his dominions, even though Austria was at war with France. On August 2nd he left Gratz for Switzerland.

Passing through Munich on his way to Basel, he handed to the French Minister at the Bavarian court a letter to be forwarded to Napoleon. It was dated August 4, 1813. Louis wrote that he had heard with sorrow the news of the disaster of Vittoria, and the accession of Austria to the Coalition. Now that the Emperor had to face a million enemies, he felt he could not himself stand aside from the crisis that was imminent. He knew that he counted for very little, but such as he was he must now belong ' to Holland, and after that to France and to his Majesty.' He was on his way to Switzerland, where he would be at the Emperor's call whenever he thought he could make use of his services, but he added a condition, ' provided that the hope of returning to Holland, when a general peace was arranged, was not to be taken from him, and that he was not to act in violation of the oath he had sworn ' when he assumed the crown of the Netherlands. He could not believe, he said, that once the old questions of trade with England were out of the way, the Emperor would wish to deprive him and his sons of their kingdom, and he was sure that, if he could be of any service to France, the Emperor would be better able than he was to choose a course for him, that would befit a brother who had become King of Holland.

The Emperor took no notice of this strange offer. Louis persisted in his idea that he had made a generous proposal to his brother. From St. Gall in Switzerland he wrote, on August 9th, to his mother that he had left Austria in order to make it easier for the Emperor to restore him to Holland.

During the autumn campaign he was travelling about Switzerland and amusing himself with writing more poems. When he heard the news of Leipzig he hurried to Basel, expecting that now at last the Emperor would call him to his aid. At Basel he met Murat. The King of Naples had left the retreating army at Erfurt on October 24th, telling Napoleon that he must hurry back to Italy in order to bring the Neapolitans to the help of Eugène against the Austrians in the north. Murat was already a traitor to the Emperor, and his wife, Napoleon's sister Caroline, was his partner in this treachery. During the campaign of Leipzig they had both been in correspondence with Austria, and it had been arranged that Murat was to save his kingdom from the wreck of the Empire by abandoning Napoleon and securing Italy for the Coalition. The secret of the conspiracy was well kept to the last, and Napoleon, though at times he suspected Murat, always returned to a blind confidence in his old comrade, to whom he had given a crown and his sister's hand.

At Basel Murat ran a serious risk by frankly telling Louis that, if he wanted to be King of Holland again, his best plan would be to give up writing long letters to Napoleon, and instead try to come to an arrangement with the Allied sovereigns of the Coalition. Louis refused this advice. He would have done the Emperor a real service if he had promptly told him of Murat's treacherous suggestion. But it never occurred to him that the man who made it must be a traitor, against whom his brother should be warned.

It was after this interview with Murat that Louis wrote the letter he sent to his brother at Mayence. It was one more plea for his restoration, and he made the serious mistake of thinking that, because the Emperor was in dire straits, he might give it almost the form of a summons to surrender Holland to him. He wrote to Napoleon that he thought that at this moment it would be advisable to withdraw the French troops from Holland, give him free passage for himself and his suite through France, and leave it to him to organise the defence of the Netherlands, where he did not doubt that he would be welcomed by the Dutch people, who would at his call rally to the aid of the Empire.

The delusion that Holland was mourning his absence, eager to welcome him back, had become a fixed idea. He was so sure that his brother would now yield all his demands, that he wrote to many leading men in Holland to inform them that he would soon be back at Amsterdam. He sent his secretary to Holland with a letter inviting his former minister Van Capellen to come to him at once, and without waiting for a reply, either from the Emperor or from Holland, he left Basel, hurried across France, and on November 3rd arrived at his mother's château at Pont-sur-Seine.

Arrived at Mayence, the Emperor had a brief breathing-time in his struggle with the Coalition, for the Allies were not yet ready for an attempt to cross the Rhine and carry the war into France. They had to reduce large French garrisons left behind in strong fortresses, reorganise the liberated German states, repair the wastage of the campaign, concentrate their armies, and accumulate supplies for the next movement and agree upon a plan of operations. There was no armistice, but there was a pause in the active operations of the war, and the diplomatists were soon at work seeking for a possible basis of settlement, Metternich having proposed on the part of Austria that peace should be made with Napoleon on the basis of leaving him France with her 'natural frontiers,' not the old France of pre-Revolution days, but a larger France, that of the treaty of Lunéville, bounded by the Rhine, Alps, Pyrenees and sea.

This tacit truce gave Napoleon time to collect new forces for a supreme effort, in case the negotiations should come to nothing; and at the same time during these anxious weeks he was busy with the claims raised by his brothers, the three dethroned kings. He arrived at St. Cloud on November 8th. He had not replied directly to Louis, but in a letter to Cambacérès he had shown what he thought of his claim to Holland. 'I send you a letter from King Louis,' he wrote, 'which seems to me to be a piece of folly. I suppose he has not come to Paris. If he comes there as a French Prince my intention is to forget all his absurdities, all that he has printed,[1] and to receive him. But if he comes as King of Holland, and means to persist in this chimerical idea, he ought not to be received. If he has committed the folly of coming, no visits should be paid to him, and he must remain incognito with Madame at Pont. Above all, the Empress should not see him.'

In a further note to Cambacérès Napoleon gave him precise instructions how to act. If Louis was content to live in France as a Prince of the Empire, he was welcome, and all the past would be forgotten; but if he was posing as King of Holland and putting forward claims 'suggested to him

---

[1] An allusion to Louis's statement of his policy and action in Holland, which he had printed and privately circulated.

z

by Austria and the enemies of France,' Madame Mère was to try to persuade him to withdraw once more. If she did not succeed, Cambacérès and the grand dignitaries of the Empire were to give him two days in which to formally resign his claims, and if he refused he was to be arrested. Louis was informed of the Emperor's intentions and at once left Pont-sur-Seine and posted back to Switzerland, where he took up his abode at Soleure. Thence he made attempts to obtain a call from Holland, by corresponding with old friends at Utrecht and Amsterdam, whom he still imagined to be devoted partisans of his rule. Their replies were disappointing.

King Jerome, too, thought that he must assert his claims to a future restoration to a throne. From Mayence the Emperor had written to him, expressing his displeasure at the way in which his reign had ended. Napoleon thought that his departure from Cassel was a little precipitate and undignified, and was annoyed at what he heard of Jerome's proceedings at Coblenz on the occasion of his first flight from his kingdom. He told him that he wished him not to return to Paris, but to remain in some place near the frontiers of his old kingdom, where the Queen would join him, and they would live quietly without giving occasion to unpleasant rumours. He suggested the château of Brühl near Cologne, famous, by the way, in history as the place of Mazarin's exile. To Reinhard, who was with him, Jerome said that he did not want to go to Paris, but would prefer Aix-la-Chapelle to Brühl as a temporary residence, and sending some of his suite in advance to prepare the palace of Aix for his reception, he left Cologne on November 5th for the old capital of Charlemagne.

There he received an angry message from his brother. The Emperor had heard of Jerome's arrangements for purchasing the estate of Stains. He reminded him that by the law no Prince who had been given a foreign crown could hold or acquire property in France, except by the Emperor's permission, and went on to say that, apart from the irregularity of his proceedings, it was ridiculous that at such a moment he should be squandering money on such private projects. In a letter to Cambacérès the Emperor said that he was indignant at finding that at a moment when all over France private individuals were making sacrifices for the defence of the country, Jerome was busy with expensive plans for his own selfish interests.

On November 8th Reinhard arrived at Aix-la-Chapelle with a mission from the Emperor to Jerome. He was only admitted to his presence after a long delay and a preliminary interview with Lecamus, Count of Fürstenstein, who, as Minister of Foreign Affairs of the King of Westphalia, received the Emperor's representative. Jerome was still reigning, though his army, his palaces, and his kingdom were all lost to him. Reinhard told him that the purchase of Stains had been cancelled by the Emperor, and that he had directed Queen Catherine to join her husband at Aix, where she and Jerome would reside for the present. Jerome was in an angry humour. Why should he not have Stains, as well as the King of Spain.had Mortefontaine ? As to the Queen, he would not allow her to come to Aix. If he could not live with her near Paris, let the Emperor give him the palace of Laeken near Brussels. The Queen could go there, but it must be himself, not Napoleon, that would send the order to his wife. In any case, he would not let her come to Aix. Her place was not on an outpost line, where a Cossack raid across the Rhine at Düsseldorf might surprise her any day.

' No fear of that,' said Reinhard, ' the Cossacks will no more come to Düsseldorf than they will come to Laeken.' ' Yes,' replied Jerome, ' that is just the talk I heard when we were at Dresden. They kept saying the enemy would not get across the Elbe.' Then he went on to complain that he was badly treated by his brother. Traitors like the Crown Prince of Sweden were assured of their kingdoms, while he lost by his fidelity. The Emperor knew very well that he might have stayed at Cassel, if he had listened to the proposals of the Allies. Even to-day he might, if he liked, recross the Rhine, and they would welcome him. He believed that at that very moment Napoleon was discussing proposals for the cession of his kingdom, without his having a word in the negotiations. Was that a way to treat a brother who was devoted to him, a fellow-sovereign ? ' Sovereign ! ' interposed Reinhard. ' Surely your Majesty is not reigning here ! ' ' Yes, I am a sovereign. here, just as I was at Cassel,' said Jerome, and then he told him that if he had any proposals to make, he had better see the ' Minister of Foreign Affairs.' So the interview ended with a touch of comedy.

On November 11th Fürstenstein (Lecamus) in a formal note informed the French envoy that ' the King ' was about to proceed to Pont-sur-Seine to visit Madame, and that the Queen would meet him there. Reinhard protested that this was against the Emperor's orders, and was met by a statement that Jerome had received verbally the consent of Napoleon through one of the royal aides-de-camp, General Wolff, who had seen him at Mayence. Reinhard still protested, but while Jerome was preparing for his journey there arrived a new despatch from Napoleon. Queen Catherine had seen him at St. Cloud, and backed by the influence of the Empress, who had taken a great liking to her, she succeeded in persuading him to allow Jerome to return to France. But he must not come to Paris, Pont-sur-Seine, or Stains. The Emperor would lend him and Catherine the palace of Compiègne.

Jerome lost no time in leaving Aix-la-Chapelle. On November 14th he arrived at Compiègne. The Queen and her suite arrived the same evening. The following days saw the coming of a long train of chamberlains, secretaries, aides-de-camp, pages and servants. The court of Westphalia was installed in the palace, but large as it was there was not room for all Jerome's courtiers, officials, and servants. Some of them had to lodge in the town.

And soon there were something like court ceremonials. The King of Spain with a long array of attendants came from Morte-fontaine to visit his brother King of Westphalia. He had been longer in France, and came to pay his respects to the latest arrived sovereign. He had been at Mortefontaine since July 30th. On the day of his arrival Julie was at Vichy, where she had spent two months. She returned home on August 2nd. There was a large household at the château of Mortefontaine. Julie's brother Nicolas Clary, the banker, lived there and had a staff of secretaries through whom he conducted his correspondence with his business houses at Paris, Marseilles, and Genoa. The Crown Princess of Sweden, Desirée Bernadotte, was on a long visit to her sister, although her husband was leading his army against Napoleon. And Joseph had brought with him a crowd of French and Spanish officials, secretaries and aides-de-camp.

During the rest of the summer and the early autumn there was a round of country amusements. Picnic parties in the park, fishing and boating on the lakes, shooting in the woods, concerts at the château. Joseph was sometimes absent. Despite the order of Napoleon that he was not to visit Paris, he would go there incognito to see the Marqueza de Monte Hermoso. The news from Spain told of Wellington's steady progress against Soult. Joseph must have found some consolation in the fact that his rival had not succeeded where he himself had failed. Then came the tidings of disaster in Germany, and the news that Jerome was at Compiègne, and Joseph hastened to visit his brother-king and discuss with him their prospects of again wearing their crowns.

Both of them, like Louis, flattered themselves with the belief that their former subjects would be ready to welcome them back. Joseph had not seen Napoleon since his return, and had no idea of the Emperor's new plans for Spain, but he had vague hopes that if a general peace were arranged, though the Allies might not consent to his restoration at Madrid, they might agree to compensation being found for him by his being given a crown elsewhere, perhaps in Italy. Jerome had ceased to expect anything from Napoleon, but he had other plans of which apparently he gave Joseph no hint. His wife, Queen Catherine, was in correspondence with her father, the King of Würtemberg. She had a diplomatic channel through which her letters could be sent without any risk of their being opened and copied in Napoleon's *cabinet noir*. Before leaving Meudon she had written to Würtemberg asking for the King's good offices with the Allies in case of a peace being concluded. Ties of blood and honour, she pointed out, had prevented her husband from throwing in his lot with the other German princes, but it would be hard if, when all the rest were peaceably secured, with at least some part of their dominions, she and Jerome should lose everything. This was followed up with a letter to her father from Compiègne on November 18th. 'I feel certain,' she said, 'that if there is still any justice left in the world, you will be able to have some influence on the peace arrangements, and then you will not forget the King, a son-

in-law who has always acted towards you in the most affectionate way.' With this influence at work Jerome felt that
he was to some extent independent of the Emperor.

Julie, titular Queen of Spain, a country she had never even
seen, was also negotiating, but it was with the Emperor, and
her husband Joseph did not yet know anything of the project
she was discussing with Napoleon. It was largely to his
marriage with Julie Clary, and the fortune she brought him,
that Joseph owed his carreer, and indirectly it had helped all
the Bonapartes. He had been the first of the brothers to rise
from the penury of the revolutionary years after the ruin of
the family in Corsica. And he had been able to aid Napoleon
in his rise to power because Julie had placed such ample means
at his disposal. She had never cared for the ostentatious
display in which the rest of the family revelled. She preferred her country home at Mortefontaine to the Tuileries,
the Luxembourg, and St. Cloud. Since the birth of her second
daughter her health had never been completely restored, and
she had found in this an excuse for remaining in France when
her husband was reigning at Naples and Madrid. She had paid
only a brief visit to Naples, against her will, because Napoleon
insisted on her going there. She had never been in Spain.
And now her chief desire was to induce her husband to renounce
all his ideas of eventually returning to Madrid, and to assume
his old rank as a French Prince and Grand Elector of the
Empire, send the crowd of Spanish and French dependants away
from Mortefontaine, and live there quietly, with occasional visits
to the Luxembourg when his official duties called him to Paris.

On November 10th, two days after the Emperor's return
to St. Cloud, Julie went to see him there. Napoleon had just
received a letter written by Marshal Soult from the Spanish
frontier a week before. The Marshal began by reminding him
of a conversation he had had with him, when they were together at Dresden before the news of Vittoria arrived. The
Emperor had then said to Soult that perhaps the best way out of
the Spanish entanglement would be to send back Ferdinand
VII. as King, arrange for his marriage with one of the Bonaparte
princesses, conclude a treaty of friendship between France and
Spain, and obtain the mutual evacuation of the country by
the French and British armies.

Soult gave it as his opinion that the time was come to attempt
to carry out this plan as a last resource. He thought he could
hold his own for a while on the frontier, but the defence could
not be indefinitely prolonged. It was likely that the English,
bound as they were to the other powers of the Coalition, would
not consent to negotiate in case the war was renewed in northern
Italy and on the Rhine, but even so he believed the plan could
be carried through. Many of the Spanish leaders, he said,
were unfriendly to the predominance of Wellington, and would
throw over the British alliance if they were assured of Ferdinand's return and the withdrawal of the French. Spain
could be rallied to the Spanish king, and Wellington would have
to retire to Portugal. This would set free a large part of the
French forces now in the Pyrenees and northern Spain for
operations on the Rhine or in Italy.

To Julie Napoleon spoke confidentially of his new plan.
She welcomed it. It would be her work a little later to persuade Joseph to resign his shadowy prospects of ever again
ruling in Spain. For the present she was to keep the Emperor's
secret. Above all, Soult's part in the suggestion must be concealed throughout. The mention of his name in this connection would drive Joseph into frantic opposition.

The Emperor discussed the matter with Roederer, his own
trusted ally since the days of the Consulate, and Joseph's
minister at Naples, and the intermediary in many negotiations
between the brothers. He asked him if Joseph seriously
expected to return to Madrid. Roederer said that Joseph
thought it might yet be made the subject of negotiations with
the Powers.

'That is an empty dream,' said Napoleon. 'The people
don't want him. They know how incapable he is.' Then
after an outburst of invective against Joseph's proceedings
in Spain, he went on : ' I have sacrificed thousands, hundreds
of thousands of men, to make him King of Spain. It has been
one of my mistakes to think my brothers were necessary to
secure the continuance of my dynasty. It is safe without
them. It will be established even in the midst of storms
by the force of events. The Empress is enough to make it
secure. She has more wisdom and political good sense than
the whole of them. At this moment I would not give a pin

to have Joseph in Spain rather than Ferdinand. The Spaniards will always be united by their interests to France, and Ferdinand will be no more opposed to me than the King.'

Roederer suggested that perhaps Joseph wished not so much for the crown of Spain, but for a kingdom somewhere or other. ' Where were they to find it for him ? ' asked Napoleon. But in further conversation he agreed with Roederer that it would be well to find some dignified occupation for Joseph away from Paris. He might be made Governor of Turin. Finally it was settled that Roederer should go to Mortefontaine, and, without giving Joseph any information, find out what exactly was his state of mind.

On November 12th negotiations were opened secretly by means of a confidential agent between the Emperor and Ferdinand, who since his deposition had been residing at the château of Valençay, a pensioner of the Emperor, and virtually a prisoner of state. There were frequent visits of Julie to St. Cloud, but she only told Joseph that she was trying to interest the Emperor in his affairs. Roederer was often called in to assist at these conferences. The Emperor heard that the Duke of Azanza, one of the Spanish grandees who had stood by Joseph throughout, and followed him to Mortefontaine, was in difficulties for money, and sent him a large sum from his privy purse. ' Those Spaniards are gentlemen. They don't come worrying one for money like the Italians,' said Napoleon. Joseph was pleased at the Emperor's unsolicited act of kindness.

At last, on November 27th, the news of the project was broken to Joseph by the Emperor himself. He was asked to come from Mortefontaine to Roederer's house in the Rue St. Honoré, and thence went to the Emperor's study at the Tuileries. It was the first meeting between the brothers since the disaster in Spain, but Napoleon had not a word of reproach for him as to the past. He told him they must now think only of the present and the future. Quite calmly, as if he were discussing some abstract problem, he explained the situation to Joseph. The most he could hope for, he said, was to obtain a peace that would leave him France with its old frontiers. All idea of maintaining the Empire beyond these limits had to be abandoned. He was facing ruin, with his armies all but destroyed. Holland was going over to the House of Nassau. Italy was trembling in the balance, for Murat, whom he had made a king, was negotiating with his enemies. Even if he did not go over to them, no help could be expected from him. The Italians, enthusiastic for the name of Napoleon in the days of prosperity, were now turning against the Empire. In Belgium and along the Rhine there were signs of disaffection. The Pyrenees were being forced by a foreign invader. What use was it at such a time to think of foreign thrones ? The most that France could be asked to do was to defend its own borders. Its people would not make sacrifices to maintain or restore French Princes in other countries. What was the necessary conclusion from all this ?

' We must give up Spain,' continued the Emperor. ' You must return to your position as a French Prince. Or if you feel that you cannot come down to this lower dignity, you must simply withdraw and be content to live in absolute retirement. I shall give back Spain to Ferdinand. I shall restore him to the Spaniards, on the one condition that they respect the frontier of France, and interpose between the English and us. After this great concession I hope that I shall be able to withdraw the army I now have in the Pyrenees, and send it against the Austrians in Italy. Anything is worth doing to obtain this result.'

To Napoleon's surprise Joseph refused to accept the inevitable, and entered into long arguments to prove that it was to the interest of both of them to try to uphold his claim to Spain, and that nothing would be gained by surrender at this moment. The interview ended without any result.

On his return to Mortefontaine Joseph wrote to his brother a long letter repeating his arguments against the new plan. The secret of his opposition was that he still believed there was a party in Spain that was devoted to him, and he argued that if at this moment Ferdinand were restored, it was too late to gain over to France those who had so far supported the Spanish prince, while all the French party would be lost for good and all. Peace would not follow. England and Spain would be united against France. There were indeed serious miscalculations in the project of Soult and Napoleon, as well as in the argument of Joseph, but his error was his blindness to the fact that whatever happened his own position in Spain was gone for ever. The resignation asked of him was a mere formal recognition of facts, and while he himself lost nothing, there was just a chance that the Emperor might gain something by the proposed new combination.

Joseph followed up this letter by summoning his friend Roederer to Mortefontaine and sending him to the Emperor with a new suggestion. Bernadotte was married to the sister of Joseph's wife, and was now, as Crown Prince of Sweden, one of the leaders of the Coalition. Joseph thought he could induce him to intervene with the Allies to secure his restoration to Spain ; or if this could not be done, Bernadotte might obtain for him territorial compensation elsewhere. Napoleon promptly dismissed the idea as impossible. England, he pointed out to Roederer, would insist on the restoration of Ferdinand VII. as the first step to peace. Austria and Russia agreed with her in this. The Prince of Sweden had acted in such a way that no Prince of the Imperial family could have any dealings with him, and, besides, he had no real influence with the Allies : he was merely one of their generals. But apart from all this, the Emperor said that France wished to be rid once for all of the Spanish entanglement. Only the idlers and gossips of Paris had any other view. To Roederer's suggestion, made by Joseph's request, that he might be sent as a plenipotentiary to take part in the pending negotiations with the Coalition, Napoleon replied that this was impossible. Joseph had been so employed at Amiens and Lunéville, but times were changed, and the ex-King of Naples and Spain could not act in this capacity. As for finding him some other throne, that was equally out of the question. Joseph must resign himself to resuming his old position as an Imperial Prince.

Joseph remained obstinate. Julie tried in vain to influence him. But Napoleon would not allow a mere formality to stand in the way of his plans. Without waiting for Joseph's abdication, he signed on December 11th the treaty of Valençay, by which he recognised Ferdinand VII. as King of Spain and agreed to promote his immediate restoration. Ferdinand in return was to use his influence to bring about a peace between France,

Spain, and the British, and it was understood that later a marriage would be arranged between him and 'the Princess Zenaïde Bonaparte, the eldest daughter of Joseph, then a girl of thirteen. Joseph's consent had not been asked, but Julie had promised her support, and it was hoped that the prospect of seeing his daughter Queen of Spain would be some consolation to Joseph for the loss of his crown. Other clauses of the treaty dealt with the release of prisoners, the provision to be made for Joseph's Spanish officials, and the repatriation of the refugees. The Emperor hoped that at last he had freed himself from the terrible burden of the Spanish adventure, but he had acted too late.

On December 2nd Caulaincourt, who had lately been appointed the Emperor's Minister of Foreign Affairs, notified the Allies that Napoleon was ready to accept as a basis of negotiation the proposals sent by Metternich from Frankfort, that France should be reduced to the frontiers marked out at the treaty of Lunéville. For a few days there seemed to be a good prospect of peace. This hope was not realised, because on the one hand Metternich did not speak for the whole Coalition, but for Austria only, and on the other hand Napoleon, by endeavouring a little later to obtain further concessions, gave an opening for those of the Allies who declared that his ambition would never be confined within the frontiers of France, and that the only hope for a lasting peace lay in his deposition and the restoration of the House of Bourbon.

While the abortive negotiations were still pending Jerome was endeavouring to obtain some support for his claim to Westphalia through the influence of his father-in-law, the King of Würtemberg, with the Allies, and Queen Catherine was busy writing letters to her father pleading her husband's cause. At the same time King Louis of Holland, from his exile in Switzerland, was writing to Caulaincourt, urging that his claim to the crown of the Netherlands should be raised at the Congress. Holland was now evacuated by the Imperial army, he said ; would the Emperor consent to his sending delegates to Amsterdam to learn the will of the Dutch people, who, he still believed, were longing for his return ? He argued also that it was to the Emperor's interest as well as his own that he, Louis, should represent Holland at the Congress, and that this position should not be left to the Prince of Orange-Nassau. He could not believe, he said, that the Emperor would prefer a foreign prince to his own brother. Caulaincourt sent a cold official acknowledgment of Louis's letter. The Emperor turned a deaf ear to his demands. As to Holland, Napoleon had no illusions. He knew that the Dutch were enthusiastic for the restoration of their old rulers of the House of Orange, and were welcoming Bülow's Prussian army as liberators. The Emperor was thinking only of securing France for himself and his son. The Bonapartist Kings of Spain, Holland, and Westphalia belonged to a policy he had abandoned, and he was wearied by their continued harping on their hopeless claims.

Before the end of December the negotiations had broken down, and the Allied armies were again on the move. Schwarzenberg's Austrian army was marching through northwestern Switzerland to cross the Jura, cut off France from Italy, and separate the north from the south of France itself by a threat against Lyons. If Louis remained any longer in Switzerland he would be in an enemy's country.

Lucien, who was watching the great struggle as an outside spectator, but a deeply interested one, wrote to Louis from Thorngrove. He told him that he thought he need not have left Gratz when Austria joined the Coalition. ' Do you really believe,' he said, ' that you would have sided with the enemies of France, if you had remained quietly in your refuge at Gratz, in the states of a sovereign who, although he is now at war with the Emperor, is allied to him by the closest ties, and all whose efforts with a view to securing a peace concur so advantageously with those of the rest of Europe. No, my brother, I regard those only as the enemies of France who prolong the war for the sake of false ideals of glory ; those who are not moved by the sorrowful cries of a million of mourning households. If Austria will give me a place of refuge, I shall go there without any idea that in so doing I am joining hands with the enemies of France. As Switzerland is no longer a neutral country, I hope soon to be with you at your philosophic retreat of Gratz, pending the time when we can go on together to that poor Rome, which is now so barbarously ill-treated, but which, thanks to the Allied Powers and its Pope, will soon be again in possession of well-secured neutrality and religious peace.

I look forward to our being together there in the summer. There I shall be once more in possession of my fortune, which will be also yours. The pleasures of literature and a blameless life will be our consolation, especially if after all the Emperor concludes a peace which will allow France, Europe, and the Church to breathe once more.'

This letter shows that Lucien counted on being soon allowed to leave England, where, though he was living quietly on his Worcestershire estate, he was a prisoner of war. He wrote as a Roman Prince, looking forward to the coming time when he could again enter into possession of Canino, and resume his old place at the court of Pius VII., whose side he had throughout taken in the conflict with the Emperor. Of the four brothers of Napoleon he alone had refused to sacrifice his independence for a tributary crown, and for years he had lived a happier and more honourable life than that of his royal brothers, whose promotion to kingly thrones had brought them only a few anxious years of nominal power ending in disaster. Louis and Joseph were thoroughly disappointed men. Jerome perhaps did not feel his downfall so much, but one can hardly admire the equanimity that comes largely from a superabundance of levity and a corresponding lack of brains and character.

On the approach of Schwarzenberg's army Louis decided that he could no longer remain in Switzerland. He drew up a final protest against the neglect of his claims to Holland, sent manuscript copies to various public men, and then packed up his belongings and started for France, travelling incognito with passports in the name of De Taverny. On Christmas Eve he arrived at Lyons, where for a few days he was the guest of his uncle the Archbishop, Cardinal Fesch. Louis might expect to find a sympathetic friend in his uncle, for since the day when Napoleon had made Pius VII. his prisoner, Fesch had been in opposition to the Emperor.

Before the end of Christmas week Louis left Lyons *en route* for Paris, where he arrived on New Year's Day 1814, and went to his mother's house. He notified the Minister of Foreign Affairs of his arrival, and in answer Caulaincourt informed him ' in the name of the Emperor ' that if he came as a French

Prince he was welcome, but if as King of Holland he could not be received.

Louis wrote in reply that now that Holland was occupied by the enemy he did not pretend to the title of King, and was quite indifferent as to whether he was so addressed or not. 'I have come,' he wrote, 'only as a Frenchman, to share the dangers of the moment, and to make myself useful in so far as I can. If Holland should again fall into the Emperor's power and he does not restore it to me, my conscience as a King would not permit me to remain in France. If, on the other hand, at the peace Holland has to be ceded to some other prince but the Emperor, and my renunciation of its crown is necessary to sanction this part of the treaty, I shall not refuse it.'

The Emperor might have diplomatically interpreted this letter as a step towards submission, a basis for a *modus vivendi* with his brother, or at least a truce. But he was angry at Louis for having come to Paris without his permission, and irritated at his persistent harping on his supposed rights. Besides this, Napoleon still hoped for an eventual peace that would make the Rhine his frontier, and in that case it might be urged that Holland was only part of the delta of the great river, so the supposition on which Louis based a possible revival of his claim might be realised. He wrote angrily to his brother on January 4th. He told him that if he posed as King of Holland he had no right to be in France. Who had given him leave to come to Paris ? ' You are no longer King of Holland,' he continued, ' since the day when you abdicated and I re-united that country to France. The territory of the Empire is invaded, and I have all Europe in arms against me. If you persist in your idea that you are a King and a Dutchman, go away forty leagues from Paris. I won't have any complicated attitude on your part, any taking up of a middle position. If you accept the position of a French Prince, write me a letter that I can print in the *Moniteur*.'

Louis would not write another line, or go a step further. Berthier and Caulaincourt came to give him the Emperor's orders either to resume his rank as a Prince of the Imperial family and Constable of the Empire, or leave Paris. He refused to obey, and denied the right of any one to expel him from his mother's house. Napoleon could not provoke the scandal that would arise from an order to arrest his brother. Besides, he had more serious matters to occupy him than a quarrel with the deposed King of Holland. Not ' the territory of the Empire,' but France itself was invaded. Blücher had crossed the Rhine on New Year's Day. Schwarzenberg was advancing from the Jura. Bülow was threatening the north. Wellington was in the south. The final crisis had come, and amidst this battle of nations Louis's passive resistance might be allowed a petty success, such as it was.

CHAPTER XXIII

JOSEPH, LIEUTENANT-GENERAL OF FRANCE

(1814)

ONE only of Napoleon's brothers was to play some part in the great events of 1814. In the last dark days of the old year, when it was evident that the war would be renewed, and that early in the New Year he would have to leave Paris and place himself at the head of his army, the Emperor turned to Joseph for help. In his absence from the capital the Empress was to preside over the Council of Regency. He wished to leave at her right hand one whom he could more thoroughly trust than any of the professional politicians and diplomatists, all of whom he had begun to suspect. All his life long, despite their many divergences of view, he had felt a singular regard for his eldest brother, to whom in early years after his father's death he had looked up as to the head of the family. More than once he had spoken to his intimate councillors of Joseph's mistakes, failures and weaknesses, but he always came back to his earlier point of view, and thought of Joseph as the brother who stood nearest to him and was most to be relied on of them all.

Lucien he rightly judged to have the keenest intelligence after his own, the firmest character, the greatest power of holding his own in a stormy debate or facing a dangerous crisis. But Lucien had been for years in open rupture with him. As for the others, they could not for a moment be compared with Joseph. Louis with his broken health, his poetic dreams, his torturing sense of grievances that made him impracticable, his quarrel with Hortense, and Jerome with his mad extravagance, the scandals, follies, and blunders of his career, were both out of the question.

Joseph, as the elder brother of the Emperor, the Grand

Elector of the Empire, was to be the guardian of the Empress and of the infant King of Rome. It was in the latter part of December 1813 that Napoleon came to this decision, but in giving effect to it he met with unexpected difficulties on his brother's part.

Joseph had refused to renounce his rights as King of Spain. He knew that there had been some arrangement with Ferdinand, but the terms of the treaty of Valençay had not been published. It was necessary first to obtain the assent of the Spanish Junta, and so make sure that they would welcome Ferdinand as the friend of the Emperor. The Duke of San Carlos had been sent to Spain on a confidential mission to persuade the patriots to fall in with the project.[1] Joseph persisted in regarding himself as King of Spain until he chose to abdicate. He had his court and his secretaries of state at Mortefontaine—a court on a very small scale, and not to be compared in splendour to the Westphalian court of King Jerome at Compiègne. Joseph had the further advantage over his brother, that while the exiled court of Westphalia was chiefly made up of Frenchmen with German titles, the titular King of Spain had a considerable body of Spaniards who had followed him into exile, some of them with him at Mortefontaine, but most of them living as refugees in the south of France. Now, useful as Joseph might be to Napoleon, it would be impossible to employ his services if he persisted in calling himself King of a country that the Emperor must abandon if he was to make peace, and there would be endless complications if he acted at the same time as a high official of the Empire and an independent sovereign.

Once more Napoleon had recourse to Julie's good offices, and his mother was also to exert her influence with her eldest son. Julie visited Paris in Christmas week, and the Emperor's requirements and the reasons for them were explained to her. On December 27th she drove back to Mortefontaine accompanied by Madame Mère. They told Joseph that the Emperor

---

[1] San Carlos failed in his mission. The treaty was to have been ratified within a month from the date of its signature (Dec. 11, 1813). The term for ratification was prolonged till the end of March 1814, in the hope of the scheme being accepted by the Spaniards and the English. Meanwhile Ferdinand was detained at Valençay. Finally Napoleon, finding that he could not obtain the assent of the Junta, let Ferdinand go, and the treaty was never ratified.

2 A

would not require him to make any formal abdication or renunciation of his claims, but what he asked him to do was to proceed at once to Paris, simply as a French Prince, go to the Luxembourg, his official residence as Grand Elector of the Empire, and thence send to Napoleon a letter, so written that it could be published, to the effect that, as the first of his subjects, he had come to take his place beside his throne in the coming crisis.

Joseph refused to act without full consideration. It was not till the 29th that he wrote his reply, and it was useless for the Emperor's purpose. ' Sire,' he said, ' the violation of Swiss territory has laid open France to the enemy. In circumstances like these I wish to convince your Majesty that my heart is entirely French. Brought back as I have been to France by the course of events, I shall be happy if I can be of any service, and I am ready to undertake anything that can prove my devotion to you.' So far so good, but then Joseph went on to assert his royal dignity in a way that, considering the whole situation, was simply ridiculous.

' I know also, Sire,' he continued, ' what I owe to Spain. I recognise my obligations, and I desire to fulfil them all. As for my rights, I think of them only as something to be sacrificed to the general good of mankind, and I shall be happy if by this sacrifice I can contribute to the pacification of Europe. I hope your Majesty will judge fit to direct one of your Ministers to discuss an arrangement for this purpose with the Duke of Santa Fé, my Minister of Foreign Affairs.'

In other words, Joseph refused to lay aside his dignity by a tacit concession. He was still King, but ready to discuss the conditions on which he would abdicate if necessary, but it must be arranged through the regular diplomatic channels, for if he had lost his kingdom he had brought his Minister of Foreign Affairs home with him to France.

His mother and his wife suggested that he should go to Paris and talk matters over with Napoleon instead of sending this letter, but he said he was unwell and could not leave home, so the two women went back to Paris with this strange document. The Emperor was disappointed, and thought of abandoning his plans for Joseph, though just at that moment his brother, with his power of ready speech and his experience of debate, could perhaps have rendered him immediate service. For Napoleon was in conflict with the Corps Législatif, where in both Chambers there were demands for constitutional reforms as the price of aid for the National Defence. Napoleon was about to prorogue the Legislature and govern without it.

This very conflict opened the way to further correspondence between the brothers. Reports reached Mortefontaine that the debates in the Chambers were likely to provoke revolutionary disturbances in the streets, and Joseph, roused to action by the idea of imminent peril, sent a messenger to Paris offering to come immediately to the Luxembourg if the Emperor required his aid. In the same letter he mentioned that the evening before his eldest daughter, Zenaïde, had had a narrow escape. Her dress had caught fire, and only for her father's prompt intervention she would have lost her life. She had escaped with some burns, painful, but neither dangerous nor disfiguring.

Napoleon did not tell him to come, but he wrote him a New Year's letter on January 1st, thanked him for his expressions of goodwill, congratulated him on Zenaïde's escape, and sent as New Year gifts for her and her sister little porcelain boxes from Sèvres mounted in gold, and with the Empress's portrait on the lid. Next day Joseph took a step which might easily have made Napoleon give up all idea of employing his services, for he wrote that he could not sacrifice his honour, and he felt bound in honour not to appear except as King of Spain till he had formally abdicated, and this abdication could only take place on the occasion of a general peace, and after having provided for any obligations of his own towards those Spaniards who had espoused his cause. It must be done by a regular treaty like that by which he had been made King at Bayonne. He must be treated as a King, or allowed to live in obscurity.

He sent two of his friends to explain his views to Caulaincourt. The minister urged the necessity of his acting as the Emperor desired. What France needed was peace. Joseph appearing as King of Spain in any public capacity at Paris would provide a telling argument for the Emperor's enemies who wished to press the war to the bitter end, on the ground that Napoleon had not really renounced the idea of foreign conquests and a wide extended Empire ; while, on the contrary, his appearance there simply as a Prince of the Imperial family and Grand Elector would be a testimony to the moderate and pacific views the Emperor really held. The envoys also saw Louis at the house of Madame Mère. He told them that he was sure that his brother's best course was to yield the point.

At an earlier interview Roederer had told Napoleon that Joseph expected to have some other state given to him as a compensation if he resigned the crown of Spain, and at the time the Emperor had said the idea was out of the question. But when on January 4th he dictated to Caulaincourt his instructions for a new attempt to negotiate with the Allies, he added to them a suggestion that if Italy was to be rearranged, Tuscany ought to be given to Joseph.[1] But he did not let him know that he had so far modified his own opinion. He had not yet decided what further course to adopt when, on the 6th, he suddenly learned that Joseph had come to Paris and taken up his residence at the Luxembourg.

Joseph's envoys had returned to Mortefontaine late on the 4th, and next day they had told him that he ought to be at Paris. There he would be in a better position to discuss his own interests and the Emperor's projects, and his absence might be misinterpreted as a shirking of a difficult, perhaps even a dangerous position, and so do him injury in the future. From the Luxembourg he wrote to the Emperor that, without in any way modifying the attitude he had felt bound to take up, he had come, because out of his affection to him he wished to be where he could perhaps do him some service. It was for the Emperor to decide whether he was to remain at the Luxembourg or go back to Mortefontaine. Next day he had his brother's reply, a remarkably clear statement of the position. After acknowledging Joseph's communication he went on to say :—

' Here is the whole question put as briefly as possible. France is invaded. All Europe is in arms against France, and still more against me. You are no longer King of Spain. I have no need of your renunciation, for I don't want either to have Spain for myself or to dispose of it in any way ; and

---

[1] In the same instructions he notes that an effort should be made to obtain an Italian principality for Jerome as a compensation for the loss of Westphalia.

further, I do not want to have anything to do with the affairs of that country, but only to live in peace with it, and set my army free.

'What do you mean to do? Are you willing to take your place beside my throne as a French Prince? You will have my friendship, your income from the civil list, and your position as my subject and a Prince of the reigning family. In that case you must act as I do, define your position, write me a plain letter that I can publish, give a reception to the authorities, and show yourself zealous for me and for the King of Rome and a hearty supporter of the Empress's regency. Is this impossible for you? Can it be that you have not enough sound judgment to take this course? In that case you will have to go to some château in the provinces, forty leagues away from Paris, and live there in obscurity. If I survive, you will live there quietly. If I die, you will be killed or arrested. You will be useless to me, to the family, to your daughters, to France. But you will be harmless to me, and you will not put obstacles in my way. Choose at once and take your course. All mere professions of affection are just now useless and out of place.'

Berthier came later to talk over the situation with Joseph. The King's secretary, Miot, joined in the conference. Joseph insisted that by an informal abdication he would be giving up all claim to act as protector of the interests of the many Spaniards who had followed him to France. Miot suggested that the opinion of the Spaniards themselves should be taken on the point, and it was arranged that there should be a council meeting of Joseph's Spanish ministers and grandees, and at Miot's further suggestion the Queen was to be present. He knew her influence would be exerted to induce her husband to give way.

So for the last time Joseph held a formal council as King, and for the first time Julie, after having been all these years Queen of Spain, sat at the council board at her husband's side —her first and last act of royal power. The Spaniards had the good sense to advise the King to do what the Emperor asked, even if it were a tacit act of abdication. And at last Joseph wrote a 'letter that could be published,' a letter probably drafted for him by Miot.

'Sire,' he said, 'the invasion of France imposes on every Frenchman the duty of hastening to defend her, and it is most of all to those whom she has raised to so high a rank that the noble prerogative belongs of being the first to hasten to the defence of throne and country. As the first of French Princes, and thereby the first of your subjects, allow me, Sire, to beg you to accept the offer of my hand and my counsels. In whatever way you may judge fit to direct, I shall consider myself fortunate if I can co-operate in restoring to that France to which I owe everything the peace and prosperity of which all Europe stands in need. In the present circumstances I think only of the dangers of our country. Every good Frenchman ought to sacrifice every other feeling. You will yet save France, Sire, if all Frenchmen will place at the service of your throne the same self-devotion as that with which I offer you my services.'

The long crisis was over. It has been worth while telling the story of it so fully on account of the curious light it throws on Joseph's character. The Emperor declared that he was satisfied, and that all his old friendship for Joseph had been restored by his generous offer. Joseph asked only that the relief to be administered to the refugees should, in order to spare their feelings, be distributed by the Duke of Santa Fé or some other Spaniard, and that he should be allowed to keep in his personal service some of the French and Spanish officers who had served him so long and faithfully and followed him to France.[1]

On January 9th the brothers had a long interview. Joseph had the satisfaction of having it settled that, although he was no longer King of Spain, his official title should still be 'King Joseph' and his wife should be known as 'la Reine Julie.' As King of Spain he had worn the uniform of a colonel of his Spanish Guard. His ceremonial dress was now to be that of an officer of the Grenadiers of the Imperial Guard. He preferred this to the stately but somewhat fantastic official costume of the Grand Elector, and it was only on very excep-

---

[1] One of these officers was a young Spanish artillery colonel, De Montijo. He had been wounded at Salamanca, and was again wounded in the defence of Paris in 1814. After his return to Spain Colonel de Montijo married and had a daughter Eugénie, who became Empress by her marriage with Napoleon III.

tional occasions that he was to wear the mantle and plumed hat, knee-breeches and court sword, which the artist David had selected as emblems of Imperial dignity. He was to fix an early date to receive at the Luxembourg the authorities of the various departments of government. The Emperor would presently decide what were to be his functions as the chief assistant of Maria Louisa when the Regency was organised. He was to be the Lieutenant of the Emperor, surely at such a moment a higher dignity than King of Naples or even of Spain.

A week later, on January 16th, there was a state reception at the Luxembourg. Joseph, in his new uniform of a general of the Imperial Guard, welcomed and was greeted by the great functionaries of the Empire, the members of the Senate, the Council of State, and the High Courts of Justice.

It was the formal recognition of his resumption of his old rank, as first Prince of the Empire.

By the end of this third week of January 1814 the invaders were pressing forward into the heart of France. Their columns were converging on Paris, marching slowly on the snow-covered highroads, all of which radiate from the French capital. Before each hostile column a French army corps, commanded by a marshal with a record of victory unbroken till these late disastrous years, fell slowly back, doing something to delay the hostile advance. As they came on the enemy's generals had to leave behind them large detachments to hold the country and besiege or blockade the fortresses. The moment was coming for Napoleon to act. His armies, terribly inferior in numbers, were concentrating as they drew nearer the capital. The Allied armies, reduced by detachments, had approached each other, but the heads of the hostile columns were spread out along a vast semicircle, and still so far apart that the Emperor, uniting his forces in a central position, could hope to strike swiftly now at one, now at another, and have a local superiority of numbers on his side.

He had patiently watched the enemy's advance, and at the end of this third week he decided that the time was come to put himself at the head of his armies.

On January 20th Blücher had blockaded Toul, and was moving on St. Dizier with Ney and Victor retiring before him. Of the 80,000 men with whom the Prussian general had crossed the Rhine on January 1st, he had now only 30,000 with him, so many had been left behind to blockade the fortresses. Southward the left column under Schwarzenberg was near the fortress of Langres,[1] with an advanced corps under Gyulai moving on Bar-sur-Aube, opposed by Mortier. On the extreme right Bülow was still in the Netherlands. The Russian armies were coming up. Winzegerode, marching to join Bülow, was at Aix-la-Chapelle. Wittgenstein, following up Blücher in the centre, was near Nancy.[2] Napoleon intended to deliver rapid blows against Blücher and Schwarzenberg before the Allies were further concentrated. His one hope was that victory might enable him to negotiate for peace on any terms that would secure his throne and the succession of his son. He was no longer dreaming of conquest. ' I call Frenchmen to the help of France,' he had said in his proclamation to the French people. ' Peace and the freedom of our territory must be our war-cry 1 '

On January 21st he held a meeting of the Council of State, at which Maria Louisa was appointed Regent, with two chief councillors—King Joseph, Grand Elector of the Empire, for military matters, and Cambacérès, the Arch-Chancellor, for civil affairs. On the 23rd there were farewell audiences. Addressing the officers of the National Guard of Paris, he told them he confided to them the guardianship of his wife and son. Louis left his books and papers, the proof-sheets of his new edition of *Marie* and his latest poems, to bid farewell to his brother, wish him good fortune in the coming campaign, and express his regret that he could not be with him in the field. There was no need of explaining why he remained behind. He was still young, not quite thirty-six, but it would not have been easy for any one who saw him that day to believe that he was the same man who had charged beside his brother in the rush for the bridge of Lodi and saved Napoleon's life when the column was riddled by the Austrian fire. For now Louis was almost a cripple, walking with difficulty, leaning on the stick his hand could just hold, with

---

[1] Langres surrendered to the invaders after a mere show of resistance.

[2] There were two other theatres of war besides that of eastern France. On the Pyrenean frontier Soult faced Wellington and the British with their Peninsular allies. In northern Italy Eugène, sadly weakened by Murat's defection, was opposed to the Austrian army of Bellegarde.

his face prematurely aged, and his voice broken by nervous weakness. Napoleon spoke kindly to him, and told him that he could still help Joseph in Paris.

Jerome was refused an audience, for his brother was angry with him. He had heard unpleasant stories of the wasteful extravagance, the endless follies of his Westphalian court at Compiègne. He would have let it pass if Jerome had remained there, for the scandals of Compiègne only found a faint echo in the capital. But on January 14th, in defiance of his express orders, Jerome had come up to Paris and established his household at the château of Stains. On the 23rd, during the farewell audiences, Jerome's Westphalian General Count von Wickenberg appeared in the circle, and told the Emperor that ' the King ' had come up from Stains and requested an audience. Napoleon replied coldly that he could not see him ; he ought not to be in Paris ; let him go back to Stains.

Next day (January 24th), before starting for Châlons, the Emperor published a decree defining Joseph's duties, and ordered the Treasury to pay him half a million of francs (£20,000) as a special gratuity to meet the extra expenses of his new position. The decree announced that Napoleon had appointed ' his well-beloved brother, King Joseph, his Lieutenant - General.' In this capacity he was to have command of the National Guards and regular troops in Paris and its neighbourhood, and, subject to the directions of the Empress Regent, the command of the detachments of the Imperial Guard left in the capital. He was to take all necessary steps to organise the defence of Paris and its environs.

Detailed instructions explaining how this authority was to be exercised were handed to Joseph. He was to organise a headquarters office and personal staff, and was allowed to appoint to these departments several of the officers who had served with him in Spain. Though this pleased Joseph, it was not a sound arrangement, for the Imperial officers were jealous of these Franco-Spanish comrades, many of whom owed their high rank, not to service in the field, but to rapid promotion due only to Joseph's friendship. There was therefore likely to be friction, at a moment when, if results were to be obtained, the whole military and administrative machine ought to work smoothly and rapidly. Joseph was not directly to command the troops. He was to concert his measures with and send his orders through General Ornano for the Imperial Guard, General Hullin (commanding the Paris military district) for the troops of the line, and Marshal Moncey for the National Guard. In case of fighting round Paris, Moncey was to have the executive command under him and act as his 'major-general' or chief of the staff.

The work to be done was enormous, but with an effective organisation and an energetic chief who had a free hand it might have been accomplished. Clarke and the employés of the War Office were available for much of it, and then there was the permanent military staff of the Paris division. The line of the barriers of the capital, and positions beyond them, were to be entrenched and barricaded. The National Guard was to be trained, and twelve legions or mobilised regiments formed out of its best elements. Twelve companies of artillery-men were to be formed out of the students of the École Poly-technique and other volunteers from the educated classes, with such of the old gunners from the Invalides as could still serve. The civil engineers were to form an engineer corps. Recruits were to be sent to fill gaps in the field army. Cannon were to be mounted, horses, harness, arms, ammunition supplies collected, in a word every preparation made for holding Paris if any column of the enemy should make a dash for the capital.

If Joseph as Lieutenant-General of the Emperor did not effect more than he actually accomplished, he was not entirely to blame. It is easy to speak of his deficiencies, and to argue, as many have done, that it was his failure to organise an effective defence of Paris that brought to a disastrous end the Emperor's brilliant combinations for the famous 'Campaign of France.' Joseph was not to blame, for he never had the full responsibility that was nominally assigned to him ; his authority was hampered in a hundred ways ; his administration was strangled in traditional red tape, and at a moment when time was all-important formalities were multiplied, so that days were wasted where the loss of hours would have been serious enough.

Strange to say, not the least obstacle to Joseph's successful fulfilment of his task was the Emperor's own extraordinary energy and activity of mind. In the midst of the most arduous of his campaigns Napoleon was not content merely to devote himself to the conduct of his armies. Even in the field he was his own Prime Minister, and insisted on everything being reported to him and submitted to his final decision. Thus, instead of being able to take immediate action, Joseph had to report to his brother's headquarters, and await his replies. There was an endless coming and going of couriers between Paris and the army, and the swift movements of the Emperor made communication sometimes uncertain. Nor were these delays the only source of difficulty. Napoleon, without informing Joseph, would send hurried orders to the War Office, or the generals and subordinate military departments in Paris, and when the Lieutenant-General of the Emperor directed something to be done, he would be answered by his nominal subordinate showing him contradictory orders received direct from the Emperor in the field. A man of even more decision of mind than belonged to Joseph's easy-going character would soon have been hopelessly embarrassed and discouraged by such a state of things.

Further difficulties and delays were caused by the routine methods of the War Office and the other military bureaux. All military systems are liable to be tied up in red tape, smothered in a vast mass of papers, official forms to be filled up, returns to be made, documents to be copied in duplicate and triplicate, docketed, registered and filed, orders to be passed from hand to hand through a long chain, with memoranda and entries to be noted at each stage in the weary progress. Every good general, every sound administrator, struggles to keep this deluge of papers within reasonable bounds, but the permanent official, the veteran whose fighting days are over, and who has installed himself in a comfortable office, revels in such formalities and almost worships the system that has grown up around him. All armies suffer from this. It was the plague of the Imperial Army in the later years of the Napoleonic Empire.

Perhaps Napoleon himself could have made an end of these exaggerations, but he was too busy in other ways, and even he himself was a little infected with the prevailing mania for formalities. This was why he rejected the proposal for a return to the methods of the Revolutionary war, and an attempt to raise France in insurrection against the invader, and left the organisation of the *levée en masse* to the officials of the War Office, at the moment when they could not make even the regular conscription effective, and tens of thousands of recruits were wandering aimlessly about the cities or were in open rebellion against the law, hiding in the woods and robbing travellers on the highroads or the dwellers in lonely farms.

Joseph soon found that for want of full authority and unfettered responsibility, he could only report on the more important matters to the Emperor, make suggestions, and await his decision. When at last an order could be given, even if it was not found to be in contradiction with some other order of which he had heard nothing, he had to watch as patiently as he could the slow machinery of the official departments giving effect to it. The wonder is not that so little was done, but that so much was accomplished, especially when we remember the further difficulties arising from the fact that Paris was honeycombed with disaffection, and even those who were not thinking of how best to make their peace with a new régime after the Emperor's downfall were discouraged, and for want of any real hope of success lacked any real energy, and worked like men who anticipated that at best the result of their efforts would be only a mere show of resistance to the invaders.

Joseph was present at the first meeting of the Council of Regency on January 26th. From this date till the end he was occupied day and night, not only with the duties directly arising from his new office, but also with interviews, negotiations, correspondence bearing on the general situation. There was a daily exchange of letters with the Emperor, and Joseph's communications were often lengthy documents dealing with matters of high politics. At Paris, surrounded by doubtful or discouraged colleagues, seeing more clearly every day that the National Guard—that is, the people of the capital—had no heart for fighting and longed only for peace, even at the price of accepting the Bourbons, Joseph realised that resistance to the Allies could not be indefinitely prolonged, for France was not answering the appeal of the Emperor, and there was not the remotest prospect of continuing the struggle once Paris was lost, for the Provinces would accept its occupation by the Allies as the end of the war. In his letters to his brother, therefore, he rightly urged him again and again not to lose any opportunity of making peace, even on worse terms than those which Metternich had suggested at the close of 1813.

Napoleon's mood, on the other hand, varied as the fortune of war changed from day to day. When he left Paris he was inclined to make very large concessions. In the first days of February, after the defeat of La Rothière, he had yielded to the arguments of Maret, Duke of Bassano, the most trusted of his councillors, and told him to help Caulaincourt to obtain a peace at any price. ' You will settle it,' he said ; ' I shall bear the responsibility. But don't ask me to dictate the terms of my own degradation.'

Then with his marvellous success against Blücher—four victories in four days—his mood changed. He cancelled the instructions giving a free hand to Caulaincourt. He fixed a minimum, beyond which he would yield nothing. The Allies talked of negotiating on the basis of old frontiers of France, such as they were in 1792 under Louis XVI., at the outbreak of the first War of the Revolution. Napoleon declared that it would be a disgrace for him to accept less than the frontiers proposed by Metternich before the Allies had crossed the Rhine—France with its natural boundaries, Rhine, Alps, Pyrenees and the sea. These changes of mind are reflected in his correspondence with Joseph. Under the excitement of victory he began to believe in a final triumph, and in this mood he regarded his brother's moderation as savouring of disaffection. He asserted that he was still the man of Austerlitz and Wagram, and with these false hopes he let slip the one chance there was of saving his throne from destruction. Joseph, placed amid more depressing surroundings, had no temptation to such illusions, and saw more clearly the realities of the situation.

Almost at the outset he was anxious to provide for eventualities which the Emperor was reluctant to admit as even possible. Napoleon's orders to his brother were that he should run no risk of the Empress and the King of Rome falling into the hands of the Allies. If Paris were in danger of being invested, Joseph was to remove the Empress Regent and her son to some city on the Loire, and take with them the Senate, the chiefs of the great departments of state, in fact the whole administration.

Joseph pointed out that the result would be to leave Paris without a government, when probably the place would be at the mercy of the party of the Bourbons, and they would organise a declaration of the capital against him, which would end any hope of rallying France to continue the war. Joseph's own view was that, even at some risk, the departure of the Empress should be delayed to the last moment, and should not in any case be accompanied by the removal of the whole machinery of the Imperial Government. He proposed that a Commission should be organised to keep control of Paris, in case of the Empress having to leave it, and suggested that an Imperial Prince should be named as its President. Louis was the only Prince available for this post, and he would have been a mere figurehead, but all the same Napoleon accepted the idea, and Joseph made Louis the offer. Instead of simply accepting it he wrote to the Emperor a long letter full of his old theories, and Napoleon told Joseph the proposal must stand over for the present. In the hurry of the campaign he never paid any further attention to it.

Jerome's name was not mentioned in the discussion, for he was still acting in open defiance of the Emperor's wishes. A week after Napoleon's departure for the army he had left Stains, and, without asking any one's permission, had taken possession of his uncle, Cardinal Fesch's house in Paris. He asked for an audience with the Empress Regent for himself and his Queen. The matter was referred to the Emperor, who replied that till Jerome had changed his whole line of conduct he should not be received by Maria Louisa either in public or in private.

The King of Westphalia must have felt that he was in a very false position. Not only was he at open variance with the Emperor, but, though he wore a general's uniform, he was idling in Paris, while Joseph was organising the defence, and a few leagues away the Emperor was risking his life, day after day, in battles with the invaders. On February 5th he wrote a formal letter to Joseph asking him ' to remind the Emperor ' that he was ready to take up any military duties that his

Majesty might judge fit to entrust to him. Though couriers were coming and going between Paris and the Imperial head-quarters, which were close at hand,[1] no reply came to this offer. On the 7th Joseph, who had repeated the request in a second letter the day before, wrote to his brother : ' Jerome feels hurt at your Majesty not having yet said anything about the request I have made on his behalf in two of my previous letters.'

Still the Emperor took no notice of Jerome's communi-cation. It was not till a fortnight later, and after Joseph had once more pressed him on the point, that he stated the condi-tions on which he would accept Jerome's services. First of all he was to become once more a French Prince. He was to lay aside his Westphalian uniform, and wear that of the Grenadiers of the Imperial Guard. He was to dismiss the Westphalian officers and servants of his household, who would be free to return home or live quietly in France. He was to select a staff composed of Frenchmen, whose names were to be submitted to the Emperor's approval, two or three aides-de-camp, one or two equerries, and one or two chamberlains for his household. The Queen was to choose two or three French ladies to attend her, and send away the Germans. The King and Queen would then be presented to the Empress and authorised to use Cardinal Fesch's house as their Paris residence. They would retain the titles of King and Queen of Westphalia, but no Westphalian was to remain in their service. It would be a merely honorary rank.

The King was then to come with his military staff to Napoleon's headquarters. As to how he was to be employed, the Emperor, remembering his conduct in the campaigns of Silesia and Russia, laid down certain conditions. ' My intention,' he wrote to Joseph, ' is to send him to Lyons,[2] to take command of the city, the department, and the army, but only on condition that he will promise me that he will be always with the vanguard and the outposts, that he will have no train of royal attendants, no luxurious display, that he will take no more than fifteen

---

[1] From February 3rd to the 5th Napoleon was at Troyes. On the 6th he was retreating towards Paris. On the 7th his headquarters were at Nogent-sur-Seine, whence he turned northwards to attack the Allies at Champaubert and Montmirail.

[2] Augereau was holding Lyons and the district with some 20,000 regulars and a large force of National Guards and new levies. He mismanaged his operations and lost the city, which the Allies occupied on March 21st.

horses with him, that he will bivouac amongst his soldiers, and that not a musket shall be fired without his being the first under fire.'

One might expect that a Prince who bore the name of Bonaparte and claimed to be a soldier would be delighted at the chance of commanding the army that held the second city of France and guarded all the south. Napoleon felt so sure of it that he wrote the same day (February 21st) to Clarke at the War Office telling him of his offer to Jerome, and asking the minister to help him to select useful officers for his staff. He added that ' to save time ' Jerome might at once send on to Lyons his baggage, campaign kit, and servants, all on the most moderate scale. Clarke was to see that he took none of the old crowd of courtly dependants with him. The Emperor hoped that at last Jerome was going to act as a soldier and make war in earnest.

But the ' King of Westphalia ' would not accept the common-sense conditions laid down for him by the Emperor. He was willing to reduce his Westphalian court, but wanted to retain some part of it, and argued that unless he maintained his dignity as the exiled sovereign of Westphalia he would have no chance of regaining his kingdom at the peace. He wished to have some of the generals of his old German army with him, and finally, if he took command he must not be expected to receive orders from any of the marshals, but only directly from the Emperor himself. Joseph reluctantly stated these counter-proposals to Napoleon. The Emperor was disappointed, and refused to continue the correspondence, and Jerome remained in a very undignified repose at Fesch's house in Paris, while the fate of the Empire and his own were being decided by the arbitrament of war.

So much for the Princes. As to the Empress and her son, Napoleon's one anxiety was that they should not become the prisoners of the enemy. In a long letter to Joseph on February 8th, before his dash at Blücher and the first series of victories, he repeated his earlier orders, and tried to allay his brother's fears for Paris. ' I tell you,' he said, ' that Paris will not be occupied by the Allies while I am alive. . . . If through unforeseen circumstances I have to retire to the Loire, I do not want to leave the Empress and my son at a distance from me, because in that case it might happen that they would be carried off to Vienna. This is still more likely if I am no longer living. If you get news of a lost battle, or of my death, send away the Empress and the King of Rome to Rambouillet. Never let them fall into the enemy's hands. Make up your mind to it that from that moment we should have no hold on Austria. She would be carried off to Vienna, given a large civil list, and, with the Empress provided for, Austria would force upon Frenchmen all that the Prince Regent of England and the Czar might suggest. You and those who attempted to prolong the defence would be treated as rebels. As for me, I would rather see my son's throat cut by them than that they should carry him off to Vienna to be educated as an Austrian Prince, and I have a sufficiently good opinion of the Empress to believe that she shares my ideas, in so far as it is possible for a wife and a mother. I have never seen *Andromaque* played at the theatre without feeling sorry for the lot of Astyanax surviving the house to which he was born, and I have thought it was no good fortune for him to survive his father.'

The letter is worth noting, as a partial explanation of Joseph's conduct later on. He replied to the Emperor that he would strictly follow his instructions in this matter. He was glad that his own communications on the subject had made Napoleon state so clearly what he wished to be done.

In these first days of February, on the eve of the successful dash against Blücher's army, Joseph had been urging almost daily the necessity of making peace at any price. ' There are circumstances,' he wrote, ' in which men are powerless to alter the course of events. When this is clearly the case, Sire, it seems to me that true glory is to be sought in preserving as much as may be of one's subjects and one's territory, and the policy of exposing a life so precious as your own to dangers that are only too obvious is not glorious, for it is of no advantage to that great mass of men who have staked their own lives and fortunes on your existence.' He assured the Emperor that his most faithful followers longed for peace, and felt that, if this were obtained, the Emperor's genius would soon repair the losses of France and secure her prosperity under his dynasty.

The Emperor seemed to be about to give way, and accept this advice, but after the four days of victory in the middle of February he wrote to Joseph that the great peril was now over, the capital was no longer in danger; it was no longer a desperate struggle, but an ordinary war with fair chance of eventual success on his side, and he therefore ' owed it to the Empire and to his own fame ' only to accept peace on conditions that would make it real and enduring.

To a fresh letter from Joseph on the same subject Napoleon replied that there was no need of preaching to him ; he was ready to sign an honourable peace, but the Allies were asking him to hand over fortresses that were still safe, as a pledge of his good faith before arranging an armistice, and there could be no armistice on such conditions. Joseph answered that he agreed with his view ; he even thought that the Emperor was right in holding out for the Rhine frontier, not the old frontier of 1792.

But as the prospect darkened again, as the tide of invasion swelled higher despite the Emperor's victories, as the news came that the south was welcoming Wellington, and the hope of organising an effective defence of Paris became less as the days went on, Joseph resumed his exhortations to peace. The Emperor, too, seemed to hesitate. At the end of February he took a step from which he had proudly shrunk till then. Two of his old marshals were arrayed against him as allies of the coalition—Bernadotte, the Crown Prince of Sweden, and Joachim Murat, the King of Naples. As yet there had been no actual fighting in Italy between the Neapolitan army and that of Eugène. Was it possible even at the eleventh hour to hold Murat back, and to persuade Bernadotte to exert his influence on the side of peace between the Allies and the Empire he had once served as a soldier ? Napoleon sought Joseph's help. His wife's sister, Desirée Clary, Crown Princess of Sweden and wife of Bernadotte, was still at Morte-fontaine. Would Joseph try to enlist her good offices with her husband in Napoleon's interest ? As for Murat, he had been Joseph's friend, and Joseph himself was supposed to have still some influence in Italy. His brother asked him to send a confidential agent to negotiate with Murat, and at the same time to remonstrate with Murat's Queen, the Emperor's sister Caroline, and try to persuade her to abandon a rebellion against her brother ' that revolted even the Allies themselves.'

Joseph did what he could, but neither negotiation had any useful result. As his envoy to Murat and Caroline he sent his friend Faipoult, who had been his Minister of Finance at Naples, and who left Paris on his mission on March 1st. It was not till the 20th that he saw Murat in southern Italy. They had several long conversations, and at the end of the month Faipoult was on his way back to France with a report that Murat might be brought to reconsider his position. But many things had happened before the envoy could rejoin Joseph, and it was useless then to pursue the negotiation.

At the same time that Faipoult started for Italy, Joseph had sent to Bernadotte's headquarters at Liége Dr. Franzemberg, an Austrian, who had entered the Marshal's service during the last French occupation of Vienna, who had for some years been acting as secretary to his wife, and who had come with her to Mortefontaine and there become very friendly with Joseph. Franzemberg spent a week at Liége and rejoined Joseph at Paris on March 13th, and reported that Bernadotte was not anxious to push matters to extremities, and would use his influence in favour of peace, if any way to it could be opened. Joseph sent him to report personally to the Emperor, and after a visit to Napoleon's headquarters he came back to Paris with a letter from the Emperor, advising that he should go again to Bernadotte. Joseph sent him off to the north, but here again the negotiation had only given hopes that could not be realised, for events were moving too fast. But it seems to have had the effect of keeping Bernadotte and his army in a state of inaction, awaiting developments.

While these efforts to win over Bernadotte and Murat were just being begun, the Emperor had taken another step, which showed that he was not so optimistic as to the chances of the campaign as he had been after his victories in the middle of February. Acting on a suggestion of Joseph's he ordered him, on March 2nd, to convoke, under the presidency of the Empress, a council at which all the great dignitaries of the Empire and the ministers would be asked to give their opinions on the question of an armistice and peace negotiations, after having all the correspondence with the Allies laid before them. ' I don't want a formal resolution,' said the Emperor, ' but I should like to have the individual opinions of those present.'

As there was a delay in forwarding complete copies of the necessary papers, the Council did not meet till March 4th. The correspondence showed that the Allies were, anxious to reduce France to the limits of 1792, while Napoleon held out for those of the treaty of Lunéville, with the Rhine frontier as a minimum. After a long discussion the Council was practically unanimous in advising the Emperor to make every concession. Joseph explained their views in a long despatch to Napoleon, in which he said :—

' All the members of the Council seemed to be under the influence of the same feeling. They considered the proposals made by the enemy to be very unfair, and they showed an absolute confidence that your Majesty would give such instructions to your plenipotentiary, as would enable France at once to reap the benefit of the immense sacrifices demanded of her, sacrifices which we know your Majesty can only accept at the last extremity. But there was a general agreement in the opinion that the reduction of French territory to what it was in 1792 ought to be accepted as a necessity, rather than expose the capital to occupation by the enemy. The Council regards such an occupation of the capital as the end of the existing order of affairs, and the beginning of strife and disturbance, of which no one can foresee the result. Unless, then, new victories enable your Majesty to insist upon the Frankfort conditions,[1] the best course would be to sign a definite treaty, which, while it would restrict France to its limits under the last of the Bourbon monarchy, would at the same time at once deliver it from the presence of the enemy, and restore the prisoners of war. Peace at an early date in one form or another is indispensable. Whether it is favourable or unfavourable, it is a necessity. . . . Without money, without arms, beyond those actually in the hands of your soldiers, what can your Majesty now accomplish ? Not to despair of what the morrow of a peace will bring—that is the true courage. That is honour—everything—for there lies the safety of the state. You will be left to France, and France will still be yours, that same France which has astonished Europe. And you, who have saved it once before, will save it

---

[1] *I.e.* the terms offered by Metternich from Frankfort in 1813—the Rhine from the Alps to the sea as the eastern frontier of France.

a second time, by to-day signing a peace and preserving yourself as well as France. Whether you gain one more victory now or not, it is all the same necessary that you should think of peace. This is the summary of what every one here thinks and says.'

When Napoleon received this report, he was making a rapid march to strike at Blücher, who had been joined by some of the Russians. On the 7th the Emperor fought the battle of Craonne, and defeated Woronzoff and Sacken. His reply to Joseph's communication was the bulletin of victory, dated from Craonne. Not one word did he say of peace.

But when Joseph heard the news, he wrote once more begging his brother to give way on the essential point. ' After this fresh victory,' he said, ' you can gloriously sign peace with the old frontiers. Such a peace will make France mistress of herself, and after the long struggle, that began in 1792, there will be no dishonour for her in accepting it, for she will have lost none of her old territory and will have successfully insisted on carrying out those interior changes which she desired.' The argument was sound, and Joseph's view, that the success that had been won could be best used to cover such concessions, was correct. He foresaw that if the war continued numbers must tell in the end.

While Joseph was actually writing this, on March 9th, the Emperor was attacking Blücher at Laon, and the two days' battle had begun which ended in the Imperial army being repulsed with heavy losses, that there was now no means of repairing. It was the beginning of the end. Once more Joseph pleaded for peace at any price. ' Your Majesty must now feel,' he wrote on the 11th, ' that now no other resource is left but peace, and peace at the earliest possible moment. Every day that is lost makes our position much worse. The misery of individuals is reaching the last extremity, and the day that people are convinced that your Majesty prefers the prolongation of the war to a peace, even on unfavourable terms, there can be no doubt that popular feeling, weary of the struggle, will turn to our opponents. I cannot be deceiving myself in this, for my view is shared by every one else. We are on the eve of a general break-up, and there is no safety except in peace.'

This outspoken advice only angered the Emperor. Hurled back from Laon, with his foes crowding round him, he was losing all clear grasp of the general situation in the excitement of the desperate fight in which he was involved, and he thought only of where he could aim the next blow. Irritated at what he regarded as a temporary failure, for which he blamed his generals, it was not only Joseph's letter that put him in ill-humour. From Méneval, one of the Empress's secretaries, he had heard that Joseph had spoken to her of its being perhaps necessary for her soon to invoke the influence of her father the Austrian Emperor to obtain better conditions for her husband, and Méneval also sent a report that he believed a number of the senators, councillors of state, and other leading men were drawing up an address to Napoleon, calling on him to make peace or abdicate in favour of his son. Méneval did not represent Joseph as responsible for these proceedings, though it was actually at Joseph's request he sounded the Emperor on the subject.

There had been almost a conspiracy among the senators to proclaim the deposition of Napoleon, and appoint Joseph Lieutenant-General of France and Guardian of Napoleon II. during the years of his minority, in the hope that under this new state of things peace could be arranged. The project had been revealed to Joseph, and he had at once rejected it ; but he had agreed to the alternative proposal of an address to the Emperor insisting on peace, and urging that if he could not make peace he should abdicate in favour of his son. But Joseph would go no further till he had Napoleon's own views, and he used Méneval's agency to obtain them.

The Emperor at once jumped to the conclusion that Joseph was at the bottom of the whole business. He wrote to him that he was sorry to see he was losing courage ; such half-heartedness would paralyse the defence of Paris ; as to his hints to the Empress of using her influence with her father, he must not talk to her in that way. ' I don't want to be protected by a woman,' he added.

But to Méneval he wrote that if any address asking for peace was presented to him, he would consider it as an open act of rebellion. To Savary, his Minister of Police, he sent an angry letter. He blamed him for not having reported the peace.

movement, the origin of which he attributed, at a guess, to Joseph's friend Miot, and he blamed Joseph himself, without making him directly responsible for it. ' There is talk,' he wrote to Savary, ' of addresses, a regency and a thousand intrigues, equally stupid and absurd, which can only be the work of a fool like Miot. All these people don't realise that it is my way to cut a Gordian knot, like Alexander, with the sword. Let them remember that I am the same man I was at Wagram and Austerlitz ; that I will have no intrigues in the State ; that there is no authority but mine ; and that in case of a sudden emergency it is the Empress Regent who has exclusively my confidence. The King (Joseph) is weak ; he lets himself be involved in intrigues that may be fatal to the State, and to himself and his plans, if his ideas are not promptly brought back to the right course. I tell you that if any address had been drawn up contrary to my authority, I would have arrested the King, the Ministry, and all those who signed it. I will have no tribunes of the people. Let them not forget that it is I who am the chief tribune.'

Blücher, though victorious and outnumbering his defeated enemy, did not pursue the Emperor as he retired from the attack on Laon. Napoleon had a brief breathing-time to rally his strength, and to warn the Government in Paris that peace was still out of the question. Then with the hostile armies all around him, in the middle of March he made his last stroke, a splendidly daring effort to rush through a gap in the closing circle of steel, reach eastern France, free the besieged garrisons, rally the insurgent peasantry, cut the enemy's communications with the Rhine, and fall upon their rear while Paris still held out against them in their front.

He knew enough to be aware that his capital was very imperfectly prepared for resistance. But he did not expect that Joseph would have to meet a serious attack by a large force, for he believed that the mere tidings that he was between the enemy and the Rhine, calling France to arms behind the Allied armies, and cutting off their supplies, would arrest the march of their huge columns. So the final phase of the hard-fought ' Campaign of France ' began.

CHAPTER XXIV

THE CATASTROPHE

(1814)

ON March 13th the Emperor had crushed the Russian corps of the émigré General St. Priest, which formed a link between the armies of Blücher and Schwarzenberg. Next day he reoccupied Rheims, which had been for some days in the hands of the invaders. He remained there till the 16th, when he began his move to the eastward, by a stroke against Schwarzenberg's flank and rear.

Now that he had turned his back upon Paris, communication with the capital would daily become more difficult, so he sent his final instructions to Joseph. They were a repetition of the earlier orders that his first care must be the safety of the Empress and the King of Rome. If the enemy approached Paris in such force that successful resistance would be impossible, they were to retire to the Loire, accompanied by all the great dignitaries of the Empire. Joseph was to go with them. ' Keep with my son,' wrote Napoleon, ' and remember that I would rather hear that he was in the Seine than in the hands of the enemies of France '

Nothing was said of Joseph's earlier proposal that a government Commission should be formed to hold Paris in this event. Everything was left vague and undecided. The Emperor confidently expected that his daring manœuvre would draw off the enemy from his capital. This was why he disregarded the fact—of which he must have been fully aware—that Paris was not prepared for a serious defence. When he marched to the banks of the Aube, and began drawing all the forces he could concentrate under his personal command into the gap between the armies of Blücher and Schwarzenberg, he left nothing between Paris and these huge columns of invaders, each a hundred thousand strong. After their unsuccessful fight at La Fère Champenoise the two weak corps of Marmont and Mortier, by a skilful and rapid retreat, again interposed themselves between Paris and the enemy. But if the two Marshals made another stand in the open they must be swept away by mere weight of numbers. The most they could do was to delay the hostile advance a little, fall back on the capital, and unite what was left of their forces with the small garrison left in the menaced capital.

If Paris had been fortified, if it had been even surrounded by hasty entrenchments, bristling with guns, well provided with ammunition and adequately manned, the situation would have been different. Though the great city was seething with disaffection, though its people were mostly weary of the endless wars of the Empire, there would have been no popular uprising so long as some kind of defence against the foreign enemy could be maintained. But the work of hasty fortification had only just been begun.

In February and the beginning of March Joseph had submitted to the Emperor various plans for these works, prepared by his military advisers. Napoleon had rejected them all. As late as March 13th, the day of his victory over St. Priest near Rheims, he had written to his brother that the plans were much too complicated, and he wanted something quite simple.

In this, as in most of his military judgments, the Emperor was quite right. Engineer officers who have become half fossilised in their arm-chairs in a War Office have a tendency to become pedants, and draw out beautiful plans for ideal fortifications without paying sufficient attention either to the time necessary for their construction, or the conditions under which they are to be actually defended. Europe is covered with the monuments of such ill-directed ingenuity. So a lot of valuable time had been lost, and at the last moment plans for a simpler system of barricades, entrenchments, and earthwork batteries were drawn up in haste and approved, but it was not till March 23rd that Joseph was at last able to give the definite order for the work to be put in hand. Even then it could only be partly taken in hand, for some of the plans had still to be sent to the Emperor's headquarters. They never reached him.

Joseph, as Lieutenant-General of the Emperor charged with the defence of Paris, has been freely blamed for not having fortified it. The blame really rests on Napoleon. He was the commander-in-chief with most absolute powers at his disposal. His neglect to entrench the approaches to the capital was, in the first place, the result of his obstinate refusal to face the possibility of its ever being seriously attacked. If he had not been so blindly optimist in his views, he would surely have made the necessary arrangements in January, before he left Paris for the army. In a few hours the main lines of the work to be done could have been settled. Labour abounded, and there would have been no need to requisition it. In the hard times of the winter of 1813-14 the workmen of the capital and the farm labourers of its environs would have been glad of this employment at a moderate rate of pay, and to occupy them would have helped to support the waning popularity of the Government. There were seven hundred guns in the arsenal, and there was time to collect or manufacture sufficient ammunition for them. An engineer general with an active staff could have been put in charge of the work, and given full powers to carry it out, working day and night if need be.

Instead of taking this course, Napoleon left all the arrangements to be elaborated in the most leisurely fashion in the military bureaux, and he introduced a further element of delay by insisting that every project, every drawing, should be hawked backwards and forwards between Paris and his headquarters, so that he might discuss even minor details. He was once more the victim of his own self-worship, his feeling that he alone was competent to direct everything, that there were no limitations to his activity. The grim record of how the unreadiness of Paris, the direct result of his own acts, paralysed his splendid dash to the eastward, and brought on the catastrophe of the campaign, is a standing warning against the folly of even the greatest man trying directly to control every detail of a vast system with his own limited powers.

On Wednesday, March 23rd, when at last, after all these delays, pick and spade began to be busy round Paris, the end was near. Though no one then realised it, there was just a week in which to prepare for the attack. And in such cases very little is done in the first days, for it needs some time to collect men, tools and materials, and for those who direct the work and those engaged in it thoroughly to settle down to their task. On this same 23rd Napoleon—after a narrow escape from destruction in the hard-fought battle of Arcis-sur-Aube two days before—was at St. Dizier on the upper Marne. Next day he was at Joinville, and his advanced cavalry had pushed on and occupied Chaumont, a few miles from Langres. The peasants were rising, and detachments of Schwarzenberg's Austrian army left behind to guard his line of communications and hold the country were in full flight. The unexpected appearance of the Emperor and his army, in what had been looked on as a conquered district, was spreading a local panic among the invaders. He expected it would have still more far-reaching consequences and hoped for success.

But now he hesitated; for reports began to reach him that seemed to indicate that Schwarzenberg and Blücher meant to disregard his action and stake everything on an immediate advance on Paris. The Austrian general had been the first to realise the drift of Napoleon's movements. For a moment he had thought of falling back, and trying to bring him to battle. Then he adopted the sounder plan of detaching only one corps to gain touch with Napoleon, and pushing on with the rest of his army, in concert with Blücher's army on his right, to seize Paris. The Allied generals were in correspondence with the malcontents in the capital from Talleyrand, the Emperor's minister, who was preparing to betray him, down to knots of obscure Royalist conspirators in the Faubourg St. Germain. They knew that the city was still unprepared for serious defence, and they anticipated that its occupation would be promptly followed by a movement for the deposition of the Emperor as the price of peace. It was thus they were able to disregard Napoleon's threat against their rearward communications.

On Friday, March 25th, Marmont's and Mortier's corps were roughly handled in a rearguard action they fought against the Austro-Russians at La Fère Champenoise. They retired on Paris, and halted before its eastern barriers on Monday the 28th. They had eluded the pursuit of the Allies, who would have been close at their heels had not the invaders been delayed by having to pass their huge columns over the single crossing of the Marne at Meaux. The Marshals were unable to give Joseph and the Council of Regency complete information as to the force of the enemy. It was still hoped that a considerable part of the invading armies had been diverted to operate against Napoleon, and that only large detachments of the main armies of Schwarzenberg and Blücher were moving on Paris. In this case there would still be some hope of making a successful stand.

On this same day, March 28th, Napoleon realised that his plan had miscarried in so far as he had failed to alarm the Allies into abandoning their advance in force on his capital. It is possible that even yet, if he had persevered in his enterprise, he might have obtained other great results, and prolonged the struggle for his throne. But he was now mastered by the danger to which he had so far closed his eyes, that Paris in the power of the Coalition would become the centre of a national movement against his rule and his dynasty, a movement for the securing of peace even with the acceptance of the Bourbons. Early in the day his army turned westward and began a forced march by Troyes for Paris. In his impatience after a while he hurried on in front of it, outstripping even his escort. If he could reach Paris, even alone, before it had fallen, he hoped at the last moment to inspire victorious energy into the defence.

Would Paris hold out? The forces at the command of Joseph and the Council of Regency were sadly inferior in numbers to the united armies of Austrians, Prussians, and Russians, who were pouring across the bridges of Meaux and would soon be in sight of the eastern suburbs. And the Army of Paris was not one organised body, but was made up of various elements of very different value. There were some 40,000 regulars. The main body of these consisted of what was left of the two corps of Marshals Mortier and Marmont, who were bivouacked outside the eastern barriers or cantoned in the suburban villages. But for their having effected their retreat to the capital there would have been a mere handful of regulars available, for Paris had been stripped of troops to reinforce the armies in the field.

As fast as conscripts and reservists arrived at the depôts

in and around the capital, they had been armed, equipped, and sent to the armies in the field. The conscripts were marched away after three or four days of drilling, during which they were hurriedly taught to form fours and to load, fire, and clean their muskets. Placed in the line of battle among veterans, these improvised soldiers fought well.[1] There remained in Paris in the depôt barracks a mass of men, for whom arms and equipment could not yet be provided, though thousands of workers were busy repairing old weapons and manufacturing equipments.

Between the last week of January 1814 and the middle of March General Hullin's reports show that 17,863 men arrived in Paris, and no less than 27,000 were sent to the front, so that seven weeks after Napoleon took the field there were 10,000 men less in the capital than on the day of his departure. Hullin's report for March 14th shows that on that day he had in the Paris infantry depôts 19,909 men, but of these only 3899 were classed as available (*disponible*). The rest were on the sick list, untrained or unarmed men. There were 7000 cavalrymen, but only 3600 horses available for them and for the artillery. There were some hundreds of guns in the Vincennes arsenal, but mostly unavailable for want of carriages, horses, and gunners. The few batteries of field artillery that had been organised had been hurried off to the field armies.

It had been intended to form twelve ' legions ' of National Guards, each 2000 strong, thus giving a total force of 24,000 bayonets. But here again the want of arms was a difficulty. On March 16th Marshal Moncey's report on the National Guard showed that he had 11,500 men in the ranks, but of these 3000 were armed only with pikes. Even amongst those who carried firearms hundreds had not a musket and bayonet, but a carbine, a shot-gun, or light fowling-piece to which a bayonet could not be fixed. The gunmakers' stores had been cleared out. In February the available supply of military weapons in Paris was made up of 11,000 muskets and bayonets fit for service, and 30,000 more stored at Vincennes which were

---

[1] In the hurry of the moment some men were sent to the front without even this rudimentary instruction. In one of the battles Marmont asked an infantryman why he was not firing. ' I would fire as well as the rest,' said the conscript, ' *if I only knew how to load!* '

out of repair, old condemned arms. These were being refitted, but the National Guard received very few of them. The infantry depôts of the regulars had the first claim. Though cartridge-making went on day and night, ammunition was very short. In these days of hand manufacture cartridge-making was a slow process. The most that could be done was to give every soldier sent to the front fifty cartridges and send after him a reserve supply of fifty more, adding every day a few more to the small reserve in Paris.

After the middle of March, and then only, the drain on the scanty military resources of Paris ceased, for men, arms, and ammunition were no longer being sent to the front. The regulars in the depôts were organised into battalions under General Hullin. Besides these there was a small *corps d'élite*, made up of the cuirassiers and depôt battalions of the Imperial Guard, left in Paris under the trusted Corsican General Ornano, to protect the Empress and the Imperial palaces. All these regular troops could be absolutely relied on to fight against any odds, and obey orders without hesitation. But the rest of the defending army counted for very little. It was made up of the battalions of the National Guard of Paris, and some few new volunteer organisations formed in the last few weeks. Of these last the most useful was the artillery regiment formed of the pupils of the Polytechnic, with some old artillery sergeants, and a number of volunteers drawn from the educated classes. The National Guard was a force of little military value. It had been deliberately neglected and disorganised during the victorious first years of the Empire, when the existence of an armed civilian force was regarded as a source of danger. Under the stress of later years the National Guard had been reorganised and used as a means of obtaining recruits for the field armies.

In the winter of 1813-14 it had been more than once proposed to Napoleon that he should arm and embody the workmen of Paris, but he had refused to adopt what he described as a revolutionary measure. When last the lower classes possessed arms, he had fought the battle against them in the streets with which his rise began. In a *levée en masse* in the capital he had seen chiefly new possibilities of disorder. So the National Guard was made up almost entirely of comfortable householders and shopkeepers and the like, who were more anxious for peace than anything else, and few of whom had any longer much enthusiasm for the Emperor and his system. They were not fully equipped; they were mostly either untrained or very imperfectly trained; many of the officers were quite incompetent to do more than march their men along a street and form them into line for one of Joseph's perfunctory parade inspections. Some old soldiers and a number of keen young men formed here and there a useful element, that made a few of the battalions of some use, but most of those citizen soldiers had never fired at anything more formidable than a rabbit, and some of them had never faced even a target. Old Marshal Moncey, who commanded them, had done his best during the opening months of 1814 to give them some training and complete their equipment, but with all his goodwill he had not been able to accomplish much.

The only effective cavalry under Joseph's command were Ornano's Cuirassiers of the Imperial Guard, 1800 fine horsemen, rather overweighted by their equipment. Want of cavalry was the weakness of the Imperial armies in 1814, and what cavalry there was was hardly ever used for reconnoitring. On the 29th it would have been useful to have had these horsemen out to the east of Paris in touch with the enemies' advance, but none of the generals seem to have asked for this, and Joseph thought only of using them as an escort for the Empress. Thus this fine force became useless for the defence.

Moncey, as senior Marshal, took charge of the actual arrangements for meeting the coming attack, reporting to Joseph, who gave him a free hand. Mortier's and Marmont's men and Hullin's depôt troops, reinforced by some of the more reliable units of the National Guard, were posted during Tuesday the 29th along a line about eight miles long, covering the east and north-east of Paris, a line on which the defensive works had hardly been begun, and only very few heavy guns had been mounted. The right rested on the Marne among the woods about the castle and arsenal of Vincennes. Thence the line stretched by the plateau of Romainville and the heights of Belleville to the hill of Montmartre (then outside the barriers of Paris), with the extreme left on the plain of St. Denis, placed there to check an attempt to work round to the west of Montmartre. The numbers available were not sufficient to fully occupy this long line, but Montmartre, regarded as the dominating point of the whole position, was strongly held. Behind at the barriers a second line was formed of National Guards, but Moncey quite realised that the capture of Montmartre and the collapse of the first line would make it impossible to continue an effective defence.

Rumours of disasters in the field, of an immediate attack on the capital, the storming of the barriers, followed by sack, pillage, and massacre caused something like a panic among the Parisians. The theatres were deserted, many of the shops put up their shutters. Carriages and postchaises conveying wealthy fugitives rolled away from the northern and western barriers. Frightened peasants with their carts and cattle came crowding to the eastern barriers. Those who could not leave the city were burying or hiding their valuables. Masons were busy all day preparing hiding-places in cellar walls. Proclamations of the Royalists, announcing the speedy downfall of 'the usurper' and the return of the King, passed secretly from hand to hand.

Now that the crisis that would decide the fate of Paris was so near at hand, and it required not a little optimism to expect that the defence of the capital could be made good for more than a few hours, the time had come for Joseph to act on the Emperor's positive orders as to the withdrawal of the Empress to a place of safety.

On the evening of the 28th he assembled the Council of Regency at the Tuileries. It was its last meeting. He laid before the Empress and his colleagues the emphatically expressed orders of the Emperor, only after every one present, except Clarke, the Minister of War, had declared his opinion that the Empress ought to stay in Paris, and that her departure would produce general discouragement, paralyse the defence, and leave the way open for intrigues against the dynasty. Earlier in the day Louis had strongly urged the same arguments in an interview with Joseph. In the presence of the Emperor's distinct orders the Council, while adhering to its opinion, decided that Joseph must obey.

According to these orders Joseph was to go away at the same time as Maria Louisa and the King of Rome. '*Ne quittez pas mon fils*—Do not separate yourself from my son,' the Emperor had written. But Joseph, with the approval of the Empress, informed the Council that, in order to mitigate the depressing effect of her removal to a place of safety, he himself would stay in Paris so long as any resistance could be made.

In the anteroom of the council-chamber Hortense was waiting to hear the decision. Jerome found her there. During these last days he had suddenly become feverishly active, and was writing letters to Joseph and to Clarke, calling on them to arm the men of the Faubourgs, the workers, against the enemy. He had come to the Tuileries to propose that the Empress should stay at all hazards, and issue a proclamation to Paris calling on the people to defend her and her son. He sent a message to Maria Louisa asking to be allowed to give his opinion to the Council, but she refused to admit him. Presently Joseph came out, and the result of the discussion was known. Hortense sent off a hurried note to her mother, the Empress Josephine. She told her that her rival was leaving Paris, and advised her not to remain at Malmaison, now that the country round it might be at any time swept by the enemy. She suggested that she should go further away from Paris for a while, but added that she herself would, for the present, remain in the capital with Julie and Joseph.

It was not till two o'clock in the morning of the 29th that the Council broke up. As the councillors separated, some of them discussed in little groups the possibility of still taking another course. ' If I were in your position,' said one of them to Savary, the Minister of Police, ' I would raise Paris in insurrection and prevent the Empress going.' Savary replied that this might be possible, but one minister could not take a responsibility that all together had shrunk from.

Joseph himself appears to have hesitated to act on the decision of the ministers and the Emperor's orders. Late as it was, after the Council broke up, he and Cambacérès had a long conversation with Maria Louisa, and suggested that she might take the responsibility of deferring her departure ; but this she refused to do. Napoleon's order was too explicit.

Early next morning Joseph sent General Clarke to the Tuileries to superintend the departure of the Empress and her son, while he himself went to inspect the defences. Crowds gathered at the sight of the 1800 Cuirassiers of the Guard, ranged in glittering lines along the Quai of the Louvre, or massed in the Place de la Concorde. In the courtyard carriages stood ready, and waggons laden with luggage rumbled out. Jerome drove up, and hurried into the palace to make a last protest, against what he described as the flight of the Imperial family, which, however, was less precipitate than his own flight from Cassel to the Rhine. The Empress refused to listen to him, and, escorted by her suite, descended the great staircase. The Grenadiers of the Guard presented arms ; there were brief farewells ; and Maria Louisa started on her journey by the Champs Elysées, the Bois de Boulogne, Sèvres and Versailles to the château of Rambouillet. It was the first stage of a longer journey, which was to end at Vienna, where her child was to be educated as an Austrian prince— the fate his father so much dreaded for him.

. The crowds who watched the long column of steel-clad cavaliers escorting the Imperial carriages down the leafless avenue of the Champs Elysées, saw in the departure of the Empress a confession, on the part of the Government, that Paris could not be held against the enemy. They were not reassured by the proclamation which Joseph, as Lieutenant-General of the Emperor, posted on the walls of the capital.

' Citizens of Paris,' he said, ' the Council of Regency has provided for the safety of the Empress and the King of Rome. I remain with you. Let us arm ourselves for the defence of this city, of its monuments, its riches, our women, our children, all that is dear to us. Let this vast capital become for a while a camp, and let the enemy find only shameful defeat before the walls that he hopes to pass in triumph ! The Emperor is marching to our aid. Support him by a brief and vigorous resistance, and let us thus maintain the honour of France ! '

In one important point Joseph had not followed the Emperor's instructions. He had directed only a few of the great dignitaries of the Empire to follow the Empress. He gave further orders to more of them next day ; but he left in Paris Talleyrand and many more who were conspiring to save their own future by desertion from the Imperial cause as soon as the Allies were in the capital. Louis followed the Empress the same day, after sending a message to Hortense to take the same course and bring her sons with her to Rambouillet. Jerome remained in Paris, anxious, it would seem, at the eleventh hour to take some part in the struggle, of which he had been so long an idle spectator.

After the departure of the Empress, Joseph was busy all day conferring with the generals, preparing for what he knew must be a disastrous day on the morrow. In the court of the Tuileries, by his orders two millions of francs in gold, part of the Emperor's savings from his civil list, were loaded on tumbrils to be sent after the Empress as a reserve for the future. There was no news from Napoleon. The great city buzzed with excitement like a disturbed hive. The National Guards were marching to the barriers to the beat of their drums. Anxious citizens whispered of storm and pillage by the Cossacks and were hiding away their valuables. The far-off reports of cannon came from the north-east. Vague rumours spread that the Allies were in sight, that they would attack that very day.

Fugitives come in from the eastward with terrible stories of the armed multitudes that were pouring towards Paris by every road, of German uhlans and Cossack spearmen plundering the outlying villages. Other fugitives of the wealthier class streamed away by the Rouen or the Orleans roads. In the churches there were special prayers for the preservation of the city from the calamities that every one vaguely feared. Meetings of workmen demanded arms and were broken up by the police. But, on the whole, Paris was orderly enough under the strain of excitement and fear. It was nearly two centuries since the great city had seen an enemy at its gates. The last time that it had been menaced from a distance many could well remember. It had been in the days of the September massacres, and even the worst enemies of the Empire were glad that Joseph and the Regency were able to make a repetition of Revolutionary disorder impossible.

Joseph was occupied till late in the evening at the Luxembourg, where that night he was to sleep for the last time. Reports from the generals told him that the Allied armies were in contact with their outposts from the Marne to near St. Denis. Shots had been exchanged here and there along the outpost line as the night closed in. The morning would see the battle. He snatched a few hours' sleep, and at three o'clock he rose, put on his uniform of a General of the Imperial Guard, made a hurried breakfast with his staff, and then mounted and rode towards Montmartre through the dimly lighted streets, where the drums of the National Guard had begun to beat the call to arms at four o'clock. At the Clichy barrier those citizen soldiers were already under arms. There Marshal Moncey and his staff joined him and rode forward with him to the shoulder of the hill.

Joseph arrived at the spot which he had selected for his headquarters, a little country house at the junction of two roads over the hill, about five o'clock. It was still near three-quarters of an hour till sunrise, but the grey twilight was growing over earth and sky, and it would soon be possible to see something of the country to the northwards. In the immediate front all was quiet, but reports from the outposts told that away to the right the enemy was moving. Joseph had sent orders to the generals the night before to meet him here, to make the final arrangements for the day, and a crowd of brilliantly uniformed officers, some of them men famed in the story of the Empire, were riding up and dismounting, till Joseph had around him a multitude of councillors. The only thing wanting was some really strong man to take command of this crowd of leaders. As it was, there was too much equality among the chiefs, and no master mind to dominate them.

There were two kings present, for Joseph found his brother King Jerome, with a staff of strangely uniformed Westphalian and Franco-Westphalian officers, eager to give his advice and offer his services. There were three marshals of the Empire: Moncey, to whom by right of seniority the chief executive command nominally belonged, and Marmont, Duke of Ragusa, and Mortier, Duke of Treviso, leaders in many a victory of the past, and to-day somewhat jealous of being under the orders of Joseph, who for all his grenadier uniform was a *pékin*, a mere civilian. There was another duke, Clarke, Duc de Feltre, the Emperor's minister, who for long years had seen war only in the bulletins that arrived in his office, and was now taking a look at the reality again. There was an Admiral, Decrès, chief of the Admiralty in the days of Jerome's naval escapades, and still Minister of Marine. He had come out to help if he could. There was Hullin, Governor of Paris, and General Ornano, glittering in his uniform of the Guard, a dark-visaged Corsican, who was here to fight for his Corsican clansmen, that had made themselves rulers of France, these wonderful Bonapartes, who called themselves Frenchmen. There was Mathieu-Maurice, Joseph's major-general and chief of the staff, owing his promotion to cousinship with Julie, and not popular with the French officers. There was a crowd of aides-de-camp and orderlies, among them some of Joseph's Spaniards, including Colonel De Montijo, whose daughter was to be an empress. It was a strange gathering. The pity was that with such a picturesque and numerous staff, there was such a small army waiting for its orders.

There was a terrible amount of talk in that crowded room at Montmartre, and as the sun rose the irregular debate was still in progress, and what was wanted was not debate but a few clear orders. Jerome, in his eagerness to prove that he meant business, quarrelled with Clarke. ' You know,' he said, ' Monsieur le Ministre, that there are arms lying idle in the arsenal at Vincennes. The men of the Faubourg St. Antoine are crying out for them. You ought to let them have them.' ' The Emperor has not directed me to take my orders from your Majesty,' replied Clarke.[1] ' And it is very lucky for you,' retorted Jerome, turning his back on the General. Then addressing Joseph, he added, ' Surrounded by men like the Minister of War, what can you expect but failure ? '

The roar of cannon opening on the right as the sun rose, and the arrival of staff officers hurrying in from other parts of the line with reports that the enemy was advancing, put an abrupt end to this inconclusive council of war. Every one had now to fight for his own hand, as best he could. Marmont, Mortier, Ornano, Hullin galloped off with their staffs to take command of their men. Joseph went out and rode to the crest of the hill with Moncey, Jerome, and a crowd of officers.

On the left and in front of Montmartre all was yet quiet. The orders which had been sent to Blücher to attack the hill

---

[1] If Clarke had cared to argue the point he might have told Jerome that the day before 3000 muskets, all that had been repaired, had been distributed to the National Guard, and that the arms still at Vincennes were unfit for service or under repair.

at five A.M. did not reach him till seven, and his columns were only preparing to march.   But far to the right the rising smoke of artillery, the deepening voice of the cannonade, told that the Allies were coming into action in the hollow of the Ourcq and along the slopes of the plateau of Romainville. Gradually the hostile battle-line extended over a front of many miles.   It was no mere detachment trying to raid Paris. It was Europe arrayed in battle against the Emperor's capital.

The details of the attack were left to the Allied generals, but the main direction of the day's operations was in the hands of the Czar, who was having ample revenge for Moscow. With him was his ally, Frederick William of Prussia. Frederick's son, Prince William, a young captain of the Prussian Guard, was taking a personal part in the attack.   More than half a century hence, as chief of united Germany, he was to see another Napoleonic Empire go down in ruin, and another taking of Paris.

For some hours the French seemed to be holding their own. The extreme right near Vincennes was driven in about ten o'clock, and the National Guards stood to their arms at the eastern barriers.   But the Austro-Russians did not push their advantage.   The French said they feared to drive the attack home against desperate men, but the fact was the Czar had ordered Schwarzenberg not to push into the Faubourgs.   He was anxious not to be involved in street fighting, and to spare Paris the horrors of a storm.   Along most of the line the object of the Allies was only to keep the French occupied, while the main attacks of their three columns were directed to the capture of the plateau of Romainville and the domi- nating heights of Belleville and Montmartre.   With their artillery once established on these hills, northern Paris would be at their mercy, and the whole line must collapse.

Blücher was so slow that the main attack on the French left about Montmartre did not begin till near eleven, and even then the fighting was round Aubervilliers and other advanced posts below the hill.   But further to the right, where Marmont was engaged, the battle raged furiously.   A staff officer, who watched the development of the attack from the top of one of the Montmartre windmills, reported to Joseph that such masses were concentrated in his front that, taking into account also the forces engaged along the whole line as far as the Marne, the main armies of the Allies must be in action. This news was confirmed by an officer, who had been captured the night before by the enemy, coming in and reporting to Joseph that he had been assured at Schwarzenberg's headquarters that the Russian, Austrian, and Prussian armies were united for the attack on Paris. He had been liberated, in order that he might convey to the French headquarters the proclamation of the three Sovereigns announcing that they had no quarrel with the people of Paris, and warred only against the Emperor.

The Czar had sent by him a further message to the effect that, if the Allies were forced to storm the barriers, it would be difficult to restrain the troops from excesses once they were involved in street fighting. The message betrayed a desire to influence the defence to abandon the idea of a fight to the finish, and a more experienced and determined leader than Joseph would have read in it a certain anxiety on the part of the Czar. But Joseph did not notice this, and was chiefly impressed with the fact that an overwhelming force was arrayed against him.

Almost from the outset he had made up his mind that the defence could not be prolonged for many hours. At eight o'clock he had sent a message to his wife, advising her to follow the Empress to Rambouillet. But she replied that she would not go unless she received a positive order. Personally she preferred to stay till the last possible moment. At ten Joseph sent the ' positive order ' by one of his aides-de-camp, and at noon Julie left Paris.

It was about eleven o'clock that Joseph, at Montmartre, received the proclamations of the Allies and the veiled threat of the Czar's message. He called a council of war, at which none of the three marshals could be present, but he was able to consult Clarke and Decrès, the Ministers of War and Marine, and Hullin and several other general officers. All of them were, like himself, sceptical as to the possibility of prolonging the defence for many hours, now that 100,000 of the enemy were coming into action against the 28,000 regulars under Marmont and Mortier, who formed the real fighting force on their own side, for they did not place much reliance on the 12,000 National Guardsmen.

After a very brief debate it was decided that if the outer line could not be held, the idea of making a stand at the barriers and in the streets must be abandoned. Once the outlying positions became untenable the marshals should arrange to save the city from the horrors of a storm, and at the same time obtain an unmolested retreat for their troops, by agreeing to surrender the capital and withdraw to the line of the Loire. In accordance with this decision, Joseph sent to the marshals the following conditional order :—

' If the Duke of Ragusa (Marmont) and the Duke of Treviso (Mortier) cannot any longer maintain their positions, they are authorised to enter into negotiations with Prince Schwarzenberg and the Emperor of Russia, who are in their front. They will retire to the Loire.' Joseph's aides-de-camp, who conveyed the note, were to add verbal explanations.

When Joseph sent this order, a few minutes after twelve, though the pressure on the right was becoming serious, the attack on the left had barely begun, and as a whole the French position was intact. When Marmont received the message, about one o'clock, he had lost part of the Romainville plateau, but he still considered he could hold his own, for he sent off one of his staff to Montmartre with a short letter to Joseph, in which he said : ' If the rest of the line is faring no worse than our part of it, there is no reason to be in a hurry to take such a fatal course. We hope to be able to hold on till night, and the night may bring some important change in our affairs.' But when Colonel Fabvier carrying this despatch reached Montmartre, Joseph had gone.

His order to Marmont and Mortier had been conditional. But it is evident that when he sent it he considered the time had come for negotiating. At one o'clock he had followed up this first step towards a capitulation by sending off an aide-de-camp to Molé, the President of the High Court, directing him to send orders to the ministers, senators, councillors of state, etc., to leave Paris at once and follow the Empress. This showed his judgment of the situation. And he had formed it on very defective evidence. Though nominally in chief command as the Lieutenant-General of the Emperor, he was, as he had been at Vittoria, a spectator rather than the director of the battle. At Vittoria he had been under fire on the main position. But at this Battle of Paris he was nearly at one end of the long line, where he could see little of the main fight, and he had received very few reports from his subordinates. As he saw the smoke of the enemy's guns advancing along the heights above the Ourcq valley, the enemy's columns forming for the attack of Montmartre, their masses of cavalry threatening to break in on the left between the hill and the Seine, he jumped to the conclusion that all was nearly over. A soldier would have held on longer, would at least have waited for a reply from Marmont. But Joseph had completely lost heart, and before half-past one he had called his staff together, and began to ride down the hill towards the Clichy barrier of Paris. Jerome had asked to be allowed to lead a counter-attack, but Joseph had little confidence in his brother's military abilities, and thought that it was better to leave the fighting to the professional soldiers. He told Jerome to come away with him.

At the barrier he found old Moncey at the head of his National Guards, and told him Marmont would soon break off the fighting, and that he himself was going to rejoin the Empress. Picking up a cavalry escort, he rode by the Boulevards and the Champs Elysées through the Bois de Boulogne to the bridge of Sèvres, which he reached about four o'clock. He had not gone to the Luxembourg, but had paused in his ride through Paris to send off messages to Miot and others. All the time the roar of cannon told him that the generals were still fighting.

Miot, Joseph's old friend and secretary, had remained in charge of the deserted Luxembourg. At half-past one General Dejean, one of the Emperor's aides-de-camp, arrived there after a long ride, and told Miot he must see King Joseph at once, for he had to inform him that the Emperor was already at Fontainebleau with part of the Imperial Guard, and would soon be in Paris. Let Joseph hold out for even a few hours, and Napoleon would take over the command of the defence. Miot sent Dejean with an orderly officer to Montmartre. When he arrived there Joseph was some time gone. Dejean followed him, overtook him in the Bois de Boulogne, gave him his message, and urged him to return and continue the resistance. Joseph listened, and answered that he saw no reason to change his plans : the defence must soon collapse and the Emperor would arrive too late.

If he had questioned Dejean at all closely, he would have found that his report was less encouraging than it seemed, for the General had left Napoleon some miles to the south of Fontainebleau. The Emperor was driving on in advance of his army. The head of the column was miles behind him. The statement that he was at Fontainebleau was the result of a calculation. The additional news that the Imperial Guard was with him was simply untrue. The troops could not pass through Fontainebleau till much later.

At four o'clock, when Joseph and Jerome were riding over the bridge of Sèvres on their way to Rambouillet, Marmont's line was being driven in from the Romainville heights. Belleville was attacked, and the defence of Montmartre was collapsing. The marshals acted on the authorisation to negotiate given them three hours before. The Allies agreed that Marmont's and Mortier's corps and the other regular troops should be allowed to march away with their arms and artillery, provided they at once evacuated Paris. The National Guard was to preserve order till the conquerors made their entry into the city. It says something for the endurance of the French regulars that, though they had been in action for hours, they were on the march southwards towards the Loire soon after sunset.

At ten o'clock that night Napoleon had stopped to change horses at the post-house and inn of the Cour de France, only ten miles south of Paris, on the road by Corbeil to Fontainebleau. In the darkness mounted men were heard approaching, and the sound indicated that they were a numerous party. There was a moment of alarm. Could it be a Cossack raid? An orderly officer galloped forward, and came back with the news that it was the vanguard of a column of French troops retiring from the lost capital. The Emperor had come too late.

General Belliard, who commanded the advanced guard, rode forward, dismounted and approached the Emperor, who was standing by his carriage. Napoleon poured out a string of sharp questions : ' How come you to be here ? Where is the enemy ? Where is the army ? Who is holding Paris ? Where are the Empress and the King of Rome ? Where are Joseph and Clarke ? ' At last Belliard was able hurriedly to explain what had happened.

Napoleon broke out into a fury : ' Has every one lost his head ? This is what comes of employing people who have neither energy nor common-sense ! That pig Joseph (*ce cochon de Joseph*), who imagines he can command an army as well as myself ! And that cursed fool Clarke, who is utterly incapable once he is taken out of his office routine ! ' Turning to Caulaincourt and the others who were with him, he went on : ' You hear what Belliard says. Come, we must go on to Paris. Wherever I am absent nothing is done but folly ! Caulaincourt, call up my carriage.'

With difficulty he was persuaded that, with the convention signed and Paris evacuated, it would be madness to go on. He had walked forward on the road while he talked. Now he turned back to the inn, after sending a message to Marmont to break off the convention if it was not yet ratified, and call the Parisians to insurrection.

He passed a sleepless night at the Cour de France. Before dawn there came a reply from Marmont. Paris was lost ; its people had not the remotest idea of renewing the resistance ; the convention for the surrender of the capital had been ratified, and there was no hope of recovering it. Reluctantly the Emperor gave the order to drive back to Fontainebleau.

Joseph and Jerome had reached Rambouillet late in the evening of the 30th. They halted there to have supper, and take a short rest. The Empress, with King Louis and Queen Catherine of Westphalia, had left the château at half-past eleven that morning, and gone on to Chartres. Julie was at Rambouillet. Hortense and her sons arrived during the night.

At Chartres the Empress was hopeful that evening, for at half-past seven Catherine had received a letter from Jerome, written early in the day from Montmartre, in which he told her that the troops were fighting well, and the Allied attacks were everywhere repulsed. In the middle of the night she was roused to read another letter. It told her that Paris was lost, and Jerome and Joseph would be at Chartres early next morning.

Such was the flight of the three Bonaparte Kings !

CHAPTER XXV

THE LAST STRUGGLE FOR THE EMPIRE

(1814-1815)

AT Rambouillet Joseph and Jerome were more than halfway from Paris to Chartres, and making an early start on the morning of March 31st, they easily reached the famous little cathedral city in the forenoon. There they found the Empress, King Louis, and the rest of the fugitives at the Prefecture. But the carriages of the party were waiting, and the Cuirassiers of the Guard were standing by their horses on every open space in the neighbourhood. The Empress was about to start for Tours, to which the seat of the Government was to be transferred.

But was there still an Imperial Government, and how long was it going to last ? Joseph had a hurried interview with Maria Louisa. There was no news from Fontainebleau, but Joseph knew that his brother had spoken of having perhaps to transfer his army to the Loire, if the first stage of the campaign went against him, and the natural conclusion was that Napoleon would unite Marmont's and Mortier's men to the troops he had brought back from the east of France, reach Orleans by a rapid march, and then renew the struggle, calling on France to rise against the invader. At Chartres the townsfolk and the National Guards had given a respectful reception to the Empress, though there was no enthusiastic display of loyalty. But it was decided that Joseph and Jerome could safely stay there, with some of the Cuirassiers to protect them. At Chartres Joseph would be better able to communicate with Fontainebleau than if he went further. So leaving him at the Prefecture, the Empress and her party with their escort drove off to Châteaudun *en route* for Tours.

The ministers who had left Paris remained with Joseph.

Not long after the Empress's departure, an officer from Fontainebleau rode into Chartres with a despatch from Berthier, the chief of the Emperor's staff, addressed to Cambacérès, who was not there. Joseph opened it, and found that it contained an order from the Emperor that the Empress was not to go to Tours, but to Orleans or Blois. A letter from Napoleon to Maria Louisa was enclosed. Joseph sent on the letter and the order to Châteaudun.

There was another letter in the packet, from Napoleon to Joseph himself, a letter that has never been published, but it seems that, while giving his brother very little imformation as to the position of affairs, it cancelled his powers as Lieutenant-General (an office that was no longer necessary now that Paris was lost, and the Emperor was taking the direct control of affairs into his own hands), and repeated his former order that he was to remain with the Empress and the King of Rome and provide for their safety.

Travelling in very leisurely fashion, Joseph left Chartres that night and reached Vendôme on Saturday, April 2nd. There he found the Empress, who had come on from Châteaudun the day before, and was about to continue her journey to Blois. He spent some hours at Vendôme, telling her he would follow her to Blois in the evening.

During this halt he wrote to the Emperor at Fontainebleau, apparently the first letter he had sent to him since the flight from Paris. At the Prefecture at Chartres the officials had told him that the Royalists were everywhere agitating in private for a Restoration that would mean peace ; that every one was weary of the war ; that if the Allied armies appeared the National Guard could not be relied on. In his letter to Napoleon he gave him his impression of the state of public feeling in the Provinces. It was such, he said, that peace on any conditions was a necessity. When he reached Blois late the same evening, he found there a letter awaiting him, which the Emperor had sent from Fontainebleau that morning. Napoleon had recovered from the first shock of defeat. He advised that the Imperial family should not all remain at Blois. They should separate as quietly as possible. Jerome ought to go to Bourges or into Brittany, Madame Mère to Nice, Julie and her daughters to their friends at

Marseilles, Louis, 'who had always liked the south,' to Montpellier. Every one must live quietly and practise the strictest economy.

Joseph did not reply till next day. He found an Imperial court already constituted at Blois. The Empress, Madame Mère, the fugitive kings and queens, were all installed at the historic castle, the scene of the tragedies of the last days of the Valois, and of the wooing of Henri Quatre and La Reine Margot. The great houses of the city were full of senators and ministers. Bearskin-capped grenadiers guarded the castle. A brilliant escort of cuirassiers attended the Empress and the royalties when they went to High Mass at the Cathedral that Sunday morning. The ministers had improvised their bureaux. Savary was busy stopping all newspapers and letters from Paris, and trying to keep, not only Blois, but every other place he could communicate with for a while in ignorance of the fact that there was a provisional government at Paris and that the abdication of the Emperor had been demanded as a first condition of peace. Clarke was busy sending orders to generals and prefects to organise further resistance.

On the Sunday afternoon Joseph wrote to his brother. Their mother, he said, was ready to go to Nice, but six months of her pension was in arrear. Could it be paid? Jerome, too, was short of cash. Could he be sent to command at Lyons? Louis was ready to go. Julie could hardly go to Marseilles. She had no longer any friends or relations there. Next day he tried to reach Fontainebleau to discuss matters personally with his brother. He got as far as Orleans. There he heard the Cossacks were out to the south of Paris and the roads were unsafe. He does not seem to have thought of calling up a few squadrons of cuirassiers and forcing his way through. On the 6th he returned to the Empress at the old castle of Blois.

The day before Maria Louisa had received a letter from the Emperor informing her that he had offered to abdicate in favour of his son, who, if the offer was accepted, would be proclaimed as Napoleon II. under the Empress's regency. He had suggested that she should secure the support of her father for the scheme, and she had accordingly sent the Duke of Cadore, who had formerly been ambassador at Vienna, with a message to the Emperor Francis.

The Empress was very hopeful of a good result, and inspired Joseph with her own optimist views, but on the morning of the 7th Major Galbois of the Emperor's staff arrived with disappointing news from Fontainebleau. He brought letters from the Emperor and his trusted friend Maret, Duke of Bassano. They told how the Allies had refused to accept the proposed succession of the little King of Rome, and had insisted on the Emperor's unconditional abdication; how Marmont had deserted with his 11,000 men, and the other marshals had refused to obey orders; and how Napoleon had, the day before, signed a formal abdication of all the rights of himself and his heirs to the thrones of France and Italy. He was to be 'Emperor of Elba.' He had stipulated that his relations should not be impoverished by his downfall, and the Allies had agreed that there should be an annual allowance of three million francs, charged on the revenues of France, to be divided among the Imperial family.

A family council met in Joseph's rooms in the castle Madame Mère was present with Joseph, his wife and daughters, and Louis and Jerome. Miot was called in and read Maret's long despatch, and then the new situation was discussed. The three ex-kings could no longer reside in France. It was decided to send Miot to Paris to ask for passports for them for Switzerland, Rome, or Germany. The strange thing is that neither the mother nor the brothers thought of going to the fallen Emperor at Fontainebleau.

Next morning (April 8th) there was a curious scene at Blois, one of those incidents for which it is impossible to suggest a reasonable explanation.[1] Joseph and Jerome suddenly announced to the Empress that Blois was no longer a safe place of residence, that she must come with them to Bourges and establish the seat of government there. When she refused to go, they threatened to use force to compel her, and she was so alarmed that she sent one of her chamberlains to call

---

[1] It has been suggested that Joseph was only anxious to carry out Napoleon's earlier instructions and prevent the Empress and the King of Rome falling into the hands of the Austrians, but this does not explain his action. For though he had been informed on April 7th of the Emperor's abdication, he proposed on the 8th to Maria Louisa to try to maintain the Imperial Government at Bourges, and on the 10th urged Napoleon to continue the now hopeless resistance. It was not merely a question of temporarily removing the Empress and her son to a place of safety.

the officers of the guard to her help. Then only the two brothers abandoned their plan, whatever it was, perhaps some wild idea of forming a new centre of resistance and insurrection at Bourges.

It would seem indeed that Joseph, during those days when all was lost, was turning over in his mind some vague plan of renewing the hopeless struggle, for two days later there is a letter of his to Napoleon, in which he tells him it is not too late to obtain the help of Austria, and to appeal to the French people, ' take a decided course, proclaim peace, abolish the conscription and the heavy direct taxation.' The letter only shows that Joseph, under the shock of the catastrophe, could no longer think clearly or realise patent facts.

Jerome had taken a more matter-of-fact view of the situation, and wrote to his sister Elisa that he meant to ask the Czar for passports for Germany as a royal prince who had lately reigned over a German kingdom, and that he would probably spend some time at his father-in-law's court at Stuttgart.

A few hours after the scene between the two brothers and the Empress, General Count Schouvaloff, an aide-de-camp of the Czar, arrived at Blois, and told Maria Louisa that the time had come to break up her court and end the Regency. He was directed to conduct her to Orleans, where she would reside for the present. She was to be given the Duchy of Parma in Italy and the position of a reigning princess.

The Empress agreed to leave Blois. The rest of the day was spent in preparations for the journey, and in closing up the offices of the ministers and packing up their papers. Early on April 9th the Empress started for Orleans, where she arrived that evening. Madame Mère and the three brothers went with her, and the party was escorted by the Cuirassiers of the Guard. In the evening there were wild scenes in Orleans. The Cuirassiers and Grenadiers of the Guard broke out of barracks, and paraded the streets, shouting ' Vive l'Empereur ! ' and threatening to murder the local Royalists. It was with difficulty that their officers at last succeeded in restoring order.

On April 18th the Emperor set out for his new dominion of Elba, where he landed on May 4th. On the 2nd Maria Louisa and her son had crossed the Rhine near Huninguen on their way to Schönbrunn. What Napoleon had so much dreaded was to be realised. His son was in the hands of the Austrians.

With the Empress's departure the party of refugees at Orleans had broken up. As soon as he arrived there on April 9th, Jerome had sent Catherine to Paris to interview her brother the Crown Prince, who was in command of the Würtemberg contingent, and Wintzingerode, her father's ambassador. She was to arrange if possible for a residence in Würtemberg for herself and her husband. Her brother refused even to see her, and wrote to her that it would be impossible for Jerome and herself to be admitted to his father's dominions. Wintzingerode saw her, and told her she would be welcomed at Stuttgart, but only on condition that she consented to a divorce from Jerome.

Catherine refused to hear of this for a moment. On the 15th she wrote to her father describing it as ' a most revolting proposal.' Jerome, she said, had been the most affectionate of husbands, and now after years of disappointment she was expecting to bear him a son. She was sure her father could know nothing of the suggestion that she should abandon him at this trying time. But the very next day she had a letter from her father making the same suggestion, so it was clear that his envoy had acted by his orders. Catherine wrote him a letter appealing to him to dismiss all such ideas from his mind. Whatever happened she would not listen to them. But while her own people were so hostile, she found a friend in her cousin the Czar. He promised to use his influence to obtain Jerome an indemnity for the loss of Westphalia, made Catherine an advance of money, and granted her a pension, and procured French passports for herself and her husband. With these she started to rejoin Jerome.

At Etampes she received a message from him, informing her that he had left Orleans for Berne, and asking her to join him there. On her way through France to Switzerland she had a disagreeable adventure and suffered a heavy loss. She was travelling in a six-horsed carriage, accompanied by Lecamus, Count of Fürstenstein, and one of her ladies, and they had with them eleven cases containing her own and Jerome's property. Near Montereau the carriage was stopped by a party of horsemen commanded by the Marquis de

Maubreuil, who had formerly been a French cavalry officer attached to the Westphalian army, and had since thrown in his lot with the Bourbons. Maubreuil was a reckless adventurer, and it is believed that he was engaged in a plot to assassinate Napoleon on his way to Elba. Catherine knew his reputation and was terrified at falling into his hands. He produced a government commission, accused her of carrying off with her state property and crown jewels, searched her boxes, and took possession of 84,000 francs in money and jewellery to the value of at least 150,000. Only when she begged him not to leave her penniless, he handed back a thousand francs. Having thus plundered her he allowed her to proceed on her journey. Though she appealed to the Czar for help, she never recovered her property.

From Berne she wrote again to her father, asking to be allowed to come to Stuttgart with her husband. The only reply was a renewal of the divorce proposal. In June Jerome and Catherine, now with very scanty resources, went to Gratz, and in August they went on to Trieste, where Catherine gave birth to a son, who, like his half-brother in America, was given the name of Jerome Napoleon.

Joseph went from Orleans to Lausanne with Louis. After a short stay there, the younger brother proceeded to Italy, where, under the name of the Count de St. Leu, he was to spend the rest of his life. Joseph bought the estate of Prangins, near Nyon, on the shore of the Lake of Geneva. The Bourbon Government had ordered that the Bonapartes should sell all their property in France within six months, so Mortefontaine had to be given up. Joseph busied himself with removing his art collections to the lakeside château, which he expected would be his home for years to come.

Julie with her daughters had obtained permission from the new government to live quietly in Paris for the present. She intended later on to go to Prangins, but, as in the days when Joseph was at Naples and Madrid, she was always deferring her departure, on the plea of ill-health. Hortense, now definitely separated from Louis, remained also in Paris. She had succeeded in winning the friendship of the Allied sovereigns and some of the leading Royalists, and she had obtained leave to remain near her mother, the Empress Josephine, whose

CATHERINE OF WÜRTEMBERG AND HER SON PRINCE NAPOLEON

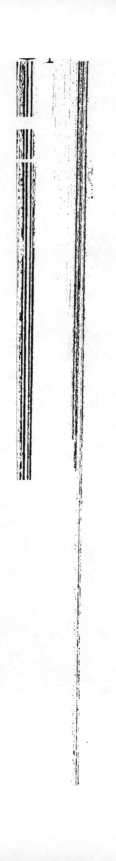

health had quite broken down, so that she had not many months to live.

Louis had written to her, asking that the elder of her surviving sons should be sent to him, but she had refused. He was further irritated against her on hearing that by letters patent, dated May 30, 1814, Louis XVIII. had conferred on Hortense the title of Duchess of St. Leu, and made over the château and estate of St. Leu [1] to her, with the further provision that her income from the estate should be made up by the treasury to the annual value of 400,000 francs. He published a formal protest against what he described as the unjustifiable alienation of his property, and began an action in the Paris courts to compel the newly made Duchess to give him the custody of his eldest son. In the youngest, the future Napoleon III., he felt no interest. The case dragged on for months, and it was not till March 7, 1815, that the Tribunal of the Seine issued its judgment by which Hortense was ordered to send her eldest son to his father within three months.

For Lucien the downfall of Napoleon and the conclusion of peace between England and France meant the beginning of a new period of prosperity. He had made a true forecast of the immediate future, when he had written to Louis in the winter that he hoped to be back in Rome in the coming year. As soon as the preliminaries of peace were signed in April he was informed that he was no longer a prisoner of war, and he at once broke up his establishment at Thorngrove and set out for Italy. Pius VII. welcomed him at Rome, and accepted the dedication of his epic poem *Charlemagne*, which had already been printed, and was published in May. He took possession again of his principality of Canino and his Roman palace, and set to work to reorganise the various works he had established years before on his estate.

Of the four brothers he was the only one who had come safely out of the storm, and he was both able and willing to help the rest. Louis came to live with him for a while in the autumn. His mother was his guest at Rome and Canino

---

[1] Before the Allied sovereigns left France, Hortense was visited at St. Leu by the Czar and the King of Prussia. Frederick William brought with him his son Prince William, the future German Emperor, who thus met for the first time Hortense's son Charles Louis Napoleon, the future Emperor of the French, then a boy of six years of age.

before she went to stay with Napoleon in Elba. To the
fallen Emperor Lucien wrote that he had forgotten and forgiven all past grievances, and that if the opportunity occurred,
he was at his disposal to protect and promote his interests.
That these were not empty words was shown by his conduct
next year.

It seemed for a while that the adventures of the Bonaparte
brothers were at an end. Napoleon had told his old soldiers
that he would devote the coming years to writing the story
of what he and they had done together, and for the present
he seemed to be entirely occupied with developing the resources
of his island empire of Elba. Jerome was living quietly at
Trieste, writing to the Czar about compensation for Westphalia, and hoping at best to be able later to settle down somewhere in Germany. Joseph seemed to be quite content with
his peaceful life on the shore of the Lake of Geneva. Lucien,
with Louis as his guest, had resumed his place in Roman
society, and was occupied with his estate and with art and
literature. From Vienna came rumours of disputes between
the Powers, possibly of a war over the new arrangement of
the map of Europe. From France reports of the endless
blundering of the restored Bourbon monarchy, which seemed
to be daily disappointing its best friends and rekindling old
animosities against its former enemies, whom the longing for
peace had for a while reconciled to it.

Suddenly everything was changed by Napoleon's splendidly
daring stroke for power. On March 1, 1815, he landed in the
south of France, at the head of a handful of men. On March
20th (the fourth birthday of the King of Rome) he was at
Paris at the head of an army rallied to him by the mere magic
of his presence, and the Bourbons were in flight. In the
proclamation which he published when he landed he had
declared that he came not to restore an absolute government,
but to defend the liberties of the people, and to free France
from the tyranny of the Bourbons, ' who had learned nothing
and forgotten nothing.' The Marseillaise, forbidden under
the Empire, was the war-song of his march on Grenoble, Lyons,
and Paris. At Grenoble he had declared that he did not
forget that all his good fortune as a soldier, as Consul, as
Emperor he owed to the people, from whom he had sprung.

The restored Empire would be a constitutional régime, based on the principles of the Revolution, an assertion of the right of France to reject a government imposed on it by foreign bayonets.

On the night of March 20th, when Paris welcomed him with an outburst of wild enthusiasm, and the Bonapartes mustered at the Tuileries, Hortense and Julie were there to greet him, both in mourning, Hortense for Josephine, who had died while Napoleon was at Elba, Julie for her mother, Madame Clary. Three of his brothers were soon at his side. Before he reached Paris the Congress at Vienna had virtually proclaimed war against him by its declaration of March 13th. The day before Maria Louisa, now the lover of Count Neipperg, had disavowed her husband's enterprise by an official letter, in which she stated that she knew nothing of his projects and placed herself under the protection of the Powers.

His son was in the hands of his enemies. They tried to prevent any of his family from joining him. The Swiss Government was asked to arrest Joseph at Prangins. Orders were sent to Trieste to secure Jerome. His sister Pauline was placed under surveillance by the Austrians in Tuscany. The Princess Elisa was conducted to the fortress of Brunn.

At the outset of his adventure the Emperor had cherished a hope that if war could not be avoided, at least he might be able to prevent all Europe uniting against him. He knew that there were fierce disputes in the Vienna Congress. He trusted that at least Austria might be held back. He declared that he had no thought of conquests ; that he would respect the arrangements made under the treaty of Paris ; that the new Empire would mean peace. After his triumphant entry into Lyons on March 10th, he had written to Joseph, asking him to inform the ministers accredited to the Swiss Government by Austria and Russia that he wished for peace, and had no dreams of winning back the provinces taken from France by the treaties of 1814. From Lyons, too, he had written in the same sense to Maria Louisa, asking her to convey the information to her father the Emperor Francis, and to use her influence with him in his behalf. He did not dream that before the letter reached her hands she would have publicly disavowed him. He also wrote to Lucien at Rome asking him to do what he could to influence diplomatic opinion in his interests.

Joseph received a timely warning that he might be arrested, and suddenly left Prangins and made his way to Paris. Jerome was also warned, and escaped from Trieste hidden on board a Neapolitan vessel, and reached the south of France by way of Naples and Corsica.[1] He was in Paris a few days after the Emperor's arrival. Lucien, who was safe from interference at Rome, at once decided to throw in his lot with his brother, but Louis refused to return to France. Alone of the brothers he was a mere spectator of the great events of 1815.

At first sight it may seem strange that Lucien, who through all the years of the Empire had been opposed to his brother, should now be so ready to abandon his secure position at Rome and stake everything on this new adventure of Imperialism. But if one looks beneath the surface of things, one sees that it was the most natural course for him to take.

In his personal dispute with his brother Lucien had triumphed. He had refused to abandon his wife for the sake of a tributary kingdom and a share in the spoils of the Napoleonic system. The system had fallen to pieces, the tributary kingdoms had all disappeared, and having taken his own course and stood apart, from motives that did him honour, he had not been involved in the general downfall. It was easy for him to make advances towards a reconciliation when Napoleon was at Elba, and when the Emperor returned to France and proclaimed a new democratic policy, Lucien, who had never quite abandoned the Liberalism of his earlier career, and who had always chafed at inaction and felt he could take a leading part in great events, welcomed the change that made it possible for him to combine loyalty to his brother with fidelity to his own democratic theories. He not only threw in his own lot with Napoleon, but helped to rally to this new popular Imperialism men who, like himself, had first come to the front as the thoroughgoing partisans of the Revolution, and whom the despotism of the earlier Empire had driven out of political life.

---

[1] After Jerome's departure the Austrians prevented Catherine leaving Trieste to follow him to Naples, and forced her to remove to Gratz with her infant son. There envoys of her father, the King of Würtemberg, arrived and summoned her to proceed with them to Göppingen in Würtemberg, warning her that if she did not go with them she would be carried off by force. During the Hundred Days and for months after she was a kind of state prisoner at Goppingen.

While Joseph and Jerome had been threatened with arrest by the Allies and had had to take special precautions in order to rejoin Napoleon in France, Lucien was able to travel from Italy to Paris without any concealment, for he came in the first instance as the unofficial envoy of his friend and protector, Pius VII. When the news reached Italy that the Emperor had landed in France and was marching on Paris, Murat, King of Naples, had at once embarked on a rash adventure, which in the end proved his own ruin and seriously damaged Napoleon's prospects, by showing that his very reappearance in France had been the signal of war in Italy. If Napoleon was changing the fate of France at the head of a thousand grenadiers, Murat thought that with the army of Naples he could revolutionise Italy and drive the Austrians over the Alps, by making the forces of Naples the centre of a national movement. Without in any way consulting Napoleon, without waiting even for his arrival at Paris, he had set his army in movement for the centre and north. He had left Naples on March 17th, and on the 19th he was at Ancona with one division of his army. Another was to march by way of Terracina and Rome into Tuscany. He had asked the Pope to give free passage through his territory to this division, and Pius VII. had refused. On the approach of the Neapolitans to Rome the Pope had left the city with the ambassadors of the Powers and taken refuge at Genoa. He sent Lucien on to Paris with a mission to Napoleon. The Emperor was to be persuaded to exert his influence with Murat to obtain the evacuation of Rome and its territory by the Neapolitans, and to disavow and discourage the projects of Murat against the Papal States.

After the utter failure of his enterprise Murat pretended that he had declared war against Austria and called Italy to arms only because he had been encouraged to this action by Napoleon. The only possible pretext for this plea was a letter from Joseph, which he might indeed have supposed to be inspired by the Emperor, but which certainly did not determine his fatal course of action, because he did not receive it until his armies were already on the march and he himself had reached Ancona.

It was a letter dated March 16, 1815, and written by Joseph on the eve of his departure from Prangins for France. Like

Joseph's former letter to Napoleon at Fontainebleau urging him to resistance in 1814, when he had already abdicated and all was over for the time, Joseph's letter to Murat is an incomprehensible document, for it was written in direct opposition to Napoleon's appeal to him to do all he could to persuade the Powers that the restored Empire meant peace, not war ; and it was more especially opposed to Napoleon's policy of trying to win the friendship, or at least the neutrality, of Austria. One can only suppose that on this, as on the other occasion, Joseph had for the moment lost his head. He called on Murat ' to support by his armies and his policy the generous movement of the French people, and to give pacific assurances to Austria, at the same time marching forward to the Alps but not passing them.' But what use were ' pacific assurances ' if he was to march his armies into provinces held by the Austrian troops, and proclaim the liberation of Italy from the control of the Viennese Government ?

Lucien reached Paris on April 10th. Jerome had not yet arrived, but Joseph, who had been there for a fortnight, and was living at the Palais Royal, introduced him to the Emperor. Napoleon had not seen Lucien for many years. He gave him the heartiest welcome, told him at once that he disapproved of Murat's mad action and would countenance no projects against the Holy See, and entrusted him with a mission to Pius VII. He was to go back to Genoa, assure the Pope of his goodwill towards him and his resolve to respect the freedom of the Church in France, and ask him to exert his influence with the Allied Sovereigns in favour of peace. The sea was not safe, for the British cruisers were already capturing French ships in the Mediterranean, and Lucien, who left Paris on April 12th, tried to reach Genoa by way of Switzerland. The Swiss authorities stopped him at Versoix on the Lake of Geneva, and after spending some days there, during which he tried to obtain leave to proceed, was busy with his correspondence, and had several interviews with Madame de Staël, whose influence he tried to win for his brother, he received a letter from Joseph recalling him to Paris.

He was again at the Tuileries on May 7th. He had another long interview with the Emperor, and when he came out of his study the courtiers in the ante-room saw that for the first time he was wearing the Grand Cordon of the Legion of Honour. Napoleon had given him the coveted decoration, told him that his position as a Prince of the Empire was now fully recognised, and assigned him the Palais Royal as his residence. Joseph was to have instead the hotel of the Prince of Condé, who had fled with the King.

Lucien's influence was exerted to make the new Empire as democratic as possible. Joseph was working to the same end, and he had already, in the first days after his arrival in Paris, done the Emperor a great service by securing for him the active support of one of the most important men among the French Constitutionalists.

This was Benjamin Constant. He had spent part of his student years in Oxford and Edinburgh, and under the Directory, when Joseph first knew him, he came to the front as an exponent of moderate Liberalism. Under the Empire he had been driven into exile for his opposition to Napoleon's absolutism. He had come back with the Bourbons, and taken a foremost place among the leaders of the Constitutional party. When Napoleon suddenly reappeared, Constant denounced him as the enemy of France and liberty, a Nero who thought only of his own ambition, a Ghenghis Khan who had devastated Europe, and sought to re-establish a government of Mamelukes. When Napoleon reached Paris, Constant believed his life to be in danger, but he refused to leave France, and after failing to join the Royalists in La Vendée, he returned to hide in Paris.

There he put himself in communication with his old friend Joseph, in order to obtain, if possible, his protection. Joseph had an interview with him at the Palais Royal. He assured Constant that he had nothing to fear ; that his brother had no desire to avenge himself on those who had opposed him, but wished to have as his friends all true lovers of France ; and that, further, he had greatly changed during the last year, and now sincerely desired to establish a Liberal régime, a crowned Republic, that under Imperial forms would secure the best results of the Revolution. A commission was to be appointed to draft the new Constitution of France. Joseph felt sure that if Constant would meet Napoleon, the Emperor would welcome his co-operation in the work.

The interview was arranged, and Napoleon convinced Constant of his good intentions. On April 6th the official journal published Benjamin Constant's nomination as a member of the Committee on the Constitution, and the mere fact that he had given his adhesion to the new system rallied a great mass of Liberals to the Empire.

The elaborate drafting of the new Constitution was necessarily a long process, but the main lines were soon marked out. There was to be a Corps Législatif, partly modelled on the British Parliament, with a *Chambre des Paires* or House of Peers, nominated in the first instance by the Emperor and the Council of State, and a *Chambre des Députés*, formed of representatives elected on a restricted franchise, but at least as likely to represent public opinion as the British House of Commons of the day, which, under the unreformed electoral laws of the time, was largely nominated by the peers and the great landowners, this system of election being tempered by the employment of paid mobs at the hustings, and bribery and corruption at the polling-booths. As a matter of fact the Chamber of Deputies of 1815 contained a strong opposition element. It was elected and the Peers were nominated before the Constitution had been completed. For Lucien, Joseph, and Constant, and many of the Emperor's best friends, urged him to lose no time in meeting the representatives of the people. The decree for the elections, dated April 30th, was published in the *Moniteur* of May 1st.

Lucien, though he had not sought election, was chosen as one of the deputies for the department of Isère (capital Grenoble), one of the districts where the enthusiasm for the Bonapartes had from the first been most ardent. He was disqualified from sitting in the lower House, because with his three brothers, Joseph, Jerome, and the absent Louis, he had been nominated to the Chamber of Peers. Their names headed the list. In official documents up to the abdication of 1814, the brothers, who had reigned in Naples and Spain, Holland and Westphalia, had always been described by their royal titles, King Joseph, King Jerome, King Louis, even though their kingdoms had been taken from them. A new style was now used, and the four brothers appeared as Princes, Prince Joseph, Prince Lucien, and so forth.

Prince Jerome did not reach Paris till May 27th. The Allies had refused to treat with Napoleon ; the forces of the Coalition were mustering for the invasion of France ; and the Emperor was making almost superhuman efforts to prepare an army to meet them. Jerome asked for, and was promised, employment in the field. But taught at last by his experience of his brother's earlier failures, Napoleon did not venture to give him any high command, and he was content to accept the promise that he would be employed as a general of division in one of the army corps then being formed.

Joseph and Lucien were to remain in Paris, and co-operate with the ministers in the general direction of affairs. There was to be no regency, no lieutenancy of France. The Emperor would govern from his camp, and a daily service of despatch-riders would keep him in constant touch with Paris.

During May, Lucien made more than one effort to persuade his brother to adopt a course which he hoped might yet secure peace and avert the dangers of a very unequal struggle with the armies of the Coalition, and in urging it on Napoleon he had the support of many of his friends. He proposed that the Emperor having proclaimed the Constitution, secured the support of France, and formed an army to defend, not merely his own personal position, but also the right of France to reject a government imposed by the foreigner, should announce to Europe that as a pledge of his pacific intentions, and a proof that he had renounced all personal ambitions, he would abdicate in favour of his son, proclaim him as Napoleon II., ask Austria to restore the boy to France, and the Chambers to appoint a Regency to govern during his minority.

Napoleon refused to adopt this course, and declared that it was useless. He was probably right in his forecast of the attitude of the Allied Powers. They were from first to last determined to restore the Bourbons. Even Austria under the influence of Metternich was thoroughly hostile to him. The only sovereign who might have wavered was the Czar, because he was angered at having discovered (through Napoleon communicating to him papers found at the Foreign Office in Paris) that during the brief Restoration England, France, and Austria had signed a secret treaty for a joint attack upon him in certain contingencies.

On June 1st there was a solemn ceremony in the Champ de Mars at Paris. In the presence of some 200,000 spectators and amid repeated salutes of artillery the Emperor, his brothers, the peers and deputies and great officers of the Empire, proceeded to a vast amphitheatre which had been erected on the parade-ground. The Emperor wore the Imperial robes of state. His three brothers were in court dresses of white velvet, and wore plumed caps and short mantles embroidered with golden bees. An altar had been erected in the middle of the open ground. The bishops and clergy were grouped round it, and the Archbishop of Tours said mass to ask a blessing on the day. Beyond the altar fifty thousand men, regulars and National Guards, were drawn up in serried ranks under the command of the marshals. Bayonets were fixed and swords drawn, and in the bright summer sunlight the armed multitude looked like a forest of glittering steel. After the mass the Emperor swore fidelity to the new Constitution, and then distributed the eagles to the regiments of his army. It was at once the solemn ratification of the new régime of constitutional Imperialism and an armed defiance to the Powers which had declared war against the restored Empire. Amongst the spectators in the tribunes near the throne were Hortense and her two sons, the youngest a boy of only seven years, the Louis Napoleon who in his later career was to be the centre of state ceremonials as brilliant as this, and to be the victim of a disaster even greater than that which was now impending over the Emperor.

Jerome left Paris to take command of a division in the 2nd *corps d'armée* under General Count Reille at Valenciennes. The concentration of the army on the Belgian frontier had begun. Instead of waiting to be attacked, Napoleon was going to try to destroy the British and Prussian armies in the Netherlands, before the Austrians and Russians were ready to advance across the Rhine. The first days of June were devoted to the final preparations for taking the field. Joseph was to act as President of the Council of Ministers, and to have a casting vote if there was an equal division. Lucien was to sit and vote at the Council. As far as possible the Emperor's opinion was to be taken on all matters of moment, but in case of emergency the Council was to act on its own initiative.

On Sunday, June 11th, all was ready for the great stroke, of which the secret had been marvellously kept. During these last few weeks the Emperor had left the Tuileries for the Elysée. He said he found it an advantage to be able to discuss business under the trees of the Elysée garden, instead of being always shut up in the rooms of the more stately palace. It was at the Elysée he spent his last evening in Paris before taking the field for his last campaign. It was the Sunday evening. He meant to spend the next Sunday as a conqueror in Brussels, but it was to be the day of Waterloo.

Early in the evening there was a family party at dinner at the Elysée. None of those who sat at table with the Emperor had any idea that it was the last time they would be all together. The Emperor's mother was there, his two brothers Joseph and Lucien, Joseph's wife the Princess Julie, and the Princess Hortense, whom Napoleon had always loved as a daughter for her mother Josephine's sake. His faithless wife and her child were in the camp of his enemies, and Louis, once his favourite brother, was sulking in Italy, but it was a long time since so many of his own people had been with him. During dinner he spoke hopefully of the future. He seemed happy, and at dessert, when Joseph's daughters and the two sons of Hortense came in, he joked with the young people as if he had no cares on his mind, no dangers awaiting him. After the dessert the party adjourned to the large salon of the palace, and there a kind of informal farewell court was held. The President of the Chamber of Deputies, the ministers, many of the peers and some old friends, came to wish all success to the Emperor. It was late when the party broke up, but every one remarked that Napoleon seemed to have regained all his old cheerfulness and confidence.

Next morning there were farewells, and Napoleon started for Avesnes on the northern frontier, where he had fixed his headquarters. The army corps were closing to the positions assigned to them. The Imperial Guard, after mobilising at Compiègne, was on the march northwards. It was Monday, June 12th. Three days later, on Thursday the 15th, the army was to cross the Sambre and march on Brussels.

CHAPTER XXVI

JEROME AT QUATRE BRAS AND WATERLOO

(1815)

JEROME BONAPARTE, who had commanded armies in the campaigns of Silesia and Russia, and who had been a King, was to serve in the campaign of Belgium as a general of division in the 2nd corps stationed on the French left.[1] It was commanded by General Count Reille, a distinguished soldier of the Empire. He had served in the campaigns of Italy, he had been promoted general of division in 1807, he had commanded a division of the Imperial Guard at Wagram, and afterwards he had been employed in Spain, where he commanded a corps under Soult in the Pyrenees, and afterwards in the south of France. Under such a chief Napoleon believed his brother was in safe hands. The 6th division under Jerome's command was made up of four regiments organised in two brigades. General Bauduin commanded the first of these made up of the 1st Light Infantry and the 3rd Regiment of the Line. The 1st and 2nd of the Line formed the other brigade under General Soye. The total strength was 7819 officers and men, a small force for a general who had been commander-in-chief of large armies, but the leadership of this division was a task much more fitted for Jerome's military capacities, and his eagerness for distinction

---

[1] The French Army of the North, about 120,000 strong, was made up of the Imperial Guard and five *corps d'armée* (the 1st, 2nd, 3rd, 4th, and 6th) with the reserve cavalry of four divisions. The 2nd corps under Reille was 25,000 strong with 36 guns. Its four infantry divisions were :—

5th Division, ...	General	Bachelu.
6th ,, ...	,,	Prince Jerome.
7th ,, ...	,,	Girard.
8th ,, ...	,,	Foy.

There was also a cavalry division under General Piré.

was a guarantee that his division would take its full share of the fighting.

There is no need to tell again the story of Waterloo. But it is of interest to follow Jerome's personal adventures in the campaign, only noting very briefly the larger events of which the actions of the 6th division formed a part.

On the evening of Wednesday, June 14th, Reille's corps was bivouacked between Avesnes and the Belgian frontier. Through the bivouacs ran the road which follows the south bank of the Sambre as far as the village of Marchiennes, just above Charleroi, crosses the river there by a narrow bridge, and a few miles further on, at the village of Gosselies, joins the main road from France through Charleroi to Brussels. This road by the Sambre was to be the line of march of Reille's corps, forming the French extreme left.

At half-past three in the morning of June 15th the Imperial army crossed the frontier in three columns. Though it was half an hour before sunrise the midsummer twilight was as bright as day. Reille's corps (the 2nd), with the 1st corps under Count D'Erlon following it, formed the left column and crossed the frontier at the village of Leers. Piré's lancers and chasseurs-à-cheval were scouting in front. Bachelu's division led the long column of infantry, and then came Jerome riding at the head of his four regiments. The road with its avenue of trees ran between unfenced fields of high corn, or passed through belts of wood that gave a welcome shade. There were glimpses of the river shining on the left. It was a hot dry morning, and the men marched in clouds of dust, but they were in good spirits and eager for fight.

They had been told that they would surprise the enemy. When the regiments fell in for the march the Emperor's final proclamation had been read to them. ' Soldiers,' said Napoleon, ' to-day is the anniversary of Marengo and of Friedland, which twice decided the destinies of Europe. Then, as after Austerlitz and after Wagram, we were too generous. Notwithstanding this, we have to-day allied against us the princes to whom we left their thrones, and they are menacing the independence and the most sacred rights of France. They have begun the most unjust of aggressions. Let us march against them. Are not we and they the same men as of old ? '

But the enemy were not surprised. Blücher and Wellington had heard of the concentration beyond the frontier, and the Prussian General Pirch, who commanded the advanced posts at Charleroi and along the Sambre, had orders to be on the alert, and to fall back fighting if the French advanced. In the early hours of the morning there was skirmishing between the heads of the columns and the Prussian outposts. Before six Piré sent back word that the village of Thuin was held by the enemy. Bachelu's infantry drove them out. Jerome was bringing up his men through the woods to support the attack when the enemy gave way.

A little after nine o'clock Marchiennes was in sight, where the column was to cross the Sambre. Again heavy firing broke out in front. Bachelu attacked the village supported by Jerome. The Prussians made a determined stand behind barricades and in loopholed houses, and it was not till noon that the bridge was stormed. The story told by some of his biographers that Jerome rushed the bridge at the head of a bayonet charge like Napoleon at Lodi is a legend. It was taken by Bachelu at the head of the 2nd Light Infantry.

The march over the narrow bridge took a long time. It was four o'clock when the last of the 2nd corps were over the Sambre and D'Erlon's corps began to cross. On the north bank the divisions had a short rest as they formed up. Meanwhile the Emperor, with the centre column, had crossed at Charleroi. Piré sent back word that the Prussians held Gosselies, and Reille, without waiting to have all his corps in hand, pushed on to drive them out, taking with him Bachelu's and Jerome's divisions and some of his guns. At three he was before the village, which was held by the 29th Prussian Regiment of the Line. After a short cannonade Reille attacked with his infantry, and the Prussians gave way and went off to the north-eastward.

Meanwhile Ney had ridden over from the Emperor's head-quarters at Charleroi and taken command of the left column. The capture of Gosselies had placed Reille on the main road to Brussels. There was still time to push on to the junction of roads at Quatre Bras, the early possession of which was all-important for Napoleon's plan of separating Blücher's army, now concentrating to the eastward, from Wellington's troops who were coming up from Brussels. But Ney, instead of pressing on with Reille's divisions, rode forward with the cavalry of the Guard, drove a hostile detachment out of Frasnes, skirmished with the weak force already at Quatre Bras, and returned to Gosselies, where he established his headquarters for the night. Jerome's division bivouacked along the edge of a wood near the village, and the Prince spent part of the evening with Ney and Reille. The day had been a good one, and the left column had fought three successful engagements. The army was safely across the Sambre, though it had not gone so far forward as Napoleon intended.

Friday, the 16th, saw two battles. The Imperial army had been divided into two great masses. While the Emperor with the right, the stronger of the two forces, drove Blücher from Ligny after hours of hard fighting, Ney was to occupy Quatre Bras, which he ought to have seized the evening before, and push on towards Brussels. In the early morning the position covering the Quatre Bras cross-roads was held only by General Perponcher's division of Dutchmen and Belgians, but the British with Wellington at their head were marching to support them. The Emperor had told Ney that if he attacked at once he was not likely to meet with much opposition. The Marshal had at his disposal for the operation Reille's and D'Erlon's corps, a division of the cavalry of the Guard under Lefèbvre-Desnouettes, and Kellerman's splendid division of cuirassiers. If he had attacked in the first hours of daylight on the Friday he would have had an easy victory. But though every hour was bringing reinforcements nearer the Netherlanders, Ney wasted time, and merely sent the cavalry of the Guard to skirmish with them, while round Gosselies the troops remained in their bivouacs.

It was not till near eleven o'clock (after seven hours of summer daylight had been wasted) that he sent orders to Reille to march on Quatre Bras. Wellington had been there since ten o'clock, had decided that the position could be held, and had sent back orders to hurry up the reinforcements. Reille wasted still more time. Only at noon the first of his troops were moving. Jerome's division did not march off till near one o'clock.

From his bivouac under the shelter of the woods near Gosselies to Quatre Bras was eight miles, but five miles would bring him to Frasnes, the village from which Ney was directing his attack. It was a blazing hot day and he took two hours to reach this point. He had not been long on the march when the sound of artillery told that the battle had begun. When at three o'clock he formed his division in line of columns to the left of the Brussels road a little beyond Frasnes, serious fighting was in progress. Reinforcements had joined the enemy. Picton's division was just coming into action. Wellington held a position roughly marked out by a brook that crossed the road between Quatre Bras and Frasnes. There was a wood (the Bois de Bossu) on the right of the position, hamlets and farms strengthened its centre and left. The gently undulating country on both sides of the road was covered with crops of yellowing corn, standing so high that till it was trampled down only the horsemen could easily see over it. Behind the line ran the road from Nivelles to Namur, and at the point where the Brussels road crossed it stood the hamlet of Quatre Bras, a large farmstead and half a dozen cottages.

Jerome's men had only a short rest before being thrust into the fight. On the right the French were making good progress : they had reached the Namur road and threatened to cut in behind the enemy's line on Quatre Bras. Ney hoped that, with their line of retreat thus menaced, the enemy would give way on their centre and right. But the Dutch-Belgians and Nassauers on the right of the position were holding their own doggedly against Foy's division. The Marshal sent word to Jerome to help Foy by driving the enemy out of the farm of Pierrepont at the south corner of the wood of Bossu, and then clearing the wood itself.

Jerome sent Soye's brigade (1st and 2nd of the Line) to attack the farm. The enemy were driven out, but fell back into the wood and held on there, and when Soye followed them into it he made slow progress. Jerome now personally intervened in the fight. He decided to advance between the wood and the Brussels road, drive in the Nassau regiment stationed there, and then help his other brigade by attacking the wood from its eastern side. Bauduin's brigade (1st Léger

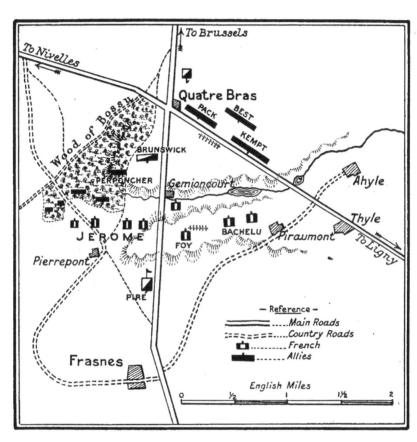

JEROME'S ATTACK AT QUATRE BRAS

and 3rd of the Line) formed for the attack, some of the Light Infantry flung out a line of skirmishers to cover the advance, and Jerome rode forward through the corn at the head of the rest of the regiment and the linesmen, with Bauduin by his side. He was hit in the bridle arm by a bullet, but bandaged the wound without dismounting, and rode on. The enemy gave way, and then a storm of cavalry came charging down on Jerome's advance between the wood and the road. The charge was led by the Duke of Brunswick, the same who had raided the Westphalian kingdom in the year of Leipsig. The two regiments rapidly formed squares and beat off the charge. Brunswick was mortally wounded by a bullet fired by one of the Light Infantrymen, and rode back supported in his saddle by one of his officers.

After this success Jerome directed his efforts against the wood, and drove the defenders out of nearly the whole of it. But this was the utmost he could do. For the rest of the day his division could just hold what it had won, and as the sun went down, the Allied position, continually reinforced from the direction of Brussels, was intact. By a series of blunders on D'Erlon's part his corps had not fired a shot during the day. It reached the battlefield of Quatre Bras only after Ney had fallen back to the ground he held in the morning about Frasnes. The attack had been repulsed.

Jerome had done well. Perhaps if, instead of giving him the command of an army in the year of Jena, Napoleon had put him at the head of a brigade, he might have made a name for himself as a soldier and won his way to higher command. He passed the night after the battle among his men in a bivouac amid the trampled corn, expecting to take part in a renewed attack next day. But in the morning Wellington heard of what had happened at Ligny. ' Old Blücher has had a damned good hiding,' he said to his staff. ' He has gone back to Wavre. As he has gone back we must go too. I suppose in England they will say we have been licked. I can't help that.' And he gave orders for the retreat to the position he had already chosen at Waterloo.

During the morning there had been only some desultory firing between the outposts of the two armies at Quatre Bras. The men in the bivouacs cleaned their arms and were inspected, and proceeded to cook and eat a leisurely meal. Ney was waiting for news and orders from the Emperor. It was only at ten o'clock that the English began to retire, leaving Lord Uxbridge's cavalry to cover the movement.

It was after one o'clock, when the Emperor had moved over from Ligny towards the Brussels road at the head of the Imperial Guard and all the troops he could spare from the pursuit of Blücher, that Ney at last prepared to move. When Jerome's division began its march along the Brussels road the weather had broken. There was a thunderstorm, followed by almost unceasing rain. The men plodded onwards under the steady downpour all through the Saturday afternoon and evening, hearing at times an outburst of artillery fire, which told that the Emperor, pursuing the Allied retreat with cavalry and horse-artillery, was in action with their rearguard. But Reille's infantry were never engaged.

After sunset Jerome's men settled down in a comfortless bivouac under the rain in the sodden cornfields north of Genappe, and several miles from the ground on which they were to fight next day. It was near midnight when the baggage-train crossed the narrow bridge over the Dyle at Genappe village, and many of the men had nothing to eat till the middle of the night. Some of them went marauding in the neighbouring farms. Jerome found shelter in a small farm-house, and his presence protected it.

The orders for next day,—Sunday, June 18th—were to concentrate for the attack on the Allied position at Waterloo. The Emperor had passed the night at the farmhouse of Caillou, about a mile and a quarter to the south of La Belle Alliance. During the night he had reconnoitred Wellington's position from the front, and formed some idea of its extent from the glare of the bivouac fires through the rain. He did not breakfast till eight o'clock. Soult, Maret, and several of the generals were with him. Ney arrived towards the end of the meal, and Napoleon spread out a map and discussed the situation. The troops were closing up to the battlefield. Jerome, having set his division in movement, rode forward with Reille to Caillou, and came into the breakfast-room during this discussion. The rain had cleared off and the sun was shining brightly.

Asked for his opinion, Soult, who knew the ground well,[1] replied that Wellington was in a strong position and it would be a serious piece of work to drive him from it. He advised that part of Grouchy's force should be at once recalled. Napoleon, who felt sure of victory, and was only afraid that Wellington might have retreated further before fighting, was annoyed at Soult's outspoken opinion. 'Because you have been beaten by Wellington,' he said, 'you think he is a great general. Well, I tell you he is a bad general and the English are poor troops. We shall make a breakfast of them.'

'I hope so,' said Soult. The Emperor asked Reille what he thought of the English army after his experiences in Spain. Reille was as frank as Soult had been. He said plainly that Wellington could hardly be successfully attacked in front in a good position, 'the calm tenacity of his infantry and the superiority of their fire would make them invincible,' but he added that the British infantry were 'less agile, less supple, less apt for manœuvring than the French, and if they could not be beaten by a frontal attack, there was no reason why they should not be outflanked and manœuvred out of their position.' Napoleon told Reille that he was wrong and broke off the discussion. He meant to hazard everything on a fierce attack on Wellington's centre. Leaving Soult to indicate to the generals where they were to place their corps and divisions, he rode out to inspect the position.

Reille's corps was to be posted on the left. Piré's cavalry protected the flank, and then on the extreme left of the main battle-line Jerome's infantry division was posted on the crest of the gently rising ground, along which the cross-road to Braine l'Alleud runs, with the wood and château of Hougomont opposite to him, the southern angle of the wood being only some three hundred yards away from his front. In those days, when a hundred yards was a long range for musketry, opposing lines of battle were placed at distances that are now only reached after hours, or even days, of fighting. Foy's division was next on Jerome's right, and behind a swell of the

---

[1] Soult had fought on the same ground twenty-one years before, as chief of the staff to Lefèbvre in his victory over the Austrians at Mont Saint Jean on July 9, 1794—an earlier and now almost forgotten battle of Waterloo. There was a fight at the village of Waterloo itself during one of Marlborough's campaigns.

ground close by Kellerman was waiting with his steel-clad squadrons of cuirassiers.

There was a long time of waiting, as two more hours of the summer morning passed by without a shot being fired. The British Guards with some Nassau and Hessian troops held Hougomont, and the red lines could be plainly seen marshalled on the rising ground of the main position beyond, nearly three-quarters of a mile away. Napoleon was said to be waiting for the ground to dry and harden, so that the guns could move easily. He rode along the line, cheered by his troops. On the left he stopped for a while to talk with his brother, and then went back to the centre near the inn of La Belle Alliance.

A few minutes before eleven the Emperor dictated to Soult an order to the effect that the battle would be begun about half-past one by an attack of D'Erlon's corps on the British centre, the objective being the village of Mont Saint Jean. Reille was to support this attack by an advance on the left—against Wellington's right. After sending off this order he followed it up with another. Reille was directed to come into action immediately against the British right, apparently with a view to misleading Wellington as to the main attack, so as to make him weaken his centre in order to reinforce his right. The order was sent verbally by a staff officer. Reille was not to drive his attack home, but only to make a demonstration. He was directed to 'occupy the approaches to Hougomont.' He was not told to capture the château. The order would seem to have meant an attack on the wood.

As Jerome was in position facing Hougomont the task fell to him, and thus it was the Emperor's brother who began the great battle. Reille sent one of his batteries to prepare the way for Jerome's advance, and this battery fired the first shot against the wood at thirty-five minutes past eleven. Three English batteries on the rising ground beyond the château replied. To support his guns Reille brought up other batteries. More guns opened on the British side. Kellerman galloped up his horse-artillery to reinforce the fire of Reille's corps, and so the cannonade gradually extended along the front towards the centre.

Reille now pushed forward Piré's lancers along the Nivelles road to protect the advance of the infantry from a possible

dash of hostile cavalry from beyond the château, and then Jerome began his attack on the wood. He first threw forward some of the dark-blue-coated sharpshooters of the 1st Light Infantry as skirmishers. The Nassauers replied from the edge of the wood, but the roundshot from the supporting batteries crashed into the trees, and the fire of the defence became unsteady. Presently Jerome, perhaps helped by a hint from his brigadier Bauduin, gave the order to storm the wood, and, as at Quatre Bras, he led the bayonet attack himself. Bauduin rode beside him. Behind them came first the Light Infantry and then the 3rd Infantry.

As they crossed the open they suffered some loss by the plunging fire of the British artillery. At the edge of the wood Bauduin was shot dead beside Jerome, but the Prince got in amongst the beech trees with the bayonets of his men around him, and then after a sharp struggle the Nassauers were driven out, and he was master of the wood. There was a good deal of undergrowth among the beech trees, and the Nassau men, reinforced by some of the Guards from Hougomont, made a dogged defence. It was an hour before they were at last forced back into the enclosures round the farm buildings of the château. Jerome had done all that was ordered in occupying the wood, but he was eager to do more, and his men were keenly excited. There was a rush at the orchard wall of Hougomont, but the steady fire of the Guards drove the French back into the wood with heavy loss, and then there was a brief lull in the fighting. Thirty yards separated Jerome's front line of sharpshooters in the wood from the Guardsmen holding the loopholed wall.

General Guilleminot, Jerome's chief staff officer, had joined him in the wood, and strongly advised him not to attempt to attack the walled orchard and the buildings till time had been given for the artillery to prepare the way. But Jerome had little experience of war, and had never studied and tried to learn from the gathered experience of others. He listened only to the promptings of his own courage, and was excited by his partial success. In the same spirit in which in his first campaign he had ordered one of his generals to storm a fortress before a single cannon shot had been fired against it, he was determined at all costs to assault Hougomont. A message from his corps commander Reille, bidding him merely to hold on under cover of the wood, did not change his opinion. He sent one of his officers back to General Soye, who commanded his other brigade, with an order to him to bring up his two battalions (1st and 2nd of the Line). His plan was to use these to continue the attack from the wood, while he himself led what was left of the first brigade round to the west of Hougomont and attacked the main gateway of the farm on that side. He kept the more dangerous attack for himself.

While Soye was occupying the wood and Jerome was leading the Light Infantry men and the 3rd of the Line round towards the Nivelles road, Napoleon had opened on the British centre with a long line of guns and was launching a mass of infantry against the farm of La Haye Sainte. In moving round to his new position Jerome lost a good many men by the fire of British guns, that opened on him from a range of about 600 yards, and by the musketry from the buildings. The garrison was reinforced by a battalion of the 3rd Guards (now the Scots Guards) under Lord Saltoun, a welcome help to Colonel Hepburn's Coldstreams. The artillery of the attack had been strengthened by a battery of howitzers, which fired not roundshot like the cannon, but shell, and more than once set the buildings on fire.

Jerome's two brigades now renewed the attack. Soye's linesmen dashed at the garden and orchard wall, tried to climb it, fired into the loopholes, sometimes even seized a musket as it was pushed out, and tried to drag it through the hole. Those who passed the wall were bayoneted, those outside were shot down. Beaten off, they rallied in the wood and came on again, reckless of loss. A British officer, who had seen all the hardest fighting in the Peninsula, said afterwards that never had he seen the dead lie as thick as they did between the margin of the wood and the enclosures of Hougomont.

On the other side Jerome attacked the buildings with equal recklessness and persistency. He was close up, with his left arm in a bandage, under a hot fire for hours, but he escaped another wound. Colonel Cubières of the 1st Léger was seriously wounded at his side. Twice it seemed that the place was about to be taken. Lieutenant Legros of the 1st Léger, a giant in stature and with a giant's strength, smashed one of the large doors of the gate with a pioneer's axe, and using it as his weapon burst in with fifty bayonets at his back. Legros was killed, most of his men shot down at close quarters or bayoneted : the rush was stopped and the gateway hastily barricaded. Then, as ammunition ran short, a party of the Guardsmen charged out of another gate, drove back the attack for a moment, but had to give way, and a number of the French forced their way back with them through the gate. Only after a fierce struggle were they driven out, and the gate closed. A brave artillery-man brought up a tumbril of ammunition through the clouds of smoke and showers of sparks from the burning farm.[1] Thanks to this help the defence continued.

Regardless of loss Jerome pressed the attack again ánd again through the afternoon, literally destroying his division before this unconquerable little farmstead of Hougomont. The dogged defence of the place by our Guardsmen has made its name proudly remembered in our own military annals. When we think of Waterloo we remember at once, not only the 'rocky squares' standing solid amid the storms of French cavalry, but also the handful of Coldstreams and Scots holding on desperately amid the burning barns and farm buildings. But the name deserves to be remembered with equal pride by Frenchmen, for the men who attacked hour after hour, round the farmhouse hand to hand, or within a stone's-throw of its walls, and heaped the ground with their dead and wounded, were of the kind that 'do not know when they are beaten.' From Prince Jerome down to the youngest conscript they fought like heroes, though with a wiser and more experienced leader than the Prince they might have been spared the test to which they so nobly responded.

While the 6th division thus shattered itself against Hougo-mont, the great battle had run its course. There had been the repeated attacks on La Haye Sainte, the capture of the other farm of La Haye, the wild cavalry onsets, the secondary battle round Planchenoit to meet the ever-increasing pressure of the Prussian advance, and then at last as the sun went down the great attack of the Imperial Guard and the victorious advance of the British line. It was when all was lost that the scanty remnant of Jerome's division abandoned the assault on

---

[1] This is the exploit which Sir Conan Doyle attributes to the old sergeant of the Scots Guards in his *Story of Waterloo*.

Hougomont, pressed at the last by Chassé's Belgian division coming up on their flank from Braine l'Alleud. They went streaming back over the heights towards the Charleroi road, the nerve of the men at last breaking down under the sense of defeat following on the long strain of the fight. Leaving one of his staff officers to rally what he could of this crowd of beaten men, Jerome rode towards the height of La Belle Alliance anxious as to his brother's fate.

He found Napoleon in the midst of a mass of fugitives, on the rear of which the British cavalry were charging. The Emperor was forming up two regiments of his Guard to check the pursuit, and the two squares of Grenadiers were like islands in the midst of the rout. Jerome rode into one of the squares with his brother, and behind the bristling hedge of bayonets they spoke together. 'It would be well,' said Jerome, 'if we who bear the name of Bonaparte could die here.' These days of toil and danger had made him a different man from the idler of Cassel and Napoleonshöhe, the Prince who had played at being a general in Silesia and Poland. As the Emperor looked at him, with his wounded arm bandaged up, his uniform torn and dust-stained, his face black with powder smoke, he felt Jerome was a better man than he had ever imagined, the man he had hoped to see him. He took his hand. '*Mon frère, je vous ai connu trop tard,*' he said,—' I have known you too late, my brother.' In the midst of the ruin of Waterloo it must have been a moment of passing happiness for both.

The brothers were not to die there in the square of the Old Guard. Soult seized the Emperor's bridle. 'They will not kill you, Sire,' he said, 'you will be their prisoner.' Some of his officers forced him out of the square, and he rode towards Genappe through the deepening twilight. Jerome remained with the Guardsmen while they met the first charge of Uxbridge's cavalry. But reckless as he had shown himself of life there was the growing certainty that the Guard could not hold its own, could not even retire unbroken. A Bonaparte must not be among the prisoners. A way was made for him to leave the square during a lull of the attack, and he became a unit in the multitude of fugitives that was moving through the darkness towards the bridges of the Sambre, with Gneisenau's Prussians in merciless pursuit.

CHAPTER XXVII

THE BROTHERS AT PARIS AFTER WATERLOO
THE ABDICATION

(1815)

AFTER the Emperor's departure for the army Paris was in anxious expectation of news from the front. On Saturday the 17th it was generally known in the capital that the Sambre had been crossed, but there were no details. Unlike the Napoleon of 1870, the Napoleon of 1815 was too used to making history on a grand scale to magnify a minor frontier engagement into a great battle, so nothing was said of the numerous successful actions of the Thursday. In the middle of the night between Saturday and Sunday, Joseph was roused from his sleep at the Elysée to receive an officer who had arrived from the front with a short despatch from the Emperor. It had been written late on Friday evening, and, treating Ligny and Quatre Bras as one battle, it told of a great victory over the Allies, but gave no particulars.

Joseph sent for Lucien, and showed him the despatch. Lucien was not sanguine as to the results of the campaign, and did not like the absence of details in the Emperor's brief despatch. He told Joseph that it would perhaps be better not to make too much of it, but to wait for further news. It might only be a first contact with the enemy, and a few hours might bring news of more serious fighting. Joseph, however, felt sure the Emperor's note meant that a really important battle had been fought, and a great success obtained.

He communicated with Davofit, the War Minister. It was considered that it would be useful to reassure public opinion by making the most of the news. A short abstract of the despatch announcing a victory won at Ligny ' over the combined armies of Wellington and Blücher ' was sent to the

Moniteur to be printed on a fly-sheet as a supplement.   This was what Joseph and Davoût had gathered from the despatch, which spoke of both the British and the Prussians having been engaged, and the victory having been won at Ligny.   Orders were sent to the Invalides to fire a salute, and early in the morning Paris woke to the echo of a hundred guns, and recognised the sound as the same that in the old days of the Empire had heralded the news of Austerlitz and Jena, Friedland and Wagram.

It was the Sunday of Waterloo, a bright sunny morning in Paris.   The crowds in street and boulevard read eagerly the *Moniteur* supplement, which was freely distributed.   There was general rejoicing.   Unofficial papers came out with wild rumours : Wellington was a prisoner, Blücher was dead, thousands of prisoners, scores of guns had been taken.   The Emperor was about to enter Brussels.   The Belgian and Dutch troops had revolted and joined him.   Any one who expressed a doubt of all this good news ran a danger of being roughly handled as a Royalist traitor or a spy of the enemy.

Next day it was known that there had been two battles on the Friday, but it was reported that Quatre Bras had been a victory as well as Ligny, though not so complete.   The Prussians had certainly been disposed of, it was said, and Wellington, with his ally beaten and the whole Imperial army upon him, must be in a hopeless position.   Until the Tuesday evening Paris was jubilantly confident, and was eagerly awaiting tidings of further success, but that evening it was reported in the cafés on the boulevards that the Government had received some disquieting news, but as yet nothing was really known to the public, and flying rumours of defeat were discredited.

It was true that the bad news had arrived.   That afternoon a staff officer had come in after a long ride from the little fortress of Philippeville on the Belgian frontier, and delivered to Joseph two letters, which the Emperor had written after reaching the place at nine o'clock on the Monday morning. One was a short formal despatch, intended to be read to the Council of Ministers.   It said that a battle had been fought and lost, but it minimised the importance of the defeat.   The other was a confidential letter from the Emperor to his brother.

It told him frankly that the army had been routed, and the remnant of it was being rallied under the protection of the frontier fortresses. But it ended with a declaration that the war would go on. ' All is not lost,' wrote the Emperor. With what was left of his army, the depôt troops, the National Guards, there would soon be 300,000 men at his command. But every one must help him, not embarrass him. The deputies must be made to see that it was their duty to unite with the Emperor to save France from the invaders. He had been too busy to write the full bulletins of Ligny and Quatre Bras, but would send them on, and they should appear in the *Moniteur*. He was coming himself at once to Paris, where he hoped to arrive on the Tuesday night or early on Wednesday morning.

Joseph showed the letters to Lucien, told all the bad news to Hortense, convoked the ministers at the Tuileries, and laid the short formal despatch before them. Secrecy was enjoined on every one, and the secret was well kept, though so many knew it. But the fact that despatches had arrived was known, and that the ministers had met hurriedly without making any public announcement. Hence the vague rumours that bad news had come from the front. The ministers had arrived at no decision, beyond expressing an opinion that it would be better for Napoleon to remain with the army. A note to this effect was sent to meet him, but never reached him, for he did not return by the direct road to Paris.

Joseph had told the Council they would meet next day in the presence of the Emperor. After a rest of a few hours at Laon that evening, Napoleon drove towards Paris all through the night, and at eight o'clock on Wednesday morning he arrived at the Elysée, haggard and weary with his journey. By that time all Paris knew that there had been a disaster. One of the newspapers had received a private letter from the frontier that told of the utter rout of the Imperial army.

Before the Council met the Emperor had a talk with Joseph and Lucien. He tried to make the best of the position, and told his brothers he would soon be at the head of another army, but he must have the support of the legislature. Joseph was depressed, and said that the Chamber of Deputies would be hostile and impracticable. Already there was a strong opposition party headed by La Fayette. It would be reinforced by all who thought that the Emperor personally was the one obstacle to peace. Lucien was more sanguine and resolute. With the Emperor wearied and discouraged and Joseph losing heart, the whole burden of the crisis fell on him. He agreed with his brother that nothing could be hoped from the deputies, but he strongly expressed the opinion that the first step should be to dissolve or prorogue the Chambers, declare the country in danger, and let the Emperor act as a dictator during the state of war.

The three brothers then went into the Council of Ministers. Napoleon made a statement as to the military situation, and then went on to say that, if France would rise against the enemy, there was no reason to despair. Then he said : ' In order to save the country it is necessary that I should be given great power, a temporary dictature. I might myself assume this power in the public interest. But it would be more advantageous, more in accordance with the national spirit, if it were entrusted to me by the Chambers.' There was a discouraging silence. No one spoke until the Emperor began to ask each minister in turn for his opinion.

Carnot and Davoût, the Minister of War, approved of the Emperor's proposal. Davoût was for acting without consulting the Chamber. Fouché, who was already intriguing for the return of the Bourbons as the price of peace, protested that the Chambers would undoubtedly assist the Emperor to defend the country. The opinions of others were divided. One of them expressed a fear that the opposition would propose and the Chamber vote for the Emperor's abdication.

Lucien, silent till then, interposed. ' If,' he said, ' the Chamber will not support the Emperor, he will do without it. The safety of the country is the supreme law. If the Chamber refuses to unite with the Emperor to save France, he must save it himself. He ought to proclaim himself dictator, declare all the country in a state of siege, and call all true Frenchmen to its defence.'

Then the Emperor said that he believed the mere presence of an enemy on the soil of France would rally the deputies to him, and he added that he had made every preparation for the event of a lost battle at the outset of the campaign. He explained his plans, enumerated the forces that could be raised, and said that in four days he would again take command of the army, which was concentrating round Laon. As for any talk of his abdicating, did they realise, he asked, what it meant ? It would be confusion and disaster, for his name alone could rally the army. ' I could understand,' he said, ' being repulsed when I landed at Cannes. But now I am a part of that which the enemy attacks, and which France must therefore defend. In giving me up she surrenders herself, acknowledges herself vanquished, encourages the audacity of the conquerors. It is not freedom, but panic, that would depose me.'

The Emperor's speech inspired the Council with something of his own courage. They protested that they would loyally support him. But the Chambers had already met, and there panic and disaffection were in the ascendant. Nearly every one thought that further resistance was hopeless, and most of the deputies and not a few of the peers were thinking how best to get rid of Napoleon and make their peace with the Allies and the Bourbons. After the routine preliminaries of the sitting had been disposed of La Fayette rose, and after speaking of himself as ' an old soldier of liberty,' moved that the Chamber should proclaim that the freedom of the nation was menaced, declare itself in permanent session, announce that whoever tried to dissolve it was a traitor to the country, call upon the National Guard to protect it, and request the ministers to present themselves in order to give any information that might be required of them. After a brief debate the resolutions were carried. One of the ministers who had gone over to the Chamber came back to the Elysée, and told the Council what had happened.

The Emperor saw at once that it was the beginning of a revolt against him. ' I ought to have sent all these people about their business,' he said, ' before I went away. It is all over. They are going to ruin France.' The ministers one after another now expressed the opinion that the whole situation was changed. Davoût thought that Napoleon might be tempted to march his Grenadiers to the Chamber, and disperse the deputies, as he had turned out the Council of Five Hundred on the day of Brumaire. As Minister of War he would be responsible, and he resolved to prevent even the

suggestion of a *coup d'état*. ' The time to act has passed,'
he said. ' The resolution of the Chamber is unconstitutional,
but it is an accomplished fact. We must not flatter ourselves with the idea of repeating the 18th Brumaire under the
existing circumstances. For my part I would refuse to be the
instrument of such a plan.'

The Emperor said that perhaps he would abdicate, but first
there must be an appeal to both Chambers. A message setting
forth briefly the proposals of the Emperor for the defence of
the country was hastily written in duplicate. The Minister
Regnaud took it to the lower House, and Carnot went with it
to the Chamber of Peers. The Chamber of Deputies refused
to discuss the Emperor's message, and remained in permanent
session with a battalion of the National Guard formed up to
protect them from interruption. The peers adjourned after
having passed a resolution approving of the action of the other
Chamber.

Under the new Constitution the Emperor had the right to
send special commissioners to represent him in either House.
He entrusted the ministers with a new message to the Chamber
appealing for their co-operation, and sent Lucien with them
as his special representative. This would give his brother
the right to speak from the tribune, and Napoleon remembered
his oratorical triumphs in the days of the Republic, and hoped
much from his intervention. ' Go,' he said to Lucien, ' and
speak to them of the interests of France, which should be dear
to all her representatives. On your return I shall take whatever course my duty may dictate.'

The Council broke up. Lucien, before going to the Chamber,
went out into the garden of the palace with Napoleon. Beyond
the low wall of the enclosure there was a crowd of people, and
seeing Napoleon among the trees they began to shout '*Vive
l'Empereur! Aux armes! aux armes!*' Lucien had been again
urging his brother to dissolve the legislature. He pointed to
the crowd and said to the Emperor: ' Do you hear those
people ? One word, and your enemies will have to succumb.
It is the same all through France. Will you abandon her to
the factions ?' According to Lucien the Emperor replied
that he did not mean to be a mere party chief and light up
civil war. ' In Brumaire,' he said, ' we drew the sword for the

good of France. To-day we must throw that sword away. Try to win back the Chambers. United with them I can do everything. Without them, I might be able to do much for myself, but I could not save the country. Go, and I forbid you as you go out to harangue those people, who are crying out for arms. I will attempt everything for France, but for myself I do not want to attempt anything.'

At six o'clock Lucien, accompanied by several of the Ministry, entered the Chamber. At his request the galleries were cleared. It was to be a private session (*en comité secret*). Lucien then read the Emperor's message, which stated that negotiations for peace would be opened, and an endeavour made to obtain terms compatible with the honour of France ; that the Emperor had sent his brother and the ministers to give any further information the deputies might require, and that he relied on their patriotism and their attachment to himself personally, and counted on their support. Lucien added in a few words a stirring appeal for union for the sake of France in the presence of the enemy.

Davoût as Minister of War, Carnot as Minister of the Interior, tried to show that there were still means of resistance ; Caulaincourt, the Minister of Foreign Affairs, said that there was good hope of successful negotiations, provided always that the army and the Chambers showed they were not ready to surrender at discretion. The other minister present was Fouché, the chief of the police department. He was silent. He had already arranged the next move with the deputy Jay, one of the speakers of the opposition.

Jay rose and said he had a motion to propose that was a perilous one for himself. Before going further he asked the ministers and Prince Lucien to say frankly if they thought France could oppose the combined armies of Europe, and if the real obstacle to peace was not the presence of Napoleon. Lucien and the three ministers who had spoken hurriedly consulted together, but before they could decide anything Fouché sprang up and said, ' The ministers have nothing to add to the reports they have already made.' Jay then went on to insist that to prolong the war was hopeless, but it was also unnecessary. The Coalition had been formed not against the independence of France, but against Napoleon personally.

2 F

The conclusion was self-evident. He turned to Lucien and went on. ' You, Prince, who have shown nobility of character in good and evil fortune alike, remember that you are a Frenchman, and that everything should give way to the love of our country. Go back to your brother. Tell him that the representatives of the people here assembled expect on his part a resolution that will do him more honour in the future than his many victories. Tell him that by abdicating he can save France, which has made such great and painful sacrifices for his sake.' He then proposed that, after Lucien had seen his brother, a deputation should go to Napoleon and request him to abdicate.

Lucien rose to protest. It was cowardice, he said, to assert that further resistance was hopeless. It was folly to say that the Allies were hostile only to the Emperor. No ! They were attacking France. They meant to invade her, ruin the people, partition the territory, reduce France to a second-rate power, and impose a government that the people had rejected. And was it at this moment that they spoke of abandoning the Emperor, the one hope of success, the one leader the enemy dreaded ? So far Lucien had done well and his audience was moved by his words, but he ended with an unfortunate phrase. If France abandoned Napoleon, he said, the nations might justly ' brand her with levity and inconstancy.'

La Fayette saw the opening for a deadly retort. He sprang up. ' That is a calumny,' he exclaimed. ' How can any one charge the French nation with inconstancy and levity towards Napoleon. They have followed him through the sands of Egypt and the deserts of Russia, and thanks to having thus followed him they have to regret the blood of three millions of Frenchmen !'

A storm of applause told Lucien he had spoiled the effect of his appeal. The debate became more hostile. Deputy after deputy rose to support the proposal of Jay, but it was decided to adjourn the division on it, and meanwhile the Chamber resolved to appoint a committee of five to act with the Ministry, and invited the peers to do likewise. At eight o'clock the public were again admitted to the galleries. The election of the committee was proceeded with, and Davoût rose and said he had just heard there was a rumour that he was arranging for the troops to march on the Chamber. That was a calumny against himself and against the Emperor. Neverthe-less General Durosnel, who commanded the National Guard, was directed to reinforce the battalion that was on duty. The deputies still feared a *coup d'état*. Even Lucien's presence reminded them of Brumaire.

At half-past eight Lucien and the ministers went to the Chamber of Peers and read the Emperor's message, and the resolution of the lower House inviting them to name five peers to act with the ministers. The peers selected two civilians and three generals. Lucien then went back to the Elysée, where he found the Emperor finishing his dinner with Hortense.

Napoleon was tired and depressed. In his conversation with Lucien he seemed undecided as to what was to be done. Now he talked of abdicating, now of forcibly dissolving the Chambers. The Emperor's trusted friend, Maret, Duke of Bassano, and Caulaincourt were called in. Both advised abdication. It was better that it should be the free act of Napoleon, not a submission to a demand from the Chambers. Lucien said the Chamber of Deputies had gone so far that it was hopeless to think of bringing it back. There was no choice but abdication or dissolution, and for his part he was in favour of the latter, by force if need be. While the Emperor was losing heart and the ministers were thinking only of how to save themselves in the coming change of government, Lucien was all courage and eagerness for decided action. He was no longer the Roman Prince with his circle of artist friends, the Worcestershire country gentleman busy with literature and science; he was the old Jacobin, the fighting politician of the day of Brumaire, ready, if his brother would but consent, to go back to the Chamber at the head of a battalion of Grenadiers.

Napoleon hesitated. He was weary with the night's journey, the agitation of the long day. He felt the sense of defeat. At another time he would have cut short these endless debates, and acted. Now he took refuge in further discussion. It was decided to hold a Council at the Tuileries at eleven o'clock that night. He remained at the Elysée. Joseph and Lucien were to represent him, and the ten delegates of the Chambers were invited to meet the ministers at the Council board.

The Council lasted from eleven at night till three in the morning. After some debate a vague resolution was adopted

to the effect that the ministers undertook to propose to the
Chambers measures for providing for the national defence and
the preservation of order.   Then, by a narrow majority of one,
a resolution was passed, which stated that at this crisis everything except constitutional liberty and the integrity of the
territory must if necessary be sacrificed.   This implied a
possible abdication.   Then one of the delegates of the Chamber
of Deputies proposed, that as the Allies would not treat with
the Emperor, the Chambers should send commissioners to
negotiate a peace.   Fouché was the only minister who accepted
this.   The two Princes, the rest of the ministers, and some of
the delegates secured its rejection.   But it was amended by
adding that the peace commissioners should be chosen with
the assent of the Emperor, and then it was carried by sixteen
votes to five.

The way had thus been prepared for a further step.   La
Fayette, who was present as a delegate of the lower House,
suggested that the Emperor should be advised at once to
abdicate.   Lucien protested and added, ' If the Emperor's
friends had thought his abdication necessary for the welfare
of France, they would have been the first to require it of him.'
' That is speaking like a true Frenchman,' said La Fayette.
' I adopt the idea.   I demand that we go all together to the
Emperor, and tell him that his abdication has become necessary
in the interest of the country.'   Cambacérès, who presided,
refused to put the resolution, and said that it was beyond
their powers.   Then the meeting broke up.   Abdication had
not been formally voted for, but it had been plainly indicated.

Napoleon had tried to sleep while the Council was sitting,
but he had many wakeful hours during that night, and in his
memoirs of St. Helena he says that more than once he thought
of rising and preparing for a *coup d'état* in the early morning :
a hurried meeting of the Council of State at the Tuileries,
the troops marching out from their barracks to disperse the
rebel parliament and arrest the leaders of the opposition,
and then a proclamation of a dictatorship while the country
was in danger.   But in the morning he felt again the horror
of civil war, of bloodshed in the streets of Paris, of giving the
Allies a new pretext for saying that they had come to free
France from a military despotism.   Tried friends who came to

see him spoke of abdication as a painful necessity. Lavalette spoke to him of a new Brumaire as a dangerous policy. ' Any thought of the kind is far from me,' said Napoleon.

Early in the day the ministers came to the Elysée and reported the resolutions of the Council held in the night. The Emperor told them to inform the Chambers that he agreed to their sending commissioners to the Allies to propose peace, and if his presence in France was really an obstacle to it, he was ready to make any sacrifice.

The ministers had hardly gone when Captain Vatry, one of Jerome's staff officers, arrived from Laon with encouraging news. He had letters from Jerome and from Marshal Soult. Soult reported that Grouchy with his army and more than a hundred guns had effected his retreat from Belgium and was on the march for Laon. The Marshal himself had 3000 of the Old Guard at Laon and some thousands of the Line. Other detachments had rallied between Laon and the frontier. Jerome's report was even more welcome, for it showed that he was doing manful service. He had rallied more than 2000 horse and foot during the flight from Waterloo, and marched into Avesnes at their head. There he had got together and organised some thousands more. He had marched to Laon with 10,000 men, and after handing them over to Soult, he would come on to Paris. The Emperor estimated that he had now 60,000 men in Laon or on the way to it. He sent Davoût to the Chamber of Deputies with the news.

The Chamber had heard the resolutions adopted at the Council and the Emperor's message, and received these communications in no friendly spirit. The opposition, now dominant, asked what was the use of sending commissioners to treat for peace with the Allies, who had solemnly declared that they could have no peace with Napoleon. His abdication was a necessity, they said, and Davoût's hopeful statement was regarded as only an attempt to bolster up Napoleon's position. The Marshal was openly told that he was misleading the House. Some of the more moderate men succeeded in carrying a resolution that, instead of demanding the Emperor's abdication, a deputation should be sent to him to persuade him to come to an immediate decision of his own accord. As the debate closed La Fayette walked up to Lucien

and said to him : ' Tell your brother to send us his abdication.
If not, we shall send him his deposition.' ' And I will send you
La Bédoyère [1] at the head of a battalion of the Guard ! '
replied Lucien, who was still defiant and hoping against hope
to inspire the Emperor with his own fighting spirit.

The delegates of the Chamber were General Solignac (who
as a regimental officer had been with Napoleon on the day of
Brumaire) and two others. Napoleon listened patiently to
their arguments, and told them he would presently send the
Chamber another message, which he hoped would content
them. Then he met his brothers and the ministers. They
told him that Davoût's report had been ridiculed, and the
majority had nearly voted for abdication. The motion had
been only temporarily adjourned.

Napoleon was irritated, and for a few moments spoke of
resisting. ' If they mean to force me,' he exclaimed, ' I shall
not abdicate. The Chamber is made up of Jacobins, hare-
brained fools, and ambitious men. I ought to have denounced
them to the nation, and turned them out. But we can make
up for lost time now ! ' He walked up and down talking to
himself. The rest looked on in silence, and as he became
calmer, Regnaud, one of the ministers, interposed. He said
it was useless to struggle against ' the invincible force of
events.' Time was running on, the enemy advancing. Was
it wise to give a pretext for saying he had made himself an
obstacle to peace ? ' Sire,' he continued, ' last year you
sacrificed yourself for the good of all—' Napoleon interrupted
him. ' I shall see what I ought to do,' he said. ' It has never
been my intention to refuse to abdicate. But I want to be
allowed to think things out in peace. Tell them to wait.'

Some of the ministers were silent. Others spoke in support
of Regnaud's advice. Carnot opposed them. Abdication,
he said, would be a signal for general surrender, a *sauve qui
peut*. Let the Emperor go to the army, declare the country
in danger, and call France to his aid.

Lucien made a last attempt to secure the adoption of his
own bold plans. The time was come, he said, for action.
Orders should be sent at once to disperse the Chamber. ' You

---

[1] La Bédoyère, the young colonel of the Guard, who had been one of the first to
join Napoleon after the return from Elba. He was executed during the ' White
Terror' after the Restoration.

did not do so badly,' he continued, ' when you followed my advice on the 18th Brumaire. The country approved our action, hailed you with acclamations. But all the same it is true that we had no legal right to take the course we adopted. It was simply a revolution. What is the difference to-day ? You have full power at your command. The foreigner is marching on Paris. Never was a dictatorship—a military dictatorship—more justifiable ! '

The Emperor turned to his brother, and speaking in a very gentle voice replied : ' My dear Lucien, it is true that on the 18th Brumaire we could only plead the welfare of the people, and all the same when we asked for a bill of indemnity a general acclamation was our answer. To-day we have every right on our side, but we ought not to take advantage of this.' He paused, and then in a different tone, a tone of command, he continued, ' Prince Lucien, write at my dictation.'

While Lucien was seating himself and preparing to write, Napoleon addressed Fouché. ' Write to those good people,' he said, ' to be quiet. They will soon be satisfied.' The message sent through Fouché seemed to show that the Emperor knew he was working against him, as he had done in 1814.

Lucien, waiting pen in hand, looked up at his brother, who was thinking how to shape his message. In the silence there came from outside the palace the cheers of the crowd that had waited since early morning crying ' *Vive l'Empereur ! Aux armes !* ' The Emperor began to dictate. Lucien had written a few lines before he realised that it was a message announcing his brother's abdication. He sprang up, dashed down the pen, flung back his chair and walked towards the door, thinking perhaps of throwing himself into the crowd and calling for a popular revolt in defence of the Emperor.

Napoleon called him back, and asked him to complete the message. It ran thus :—

'When I began the war to uphold the national independence, I counted on the union of the efforts and the wills of all, and on the support of all the national authorities. I had reason to hope for success. Circumstances seem to me to have changed. I offer myself as a sacrifice to the hatred of the enemies of France. It is to be hoped that they will prove to be sincere in their declarations, and hostile only to me personally. Unite yourselves to secure the welfare of the people and its continuance as an independent nation.'

This was all. Lucien, supported by Carnot, remonstrated with the Emperor. He must say more, they urged. Under the Constitution, if he ceased to be Emperor, his son succeeded. This should be insisted on. Surely it was not necessary to abolish the dynasty. One of the ministers suggested that unless Napoleon II. was named, it was simply opening the door for the Bourbons. 'The Bourbons!' exclaimed Napoleon. 'Well, at any rate they will not be under the rod of Austria.' It was the idea that his son was in foreign hands that had made him hesitate to proclaim him as his successor. But at last he gave way to Lucien's arguments, and dictated this addition to his message :—

'I proclaim my son, under the name of NAPOLEON II., Emperor of the French. The Princes Joseph and Lucien and the Ministers now in office will form a Provisional Government Council. On account of my interest in my son I feel I must ask the Chambers to lose no time in passing a law to create a Regency.'

Maret suggested that the names of the two princes might give rise to discussion in the Chambers, and Napoleon crossed them out. The message was copied in duplicate. Carnot was to communicate it to the Chamber of Peers, Fouché to the Chamber of Deputies.

Lucien, once more hopeful, left the Elysée, after telling his brother that he was going to watch the reception of the message in the Chambers, and interpose in the debates if necessary. Napoleon was calmer than he had been since his return from Waterloo. He had taken a great decision. His second reign had closed, but he believed his career was not over. France might yet rally to the name of his son, and the Allies might, under the influence of Austria, stay their march rather than carry on a war against a nation asserting its right to choose its own rulers, that choice being now the son of Maria Louisa. For the present Napoleon must keep in the background, but surely he would have a great part to play in coming years. Perhaps, if the war went on, he might still lead the armies of France as commander-in-chief for Napoleon II.—the child who was that day playing in the gardens of Schönbrunn, all unconscious that he was an Emperor.

CHAPTER XXVIII

NAPOLEON II.—THE DAYS OF EXILE

(1815-1817)

THERE can be no doubt that so far as there was any legality in the Constitution of the Empire, the reign of Napoleon II. legally began on June 22, 1815—a reign destined to last only a few days. But most of those who had called for the abdication of Napoleon I. had no idea of the Empire surviving his downfall. As the price of peace they were again ready to accept the Bourbons, though some hoped to see royalty restored in the person of the Duc de Chartres, the representative of the Orleans line, the soldier of Jemappes and the son of Philippe Egalité.

Both Chambers, without making any reference to the claims of the King of Rome, sent deputations to thank the Emperor for his act of patriotic self-sacrifice, and at once proceeded to appoint a Commission—practically a Provisional Government—formed of the ministers and of delegates from both Houses.

To both the deputations Napoleon pointed out that he had only abdicated conditionally, leaving the Empire to his son under a Regency. To the delegates of the Peers he said, ' If the Chambers do not proclaim my son, my abdication is null and void.'

When the Chamber of Peers reassembled at half-past eight that evening, Lucien took his seat with Joseph and Cardinal Fesch beside him. The President read a very guarded report of the interview with Napoleon, and then Lucien at once raised the question of the succession. Going to the tribune he began by repeating an adaptation of the old formula of the days of royalty : ' The Emperor is dead ! ' he proclaimed. ' Long live the Emperor ! The Emperor has abdicated ! Long live the Emperor! There can be no interval between the Emperor who dies or abdicates and his successor. I demand that in virtue of the continuous force of the Act of the Constitution the Chamber of Peers shall, without debate and by a spontaneous and unanimous vote, declare that it recognises Napoleon II. as Emperor of the French. I give the first example, and I swear fidelity to him.'

There were some cries of ' *Vive l'Empereur!* ' but there were also murmurs of dissent. One of the orators of the opposition, Pontecoulant, rose to protest against Lucien's action. He said that personally he was devoted to Napoleon, he owed him everything, but this was no reason why he should adopt a policy that he considered a mistake. As for Prince Lucien, by what right did he speak for the Chamber ? ' Is he a Frenchman ? ' he asked; and he went on, ' I do not regard him as such. He invokes the Constitution, but he has no constitutional right to be here. He is a Roman Prince, and Rome is no longer a part of the Empire.'

Lucien, who could easily have demolished this quibble, sprang up exclaiming, ' I am going to reply to that.' But Pontecoulant went on : ' You will reply, Prince, after I have done. Respect that equality of which you have so often yourself given the example.' Then he went on to protest that Lucien's proposal could not be accepted without treason to their duty to the country. ' I declare,' he said, ' that I will never recognise as my sovereign a child, an individual who does not reside in France. To take such a resolution would be to close the door against any useful negotiations.'

Lucien answered with a brief speech. He held his place among the peers by precisely the same title as the last speaker. ' If I am not a Frenchman in your eyes,' he said, ' I am such in the eyes of the whole nation. The moment Napoleon abdicated, his son succeeded him. Don't let us ask the foreigner to choose our rulers for us. In recognising Napoleon II. we do what is our duty ; we call to the throne him who is called to it by the Constitution and the will of the people.'

The debate went on. There was a grave argument by Joseph, a fiery· speech by the young General De la Bédoyère, who within a few weeks was to be condemned to death by a Bourbon court-martial. Roederer, Maret, Duke of Bassano, Flahault,

Ségur, all devoted friends of the Emperor, intervened, but each was answered in turn by a hostile speech, which was more loudly applauded than the pleas of the Emperor's partisans. Finally the debate was adjourned, and the peers proceeded to elect their delegates to the Government Commission or Provisional Government. An attempt to secure the election of Lucien as a member of it was defeated by fifty-two votes against eighteen. This showed how strong was the opposition to the Emperor. The Chamber of Deputies had refused to debate the proclamation of Napoleon ii., and had passed on at once to the selection of its representatives on the Government Commission.

In Paris the news of the abdication had spread abroad, and there was an outburst of popular agitation that made the opposition leaders not a little anxious. Angry crowds with officers and soldiers among them paraded the Boulevards, protesting that the Emperor was betrayed, that he must not go. In the Place Vendôme a cheering crowd surrounded the column. Before the Elysée the people gathered hoping to catch a glimpse of their hero. Round the palace of the Chamber of Deputies there was a threatening multitude, held back by the ordered lines of the National Guard. Lucien thought of an appeal to the people of Paris, of another day like those of the Revolution, but he held his hand in deference to his brother's protest against provoking civil war and bloodshed in the streets.

On the morning of June 23rd the Government Commission met and chose Fouché as its president, and henceforth he directed affairs. He was alarmed at the agitation in Paris, and with a view to calming it, he secured the same day, after a stormy debate, the recognition of Napoleon ii. by the Chamber of Deputies. He told his friends that, when it became advisable to do so, it would be just as easy by a similar vote to substitute another sovereign for the child-Emperor. The Chamber then proceeded to discuss a new Constitution. ' It is like the Greek Empire,' said Napoleon, when he heard of it. ' Poor wretches, they keep on debating, with the enemy at their gates! '

Jerome arrived in Paris that afternoon, and went to stay with his uncle Cardinal Fesch. He saw Napoleon at the Elysée, and had the pleasure of hearing his brother warmly praise his conduct in the field, and the way in which he had rallied so many thousands from the rout of Waterloo, and led them to reinforce the army at Laon.

Joseph and Lucien came in, and the brothers discussed the future. Lucien was hopeful. Napoleon II. reigned now by right of succession and by the vote of the Chambers. There would be a Regency, and peace by the intervention of Austria, and there would still be great days for the Bonapartes. Neither Joseph nor Napoleon was so sanguine. The ex-Emperor knew that his continued stay in France would be as great an obstacle to peace as if he still reigned. He must go away, at least for a while. He spoke of going to America, the land of refuge to which so many of the Bonapartes turned in the days of exile. There were two frigates at Rochefort ready for sea, the *Saale* and the *Méduse*. That very evening he wrote to Decrès, the Minister of Marine, asking that they should be placed at his disposal to convey him to some port in the United States.

All that day and the next excited crowds of soldiers and civilians surrounded the Elysée, crying ' *Vive Napoleon II.!* ' ' *Vive l'Empereur!* ' ' *Death to the Royalists!* ' ' *Give us arms!* ' To a deputation which forced its way into the courtyard Napoleon said, ' You shall have arms, but only to use against the foreign enemy.' Fouché had good reason to fear an outbreak. At his suggestion the Government Committee ' invited ' the Emperor to withdraw from Paris, ' where his presence gave rise to a dangerous agitation.' He decided to retire to Malmaison, where he had spent so many happy days with Josephine, and went there on the 25th, slipping out of the Elysée by a side-door to escape a popular demonstration. Next day Fouché, on the part of the Government, ' invited ' Jerome to follow his brother's example and withdraw from the capital, ' in the interest of the tranquillity of the state and of his own.' Joseph and Lucien had already left Paris on the 24th.

The three brothers were with Napoleon at Malmaison on the afternoon of the 25th, the day of his arrival there. Napoleon was surprised at the delay in authorising his voyage from Rochefort, and soon began to suspect a possible plot against him. At Vienna there had been talk of deporting him to some distant island of the ocean, Santa Lucia or St. Helena—this while he was still at Elba. He might be handed over to the vengeance of the French Royalists, who were threatening a new terror. The Prussians, who were now advancing on Paris, were eager to make him their prisoner, and talked of a summary execution if he fell into their hands. An English minister had written that it would be a good thing if Louis xviii. could get hold of him, and shoot or hang him. For the present he was protected at Malmaison by a small detachment of the Guard under General Becker, but the General's orders showed that Fouché and his party regarded the Emperor as their prisoner, a possible hostage for their own safety in the coming days of the Restoration. It was an anxious time. Joseph told his brother that, as soon as he was safely on the way to America, he would follow him there. For the moment he occupied himself with arranging an alternative means for Napoleon's escape across the Atlantic, in case the Provisional Government should refuse the frigates or play a treacherous part. Lucien expected to return to Rome, where he could be of use to the rest of the family. Jerome still hoped to be allowed to rejoin Catherine in Germany.

On June 28th, the fourth day of his stay at Malmaison, permission at last arrived for the Emperor to proceed to Rochefort. The Government's decision had been taken only when the Prussian cavalry were sweeping round to the southeast of Paris, and there was danger that if Napoleon remained longer at Malmaison he would be their prisoner. That day a number of visitors came from Paris to say good-bye, Madame Mère, Cardinal Fesch, Joseph, Maret, the Countess Walewska among them. Joseph spent the night at Malmaison with his brother.

That afternoon the dull reports of cannon were heard in the distance. Davoût's troops were in touch with the Prussians. At the familiar sound the Emperor became eager to fight once more. He sent off an appeal to the Provisional Government to allow him, merely as a French general, to direct the operations against the Prussians and the British round Paris. He pledged his honour that once the fight was over he would leave France. Next morning he put on his uniform, belted on his sword, had his horses and his staff officers ready. The booming of the distant guns told that the action had been resumed. Napoleon hoped he would soon be in the midst of it. But from Paris came a refusal of his petition. Fouché shrank from the danger of letting the Emperor again appear at the head of an army. He told him that the Government could not consent to his delaying his departure. The fallen Emperor laid his sword aside, changed his uniform for a civilian dress, and drove to the château of Rambouillet, where he spent the next night. It was the first stage of the journey to St. Helena.

He reached Niort on July 2nd, and there he was rejoined by Joseph, who had waited a day in Paris to arrange various money matters. The Emperor's private fortune had been entrusted to the banker Lafitte, and Joseph had brought to Niort a considerable sum in gold, for the emergencies of the moment. Next day the brothers went on to Rochefort. It was the day of the second capitulation of Paris, July 3, 1815, a fortnight after Waterloo.

The two frigates, the *Saale* and *Méduse*, still flying the tricolour, lay in the port, but English cruisers were watching the coast, and the Government had given orders that the cruisers were not to go to sea unless there was a certainty of evading them, or alternatively unless the English admiral agreed to give them free passage. Napoleon found himself thus a prisoner at Rochefort. Various projects were discussed. Some of his friends begged him to rejoin the French army now retiring behind the Loire, and call France once more to arms, but he refused to hear of a plan that must lead to civil war.

Joseph set to work to arrange for his running the blockade in some trading ship, either from Rochefort or an adjacent port, or for the unauthorised use for this purpose of one of the lighter craft of the navy. From these projects, however, Napoleon shrank. To go to sea with two frigates, which could if necessary protect him from capture, was one thing. To run the risk of being made prisoner by the English, while hiding in a blockade-runner, was something very different. He asked the permission of the Government to communicate with the English squadron, in order either to negotiate for a free passage or, if that failed, to surrender to a British officer. He had already formed the project of throwing himself on the generosity of the English people, if all else failed, and asking the Prince Regent to allow him to live as an exile under the protection of British law.

On July 7th the Provisional Government was dissolved after arranging for the restoration of the Bourbons, and next day Louis XVIII. entered Paris, which, since the capitulation, had been occupied by the armies of the Allies. Napoleon was still at Rochefort. On the day of the royal entry into Paris he had gone on board the *Saale*, but the British cruisers were sighted off the port, and the authorities refused permission for the frigates to sail, though their captains expressed their willingness to try to run the blockade, or even to fight their way out to sea. Napoleon disembarked, and at the request of the local authorities, who were alarmed at the rising agitation in his favour at Rochefort, left the town for the neighbouring Île d'Aix.

Some of the naval officers had secretly equipped a quick-sailing lugger as a blockade-runner, provisioned her for a long voyage, and asked the Emperor to entrust himself to them. For a while he seemed inclined to adopt this resource. Joseph was busy with another project. He had remained at Rochefort, where he had entered into negotiations with a shipowner named Pelletreau, who was agent for an American ship then lying at Bordeaux. He agreed to charter this ship for his own voyage to America. He also arranged that a small sailing craft should lie at Royan at the mouth of the Gironde, ready to convey him to Bordeaux. This settled, he went to see Napoleon at the Île d'Aix, on the morning of July 13th, to propose to him that he should accept the means of escape he had prepared for himself.

Generals Montholon, Marchand, and Lallemand, all trusted retainers of the Emperor, were called in to the council that was held that morning. Joseph showed his brother a letter he had received from Julie, who was still in Paris. She told of the entry of Louis XVIII., and the rising cry of the Royalists for vengeance, a cry to which Ney, La Bédoyère and many more were soon after sacrificed. The tricolour still flew at the Île d'Aix and Rochefort, but it would soon be replaced by the Bourbon flag, and Napoleon, closely guarded even now by his nominal escort, would be the prisoner of the vengeful Bourbons. The authorities had so far only put obstacles in the way of his attempting to get out to sea. The British cruisers were watching the outlets near Rochefort.

Joseph insisted that for Napoleon the situation was growing dangerous, and in order to favour his brother's escape he showed he was ready to take considerable risks himself. He had an official permit enabling him to pass out of the fortress of the Île d'Aix, and embark for Rochefort that evening. He had a carriage ready outside the town of Rochefort, where there would be no barriers to pass. His boatmen could be trusted to obey orders. Though he was a little taller than his brother, he might be easily mistaken for him in twilight and darkness. That afternoon it was to be reported that the Emperor was ill. Joseph was to take his place, and Marchand undertook to use the plea of illness to prevent any one entering his room for twenty-four hours. Meanwhile Napoleon, muffled in Joseph's cloak and using his pass, would cross over to the mainland, drive in the night to Royan, and embark there. The American clipper would come down the Gironde and pick him up.

Napoleon generously refused to expose his brother to the vengeance of the Royalists. Joseph tried in vain to persuade him. Napoleon insisted that at the worst he could take refuge in England. Joseph argued that this was a mistake. He would only be the prisoner of his enemies, less hostile and vindictive than the Bourbons, but enemies all the same. At last, seeing he could not move the Emperor from his fixed idea, he said he would remain with him. But this Napoleon would not hear of. Joseph, he said, could be most useful to him as a free man in the United States. If he remained in France he would be in danger to no purpose. At last Joseph agreed to go.

That evening there was a sorrowful farewell. Joseph recrossed to the mainland, and was at Royan before morning. He had a passport in the name of ' Monsieur Bouchard, commercial traveller, about to leave France on business.' On the morning of July 14th he was afloat in the Royan fishing-boat. A few hours later he was on board the American trader, sailing down the Gironde under the protection of the Stars and Stripes, and bound for New York.

Next day, July 15th, Napoleon went on board the *Bellerophon* and surrendered to Captain Maitland. Long before Joseph reached New York his brother was also on the Atlantic, a prisoner on board the British warship *Northumberland* bound for St. Helena.

The first period of the greatness of the Bonapartes had closed. It had lasted twenty years, from the day of Vendémiaire in 1795, when Napoleon scattered the National Guard of Paris with his cannon, to the day of Waterloo. These years had changed the face of Europe, and all the four brothers of the Emperor had taken their part in the 'making of history' on a grand scale. But now they had been swept aside in the general collapse of the Imperial system. The day of exile, the time of small things, had begun for them, with only the vaguest prospect of their ever again being called to play a great part in the world. Their story for some years to come can be told within much narrower limits than the record of what was now for them the memory of vanished greatness.

With Napoleon, a prisoner without hope of escape at St. Helena, there was no chance of another venture like the raid on France from Elba. His son—the child who had nominally reigned for a few days as Napoleon II.—was to be educated as an Austrian Prince. Maria Louisa, now Duchess of Parma, thought little of the prisoner of St. Helena or even of her boy at Schönbrunn. Joseph was in America. Lucien, Louis, and Jerome were all exiles from France. The Allied Powers had agreed to exercise a surveillance over all the members of the Bonaparte family. None of their ambassadors was to give a passport to any of them without the assent of his colleagues. Till after the death of Napoleon they were all carefully watched.

In the dark days after Waterloo Lucien had been the boldest and most active of his brother's partisans. When all was lost and the deposed Emperor was on his way to Rochefort, Lucien recognised that he himself was no longer safe in France, where the Royalist extremists were calling for a general proscription of the Bonapartist leaders, and in many places Bourbonist mobs were organising a *jacquerie* of the Imperialists. He secured passports in an assumed name, and set out for Rome by way of northern Italy. He had no sooner crossed the pass

2 G

of Mont Cenis than he was arrested by the Piedmontese Government, and for three months he was kept a close prisoner in the citadel of Turin. It was only thanks to the intervention of his friend Pius VII. that his liberation was at last secured. Notwithstanding his action in the Hundred Days the Pope welcomed him at Rome, and reinstated him in his principality of Canino.

Louis, whom in any case his broken health would have disqualified for taking any prominent part in public affairs, had remained in Italy, a distant spectator of the great events of 1815. His brother had placed his name on the list of his new Chamber of Peers, but he had not asked for Louis's consent before doing so, and the ex-King of Holland had expressed no sympathy with the adventurous bid for Empire, and had from the first predicted the failure of the enterprise. It was a new grievance for him against Hortense that she took no notice of the judgment of the Tribunal of the Seine, published on the eve of Napoleon's return, and refused to send his eldest son tò him in Italy.

After the Emperor's departure for Rochefort, Hortense found· that her position in France had become impossible. She too must go into exile. Her action during the Hundred Days had for ever lost her the favour of the Bourbons, to whom she owed her title of Duchess of St. Leu and the possession of the St. Leu estate. Even if they could have forgiven her her devotion to Napoleon and again invited her to the Tuileries, she could not have shown herself in a court circle so bitterly hostile to the Emperor and all who were in any way related to him. But it was not so easy to find a place of refuge abroad. For nearly two years she led a wandering life with her sons, and found that government after government objected to her establishing herself in its territory. She was for a while at Carlsruhe and Augsburg. At last the authorities of the canton of Thurgau invited her to take refuge within their borders, and she found a home in Switzerland. On February 10, 1817, she bought the villa and estate of Arenenberg on the shore of the Lake of Constance. She lived there very quietly, devoting herself to the education of her sons. Arenenberg became in later years the starting-point of the revival of Bonapartism.

After bidding farewell to Napoleon at Malmaison, Jerome had returned to Paris. It was forbidden ground to him in consequence of Fouché's order of June 26th, politely requiring him to withdraw from the capital. He therefore took care not to show himself in public, and remained hidden in the house of a poor Corsican shoemaker, on whose fidelity he could absolutely rely. Here a friendly doctor secretly visited him, for the slight wound he had received at Quatre Bras was giving him trouble and his general health was not good. He had come back to Paris, and taken all the risk this implied, in order to try to see the envoy of Würtemberg and endeavour to arrange terms with his father-in-law, the King, so as to be able to rejoin Catherine. After a few days he found that there was no chance of doing anything in this direction, and he was warned that his presence in Paris had become known to the Provisional Government, and that if he stayed longer he might be arrested.

He endeavoured to join Napoleon and Joseph at Rochefort, but he got no further than Niort, where he heard that the Emperor had surrendered himself to the English. Meanwhile he had learned that he would be allowed to enter Würtemberg, provided he undertook to reside in the place assigned to him by the King, and not to leave it without his permission. At the same time he was warned that the restored Bourbon Government was anxious to secure his arrest. Disguised, and with the help of a passport belonging to a friend, he made his way across France to Switzerland. The journey was not without its dangers, for although Fouché was really anxious to favour his escape, and had no wish to make a prisoner of one of Napoleon's brothers, there were plenty of the Royalists who would have been eager to lay hands on him, and in many districts the mob was hunting down the partisans of the old régime. The ' White Terror ' had begun. Marshal Brune had been murdered by the mob at Avignon, and other prominent Bonapartists were in prison awaiting trial on capital charges.

Jerome, however, escaped all danger and reached Switzerland safely, and then travelled on to Würtemberg, where on August 22nd he rejoined Catherine and her infant son at the castle of Göppingen. Here he found himself practically a state prisoner, as his wife had been since she was brought there from Gratz in the spring. Shortly after Jerome and Catherine were removed to Elvangen, but here too they were kept prisoners within narrow bounds. For two years this state of things continued. Again and again Catherine was informed that she would be restored to her father's favour, and Jerome would be given a pension and allowed to live wherever he liked abroad, provided she would agree to a divorce. She indignantly rejected all these proposals. Devoted as she was to her husband, this period of semi-captivity with him was not the least happy of her life.

Jerome's first wife, Elisabeth, had sailed from New York for Europe during the Hundred Days, leaving her son Jerome at school at Mount St. Mary's College, Emmetsburg, Maryland. She landed in England, and arrived in London just after the downfall of the Emperor. It was a disappointment, for she had hoped for a renewal of his bounty, and for honours for herself and her son if he succeeded in re-establishing himself upon his throne. But there were some minor consolations. From London, on August 22, 1815, she wrote to her father that she had been agreeably surprised by the friendly and flattering welcome she had received in English society. She added that she thought of bringing her son to England to complete his education. She mentioned that Napoleon had just set sail for St. Helena.

From London she went on to Paris, where also she found a welcome in fashionable circles. She declined an invitation to be presented to Louis XVIII. at the Tuileries. For one who claimed to bear the name of Bonaparte, that would have been going too far. But short of this, she made no scruple of meeting in society those who had wrought the Emperor's ruin. In her letters to Baltimore she mentioned conversations with Wellington and Talleyrand. Other acquaintances were Châteaubriand, Madame de Staël, and the historian Sismondi. In a letter to her father, on February 22, 1816, she spoke of her husband. ' The ex-King of Westphalia,' she wrote, ' is at present living at the court of Würtemberg. He has a great fortune, but he is so mean as to do nothing for the support of his son. He ought at least to repay you your money.' In the summer of 1816 she left Paris and returned to Baltimore.

When Elisabeth wrote thus of Jerome's supposed wealth and position at his father-in-law's court, he was still in semi-durance at Elvangen, and nearer poverty than he ever was in his life. It was not till 1817 that the King of Würtemberg at last realised that he could not break down his daughter's resolution and that his treatment of her was becoming a public scandal. He entered into negotiations, and it was agreed that Jerome and Catherine should be set at liberty on condition that for some time to come they should live in Austrian territory. Catherine had already a pension from the Czar. The King her father consented to grant her a further annual allowance, though he knew this was practically giving it to Jerome, whom he now hated. Husband and wife were not to use the title of Prince and Princess, but were to be known as the Count and Countess de Montfort. With what Jerome had saved from the wreck, and Catherine's two pensions, they would have an income of about £3000 a year.

After this victory of Catherine's she settled down with her husband and child at Trieste, where two of Jerome's sisters, Elisa and the widowed Caroline Murat of Naples, were also living in 1817. Lucien and Louis were near at hand in Italy, where Madame Mère had also found refuge. The two elder brothers were beyond the seas—Napoleon in his island prison, Joseph in the United States.

CHAPTER XXIX

THE BONAPARTES IN EUROPE AND AMERICA—
FIRST YEARS OF LOUIS NAPOLEON (THE FUTURE
NAPOLEON III.)

(1815-1830)

WHILE Lucien, Louis, and Jerome remained in Europe, their eldest brother had shown more enterprise, and had made a new start in life among surroundings that presented the strongest contrast to the scenes of his past greatness. When he landed at New York in 1815, Joseph had assumed the title of Comte de Survilliers, taking the name from a little place on the Mortefontaine property. He had sold Prangins and arranged for the proceeds and other considerable sums to be remitted to him in addition to what he had brought with him. He was made heartily welcome at New York. There were sufficient reasons for this. He was wealthy ; he had been a king ; he was the brother of the most famous man of his time. No wonder he found plenty of people ready to be called his friends.

He lived for a few weeks at a country house on the bank of the Hudson. It then stood among woods and fields. It still exists, but the great city has long since extended beyond it, and it is now a hotel—' The Claremont '—at the river end of 123rd Street.

During this stay in the suburbs of New York he was not only making friends, but also looking out for an estate where he could set up housekeeping. He had no intention of pioneering in half-settled districts, and he selected a property of several hundred acres near Bordentown in the State of New Jersey. There was a large old-fashioned house dating from colonial days, and most of the estate was well-developed farmland.

Joseph had had a liking for country pursuits since the days when, as a youth, he managed the family property near Ajaccio. He spent large sums in improving the Bordentown estate, adding to the accommodation of the house and erecting ranges of farm buildings and stables. Julie had remained in Europe with her daughters, and pleaded ill-health as a reason for declining to make a voyage across the Atlantic. But Joseph had always guests at his Bordentown mansion, and was soon known as a hospitable, open-handed, country gentleman, with progressive ideas on scientific farming, literary tastes, and a rich store of anecdotes of the great days he had lived in Europe. It is to his credit that twice, first in 1817 and again in 1819, he wrote to Napoleon offering to leave his pleasant life at Bordentown and share his captivity at St. Helena. Lucien made similar offers from Rome. Correspondence with St. Helena was not easy, but at last replies came from Napoleon refusing to accept his brothers' self-sacrificing offers.

Joseph purchased another property in Jefferson County, in the State of New York. It was a huge tract of wild country, a hunting-ground where he went from time to time on shooting expeditions, sometimes taking a party of friends with him. He called it his ' wilderness.' Before long he had a visitor from Europe in the person of his nephew, Prince Lucien Murat, a son of his sister Caroline and her husband, the famous cavalry leader who had succeeded Joseph as King of Naples, and had been summarily executed by sentence of a court-martial when he raided his old kingdom in October 1815. Young Murat was at first very welcome at Bordentown, but he was soon a source of endless trouble to his uncle. He was a wild, reckless youth, who spent his days riding and hunting, and many of his nights drinking and card-playing. When he had lost the little he had brought with him, he asked Joseph for help, and was given money and good advice. He neglected the good advice and squandered or lost the money, and then appealed to Joseph again. Thanks to his uncle's easy-going good-nature he was able to repeat this proceeding many times, till at last there was an open breach between the ex-King and the young Prince. It was not the result of Murat's extravagance, but of his eloping with Miss Caroline Georgiana

Fraser, the daughter of a Southern planter who was one of Joseph's guests. Murat married her in defiance of her father. She had a small fortune in her own right, and Murat soon squandered it. He was living in a little house in Bordentown, and there his wife set up a school to support herself and her spendthrift husband. Joseph occasionally helped her when times were hard, but refused any further supplies to his nephew. The Bordentown school went on till an unexpected turn in the fortunes of the Bonapartes recalled Prince Lucien Murat to Europe, and the Bordentown schoolmistress appeared as a Princess at the Tuileries. Her daughter Anne, born at Bordentown, became Duchess de Mouchy.

Lucien Murat's elder brother, Achille, also crossed the Atlantic. But he was a man of a different stamp. After a short visit to Joseph at Bordentown he went south, and purchased a plantation in Florida. There he married Catherine Willis, a grand-niece of Washington. His venture prospered and he became a wealthy planter, but he did not survive to see the renewed greatness of the Bonapartes.

Julie Bonaparte had remained in Europe and was living in Italy. Joseph had been separated from her for many years, except during the few months he spent in France after Vittoria and during the Hundred Days of 1815. In Naples he had put an Italian duchess in her place. In Spain he had been the lover of the Marquesa de Monte Hermoso, who had followed him to France. During these years in America he formed another irregular connection.

In 1822 he built a villa among the woods on his ' wilderness ' estate in Jefferson County, New York. Till he left America in 1832, he divided his time between Bordentown and his house in the ' wilderness,' and he installed as mistress of the villa in the woods Annette Savage, the daughter of a Quaker family of Philadelphia. When he returned to Europe he left Annette in America, after making a provision for her and the daughter she had borne to him. More than thirty years after Joseph's daughter and her husband, a Mr. Benton, came to Europe, and visited the Paris of the Second Empire. Napoleon III. received them at the Tuileries, and granted a pension to Mrs. Benton. She returned to America, but after Sedan the pension ceased, and her husband was dead, so for twenty years she supported herself by teaching music at Utica and Watertown. She died in humble lodgings at Richfield Springs in New York State in 1891.

At Bordentown Joseph received more than one visit from another woman who had been deeply wronged by a Bonaparte. This was Jerome's American wife Elisabeth, the daughter of William Patterson of Baltimore. Joseph had taken her side in the first years after Jerome's marriage, and tried to make peace with the Emperor in her interest. When he first saw her in America it was after her return from the visit she paid to Europe in the year of Waterloo. He welcomed her, and promised her a friendly reception from the Bonaparte family in case she again crossed the Atlantic.

In 1819 Elisabeth, thus encouraged, reappeared in Europe with her son, who was now fourteen years old. She intended that he should complete his education in a French-speaking school, and she hoped to come to some arrangement with the Bonapartes that would secure him an income and a future position. In July she landed at Amsterdam, and applied for passports for France, which the French Government refused. She then travelled by way of Germany to Geneva, where she lived for two years, her son Jerome continuing his studies at a local college. The boy was a thorough American, and disliked Europe and European ways. From his school at Geneva he wrote to his grandfather Patterson : ' I have never had any idea of passing my life on the Continent. On the contrary, as soon as I have finished my education I shall go back to America, which I have always regretted since I came here.' From Geneva Elisabeth made more than one excursion into Italy, and met with a most friendly welcome on the part of Madame Mère, Lucien, and Louis.

Jerome and his German wife were still living at Trieste. In 1821 Elisabeth wrote of him to her father : ' He is entirely ruined, his fortune, capital, income, entirely spent, and his debts so large that his family can do nothing for him if they were inclined, which they are not.' Her report as to Jerome's financial position was quite accurate. With his income (chiefly his wife's allowances from Russia and Würtemberg), which amounted to about £3000 a year, he might have lived very comfortably at Trieste, kept up some of the state which he considered befitted an ex-king, and still paid his way. But it seemed to be part of his nature to squander money uselessly, and he was soon in debt. He appealed to his mother for help. At first she gave him some assistance, but she found that the money was quickly spent and then more was asked for. She sent him some good advice. ' Imitate me,' she wrote, ' cut down your expenses. I am sorry I cannot impart some of my own character to you. It would be more honourable to struggle against and conquer adversity, and I am sure that Catherine is strong-minded enough to economise as closely as possible.' Catherine was ready enough to do this, but Jerome, Count of Montfort, could not forget that he had been Jerome, Prince of the Empire and King of Westphalia, and insisted on keeping up a numerous and expensive household.

Catherine's second child, Mathilde, afterwards the Princess Demidoff, was born in 1820, and a few months later Jerome's sister Elisa died. News of Napoleon's illness had come from St. Helena, and Catherine had generously written to the English Government, begging for permission to go to the island in order to take care of him. ' I should consider myself most happy,' she said, ' if I could by my care help to alleviate the rigour of his captivity.' The reply was a cold official refusal.

On May 5, 1821, Napoleon died at St. Helena. It was more than two months before the news reached Europe. It was a blow to the Bonapartes, but at the same time it indirectly improved their position. The general opinion among the statesmen of Europe was that with the death of the great Emperor Bonapartism had ceased to exist as a factor in politics, and there was therefore no longer any reason for keeping the members of his family under strict surveillance. While he was at St. Helena, carefully as he was guarded, and remote and difficult of access as his island prison was, there had been a haunting fear that he would achieve the apparently impossible, and regain his liberty. There had been, indeed, more than one plot in America for carrying him off, and Joseph had been consulted on the subject by more than one daring

adventurer.[1] But now that the Emperor was dead, the Bonapartes were supposed not to be any longer dangerous. His
heir was a weakly youth, who was being educated at Vienna
by his grandfather, and had been given in 1818 the title of the
Duke of Reichstadt. If he lived he would be an Austrian
general. Louis, who stood next in succession, was a broken
invalid, happy enough in being allowed to live quietly in
Italy, and devoid of any ambition.

The first result of this relaxation of the strict watch that
had so far been kept on the Emperor's relations was that
Jerome and Catherine were informed that they were no longer
bound by the restriction of having to live in Austrian territory.
They took advantage of this to go across to central Italy,
and visit the other members of the family at Rome and
Florence. Jerome's wife Elisabeth was also in Italy. When
she heard of the Emperor's death, she had left Geneva in order
to visit Madame Mère and her sons Lucien and Louis, to offer
them her condolence, and at the same time to suggest that,
now that the Emperor's inheritance was to be divided among
the family, some provision should be made for her son. She
brought the boy with her, and every one was pleased with him.
Madame Mère took a special interest in her American grandson, and became a keen advocate of a project for providing
for him by arranging a marriage, a few years hence, between
him and Joseph's daughter Zenaïde.

For a while the matter was looked upon as almost a settled
thing. Elisabeth wrote to her father at Baltimore :—
' Madame, knowing the state of Jerome's finances, and the
impossibility of his ever doing anything for any one, wishes
Joseph to provide for this child by marriage. I have given
my consent.' The Emperor's sister, Pauline, Princess
Borghese, promised to give Zenaïde and Elisabeth's son a
present of 300,000 francs on the day of their marriage.
Joseph, however, did not agree to the proposal, and in 1822
Zenaïde was married to her cousin Charles Lucien, the eldest
son of Lucien, and the heir to the principality of Canino. He
went with Zenaïde to America and visited Joseph at his Borden-

---

[1] In one of these wild projects a submarine of the type invented by Fulton was to
have played a part. It was to have been used to convey the Emperor secretly past
the guardships to an American vessel lying well out at sea.

town estate.   He was nearly six years in the United States,
devoting himself to serious studies, and in 1825 he published
the great work on American Ornithology which won him a
high reputation as a scientific naturalist.[1]

Jerome Patterson Bonaparte also returned to America to
follow a three years' course of study at Harvard University.
His mother remained for a while in Europe, living sometimes
in Switzerland, sometimes in Italy.   Once only she saw her
husband.   She was one day looking at the pictures in the
Pitti Palace at Florence, when Jerome and Catherine, who
were also visiting the city, came into the gallery.   For a
moment Jerome and the woman he had deserted were face to
face.   They said nothing, Jerome whispered an explanation
to Catherine, and hurried away with her.

But in 1826, when the American Jerome returned to Europe
after his course at Harvard, he met his father and Catherine.
After the birth of their second son, Napoleon Joseph Charles
Paul—the ' Prince Napoleon ' of the Second Empire—who
was born at Trieste in 1822, Jerome and Catherine had left
the Austrian city and settled down in Rome.   Elisabeth was
living at Florence when her son returned from America, and
it was arranged that he should pay a visit to his father at Rome.
Jerome, and even Catherine, gave him a welcome, and his
grandmother and the other Bonapartes were as friendly as
they had been on the occasion of his first visit.   So staying
now with one now another member of the family, he spent
three months in or near Rome.   To his grandfather, Mr.
Patterson of Baltimore, he wrote : ' From my father I have
received the most cordial reception, and am treated with all
possible kindness and affection. I have not seen mamma
for two months.   She is still at Florence.'   As to any material
result from his visit he was not sanguine.   He wrote that all
his Bonaparte relations, except thrifty Madame Mère, appeared
to him to be living beyond their means, and it was most unlikely
that any of them would be able or willing to do anything to
provide for his future.   But he was not disappointed.   He

---

[1] The *American Ornithology* appeared in three volumes in 1825.   After his return
to Europe in 1828 Charles Lucien Bonaparte published other important zoological
works, among them *Iconografia della Fauna Italiana* (1833-1841), *Mammifères
Européens* (1845).

liked Europe no more than he had done on his first visit, and he meant to live as an American citizen in the United States. Next year he returned to Baltimore, and in 1829 he married Susan May Williams, the daughter of a family that had long been on terms of close friendship with the Patterson household. He became a lawyer, had a prosperous career, and founded a family whose present representative was for some years a member of Mr. Roosevelt's administration.

When the young American Bonaparte remarked that his European relations were living beyond their means, he was probably impressed by a way of life that had made more show of wealth than he had ever seen in quiet Baltimore. Jerome was extravagant enough. Lucien and Louis were living up to their income, but not exceeding it. Louis, as an invalid, had little temptation to squander money. In 1826 he left Rome for Florence, where he passed the rest of his life. Lucien was the wealthiest of the family. In his Roman palace, his villa at Tivoli and his *castello* at Canino he kept up something of his former state, and delighted in posing as a patron of art and literature.

In 1819 he had published his second epic, the *Cyrneïde*, the story of the deliverance of Corsica from its Moorish oppressors, with the help of the fleet of Pisa, in the eleventh century. It was the sequel to his *Charlemagne*, ' the *Odyssey* of his *Iliad*,' as he somewhat presumptuously described it. He found a constant pleasure in his excavations at Canino. The place must have been the site of an old Etruscan settlement, and every year added something to his valuable collection of the remains of this early race. Then he had the pleasure of witnessing the success of his eldest son as a scientific writer, and directing the studies of his third son, Louis Lucien, who was making a speciality of languages and philology, a science of which he proved later to be a master. There were two younger sons, Pierre and Antoine, born in 1815 and 1816. Pierre was wild and intractable. His was to be a stormy life.

The career of the second son Paul came to an untimely end. The young man had gone to fight for the cause of Greek independence, and lost his life by an unfortunate accident. One day in 1827 he was on board of Cochrane's flagship in the Gulf of Corinth. Some Turkish warships hove in sight, and the flotilla got under way to attack them. Paul Bonaparte went to his cabin to prepare for action. He had belted on his sword, and was taking up his pistols, already loaded, when one of them went off and mortally wounded him.

This unlucky adventure of Paul's was the only excursion of the Bonapartes into the region of active politics for some time to come. The brothers of Napoleon seemed to have resigned all idea of the family ever again claiming its old place among the sovereigns of Europe. They had some Platonic relations with the Italian Liberals, but they lived mostly in their past so far as politics were concerned, Louis, Lucien, and Joseph giving some time to the composition of their memoirs. As for the present and the future, they seemed to be content with the easy life and the acknowledged princely rank which the active years of their earlier lives had secured for them.

Nor did their ambitions for their children turn their thoughts in the direction of political agitation. The most they hoped for was to arrange advantageous marriages for them. Lucien's dream of the future for his family was that it would have a permanent position among the princely houses of Rome, perhaps some day there would be a Cardinal Bonaparte, who might be Pope. Joseph was content to marry his two daughters to cousins bearing the name of Bonaparte. Jerome hoped his sons would have a career in Germany, as princes connected with the royal house of Würtemberg. The sorrow of Louis's life was that he was separated from his two surviving sons. The elder had been with him for only a few years. They were growing up at Arenenberg on Lake Constance under the care of their mother Hortense, and all he could do was to correspond with them.

But it was on one of these youths that the future of the Bonapartes depended, and Hortense was the only one of the family who had high ambitions, with which she inspired her sons. The younger of them, Charles Louis Napoleon, was, except the Duke of Reichstadt, the only Prince of the Imperial family who had been born in Paris amid the splendours of the Empire. When Napoleon died he was a boy of thirteen living at Arenenberg with his mother and his tutors. He had vague childish recollections of the great Emperor, but had begun to know something more of him through his mother's frequent talks about Napoleon and his wonderful exploits. Hortense was an enthusiast for his memory, and sought to inspire her son with her own ideas. For her he was an attentive pupil, though with his ordinary studies he gave his tutors trouble. They thought he lacked, not intelligence, but application; that he was too much of a dreamer. And Hortense suggested dreams of future greatness. ' With the name you bear,' she said, ' you will always be something, either in old Europe or in the New World.'

He received a good education. Like so many of the Bonapartes, he early showed strong leanings to literature. But his teachers did not keep him busy only with books. He was taught to ride and fence ; he was a bold swimmer ; and when a mere boy he won prizes for shooting at the local rifle meetings of the canton of Thurgau. He could use his pencil too, and without being an artist could sketch cleverly. He filled whole sketch-books with artistic impressions of the places he visited when, in the autumn of 1823, he made a tour in Italy with his mother.

By that time he had a military tutor, Colonel Arimàndi, with whom he visited some of the famous battlefields where his uncle had won the victories of 1796. At Rome he saw his grandmother Letizia, his uncle Lucien, and his father and his elder brother, and it was agreed that the two boys should go back together to Arenenberg, to complete their education there.

Hortense and her sons paid another visit to their relations in Rome in 1824. During the following years Louis Napoleon was completing his military education by drilling with a Baden regiment in garrison at Constance, and paying prolonged visits to Thun to follow the artillery course of instruction given to officers of the Swiss army. His uncle had begun his career as an artillery officer, and with a view to the future he was devoting special attention to qualifying himself in the same branch of military science. English dislike to his policy in later years has led to an unjust depreciation of his whole career, with the result that few people realise that he was an expert in artillery questions, and that to his initiative in the days when he was in power was due the appearance of ironclad warships on the sea and rifled cannon on the battlefield.

Still looking to the future, he was eager, as he arrived at
manhood, to win a reputation as a soldier. He thought first
of the near East. Byron had made the cause of Greece popular
with all the young men of Europe. When Russia was about
to intervene in 1829, Louis Napoleon wrote to some of his
friends who had influence at St. Petersburg, to obtain an
appointment as a staff officer under General Diebitch. But
his father vetoed the proposal, to which Hortense was also
opposed. But next year the future Emperor had his first
warlike adventures, not with a regular army, but in the ranks
of an insurrectionary band.

The revolution of February 1830 in Paris, which drove
out the Bourbons of the elder branch, called the house of
Orleans to reign in the person of Louis Philippe, and restored
the tricolour as the national flag of France, had its echo in
revolutionary movements in other countries. It changed
the course of events in the Spanish peninsula and in the
Netherlands, and led to a series of Nationalist risings in Italy.

Louis Napoleon and his elder brother were already in
relations with the revolutionary party in the Papal States.
During a visit to Rome they had been initiated into a masonic
lodge, and masonry in Italy was identified with the advanced
Liberal movement. It has been asserted that they were
also members of a Carbonarist *venta*. This is possible, and
even likely, but even if they were not actually enrolled among
the Carbonari, they were certainly in touch with men who
belonged to that society. Arimandi, their military tutor, was
in touch with the organisation, and men who were leaders in
the movement paid flying visits to Constance and Arenenberg.
The name of the great Napoleon had become so associated
with the hopes of the Liberals of Italy, that it was considered
a gain to win the sons of King Louis as recruits to the cause.
Menotti himself invited them to take the field when next a
rising was attempted.

Hortense and her sons were in Rome when the news of the
February revolution arrived from Paris. It precipitated a
movement in Italy. The conspirators had intended to attempt
a rising in Rome itself, but the Government was informed
in time, and anticipated the plans of the revolutionists by a
series of arrests that paralysed the organisation. Louis

Napoleon was warned one morning by a Carbonarist friend that he had better conceal himself if he wished to escape arrest. He disregarded this friendly advice. In the afternoon the Roman police surrounded the palazzo, and an officer informed Hortense and her sons that they were expelled from the Papal territory. He had orders to conduct them to the frontier. They went to Florence, where the ex-King of Holland had been residing since 1826.

They had hardly arrived there when news came that a rising had begun in the Romagna. A message from Menotti reminded the Princes that he counted on their help, and leaving their mother in Florence they hurried to the scene of the insurrection.

They reached Bologna just as the provisional government was being formed. It was short-lived, for the rising was a half-hearted, ill-organised business, the general movement in Italy had been damped down by the vigilance of the authorities, and the Austrian armies were on the move. The two Bonapartes went into central Italy with a band of insurgents, who possessed as their artillery a light field-piece, which was entrusted to Louis Napoleon, thanks to his studies at Thun. They occupied Città Castellana after a skirmish, but had to abandon it on the approach of a flying column of Austrians. They fell back by Forli towards Ancona, and there were some small engagements on the way. Arimandi was with them, and probably acted as the real commander, while giving his pupils what credit there was in the guerilla campaign. To Hortense he wrote afterwards that she had a right to be proud of the soldierly qualities of her sons.

But the affair ended soon in disaster. In a bivouac near Forli, Napoleon Louis, the elder of the princes, was seized with a fever. At first it was supposed to be only a passing attack of malaria, but it proved to be smallpox, and ended in his death. His brother Louis Napoleon caught the infection, though the attack was not so serious. The band dispersed, and Arimandi conveyed the sick man to Spoleto, where he was protected from arrest and cared for in the palace of the Bishop, Monsignor Mastai-Feretti, the future Pius IX., and furnished with guides as soon as he could move. In after years Louis Napoleon showed scant gratitude to the prelate

2 H

to whose generous hospitality he owed freedom and life in this first adventure of his career.

Hortense had hurried from Florence on hearing of the failure of the movement and the illness of her sons. At Forli she heard of the death of Napoleon Louis. At Pesaro she joined Louis Napoleon, who was endeavouring to reach Ancona, where he hoped to embark for a place of safety. The Austrians were approaching. Hortense had provided herself with a passport, in which she was described as an English lady travelling with her two sons. When she left Pesaro for Ancona, in order to avoid explanations as to this passport, she took with her, as well as her surviving son, one of his comrades, the young Marchese Zappi.

At Ancona she provided part of the expense of sending off to Corfu two coasting craft, in which a number of the insurgents made their escape before the entry of the Austrians into the city. It was intended that Louis Napoleon should go with one of these parties, but his illness had increased, so that it was impossible for him to embark. Hortense concealed him in one of the rooms of the house she had taken, and arranged that one of her servants should be carried on board the ship with the refugees, and that the report should be spread that this was her son.

When the Austrians arrived General Geppert, their commander, took up his quarters in the same building. Hortense flattered herself that the presence of the invalid was unknown, and told the General that she would like soon to leave Ancona for Leghorn, where she intended to embark for Malta in order to rejoin her son there. He had sailed for Malta, she said, by way of Corfu. Geppert was very polite, asked no questions, took or seemed to take Hortense's elaborate fiction for fact, and told her he would give her a passport with the names in blank whenever she asked for it. She could fill it in as she liked. In a week Louis Napoleon was better, and Hortense, having obtained the passport, left Ancona for Tuscany, with her son Louis disguised as a servant in livery until the frontier was passed.

Travelling by Modena, Pisa and Genoa, the Prince and his mother entered France by way of the Riviera, and went on to Paris under assumed names. In official France it was generally believed that the fugitives were at Corfu. Arrived in Paris, they took lodgings in the Rue de la Paix. Hortense, as Duchess of St. Leu, asked to be received at court. Louis Philippe wrote to her in reply that it was impossible, and added that it was very imprudent for her and her son to come to a country from which they were banished by law. Next day Casimir Perier, who was then President of the Council, came to see her, and on the understanding that she and her son were taking no part in French politics, it was arranged that the King would give her a private audience.

She was received at the Tuileries by the King and Queen Amélie. Louis Philippe spoke in a very friendly way of the Bonapartes, but expressed the hope that the presence of Louis Napoleon in Paris would not become generally known. It would be embarrassing for both the King and the Ministry. Hortense told him that he need not be anxious on this point, for her son was still suffering from recurring attacks of fever, and stayed in his lodgings and saw no one. Next day Casimir Perier startled the King by telling him that he had police reports to the effect that, at the very time Hortense was talking about her son's illness, Louis Napoleon was attending a secret conference of some of the leading members of the Republican party. The report was probably untrue, for the Prince was really ill. But rumours of the wildest kind were in circulation, talk of a Bonapartist plot, of a popular demonstration at the Vendôme column on the anniversary of Napoleon's death, a demonstration in which Louis Napoleon would take part. The Government sent to Hortense and her son a 'request' that they would leave France at the earliest possible moment. They started from Paris on May 6th, and after a trying journey and a rough passage across the Channel reached London.

They made only a short stay in England, but during this time Louis Napoleon was introduced to many leading men in English society who were his friends during his later residence in London. Hortense was anxious to return to Arenenberg. Talleyrand, who was then the French ambassador in London, made the journey easier by providing passports, which enabled the exiles to take the shorter route through France, instead of travelling through Belgium and Germany.

They were back at Arenenberg in August. The Prince

rapidly regained his health amid the country life of his Swiss home, and resumed his studies. There were many visitors coming and going at the villa, tourists, French men of letters, and old friends and allies of the Bonapartes. Thus the foundation was laid for a wide correspondence with France. It was well known that the Duke of Reichstadt, the son of the great Emperor, was a hopeless invalid slowly dying of consumption. Louis Napoleon already regarded himself as the heir of the great Emperor. On July 22, 1832, the son of Napoleon and Maria Louisa died at Schönbrunn, aged just twenty-one years. For a few days in 1815, in virtue of the vote of the Chambers and his father's abdication, he had been Napoleon II. As the direct line of the Bonapartes died with him, and Joseph had no sons, Louis the ex-King of Holland, now an invalid busy with books and poems in his palazzo at Florence, stood next in succession. But he had already renounced his claim in favour of his sons, of whom Louis Napoleon was the only survivor. Thus the young Prince at Arenenberg became the heir of the vanished Empire, Napoleon III. *de jure*, so far as any legal rights could be claimed for a Bonaparte.

CHAPTER XXX

DEATH OF 'NAPOLEON II.'—STRASBURG-
DEATH OF HORTENSE

(1830-1837)

THE Duke of Reichstadt, the 'Napoleon II.' of 1815, died of consumption at Schönbrunn on July 22, 1832. His mother, the ex-Empress Maria Louisa, Duchess of Parma, had been with him for the last few days of his life, but during the long years from 1815 to 1832 she had seen little of him, and seemed almost to have forgotten him. She was a thoroughly selfish woman. During Napoleon's captivity at St. Helena she had not even written to him. No sooner did she hear of her husband's death than she married her lover, Count Neipperg. When he died she found another consort in Rombelles, the chief of her household at Parma. She thought more of the children of Neipperg than of the son of the Emperor.

The short life of the second Napoleon had been a lonely one. He was purposely cut off from all intercourse with the Bonapartes. His grandfather, the Austrian Emperor, who was very fond of him, took care that he had a good military education, and before he was of age he was colonel of a Hungarian cavalry regiment. The young man was devoted to his father's memory, a keen student of his campaigns, and ambitious of military distinction. Despite his weak health, he spared no effort to qualify himself for future command. Often he would talk to his few friends of his hopes that, if he was not recalled to France, he would, like Prince Eugène of Savoy, be a successful French general in the Austrian service and do deeds worthy of his name. There were vague proposals to find a throne for him elsewhere than in France. As Greece, Poland, Belgium became the centre of revolution, it was suggested that the young Napoleon might be called to found a new dynasty in one or other of these countries. But these suggestions never assumed a practical form.

Even before 1830 there had been more than one abortive conspiracy in France for his restoration. Joseph regarded this as the one hope of the family, and when it became clear that the throne of Charles x. was in danger, he exerted himself in his nephew's interests. He sent agents to Vienna to propose a restoration of the Empire to Metternich. France, he urged, would be a firm ally of Austria under a sovereign who was the grandson of the Emperor Francis. To the Emperor himself he wrote, during the crisis of 1830, that if he would entrust young Napoleon to him, he would return from America and take him to France, where he would be received with enthusiasm. He urged the Bonapartists in France to action. After Louis Philippe had been proclaimed, Joseph in September 1830 addressed a protest to the Chamber of Deputies. They had made a mistake, he argued, in neglecting the claim of Napoleon II. ' I have the best reason to know,' he said, ' that Napoleon II. would be worthy of France. The son of the great Napoleon, the man of the nation, could unite all parties under a really Liberal Constitution, and so secure the peace of Europe.' For a moment during the crisis of 1830 there was a chance of a military pronunciamento for Napoleon II. A number of generals, including the commandant of Strasburg, had given their adhesion to a plot for proclaiming him. But they had laid down as the first condition for action that the young man should be brought from Schönbrunn to Strasburg, whence they would escort him in triumph to Paris, and he was far too carefully guarded at Vienna for the attempt to be made.

Of all these efforts in his favour the young man knew nothing. In the days when his health was thoroughly broken and the end was approaching, he was allowed to see a letter from his cousin Louis Napoleon, in which he expressed the wish to come to Vienna to be his companion. But he was informed that this could not be permitted. He died at Schönbrunn in the same room that his father had occupied during the campaign of Wagram, the room in which he had first discussed with his intimate councillors the divorce of Josephine and the marriage with an Austrian archduchess. There was a Nemesis hanging over the son of this union, to which he sacrificed poor Josephine. The fate he had dreaded for the King of Rome had fallen upon him. He had been educated as an Austrian prince. He was buried in the white uniform of his Austrian regiment. And it was a grandson of Josephine, the son of Louis Bonaparte and her daughter Hortense, who became the heir of the Empire.

Except this young man, the dreamy Swiss artillery officer at Arenenberg, none of the Bonapartes had now any hope for the political future of the family. The untimely death of the great Emperor's son seemed to have set the seal on the extinction of his dynasty. But Louis Napoleon still looked forward to power in the future, and now that he was the heir of French Imperialism, he determined to strive to the utmost to make his hopes into realities.

There were already signs that Bonapartism might again become a power in French politics. The story of the splendours of France under Napoleon was becoming a legend. A generation was growing up that had known nothing of the oppression and the miseries of the Empire, and remembered only that it had made France the mistress of Europe. There was a literary and artistic cultus of Napoleon. The great days of the Empire were made the subject of popular dramas. There was hardly a house in France that had not now the Emperor's bust or his picture. The Government of Louis Philippe, following the trend of popular opinion, was replacing on the Vendôme column the statue of the Emperor which had been removed at the Restoration, and was completing the Arc de Triomphe.[1] There were already proposals that the remains of Napoleon should be brought back from St. Helena and laid to rest in a worthy sepulchre ' on the banks of the Seine,' where in his last will he had asked that he should be buried.

Louis Napoleon showed a ripe political judgment in at first abstaining from posing as a pretender. Instead of talking of the restoration of the Empire, he tried to establish friendly relations with the Republican party in France. It was through the Republic his uncle had risen to power, and in the first years of the Empire certain Republican forms were retained,

---

[1] It was finished in 1836, the year of Louis Napoleon's attempt at Strasburg.

as had been done by the Roman Cæsars, who were Consuls as well as Imperatores. On the earlier Imperial coins of Napoleon one reads on the obverse *Napoléon Empereur* and on the reverse *République Française*. The nephew of Napoleon saw in a Republic the means of securing a leading place in French political life, a stepping-stone to Empire. But he was haunted, too, by dreams of repeating the return from Elba, of presenting himself to a French regiment, calling upon them to add the victorious eagle to the tricolour, and provoking a military pronunciamento in favour of the representative of the name which the army still associated with years of glory, that some of the older officers and sergeants had shared.

Meanwhile, whether he meant to rise to power through a Republican movement or through a sudden appeal to the army as the heir of its greatest and most beloved chief, it was necessary for him to keep his name before the public mind in France. His pen supplied the means of doing this. He inherited literary tastes from his father. Most of the Bonapartes had this tendency to authorship. Napoleon had been a pamphleteer in the days when he was an unknown officer of artillery in the Revolutionary army. His brothers, Joseph, Lucien, Louis, had sought literary distinction. In these years at Arenenberg, after his adventures in the Italian insurrection, Louis Napoleon produced a whole series of little books and one important scientific treatise. First came a volume of *Rêveries Politiques*, a bid for the support of the Republican party, with incidentally an attempt to show that in France Bonapartism and Democracy were much the same thing. Then there was a controversial pamphlet addressed to Châteaubriand, who had been a visitor at Arenenberg; a little later an essay on the civil and military institutions of Switzerland; and finally a book that was intended to make for its author friends in the French army—the *Manuel d'Artillerie*. It was the result of his studies at Thun, and though ostensibly a purely technical work, it was as much an instrument of propaganda as if it had been a political pamphlet. Napoleon had served at first in the French artillery, and his handling of great masses of guns had been a feature of his battles. Louis Napoleon wished to show that he had a real knowledge of the branch of military science of which his uncle had been such a master. He sent scores of copies of the book to officers of rank in the French army, each accompanied by a gracefully phrased letter, that in many cases laid the foundation of a friendly correspondence.

Since the rising of the Romagna Italy was forbidden ground for Louis Napoleon. For some years his communications with his father were only by letter. He told him very little of his hopes and projects, and the ex-King of Holland always felt a mistrust of him as the pupil of Hortense, and was continually warning him against the friends he had chosen for himself. He regarded his son as a light-headed young man, who was only too likely to be led into further revolutionary escapades. His uncle Joseph was a more sympathetic correspondent. He had left America in 1832, hoping that the Liberal Government of Louis Philippe would revoke the decree of exile, and allow him to re-establish himself in France. He had come to London, whence he addressed a long correspondence to the French Government without obtaining any result. In the summer of 1835 he wrote to his nephew Louis Napoleon asking him to come and see him in London. He would go to Arenenberg, he said, but his years and failing health made him dread the long journey.

Louis Napoleon went to London by way of the Rhine and Belgium, stopping in Brussels to visit the field of Waterloo. He had with him as his travelling companion the young Milanese Count Arese. King Louis wrote to him that he was ill-advised in choosing for his companion a noted adherent of the Italian revolutionary party, and expressed a fear that the journey to London was connected with some dangerous project. The Prince replied that it was painful to him to be always blamed by his father, whatever he might do. As for Arese, he had mentioned in letters written six months before that he was at Arenenberg, and the ex-King had made no remark. He had taken him on the journey because there was no one else who was ready to go with him. The visit to London, he said, had no political significance. He had come only to give his uncle Joseph the pleasure of seeing him again after so many years. Finally, he reminded his father that he was no longer a child. He was twenty-five years of age, old enough to choose his friends.

Of what passed between Joseph and his nephew we have no reliable record. The young man received many invitations, and mingled freely in London society, which was then more exclusive than it is at present. At one evening party he met Talleyrand, who was still ambassador to England. In a letter to Arenenberg Louis Napoleon tells how Talleyrand tried to snub him, by pretending not to recognise him. The ambassador was talking to Lady Tankerville. In order to show he was not embarrassed by his action, the Prince went up to them and spoke to the lady without taking any notice of the ambassador. He made other friends who were not in society, useful adherents among the refugees of Soho. The most important was Fialin, better known by his later name of the Count de Persigny. Persigny was a journalist and an adventurer. He was a born conspirator. He told Louis Napoleon that he had a thorough faith in his future, and from the day they met he worked to realise the resurrection of the Empire, which was to make his own fortune as well as that of the heir of the Bonapartes.

After a brief stay in London Louis Napoleon and Arese returned to Switzerland. Persigny, the new recruit, was with them. His was most likely the mind that thought out the plans on which the Prince ventured in the coming year. There had been abortive Bonapartist *émeutes* in various garrisons under the Restoration: at Grenoble in 1816, at Vincennes in 1820, at Belfort and Saumur in 1823. In more recent years there had been military pronunciamentos that had changed the course of events in Spain and Portugal. The plot of Fieschi in Paris in 1834 had shown that the Government of Louis Philippe had active enemies. There was the growing popularity of Bonapartism to suggest that possibly, if one garrison declared for the Emperor's nephew, he might repeat the exploit of the return from Elba, and the unopposed march from Cannes and Grenoble to Paris.

For the conspirators of Arenenberg the nearest important French garrison was Strasburg. Between Arenenberg and Strasburg was Baden, then the Monte Carlo of Europe, a city of pleasure, where the mineral springs were a much less attraction than the *Rouge-et-Noir* tables. In the twelve months between the autumn of 1835 and October 1836 Louis Napoleon paid frequent visits to Baden, and during these visits he made many excursions to places along the frontier, amongst others to Kehl, the German town that stands on the German bank of the Rhine opposite Strasburg, and is now included in the circle of its outlying forts. Persigny was often his travelling companion. At the tables at Baden they met French officers from Strasburg. There were other interviews during the visits to Kehl, and at quiet hotels on the Rhine. At first these were mere social conversations, but soon the Prince and his new friends began to talk politics. Some of them became his correspondents when he sent them his handbook of artillery. The 4th Artillery, in which the great Napoleon had served as a regimental officer, was in garrison at Strasburg.

Early in 1836 Louis Napoleon and his ally Persigny had so far prepared the ground that they were able to talk openly to some of the officers of their project for proclaiming the Empire at Strasburg before the year was over. The first recruits won to the plot did not come from the artillery. They were officers of the 16th Infantry, Captain Raindre and Major de Franqueville. Persigny hinted to them that General Voirol, who commanded the garrison, had been sounded and would not be hostile to the movement. He might even join it. This appears to have been a piece of fiction, intended to encourage the younger men. It was considered, however, that the most important man to gain over was not Voirol, but Colonel Vaudrey of the artillery.

Vaudrey commanded at Strasburg a brigade made up of the 3rd and 4th Regiments of Artillery and a battalion of Pontonniers. He was just fifty years of age, and he was a disappointed man. He saw no prospect of promotion, and two petitions he had lately sent to the Government had been rejected—one asking for a place at a military school for his son, the other an application for an appointment as aide-de-camp to the Duke of Orleans, which would have opened the way to promotion to the rank of General. Men younger than himself and with less brilliant records of service had been promoted. He had entered the Imperial army at the age of twenty and served under King Joseph as an artillery officer in Naples and Calabria. He had bad luck in the campaign of Eckmühl, where he was wounded and taken prisoner, but he had fought so well that he was promoted as soon as he

was released.   In 1813 he had won the Cross of the Legion on
the battlefield.   At Waterloo he had commanded a group of
three batteries.   Then came the years of peace, and he was
growing old in a provincial garrison.   The reward of a successful revolt at Strasburg would be the rank of General.

There are some ugly features of these Bonapartist plots.
Louis Napoleon had few scruples as to the means to be used.
Persigny had none.   At Baden the latter was living with a
Madame Gordon, a French opera-singer who had married an
English officer, and had soon been left a widow with a moderate
fortune.   Vaudrey was a man of loose life, and Madame Gordon
was employed to entrap him.   She temporarily left Persigny
and played the lover, and Vaudrey was soon ready for anything she suggested.   He met Louis Napoleon, and was
initiated into the conspiracy.   He was soon looking forward
to being a Marshal of a restored Empire.

In August 1836 Louis Napoleon entered into correspondence
with General Voirol, and hinted at possibilities of the immediate
future in such frank terms that many suppose that by this
time Voirol was really not an entire stranger to the plot, but
was prudently waiting to see how far it would go before he
declared himself.   He had to be left out of the scheme.   The
conspirators thought they could count on the infantry, of
which many officers had been won over, and on the artillery,
thanks to Vaudrey.

The Empire was to be proclaimed at Strasburg.   An effort
was then to be made to secure the support of the garrisons
of Metz, Nancy, and the minor fortresses of Alsace-Lorraine.
The population, who had been devoted adherents of the First
Empire, were expected to acclaim the movement.   There were
no railways in eastern France, no telegraphs.   It would be
some days before the rest of the country was even aware of
the revolt.   There were 50,000 troops in the east of France.
This was the army with which the conspirators hoped to march
on Paris.   The plot failed.   Kinglake and others have poured
ridicule upon it, but success was quite possible.   It was not
by any means the mad enterprise that it appears in the light
of failure.

On October 24, 1836, in the evening, Louis Napoleon told
his mother that he was leaving Arenenberg next morning to

spend a few days in a hunting excursion in Baden. Hortense probably knew or suspected that something more important was in hand. She took from her finger a ring she had worn for years, the wedding-ring of her mother the Empress Josephine, and put it on the little finger of her son. ' If you are in any danger,' she said, ' this will be your talisman.'

Next day he was at Freiburg, where he was joined by Colonel Vaudrey on leave from Strasburg, and Persigny and Madame Gordon. On the 28th the party crossed the Rhine and went in a travelling-carriage by way of Neuf-Brisach to Colmar, where they took the road to Strasburg. Vaudrey had gone on in advance. Napoleon went to apartments at a private house in the town, which Persigny had taken under the name of Monsieur Manuel the month before. Other agents in the plot had already arrived. The final details were settled next day at an interview with Vaudrey.

This interview took place soon after nightfall in the moonlight on one of the quays by the river. The Prince returned from it, not to Persigny's lodgings, but to rooms in another house that had been taken two days before by one of the conspirators. Here, late in the evening, he held a secret meeting of some of his friends and of the officers who were in the plot. He was anxious to make it appear that the movement was not intended to be a mere military revolt, but an appeal to the democracy as well as the army. In a letter to his mother, written that same night, he called God to witness that he was not acting from mere personal ambition, but ' because he thought he had a mission to fulfil.' Perhaps he had persuaded himself that it was so. In any case, he tried to give his friends the idea that he was inspired with a patriotic ambition to give France a government that would protect both the interests of the people and the national honour more effectually than the ministers of Louis Philippe had done. He read to the assembled conspirators three rather long-winded proclamations : ' To the French people,' ' To the Army,' ' To the inhabitants of Strasburg.' To the people he proclaimed that they were betrayed. The Government of 1830 had been created without any appeal to the people through a Constituent Assembly. They were governed by the

'traitors of 1814 and 1815, the murderers of Ney, the dupes
of the Holy Alliance,' by men who shot down workmen in the
streets, and were surrounding Paris with forts, not to defend,
but to terrorise it. He appealed to them in the name of the
great man who had brought glory and prosperity to France.
He came 'with the last will of Napoleon in one hand, the
sword of Austerlitz in the other.' He called on them to rally
to the eagle, and constitute a free government under this
emblem of glory and liberty. To the army he spoke of resuming as its standard the Imperial Eagle associated with so
many triumphs. 'The lion of Waterloo still stands on our
frontiers,' he said; 'Huningen has no defences; the Cross
of the Legion is lavished on intriguers and refused to the
brave.' Let them rise against traitors and oppressors. Let
the soldiers of the Empire and the Republic rally round him,
and with them the younger men who, like himself, were born
to the sound of the cannon of Wagram. From heaven the
shade of Napoleon would look down upon them and guide
them. The people of Strasburg were reminded how their
trade had suffered by the treaties of 1815, and called upon
to inaugurate the new revolution. All three documents were
very theatrical compositions, not like the trumpet notes of
the great Emperor's calls to arms.

The meeting showed no inclination to revise them. A few
of those present remained with the Prince, the rest went
back to spend an anxious night in their quarters. The
attempt was to be made at six A.M. on Sunday the 30th, an
hour after réveillé at the barracks. The weather had changed
during the night. At six it was wretchedly cold. A cloudy
sky made the darkness deeper, and snow was falling.

Colonel Vaudrey had gone at five A.M. to the Austerlitz
barracks, where the artillery were stationed. He paraded
the regiment, distributed cartridges, sent a party to bring
the horses for his guns from the stables. The officers who
were in the plot passed along the lines and prepared their
men for what was coming. They were apparently led to
believe that a revolution was in progress throughout France,
and that they would not be isolated. Six o'clock had not yet
struck when a party of men with a standard rolled round its
staff appeared at the barrack gate, and were admitted to the

parade-ground. Vaudrey posted himself in front of the regiment and called it to attention.

The newcomers were all dressed in various military uniforms. Some of them were officers, others, like Persigny, held only rank by appointment of their leader, Louis Napoleon. After the failure of the plot the fact that so many of the pretender's civilian allies had appeared as officers in uniform was made a subject of cheap wit. But in most insurrections the leader gives irregular commissions ; those who accept them do not take the field in frock-coats and top-hats ; and if success comes, their grades are confirmed. It was said that Louis Napoleon was dressed up to represent the great Emperor as he appeared in the popular portraits of the ' little corporal.' But Napoleon's campaigning dress was the uniform of the Chasseurs of the Guard, and Louis Napoleon at Strasburg wore the uniform of the French artillery, with a colonel's badges of rank and the Legion of Honour. Only the cocked hat with its tricolour cockade suggested the dress associated with his famous uncle.

Vaudrey saluted the Prince, and turning to his men told them that a revolution was to begin that day. The nephew of Napoleon stood before them ; he had come to give back the eagles to the army and a free government to France. He ended by waving his sword and crying ' Vive l'Empereur ! ' The cry was taken up by the soldiers. The Prince took the tricolour with the eagle on its staff and unfurled it. Addressing the regiment he told them he counted on them. It was in the 4th Artillery that Napoleon had served for years. It was the same regiment that welcomed him at Grenoble when he returned from Elba. A great enterprise had begun that day. Theirs was the honour of being the first to salute the eagle, the standard of Austerlitz and Wagram, the emblem of glory and freedom. ' Soldiers,' he said, ' will you not rally to the standard that in fifteen glorious years was carried into every capital in Europe ? Will you not march with me against the betrayers and oppressors of our country, to the cry of ' Vive la France ! Vive la Liberté ! '

·· He handed the eagle to Colonel Vaudrey amid repeated cries of ' Vive l'Empereur ! ' It seemed that the movement was going to be a success. Parties were told off to go to a printing-office

and see the proclamations printed ; to go to the barracks
of the 3rd Artillery and the Pontonniers and secure their
adhesion ; and to arrest the prefect of the department at the
prefecture. Persigny headed this party. Louis Napoleon
himself took command of the main body. He gave the order,
' Form fours right,' and the regiment marched out into the
city, where most of the people were still asleep. Early risers
going to their work or to mass echoed the cheers of the
soldiers, and followed the column shouting ' *Vive l'Empereur !* '

' At last I have the happiness of commanding French troops,'
said Napoleon to one of his friends. So far all had gone well,
but now he made his first mistake. The column halted at
General Voirol's house.   The sentry at the door presented
arms and cried ' *Vive l'Empereur !* ' The door was opened, and
Napoleon entered with some of his officers. He felt quite
sure the General would declare for him and thus bring over the
rest of the garrison.

Voirol was in bed. He was roused by the cheers of the
soldiers and workmen in the street, sprang up and began to
dress. He was half dressed when the Prince entered his room.
' General,' he said, ' I would be sorry to raise your old flag
without having a brave soldier like you on my side. The
garrison has declared for me. Make up your mind and follow
me.' ' No, no,' replied Voirol, ' the garrison is not for you, or
if it is, it will soon recognise its mistake.' The Prince pressed
the point. ' Come, my brave general,' he said, ' recognise me
as Napoleon II.,' [1] and he held out his hand. Voirol would not
take it. Some of the artillery officers and a few of the gunners
were at the open door. Captain Parquin urged Voirol to declare for ' the Emperor.' ' Silence ! ' said Voirol. ' You have no
business here,' and he ordered the gunners to arrest the officer.
They replied with a shout of ' *Vive l'Empereur !* ' Instead of
making Voirol prisoner on the spot, the conspirators hustled
him into another room. But it had an inner door opening
on the staircase, down which he made his escape, pursued by
Parquin and others. But here the General met some officers
of his staff who were coming to his help. Surrounded by
these he made his way through the crowd at the door, and

[1] So said the witnesses at the subsequent trial. It was not till later that Louis
Napoleon realised the advantage of counting himself the Third of the Napoleons.

some of the revolted gunners, who had been told the General would join them, lost heart and went away with him.

Louis Napoleon came out and marched off towards the infantry barracks. On the way he learned that Persigny had secured the prefect in safe custody, and that the proclamations were being printed, but that the 3rd Artillery and the Pontonniers had refused to join in the revolt. Everything now depended on obtaining the support of the infantry.

The Prince and Vaudrey's gunners marched into the barrack-yard shouting ' Vive l'Empereur ! ' and officers and soldiers of the infantry crowded on to the parade-ground without falling in. Some of them refused to have anything to do with the revolt. ' You have served a long time, my fine fellow,' said Louis Napoleon to an old sergeant. ' Twenty-five years, and with honour,' was the reply. ' Well, you must join me, I am the Emperor's heir,' said the Prince. ' The son of the Emperor is dead, and I recognise only the King,' was the disappointing answer. But though some were thus openly hostile and others hesitated, the men began to fraternise with the gunners, and more and more of them cried ' Vive l'Empereur ! ' At this moment a quick-witted officer turned the tide against the pretender. ' Soldiers,' he shouted, ' you are deceived ! The man they are presenting to you as the heir of the Emperor is nothing but a dressed-up actor—he is only Colonel Vaudrey's nephew.' There was an immediate change of opinion among the infantrymen. In vain Colonel Vaudrey protested that it was a lie. In vain he shouted out, ' We proclaim the Emperor Napoleon II. Join us and cry " Vive l'Empereur ! " Colonel Taillandier, who commanded the infantry, appeared on the parade, and when he told his men to fall in, he was at once obeyed. He gave the order to arrest the Prince. Louis Napoleon set his back to the barrack wall, surrounded by a group of officers, with the artillerymen in front of them. Swords were drawn. The two regiments faced each other and bloodshed seemed imminent. An infantry captain, pressing forward followed by his company, was disarmed by the gunners, and there was some hustling, but on both sides the officers hesitated to give the order to fire.

There was another attempt made by the linesmen to force a way through the gunners, and Louis Napoleon, sword in hand, had to parry blows aimed at him. From the neighbouring rampart which overlooked the yard a crowd of workers threw stones at the linesmen. Taillandier fired a volley into them, and they dispersed, all except one man, who took cover and kept up the stone-throwing.

The volley showed that matters were becoming serious. Some of the officers told Louis Napoleon that if he gave the word, they would cut a way for him through the infantry, but to his honour he refused to risk useless bloodshed. He told them he was ready to surrender. Taillandier came forward to parley, and Vaudrey gave his gunners the order to return quietly to their quarters. Voirol had arrived with reinforcements. Louis Napoleon, Vaudrey, and the other leaders of the revolt gave up their swords and were marched off to prison under escort. Madame Gordon and other conspirators were arrested a little later. Persigny escaped to Kehl. At eight o'clock the revolt was at an end.

From his prison Louis Napoleon wrote to his mother telling her of his failure and asking her to send on the news to his father. He was glad, he said, that no French blood had been shed, and anxious only as to the fate of his companions. Under the strict letter of the law the Government might have brought the pretender to trial before the Chamber of Peers, and executed him if he was convicted. But Louis Philippe and his ministers hesitated to take this course. Several of the peers expressed their unwillingness to be the Prince's judges. It was not even certain that a conviction would be secured. In any case the trial would, it was thought, give a new impetus to the Bonapartist movement. It was at last decided merely to send the Prince into exile.

On November 9th General Voirol came to the prison and took Louis Napoleon with him in his carriage to the Prefecture. There he was handed over to the custody of two officers of gendarmes, and informed that he would be conveyed to a French port and transported to America. He wrote a farewell letter to his mother, asking her to see that funds were provided for the defence of his fellow-prisoners, and to assist the wife and sons of Colonel Vaudrey, who were at Paris. He was conveyed to L'Orient, where he arrived on November 15th, and was imprisoned in the citadel. A few days later he embarked on board of the frigate *Andromède*, bound for America, the place of exile of so many of the Bonapartes.

On January 6, 1837, seven of his accomplices were brought to trial before the Court of Assizes of Strasburg. Most of them were officers with a splendid record of service. There was Colonel Vaudrey, the soldier of Waterloo ; Parquin, who had to his credit eleven campaigns under the Empire and eleven wounds ; Laity, a young officer who had been involved in a revolt at Quimper five years before ; De Bruc, who had won the Cross of the Legion under Napoleon at Montereau ; De Gricourt, de Quérelles, and Madame Gordon. Popular feeling was strongly on their side. The trial lasted for several days. In their examination most of the accused boldly avowed that in the presence of a Bonaparte they could not act otherwise than they had done. Parquin said he felt he was still bound by the oath of fidelity he had taken years ago to the great Emperor. ' I am not like a famous diplomatist,' he added, ' who has sworn loyalty to thirteen governments,' an allusion to Talleyrand, at which the audience laughed. Their counsel fiercely attacked the Government. But the facts were clear, conviction seemed inevitable. On January 18th the jury at last withdrew to consider their verdict. As they retired the audience cried out, ' Acquit them ! acquit them ! ' After twenty-two minutes of deliberation they came back, and announced that on all counts they had found the accused not guilty.

It was a political verdict, a verdict against the evidence, but still more against the Government. The jury and the released prisoners were made the objects of a popular ovation, in which numbers of the soldiers of the garrison joined. All day the city was *en fête*. In official circles in Paris the news was received with dismay. The attempt of Strasburg had not been after all an utter failure. It showed that Bonapartism was still a force to be reckoned with.

Louis, the ex-King of Holland, took quite unnecessary trouble to explain that he had no part in his son's escapade at Strasburg. Joseph, though he had lately seen his nephew in London, had no hint of what was coming, and after the event he wrote to him strongly condemning his action. Lucien and Jerome were not in intimate correspondence with Arenenberg.

The French Government, having decided on the deportation of the Prince to America, appears to have been anxious to delay for some time before setting him at liberty in the United States.   From L'Orient the *Andromède* steered for Rio Janeiro, and lay in the harbour day after day without allowing Louis Napoleon to communicate with any one on shore.   The absence of news in France of his expected arrival in the United States, or of the movements of the frigate, led to rumours that the ship had been lost at sea.   During the voyage and at Rio the Prince was treated in the most friendly way by the captain and officers of the *Andromède*, and some of them owed promotion in the days of the Second Empire to a friendship which began at this time.   It was not until the end of the year that the *Andromède* left Rio and steered for New York, where Louis Napoleon at last landed on a bitterly cold day of January 1837.

He took up his quarters at the Old City Hotel in Broadway ˙ and soon made many friends.   His cousins Achille and Lucien Murat came to see him.   General Scott of the United States army, and Halleck the poet, were the most notable among his American acquaintances.   The French Government had exacted no pledge as to the duration of his absence in America. He intended to stay there a year, make a tour of the chief cities, and then return to Europe.   But a letter from Arenenberg, received in the early summer, led him to change his plans.   His mother was dangerously ill.   If he did not return at once he might not again see her alive.

Before leaving New York on June 6th he addressed a formal letter of farewell to the President, Van Buren.   ' I am unwilling,' he wrote, ' to leave the United States, without expressing to your Excellency my regret at having been unable to make your acquaintance in Washington.   Although taken to America by a fatality, I hoped to employ my exile profitably in studying its great men ;   I would have liked also to have studied the manners and institutions of a people who have made more conquests by commerce and industry than we in Europe have made by wars.   An imperious duty recalls me to the Old World.   My mother is dangerously ill, and no political considerations detaining me here, I am starting for England, whence I shall try to reach Switzerland.   It is with pleasure, Mr. President, that I enter into these details with you, who may have given credence to certain calumnious rumours representing me as under engagements to the French Government. Appreciating the attitude of the representatives of a free country, I should be happy to have it well known that with the name I bear it would be impossible for me to depart for a moment from the path laid down for me by my conscience, my honour, and my duty.'

On June 27th he sailed for England on board of an American passenger ship, the *George Washington*, and landed at Liverpool. In London he found Persigny, who had been busy writing pamphlets and newspaper articles in defence of the affair of Strasburg. One unpleasant result of this affair was that the Prince found it difficult to persuade any of the ambassadors of the Powers in London to give him passports for his journey to Switzerland. Every route seemed closed by their suspicions that, under the pretext of hurrying to his sick mother's side, he was planning some new adventure. He spent some time in London in fruitless negotiations. It was during this time he wrote to his father at Florence :—

' If you only knew, my dear father, how wretched I am in the midst of all this tumult of London, with relatives who avoid me, and enemies who suspect me. My mother is dying, and I am not able to go to her and console her as a son should do ; my father is ill, and I cannot hope to go to see him once more. What have I done, to be thus made the pariah of Europe and of my own family ? I have displayed the flag of Austerlitz for a moment in a French city. Blame me if you will, but do not refuse me your affection.'

At last, tired of waiting, he decided to risk arrest, and made use of a passport he had secured in America in the name of Robinson, and had it visaed by the Swiss consul. French police agents were watching him, but he threw them off the track by leaving his hotel for Richmond one Saturday evening, after saying he would spend the Sunday there. Starting from Richmond on the Sunday he drove to a point on the river, where he took a boat and boarded a ship bound for Rotterdam. Thence he went by steamer up the Rhine, left the river at Mannheim, and hired a postchaise, in which he reached Arenenberg on the evening of August 4th.

He found his mother very ill, but she lived for three months longer. She died on October 5th. Almost her last word was a request to Dr. Conneau, who had long resided at Arenenberg, to take care of her son, and never be separated from him.

Louis wrote to his son from Florence condoling with him in his loss, and assuring him of his warm affection. Louis Napoleon replied on October 31st, expressing the hope that before long he would be allowed to visit his father in Italy. 'My mother has left a will,' he said. 'The only words that refer to you are these,—" Let my husband give a thought to my memory, and let him know that my greatest regret has been that I was not able to make him happy."—This new misfortune,' he added, ' has induced my family to give me some marks of their affection. My uncles Joseph and Lucien have written to me. My uncle Jerome is the only one who has not deigned to do so.' The expressions used by the writer show how isolated he had been from his uncles, the brothers of the Emperor, who did not believe in his schemes and disapproved of his policy.

CHAPTER XXXI

FROM ARENENBERG TO THE PRISON OF HAM

(1837-1840)

AFTER his mother's death Louis Napoleon continued to reside at Arenenberg, making occasional visits to Baden, where he met many French people, who came there either for the ' cure ' or for the excitement of the gaming-tables. Other French visitors came and went at Arenenberg. Lieutenant Laity, who had joined the Strasburg plot and been acquitted by the assize court, spent some time there in the spring of 1838, and with the help of his host drew up a narrative of the Strasburg affair, which was published in France in the following June. Laity was prosecuted, and condemned to five years' imprisonment, and the French Government followed up this prosecution by demanding the expulsion of Louis Napoleon from Switzerland. The French ambassador, who presented this demand to the authorities at Berne, was no other than the Duke de Montebello, the son of Marshal Lannes, who owed his title and the position of his family to the Emperor.

To its honour the Federal Government refused to grant this demand. It based its refusal on a double ground. First on the right of hospitality, which Switzerland had long granted to refugees from other lands ; secondly, on the fact that Louis Napoleon had been adopted as a citizen by the canton of Thurgau, and could not be molested in any way as long as he obeyed the law. There was an outburst of patriotic enthusiasm in Switzerland. Other cantons voted their honorary citizenship to the Prince. The Swiss papers told of all he had done for his own canton. He had founded schools near Arenenberg. He had contributed to various public funds. He had served in the cantonal militia, and when

Thurgau raised a force of artillery, he had made the canton a present of two field-pieces fully equipped. He was the President of the cantonal rifle club. Twice he had been publicly honoured by the local authorities for saving lives on the Lake of Constance at the risk of his own.

The French Government insisted, and mobilised an army corps on the Swiss frontier. Prussia, Austria, Baden, and Würtemberg gave their diplomatic support to the demand. Switzerland prepared for war. The Government of Louis Philippe had spoken of Louis Napoleon as an insignificant adventurer. Now it was making his presence in a neighbouring country to France an international question. Louis Napoleon took a wise course. He had much to gain by his name being the centre of a serious international dispute, but having gained this, at the last moment he wrote a dignified letter to the authorities of Thurgau, thanked them for their hospitality, congratulated Switzerland on its fearless assertion of his own rights and the independence of the country, and then announced that, in order to spare the cantons the horrors of war, he was about to retire to London. There he would be near enough to France and safe from interference, for it was not likely that Paris would venture to address such a demand to Lord Melbourne and Queen Victoria's government.

On his arrival in London, after a short stay at a West End hotel, he took first lodgings in King Street, St. James's, and later set up as a householder on a grand scale at No. 17 Carlton House Terrace, which he rented from Lord Cardigan. He had brought with him to London half a dozen of his adherents, a kind of personal staff, including Count Arese, Colonel Vaudrey, Persigny, and Dr. Conneau. He had already many friends in England, and he made more during his two years' stay. For the first year he was a kind of social lion, and had endless invitations to good houses in London and in the country. He was made a member of several clubs. In his second season in London he fell a little into the background. He mingled in more Bohemian society, and was a frequenter of the literary gatherings at Lady Blessington's. There he met many of the prominent men of letters of the day, and made the acquaintance of Disraeli and the Count d'Orsay. The ladies to be found in Lady Blessington's salon were those who were not very careful as to the society they frequented. Among them was a Miss Howard, who for some years to come irregularly linked her fortunes with those of the Prince. He gave her a title and a fortune when he became Emperor, but not the wedding ring and the Imperial crown to which she rashly aspired.

At the Eglinton tournament in Scotland Louis Napoleon figured as one of the champions, masquerading in mediæval armour by day and in a quaint court dress in the evening. He was nearly involved in a more serious combat, which might well have ended his career and changed European history. He was challenged by a noted French duellist, who claimed to be his cousin and a son of the first Napoleon, and who had already killed his man in an earlier encounter. The parties met on Wimbledon Common. A dispute as to formalities delayed the affair, and the police arrived just in time to stop it.

While amusing himself in society and in less exclusive circles, and posing as an idle dandy and man of fashion, he was all the time hard at work. He produced another book, *Idées Napoléoniennes*, a somewhat high-flown essay on the policy of his famous uncle. It was an attempt to prove that the Empire was not necessarily, or primarily, based on military power and committed to warlike enterprises. He tried to show that Napoleon's campaigns and victories were the least part of his life-work : that war had been forced upon him, but that he was essentially a reconstructive, organising force in France and western Europe, endeavouring to preserve and consolidate the gains of the Revolution and to promote the prosperity of the people, while securing at the same time the reign of organised order and law. The book was meant to shadow forth his own policy, and to reassure those who feared that his accession to power in France would inaugurate a new period of international conflicts in Europe. It was an anticipation of his declaration in later years that ' the Empire meant Peace.'

His residence at Carlton House Terrace was the centre of a permanent conspiracy. The rooms to which visitors were admitted were adorned with works of art and personal relics, reminding them of the First Empire. The Prince and his staff of assistants were in correspondence with men of all classes in France, especially with journalists, men of letters, and soldiers.

There was an elaborate record kept of every notable man in the army and in politics. The work done every day kept a whole bureau of assistants busy, and it was concealed under an air of idleness on the part of the man who was the centre of it all. Louis Philippe's government tried to keep a watch on these proceedings, but its London agents sent such endless reports of plots and imminent raids on France that, as the months went by and nothing happened, the agents themselves were discredited, and official Paris came at last to believe that the Prince was amusing himself in London, and waiting for a change in the whole political situation, before again risking any such adventures as that which had ended in failure at Strasburg in 1836.

But he had not been twelve months in London before he began to prepare seriously for another attempt to make himself master of France. The internal difficulties that embarrassed the Orleanist Government, the activity of the opposition, the sense of national humiliation at the failure of French policy in Syria, and the success of the rival policy of England, Austria, and Russia, and with all this the ever-growing popularity of the memories of the great Napoleon and the glories of the Empire, led him to believe that a revolution was possible. A French adventurer, who had long dabbled in the secret ways of diplomacy, and been the paid agent of more than one power, encouraged him by persuading him that Russia would hasten to recognise him, and offer him the hand of a Grand Duchess as the price of a French alliance. A Bonapartist committee in Paris, which claimed to have as its chief one of the old marshals of the Empire, assured him that it had secret relations with all the garrisons in France, and that many of the regiments were ready to declare for the Empire, if he would raise its standard anywhere on French soil. Articles in the press and a flood of pamphlets kept up the literary propaganda of the movement. Not a few of the Republican party were drawn into sympathetic relations with Bonapartism by Louis Napoleon's repeated declarations, that according to his ideals the Empire would be a democratic state, a Republic in all essentials, with the Emperor as its permanent chief executive officer. In any case, he said, what he aimed at in the first instance was to give France an opportunity of declaring its will, and setting up whatever precise form of government it might choose. These declarations were mingled with invectives against the Orleans régime, which he persisted in representing as having been imposed on France by a handful of lawyers and intriguers in Paris in 1830, without any appeal to the electors, without a plébiscite, such as those which had accepted the various modifications of the old Napoleonic system.

The Strasburg attempt was to be the model of the new enterprise. The first starting-point chosen for it was Lille, on the Belgian frontier. General (afterwards Marshal) Magnan commanded there, and it was thought that he could be induced to be a party to the scheme. Two of Napoleon's emissaries, both of them accomplices in the Strasburg plot, arrived at Lille, and formed friendly relations with many officers of the garrison. They approached Magnan, and soon ventured to make him open offers in return for his co-operation. In his subsequent evidence before the courts Magnan declared that he indignantly rejected these proposals, but the strange thing is that he did not break with the conspirators who had tempted him, or interfere with their propaganda at Lille and in other garrisons of the north of France.

At the beginning of 1840 it was believed, at the headquarters of the conspiracy in Carlton House Terrace, that things were sufficiently advanced for the attempt to be made that year. Louis Napoleon and his friends were to land in the north of France, and secure the adhesion of one of the minor garrisons. At the news there would, it was hoped, be movements in other garrison towns of the north. The march on Paris would follow, and his friends there would organise a rising. It was expected that Vincennes could be secured by a military revolt. The plot had certainly wider ramifications. Louis Napoleon was not a genius, but he was not a fool, and he did not venture to land in France in the mere expectation that his very presence would provoke a revolution, as the mere appearance of the great Napoleon had done in 1815.

There was a new inducement to action in the fact that the Orleanist Government had decided to bring back the remains of Napoleon from St. Helena before the end of the year. England had given her consent, and the preparations for this climax of the national hero worship of the great Emperor were in progress. So in the proclamations, which Dr. Conneau printed on a hand-press in London, to be distributed on the landing in France of the Emperor's nephew, the French people were told that the ashes of Napoleon should be restored to a regenerated France, freed from a government that would pay them only a hypocritical homage. ' Liberty and glory must greet the coffin of the great Emperor, and the traitors to the fatherland must be driven away.'

Not only rhetorical proclamations to the French people, the army, the inhabitants of the northern departments, were prepared and printed in secret, but also a decree to be issued as soon as the conspirators had secured a footing in France. It did not proclaim the Empire, but it announced that the ' dynasty of the Orleans Bourbons had ceased to reign '; that the Chambers were dissolved ; and a ' National Congress ' would be convoked to decide on the future government of France. M. Thiers was invited to assume the presidency of the Provisional Government, and Marshal Clausel was appointed Commander-in-chief of the Army of Paris.

Thiers had certainly no knowledge of the plot. But it was hoped that the man who had done so much to revive the national Napoleon worship would accept accomplished facts, and lend the prestige of his name to the movement once its success was at least probable. It is not so certain that Marshal Clausel was outside the conspiracy. In July he went to Eaux Bonnes in the Pyrenees and arranged to make a prolonged stay there. In the first week of August he suddenly left the place for Paris.

In July it was decided that the landing-place should be Boulogne. It had a garrison of only two companies of the 42nd Infantry, one of whose officers was deep in the plot. The expedition was made up of fifty-six individuals. There were Napoleon and his servants and his personal staff, and then a number of Polish and French refugees enlisted in the neighbourhood of Leicester Square and Soho. Uniforms were procured from France. Arms were brought from Birmingham. An excursion steamer, the *Edinburgh Castle*, Captain James Crowe, was chartered for a month ' for a party of pleasure.' From July 6th to August 6th she was to be at the orders of the Prince, whose name, however, did not appear in the business. Cases of arms and equipments were put on board of her in the Thames without exciting any suspicion. Those who were enlisted for the expedition were kept in the dark as to what was intended.

The start was made on the night of August 3rd. As the steamer went down the Thames she picked up the expedition in small parties at Wapping, Gravesend, Greenwich, Chatham, and Margate. Parquin, one of the adventurers of Strasburg, was in charge of the Wapping detachment. While waiting for the steamer he saw a small eagle on sale in a cage at an East End bird-fancier's, and bought it and took it on board. He knew that Louis Napoleon was inclined to be superstitious, and had a theatrical element in his character, and he thought that the setting free of the eagle on French soil would strike him as a good omen.

Louis Napoleon himself, with Count Montholon, who had been with the Emperor at St. Helena, joined the party at Margate on the 4th. For more than twenty-four hours the *Edinburgh Castle* was steaming about the channel, keeping out of sight of the French coast. On the afternoon of the 5th she was headed for Wimereux, near Boulogne. Louis Napoleon assembled the party on deck and told them the object of the expedition. He had friends in France, he said, who only awaited his arrival to act. ' As sure as the sun is shining,' he added, ' we shall be in Paris in a few days.' Uniforms were put on, the rank and file of the expedition, who were to form the escort of the staff, appearing as soldiers of the 40th Regiment of the Line.

Soon after midnight the steamer anchored off Wimereux. Less than four miles away to the southward the harbour lights of Boulogne shone through the darkness. The disembarkation began at two A.M. The first party that landed was met by Lieutenant Adalenize of the 42nd Regiment, and two of his friends. Some custom-house officers came up to make inquiries and were told that the new arrivals were a party of the 40th Regiment on their way by sea from Dunkirk to Cherbourg ; their steamer had broken down and was putting them ashore. At first the officers were satisfied, when they became suspicious they were made prisoners.

At five A.M., in bright daylight, the party marched on Boulogne, one of the leaders displaying a tricolour embroidered with the names of Napoleon's victories, and with a bronze eagle on the flagstaff. At the barracks an attempt was made to induce the two companies of the 42nd to declare for ' Prince Napoleon.' Some of the men cried ' *Vive l'Empereur !* ' but most hesitated, and the officers succeeded in steadying them, and tried to arrest the leaders of the expedition. There was a scuffle, in which Louis Napoleon shot one of the soldiers. His party succeeded in preventing his arrest, and leaving the town, marched out to the column of the Grand Army, still expecting that their friends in Boulogne would rise and join them. Instead of this the two companies of regulars marched out against them, supported by the local battalion of the National Guard, shouting ' *Vive le Roi !* '

The invaders fled to the shore, hoping to be taken off by their steamer ; but she had been captured by a coastguard boat sent out from Boulogne, and was steaming for the port. They launched a boat which was on the beach, and some of them were clambering into her when she overturned. The National Guard opened fire on the men in the water. The Prince ran the risk of being shot or drowned. Two bullets tore his clothes. One of his party was killed beside him, others were wounded. He waded ashore and surrendered. Forty-five of his followers were taken with him, and by eight o'clock they were all safely lodged in the prison of Boulogne. It was a far worse failure than Strasburg.

The Boulogne fiasco was made the text of articles in most of the European papers, in which the name of Louis Napoleon was covered with contemptuous ridicule,[1] and it was confidently predicted that the cause of Bonapartism was lost for ever. In France one of the leading opposition papers, the *National*, stood alone in declaring that the Prince might be still a force in European politics.

The Government was not going to repeat the mistake of setting him at liberty and indicting only his accomplices.

---

[1] There were many poor jokes about Parquin's tame eagle, which was said to have been set free and to have flown to the top of the Grand Army monument. It had been left on board the *Edinburgh Castle*, and became a trophy of the coastguards who took her into Boulogne harbour.

It was decided to put him on his trial before the Chamber of Peers. After the experience of the Strasburg trial the jury of an assize court was not to be trusted. He was removed from Boulogne to the fortress of Ham, in north-eastern France, and thence on August 12th he was transferred to the prison of the Conciergerie [1] at Paris, where he was confined in the cell occupied five years before by the would-be regicide Fieschi. During these movements he was guarded by strong military escorts, for the Government, though it affected to regard the Boulogne attempt as a ridiculous failure, was seriously alarmed at the evidence it had obtained as to the ramifications of the conspiracy, and had begun to disperse the northern divisions of the army among various garrisons in the south.

Louis, ex-King of Holland and Count of St. Leu, intervened in the affair, by addressing to the newspapers a letter in which he tried to throw on others the blame for his son's conduct. The letter, dated from Florence on August 24, 1840, was to this effect : ' Allow me to ask you to find a place for the following declaration. I know that it is an unusual, and hardly the proper method, for me to have recourse to the newspapers ; but when a father, who is afflicted, broken with years and infirmities, and legally expatriated, can in no other way come to the aid of his unfortunate son, such a course cannot fail to meet with the approval of all who have the feelings of a father. Convinced as I am that my son, the only one now left to me, is the victim of an infamous intrigue and misled by vile flatterers, false friends and perhaps treacherous advice, I could not keep silence without laying myself open to the most bitter reproaches.—I declare therefore that my son, Louis Napoleon, has for the third time fallen into a terrible snare, a horrible trap prepared for him, for it is impossible that a man who is not without resources and some common-sense, should fling himself light-heartedly over such a precipice. If he is guilty, far more guilty and the real culprits are those who have misled him and set him astray. I declare above all with a holy horror that the insult that has been put upon my son by confining him in the

---

[1] When Queen Victoria was his guest in Paris, as he drove with her over the Pont Neuf, he pointed to the towers of the Conciergerie and said with a smile, ' I was once in prison over there.'

cell of an infamous assassin, is a monstrous cruelty, an act un-
worthy of Frenchmen, an outrage as base as it is treacherous.
As one who is in deep affliction, as a good Frenchman who has
suffered the trials of thirty years of exile, as the brother, and
if I may venture to say it, the ,pupil of him whose statues
France is now replacing on their pedestals, I recommend my
son, who has been misled and seduced by others, to the goodwill of his judges, and of all those who have the heart of a
Frenchman and of a father.   LOUIS DE ST. LEU.'

The Bonapartists tried to make out that this letter, in which
the Prince was not put in a very favourable light, was a forgery,
intended to injure him by representing him as the weak victim
of others. But Louis never denied its authorship, and it was
a composition that was characteristic of him. Others tried
to make out that Louis was acting under the influence of his
brother Jerome, who was just then trying to take advantage
of the official patronage of Napoleon's memory in France in
order to persuade the Government to allow him to return from
exile, and even to grant him a pension. He was naturally
annoyed at his nephew's escapade, which upset his own plans,
but it is not likely that he influenced Louis.

The French Ministry replied to Louis's letter by sending
a *communiqué* to the editors who had published it, in which
they explained that it was a mere chance that Louis Napoleon
occupied the room of Fieschi. It had been completely remodelled since the famous assassin was confined in it ; it had
been used as the lodging of one of the officials of the prison,
and had been given to the Prince because it was one of the best
rooms in the building.

It was not till September 28th that Louis Napoleon and
eighteen of his companions were indicted before the Chamber
of Peers at the Luxembourg. Amongst the accused were
Count Montholon, Persigny, and Dr. Conneau. The Prince
had secured for his defence the services of Berryer, the eloquent
leader of the French bar, who, though opposed to him in politics,
was quite ready, as a Legitimist, to make the defence an in-
dictment of the Orleanist Government. In his examination
Louis Napoleon explained that he had raised no claim to
govern France unless the people by universal suffrage called

him to do so. Since 1789 universal suffrage was the only source of legitimate authority in France. His action was a protest against a government that ruled in defiance of this principle, an effort to secure for the people the opportunity of declaring their will. To rule with their consent, and in their interest, had been the tradition of his family. ' I am the son of a father,' he said, ' who left his throne without regret, on the day when he saw it was no longer possible to reconcile with the interests of France those of the nation he had been called to rule. The Emperor, my uncle, preferred to abdicate the Imperial crown rather than accept treaties that narrowed the frontiers of France, and thus exposed her to the insults and menaces in which the foreigner indulges to-day. I do not forget such examples.' Louis Napoleon was no orator, and it was generally believed that his statement to the court had been written for him by Berryer.

Berryer's own speech for the defence was a masterpiece of forensic eloquence. He reminded the judges that he was an adherent of the Legitimist party, and as such opposed to his client's views, but he said this did not prevent him from defending him and putting these views forward, just as after Waterloo he had defended and secured the acquittal of the Bonapartist Cambronne. He reminded the court that the recent history of France was made up of changes of government. When men had sworn fealty to half a dozen different systems in the course of their career, was it to be expected that to attempt to subvert any particular form of government would be regarded as a grave crime ? After all, the accused Prince was the heir of a ruler who had been acclaimed by the votes of four millions of Frenchmen. The existing government was itself based on a Revolution, and had at most the votes of 200,000 electors to approve its violent seizure of power. By what right did it seek to brand Louis Napoleon as a criminal for having sought to subvert it by the same methods that had brought it into being ? They had before them not a criminal and his accuser, but the representatives of two rival parties.

And who were they who sat as his judges ? Peers of France, for the most part dukes, barons, and counts of the new nobility that dated from the Empire. At this very moment France was preparing to do the highest honour to the great Emperor.

2 K

Under the strict letter of the penal code his nephew, his heir, his representative was doomed to death. For no one denied that he had ventured on acts of open insurrection. But, he went on, there would be no sentence of death. Could they dare in the same year to enshrine one Bonaparte in a splendid monument as the idol of the people of France, and send another to the scaffold? No, there would be no sentence of death. They could not carry out the prescriptions of the law and pronounce a legal sentence. Their judgment, whatever it might be, would be only a pronouncement of a political opinion, a political sentence of one party against another. It could inflict no disgrace upon its victim, and his cause and his motives would be judged by honourable men quite apart from it. He appealed to them not to be the tools of a party, but to have the courage to pronounce by their judgment that Louis Napoleon might indeed be mistaken, but had been guilty of no crime.

Before the proceedings closed the Prince intervened to tell the court that he did not wish his case to be separated from that of his companions. If any were guilty, he was guilty, and he wanted no acquittal unless all went free.

On October 6th the court pronounced its decision. The Chamber of Peers then consisted of 312 members. Of these only 167 took any part in the proceedings, and only 152 voted. The prisoners were all found guilty. Only one of the peers voted for a sentence of death. The judgment was that Louis Napoleon should be imprisoned ' in perpetuity.' The rest were sentenced to various terms of imprisonment, to be followed by police surveillance for the rest of their lives.

The prisoners were not in court when the judgment was pronounced. Their sentences were read to them in prison. When Louis Napoleon was told that he was to be imprisoned ' in perpetuity,' he asked with a smile, ' *How long does perpetuity last in France?* ' Next day, October 7th, he arrived at the fortress of Ham, which had been selected by the Government as his prison for life. On the very same day the frigate, *La Belle Poule*, commanded by the Prince de Joinville, anchored in the roadstead of St. Helena, and exchanged salutes with the shore batteries. She had come to carry back to France the remains of Napoleon. The Government that had sent his nephew to prison was preparing to celebrate the glories of the Empire, and calling all France to do honour to the name of Bonaparte.

Louis Napoleon was a prisoner of state in the old feudal castle of Ham from October 7, 1840, to May 25, 1846. In this case 'perpetuity' amounted to about five and a half years. He had nothing to complain of in his treatment. He was allowed to furnish his rooms, to obtain books and papers from outside, to carry on literary work, and, subject to the inspection of the commandant, a large correspondence. Within the limits of the castle he had a certain amount of liberty. He enjoyed the society of his fellow-prisoners, Count Montholon and Dr. Conneau, and sometimes was allowed to receive visitors. In a courtyard near the outer rampart he amused himself by cultivating a little garden.

The expenses of the Boulogne raid, of the trial that followed it and the literary campaign that had preceded it, joined to the outlay he honourably incurred in making provision for those who had been reduced to poverty by throwing in their lot with his, had made great inroads on his fortune, and he had reluctantly to consent to the sale of Arenenberg. But he had in his nature something of the optimist fatalism of his uncle, and he spoke confidently of regaining everything, and winning much more to add to it, before very long. Meanwhile he occupied his abundant leisure with literary work, in order to keep his name before the French public and prepare the way for yet a third bid for power and fortune when the opportunity came. As a diversion from work at his desk he gave some time to the study of physics, electro-magnetism, as it was then called, and chemistry. M. Acar, a chemist of Ham, was allowed to come regularly to assist him in his experiments, for which a laboratory was fitted up.

The first product of his literary activity was a small book of less than one hundred and fifty pages, published in 1841, *Fragments Historiques*, a political essay, disguised as a study of the English Revolution of 1688. He revised and brought up to date his treatise on artillery, and with a view to conciliating the opinion of the working classes in France and gaining the support of the Republicans, who were dabbling in state socialism, he produced an elaborate scheme for the ' Extinction of Pauperism.' A great part of the work was devoted to a proposal for co-operative agricultural colonies in France, but incidentally he took care to set forth a detailed account of what the Empire had done for the peasant and the working man. A minor essay in economics was a pamphlet on the *Question des Sucres*, the cultivation of the beetroot and the development of the manufacture of beetroot sugar in France. At first sight one does not realise that this had anything to do with Bonapartism, but he could claim that his uncle was the founder of this new industry in France, an industry that was a gain to both the peasant and the factory-hand. It was when the continental blockade and the activity of the British cruisers had made West Indian cane-sugar almost unobtainable in France, that Napoleon set a group of practical men and scientific experts to work to devise efficient methods of extracting sugar from beet. He was so proud of the result that for a long time a tiny cone of beet sugar was the chief ornament of his study mantelpiece at St. Cloud.

But while losing no opportunity of putting forward the claims of the Empire to the gratitude of France, he took care never openly to assert any personal ambition to claim for himself the Imperial purple. He insisted that, while proud of the name he bore, he asked only to be allowed to serve France in any capacity. A prisoner, he could only do so by his writings. In a note on the *Fragments Historiques* he had said that he did not wish to be regarded as merely one more of those scions of a fallen family that had once reigned, who thought only of wasting their time in asserting their pretensions. In the essay on the 'Extinction of Pauperism' he wrote : '*Je suis citoyen avant d'être Bonaparte*' ('I am a citizen in the first place, a Bonaparte only after that ').

Through visitors, and through his correspondents, he was able discreetly to keep in touch with the partisans of Bonapartism in France. Letters, too, passed in and out which the commandant never saw. Sometimes a visitor was the intermediary, but oftener his valet, Thélin, who after a few months was allowed to make expeditions into the town. Louis Napoleon was always more or less in touch with a Bonapartist propaganda in the opposition press, and had helped to find money for more than one journal whose programme was the restoration of the Empire. The time might before long be ripe for renewed action. There was in France a growing discontent with the methods of government of the Citizen King and his minister Guizot. France had still the restricted franchise of 1830, and while England had changed its whole system by a wide extension of the right to vote, the millions of France were represented only by a Chamber chosen by less than a quarter of a million of electors on a high property qualification. The agitation for reform made Republicans, Bonapartists, and Liberal Monarchists confederates for a time. Even the Legitimists might be tempted by dislike for the Orleans monarchy to join forces with these discordant allies.

Five years of imprisonment made the studious prisoner of Ham anxious to find some means of regaining his liberty without pledging his freedom of action. In 1846 the illness of his father determined him to make an effort to escape, just as years before the illness of his mother had decided him to return from his exile in America.

CHAPTER XXXII

DEATHS OF THE ELDER BROTHERS—JEROME THE SOLE SURVIVOR—LOUIS NAPOLEON RESTORES THE FAMILY FORTUNES

(1840-1848)

LUCIEN, Prince of Canino, had died in 1840, the year of the Boulogne fiasco, leaving his principality to his son. The only one of the brothers who had never worn a crown, Lucien's career had been on the whole that of a successful man. The resolute courage with which he had braved the anger of Napoleon, and refused even a kingdom and a great career, rather than disavow his wife and his children, or inflict even a shadow of dishonour on them, ennobled all his later life and made men forget the less creditable episodes of his first rise to fortune. The Emperor was probably right in regarding him as by far the ablest of his brothers, and the story of the Empire might have been different if Lucien had been his right-hand man in directing affairs in Paris during the years of victory. But by his own despotic claim to dictate a line of private conduct to his brother, Napoleon deprived himself of Lucien's courage and skill, and had his help only in the last desperate struggle for Empire.

Joseph, whom Napoleon had esteemed less but loved more than Lucien, had been allowed to return to Italy in 1841, and after long years of separation rejoined his wife Julie at Florence. He had her affectionate care in the few years that remained to him, years of rapidly declining health. He died in 1844, and his wife survived him only a few months. He was a man of moderate ability, forced into positions that demanded something like genius to command success. And he had the further misfortune to be handicapped by the fact that he was never given a free hand, but was continually overruled or opposed by those on whom he counted for support. That he failed in Spain was not wholly his fault. He has been made the scapegoat of the mistakes of others. At Paris in 1814 he was not really responsible for the collapse of the defence. He might have been more useful to his brother if Napoleon had not insisted on making him a King. His life would certainly have been happier if he had remained in France as the seigneur of Mortefontaine, presiding at state functions, and appearing at European congresses as the envoy of France.

The deaths of his brothers were warnings to Louis, ex-King of Holland, that for him too the end could not be far off. They were his seniors, but then they had always enjoyed robust health compared to him. For a great part of his life he had been an invalid. Increasing years added to his infirmities. The brilliant soldier of the first campaign of Italy was now a paralysed cripple, spending his days on a couch or in a wheeled chair in the garden of his villa at Florence, or at Leghorn, where he was taken for the sake of the sea air. The imprisonment of his only surviving son, the apparent destruction of all his hopes for the future of Louis Napoleon, had been a severe blow to him. He found some consolation for his sufferings and disappointments in a return to the practice of the religion in which he had been educated.

Towards the end of 1845 the doctors warned him that the end could not now be long deferred. He had a great longing to see his son once again. He wrote to Louis Napoleon on the subject, and sent letters to three of the French Ministry asking them to arrange, if possible, for an amnesty for his son, or if this was out of the question, at least for his temporary release on parole. The friendly intervention of many prominent men who had influence at Paris—amongst them Lord Malmesbury and Lord Londonderry—was procured by Louis Napoleon in support of his father's petition. But the ministers refused to advise the King to exercise his prerogative of mercy. It was hinted that a different course might perhaps be taken, if Louis Napoleon would present a petition for pardon, in which he would acknowledge that he had been guilty of a criminal attempt, and would pledge his

word of honour to abstain from all political action in France
for the future.

The Prince would not hear of this. It would be dishonour,
he said. But on January 14, 1846, he wrote from Ham
a personal letter to the King, which was presented to Louis
Philippe by the son of Marshal Ney. He asked only for a
brief period of liberty in which to visit his dying father. He
was ready to pledge his word that he would return and recon-
stitute himself a prisoner as soon as the French Government requested him to do so. ' I am convinced,' he said,
' that your Majesty will appreciate as it deserves a step·that
will give you a claim upon my gratitude, and that, touched
by the isolation in a foreign land of a man who when on a
throne won the esteem of Europe, you will grant my father's
petition and mine.'

The King told Ney that personally he thought the pledge
offered by Louis Napoleon was satisfactory enough, but he
must refer the matter to his ministers. But they still refused
to advise any concession. They repeated this refusal when
an appeal was made to them by a deputation of members of
the Legislature in support of the petition. At the end of
February Louis Napoleon wrote to a friend that he had to
give up all hope of being allowed to leave the fortress.

When the spring came, a pathetic letter from King Louis,
telling of a marked increase of his infirmities, led the prisoner
to think seriously of devising some means of escape. Dr.
Conneau became his accomplice, and the valet Thélin, being
able to pass in and out, procured a workman's dress to serve
as a disguise. Some repairs were being carried out in the
fortress and numbers of workmen were coming and going.
It was decided that the Prince should escape disguised as one
of them.

On May 24th he kept to his room, and Conneau said he was
unwell. Early next morning he walked boldly out un-
challenged by the sentinels. He wore a rough cap and a pair
of heavy shoes, with a workman's blouse and a loose pair of
trousers over his other clothes. He had shaved off his
moustache and painted his face, and as a means of partly
hiding it he carried over his shoulder a plank, a long shelf
taken from his library. Thélin slipped out after him, procured

a carriage in the town, and drove to a point on the road outside it, where he found the escaped prisoner waiting for him.

They drove by St. Quentin to Valenciennes. Thélin had brought in a bundle a hat, shoes, and an overcoat, and the Prince got rid of his disguise on the way. At Valenciennes he caught the express train for Brussels, where he arrived early in the evening.

His escape was not discovered till seven P.M., when he was safe in Belgium and all pursuit was useless. Dr. Conneau had succeeded in keeping up the fiction that Louis Napoleon was too ill to leave his bed, and even prevented the commandant from entering the room, when he came on his round of inspection, by protesting that his patient was asleep, and must not be disturbed. It was not until seven o'clock in the evening that the commandant insisted on seeing his prisoner, and the truth became known. Conneau was handcuffed, taken to Péronne, and condemned to three months' close imprisonment. His original sentence for the Boulogne affair had expired, and at the end of the three months he was at liberty. He had kept the promise he had made to Queen Hortense on her deathbed that he would be a faithful friend to her son.

From Brussels Louis Napoleon crossed over at once by Ostend to London, whence he wrote to King Louis on May 27th :—

'MY DEAR FATHER,—The desire to see you again has made me attempt what otherwise I would never have done. I have eluded the vigilance of four hundred men, and arrived safe and sound at London. I have powerful friends here. I am going to make use of them in order to endeavour to come to you. I beg you, dear father, to do all you can to facilitate my soon being with you. NAPOLEON-LOUIS B.

'My address is "Count d'Arenenberg, Brunswick Hotel, Jermyn Street, London."'

At the same time he wrote to the French ambassador in London, informing him that he had escaped from Ham only when, after repeated refusals to allow him to go out on parole, there was no other course open to him, if he meant to see his dying father again. 'I give you the formal assurance,' he added, ' that if I have left my prison, it is not to occupy myself with politics, or to attempt to disturb the peace that Europe' enjoys, but only to fulfil a sacred duty.'

But he found it impossible to obtain passports for Florence. The Austrian ambassador replied to a request for a permit for a journey by the Tyrol and northern Italy, that out of deference to the French Government, his own could not allow the Prince to pass through the Austrian dominions. The French route was of course impossible. A sea voyage to Italy was then thought of, and Leopold, the Grand Duke of Tuscany, was approached by influential friends of the Prince with a view to arranging for Louis Napoleon spending even a few days in his dominions. But here again French and Austrian official hostility barred the way, and the Grand Duke replied that he could not give the Prince leave to appear in his territory even for twenty-four hours.

The aged King Louis was too broken in health for even a short land or sea journey, otherwise he might have been removed to Rome or to Malta to meet his son. He had to give up the hope of seeing him again. He died at Florence on July 25, 1846, aged sixty-eight years.

Jerome, ex-King of Westphalia and Count de Montfort, was now the sole survivor of the Bonaparte brothers. His devoted wife, Catherine of Würtemberg, had died in 1834. ' What I loved most in the world was you, Jerome,' she said to him as she lay dying. ' I only wish I could have said this farewell to you in France.' With her death the pensions from Würtemberg and Russia ceased, and Jerome was for some time to come nearly resourceless. He had left Rome for Florence, where he had a palazzo. This he had now to give up, and retire to a small villa in the suburbs, living in what to him was poverty.

In 1836 he was with Lucien at his mother's deathbed. He hoped that he would inherit a large sum from her, but she divided what was left of her savings among all her relations, and very little came to Jerome. He tried to make peace with the Orleanist government in France, and hoped to be allowed to return from exile, and to receive at least a military pension, as a general who had commanded French troops in the field. But his efforts were without result, and he attributed their failure to the escapades of his nephew Louis Napoleon, and regarded him as a wild dreamer who was ruining the prospects of the family.

At last in 1840 Jerome's difficulties came to an end. His daughter Mathilde married the wealthy Russian Prince Anatole Demidoff and was able to make him a handsome allowance, and then he himself contracted a third marriage. The bride was a rich widow living in Florence, the Marchesa Bartolini-Badelli. She was a handsome woman of forty—fifteen years younger than her husband—and she was of a gentle, affectionate disposition, and known for her charity to the poor of the city. Though Jerome was deep in debt, he remembered that he had been a King and was still a Prince, and he considered the union with a mere Marchesa was below his dignity; so it was arranged that though there was a marriage, it should be ' morganatic,' and the Marchesa should not become a Princess. To the last her husband always spoke of her as ' Madame la Marquise.' Of course, though Jerome would not have admitted this, the marriage was also bigamous, for all the while there was his abandoned first wife living in the United States.

Besides his daughter Mathilde, Catherine of Würtemberg had left him two sons. The elder was living with him in Florence; the second, born in 1822 at Trieste, bore the name of Napoleon and had a remarkable likeness to the great Emperor. When he was fifteen, through the influence of friends of his mother, he was given a commission in the Würtemberg army by his uncle, who had succeeded Catherine's father on the throne. He went to Stuttgart, and a few years' peace service gave him something of a military education. He took his holidays in Italy. It was during one of these excursions that he passed with his father through the territory of Parma, now a Duchy ruled by the ex-Empress Maria Louisa, who had married the Austrian Neipperg, with whom she had lived for years while her husband was a prisoner at St. Helena. Another carriage passed on the road with a lady in it. ' Look, look ! ' exclaimed Jerome, seizing his son's hand, ' that is the Empress Maria Louisa.' ' No,' replied his son scornfully, ' she is no longer the Empress. It is only Madame Neipperg.'

After a few years Prince Napoleon retired from the army, with a liberal pension granted by his uncle King William of Würtemberg, who had taken a great liking to the young man.

He travelled about Europe, and was even allowed to visit France. But he did not give up his military studies, which now took the form of reading everything that was published about his uncle's campaigns, and conversing about them with the veterans who had taken part in them, either as the followers or opponents of the Emperor. At the same time be began to pay attention to political questions. He had made up his mind that to attempt the restoration of the Empire in France was a mistaken and hopeless policy. He thought that the best prospect for his family would be opened up by the advent of a second French Republic, which would accept the services of the Bonapartes in the army and in its civil administration, and give them a career as leading citizens, not masters, of the state.

But it was not only on account of these politic considerations that his sympathies turned to the Republican party in France, and were opposed to the ambitions of his cousin Louis Napoleon. He was a Radical by temperament, and in later years, as a Prince of the new Empire, he always leant towards the Liberal Opposition. In the Paris of Louis Philippe, as a young man, he was imprudent enough to alarm the authorities by his intimate relations with and unconcealed sympathy for the leaders of the Republican party, and this led to his expulsion from France in 1845.

Two years later Jerome, his wife the Marchesa, and his son Prince Napoleon were allowed to settle in Paris. Louis Philippe's Government withdrew the ban of exile under the influence of many friends who exerted themselves on Jerome's behalf. Amongst these was Victor Hugo.[1] Perhaps the known hostility of both father and son to Louis Napoleon made the Orleanist Government more willing to allow them to

---

[1] Victor Hugo, the fierce opponent of the Second Empire, was in his earlier years Bonapartist in his sympathies, as the result of his admiration for the great Napoleon. In 1830 he was in correspondence with Joseph and a partisan of the restoration of Napoleon II. In a letter to Joseph he referred in these terms to the Duke of Reichstadt: 'It is because I am devoted to France, devoted to liberty, that I have faith in the future of your royal nephew. He can be of great service to our country. If he gives, as I have no doubt he will, all necessary guarantees for the ideals of emancipation, progress, and liberty, no one will rally to this new order of things more heartily and more eagerly than myself, and with me, Sire, I will venture in its name to answer for the support of all the youth of France, who venerate the name of the Emperor, and on whom, obscure as I am, I have perhaps some influence.'

return. So Jerome saw Paris again after thirty-two years of banishment. His eldest son had died just before he left Italy.

Louis Napoleon regarded the acceptance of any concession from the royal Government of France as a surrender. Despite his repeated failures, he was the one man among the Bonapartes who looked forward with unshaken confidence to a great future for himself and his kindred. Like his uncle the Emperor he spoke of his destiny, and waited patiently for the course of events in France to shape an opportunity for him. He had not long to wait.

Meanwhile he abstained from any further active attempts to assert his claims. For he had not only on his arrival informed the French ambassador that this was his intention, but he had also given assurances to the British Government that while he remained in England he would take no step that could give ground for a protest from Paris against the hospitality afforded to him in London.

He occupied himself with a new edition of his Artillery Manual, and went to stay for a while at Bath. There he made the acquaintance of Walter Savage Landor, who told him in his characteristically frank style what he thought of his ambition to rule as an Emperor. The Prince had given him one of the first copies of the new edition of his book, writing a few words on the flyleaf to express his esteem for him ' notwithstanding the opposition of our ideas.' Landor wrote to a friend : ' I told him if ever he were again in prison I would visit him there ; but never, if he were on a throne, would I come near him. He is the only man living who would adorn one, but thrones are my aversion and abhorrence.'

Early in 1847 he was back in London, where he took a house in King Street, St. James's, now marked by a tablet commemorative of the fact. He had many friends in London, from serious politicians in both Houses of Parliament down to the members of such Bohemian coteries as that which met in Lady Blessington's drawing-room. He kept up an extensive correspondence with his supporters in France, and maintained in London the group of adherents that formed a kind of headquarters staff, with Persigny for its chief. He was not conspiring, but he was keeping the elements of a possible combination for a new attempt ready for the favourable moment, and watching with keen interest the growing difficulties of the Government in France, and the rising power of the movement for the extension of the franchise. Public meetings are not a French institution, except at election times. The Opposition leaders used instead, as the methods of their propaganda, a series of 'banquets,' at which fiery speeches were delivered against the Orleanist Government and reported in the press. Many new journals were founded, some of them openly Bonapartist; in fact newspapers grew up like mushrooms, and at the same time thousands of pamphlets were poured out from the printing-presses of Paris. The main drift of the opposition movement was clearly Republican. The voice of the people at large was to be substituted for that of a small bourgeois class of voters, a large number of whom were employés of the administration or otherwise personally interested in keeping the Ministry in power. It was as a citizen of the coming Republic that Louis Napoleon looked forward to gaining a footing in France. After that anything would be possible.

Kinglake, and other writers who shared the same views of bitter hostility to Louis Napoleon and the Second Empire, are responsible for having created the legend that during this stay in London he was in desperate financial straits. They tell of the group of middle-aged men living a Bohemian life as refugees in London, short of cash and with no prospects for the future, a group of which Louis Napoleon and ' Fialin *alias* Persigny ' were the centre, and of how they put their heads together to make their fortunes at the expense of the French people by getting up a second-rate imitation of the Empire of Napoleon. But as a matter of fact Louis Napoleon was never without considerable financial resources. The fortune left him by Hortense had disappeared in the ' shipwreck ' of Boulogne, and even Arenenberg had had to be sold to provide for the state trial and the help given to those who had lost all in embarking with the Prince in that disastrous venture. But he had been left a considerable sum and some landed property by his father, and though he spent money freely he had £7000 to his credit in one of his banking accounts in London in the autumn of 1847. He had always friends ready to assist him, because they believed that sooner or later he would be able more than to repay them. Before he left Ham the exiled Duke of Brunswick had placed a large sum at his disposal, and one of the greatest banking-houses in London had told him that if he needed money he had only to ask for it.

He would have had abundant supplies always in his possession if he had not amused himself with betting and cards. In this way he squandered some thousands, but he was always able to pay his losses at once. A large allowance to Miss Howard was another drain on his purse, and he spent still larger sums in providing means for his headquarters staff, and allowing pensions to those who had been ruined in his service or to their relatives. When he borrowed it was for his political propaganda. Money was sent to France to keep journalists and pamphleteers at work in his interest, and to distribute broadcast newspapers started to prepare the way for his reappearance.

On February 22, 1848, the resistance of Louis Philippe and his minister Guizot to the growing demand for electoral reform was challenged by the raising of barricades in the streets of Paris. Brought face to face with a popular insurrection, the Government for three days made half-hearted attempts to put down the rising. The King dismissed Guizot, but the surrender came too late. As ' Mr. Smith,' carrying the historic umbrella, the Citizen King slipped out of his palace, reached Dieppe, and took a ticket for Newhaven, while Lamartine proclaimed the Provisional Government of the Republic at the Hôtel de Ville.

On the news that there were barricades in Paris, Louis Napoleon prepared to leave London. As soon as he heard that Louis Philippe had fled, he started for Paris. On February 28th he announced his arrival by this letter to the Provisional Government :—

'GENTLEMEN,—The people of Paris having by their heroism destroyed the last vestiges of a foreign invasion, I hasten back from exile to place myself under the flag of the Republic which you have just proclaimed. Without any ambition but that of being of service to my country, I announce my arrival to the Provisional Government, and beg to assure them of my devotion to the cause which they represent, and of my goodwill to themselves as individuals. Accept, gentlemen, this assurance of my sentiments. LOUIS NAPOLEON BONAPARTE'

There was a disappointing reply. The Government did not feel sufficiently sure of their own position to welcome the support of a would-be ally with such a dangerous name and such a compromising record. They thanked him for his letter, and asked him to be so good as to withdraw from France, where his presence at this crisis might be embarrassing and might be open to mistaken interpretations. Next day (February 29) he left Paris to return to London, after sending the Government another letter in which he said : ' I thought that after thirty-three years of exile and persecution, I had at length the right to find a home in my native country. You think my presence in Paris at this moment may prove embarrassing to you. I therefore withdraw for the present. You will see in this sacrifice a proof of the purity of my intentions and of my patriotism.'

His uncle Jerome had also hastened to give his adhesion to the Provisional Government. ' Gentlemen,' he wrote to them from his new home in Paris, ' the nation has at length torn up the Treaties of 1815. The old soldier of Waterloo, the last surviving brother of Napoleon, returns at this moment to the bosom of the great family. For France the era of dynasties has passed. The law of proscription, which struck me down, has gone with the last of the Bourbons. I ask the Government of the Republic to decree that this proscription was injurious to France, and that it has disappeared with all else that the foreigner forced upon us. Pray be assured of my respect and devotion.—JEROME BONAPARTE.'

In his enthusiasm for the new Republic, his son, Prince Napoleon, wrote to the King of Würtemberg signing himself ' Citizen Bonaparte,' and his royal uncle immediately stopped his pension of 30,000 francs a year, writing to his nephew that he felt sure so sincere and ardent a republican would feel pained at receiving money from a King.

His cousin, Louis Bonaparte, was again watching the course of events from London, and waiting for his opportunity. This time he had reason to feel certain that his stay in England would not be much prolonged. His friends kept his name before the French public in the press. His spirit of loyal abnegation in leaving France was eulogised. His books on the democratic ideals of Napoleon and on the project for the extinction of pauperism were quoted, and were largely circulated. Persigny and others urged him to put himself forward as a candidate at the elections for the Constituent Assembly on April 23rd. With a wise discrimination he decided that the time was not yet ripe for this step, but three of his cousins were nominated for various constituencies. These were wild Pierre Bonaparte, a son of Lucien and brother of the actual Prince of Canino ; Napoleon Bonaparte, the ex-Würtemberg officer and son of Jerome ; and Lucien Murat, a son of the great cavalry leader who had ruled in Naples and of the Emperor's sister Caroline. All three were elected as supporters of the Republic, and took their seats in the Assembly without any question being raised.

There was a movement in progress in Paris which was indirectly preparing the way for the restoration of the Empire by leading up to a crisis, the terrible memories of which for years after made all who had anything to lose in Paris and in France the advocates of a strongly organised Government that could secure order and property. Under the influence of the Socialist wing of the Republicans the Government admitted the right of every man who asked for it to be employed by the state. National Workshops were opened for the unemployed. But soon it became known that in the workshops men could put in a very slack day's work under foremen who did not dare to call them to order, and who having no power to dismiss them could not enforce discipline. In every trade in Paris the malcontents began to strike, and went off to the National Workshops for employment. The numbers on the pay-list rose steadily, until after a few weeks 120,000 men were idling at the expense of the taxpayers. It was soon recognised that the National Workshops could only be kept open at the cost of a gradual ruin of the industry of Paris. But the Socialist leaders defied the Government to close them, and declared the workmen were the masters of the situation.

In May, when this critical state of things was causing anxiety to all who had a thought for the future, supplementary elections were announced to fill a number of vacancies in the Assembly. Louis Napoleon's friends nominated him as a candidate in Paris and three of the departments. On a report that even

2 L

if he were elected the law of exile would be enforced against him, his friend Pietri, a Corsican deputy, moved in the Assembly the revocation of the decree of banishment issued by the Orleanist Government in 1832.   He argued that as three of the Bonaparte family already sat in the Assembly, the decree had already been practically abrogated.   His opponents replied that Louis Napoleon's case was different from that of his cousins : they had not been involved in armed attempts to proclaim the Empire, and their names were not, like his, the rallying cry of a party that had worked openly for this end.   The debate, begun on June 2nd, was adjourned to the 8th. By that time the elections had taken place, and the Prince had been elected by Paris and the departments of the Seine, Yonne, and Charente-Inférieure.   On the resumption of the debate the Assembly voted that the decree of exile had no longer any effect and that the elected member was free to take his seat.   The Government had to cancel a warrant for his arrest which they had already issued.

But some of his indiscreet supporters had already, in their enthusiasm at his election, acted in a way that seemed to justify the suspicions of the Government against him.   Bonapartist writers in the press spoke of him as a candidate for the Presidency and the man who would restore France to its old position in Europe.   A regiment on parade at Troyes cheered at the news of his election.   A crowd in Paris on the Place de la Concorde raised the cry of ' Vive Napoléon ! Vive l'Empereur ! ' and a shot was fired at the National Guard which dispersed it.   The Prince's opponents in the Chamber declared that there was an organised plot to make his appearance in Paris the signal for a revolt.

Louis Napoleon was preparing to leave London in order to take his seat in the Assembly, when he heard that Paris, already endangered by the crisis of the National Workshops, was agitated by further fears of a Bonapartist attempt against the Government.   Once more he showed that he knew how to wait.   He resigned his seat and wrote to the President of the Assembly conveying to him this decision in a letter in which he said :—

' I was proud of being elected a representative for Paris and three departments.   It was in my eyes an ample reparation for thirty years of exile and six of imprisonment. But the unjust suspicions to which my election has given rise, the troubles of which it has been the excuse, and the hostility of the executive government impose upon me the duty of declining an honour which I am supposed to have obtained by intrigue. I desire order and the maintenance of a wise, great, and intelligent Republic ; and since against my will my name is made the excuse for disorder, I place, not without deep regret, my resignation in your hands. I hope that before long things will be again quiet, so that I shall be able to return to France as the most unassuming of her citizens, but also as one of the most devoted to the peace and prosperity of my native country.'

It was a wise step to take. He could watch from London the wild storm of the Red revolt of June 1848, when, on the closing of the National Workshops, the army of Socialism raised the barricades, and only succumbed after days of hard fighting which cost a heavy loss of life. Cavaignac, the conqueror of the Reds, governed as a military dictator. Louis Napoleon had had the good fortune to be a neutral in the civil strife, and had made no enemies.

On the morrow of the struggle he refused a seat in the Assembly offered by Corsica. It was not till the state of affairs in France had again become normal that he allowed his name to be put forward as a candidate at the supplementary elections in September. He was elected by five departments, and returning to Paris he took a suite of rooms at the Hôtel du Rhin in the Place Vendôme. His windows looked towards the column crowned by the Emperor's statue. His own rise to power had at last begun.

He had arrived in Paris on September 26th. Next day he took his seat in the Assembly. He came in with an old friend M. Vieillard, shook hands with a few whom he recognised among the members, took the oath to the Republic, and said a few words protesting against the 'calumnies' of those who represented him as intriguing for its overthrow. It cannot be said that he was a success as a deputy. He was no orator. A touch of a German accent told against him. He spoke seldom and was irregular in his attendance at the debates, the chief subject of which was the drafting of the new constitution. His first important speech was a distinct failure. It was in opposition to a motion which would have excluded members of houses that had ruled in France from the Presidency. Some of those who saw in him a wily conspirator suggested he had failed purposely. In any case the speech made many jump to the conclusion that the speaker was not a man likely to count for much in French politics. The motion that would have excluded him was rejected.

The new constitution was formally promulgated on November 12th. It had been decided that the President of the Republic should be elected by universal suffrage. The vote was to be taken on December 10th. The Prince's friends had been busy all over France carrying on a propaganda in his favour. His only serious opponent was General Cavaignac, and all the blunders of the Government told against its head. Even his stern repression of the Red revolt did not help him with the friends of order, while it made him unpopular with the workers. It was said that France did not want a military dictator. Louis Napoleon was represented as the friend of the working classes, and at the same time the pledged adherent of a moderate, law-abiding Republic that would be the guarantee of order and progress. He had made friends in all parties. His election address, issued on November 27th, was welcomed by newspapers representing many shades of political opinion. With his characteristic optimism he declared that he counted with certainty on a majority.

The result of the polling was announced on December 19th. Cavaignac had obtained 1,448,302 votes. Louis Napoleon had defeated him by a majority of more than four millions with a poll of no less than 5,534,520 votes. With all his optimism he had never ventured to hope for such a triumph.

Charles Greville noted in his diary next day the impressions produced by the news : ' The result of the French election for President,' he wrote, ' has astonished the whole world. Everybody thought Louis Napoleon would be elected, but nobody dreamt of such a majority. Great alarm was felt here (in London) at the probable consequences of Cavaignac's defeat and the success of his rival, and the French funds were to rise if Napoleon was beaten, and to fall if he won. The election has taken place ; Napoleon wins by an immense majority, the funds rise, confidence returns, and people begin to find out that the new President is a ·marvellous proper man. . . . Van de

Weyer, who is here, says that he has long known him and well, that he is greatly underrated here, and that he is really a man of considerable ability.'

It was on the evening of the 19th that the result was proclaimed in the Chamber, and it was formally announced that ' Citizen Louis Bonaparte ' was President from that day until May 1852. He took the oath : ' In the presence of God, and before the French people, I swear to remain faithful to the democratic Republic and to defend the Constitution.' Then unfolding a paper he read a speech which began with the words : ' The votes of the nation and the oath I have just taken will direct my future conduct and indicate my duty to me. I shall count as the enemies of the country all who may endeavour by illegal means to change the form of Government you have established.'

Then he took possession of the Elysée, which had been assigned to him as his official residence. It was the palace where the Emperor had signed his abdication. For his nephew his entrance into it was the first great step to imperial power.

CHAPTER XXXIII

EMPIRE-MAKING AGAIN

(1848-1851)

'THE Government will be neither Utopian nor reactionary,' the new President had said in his inauguration
speech. 'We shall try to secure the prosperity of the
country, and we hope that, with the blessing of God, even if
we do not accomplish great things, we shall endeavour to do
good things.'

He formed a coalition Ministry, including representative men
of all parties except the extreme Left, but he soon showed that
he meant to be his own Prime Minister. He insisted on seeing
all important despatches and reports, and discussed every detail
with the ministers. The extreme wing of the Republican
party, amongst whose leaders were men who won an evil fame
in the days of the Commune more than twenty years later,
accused him of playing the autocrat, and declared that the
Assembly should reduce him to the position of its obedient
executive officer. A dangerous agitation began in Paris. In
January 1849 the closing of some Socialist clubs was met by
threats of armed insurrection. On the 29th General Changarnier, whom the Prince-President had put in command of
the troops and National Guards of the capital, nipped in the bud
a formidable attempt at rebellion. 'The men who raise the
paving-stones will not be given time to build them into
barricades and will not live to replace them,' said the stern
soldier.

The Prince had been elected by a coalition of all the moderate
parties, helped by unexpected allies, for even the Legitimists
had supported him as the protector of order. But there were
now divisions in the ranks of his supporters. More or less
critical and even hostile groups formed in the Assembly.

Republican and Monarchist parties began to pursue policies of their own.

He had appointed as ambassador at Madrid his cousin Prince Napoleon, though it was well known that the son of Jerome was at best a doubtful ally. At Bordeaux on his way to Spain the newly appointed ambassador made a speech in which he said that his cousin the President was not master of his own policy, that he was dominated by a reactionary group and anxious to escape from their tutelage, and that the best thing for France and for the President himself would be to try to return to the new Assembly, soon to be elected, a number of good Republicans, members of the Opposition, not time-serving Moderates.

The extremists rejoiced, and proposed to nominate Prince Napoleon for twenty departments. Instead of at once recalling him from his post, the President wrote him a friendly letter, in which he patiently explained to him that it was a mistake to indulge in oratorical escapades that could only lead to serious trouble in the end, and begged him to assist instead of opposing his policy. Prince Napoleon was to the end from time to time a source of anxiety to Louis Napoleon, under Republic and Empire alike, but somehow he always managed to reap the fruits of his cousin's success, and, while coquetting with the Republican and Liberal opposition, sought and obtained place, power, and wealth from the man he was so ready to criticise and almost to denounce.

Did Louis Napoleon intend to keep the oath of fidelity to the Republic which he had taken ? Was he sincere in his protests that those who accused him of disloyalty to it were calumniating him ? The most one can say is that this is possible. It may have been that he was for the time quite content to be the head of a Republican France, and had laid aside his earlier projects of a restoration of the Empire. As President of the Republic with a highly centralised administration, a system that made him really his own Prime Minister, and the army at his command, he had all the reality of power. The enormous majority he had secured at his election made him believe that he was sufficiently popular in France to be able at any moment to overrule the Chamber, if it should oppose his views. As

for the constitution, he who had asked ' How long does perpetuity last in France ? ' knew well that it was open to revision
by the same powers that had made it, and no doubt he persuaded himself that his oath to uphold it did not bar a legal
evolution towards an Imperial system by successive revisions,
any more than it would oblige him to resist proposals made in
the new Assembly to introduce amendments to the existing
scheme of Government. There is no need of assuming that
Louis Napoleon perjured himself, and consciously resolved
from the outset to betray the Republic, of which he had been
chosen the chief magistrate.

His apologists maintain that he was driven into violent
action against the Assembly by three years of factious opposition, in which the self-styled defenders of the Republic themselves mutilated its constitution, and leagued themselves
now with the Red propagandists of armed revolt, now with
the Legitimist or Orleanist irreconcilables, to thwart the policy
and the enlightened activity of the Prince-President. This
was undoubtedly his own view, but how far it can be justified
by the cold facts of history is another question. To answer
it one would have to analyse in detail the complicated tangle
of French politics in 1849, 1850, and 1851. We may leave
this question unsettled, and note only some of the leading
points in the personal history of Louis Napoleon in the days
when, according to his friends, he was being forced by a kind
of fate to follow the path of the first Napoleon, and to pass
from the position of temporary head of the Republic to that
of its permanent chief, and then to Empire. His 18th of
Brumaire was December 2, 1851, the anniversary of Austerlitz and the day of the *coup d'état.*

As the only surviving son of Louis, he was by the constitution
of the Empire Napoleon's heir. But the very theory of
Bonapartism was that there could be no mere hereditary
claim to Imperial power without the call of the nation. If
he meant to bring about a successful appeal to France for the
restoration of the Empire, he would have to do it without
any help from the other Bonapartes. They had stood aloof
when he was striving single-handed to restore the political
fortunes of the family. And now that he was President of
the Republic and ruler of France, they left him in a kind of

isolation. On none of his three cousins who had been elected to the Constituent Assembly could he count as an ally. Wild Pierre Bonaparte, politic Lucien Murat, both took care not to be too closely identified with his views, and Napoleon, the son of Jerome, on whom he had bestowed an embassy, was almost ostentatious in his Radical independence. Jerome himself, who had ' made history ' on a grand scale in days of the Revolution and the Empire, was too selfishly occupied with his own melancholy kind of pleasures to give any time to aiding his nephew and strengthening his position. Jerome was not at all sure that the new fortune of the family would last long, but he was old enough to anticipate that it might well last his time. He was now sixty-five years of age. The Republic had conferred on ' the old soldier of Waterloo ' the Governorship of the Invalides, where he lived in a fine suite of rooms, as commandant of the veterans, many of whom were survivors of the wars of the Empire, proud to see a Bonaparte at their head. He had squandered the fortune of his Italian wife, the Florentine Marchesa Bartolini-Badelli, who was living an unhappy life at the Invalides, neglected by her husband and hated by her stepson, Prince Napoleon.

The appointment to the Governorship of the Invalides had done something to repair Jerome's fortunes, for it carried with it an income of 45,000 francs. Louis Napoleon added to his uncle's dignities and resources by making him a General with a further allowance of 12,000 francs a year, and providing for his son. One of the President's anxieties arose from the necessity of helping a crowd of needy relatives. Once, when Jerome in a fit of bad humour told him he had nothing of the great Emperor about him, he replied with a smile, ' Pardon, I have always his family.'

To have Jerome nearer him in Paris was no help. It was more likely to be a source of discredit and embarrassment. The old King was, it is true, a link with a famous past, and at reviews and military inspections Jerome in his general's uniform, looking somewhat like the great Emperor might have been had he lived to an advanced age, was a very ornamental and not unpopular figure. On these occasions and at other state gatherings he wore, beside the Legion of Honour, his own order of the crown of Westphalia. Perhaps he was the only living man who still treasured the decoration.

With his old-world courtly manners this man, who had been King, was a dignified figure in the President's circle at the Elysée, and when he himself received guests at the Invalides. But there his dignity ended. The spoiled child of the Bonapartes, his life had been one long dissipation. Vicious habits and tastes had become a part of his nature. Once he was away from official circles and ceremony-loving society his manners became rude, his language coarse. He had been false to Elisabeth Patterson, false to Catherine, and he was now unfaithful to the poor Marchesa. The old roué was still chiefly interested in belated amours which were the gossip of scandal-loving Paris. He still squandered his money freely, and could not have paid his way if his daughter Mathilde, the Princess Demidoff, had not again helped him. His most harmless amusement was to escape from a formal dinner at the Elysée or the Invalides and go off in plain clothes with his aide-de-camp, Du Casse, to dine at a restaurant and finish the evening at some theatre, often of the minor music-hall type. One evening, when in a popular drama Napoleon appeared on the stage, giving a sharp scolding to the King of Westphalia for his doings at Cassel, the attention of the audience was attracted by an old gentleman in one of the boxes who was convulsed with laughter. They burst into loud applause as they recognised the ex-King himself, whose earlier years were made to give a comic interest to the play.

Until Louis Napoleon was at last the absolute ruler of France, old Jerome could hardly believe seriously in his nephew. All through the anxious years of the Presidency he took care to keep in such friendly touch with several of the Opposition leaders that, even if the President had to disappear into private life, he himself would still have advocates to maintain him in his comfortable post at the Invalides. Kinglake has represented him as one of the accomplices in the *coup d'état*, and told how he was posted beside Louis Napoleon at the Elysée to see that no disquieting news of dangerous resistance could reach him. This is a baseless legend. Jerome had been quite satisfied with the 'independent' attitude of his son, and was very anxious as to how his nephew's ambitious policy would end; and in the days of the *coup d'état* he expected failure, and in concert with Prince Napoleon took such precautions as to be able to deny all responsibility for the bold stroke, if it should miscarry.

But if Louis Napoleon found no reliable supporters among the Bonapartes, he had kept around him a band of faithful confederates of the days of adversity, and rallied to them many fresh allies. Persigny was still his right-hand man, and recruited several of these new adherents. De Morny, a prominent figure in Parisian society under Louis Philippe, and a successful man of business, was an early recruit. Rumour said that he was a half-brother of the Prince-President, a son of Queen Hortense. De Maupas, Colonel Vaudrey's son-in-law, was another useful adherent. Other new allies were Eugène Rouher, an able lawyer and a born politician, and many ambitious soldiers from the Algerian army, like Fleury and St. Arnaud. The men who made the Empire anew were not a set of ruined gamblers. They had no small measure of ability and courage, and if some among them were unscrupulous intriguers, others were men of character who believed that after a long succession of Revolutions the safety of France lay in an intelligent absolutism. And for many years a great majority of the French people were of the same opinion.

The events of 1849 helped to strengthen the President's influence with the army, and at the same time to maintain his hold on his more Conservative supporters, who saw in his policy a safeguard against disorder. The expedition to Rome under Oudinot had for its primary object the restoration of French influence in Italy. The armed conflict with the Roman Republicans had not been foreseen when the expedition was despatched. Its policy had some similarity to that of Louis Napoleon's later intervention in the affairs of Italy. It was primarily an effort to substitute French for Austrian influence in central Italy. It was hoped that the Roman Republicans would accept a French occupation, and so allow France to become mistress of the whole situation. When they attacked Oudinot before the gates of Rome, and drove the French back with heavy loss, the President resolved that at all costs the defeat must be wiped out by the capture of Rome. The object of the expedition then became the restoration of Pius IX. In taking this course Louis Napoleon offended the Republican opposition, but he not only rallied to his support much of the Conservative element in France, but what was much more important for him, he secured the thoroughgoing support of the army.

All who feared the Red Socialist movement were further rallied to the President by an ill-directed attempt of the Extremists to overthrow him. In June a group of these men, headed by Ledru-Rollin, posted proclamations declaring the President and ministers outlaws, and calling the workmen of Paris to arms. There was only a feeble response. After causing widespread alarm the movement was quickly trampled out in Paris, but at Lyons there was a more serious outbreak, which was not suppressed without much bloodshed.

In the autumn he made a progress through the provinces, and was everywhere received with enthusiasm. At Amiens he spoke of the treaty of 1802 and of his policy of friendship with England. Speaking of the welcome given to him, he said: ' I have done so little as yet for my country, that I am at once proud of, and perplexed by, this reception, which I attribute to my name rather than to myself.' The most interesting incident of the tour was his visit to Ham, where he had spent so many years in the old castle. Conneau, who had aided him so well in his escape, was with him, as well as Persigny, Vaudrey, and Laity. There were triumphal arches in the streets, and the guns of the prison fortress fired a welcoming salute. He went to his old rooms, and found there a prisoner of state, the Arab chief Bou-Maza, and exercised his prerogative of pardon by at once setting him free, and arranging for his return to his tribe in Algeria. There was another enthusiastic reception for the President at Strasburg, the scene of his first attempt to win power in France.

There is no doubt that these journeys through France, begun in 1849 and repeated in 1850 and 1851, helped to increase the personal popularity of the Prince-President, and to prevent his having to depend too largely for support on popular feeling in Paris. He spoke everywhere of his plans for promoting the general prosperity of France, and showed a special interest in the development of the new railway system, which was still in a very rudimentary condition ; he took care, according to the local interests of the places he visited, to insist on his anxiety to develop the agriculture, industry, and commerce of the country. Again and again he referred to the name he bore, and summarising the theory he had upheld in the *Idées Napoléoniennes*, he protested that the name of Napoleon meant not war and conquest, but also the organisation of law, order, and peace.

If he were to be looked upon as the man who was to realise them, whatever hopes he thus aroused and encouraged were overshadowed by the fact that, under the constitution, his term of power must be a very short one. There would be another Presidential election early in 1852, and under the constitution the existing President was incapable of re-election. Men said that when the time for the momentous choice came, there would be a scramble for power among the party leaders, and most likely another Revolution. In the Legislative Assembly, elected to succeed the Constituent Assembly of 1848, the gaps made by abortive insurrections in the ranks of the Extreme Republicans had crippled their party, and the Legislature was mainly made up of Moderate Republicans and Conservatives, with a majority that was composed of men who were either openly Royalist or Orleanist, or who would have no great difficulty in accepting the return of a King. Changarnier, who commanded the Army of Paris, was believed to be not unwilling to play the part of General Monk if the opportunity presented itself. His relations with the Orleanists became more and more friendly. As for the thoroughgoing Republicans of the extreme Left, they were in the popular mind connected with the Red Revolution, civil war and disorder, and sporadic outbreaks in various parts of France kept alive the alarm they had excited.

It was the fear of the party of disorder that was used as the chief argument for the proposal brought forward in the Assembly in May 1850 to modify the constitution by abolishing, or as some put it ' suspending,' universal suffrage, which was its very basis. Instead of manhood suffrage, the vote was to belong only to registered voters, who could show that they had resided continuously for three years in their electoral district. It was argued that this would keep the vote in the hands of

good citizens, who had a settled abode, and get rid of the vaga-
bond army of disorder.   The proposal became law, and out of
some ten millions of French electors it disfranchised three
millions, most of them working men who had to move from
place to place for the sake of employment.   The President
gave his official consent to the new law, though it was directly
opposed to the principle he had so perseveringly put forward
as the necessary basis of government, and to which he owed
his own position—the principle of universal suffrage.   His
apologists after the *coup d'état* maintained that it was not he
who had destroyed the constitution of 1848, but that the
Assembly had already swept away its essential principle by
this vote of May 31, 1850.   The argument reminds one of
his uncle's telling the Legislature, on the day of Brumaire,
that they had already destroyed by their own acts the constitution of the Year III.   Louis Napoleon certainly took no step
to prevent, or protest against, the disfranchisement of the
three millions.   Later on his friends argued that it was the act
of the Assembly only, inspired by Thiers and the Orleanists,
and that the President was helpless.   ' He had no veto ;
he could only suspend the publication of a law, and ask for its
reconsideration ; but if reconsidered, if passed by a bare majority, it became a law absolutely.   This law was passed by such
a large majority that it was deemed wholly useless to exercise
this suspensive power.'[1]   But surely to send the law back for
reconsideration, and only accept it when the Assembly voted it
anew, would have served to divest the President of any responsibility for it.

But if the constitution could thus be modified in its essential
basis without an appeal to the country, it was obvious that its
details were open to revision.   The year 1851 opened with a
movement for revision, in favour of which petitions were got
up in all parts of France.   In the minds of vast numbers of
those who signed these petitions, and in that of a still larger
proportion of those who organised them, the chief object in
view was to eliminate the clause that forbade the re-election
of the President.   There were other motives for revision, but
this was not the least of them.

[1] Blanchard Jerrold, *Life of Napoleon III.*, vol. iii. p. 127.   The passage is a
quotation from an American defence of Louis Napoleon's conduct in 1850.

But to carry a revision resolution there must be a three-fourths majority. When the vote was taken on July 19th, 724 members were present. The minimum to give the required majority was a vote of 543 members in favour of revision. The resolution only obtained the votes of 446. The minority of 278, which rallied against it, was therefore victorious. The resolution was followed by a vote of want of confidence in the Ministry, carried by a narrow majority of 13.

The Chamber had already on more than one occasion shown hostility to the President. It had rejected a vote of money for the expenses of his tours. When, after hearing that Changarnier was plotting with the Orleanists, Louis Napoleon had dismissed him from the command of Paris, the General had received an ovation from the deputies. Prominent in the ranks of the extreme opposition was Louis Napoleon's cousin, Prince Napoleon. He had no support from his family. Rather they were an embarrassment to him. Pierre Bonaparte, Lucien's erratic son, had been the hero of many escapades. In order to remove him from Paris Louis Napoleon had given him a commission in the Foreign Legion, but he presumed on his relationship to the President to indulge in acts of open indiscipline, and had to be deprived of his rank. But if he had no help from his cousins, Louis Napoleon had the old guard of fellow-adventurers and friends now recruited by some of the ablest men in France. These rallied round him, determined to fight for his cause and their own, and secure the prolongation of his power in the coming crisis.

The first thing to be done was to form a new Ministry. The two most important men in it held portfolios for the first time. They were Vaudrey's son-in-law, M. de Maupas, who was given the Ministry of the Interior, and General Le Roy de Saint-Arnaud, who had just distinguished himself in a hill campaign in Algeria, and whom his friend and comrade Colonel Fleury, the President's trusted aide-de-camp, persuaded to accept the Ministry of War. General Baraguay d'Hilliers, the son of a Marshal of the Empire, and who had himself served as a young officer under the great Napoleon, was in command of the Army of Paris. Though the Assembly had given a majority for revision it was insufficient, but the Councils-General of the French Departments had all but unanimously declared for it.

It was now too late to carry it by an ordinary procedure before the crisis of the Presidential election of 1852. Every one in France who knew what was going on realised that it was most unlikely that this would be allowed to follow the normal course. Rumour already whispered that the President and his friends would make some bold stroke to avoid the substitution of another head of the state by election. The ultra-Republicans were planning a rising. The two wings of the Royalist party, Legitimists and Orleanists, were both hoping that with the help of the majority in the Chamber one or the other of them would secure a royal restoration. The Orleanists were most active, and were undoubtedly conspiring. Their avowed policy was to secure the election of an Orleanist President as a first step, and they counted on several of the generals.

The impatience of the Red party helped to precipitate the crisis. In the departments of the Cher and the Nièvre outbreaks were followed by the declaration of a state of siege in the interests of the defence of life and property. In Paris some of the chiefs of Socialist clubs were arrested, and there was a scare among the propertied classes and the shopkeepers.

When the Assembly met again in November, Louis Napoleon took a politic step in proposing in his message to the Chamber that the voter's qualification should be reduced from three years to six months' residence. The restriction of the franchise, he said, was too sweeping. The Chamber showed at once its hostility to the proposal, and the President secured thus the support of more than two millions of the disfranchised.

The debates that followed showed how wide was the rift between the Assembly on the one side, and the Executive, composed of the President and his ministers, on the other. Neither party meant to wait for the elections of 1852. Each was plotting against the other. The Royalist majority in the Chamber was in close communication with the exiled Orleanist princes, and a plan of action had been arranged. The Republicans were less forward with their plans. Louis Napoleon and his friends at the Elysée were preparing for a bold stroke, which in their eyes was justified by the view that it was an anticipation of hostile action against them, and was to be followed by an appeal to universal suffrage to approve or repudiate it.

The serious question was, who would have the command and support of the army in the coming struggle ? General Changarnier, when he was still commandant of Paris, had told his friends that he could any day he liked send the President to Vincennes in a prison-van. When he was deprived of the command and it was given first to Baraguay d'Hilliers and then to Magnan, it did not seem to occur to him that the army was equally in their hands. He told his colleagues in the Assembly that if the President tried to use the army to overrule the Legislature, he would not be obeyed. M. Thiers, the most prominent figure among the Orleanist deputies, speaking to one of his friends and alluding to the President, said, ' Within a month we shall have him locked up in Vincennes.' ' Take care he does not put you there,' said the other. There was the some optimism in the Assembly. ' The soldiers love the Republic and would rise as one man against any one who assails it,' said M. Crémieux, one of the Republican chiefs, and there were cries of ' The army is with us.'

An effort was made to carry a resolution that would give the Assembly, through its President, the right of sending orders directly to the troops, without transmitting them through the Minister of War. The attempt was based on the right of the Assembly to call for military protection for its place of meeting. The resolution was defeated through the Republicans rallying against it in their fear of putting a strong weapon in the hands of the Orleanists. It was reported that if it had been carried the President would have at once forcibly dissolved the Assembly, and the question now was how long he was likely to wait before taking some decisive action to prolong his power. At the end of November General Changarnier discussed the outlook with his friends, and confidently predicted that nothing would happen till after New Year's Day. ' We have at least a month before us,' he said. ' Louis Napoleon will not make enemies of all the small dealers of Paris by upsetting their New Year trade.'

But the move was already arranged, and the date fixed for it, by the small group which formed the Prince-President's inner circle of adherents. The plan was Morny's. During the recess, when there was some talk of dissolving the Assembly, he had opposed the idea of anything being done while the

2 M

deputies were scattered all over France. In the departments
and the great cities some of them might easily form centres
around which resistance could be organised. Better wait
till they were all in Paris. Then resistance could be paralysed
by the simultaneous arrest of the leaders. ' In troublous
times,' he had said, ' to arrest a party man is to do him a
service. You cover his responsibility to his own party, and
you keep him out of personal danger.'

The 2nd of December, the anniversary of Austerlitz, had
been selected as the day for the revolution which was to be
for Napoleon III. and the Second Empire what the *coup d'état*
of Brumaire had been for Napoleon I. There were vague
rumours in Paris that something was going to happen, even
the day of Austerlitz was talked of as one that might be anything but peaceful. But what discredited all these alarmist
reports was the air of undisturbed routine that pervaded
the Elysée, where Louis Napoleon and those who were known
to be his most intimate advisers were all going about their
ordinary occupations, as if they had nothing in the world
to make them more busy or anxious than usual.

Louis Napoleon seemed to be in particularly good spirits.
He issued invitations for a large dinner-party at the Elysée
for the evening of Monday, December 1st. That morning
he seemed to have plenty of time to spare. He gave a long
interview to the Hon. Mrs. Norton, whom he had known in
London, and who was passing through Paris, and he took
some trouble about arranging for a friend of hers to have
access to documents at the Bibliothèque Nationale.

The dinner-party was particularly brilliant and gay. De
Morny left early and went to the Opéra, where he passed from
box to box to chat with friends. ' It is said they are going to
sweep out the Assembly. What will you be doing, M. de
Morny ? ' said one of them. ' I shall try to be on the same
side as the broom,' was the answer. The same evening St.
Arnaud was told that the Assembly meant to summon him
to answer a string of questions next day. ' My reply is ready,'
said the General.

A reception followed the dinner at the Elysée. The rooms
were crowded, and the President walked from group to group
of his guests with a pleasant word for every one. In one of

his own private rooms his secretary, M. Mocquard, was busy sorting out and arranging the papers and orders for the work of the night and the next morning. Once or twice Louis Napoleon came in to smoke a cigarette with him, and see how he was getting on. 'No one has any suspicion,' he said to his secretary. 'Some of them are talking about a *coup d'état*, but it is not ours. It is the move the National Assembly is planning against me.'

A little after ten o'clock the guests went away. A few minutes after Louis Napoleon met in his study the men who were to carry through the *coup d'état* that was to make him master of France. He had arranged his memoranda and orders and the copies of his proclamations on a table ornamented with Roman mosaic inlaying—a table with a history, for it was at the Elysée in June 1815. Lucien had sat at it to write at the first Napoleon's dictation the message by which he abdicated in favour of his son, and bending over the table the Emperor had signed it. Perhaps his nephew, with the touch of superstition that ran through his life, thought it was 'lucky' to gather his staff for the new Brumaire round the mosaic table. Persigny, his right-hand in so many schemes, was the first to arrive. Then came De Maupas, Prefect of the Police, General St. Arnaud, Minister of War, and De Morny.

One of the legends of the *coup d'état* is that at this last moment Louis Napoleon lost his nerve and talked of adjourning the attempt, and that Colonel Fleury drew a pistol and threatened to blow his brains out if he did not go on. Kinglake tells the story. But Fleury was not even present at the council at the Elysée. He had only a vague knowledge of what was going on, and did not meet the President till he reported himself for duty as his aide-de-camp next morning. Fleury was regarded as a little hot-headed, and the conspirators kept him in the outer circle, for fear he might by some thoughtless word give an enemy an inkling of what was coming.

There was no discussion at this meeting at the Elysée, no debate as to whether action was to be taken or not. Everything was already arranged. The proclamations and the orders were read over to make sure that each one understood his part. At eleven the President shook hands with his friends, wished them good luck, and went away to go to bed.

De Morny had nothing to do till next morning. He went to play cards at the Jockey Club, where his appearance seemed a proof that nothing was going to happen. Persigny sat up at the Elysée, ready to wake the President if there was any hitch in the execution of the plan. De Maupas with his police, and St. Arnaud with the soldiers had all the work to do.

The Director of the Imprimerie Nationale had been ordered to have a staff of printers ready at eleven to do some emergency work. This often happened, and aroused no suspicion. De Maupas (having first surrounded the printing-office with a cordon of gendarmes, with orders to let no one leave it or send out any message) handed the director the proclamations, and had them cut up into small pieces of copy, so that very few of the printers knew the full meaning of what they were setting up. This done, he went to the Prefecture of Police, whence in the small hours of the morning fifty parties of police agents issued out, and while Paris slept arrested and conveyed to the Mazas prison the leaders of the Assembly, the generals who were members of it, and who might perhaps influence the troops, and certain active politicians who, though not in the Assembly, might try to organise resistance. Generals Changarnier, De Lamoricière, and Le Flo, M. Thiers and M. Crémieux, and nearly threescore more of Legitimists, Orleanists, Moderate Republicans and Socialists were roused from their beds to be driven off to prison.

Parties of police stopped the issue of the newspapers, prepared to close at dawn clubs and cafés that were the resort of the working-men leaders, and, in order that Paris might not be short of food, saw that the market carts were rapidly unloaded at the Halles, and then sent away before they could be used as material for barricades. Before the sun rose the proclamations, printed secretly in the night, were posted in all places of public resort. Paris woke to find that a new Government had been formed while it slept. De Maupas's part in the *coup d'état* had been executed without the least hitch.

From the Elysée St. Arnaud had driven off to see General Magnan, the commander of the troops in Paris. Magnan had refused to take any part in the deliberations at the Elysée, but he had said he would obey without hesitation any order received from St. Arnaud as Minister of War, and he had fully discussed with him already the steps to be taken to preserve order in Paris, in case of a forcible dissolution of the Assembly. He now despatched his detailed orders. Soon after midnight a cordon of troops surrounded the palace of the Assembly, to prevent any attempt to hold a meeting there in the early morning. Before dawn all the garrison of Paris was under arms, and messages had been sent to call in reinforcements from neighbouring towns. The railway stations and telegraph offices, open spaces and other important points were occupied, and guards were posted at the offices of the ministers.

The proclamations to the Army and the People, posted in Paris in the night of December 1st-2nd, were despatched early next day to be published throughout France. The proclamation to the French people announced the dissolution of the Assembly. Despite the efforts of a patriotic minority, said the President, it had become a hotbed of conspiracies, and was promoting civil war. It had tampered with the constitution ; it was intriguing with the counter-Revolution. He could not see the ship of the state being run into peril without taking the helm in his own hands. He appealed to universal suffrage to justify his action. If the votes of the nation disapproved of it he was ready to retire. But he asked France to put an end to a period of unrest and danger by repeating its former act of confidence in him, and accepting the plan which would be as soon as possible submitted to the decision of a plébiscite. His proposals (borrowed almost entirely from the system of the First Consul, and intended to give him the same degree of power) he set forth as follows :—

'Persuaded that the instability of the executive authority and the predominant power of a single Assembly are permanent causes of disturbance and discord, I submit to your votes the following fundamental bases of a constitution which the Assemblies will elaborate later on :—

1. A responsible chief elected for ten years.
2. Ministers responsible only to the Executive.
3. A Council of State, composed of distinguished men, who will prepare drafts of laws and support them in debate in the Legislative Assembly.
4. A Legislative Assembly elected by universal suffrage.

5. A Second Chamber composed of the illustrious men of the country, a deliberative body, the guardian of the basis of the constitution and of public liberties.'

The army was called on to preserve order, and enable the nation to vote in peace, and the right of voting was given to the soldiers. Finally a list of a brand-new Ministry was published. Eugène Rouher was Prime Minister ; De Morny went to the Ministry of the Interior ; St. Arnaud remained at the War Office ; Achille Fould, an eminent authority on the subject, became Minister of Finance ; Turgot, the bearer of a historic name, was Foreign Minister ; Magne, who had already been Minister of Public Works in an earlier Government, resumed the post. It was a fairly strong combination.

On the morning of December 2nd Louis Napoleon was up early. At seven Persigny, who had been out to make a rapid tour of Paris, came back with the report that everything was quiet. It had been arranged that early in the day the President should show himself in central Paris at the head of his staff, and messages were sent off asking his friends to join him in this ride. By eight o'clock they began to arrive—old adherents and new supporters eager to do homage to the rising sun.

When King Jerome received the invitation at the Invalides, his son Prince Napoleon was with him. They had discussed the news of the morning, and it was agreed that the family fortunes should be secured whatever happened, by the old King proceeding to the Elysée, and the Prince putting himself in communication with the remaining leaders of the Radical Republicans and finding out what were the prospects of resistance. Jerome put on his general's uniform and rode to the Elysée with a couple of his aides-de-camp. On his way he was joined by a veteran of the First Empire, one of the very few survivors of Napoleon's generals, old Count Exelmans, a soldier of the wars of the Revolution and the Consulate, whom Louis Philippe had made Chancellor of the Legion of Honour, and on whom the President bestowed a Marshal's bâton. The King was anxious and somewhat gloomy, the Marshal delighted at seeing the nephew of his old master making a bold stroke for power.

At half-past nine the cavalcade rode out. First came the President in a general's uniform, with a smiling, confident look on his face ; then the old King and the veteran Marshal followed by a numerous staff. The troops stationed round the Elysée broke out into cries of ' *Vive Napoléon !* ' The party rode first to the Place de la Concorde, where several batteries of artillery were drawn up. Here, in the cheers of the soldiers, ' *Vive l'Empereur* ' mingled with ' *Vive Napoléon.*' He then rode along the Boulevards. Everywhere the troops cheered wildly. Civilian opinion was divided, but there is evidence enough that large numbers of the bourgeois and working men joined in the acclamations that greeted him. The personal impression he produced helped to turn opinion in his favour. He returned to the Elysée by the Place du Carrousel, the quays and the Champs Elysées.

At the Elysée there were numerous callers, among them the Russian and English ambassadors, the latter with a friendly message from Lord Palmerston. Reports sent in by the energetic Prefect of Police, De Maupas, and by De Morny from the Ministry of the Interior, and St. Arnaud from the War Office, were all encouraging.

There had been several attempts to organise resistance, but the steps taken in the night had made any movement in Paris exceedingly difficult. An attempt of some of the deputies to meet at the Palais Bourbon had been prevented by the troops on guard. The President of the Assembly, who had not been arrested, had given them discouraging advice. ' Of course,' he said, ' the constitution is being violated. We have right on our side ; but then we are the weaker party.' About three hundred members met later at one of the Mairies. They passed a resolution declaring Louis Napoleon an outlaw, establishing a Provisional Government, and naming General Oudinot commander of the Army of Paris. Some troops arrived, called on them to disperse, and treated Oudinot's counter-orders with contempt. The deputies declared they would only yield to force. Some two hundred of them were then arrested, and marched off surrounded by bayonets to the barracks of the Quai d'Orsay on the south bank of the Seine, where they were temporarily imprisoned in the officers' quarters.

Some active supporters of resistance printed, and even posted on the walls, the decree of the dispersed Assembly outlawing the President. The High Court of Justice hastily assembled, and had just drafted another decree of outlawry, when they were dispersed by a battalion of Municipal Guards. But somehow their unsigned decree was printed and placarded.

Crowds gathered in eastern Paris, especially in the old citadel of insurrection the Faubourg St. Antoine, but they were easily dispersed by the police, who made numerous arrests. There was no organised rising. Most of the shops were open all day. On the main Boulevards curious crowds were kept on the move. In the evening the theatres and music-halls had good audiences.

At the Elysée the President had invited his new Minister of Foreign Affairs, M. de Turgot, and some of the diplomatic corps to dine with him. He told them that the most dangerous day was peacefully past, and there was now not much fear of disturbance. The news had hardly reached the provinces, but there too all was quiet.

But late on the 2nd a Republican Committee of Resistance was formed. An attempt to organise a rising for that evening proved a failure, but proclamations, signed by Baudin and other deputies and by Victor Hugo, were posted calling the people of Paris to arms. The rising was fixed for the morning of Wednesday the 3rd. Two days of street fighting and bloodshed, chiefly in eastern Paris, followed. The only hope of the insurgents, mostly working men, was that the troops would not obey orders to act against them, or that help would come from generals in the provinces, who were not prepared to accept the new state of things. Both hopes were disappointed.

Early on the 3rd Baudin was killed at a barricade, which he had had erected in the Faubourg St. Antoine. Through the morning there was desultory fighting from the Faubourg to Montmartre. Barricades were erected, stormed, and abandoned, but others rose up to take their place. In the afternoon a considerable area was in possession of the insurrection, and St. Arnaud and Magnan withdrew the troops from actual conflict, and contented themselves with establishing a cordon round the rebel districts, in order to prevent the insurrection spreading. It had been decided that instead of involving the army in a series of isolated street fights, it would be better to allow the party of resistance to erect their barricades and collect their forces during the remaining hours of the short December day, let them weary themselves with waiting and watching for an attack during the night, and then, after giving the troops a good rest, make a combined attack by converging columns on the 4th, and thoroughly stamp out the rising, bombarding the barricades with artillery and carrying them with bayonet charges. This thorough sweeping of the insurrectionary quarters would, it was calculated, put an end to all chance of revolt in Paris for years to come.

During the anxious hours of December 3rd the President had shown unbroken confidence in final success. He even drove out in a carriage without an escort, and made his appearance at the west end of the Faubourg St. Antoine, where it was noticed that groups of workmen joined in the cheers of the troops at his appearance. Reports of minor disturbances in the provinces had reached the Elysée, but they were taking the form of riotous attacks on priests and churches, chateaux and landed proprietors, and this abortive Jacquerie only strengthened the position of Louis Napoleon, by increasing the fears of the large numbers of Frenchmen who thought they saw in his strong rule a barrier against a Red Socialistic rising. The reports also served to make the insurrection in Paris appear like the Red Revolt of June 1848, still remembered with terror by every investor and every shopkeeper.

In the absence of newspapers in Paris all kinds of wild rumours circulated. The temporary suppression of the daily papers was in fact a mistake and a source of trouble. In the afternoon of the 3rd some of these reports were carried to King Jerome at the Invalides by Prince Napoleon, who, without compromising himself with the insurrection, kept in friendly touch with its leaders and closely watched events. He found his cousin Lucien with his father, and said to them : ' Well, it is not all over yet. The barricades are going up, the clubs are moving, the Faubourgs are all excitement. General Neumayer is marching on Paris with 15,000 men to help the rising. The Court of Appeal has met to indict and condemn Louis Napoleon. Things are getting warm.' Later in the day he sent his father a report that the provinces were declaring against his cousin, and that by next day Louis Napoleon would be a prisoner of state at Vincennes. Jerome kept quiet, waiting to see how it would all end.

The end came swiftly on Thursday, December 4th. By eight

o'clock masses of troops were moving to reinforce the thin cordon that had barred the outlets of the insurgent districts. A column massed at Vincennes was to attack from the eastward, while other attacks were directed from the Paris side down every thoroughfare opening into the scene of the revolt. The attack was organised in a very leisurely fashion. The general advance did not take place till two P.M. Proclamations had been posted and sent into the revolted quarters, signed by the Minister of War, warning those who held the barricades that insurgents taken with arms in their hands would be shot without trial. There was only a half-hearted resistance. Many of the barricades were abandoned without even a show of defence. A few salvoes of artillery followed by bayonet charges cleared the rest.

On the main line of the Boulevards there was an unfortunate incident, near the Rue Montmartre. A long column of infantry was standing in fours, waiting to support an attack on a barricade further east. It is alleged that some shots were fired from a window, but however this may be, the men were seized with a sudden alarm, and firing began at the head of the column and ran down the line, the men shooting some at the windows, some at the crowd on the side-walks. There was a deplorable loss of life. It was represented by the President's opponents to be a deliberate massacre of peaceful citizens intended to inspire terror. The idea is too wild to require formal refutation. Such incidents have occurred in other places in times of excitement.[1]

By nightfall the insurrection was crushed out. All the leaders were in prison, in flight, or among the dead and wounded. Their followers had suffered heavily in the fighting, and some thousands were huddled together in prisons and barracks. On the morning of the 5th a handful of desperate men tried to renew the fight, but could only get up a few street rows. France accepted the verdict of events in Paris, and in the eyes of most Frenchmen it was deliverance from a period of endless agitation and uncertainty.

[1] For instance, at the beginning of the American Civil War a column from St. Louis marched out, broke up a Confederate camp, and was returning escorting a number of prisoners, when, as it marched through a hollow way, the troops were somehow seized with the idea that the crowds who lined the banks were hostile, and fired on them, killing many unarmed and friendly citizens.

Before the plébiscite, which was fixed for December 20th, there was little doubt about the result. Montalembert rallied the Conservatives of France to the cause of the President by a manifesto, in which he represented the *coup d'état* as a victory over the forces of disorder. ' To vote for Louis Napoleon,' he said, ' is not to approve all he has done ; it is only to choose between him and the total ruin of France.' The country was tired of revolutions. Royalists, Bonapartists, Moderate Republicans united their forces, and the most active leaders of a possible opposition had disappeared. On December 20th the plébiscite was taken by ballot and with universal suffrage. 8,116,773 votes were given, and of these 7,439,216 approved of the new policy of Louis Napoleon. On December 31st the Commission charged with carrying out the plébiscite formally announced the result to the President at the Elysée. ' I left the limits of legality,' he said, ' in order to re-establish lawful right. More than seven million votes have absolved me, thus justifying an act which had only one object, that of saving France, and perhaps Europe, from years of disorder and misery.'

So ended the Brumaire of the Emperor's nephew. He had reached the stage of the Consulate. There was only one step more to Empire.

CHAPTER XXXIV

THE SECOND EMPIRE—THE LAST YEARS OF JEROME (1852-1860)—THE BONAPARTES OF TO-DAY

ONCE the success of the *coup d'état* was assured no one was more profuse in his congratulations than Jerome Bonaparte. His son, Prince Napoleon, gave a more guarded adhesion to the new order of things. Both were to benefit largely by the changes now impending in France.

Instead of having to look forward to an election in the spring of 1852, at which he could not even be a candidate, Louis Napoleon was now President for ten years, with almost arbitrary powers. The constitution, outlined in the programme approved by the plébiscite, would give a very limited authority to the new Chambers. The Legislature would be under the control of the Executive, and the Executive would be at the beck of its chief. The new régime did not last a year. Almost from the outset it was evident that it was only the prelude to the Empire.

Though the Prince-President still spoke of maintaining and consolidating the Republic, every one felt that the Presidency, with the practically autocratic powers he now had in his hands, would be for him what the Consulate had been to his uncle. With the leaders of the Opposition in prison or in exile the elections gave him a majority, and when the Corps Législatif met on March 29, 1852, the supporters of the Government were all-powerful. Jerome was appointed President of the newly nominated Senate, with the Luxembourg for his official residence. At the Elysée Louis Napoleon maintained a more than royal state. A great household was organised. The liveries of the First Empire reappeared. There was a hunting establishment with parties for the chase at Fontainebleau and Compiègne. It was at these parties that the President made

PRINCE NAPOLEON

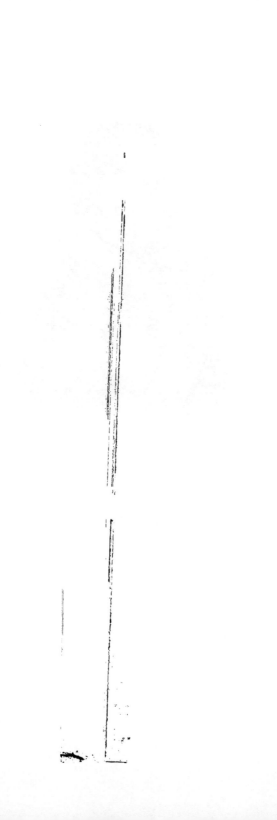

the acquaintance of Mademoiselle Eugénie de Montijo, the daughter of a soldier of the First Empire. She was a splendid rider, and this was what first brought her and the Prince-President together. Devoted to the memory of the Emperor, for whom her father had fought, she had made Louis Napoleon one of her heroes, and during the crisis before the *coup d'état*, she had told one of her Bonapartist friends that she would be glad, if it was required, to put her private fortune at the disposal of the party. Louis Napoleon was not aware of this offer till much later.

The old cry of *Vive l'Empereur* was now heard at reviews. The press, subject to a censorship and therefore under strict control, began an agitation for the restoration of the Empire. Petitions for the same end began to come to the Elysée from public bodies all over France. In a progress through the departments the President was acclaimed as the future Emperor. At Bordeaux he announced that he would yield to the 'wish of France,' and make the restoration of the Empire the subject of a new plébiscite. ' The Empire means peace,' he said. He had no ambitions for conquest. His task, his glory would be to develop the resources of France, and make her people prosperous and happy.

The plébiscite gave the result that every one expected. Nearly eight millions of votes called for the restoration of the Empire, only a quarter of a million opposed it. With a studious care to link the new Empire with the traditions of the past, Napoleon went to St. Cloud during the plébiscite. It was there that the delegates of the Assembly had offered the Imperial crown to his uncle. It was there that he was officially informed by the delegates of the Senate and the Corps Législatif of the result of the vote. On December 2, 1852, he was proclaimed as ' Napoleon III., Emperor of the French,' and took possession of the Tuileries.

One of his earliest acts as Emperor was to announce to the Corps Législatif his coming marriage with Eugénie de Montijo. The marriage was celebrated at Notre Dame with a magnificent display of ecclesiastical, ceremonial, and Imperial state. The Empress won the hearts of the Parisians by a graceful act. The municipality had voted a sum of 600,000 francs to present her with diamonds on her wedding day. She thanked them for their goodwill, but said that she would be sorry to think that, for the sake of making her a wedding present, so large a sum should be taken from the funds of the city, and paid by the taxpayers. But she would not altogether refuse their gift. It would be a pleasure to her if, instead of spending it on diamonds, they would devote it to founding some public work of charity. The money was used to found an orphanage. Amongst her husband's gifts to her on her wedding day was a sum of a quarter of a million francs. This too the Empress at once gave to the poor of Paris.

The new Emperor had been granted a civil list on the most generous scale, and he made a liberal provision for all the members of his family. Jerome was always anxious for money, always more or less in debt. As President his nephew had restored him to his rank as a general. As Emperor he gave the ex-King of Westphalia the marshal's bâton, which carried with it an income of 30,000 francs a year in addition to his allowance from the civil list as an Imperial Prince, and his salary as Governor of the Invalides. His daughter, Princess Mathilde, had for some years given him out of her fortune an annual grant of 40,000 francs. Thinking that he was now so well off that he ought not to need her help, she informed him that the allowance would be no longer paid. The result was a fierce quarrel. Jerome told her she was a heartless, ungrateful daughter.

The ex-King of Westphalia, now His Imperial Highness Prince Jerome, Marshal of France, was a living link with a glorious past. But unfortunately for Napoleon III. the surviving brother of the great Emperor was the least reputable member of his family. He was that most contemptible of beings, a selfish, vicious old man. And he soon became the centre of scandals that gave endless anxiety to his nephew.

Jerome had already squandered the fortune of his third wife, and he and his son, Prince Napoleon, both showed the unfortunate Marchesa Bartolini that they disliked her. Jerome had fallen under the influence of an adventuress, a married woman, whose husband added to the scandal by being one of Jerome's hangers-on at the Invalides. In 1853 the ex-King of Westphalia's matrimonial affairs came to a crisis. He believed, or affected to believe, a horrible accusation trumped up against his wife, who was certainly as faithful to him as he was faithless to her. To the charges brought against her she replied with tearful denials, and left Paris for Florence. Napoleon insisted on Jerome repaying her the fortune he had wasted, and after her husband's death he allowed her a pension. Even her stepson, Prince Napoleon, made some amends for his ill-will to her by paying the rent of her palazzo at Florence. Jerome up to the year of his death was in the toils of the woman who had displaced her.

All this time Jerome's first wife, Elisabeth, was living at Baltimore. In 1854, the year after he had driven the Marchesa Bartolini from Paris, he was reminded of Elisabeth's existence and his own past by the arrival in Paris of Jerome Bonaparte of Baltimore, the son of his first marriage.

Napoleon III. had met Jerome of Baltimore in Italy in his young days, and had seen him again during his visit to America after the Strasburg attempt. Jerome was a prosperous lawyer, and before coming to Paris he had forwarded to the new Emperor all the documents bearing on his mother's marriage, and the record of his own birth. Napoleon had put these papers in the hands of his Minister of Justice, and on the very day that Jerome reached Paris, he invited him to dine with him at St. Cloud, and after dinner showed him a report on his claims, signed by M. Abbatucci, the Minister of Justice, M. Troplong, President of the Senate, and M. Baroche, President of the Council of State.

For the son of Elisabeth it was a most satisfactory document. The conclusions of the three eminent authorities who had drawn it up were : ' 1. M. Jerome Bonaparte has the right to be regarded in France as of legitimate birth. 2. He is a Frenchman by birth, and if he has resigned this nationality it can be restored to him by a decree according to the terms of Article 18 of the Civil Code.' A few days after, on August 30th, Napoleon III. signed a decree giving all the rights of French subjects to Jerome Bonaparte, and to his sons, Jerome and Charles. Charles was following his father's profession. Jerome junior was a young officer in the United States army. He was anxious to serve in that of his cousin the new Emperor. On September 5th a second decree granted Jerome Bonaparte the rank of lieutenant in the 7th Dragoons. He had come to Europe with his father, and at once joined his French regiment.

Jerome, the ex-King of Westphalia, now came upon the scene with a formal protest. According to the *Statut de Famille* of Napoleon I., that was now part of the constitution of the Second Empire, Napoleon III. stood at the head of the family as the representative of Louis, King of Holland. If the line of Louis should fail, that of Jerome came next, and till the birth of the Prince Imperial Jerome's son, Prince Napoleon, was the heir of the Empire, unless indeed his father survived the Emperor and Napoleon III. left no heir. It is in virtue of this arrangement of Napoleon I. that a grandson of Jerome, a son of Prince Napoleon, is now the head of the Bonapartes. If these American Bonapartes were to be recognised, Jerome Bonaparte of Baltimore or his son might claim to be the heir of the French Empire, and Prince Napoleon was thrown out of the succession.

Old Prince Jerome handed his formal protest to the Emperor. ' Your decrees,' he wrote, ' dispose of my name without my consent. They introduce into my family, without my having even been consulted, persons who have never formed any part of it. They make the legitimacy of my children doubtful in the eyes of the French people, and open the way for a scandalous lawsuit being brought against them, when the time comes for the succession to my property and rights to be dealt with. They are an attack on my honour, and on that of my brother, the Emperor, for they annul the solemn engagements we entered into with the King of Würtemberg and the Emperor of Russia as a condition of my marriage with Queen Catherine.'

Jerome had thought little then, and thought as little now, of the solemn engagements he had contracted with Elisabeth Patterson, and of his repeated protests that he regarded them as binding on his honour and conscience. He was anxious only to bury his past in the interest of the son of Catherine of Würtemberg. His nephew, Napoleon III., had apparently not fully realised the effect of his decrees on the question of succession, and he now tried to persuade Jerome Bonaparte of Baltimore to consent to renounce all claims based on his

mother's marriage, and accept as compensation the title of
Duc de Sartène, and the grant of an estate in France, with
the succession to the title and property for his son, the cavalry
officer. The American Bonaparte refused these offers, and
stood upon his rights. Prince Napoleon and the Princess
Mathilde then intervened by a joint petition to the courts to
forbid the American to use the name of Bonaparte. The
judgment was that ' the defendant had the right to use the
name of Bonaparte, by which he had always been known,'
but it was added that this left the question of legitimacy open.
The decision was in contradiction with the formal opinion
given by Abbatucci and his colleagues. But Jerome of Baltimore failed to get anything further from the courts at this
stage, and went back to America resolved to reopen the
question after his father's death. The official opinion of the
minister and his colleagues was regarded by Elisabeth as a
victory, and she was pleased at her grandson being given the
commission in Napoleon's army.

The ex-King of Westphalia survived for nine years of the
new Empire, its most successful years, when to many it seemed
that the dynasty of Napoleon had won a permanent place
among the ruling families of Europe. To Jerome it must
have seemed as if the old times of his youth had come again.
Although Napoleon III. had declared that the Empire meant
peace, the Imperial army soon went forth to war. The
cannon of the Invalides again roared out news of victory,
Alma, Balaclava, Inkerman, Tchernaya, Sebastopol. Again
a marshal of France took a ducal title for victory won, when
Pelissier was created Duc du Malakoff. Jerome's son Napoleon
had shared the military glories of the new Empire. He had
commanded a division of the French ' Army of the East,'
at the Alma and Inkerman. He rode among the victors
the day that Napoleon III., with Marshal Prince Jerome among
his staff, took his place beneath the column of Napoleon I.
in the Place Vendôme to see the returned Army of the East
march past in triumph.

Sebastopol had blotted out the memories of Moscow. Then
came the Italian war. It was still more like the old days.
Napoleon himself took the field. The French army fought on
the very ground where in Jerome's boyhood his brother, as a

2 N

General of the Directory and then as First Consul, had led France to victory. The marshals of Napoleon III. defeated the Austrians on some of the very battlefields where Napoleon I. had routed them more than half a century ago. The Napoleonic policy of making France dominant in Italy had been revived. There was even an attempt at Napoleonic king-making, though Cavour had quietly counter-checked it. Jerome's son, Prince Napoleon, had not shared the glories of the Lombard campaign, but he had commanded the army corps that occupied Tuscany, Parma, and Modena. On the eve of the war he had been married to the Princess Clotilde, the daughter of Victor Emmanuel. It had been intended that he should be King of Tuscany in a federated Italy. The scheme had to be abandoned under pressure of the new Italian unionist movement.

Still Jerome's son was the son-in-law of the King of Italy, and only a single life, that of the Prince Imperial, born in 1856, stood between him and succession to the Empire, which was now regarded as the most formidable military power in Europe, and was launching out on schemes of conquest in Asia and Africa. It must have seemed to Jerome something like a miracle that all this had come after the long years of exile, and the strange shifts and turns to find the means of living in foreign cities. The trouble was that he was old and broken in health at last. His son could enjoy the good times that had come again. He had warnings that he must soon leave them. He had lived for three-quarters of a century, but the end had come at last.

In the spring of 1860 he was seriously ill, and by the advice of the doctors he was moved from Paris into the country, to the château of Villegenis. His son and daughter, Prince Napoleon and the Princess Mathilde, were with him. It was only on the eve of leaving Paris that he was separated from the woman who had been the evil genius of his later years. Face to face with death, he sent for a priest and received the last rites of the Church. He died on June 24th.

He was buried beside his famous brother at the Invalides. Paris saw that day a splendid display of military pomp— for the funeral procession passed through streets lined with troops, escorted by cuirassiers, artillery, and grenadiers of the

Imperial Guard. Veterans of the wars of the First Empire paraded at the Invalides. The boom of cannon sounded from the Champ de Mars. It was the funeral of a Marshal of France, a Prince of the First and Second Empire, an ex-King, and the last of the brothers of Napoleon.

The orator who pronounced the funeral discourse from the pulpit dwelt chiefly on the most creditable episode in his long career, his fight for France in the campaign of Waterloo. Most of his life was no topic for oratory of any kind. In the crowd who looked on there was a woman muffled in mourning, who, as the ceremony ended, made her way to his tomb and fell weeping before it. She was the poor Marchesa Bartolini, the woman he had so cruelly treated. Yet womanlike she thought only of the time when he had loved her, and she had come from her home in Florence to mourn for him.

When the news of Jerome's death reached Baltimore, the lawsuit he had foreseen was begun in the French courts. The plaintiffs were described in the proceedings as ' Monsieur Jerome Napoleon Bonaparte and Madame Elisabeth Patterson, divorced wife and widow of His Imperial Highness Prince Jerome ' ; the defendants were Prince Napoleon and the Princess Mathilde. M. Berryer appeared as leading counsel for Elisabeth and her son. The case was heard in Paris in 1861. Berryer maintained that Elisabeth Patterson was the only lawful wife of Prince Jerome, and that her son was the heir to all rights that he possessed and to a due share of his property. His speech was a bitter attack on Jerome's conduct, and on the policy of the first Napoleon, and indirectly damaging to the existing Imperial system. The case thus became a state trial, into which an immense amount of political feeling necessarily was introduced. The court gave its decision against the validity of the Baltimore marriage, denied the legitimacy of Jerome, and declared that he and his mother had no claim to the inheritance of Prince Jerome. It was a decision that it would be difficult to justify, on any broad ground of morality and equity. It depended entirely on the provision of the French Code that requires the consent of a parent to the marriage of a son, a condition that has been the reason for so many irregular connections in France.

Jerome's son retired from the French army with the rank

of Colonel of cavalry and returned to America. Jerome died in the United States in June 1870. His mother, the first wife of Prince Jerome, survived for nine years longer. She died at Baltimore on April 4, 1879.[1]

When Prince Jerome, the last of Napoleon's four brothers, passed away, the Second Empire was at the height of its power, but it was only to last ten years. The unfortunate Mexican adventure began in 1861. The fate of that attempt at Empire-making beyond the Atlantic was decided when the Federal army conquered at Gettysburg. The withdrawal of Bazaine and the Imperial troops from Mexico was the prelude of disaster at home. The Italian policy of Napoleon III. prepared an ally for Prussia, and helped to the rise of the new Bismarckian Germany. The Emperor's failure to read the signs of the times in central Europe made the downfall of Sedan all but inevitable.

There was a strange parallel between the ending of the two Empires. Like Napoleon I. before Waterloo, Napoleon III. on the eve of the disastrous war with Germany introduced Liberal institutions into the Imperial system. The change had come too late. The Second Empire went down in ruin amid defeats more overwhelming even than Waterloo, and after his captivity at Wilhelmshöhe (the Napoleonshöhe of Jerome's gay Westphalian days), Napoleon III. came to England to die.

His son, who had been the hope of the new Empire, and on whom the chances of an Imperial restoration centred, lost his life in an obscure skirmish in Zululand. On his death Prince Napoleon, the son of Jerome, became the head of the family. He died in Rome in 1891, leaving two sons and a daughter, the children of his wife, the Princess Clotilde of Italy.

The eldest son, Victor Napoleon, is now the representative of the Bonaparte dynasty, but he appears to have no political ambition, and is quite content with his fortune and his recognised princely rank without troubling himself with dreams of substituting a Third Empire for the Third Republic. His younger brother, Louis Napoleon Bonaparte, is an officer in the Russian army. When the French President visited Russia after the conclusion of the Franco-Russian alliance, Louis

[1] See Appendix, p. 569: Note on the American Branch of the Bonaparte Family.

PRINCE VICTOR NAPOLEON

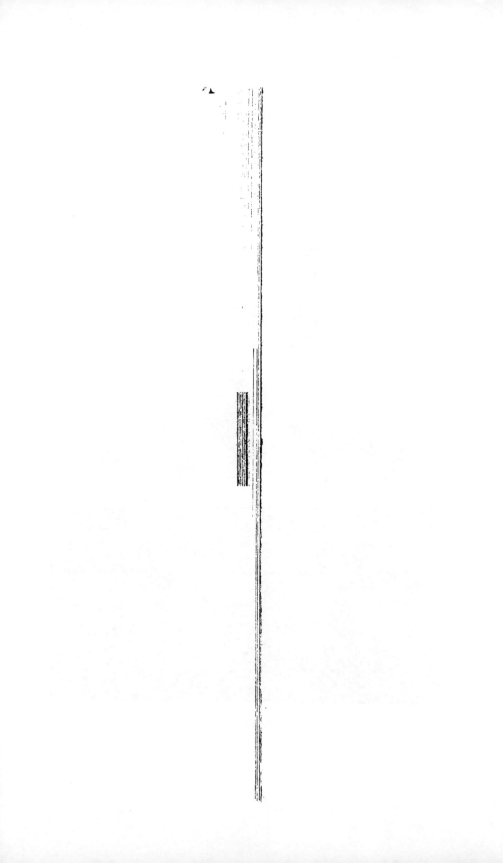

Napoleon Bonaparte was the Colonel of a cavalry regiment. At the great review near Moscow he led his regiment in the march past, and Colonel Bonaparte saluted the President of the Republic. He has since been promoted to the rank of General, and was with the cavalry in the Far East during the Russo-Japanese War. Those who know him say that, unlike his elder brother, he is ambitious, and hopes to see the Empire restored in France. If he were the elder brother, they say, General Bonaparte would try to repeat history and make himself Emperor, but he has a loyal affection for Victor, and would regard any step towards posing as a Pretender as a violation of his rights.

The Bonapartes of to-day are, like Prince Victor, without Empire-making ambitions. There is a Bonapartist party in France, but its prospects are not brilliant. It is paralysed by the absence of an active leader. The family is represented by a number of grandchildren and great-grandchildren of the Emperor's brothers, and has married into many of the princely and noble houses of Europe. There have been more daughters than sons, so that as the women marry and take another name there are fewer and fewer Bonapartes.

The direct line of the Emperor ceased when the Duke of Reichstadt died in 1832. Of his brothers, Joseph left only daughters, and the line of Louis, King of Holland, ended with the death of the Prince Imperial in Zululand on June 1, 1879. Lucien left four sons. The elder line ended with Cardinal Lucien Bonaparte, only son of the second Prince of Canino. The Cardinal died in 1891. Paul, the second son, lost his life by an accident in the Greek War of Independence. Louis Lucien, the third son of the first Prince of Canino, passed most of his life in London, devoting himself to linguistic studies. He was one of the greatest authorities on the Basque language and on the English dialects, and he wrote or edited during his long and active life more than two hundred volumes. He had been made a Senator of the Second Empire by his nephew Napoleon III., but he troubled himself little with politics, and was prouder of his membership of most of the leading scientific societies of Europe. In 1883 he accepted a civil list pension from the British Government in recognition of his contributions to the study of the English dialects. He died at Fano on the Adriatic in 1891.

The fourth son of Lucien, Prince of Canino, Pierre Bonaparte, had a stormy career. He was a Corsican soldier of fortune. In the days before the rise of the Second Empire he had fought in revolutionary outbreaks in South America and in Albania, and mixed in a Carbonarist conspiracy in Rome, and escaped arrest by shooting two papal gendarmes. For a while he led a wild life in the United States. After the Revolution of 1848 he came back to France and was elected a deputy for Corsica. After Pierre had been mixed up in various scandals, including a violent assault on a fellow-deputy, his cousin, now President, got him out of the way by giving him a commission in the Foreign Legion in Algeria. He came back to France without leave and was promptly cashiered. Under the Empire he was given a pension of 100,000 francs on condition that he would keep quiet.

In 1858 Prince Pierre contracted an irregular marriage with a Parisian girl of humble birth, Justine Ruffin. They had two children, a boy, Roland, and a girl. Pierre was in disgrace at the Tuileries, and little was heard of him, until in January 1870 he sprang into sudden notoriety by shooting the opposition journalist, Victor Noir, dead in his own rooms in Paris. Noir had come to him with a challenge to a duel. Prince Pierre asserted that the journalist had begun the quarrel by striking him. It was with difficulty that his acquittal was secured when he was brought to trial on the charge of murder, and the affair helped to the downfall of the Empire.

After Sedan Pierre was married according to French law to Justine at the French Republican Legation at Brussels. This act made Justine Princess and legitimatised her children, and gave them also recognised princely rank. For a while the Pierre Bonaparte family lived in London, in open rupture with all their relations, and in such straitened circumstances that the Princess Justine Bonaparte supported her husband and children by going back to her old trade and keeping a milliner's shop under an assumed name. But presently peace was made with the family and the business was sold.

For there had been a wonderful stroke of good fortune. Pierre's son, Prince Roland Bonaparte, married the daughter of

M. Blanc, the Savoyard waiter, who out of money made at Baden found the means to create the gambling city of Monte Carlo. Mademoiselle Blanc brought her husband a dowry of a million sterling and a palace on the shore of the Mediterranean. Prince Pierre only survived this change of fortune for a year. Next year (1882) Princess Roland died, four weeks after giving birth to a daughter, Princess Marie Bonaparte. In the autumn of 1907 this granddaughter of wild Pierre and the enterprising Blanc of Monte Carlo gave her hand and her fortune to Prince George, the second son of the King of Greece.

As has been already noted, the line of Jerome is represented by Prince Victor, the legal heir of the Empire, and General Louis Napoleon Bonaparte of the Russian army. There is another offshoot of the Bonapartes in the American family that is descended from Jerome's first marriage with Elisabeth Patterson. Its chief representative is the Hon. Charles Joseph Bonaparte, for several years a member of President Roosevelt's administration, and one of his most trusted friends. The American Bonaparte has never troubled himself about claims derived from his royal grandfather and his cousinship with Imperial princes, and one of his favourite sayings is that ' he who serves his country well need not boast of ancestry.' One service that he has done his country has been to assist in the rapid development of her sea power when he was for a while at the head of the Navy Department—a curious link with Jerome's early career as a naval officer. But unlike the young *capitaine de vaisseau* who became a king, the American Bonaparte has never been a trifler. Everything he puts his hand to he counts as serious work ; he has taken a distinguished part in social and benevolent activity of many kinds as well as in the arduous field of politics ; and even the most bitter opponent has never thrown a doubt on his high standard of political honour.[1]

It is remarkable that it should be on the other side of the Atlantic that a Bonaparte holds a prominent place in public affairs, while in Europe the course of events has excluded the family from the land associated with their days of greatness. After living for the better part of a century on the fame of Napoleon, they hold now the position of a princely family,

[1] See in the Appendix an account of the American branch of the Bonapartes and of Charles Bonaparte's career.

connected by marriage with more than one of the reigning houses of Europe, but debarred by their name and traditions from any prospect of taking part in directing the fortunes of France, unless changes as yet unforeseen and beyond the range of probability take place in that country.   The Imperial system imagined by Napoleon belongs now to the record of far-off years.   The memories of Sedan stand in the way of any hope of a revival of the system, and the tributary kingdoms of Napoleon's brothers have left no trace in the present political map of Europe.   Their history is at best the story of a failure.

APPENDIX I

NOTE ON THE AMERICAN BRANCH OF THE BONAPARTE FAMILY

I OWE to the courtesy of the Hon. Charles J. Bonaparte of Washington, U.S.A., some notes on which I have based the following information as to the American branch of the Bonaparte family and its living representatives.

Jerome Napoleon Bonaparte (the son of the Emperor's youngest brother), who was born at Camberwell, June 17, 1805, and died at his residence in Baltimore, June 17, 1870, married on November 3, 1829, Susan Mary Williams of Baltimore. She was the daughter of Benjamin Williams, originally of Roxbury, Massachusetts, who lived for many years in Baltimore.

Of this marriage there were born two sons—Jerome Napoleon Bonaparte, who was born at Baltimore, November 5, 1830, and died at Prides Crossing, Massachusetts, on September 3, 1893; and Charles Joseph Bonaparte, born at Baltimore, June 9, 1851, who is still living.

The elder of these two grandsons of Prince Jerome married on September 7, 1871, Caroline Le Roy Edgar, widow of Newbold Edgar, and daughter of Samuel Appleton of Boston.

Of this marriage there were born (1) a daughter, Louise Eugénie Bonaparte, born at Baltimore in February 1873, who married in December 1896 Adam, Count Moltke-Huitfeldt of Denmark; and (2) a son, Jerome Napoleon Charles Bonaparte, born in Paris, February 1878, and now living in the United States.

The younger grandson of Prince Jerome, Charles Joseph Bonaparte, married at Newport, Rhode Island, on September 1, 1875, Ellen Channing Day, daughter of Thomas Mills Day of Hartford, Connecticut. There are no children of this marriage.

There are thus two surviving representatives of the Bonapartes in the United States, a grandson and a great-grandson of the Emperor's brother. The former of these, the Hon. Charles Joseph Bonaparte, has had a very distinguished career. He graduated at Harvard in 1871, and at the Harvard Law School in 1874. In the autumn of this year he was admitted to the Bar of Maryland, and entered on the regular and successful practice of his profession.

In the autumn of 1895 he was Supervisor of Elections for Baltimore City. In 1904 he was a member of the Board of Commissioners of Indian Affairs, and in the same year he was chosen as a Presidential Elector for Maryland. Next year he was appointed to the important position of Secretary to the Navy, or chief of the naval administration of the United States (July 1, 1905). He held this position for a year and a half until, on December 17, 1906, he exchanged it for that of Attorney-General of the United States.

Besides these political appointments he has held, or still holds, various offices which prove both the wide range of interests to which he has found time to devote himself, and the confidence of all classes of his fellow-citizens. For the twelve years 1891 to 1903 he was an Overseer of Harvard University, and for two years he has been a Trustee of the Catholic University at Washington. He has been since its foundation a Trustee of the Enoch Pratt Free Library of Baltimore, and for many years a Trustee of the Catholic Cathedral of the same city. He has taken a prominent and useful part in many public movements, such as the National Civil Service Reform League, the National Municipal League (of which he is President), the Baltimore Reform League, the Society for the Suppression of Vice, and the American Charity Organisation Society, and several others of the same type having for their objects the purification of political life and the improvement of social conditions.

His nephew, Jerome Napoleon Charles Bonaparte, was educated at the Jesuit College of Georgetown University, whence he went to Harvard, where he graduated in 1900. He was for some years connected with the American Security and Trust Company of Washington, but retired in the spring of 1908. He is still unmarried, and has not yet held any public office. He resides with his mother at Washington.

APPENDIX II

NOTE ON SOME SOURCES AND AUTHORITIES FOR THE STORY OF THE EMPEROR'S BROTHERS

So much of the story of Joseph, Lucien, Louis, and Jerome is closely linked with that of Napoleon that the standard authorities for the history of the latter, his correspondence, and the memoirs of his intimate associates, are also sources for the history of his brothers.

But there is also a considerable amount of literature bearing specially upon their careers. Joseph and Lucien left lengthy memoirs, Louis a very full *ex parte* treatment of the most important episode in his life, and Jerome an extensive correspondence, out of which and other documents his memoirs were prepared after his death by a semi-official writer under the régime of the Second Empire.

Baron Du Casse, aide-de-camp to Jerome during his last years in Paris, and an indefatigable worker, edited Joseph Bonaparte's memoirs in ten volumes : *Mémoires et Correspondance politique et militaire du Roi Joseph, publiés, annotés et mis en ordre par le Baron P. E. A. Du Casse* (Paris, 1853).

Jerome's correspondence, his Queen Consort's letters, and a connecting narrative, were published in seven volumes under the title of *Mémoires et Correspondance du Roi Jérôme et de la Reine Catherine* (Paris, 1861-66). Du Casse long after added to these another series of letters : *Correspondance inédite de la Reine Catherine de Westphalie* (Paris, 1893).

Lucien's memoirs, begun during his stay in England, were not published till long after. The *Mémoires de Lucien Bonaparte écrits par lui-même* appeared in London in 1836, and the publication of a translation into English 'made under the supervision of the author' was begun at the same time. The memoirs have been re-edited, completed from other sources, commentated and made the basis of a completely new work by H. F. T. Jung : *Lucien Bonaparte et ses Mémoires d'après les papiers déposés aux archives étrangères et d'autres documents inédits* (Paris, 1882 and 1883, three volumes).

Louis Bonaparte's memoir's deal with his connection with Holland, the conflict with his brother, and his own abdication and its results. They were written in exile some years after the events they describe, and while their author was in very poor health. They are an elaborate defence of his own policy and conduct, but the narrative cannot always be relied on—sometimes there is a failure of the ex-King's memory, and at others he is obviously straining the facts to fit them into his theory, or reading into his actions ideas inspired by subsequent events. The French original was issued at Ghent in 1820 under the title of *Documents Historiques et Réflexions sur le Gouvernement de la Hollande*, in three volumes. A Dutch translation was published, the same year, at Deventer, and an English version in London (*Historical Documents and Reflections on the Government of Holland*).

Dutch views of Louis's conduct as King are to be found in Jorissen's *Napoléon I. et le Roi de Hollande*, and Wichers' *De Regeering van Koning Lodewijk Napoleon*, and much information reflecting contemporary gossip is summed up in Garnier's *Mémoires sur la cour de Louis Napoléon et sur la Hollande* (Paris, 1828). In the same way there is a budget of gossip on Jerome's reign in *Le Royaume de Westphalie, Jérôme Bonaparte et sa Cour, par un Témoin Oculaire* (Paris, 1820). Among studies of the episode from a German standpoint are Von Kaisenberg's *König Jérôme Napoléon, ein Zeit- und Lebensbild*, and Von Lehnsten-Dingelstadt's *Am Hofe König Jérômes*. An English writer has given a lively sketch of Jerome's career in his book, *The Burlesque Napoleon, Jerome Bonaparte, King of Westphalia* (London, 1905), but has perhaps made the 'burlesque' element too prominent in his narrative.

Baron du Casse summed up his recollections and impressions of the ex-King of Westphalia in his *Souvenirs d'un aide de camp du Roi Jérôme* (Paris, 1890). While Jerome was still living Du Casse edited for him elaborate records of his Silesian and Polish campaigns. These appeared under the titles :—

Opérations du Neuvième Corps de la Grande Armée en Silésie sous le commandement-en-chef de Son Altesse Impériale le Prince Jérôme Napoléon, 1806-7 (Paris, 1851, two volumes and a folio atlas of maps and plans).

Mémoires pour servir à l'Histoire de la Campagne de 1812 en Russie, suivis des Lettres de Napoléon au Roi de Westphalie pendant la Campagne de 1813 (Paris, 1852).

Du Casse supplies some further material in his book *Les Rois Frères de Napoléon* (Paris, 1883). Certain episodes in Lucien's career are the subject of Marmottan's *Lucien Bonaparte et Napoléon en 1807*, and of his own statement in *La Vérité sur les Cent Jours* (Paris, 1835). On the artistic side of his character light is thrown by his catalogues of paintings and his reports on his excavations and Etruscan discoveries at Canino.

On all four brothers there are abundant details in M. Frédéric Masson's elaborate work on *Napoléon et sa Famille* (nine volumes issued, bringing the narrative down to 1814). Much of the work is devoted to Napoleon's sisters and to the family connections by marriage —Eugène Beauharnais, Bernadotte, Murat, etc.— and throughout the brothers are considered in their relation with Napoleon, and M. Masson's view of them is coloured by a theory that they were always inclined to combine and conspire against the Emperor, and that his downfall and their failure were due to their disloyalty as well as their incapacity.

M. Henri Houssaye's masterly studies of the events of 1814-15 (1814: *Campagne de France*—1815: *Le Retour de l'Ile d'Elbe—Les Cent Jours—Waterloo—La Terreur Blanche*) are important in connection with the part played by the brothers in these events: Joseph's Lieutenancy, the Defence of Paris and its evacuation, his and Lucien's action in the Hundred Days, and Jerome's share in the Waterloo campaign, etc.

Joseph's stay in the United States after Waterloo is dealt with in Bertin's *Joseph Bonaparte en Amérique*. I have also used some notes on the subject supplied by an American correspondent. On the fortunes of the Bonapartes in Europe after Waterloo and the restoration of the Empire there are interesting details in Welschinger's *Roi de Rome*; in B. Jerrold's *Life of Napoleon III.*, a work written from the point of view of the family; and in André Lebey's more impartially inspired *Trois Coups d'Etat de Louis Napoléon Bonaparte*.

The map of the Jena campaign is based on an outline sketch map in Otto Berndt's *Zahl im Kriege*; that of the dispersion of Jerome's army in Poland is based on part of one of the large-scale maps in General von Horsetzky's *Feldzüge der Letzten Hundert Jahre*; and the plan in outline of Jerome's attack at Quatre Bras is simplified from the beautifully detailed map of Quatre Bras and Ligny in Colonel James's recently published *Campaign of 1815*.

THE BON

(This Genealogical Table contains the names o

CHARLES BUONA

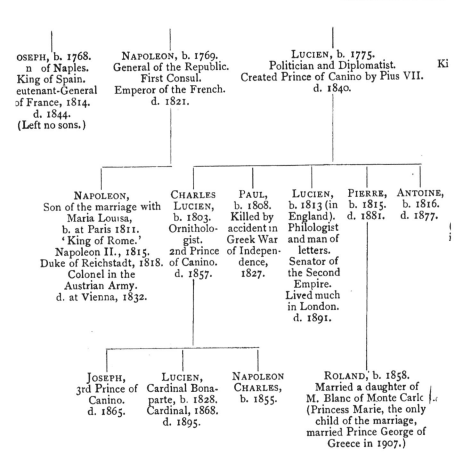

OSEPH, b. 1768.
n of Naples.
King of Spain.
eutenant-General
of France, 1814.
d. 1844.
(Left no sons.)

NAPOLEON, b. 1769.
General of the Republic.
First Consul.
Emperor of the French.
d. 1821.

LUCIEN, b. 1775.
Politician and Diplomatist.   Ki
Created Prince of Canino by Pius VII.
d. 1840.

NAPOLEON,
Son of the marriage with
Maria Louisa,
b. at Paris 1811.
'King of Rome.'
Napoleon II., 1815.
Duke of Reichstadt, 1818.
Colonel in the
Austrian Army.
d. at Vienna, 1832.

CHARLES
LUCIEN,
b. 1803.
Ornitholo-
gist.
2nd Prince
of Canino.
d. 1857.

PAUL,
b. 1808.
Killed by
accident in
Greek War
of Indepen-
dence,
1827.

LUCIEN,
b. 1813 (in
England).
Philologist
and man of
letters.
Senator of
the Second
Empire.
Lived much
in London.
d. 1891.

PIERRE,
b. 1815.
d. 1881.

ANTOINE,
b. 1816.
d. 1877.

JOSEPH,
3rd Prince of
Canino.
d. 1865.

LUCIEN,
Cardinal Bona-
parte, b. 1828.
Cardinal, 1868.
d. 1895.

NAPOLEON
CHARLES,
b. 1855.

ROLAND, b. 1858.
Married a daughter of
M. Blanc of Monte Carlo
(Princess Marie, the only
child of the marriage,
married Prince George of
Greece in 1907.)

PARTE FAMILY

he men of the family with some brief biographical notes.)

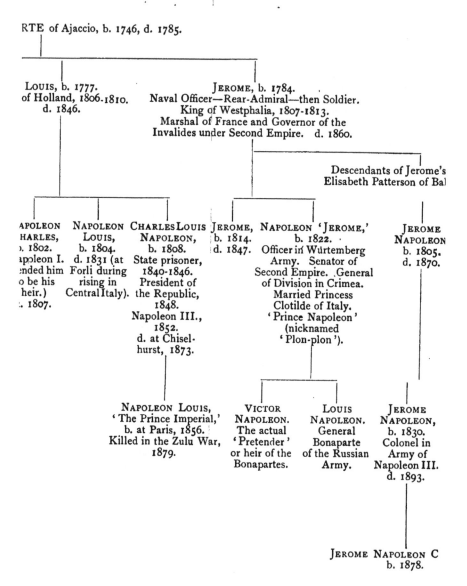

RTE of Ajaccio, b. 1746, d. 1785.

LOUIS, b. 1777.
of Holland, 1806.1810.
d. 1846.

JEROME, b. 1784.
Naval Officer—Rear-Admiral—then Soldier.
King of Westphalia, 1807-1813.
Marshal of France and Governor of the
Invalides under Second Empire.   d. 1860.

Descendants of Jerome's
Elisabeth Patterson of Bal

APOLEON
HARLES,
). 1802.
ıpoleon I.
:nded him
o be his
heir.)
:. 1807.

NAPOLEON
LOUIS,
b. 1804.
d. 1831 (at
Forli during
rising in
Central Italy).

CHARLES LOUIS
NAPOLEON,
b. 1808.
State prisoner,
1840-1846.
President of
the Republic,
1848.
Napoleon III.,
1852.
d. at Chisel-
hurst, 1873.

JEROME,
b. 1814.
d. 1847.

NAPOLEON 'JEROME,'
b. 1822. ·
Officer in Würtemberg
Army. Senator of
Second Empire. General
of Division in Crimea.
Married Princess
Clotilde of Italy.
'Prince Napoleon'
(nicknamed
'Plon-plon').

JEROME
NAPOLEON
b. 1805.
d. 1870.

NAPOLEON LOUIS,
'The Prince Imperial,'
b. at Paris, 1856.
Killed in the Zulu War,
1879.

VICTOR
NAPOLEON.
The actual
'Pretender'
or heir of the
Bonapartes.

LOUIS
NAPOLEON.
General
Bonaparte
of the Russian
Army.

JEROME
NAPOLEON,
b. 1830.
Colonel in
Army of
Napoleon III.
d. 1893.

JEROME NAPOLEON C
b. 1878.

INDEX

Printed by T. and A. CONSTABLE, Printers to His Majesty
at the Edinburgh University Press

Lightning Source UK Ltd.
Milton Keynes UK
UKHW02f2116170818
327336UK00009B/419/P